International Tax Aspects of Sovereign Wealth Investors

Series on International Taxation

VOLUME 67

Series Editors

Prof. Ruth Mason, University of Virginia School of Law
Prof. Dr Ekkehart Reimer, University of Heidelberg

Introduction & Contents

The Series on International Taxation deals with a wide variety of topics in the global tax arena. The authors include many of the field's leading experts as well as talented newcomers. Their expert views and incisive commentary have proven highly useful to practitioners and academics alike.

Objective

The volumes published in this series are aimed at offering high-quality analytical information and practical solutions to international tax practitioners.

Readership

Practitioners, academics and policy makers in international tax law.

Frequency of Publication

2-3 new volumes published each year.

The titles published in this series are listed at the end of this volume.

International Tax Aspects of Sovereign Wealth Investors

A Source State Perspective

Richard Snoeij

Published by:
Kluwer Law International B.V.
PO Box 316
2400 AH Alphen aan den Rijn
The Netherlands
E-mail: international-sales@wolterskluwer.com
Website: lrus.wolterskluwer.com

Sold and distributed in North, Central and South America by:
Wolters Kluwer Legal & Regulatory U.S.
7201 McKinney Circle
Frederick, MD 21704
United States of America
Email: customer.service@wolterskluwer.com

Sold and distributed in all other countries by:
Air Business Subscriptions
Rockwood House
Haywards Heath
West Sussex
RH16 3DH
United Kingdom
Email: international-customerservice@wolterskluwer.com

Printed on acid-free paper.

ISBN 978-90-411-9431-2

e-Book: ISBN 978-90-411-9433-6
web-PDF: ISBN978-90-411-9434-3

© 2018 Richard Snoeij

All rights reserved. No part of this publication may be reproduced, stored in a retrieval system, or transmitted in any form or by any means, electronic, mechanical, photocopying, recording, or otherwise, without written permission from the publisher.

Permission to use this content must be obtained from the copyright owner. More information can be found at: lrus.wolterskluwer.com/policies/permissions-reprints-and-licensing

Printed in the United Kingdom.

For Lien

Table of Contents

List of Abbreviations   xix

Acknowledgements   xxi

CHAPTER 1
Introduction   1
1.1   Subject   1
1.2   Focus and Purpose   2
1.3   Approach and Further Scoping   5
1.4   Outline of the Study   10

CHAPTER 2
Sovereign Wealth Investors   13
2.1   Introduction   13
2.2   The Santiago Principles   14
      2.2.1   What Are the Santiago Principles?   14
      2.2.2   International Forum of Sovereign Wealth Funds   15
2.3   Definitions and Classification of SWFs   16
      2.3.1   Introduction   16
      2.3.2   US Department of Treasury   16
           2.3.2.1   Definition   16
           2.3.2.2   Classification   17
      2.3.3   State Street   17
           2.3.3.1   Definition   17
           2.3.3.2   Classification   17
      2.3.4   The IWG and the IMF   18
           2.3.4.1   Definition   18
           2.3.4.2   Classification   19
      2.3.5   Other Attempts   22
      2.3.6   Analysis and Working Definition of SWFs   23

Table of Contents

2.4	Governance Structure of SWFs		25
	2.4.1	Owner	25
	2.4.2	Governing Body/ies	25
	2.4.3	Operational Management	25
2.5	SWFs by Region		26
2.6	Definition of SWEs		26
2.7	Investment Trend		27
2.8	Legal Framework of Sovereign Wealth Investors		27
	2.8.1	SWFs	27
	2.8.2	SWEs	28
	2.8.3	SWFs and SWEs Combined	28
2.9	Selected Examples of Sovereign Wealth Investors		29
	2.9.1	Government Pension Fund Global (Norway)	29
		2.9.1.1 Incorporation & Objective(s)	29
		2.9.1.2 Legal Form & Governance	29
		2.9.1.3 Funding & Portfolio	30
	2.9.2	Temasek Holdings (Private) Limited	30
		2.9.2.1 Incorporation & Objective(s)	30
		2.9.2.2 Legal Form & Governance	30
		2.9.2.3 Funding & Portfolio	31
	2.9.3	Abu Dhabi Investment Authority	31
		2.9.3.1 Incorporation & Objective(s)	31
		2.9.3.2 Legal Form & Governance	32
		2.9.3.3 Funding & Portfolio	32
	2.9.4	China Investment Corporation	33
		2.9.4.1 Incorporation & Objective(s)	33
		2.9.4.2 Legal Form & Governance	33
		2.9.4.3 Funding & Portfolio	33
2.10	Home State Tax Status of Sovereign Wealth Investors		34
2.11	Conclusions		36

CHAPTER 3
Tax Policy Considerations and Approaches to Taxation of Foreign Sovereign Wealth Investors 39

3.1	Introduction		39
3.2	Tax Treatment of Foreign Sovereign Wealth Investors and Other Investors		40
	3.2.1	Tax Treatment of Investment Income Derived by Residents	40
		3.2.1.1 Regular Investors	40
		3.2.1.2 Sovereign Wealth Investors and Other State Entities	41
		3.2.1.3 Collective Investment Vehicles	41
		3.2.1.4 Pension Funds	42
		3.2.1.5 Not-for-Profit Organizations	43

					Page
		3.2.1.6	Comparison		43
	3.2.2	Tax Treatment of Investment Income Derived by Non-residents			44
		3.2.2.1	Regular Non-resident Investors		44
		3.2.2.2	Foreign Sovereign Wealth Investors		45
		3.2.2.3	Non-resident Collective Investment Vehicles		47
		3.2.2.4	Non-resident Pension Funds		48
		3.2.2.5	Non-resident Not-for-Profit Organizations		48
		3.2.2.6	Comparison		49
3.3	Identifying the Main Attributes of International Tax Policy				49
3.4	International Neutrality (Efficiency)				51
	3.4.1	General			51
	3.4.2	Capital Export Neutrality			52
		3.4.2.1	The Concept Explained		52
		3.4.2.2	Considerations Regarding Foreign Sovereign Wealth Investors		53
	3.4.3	Capital Import Neutrality			53
		3.4.3.1	The Concept Explained		53
		3.4.3.2	Considerations Regarding Foreign Sovereign Wealth Investors		54
	3.4.4	Capital Ownership Neutrality			56
		3.4.4.1	The Concept Explained		56
		3.4.4.2	Considerations Regarding Foreign Sovereign Wealth Investors		59
3.5	Equity (Fairness)				60
	3.5.1	General			60
	3.5.2	Inter-taxpayer Equity			60
		3.5.2.1	The Concept Explained		60
		3.5.2.2	Considerations Regarding Foreign Sovereign Wealth Investors		62
	3.5.3	Inter-nation Equity			64
		3.5.3.1	The Concept Explained		64
		3.5.3.2	Considerations Regarding Foreign Sovereign Wealth Investors		65
3.6	International Attractiveness (Instrumentalism)				66
	3.6.1	General Considerations			66
	3.6.2	Considerations Regarding Foreign Sovereign Wealth Investors			68
3.7	Is There a Clear Hierarchy among the Tax Policy Principles and Objectives?				70
3.8	Conclusions				73

Table of Contents

CHAPTER 4
Sovereign Immunity and Taxation of Foreign Sovereign Wealth Investors — 75
- 4.1 Introduction — 75
- 4.2 The Sovereign Immunity Principle — 77
  - 4.2.1 Some General Remarks — 77
  - 4.2.2 Rational Basis and Origin of Sovereign Immunity — 79
  - 4.2.3 Scope of Sovereign Immunity — 80
    - 4.2.3.1 Material Scope of Immunity from Jurisdiction — 80
    - 4.2.3.2 Material Scope of Immunity from Measures of Constraint — 83
    - 4.2.3.3 Personal Scope of Sovereign Immunity — 84
  - 4.2.4 Jurisdictional Immunity Legislation of Australia, Canada, the UK and the US — 84
    - 4.2.4.1 Australia — 85
    - 4.2.4.2 Canada — 85
    - 4.2.4.3 UK — 85
    - 4.2.4.4 US — 86
- 4.3 Tax Immunity and Income Derived by Foreign Sovereign Wealth Investors — 86
  - 4.3.1 Immunity from Source Taxation in Australia, Canada, the UK and the US — 86
    - 4.3.1.1 Australia — 86
    - 4.3.1.2 Canada — 87
    - 4.3.1.3 UK — 88
    - 4.3.1.4 US — 88
  - 4.3.2 Comparison Between the Tax Immunity Regimes and the Rules on Jurisdictional Immunity in Civil Proceedings — 90
  - 4.3.3 Customary International Law Aspects in the Field of Taxation — 92
    - 4.3.3.1 Do Tax Immunities Logically Follow from the Sovereign Immunity Principle? — 92
    - 4.3.3.2 Constitutive Elements of Customary International Law — 94
      - 4.3.3.2.1 State Practice — 95
      - 4.3.3.2.2 *Opinio Juris* — 95
    - 4.3.3.3 Analysis — 96
- 4.4 Immunity from Measures of Constraint and Source State Taxation of Income Derived by Foreign Sovereign Wealth Investors — 97
  - 4.4.1 Introduction — 97
  - 4.4.2 Personal Scope — 98
  - 4.4.3 Material Scope — 99
    - 4.4.3.1 Property Serving Sovereign Purposes — 99
    - 4.4.3.2 Property Belonging to SWFs — 100

		4.4.3.3	Sovereign Wealth Investors Constituted by a Pool of Assets Within a Central Bank	101
	4.4.4	Analysis		102
4.5	Impact of the Sovereign Immunity Principle on Achieving Neutrality (Efficiency), Equity (Fairness) and International Attractiveness in Relation to Foreign Sovereign Wealth Investors			102
4.6	Conclusions			103

CHAPTER 5
Tax Treaty Aspects of (Foreign) Sovereign Wealth Investors 107
5.1 Introduction 107
5.2 The Interpretation Rule (Article 3(2)) 108
    5.2.1 General 108
    5.2.2 'Unless the Context Otherwise Requires' 109
    5.2.3 Relationship Between Article 3(2) and the Vienna Convention on the Law of Treaties (1969) 109
5.3 Tax Treaty Access (Articles 1, 3 and 4) 110
    5.3.1 General 110
    5.3.2 The Definition of 'Person' (Article 3(1)(a)) 110
        5.3.2.1 Introduction 110
        5.3.2.2 'Company' and Article 3(2) 111
        5.3.2.3 States, Political Subdivisions and Local Authorities and 'Person' 112
        5.3.2.4 Application to Sovereign Wealth Investors 113
            5.3.2.4.1 (i) Sovereign Wealth Investors Constituted by a Pool of Assets Within the State 113
            5.3.2.4.2 (ii) Sovereign Wealth Investors Established as or Within a Separate Legal Entity Other Than the State Itself 114
            5.3.2.4.3 (iii) Sovereign Wealth Investors Organized as a (Legal) Entity Without a Separate Legal Personality 114
    5.3.3 Residency (Article 4) 114
        5.3.3.1 Introduction 114
        5.3.3.2 Relationship Between 'Liable to Tax' and the Interpretation Rule of Article 3(2)? 115
        5.3.3.3 Relevance of the Connecting Criteria for the Meaning of 'Liable to Tax' 117
        5.3.3.4 'Liable to Tax' as (the Most) Comprehensive Taxation 118

	5.3.3.5	A Source State Perspective on 'Any Other Criterion of a Similar Nature'?	121
	5.3.3.6	Liable to Tax Versus Subject to Tax	122
	5.3.3.7	Application to Sovereign Wealth Investors	123
		5.3.3.7.1 Tax Treatment of Sovereign Wealth Investors in Their Home State	123
		5.3.3.7.2 Relationship Between 'Liable to Tax' and the Interpretation Rule of Article 3(2)?	125
		5.3.3.7.3 (1) Liable to Home State Taxation on Worldwide Income	125
		5.3.3.7.4 (2) Liable to Territorial Based Home State Taxation	125
		5.3.3.7.5 (3) Subjectively Exempt from Home State Taxation	126
		5.3.3.7.6 (4) Income Tax Legislation Has Been Enacted, but Is Not Enforced	127
		5.3.3.7.7 (5) Carved Out from Their Home State's Tax Statute as a Person	128
		5.3.3.7.8 (6) No or a Very Limited (Corporate) Income Tax System in Place	129
		5.3.3.7.9 Comment	129
5.3.4	'[T]hat State and Any Political Subdivision or Local Authority Thereof' (Article 4(1))		130
	5.3.4.1	Introduction	130
	5.3.4.2	History	130
	5.3.4.3	Integral Part of the State, Etc.	131
	5.3.4.4	Application to Sovereign Wealth Investors	131
		5.3.4.4.1 When Are Sovereign Wealth Investors an Integral Part of a State?	131
		5.3.4.4.2 (i) Sovereign Wealth Investors Constituted by a Pool of Assets Within a State	133
		5.3.4.4.3 (ii) Sovereign Wealth Investors Established as or Within a Separate Legal Entity Other Than the State Itself	133
		5.3.4.4.4 (iii) Sovereign Wealth Investors Organized as a (Legal) Entity Without a Separate Legal Personality	134

5.4	Dividends (Article 10) and Interest (Article 11)		134
	5.4.1	Introduction	134
	5.4.2	Dividends	135
	5.4.3	Interest	136
	5.4.4	Application to Sovereign Wealth Investors	136
5.5	Capital Gains (Article 13)		137
	5.5.1	Introduction	137
	5.5.2	Application to Sovereign Wealth Investors	137
5.6	Non-discrimination (Article 24)		138
	5.6.1	Introduction	138
	5.6.2	Sovereign Wealth Investors and Article 24(1)	138
	5.6.3	Sovereign Wealth Investors and Article 24(5)	139
5.7	Impact of Tax Treaties on Achieving Neutrality (Efficiency), Equity (Fairness) and International Attractiveness in Relation to Foreign Sovereign Wealth Investors		140
	5.7.1	Neutrality (Efficiency)	143
		5.7.1.1 Capital Export Neutrality	143
		5.7.1.2 Capital Import Neutrality	143
	5.7.2	Equity (Fairness)	145
		5.7.2.1 Inter-taxpayer Equity	145
		5.7.2.2 Inter-nation Equity	148
	5.7.3	International Attractiveness	149
5.8	Conclusions		150

Chapter 6
European Tax Law Aspects of Foreign Sovereign Wealth Investors   155

6.1	Introduction		155
6.2	European Law: A Basic Introduction		156
	6.2.1	The EU and the Internal Market	156
	6.2.2	How the Internal Market Is Achieved	157
		6.2.2.1 Integration	157
		6.2.2.2 Fundamental Freedoms	157
		6.2.2.3 State Aid Rules	158
		6.2.2.4 Directives in the Field of Direct Taxation	159
	6.2.3	The European Economic Area and the Extension of the Internal Market	159
	6.2.4	Code of Conduct for Business Taxation	160
6.3	Freedom of Establishment, Freedom of Capital Movement and Foreign Sovereign Wealth Investors		162
	6.3.1	Introduction	162
	6.3.2	Step (1): Access to the TFEU or EEA Agreement and the Freedom of Establishment and Freedom of Capital Movement	162
		6.3.2.1 Purely Domestic Situations	162

Table of Contents

		6.3.2.2	Freedom of Establishment	163
			6.3.2.2.1 Personal and Territorial Scope	163
			6.3.2.2.2 Material Scope (Acts of Establishment)	163
			6.3.2.2.3 Application to Sovereign Wealth Investors	165
		6.3.2.3	Freedom of Capital Movement	167
			6.3.2.3.1 Personal and Territorial Scope	167
			6.3.2.3.2 Material Scope (Capital Movements)	168
			6.3.2.3.3 Standstill Provision TFEU	170
			6.3.2.3.4 Application to Sovereign Wealth Investors	172
		6.3.2.4	Freedom of Establishment Versus Freedom of Capital Movement: Order of Precedence	174
	6.3.3	Step (2): Comparability		176
		6.3.3.1	Vertical Comparability	177
		6.3.3.2	Horizontal Comparability	181
		6.3.3.3	Application to Sovereign Wealth Investors	184
			6.3.3.3.1 Vertical Comparability	185
			6.3.3.3.2 Horizontal Comparability	190
	6.3.4	Steps (3)–(5): Justification Test		193
		6.3.4.1	Relevant Justification Grounds	193
		6.3.4.2	Need for Effective Fiscal Supervision in Relation to Third States	194
		6.3.4.3	Application to Foreign Sovereign Wealth Investors from Third States	194
6.4	State Aid and Foreign Sovereign Wealth Investors			195
	6.4.1	General Aspects		195
	6.4.2	Constitutive Elements		197
		6.4.2.1	Advantage	197
		6.4.2.2	State Resources	198
		6.4.2.3	Undertaking (and Economic Activity)	198
		6.4.2.4	Selectivity and Justification	202
		6.4.2.5	Effect on Trade and Competition	203
	6.4.3	EC Decision on the Former Dutch Corporate Income Tax Regime for Public Enterprises and the Belgian and French Corporate Income Tax Regime for State-Owned Ports		203
	6.4.4	Could Preferential Tax Treatment Accorded to a Sovereign Wealth Investor Constitute State Aid?		205
		6.4.4.1	Preferential Tax Treatment	205
		6.4.4.2	Foreign Sovereign Wealth Investor as a Direct Beneficiary	205

			6.4.4.2.1	State Aid Recovery and Sovereign Immunity	206
			6.4.4.2.2	Undertaking (and Economic Activity)	206
			6.4.4.2.3	Selectivity and Justification	208
			6.4.4.2.4	Effect on Trade and Competition	211
		6.4.4.3	Indirect Beneficiaries		213
			6.4.4.3.1	External Asset Managers	213
			6.4.4.3.2	Investment Targets	213
		6.4.4.4	Conclusion		214
6.5	Parent-Subsidiary Directive and Interest & Royalties Directive				215
	6.5.1	Parent-Subsidiary Directive			215
		6.5.1.1	Main Features		215
		6.5.1.2	Some Comments Regarding Foreign Sovereign Wealth Investors		216
	6.5.2	Interest & Royalties Directive			216
		6.5.2.1	Main Features		216
		6.5.2.2	Some Comments Regarding Foreign Sovereign Wealth Investors		217
6.6	Impact of European Law on Achieving Neutrality (Efficiency), Equity (Fairness) and International Attractiveness in Relation to Foreign Sovereign Wealth Investors				218
	6.6.1	Neutrality (Efficiency)			220
		6.6.1.1	Capital Export Neutrality		220
		6.6.1.2	Capital Import Neutrality		221
	6.6.2	Equity (Fairness)			222
		6.6.2.1	Inter-taxpayer Equity		222
		6.6.2.2	Inter-nation Equity		224
	6.6.3	International Attractiveness			226
6.7	Conclusions				227

CHAPTER 7
The Framework Applied to The Netherlands 235
7.1	Introduction				235
7.2	Dutch International Tax Policy Considerations				236
7.3	Sovereign Immunity				240
7.4	OECD MTC Based Treaties				240
7.5	European Law				241
	7.5.1	Introduction			241
	7.5.2	Dutch Corporate Income Tax Regime			242
		7.5.2.1	Introduction		242
		7.5.2.2	Public Enterprises		242
		7.5.2.3	Collective Investment Vehicles		244

Table of Contents

			7.5.2.3.1	*Fiscale beleggingsinstelling* (Fiscal Investment Institution)	244
			7.5.2.3.2	*Vrijgestelde beleggingsinstelling* (Tax-Exempt Investment Institution)	245
		7.5.2.4	Pension Funds		246
		7.5.2.5	Not-for-Profit Organizations		246
		7.5.2.6	Application to Foreign Sovereign Wealth Investors and Comparison to Other Investors		247
			7.5.2.6.1	Tax Regime for Public Enterprises	247
			7.5.2.6.2	Tax Regimes for Collective Investment Vehicles	249
			7.5.2.6.3	Tax Regime for Pension Funds	250
			7.5.2.6.4	Not-for-Profit Organizations	250
			7.5.2.6.5	Tax Regime for Regular Corporate Investors	251
			7.5.2.6.6	Tax Regime for Individuals	251
		7.5.2.7	Conclusion		251
	7.5.3	Dutch Dividend Withholding Tax Regime			252
		7.5.3.1	Introduction		252
		7.5.3.2	The Dividend Withholding Tax-Exemption Regime (Article 4 DDWTA 1965)		253
		7.5.3.3	The Dividend Withholding Tax Refund Regime (Articles 10 and 10a DDWTA 1965)		254
			7.5.3.3.1	Entities Which Are Not Subject to Corporate Income Tax	254
			7.5.3.3.2	Legal Persons of Public Law and Legal Persons of Private Law Owned by a Legal Person of Public Law	255
			7.5.3.3.3	Non-resident Individuals and Non-resident Entities Faced with a Higher Dutch Tax Burden	256
		7.5.3.4	Application to Foreign Sovereign Wealth Investors and Comparison to Other Investors		258
		7.5.3.5	Conclusion		262
	7.5.4	Dutch Tax Treaties			264
		7.5.4.1	General		264
		7.5.4.2	Selectivity		265
		7.5.4.3	Conclusion		266
7.6	Conclusions				266

Table of Contents

CHAPTER 8
Summary and Conclusions 269
8.1 Introduction to This Study 269
8.2 Sovereign Wealth Investors 272
8.3 Tax Policy Considerations and Approaches to Taxation of Foreign Sovereign Wealth Investors 273
  8.3.1 Introduction 273
  8.3.2 Neutrality (Efficiency) 274
    8.3.2.1 Capital Export Neutrality 274
    8.3.2.2 Capital Import Neutrality 275
    8.3.2.3 Capital Ownership Neutrality 276
  8.3.3 Equity (Fairness) 277
    8.3.3.1 Inter-taxpayer 277
    8.3.3.2 Inter-nation Equity 278
  8.3.4 International Attractiveness 279
  8.3.5 Conclusion 280
8.4 Sovereign Immunity Principle 282
  8.4.1 Introduction 282
  8.4.2 Main Findings 282
  8.4.3 Conclusion 283
8.5 Tax Treaties 283
  8.5.1 Introduction 283
  8.5.2 Main Findings 284
  8.5.3 Conclusion 286
8.6 European Law 286
  8.6.1 Introduction 286
  8.6.2 Main Findings 287
8.7 The Framework Applied to the Netherlands 292
8.8 Final Conclusion and Final Remarks 293

APPENDIX
Dutch Tax Treaties 297

Bibliography 305

Table of Cases 317

Table of Treaties and Other Instruments 325

Table of National Instruments 329

Miscellaneous 333

Index 339

xvii

List of Abbreviations

ADIA	Abu Dhabi Investment Authority
AIKOM	Association of Italian Knights of the Order of Malta
ATO	Australian Taxation Office
BIT	Bilateral Investment Treaty
CEN	Capital Export Neutrality
CFI	Court of First Instance
CIC	China Investment Corporation
CIN	Capital Import Neutrality
CIVs	Collective Investment Vehicles
CJEU	Court of Justice of the European Union
CON	Capital Ownership Neutrality
DCITA 1969	Dutch Corporate Income Tax Act (1969)
DDWTA 1965	Dutch Dividend Withholding Tax Act (1965)
EC	European Commission
ECHR 1950	European Convention on Human Rights (1950)
ECtHR	European Court of Human Rights
ECSI 1972	European Convention on State Immunity (1972)
EEA	European Economic Area
EFTA	European Free Trade Association
EU	European Union
FBI	*Fiscale beleggingsinstelling*
GAPPs	Generally Accepted Principles and Practices
GPFG	Government Pension Fund Global (Norway)
HRC	UN Human Rights Committee

List of Abbreviations

ICCPR 1966	International Covenant on Civil and Political Rights (1966)
ICJ	International Court of Justice
IFSWFs	International Forum of Sovereign Wealth Funds
ILC	International Law Commission
IMF	International Monetary Fund
IRC	Internal Revenue Code
IWG	International Working Group of Sovereign Wealth Funds
KIA	Kuwait Investment Authority
MENA	Middle East and North Africa
MFN	Most-Favoured-Nation
NBIM	Norges Bank Investment Management
NT	National Treatment
OECD	Organisation for Economic Co-operation and Development
OECD MTC	OECD Model Tax Convention on Income and on Capital
SOEs	State-Owned Enterprises
SPRF	Sovereign Pension Reserve Fund
SSRF	Social Security Reserve Fund
SWE	Sovereign Wealth Enterprise
SWF	Sovereign Wealth Fund
TFEU	Treaty on the Functioning of the European Union
UAE	United Arab Emirates
UK	United Kingdom of Great Britain and Northern Ireland
UN	United Nations
UN MTC	United Nations Model Double Taxation Convention between Developed and Developing Countries
UNCSI 2004	United Nations Convention on Jurisdictional Immunities of States and their Property (2004)
US	United States of America
VAT	Value-added tax
VBI	*Vrijgestelde beleggingsinstelling*
VCLT 1969	Vienna Convention on the Law of Treaties (1969)

Acknowledgements

A dissertation is a 'proof of competence in independently conducting scientific research'.[1] Drawing parallels with successfully completing a first marathon or '*hemelbestorming*'[2] will raise some eyebrows, I presume. Nevertheless, the road towards a completed dissertation somehow reminds me of this. Just like completing these athletic endeavours, finishing a thesis requires endurance, patience, stubbornness, resilience, good planning, sacrifice and being somewhat odd. Both are accompanied by unknown peaks and valleys; the condition of which is continuously determined by their relative magnitude. My road has not been without obstacles, neither in my private life, nor in my working life. I will forever be deeply affected by the (sudden) loss of my beloved father – who I so deeply miss. I know my grandmothers would have been so proud as well. At the same time, I feel strengthened by the support and love of my dearest Lien, my mum and dad, my brother (Jeff), Willem, Huub & Jen, and many others. I have underestimated writing a thesis, being a tax advisor and being a lecturer at the same time. With the help of Loyens & Loeff – for which I am most grateful – this was changed in a formula that has proved successful for me.

Nobody gets to the finish without support. I would therefore like to express some words of gratitude; in particular to Prof. Ton Stevens and Prof. Reinout Kok, for your pleasant supervision and constructive feedback, and for your patience; to Sjaak Janssen, (again) Ton and Prof. Sigrid Hemels, for giving me the opportunity to write this thesis; to Loyens & Loeff, in particular Wil Martens, Marcel Buur, Paul Simonis, François Hoenjet, Bart Rubbens and Rob Cornelisse, for facilitating the process, your trust in me and your patience; to Maarten de Wilde, for the endless conversations, inspiration, insights and stimulating my imagination; to the members of the thesis committee (Prof. Arnaud de Graaf, Prof. Peter Kavelaars en Prof. Daniël Smit), for being critical and for taking this thesis to a higher level; to the other members of the

---

1. Translation from Dutch: 'proeve van bekwaamheid tot het zelfstandig beoefenen van de wetenschap'. Art. 2.1 Promotiereglement 2015 Erasmus Universiteit Rotterdam (version 13 March 2015).
2. The Dutch term '*hemelbestorming*' is derived from *2Doc: Hemelbestormers*, 27 June 2016, EO, NPO 2.

Acknowledgements

plenary committee, for your time and your willingness to discuss my thesis; to Prof. Henk van Arendonk, for sharing your opinion on my thesis; to Prof. Raymond Luja and Anna Gunn, for commenting on the chapter on State aid; to Prof. Ellen Hey, for providing input on my initial analysis regarding sovereign immunity; to Renee Louman, for checking my maths; to Fenneke van Dam, for your assistance; to my family and friends, for your support and encouragement. Special thanks go to Lien, my love, for never having to walk alone.

Richard Snoeij
Rotterdam, February 2018

CHAPTER 1
Introduction*

1.1 SUBJECT

In addressing the purpose of the nation State, political philosophers often refer to the 'supreme good',[3] the 'general good',[4] 'the common good',[5] or the 'common essence'[6] of its citizens. At first sight, these terms seem to share common ground, but, in fact, may be understood differently by political philosophers. Their understanding seems to correlate with the functions they attribute to the State. Some (liberal) philosophers, such as John Locke and Adam Smith, focus on individual citizens. In their view, the State should merely facilitate individual citizens in their strivings for private (economic) interests, as this would serve the general interest.[7] To them, the term common

---

* Materials have been included up to 17 December 2017.
3. Aristotle, *Politics*, trans. H. Rackman, in *Aristotle: in Twenty-Three Volumes*, Vol. XXI, (Cambridge, Massachusetts: Harvard University Press, 1967), p. 3: 'Every state is as we see a sort of partnership, and every partnership is formed with a view to some good (since all the actions of all mankind are done with a view to what they think to be good). It is therefore evident that, while all partnerships aim at some good, the partnership that is the most supreme of all and includes all the others does so most of all, and aims at the most supreme of all goods; and this is the partnership entitled the state, the political association.' Underline added.
4. John Locke, *Two Treatises of Government*, ed. P. Laslett, (Cambridge: Cambridge University Press, 1988), p. 305: 'For *Law*, in its true Notion, is not so much the Limitation as *the direction of a free and intelligent Agent* to his proper Interest, and prescribes no farther than is for the general Good of those under that Law. (...) [T]he end of Law is not to abolish or restrain, but *to preserve and to enlarge Freedom* (...).' Underline added.
5. Cicero, *De Re Publica, De Legibus*, trans. C. Keyes, (Cambridge, Massachusetts: Harvard University Press, 1966), p. 65: 'Well, then, a commonwealth is the property of a people. But a people is not any collection of human beings brought together in any sort of way, but an assemblage of people in large numbers associated in an agreement with respect to justice and a partnership for the common good.' Underline added.
6. Karl Marx, 'On the Jewish Question', ed. D. McLellan, in *Karl Marx: Selected Writings* (Oxford: Oxford University Press, 1977), p. 47.
7. Adam Smith, *The Theory of Moral Sentiments*, (1759, 1799, 6th edn.), ed. D. Rapheal & A. Macfie, (Glasgow Edition, Vol. I), (Oxford: Clarendon Press, 1976), IV, I, 11, pp. 185–186.

good and related terms refer to what is common to each citizen, that is, the individual well-being. In this theory, the function of the State should be limited to protecting the life, freedom and property of each citizen. Other philosophers, such as Karl Marx, focus on the multitude of citizens where the term common good and related terms refer to what is common to the whole people, that is, their collective well-being.[8] In their view, the State should have a far greater power over its citizens and be much more involved in public and private life, as is necessary to achieve the common good.

Either way, the nation State needs resources to strive for the supreme good, the general good, the common good, or the common essence. Traditionally, States collect taxes, issue government bonds, sell available natural resources, etc., to fund public expenditure. More recently, an increasing number of States have entered the market looking to invest resources in domestic and, even more so, foreign assets. They do so to achieve financial objectives, serve a variety of macroeconomic purposes and, as some would argue, to contribute to the common good. Their investments are, more often than not, structured through special purpose investment funds or arrangements, known as sovereign wealth funds ('SWFs'), or investment entities owned by SWFs, known as sovereign wealth enterprises ('SWEs'). The total value of assets under the management of SWFs and SWEs – together referred to as 'sovereign wealth investors' in this study – is currently estimated at US$ 7.6 trillion (February 2018), which is an increase from US$ 5.8 trillion as in March 2012 and US$ 3.9 trillion as in March 2008.[9] This development of States acting as investors, managing the wealth of a nation, and competing in the marketplace with other (private) investors, raises many interesting questions in various fields. This study is concerned with international tax aspects of sovereign wealth investors.

1.2 FOCUS AND PURPOSE

SWFs and their 'local' SWEs[10] are generally not taxed in the State in which they have been set-up (i.e., generally no taxation in their home State). However, in a cross-border context, income (including capital gains) from investments of such sovereign wealth investors may be taxed in the investment recipient State ('the source State'). The more tax a foreign sovereign wealth investor pays in a source State, the smaller the return and revenue available to its home State. Therefore, this study will primarily focus on a source State perspective, but that does not mean that the tax treatment of sovereign wealth investors in their home State cannot be relevant for the international tax analysis of such investors, from a source State perspective. Thus, the home State tax treatment of sovereign wealth investors will also be looked at. The reasons for concentrating on sovereign wealth investors will be explained below.

---

8. Karl Marx, 'On the Jewish Question', ed. D. McLellan, in Karl Marx: Selected Writings (Oxford: Oxford University Press, 1977).
9. SWF Institute, Sovereign Wealth Fund Market Size, available at < http://www.swfinstitute.org/sovereign-wealth-fund-rankings/ >.
10. A 'local' SWE of an SWF is an SWE which has been established in the same State as the SWF which owns the SWE.

Chapter 1: Introduction

In recent years, sovereign wealth investors have established themselves as an important class of investors and will continue to be so.[11] They are widely regarded as a separate group of investors in various fields of law, including international investment law[12] and international tax law,[13] by academics and policymakers. Addressing sovereign wealth investors separately from other investor groups can essentially be traced back to the following developments and distinctive features. First, sovereign wealth investors own and invest extreme amounts of money, and their investment activity increases rapidly. They have increased in both number and size and will continue to look for cross-border investment opportunities in the years to come. Second, sovereign wealth investors are owned, controlled and funded by States. This link has not only raised political and security concerns in source States,[14] but also raises questions as to the scope of the international law doctrine of sovereign immunity. Based on this doctrine, a foreign State, and its entities, can be held immune from the jurisdiction or enforcement power of a source State. A number of source States also apply the doctrine of sovereign immunity to taxation.[15] By its nature, this doctrine cannot apply to other investor groups. In addition, the fact that sovereign wealth investors are owned, controlled and funded by States, means that the home State tax treatment of such investors is based on a different rationale,[16] compared to the tax treatment accorded by home States to other groups of resident investors, such as pension funds and collective investment vehicles ('CIVs').[17] A third reason for addressing sovereign wealth investors separately, may be found in a recent investment trend concerning this group of investors. Whereas sovereign wealth investors traditionally invested as *passive* investors, for example in listed shares or government bonds (portfolio investments), they are increasingly operating as *active* investors by making long-term investments, for example in real estate, infrastructure and private companies (direct investments).[18] This move from traditional asset classes to alternative (less

---

11. A. Sandor, 'Leveraging International Law to Incentivize Value-Added Shareholding: Why Foreign Sovereign Wealth Funds *Still* Matter and How They Can Improve Shareholder Governance' (2015) 46 *Georgetown Journal of International Law* 948, pp. 948–950.
12. For example, F. Bassan (ed.), *Research Handbook on Sovereign Wealth Funds and International Investment Law* (Cheltenham: Edward Elgar Publishing, 2015).
13. For example, *Notitie Fiscaal Verdragsbeleid 2011, Tweede Kamer*, 2010–2011, 25 087, No. 7, p. 33 & p. 76; Joint Committee on Taxation, *Economic and U.S. Income Tax Issues Raised by Sovereign Wealth Fund Investment in the United States* (June, 2008), available at: <http://www.jct.gov/x-49-08.pdf>; M. Kandev, 'Sovereign Wealth Funds: Are They Welcome in Canada?' (2010) 64 *Bulletin for International Taxation* 649; J. Bird-Pollan, 'The Unjustified Subsidy: Sovereign Wealth Funds and the Foreign Sovereign Tax Exemption' (2012) 17 *Fordham Journal of Corporate & Financial Law* 987; R. Snoeij, 'Sovereign Immunity and Source State Taxation of Sovereign Wealth Funds: Is It Time to Re-Evaluate?' (2016) 8 *World Tax Journal* 225.
14. A. De Luca, 'The EU and Member States: FDI, Portfolio Investments, Golden Powers and SWFs', Chapter 7 in: F. Bassan (ed.), *Research Handbook on Sovereign Wealth Funds and International Investment Law* (Cheltenham: Edward Elgar Publishing, 2015).
15. The application of the sovereign immunity principle in tax matters will be discussed in Chapter 4.
16. Discussed in Section 2.10.
17. *See* in more detail, Section 3.2.
18. M. Castelli & F. Scacciavillani, 'SWFs and State Investments: A Preliminary General Overview', Chapter 1 in: F. Bassan (ed.), *Research Handbook on Sovereign Wealth Funds and International Investment Law* (Cheltenham: Edward Elgar Publishing, 2015), pp. 20–22; PwC, *Sovereign*

liquid) assets is, to a large extent, driven by the current economic environment of low-interest rates and slow economic growth.[19]

Given the increasing significance of sovereign wealth investors, and taking into account their distinctive features, there has been surprisingly little research on sovereign wealth investors in a tax policy context. Most of the existing research focused on source taxation of foreign sovereign wealth investors from the perspective of a particular State, notably Australia,[20] Canada,[21] Singapore[22] and the United States ('US'),[23] but not from any Member State of the European Union ('EU Member State'). Of wider relevance are the 2009 proposals of the Organisation for Economic Co-operation and Development ('OECD') Committee on Fiscal Affairs on tax treaty residency of SWFs,[24] as reflected in the 2010 update of the OECD Commentary, and other tax research, focusing on specific tax topics in relation to foreign sovereign wealth investors, such as sovereign immunity (Snoeij, 2016),[25] sovereign immunity in the context of tax treaties (Joseph, 2015),[26] and jurisdictional taxing rights of sovereign wealth investors (Joseph, 2015).[27] This study provides the first comprehensive academic work on foreign sovereign wealth investors in a tax policy context, and focuses on income tax. Its relevance is not limited to a particular source State, nor is it limited to a specific tax topic.

Investors 2020: A growing force (April, 2016). In January 2015, one of China's SWFs even established a separate investment vehicle for making 'direct investments'.
19. *Ibid*.
20. S-A. Joseph, M. Walpole & R. Deutsch, 'Taxation of Sovereign Wealth Funds – A Suggested Approach' (2015) 10 *Journal of the Australasian Tax Teachers Association* 119, available at: < https://www.business.unsw.edu.au/About-Site/Schools-Site/Taxation-Business-Law-Site/Journal%20of%20The%20Australasian%20Tax%20Teachers%20Associati/JATTA-2015_all_articles.pdf >.
21. M. Kandev, 'Sovereign Wealth Funds: Are They Welcome in Canada?' (2010) 64 *Bulletin for International Taxation* 649.
22. S-A. Joseph, 'Taxing Sovereign Wealth Funds Mark II: Looking to Singapore for Inspiration', Australasian Tax Teachers Association Conference Papers, 2016, available at: < https://www.business.unsw.edu.au/About-Site/Schools-Site/Taxation-Business-Law-Site/Documents/Joseph_ATTA-2016-Sally-Joseph.pdf >.
23. Joint Committee on Taxation, *Economic and U.S. Income Tax Issues Raised by Sovereign Wealth Fund Investment in the United States* (June, 2008), JCX-49-08; M. Melone, 'Should the United States Tax Sovereign Wealth Funds?' (2008) 26 *Boston University International Law Journal*, pp. 143 et seq.; V. Fleischer, 'A Theory of Taxing Sovereign Wealth Funds' (2009) 84 *New York University Law Review* 440; V. Fleischer, 'Should We Tax Sovereign Wealth Funds?' (2008) 118 *Yale Law Journal Pocket Part* 93; M. Knoll, 'Taxation and the Competitiveness of Sovereign Wealth Funds: Do Taxes Encourage Sovereign Wealth Funds to Invest in the United States?' (2009) 82 *Southern California Law Review* 703; J. Bird-Pollan, 'The Unjustified Subsidy: Sovereign Wealth Funds and the Foreign Sovereign Tax Exemption' (2012) 17 *Fordham Journal of Corporate & Financial Law* 987.
24. OECD (2009), *Discussion Draft on the Application of Tax Treaties to State-Owned Entities, Including Sovereign Wealth Funds*.
25. R. Snoeij, 'Sovereign Immunity and Source State Taxation of Sovereign Wealth Funds: Is It Time to Re-Evaluate?' (2016) 8 *World Tax Journal* 225.
26. S-A. Joseph, 'Do Tax Treaties Embody Sovereign Immunity? – An Assessment with Regard to Sovereign Wealth Funds' (2015) 69 *Bulletin for International Taxation* 637.
27. S-A. Joseph, 'Jurisdictional Taxing Rights of Sovereign Wealth Funds' (2016) 70 *Bulletin for International Taxation* 146.

Given the increasing significance of sovereign wealth investors and taking into account their distinctive features, source States may wish to introduce new tax policy, or evaluate or reconsider their existing tax policy vis-à-vis foreign sovereign wealth investors. The purpose of this study is to assist source States in doing so, by developing a conceptual framework.

1.3 APPROACH AND FURTHER SCOPING

This study will use two main ingredients to develop the conceptual framework: (i) international tax policy principles and objectives, and (ii) international law.

Basic principles and objectives often underlie a State's international tax policy and its international tax rules design. A State's international tax policy choices, and the underlying basic principles and objectives, may depend on various factors – such as the size and nature of its economy, public interests, societal values, as well as tax policy choices of other States – and may change over time. International tax policy principles and objectives can serve as a useful and important starting point for source States when introducing new tax policy or reconsidering existing tax policy vis-à-vis foreign sovereign wealth investors. This study identifies as today's three main 'substantive' attributes[28] of international tax policy: (i) neutrality (efficiency), (ii) equity (fairness), and (iii) international attractiveness. It will discuss and present the key theoretical implications of these policy principles and objectives for the design of international tax rules, focusing on foreign sovereign wealth investors. This presentation will then be used to measure approaches to source taxation of foreign sovereign wealth investors by their neutrality, equity and international attractiveness. Before being able to do so, it is necessary to consider the taxation of foreign sovereign wealth investors by source States, and how such taxation compares to the taxation of other investor groups, such as CIVs and pension funds. This comparison puts things into perspective and is relevant for the international law analysis, the second main ingredient.

International law may impact the ability of source States to achieve tax policy objectives. Because of the obligations it can impose on a source State in the field of taxation, international law could restrict or limit, to a greater or lesser extent, a source State's sovereign power (i.e., its ability) to implement (or promote) a tax policy principle. So, this study will examine and, sometimes, explore its possible impact on source States' ability to achieve tax policy objectives in relation to foreign sovereign wealth investors.[29] With respect to the international law analyses, this study will consider the (possible) impact of: (1) the sovereign immunity principle, (2) tax treaties, and (3) European law.

---

28. 'Substantive' tax policy principles should be distinguished from 'procedural' tax policy principles. *See* in more detail Section 3.3.
29. In addition, constitutional restrictions on the ability to achieve tax policy objectives may apply in some source States.

Tax treaties form a part of 'traditional' public international law, which governs the relations between sovereign States.[30] In the field of international taxation, relations between sovereign States may also be governed by public international law other than (tax) treaties.[31] The OECD Commentary notes that some States apply the so-called sovereign immunity principle in tax matters.[32] According to this principle of customary international law, one sovereign State is, as a general rule, immune from the jurisdiction and enforcement power of another sovereign State. Some source States grant other States immunity from their taxing power based on the international law concept of sovereign immunity. This study will examine what impact the sovereign immunity principle could have on the ability of source States to achieve tax policy objectives in relation foreign sovereign wealth investors.

Tax treaties govern relations between States, in that these international instruments allocate taxing rights between States, which may allow one State and prevent another from taxing the same income. Like non-tax treaties, tax treaties are generally based on (some form of) reciprocity. Many bilateral tax treaties are based on the *OECD Model Tax Convention on Income and on Capital* ('OECD MTC'), or the *UN Model Double Taxation Convention between Developed and Developing Countries* ('UN MTC'). Both models apply to persons who are 'liable to tax', but also to the State itself and its political subdivisions and local authorities. With respect to tax treaties, and

---

30. In a traditional sense, public international law used to be defined as the body of law governing the relations between States. Under this traditional definition, only States were regarded as the *subjects* of public international law, i.e., only States were considered to have rights and/or obligations under public international law. Although public international law could also be concerned with others than States, such as individuals, they were merely seen as *objects* of international law, in that the burden and/or benefit international law had on/for these *objects* was passed on through the State. Modern public international law has been defined as the body of law that is concerned 'with the conduct of states and of international organizations and with their relations *inter se*, as well as with some of their relations with persons, whether natural or juridical.' Under the modern definition of public international law, States remain the primary *subjects* of public international law, but no longer are they the only ones. Individuals and international organizations are now generally regarded as other examples of *subjects* of public international law. See P. Malanczuk, *Akehurst's Modern Introduction to International Law*, 7th edn., (London: Routledge, 1997), p. 1; *Oppenheim's International Law* ed. by R. Jennings & A. Watts (Vol. I, 9th edn.) (London: Longman, 1992), p. 4 & pp. 16 et seq.
31. As regards the relationship between treaties and domestic law, a distinction can be made between monist systems and dualist systems. Under a 'pure' monistic system, (tax) treaties become a part of domestic law when they are ratified; they do not need to be transformed into domestic law, so that treaty provisions can be directly invoked by individuals and entities, and be directly applied by national courts. On the other hand, under a 'pure' dualistic system, (tax) treaties must be transformed into domestic law by legislative steps before they become a part of the domestic legal order. However, in practice, many constitutions contain both monistic and dualistic features. For example, in some States some treaties need to be implemented into domestic law, while other treaties do not. As regards the relationship between customary international law and domestic law, it is noted that, even in many dualist States, customary international law has domestic legal force, or it is applied by courts directly. *See* L. Wildhaber & S. Breitenmoser, 'The Relationship between Customary International Law and Municipal Law in Western European Countries' (1988) 48 *Zeitschrift für ausländisches öffentliches Recht und Völkerrecht* 163; D. Sloss, 'Domestic Application of Treaties' (2011), available at: <http://digitalcommons.law.scu.edu/facpubs/635>.
32. Para. 52 of the Commentary on Art. 1 of the OECD MTC.

Chapter 1: Introduction

their application to foreign sovereign wealth investors, this study will primarily focus on the OECD and UN MTC, although specific bilateral tax treaties will also be referred to.

From a source State perspective, the European law analysis will only be relevant to the EU Member States and (other) members to the *Agreement on the European Economic Area*[33] ('EEA Agreement'). This study will consider primary European law, notably the fundamental freedoms and State aid rules included in the *Treaty on the Functioning of the European Union* ('TFEU') and the EEA Agreement, which can all apply in (direct) tax matters. An important reason for including the EEA Agreement is that Norway, a member to this agreement, hosts currently the largest sovereign wealth investor in the world in terms of assets under management (US$ 1.032 billion as in February 2018).[34] As regards the fundamental freedoms, it is noted that the freedom of capital movement, rather than the freedom of establishment, potentially has the most relevance in relation to foreign sovereign wealth investors. The first reason for this is that, although sovereign wealth investors increasingly operate as long-term, active investors, they are still predominantly (passive) portfolio investors (to which the free movement of capital has the most relevance). The second reason is that most sovereign wealth investors reside outside the European Union ('EU'). Importantly, the personal and territorial scope of the free movement of capital in the TFEU is not limited to EU Member States; it has universal personal and territorial scope. As a result, the free movement of capital in the TFEU, as opposed to its counterpart in the EEA Agreement, may be relevant in relation to sovereign wealth investors from so-called third countries. Nevertheless, because sovereign wealth investors are increasingly operating as active investors, and may reside inside EU Member States and (other) members to the EEA Agreement, the freedom of establishment will be considered as well. The freedom to provide services is in principle not relevant, because the activities of foreign sovereign wealth investors should already be covered by another freedom, and the activities are normally not provided for remuneration.[35] As regards the State aid rules, the analysis will be a first general analysis in the context of foreign sovereign wealth investors, aimed at identifying potential issues in this complex and rapidly developing area of European law. This study will, furthermore, consider the implications of secondary EU law, notably the Parent-Subsidiary Directive and Interest & Royalties Directive, which can in principle only apply to EU based sovereign wealth investors.

Although the non-discrimination provisions in human rights conventions, most notably the *Convention for the Protection of Human Rights and Fundamental Freedoms* (1950) (better known as the European Convention on Human Rights ('ECHR 1950')) and the United Nations ('UN') *International Covenant on Civil and Political Rights* (1966) ('ICCPR 1966') should also apply to taxation,[36] these provisions currently appear

---

33. *Agreement on the European Economic Area*, Official Journal of the European Union, Vol. 37, L 1, 3 January 1994, p. 3.
34. < http://www.swfinstitute.org/sovereign-wealth-fund-rankings/ >.
35. Article 57 TFEU.
36. According to the European Court of Human Rights ('ECtHR'), Art. 14 of the ECHR 1950 (in conjunction with Art. 1 First Protocol; protection of property) also applies to taxation (*see* ECtHR, 23 October 1990, No. 17/1989/177/233 (*Darby*), Para. 30). Although the UN Human

7

to have rather limited relevance in relation to non-resident taxpayers, including foreign sovereign wealth investors. First, these non-discrimination provisions do not normally seem to be concerned with differences in treatment on the basis of residence.[37] Second, even if these non-discrimination provisions would be concerned with differences in treatment on the basis of residence, in the field of taxation, party states, 'enjoy a wide margin of appreciation in assessing whether and to what extent differences in otherwise similar situations justify a different treatment'.[38] In tax matters, this wide margin of appreciation means that it would normally be easy for party states to justify differences in treatment: (i) between resident and non-resident investors,[39] and (ii) among and between non-resident investors (i.e., no most-favoured-nation ('MNF') treatment).[40] Therefore, the non-discrimination provisions in human rights

---

Rights Committee ('HRC'), the body monitoring the implementation of the ICCPR 1966, has not explicitly held that Art. 26 ICCPR 1966 applies to taxation, support for a confirmative view can be found in *Broeks*, regarding social security, in which the HRC considered that '[a]lthough article 26 requires that legislation should prohibit discrimination, it does not of itself contain any obligation with respect to the matters that may be provided for by legislation. Thus, it does not, for example, require any State to enact legislation to provide for social security. However, when such legislation is adopted in the exercise of a State's power, then such legislation must comply with article 26' (*see* HRC, 9 April 1987, No. 172/1984 (*Broeks*), Para. 12.4). Although Art. 14 of the ECHR 1950 and Art. 26 of the ICCPR 1966 list similar grounds of discrimination, such as sex, race, colour, language and birth, the first non-discrimination provision is limited to the rights and freedoms secured by the ECHR as such, whereas the second provision is more general in character. The optional Twelfth Protocol to the ECHR 1950 provides for a more general prohibition of discrimination, which is much more in line with Art. 26 of the ICCPR 1966; however, many ECHR party states currently have not ratified the Twelfth Protocol. This fact should have no significant impact, though, since all ECHR party states are also party to the ICCPR 1966 and have accepted Art. 26 ICCPR 1966.

37. In this respect, the ECtHR has held that the non-discrimination provision of the ECHR 1950 is only concerned with differences 'having as their basis or reason a personal characteristic ("status") by which persons or a group of persons are distinguishable from each other' (*see* ECtHR, 13 September 2005, No. 42639/04 (*Victor Jones against the UK*), Para. 5). The decision of the UN HRC, the body monitoring the implementation of the ICCPR 1966, in *De Vos* seems to point in the same direction (*see* HRC, 25 July 2005, No. 1192/2003; *see also* HRC, 30 March 1989, No. 273/1988 (*B. d. B. et al. v. The Netherlands*), Para. 6.7). In the author's view, it can be argued that 'residence' as such is not a personal characteristic in the same way that, for example, sex, race, colour, language and birth are personal characteristics. Therefore, foreign sovereign wealth investors would not normally be comparable to resident investors. *See also*, in more general terms, P. Baker, 'Taxation and the European Convention on Human Rights' (2000) 4 *British Tax Review*, pp. 211–377.

38. Regarding Art. 14 of the ECHR 1950, *see* ECtHR, 22 June 1999, No. 46757/99 (*Della Ciaja et al. against Italy*). The limitedly available domestic case law suggests that a wide margin of appreciation should also apply in the context of Art. 26 ICCPR 1966 (*see*, e.g., Dutch Supreme Court, 22 November 2013, No. 13/016222, *BNB* 2014/30; Dutch Supreme Court, 2 March 2007, No. 42.144, *BNB* 2007/240). *See also* R. Attard, 'Discriminatory Taxation and the European Convention on Human Rights', Chapter 9 in: D. Weber & P. Pistone (eds) *Non-Discrimination in Tax Treaties: Selected Issues from a Global Perspective*, IBFD 2016, Online Books IBFD, sec. 9.6.3.

39. P. Baker, 'Taxation and the European Convention on Human Rights' (2000) 4 *British Tax Review*, pp. 211–377.

40. According to the Dutch Court of Appeal, Art. 26 ICCPR 1966 is, in any case, not concerned with differences in treatment between non-resident taxpayers resulting from different bilateral tax treaties (*see Gerechtshof 's-Hertogenbosch*, 12 May 2000, No. 97/0437, *BNB* 2001/426).

Chapter 1: Introduction

conventions currently appear to have rather limited relevance for taxation of foreign sovereign wealth investors.

The same conclusion applies to bilateral investment treaties ('BITs').[41] In general, the non-discrimination provision in BITs comprises at least one of the following two standards: (i) the national treatment ('NT') standard; requiring the source State to accord to non-resident investors treatment which is no less favourable than that accorded to domestic investors in the same or similar circumstances, and (ii) the 'MFN' standard; requiring the source State to treat non-resident investors no less favourably than investors from any third country (in similar circumstances). However, the overwhelming majority of BITs contain full or limited carve-outs with respect to direct taxes.[42] The most common practice is to exclude MFN standards with respect to tax benefits accorded to domestic investors or third country investors on the basis of bilateral tax treaties or other international tax arrangements, such as European tax directives.[43] Such carve-outs also very regularly apply to the NT standard.[44] Several more recent BITs even contain a general exception to taxation, thus also in respect of tax benefits accorded to domestic investors or third country investors on the basis of domestic legislation of the source State.[45] BITs may have implications for source State taxation of non-residents, including foreign sovereign wealth investors, in individual cases where the NT standard applies in tax matters, but even then it may still be unclear whether non-resident taxpayers are in the same or similar circumstances as resident taxpayers. Overall, the implications of BITs for direct taxation of non-residents, including foreign sovereign wealth investors, appear to be rather limited as well.[46]

For the above-mentioned reasons, human rights conventions and BITs will not be further considered in this study, although they may have an impact in very specific situations.

The approach of measuring a source State's tax treatment of foreign sovereign wealth investors against the three main 'substantive' attributes of international tax policy (i.e., (i) neutrality, (ii) equity, and (iii) international attractiveness), and examining the possible impact international law could have on achieving tax policy objectives based on these attributes, will produce the conceptual framework.

---

41. A. Kardachaki, 'Tax Aspects of International Non-Tax Agreements' (2012–2013), *IFA Research Paper*. United Nations Conference on Trade and Development, *Bilateral Investment Treaties 1995–2006: Trends in Investment Rulemaking* (UN, 2007), pp. 42–43 & pp. 81–83, available at <http://unctad.org/en/docs/iteiia20065_en.pdf>.
42. *Ibid.*
43. *Ibid.*
44. *Ibid. See*, e.g., the Dutch Model BIT (2004).
45. *Ibid.*
46. C. Hoyos Jiménez, 'Non-Discrimination on the Basis of Nationality in IIAs: A Latin American Tax Perspective', Chapter 2 in: D. Weber & P. Pistone (eds) *Non-Discrimination in Tax Treaties: Selected Issues from a Global Perspective*, IBFD 2016, Online Books IBFD, sec. 2.5.

1.4 OUTLINE OF THE STUDY

The central question in this study is as follows:

> What impact, if any, does international law have on source States' ability to achieve (or promote) tax policy objectives in relation to foreign sovereign wealth investors?

This question will be answered by discussing the following five sub-questions:

(1) Who are sovereign wealth investors, why do they exist, what do they do, what (legal) forms can they take, and what is their home State tax status?

The first sub-question will be discussed in Chapter 2. The purpose of this chapter is to come to a working definition of SWFs and SWEs that will be used throughout this study, as well as for the reader to get a better understanding of sovereign wealth investors. Chapter 2 is based on information derived from a variety of organizations, such as the OECD, the International Monetary Fund ('IMF'), the US Department of Treasury, an international working group of SWFs and the SWF Institute, as well as information derived from literature and information made available by sovereign wealth investors themselves.

(2) How do source States tax foreign sovereign wealth investors (in comparison to other investor groups), and how does such taxation relate to generally accepted attributes of international tax policy?

The second sub-question will be discussed in Chapter 3. The main purpose of this chapter is to discuss tax policy considerations and to measure source States' tax treatment of foreign sovereign wealth investors against generally accepted attributes of international tax policy. Chapter 3 will first consider the approaches of source States to taxation of foreign sovereign wealth investors, and how they are treated in comparison to other investors. Based on a review of State practice and literature, Chapter 3 will then identify as today's three main 'substantive' attributes of international tax policy: (i) neutrality (efficiency), (ii) equity (fairness), and (iii) international attractiveness. This will be followed by a discussion and presentation of the main theoretical implications of these policy principles and objectives for the design of international tax rules, which will enable to measure approaches to source taxation of foreign sovereign wealth investors by their neutrality, equity and international attractiveness.

(3) What impact, if any, does the sovereign immunity principle have on source States' ability to achieve tax policy objectives in relation to foreign sovereign wealth investors?

The third sub-question will be examined in Chapter 4. This chapter will deal with the sovereign immunity principle and will focus on four areas in which the sovereign immunity principle can manifest itself: (1) immunity from the jurisdiction of the courts of a State in civil proceedings, (2) immunity from taxation, (3) immunity from the jurisdiction of the courts of a State in tax proceedings, and (4) immunity from measures of constraint (enforcement power). The analysis in Chapter 4 is primarily based on multilateral instruments, such as the *United Nations Convention on Jurisdictional*

Chapter 1: Introduction

Immunities of States and Their Property (2004) ('UNCSI 2004'), the preparatory work of the International Law Commission ('ILC') and national practice of States, including (tax) legislation, (tax) cases and administrative (tax) practice of States in the field of sovereign immunity.

(4) What impact, if any, do tax treaties (in particular those based on the OECD and UN Model) have on source States' ability to achieve tax policy objectives in relation to foreign sovereign wealth investors?

The fourth sub-question will be discussed in Chapter 5. This chapter will focus on OECD and UN MTC based treaties, in particular on the resident article (Article 4), the dividend and interest article (Articles 10 and 11), the capital gains article (Article 13) and the non-discrimination article (Article 24). Chapter 5 is based on an analysis of the Commentaries on both models, case law, literature and other publicly available information.

(5) What impact, if any, does European law have on source States' ability to achieve tax policy objectives in relation to foreign sovereign wealth investors?

The fifth, and final, sub-question will be discussed in Chapter 6. Chapter 6 will consider primary European law, notably the fundamental freedoms and State aid rules included in the TFEU and the EEA Agreement, as well as secondary EU law, notably the Parent-Subsidiary Directive and Interest & Royalties Directive. As explained, with respect to the fundamental freedoms, the focus will be on the freedom of capital movement and the freedom of establishment. The comparability analysis applied to foreign sovereign wealth investors, which is relevant under the fundamental freedoms as well as the State aid rules, lies at the heart of this chapter. Are foreign sovereign wealth investors objectively comparable to other investors, if any at all? It is also examined whether existing justification grounds should apply any differently in relation to foreign sovereign wealth investors. It will then provide a first general analysis of the application of the State aid rules in the context of foreign sovereign wealth investors, aimed at identifying potential issues in this complex and rapidly developing area of European law. Finally, Chapter 6 will consider the implications of secondary EU law, notably the Parent-Subsidiary Directive and Interest & Royalties Directive, which can in principle only apply to EU based sovereign wealth investors. Chapter 6 builds on existing European case law and connects with other fields, such as sovereign immunity.

Chapters 3–6 together constitute the conceptual framework. In Chapter 7, the framework will be applied to the Netherlands, as an illustration. By giving an overview of selected tax treaties concluded between the Netherlands and States that are home to sovereign wealth investors, the Appendix provides relevant background information for the analysis in Chapter 7. The Netherlands has been selected for several reasons. First, the primacy of Dutch international tax policy in relation to sovereign wealth investors is international attractiveness. This policy has found its way into Dutch tax treaties; the Netherlands has concluded several tax treaties containing favourable provisions for sovereign wealth investors. Second, the Netherlands is an OECD Member State, as well as an EU Member State, which means that the international law analysis will have to be considered in full. Third, the application of the framework requires in-depth knowledge of a tax system and a certain level of information. The author is familiar with Dutch tax law, whereas political decision-making in the Netherlands happens in a transparent way, and tax policy information, legislative information and other relevant information is publicly available.

Chapter 8 will provide a summary and set out the main conclusions of this study.

CHAPTER 2
Sovereign Wealth Investors

2.1 INTRODUCTION

With the value of assets under management estimated as high as US$ 7.6 trillion (February 2018),[47] SWFs and their SWEs (i.e., together, sovereign wealth investors) are among the important players in the international financial markets. Sovereign wealth investors have been around for decades, but their rapid increase in both number and size since 2000[48] (due to the commodity boom and the rise of the emerging markets), and their billion dollar investments in troubled companies during the beginning of the (most recent) credit crisis,[49] has attracted growing and wide attention. Sovereign wealth investors can typically be found in emerging and developing countries that have shifted from net foreign debt to net foreign asset positions.[50] Who are SWFs and SWEs, and what particularities make them a topic of much debate?

The purpose of this chapter is twofold. Its first purpose is to come to a working definition of SWFs and SWEs, to use throughout this study. The second purpose is to get a better understanding of these sovereign wealth investors. Who are they? Why do they exist? What do they do? What (legal) forms do they take? How can their

---

47. < http://www.swfinstitute.org/sovereign-wealth-fund-rankings/ >.
48. J. Santiso, 'Sovereign Development Funds: Key Financial Actors of the Shifting Wealth of Nations' (2008), *OECD Emerging Markets Network Working Paper*, p. 7, available at: < http://www.oecd.org/dev/41944381.pdf >. This includes the establishment of (a) (relatively large in size) SWF(s) by China (in 2007) and Russia (in 2008). *See also* M. Maslakovic, 'Sovereign Wealth Funds 2010' (2010) *International Financial Services London Research*, p. 2; African Development Bank, 'The Boom in African Sovereign Wealth Funds' (2013), available at: < http://www.afdb.org >.
49. M. Maslakovic, 'Sovereign Wealth Funds 2010' (2010) *International Financial Services London Research*, p. 2.
50. J. Santiso, 'Sovereign Development Funds: Key Financial Actors of the Shifting Wealth of Nations' (2008), *OECD Emerging Markets Network Working Paper*, p. 4 & p. 11.

governance structure look like? What is their home State tax status? As SWEs are merely a component of some SWFs, this chapter will mainly focus on SWFs.[51]

2.2 THE SANTIAGO PRINCIPLES

2.2.1 What Are the Santiago Principles?

In October 2008, at its third meeting in Santiago, Chile, the International Working Group of Sovereign Wealth Funds ('IWG') agreed on a voluntary set of Generally Accepted Principles and Practices ('GAPPs') for SWFs (but not for SWEs), known as the 'Santiago Principles'.[52] The IWG was initiated by the IMF and established during a meeting held at the headquarters of the IMF in Washington D.C. from 30 April – 1 May 2008[53] between representatives of twenty-six IMF member countries with SWFs,[54] investment recipient States, the OECD, and the European Commission ('EC'). The Santiago Principles are a response to concerns raised by investment recipient States about investment objectives of SWFs. It was argued that SWFs, being State-owned investment funds, might (also) pursue political objectives rather than purely economic and financial ones.[55] According to the IWG, the Santiago Principles should take away this concern:

> Publication of the GAPP should help improve understanding of SWFs as economically and financially oriented entities in both the home and recipient countries.

---

51. < http://www.swfinstitute.org/statistics-research/sovereign-wealth-enterprise-swe/ >.
52. International Working Group of Sovereign Wealth Funds, *Sovereign Wealth Funds: Generally Accepted Principles and Practices 'Santiago Principles'* (October, 2008), available at: < http://www.ecgi.org/codes/documents/iwg_santiago_principles_oct2008_en.pdf >.
53. 'International Working Group of Sovereign Wealth Funds is Established to Facilitate Work on Voluntary Principles' (May, 2008), Press Release No. 08/97.
54. The twenty-six IMF member countries were: Australia, Azerbaijan, Bahrain, Botswana, Canada, Chile, China, Equatorial Guinea, Islamic Republic of Iran, Ireland, South Korea, Kuwait, Libya, Mexico, New Zealand, Norway, Qatar, Russia, Singapore, Timor-Leste, Trinidad and Tobago, the United Arab Emirates and the US, with Oman, Saudi Arabia and Vietnam as permanent observers.
55. The OECD's Investment Committee Report, 'Sovereign Wealth Funds and Recipient Country Policies' (4 April 2008), p. 4 more specifically states that SWFs: '(...) can raise concerns with respect to foreign government control or access to defence related technologies – for example, that such investments could provide a channel for the acquisition of dual-use technologies for military purposes by the acquiring country or for denying technology or other assets critical for national defence to the recipient government itself, or for aiding the intelligence capabilities of a foreign country that is hostile to the host country'. *See also* Joint Committee on Taxation, *Economic and U.S. Income Tax Issues Raised by Sovereign Wealth Fund Investment in the United States* (June, 2008), JCX-49-08, p. 1 & p. 30; D. Markheim, 'Sovereign Wealth Funds: New Voluntary Principles a Step in the Right Direction' (2008), The Heritage Foundation, WebMemo No. 2175, p. 1; OECD, 'Foreign Government-Controlled Investors and Recipient Country Investment Policy: A Scoping Paper' (2009), p. 6, available at: < https://www.oecd.org/daf/inv/investment-policy/42022469.pdf >.

This understanding aims to contribute to the stability of the global financial system, reduce protectionist pressures, and help maintain an open and stable investment climate.[56]

The GAPPs, twenty-four in total, are broadly divided into the following parts: (i) the legal framework of SWFs, their objectives and macroeconomic linkages, (ii) the institutional framework of SWFs and their governance structure, and (iii) the investment and risk management framework of SWFs. The Santiago Principles as such do not deal with tax.

2.2.2 International Forum of Sovereign Wealth Funds

The IWG was only established to draft the Santiago principles and has been replaced by the International Forum of Sovereign Wealth Funds ('IFSWFs'), a voluntary group of SWFs. The IWG recognized that the Santiago Principles could benefit from a continuing exchange of ideas and views among SWFs themselves and with others,[57] and, therefore, agreed to explore the possibilities of establishing a standing group of SWFs.[58] On 6 April 2009, the IWG reached consensus in Kuwait City to establish the IFSWFs.[59] IFSWFs' purpose is to 'meet, exchange views on issues of common interest, and facilitate an understanding of the Santiago Principles and SWF activities'.[60]

---

56. International Working Group of Sovereign Wealth Funds, *Sovereign Wealth Funds: Generally Accepted Principles and Practices 'Santiago Principles'* (October, 2008), p. 4.
57. Ibid., p. 6.
58. Communiqué of the International Monetary and Financial Committee of the Board of Governors of the International Monetary Fund (2008), Para. 8.
59. International Working Group of Sovereign Wealth Funds, '"Kuwait Declaration": Establishment of the International Forum of Sovereign Wealth Funds' (April, 2009). Its current members are: Fundo Soberano de Angola, The Future Fund (Australia), State Oil Fund of the Republic of Azerbaijan, The Future Generations Reserve Fund (Bahrain), The Pula Fund (Botswana), Alberta Heritage Savings Trust Fund (Canada), Economic and Social Stabilization, and Pension Reserve Funds (Chile), China Investment Corporation, Fund for Future Generations (Equatorial Guinea), National Development Fund of Iran, Ireland Strategic Investment Fund, JSC National Investment Corporation of the National Bank of Kazakhstan, JSC Samruk-Kazyna (Kazakhstan), Korea Investment Corporation, Kuwait Investment Authority, Libyan Investment Authority, Khazanah Nasional Berhad (Malaysia), Budgetary Income Stabilization Fund (Mexico), New Zealand Superannuation Fund, Government Pension Fund Global (Norway), State General Reserve Fund (Oman), Palestine Investment Fund, Fondo de Ahorro de Panamá, Qatar Investment Authority, Russian Direct Investment Fund, Agaciro Development Fund (Rwanda), Government of Singapore Investment Corporation Pte. Ltd. and Temasek Holdings (Private) Limited (Singapore), Timor-Leste Petroleum Fund, The Heritage and Stabilization Fund (Trinidad & Tobago), Turkiye Wealth Fund (Turkey), Abu Dhabi Investment Authority (United Arab Emirates) and Alaska Permanent Fund Corporation (the US).
60. Ibid.

2.3 DEFINITIONS AND CLASSIFICATION OF SWFs

2.3.1 Introduction[61]

Although the roots of the oldest SWF, today known as the Kuwait Investment Authority ('KIA'), traces back to 1953,[62] the term SWF was introduced only as recently as 2005.[63] It has been said that no universally agreed definition of SWFs exists.[64] The term SWF can have a different meaning to different persons. Illustrative in this respect is an exchange between Henry Paulson, US Treasury Secretary, and the Prime Minister of Russia, Vladimir Putin, during a meeting in Russia in 2008. Paulson told Putin he had had a productive discussion with the Russian Finance Minister about Russia's SWF, to which Putin replied, '[s]ince we do not have a sovereign wealth fund yet, you are confusing us with someone else'. Paulson responded by saying '[w]e can discuss what you have called the "various funds" but we very much welcome your investment'.[65]

Numerous attempts have been made to define and classify SWFs, some of which are discussed below. Classification of SWFs can be helpful in, for example, determining an SWF's risk profile and (interrelated to this) the composition of its portfolio.

2.3.2 US Department of Treasury

2.3.2.1 Definition

In June 2007, the US Department of Treasury described an SWF as:

> a government investment vehicle which is funded by foreign exchange assets, and which manages those assets separately from the official reserves of the monetary authorities (the Central Bank and reserve-related functions of the Finance Ministry). SWF managers typically have a higher risk tolerance and higher expected return than traditional official reserve managers.[66]

---

61. Some of the definitions discussed in this chapter refer to the government (or Ministry of Finance) as owner of the SWFs. This is not always correct from a legal perspective, since governments (or Ministry of Finance) do not always have legal personality, in which case the State is the owner in a legal sense. Nevertheless, the terms State and government (as representative of the State) are used interchangeably.
62. R. Kimmitt, 'Public Footprints in Private Markets: Sovereign Wealth Funds and the World Economy' (2008) 87 *Foreign Affairs* 119.
63. The term SWF was introduced by Rozanov. A. Rozanov, 'Who Holds the Wealth of Nations?' (2005) 15 *Central Banking Journal* 52.
64. Joint Committee on Taxation, *Economic and U.S. Income Tax Issues Raised by Sovereign Wealth Fund Investment in the United States* (June, 2008), JCX-49-08, p. 22; R. Beck & M. Fidora, 'The Impact of Sovereign Wealth Funds on Global Financial Markets' (2008), *ECB Occasional Paper No. 91*, p. 6, available at: <https://www.ecb.europa.eu/pub/pdf/scpops/ecbocp91.pdf>; A. Monk, 'Recasting the Sovereign Wealth Fund Debate: Trust, Legitimacy, and Governance' (2009) 14 *New Political Economy* 451, p. 454.
65. Derived from A. Monk, 'Recasting the Sovereign Wealth Fund Debate: Trust, Legitimacy, and Governance' (2009) 14 *New Political Economy* 451, p. 454.
66. US Department of the Treasury, Office of International Affairs, *Semiannual Report on International Economic and Exchange Rate Policies* (June, 2007), Appendix 3: Sovereign Wealth Funds.

2.3.2.2 Classification

In classifying SWFs, the US Department of Treasury distinguished between SWFs by reference to the source of funding.[67] Under this approach, SWFs are grouped into commodity funds and non-commodity funds. The first group of funds are established through transfers of receipts resulting from (taxes on) commodity export(er)s (e.g., Norway's Government Pension Fund Global ('GPFG') and various Middle Eastern SWFs), whilst the second group of funds are typically established through transfers of foreign exchange reserves generated by trade surpluses (most prominently, the China Investment Corporation ('CIC')).

2.3.3 State Street[68]

2.3.3.1 Definition

As an alternative to the previous definition, State Street (in 2008) defined SWFs by exclusion. According to State Street, SWFs are:

> sovereign-owned asset pools that are neither traditional public pension funds nor traditional reserve assets supporting national currencies.[69]

Under this definition, foreign exchange reserves held by the monetary authorities/central banks for traditional balance of payments and/or monetary policy purposes cannot be viewed as SWFs. This is different to the extent foreign exchange reserves exceed an amount that is reasonably required for such purposes.[70]

2.3.3.2 Classification

In classifying SWFs, State Street distinguishes between SWFs by reference to their liability.[71] Under this approach, four types of SWFs are distinguished:

---

67. US Department of the Treasury, Office of International Affairs, *Semiannual Report on International Economic and Exchange Rate Policies* (June, 2007), Appendix 3: Sovereign Wealth Funds. Similarly, see R. Kimmitt, 'Public Footprints in Private Markets: Sovereign Wealth Funds and the World Economy' (2008) 87 *Foreign Affairs* 119, p. 120. See also R. Gilson & C. Milhaupt, 'Sovereign Wealth Funds and Corporate Governance: A Minimalist Response to the New Mercantilism' (2008) 60 *Stanford Law Review* 1345, pp. 1354–1355; H. Reisen, 'How to Spend It: Commodity and Non-Commodity Sovereign Wealth Funds' (2008), *OECD Development Centre Policy Brief No. 38*.
68. State Street is the second oldest financial services institution in the US and offers custodian and asset management services, investment management services and investment research and trading services.
69. J. Nugée, 'The Growing Role of Sovereign Wealth Funds', Chapter 2 in: State Street, *Sovereign Wealth Funds: Assessing the Impact* (2008), Vol. III, Issue 2, p. 5.
70. Ibid.
71. A. Rozanov, 'A Liability-Based Approach to Sovereign Wealth', Chapter 3 in: State Street, *Sovereign Wealth Funds: Assessing the Impact* (2008), Vol. III, Issue 2, pp. 17–18.

(1) Contingent liability funds

> Contingent liability funds are stabilization funds set-up by commodity-rich countries to cover for liabilities that may arise from fluctuations of commodity prices.

(2) Fixed liability funds

> Fixed liability funds are established to meet a country's future liabilities that will crystallize in, for example, twenty to thirty years' time. The liability relates to a projected shortfall in the public pension system.

(3) Mixed liability funds

> Mixed liability funds have, on the one hand, a fixed obligation to make payments into the budget (i.e., fixed liability), whilst, on the other hand, these funds have no fixed termination date (i.e., they exist in perpetuity).

(4) Open-ended liability funds

> Unlike contingent liability funds, fixed liability funds and mixed liability funds, open-ended liability funds have no readily identifiable or contractually defined liabilities.

2.3.4 The IWG and the IMF

2.3.4.1 *Definition*

The (descriptive) definition provided by the IWG, which was also adopted in the 2010 update of the OECD MTC Commentary,[72] reads as follows:

> SWFs are defined as special purpose investment funds or arrangements, owned by the general government. Created by the general government for macroeconomic purposes, SWFs hold, manage, or administer assets to achieve financial objectives, and employ a set of investment strategies which include investing in foreign financial assets. The SWFs are commonly established out of balance of payments surpluses, official foreign currency operations, the proceeds of privatizations, fiscal surpluses, and/or receipts resulting from commodity exports.

According to the IWG, the funding of SWFs with receipts resulting from commodity exports, on the one hand, and the funding of SWFs with balance of payments surpluses, official foreign currency operations, the proceeds of privatizations and fiscal

---

72. Paragraph 8.5 of the Commentary on Art. 4 of the OECD MTC.

Chapter 2: Sovereign Wealth Investors

surpluses (together referred to as 'excess reserves'), on the other hand, reflects the distinction between the traditional and the more recent background to the creation of SWFs.[73]

The IWG discusses three key elements that, in their common view, define an SWF:[74]

i. Ownership: the ownership of the fund or arrangement is in the hands of the general government, which encompasses both the central government and governments at the sub-national level. From a legal perspective, the fund or arrangement can be owned by the State, its government (as a representative of the State) or the Ministry of Finance (as a direct representative of the government), while it is also possible that the arrangement is owned by a central bank.
ii. Investments: investments by the fund or arrangement include investments in foreign financial assets. Funds or arrangements that invest in domestic assets only, cannot be regarded as SWFs.
iii. Purposes and objectives: the fund or arrangement has been established for macroeconomic purposes and pursues financial objectives. As the liabilities of the fund or arrangement are only broadly defined, SWFs are allowed to apply a wide range of investment strategies. In this respect, assets solely held by central banks for traditional balance of payments purposes/monetary policy purposes, cannot be viewed as SWFs, as SWFs serve a different purpose. Assets held by central banks for other purposes than traditional balance of payments/monetary policy purposes, can constitute an SWF.

In the view of the IWG, its definition further excludes: (i) operations of State-owned enterprises ('SOEs') in the traditional sense,[75] (ii) government-employee pension funds, and (iii) assets managed for the benefit of individuals.

2.3.4.2 Classification

In classifying SWFs, the IMF distinguishes between SWFs by reference to their objective. On that basis, five types of SWFs are distinguished:[76]

---

73. International Working Group of Sovereign Wealth Funds, *Sovereign Wealth Funds: Generally Accepted Principles and Practices 'Santiago Principles'* (October, 2008), Part III, Appendix I. Defining Sovereign Wealth Funds, p. 27.
74. *Ibid.*
75. *See* the definition of SOEs as used by the OECD in 'Foreign Government-Controlled Investors and Recipient Country Investment Policy: A Scoping Paper' (2009), p. 6, which reads as follows: '[t]he term "SOEs" refers to enterprises where the state has significant control, through full, majority, or significant minority ownership. State-Owned Enterprises are often prevalent in utilities and infrastructure industries, such as energy, transport and telecommunication, whose performance is of great importance to broad segments of the population and to other parts of the business sector. The rationale for state ownership of commercial enterprises has varied among countries and industries and has typically comprised a mix of social, economic and strategic interests'.
76. International Monetary Fund, *Global Financial Stability Report: Financial Market Turbulence: Causes, Consequences, and Policies* (October, 2007), Annex 1, pp. 46–47; International Monetary Fund, Monetary and Capital Markets Policy Development and Review Departments, 'Sovereign Wealth Funds – A Work Agenda' (29 February 2008), p. 5.

(1) Stabilization funds

>The primary objective of stabilization funds is to guard the budget and economy against the volatility of commodity prices and the (often highly) discontinuity of commodity quantities.[77] Hence, these funds are typically commodity funded. As stabilization funds typically have a short-term or uncertain investment horizon, their portfolio intends to be dominated by cash and fixed income assets,[78] such as government securities.[79]

(2) Savings funds

>The primary objective of savings funds is to share wealth across generations by converting non-renewable assets (e.g., oil or proceeds of privatizations) into a diversified portfolio of international (financial) assets from which future income streams can be derived. Investment income from non-renewable assets abroad also mitigates the effects of the so-called Dutch disease.[80] As savings funds typically have a long-term investment horizon, their assets are more likely to consist of equity assets[81] and alternative assets, such as real estate and infrastructure.

---

77. U. Das, Y. Lu, C. Mulder & A. Sy, 'Setting Up a Sovereign Wealth Fund: Some Policy and Operational Considerations' (2009), *IMF Working Paper No. 09/179*, p. 9, available at: < https://www.imf.org/external/pubs/ft/wp/2009/wp09179.pdf >.
78. P. Kunzel, Y. Lu, I. Petrova & J. Pihlman, 'Investment Objectives of Sovereign Wealth Funds – A Shifting Paradigm' (2011), *IMF Working Paper No. 11/19*, p. 7, available at: < https://www.imf.org/en/Publications/WP/Issues/2016/12/31/Investment-Objectives-of-Sovereign-Wealth-Funds-A-Shifting-Paradigm-24598 >.
79. A. Al-Hassan et al., 'Sovereign Wealth Funds: Aspects of Governance Structures and Investment Management' (2013), *IMF Working Paper No. 13/231*, p. 5, available at: < https://www.imf.org/en/Publications/WP/Issues/2016/12/31/Sovereign-Wealth-Funds-Aspects-of-Governance-Structures-and-Investment-Management-41046 >.
80. 'Dutch disease' refers to the situation where the increased supply of foreign currency or an increased domestic aggregated demand due to, for example, a boom in the commodity sector, results in an appreciation in the real exchange rate. In such cases, a country's export competitiveness is weakened, which may affect long-term growth. This phenomenon occurred in the Netherlands when large natural gas deposits were discovered in the North Sea in the 1960s. These potential effects can be mitigated by investing in foreign currency denominated (financial) assets. C. Ebrahim-zadeh, 'Dutch Disease: Too Much Wealth Managed Unwisely' (2003) 40 *Finance & Development*, International Monetary Fund, available at: < http://www.imf.org/external/pubs/ft/fandd/2003/03/ebra.htm >.
81. P. Kunzel, Y. Lu, I. Petrova, & J. Pihlman, 'Investment Objectives of Sovereign Wealth Funds – A Shifting Paradigm' (2011), *IMF Working Paper No. 11/19*, who write on p. 5 that: '[t]he traditional [strategic asset allocation] literature suggests that, on longer horizons, equities are less volatile than short-term instruments because of the reinvestment risks associated with short-term investments. In addition, historical data suggest a fairly consistent equity return premium over longer horizons. Hence, a larger share in equities for investors with long investment horizons is appropriate'.

(3) Reserve investment corporations

Reserve investment corporations aim to increase returns on reserve assets.[82] As reserve investment corporations can be called upon in case of balance of payment deficits, a certain portion of its portfolio will be held in liquid assets.[83]

(4) Development funds

Development funds typically aim at funding '(...) socio-economic projects or promote industrial policies that might raise a country's potential output growth'.[84]

(5) Contingent pension reserve funds

Contingent pension reserve funds aim to provide for the government's contingent unspecified future pension liabilities. These higher liabilities are often the result of pay-as-you-go pension plans.[85] Importantly, contingent pension reserve funds are not funded by individual pension contributions.

In relation to public pension reserve funds, a distinction is (sometimes) made between social security reserve funds ('SSRFs'), which are set-up as part of the overall social security system, and sovereign pension reserve funds ('SPRFs'), which are directly established and owned by the government apart from the social security system.[86] SSRFs are most likely regarded as the type of government-employee pension funds that should not qualify as SWFs according to the definition of the IWG. Because SSRFs are predominantly funded by mandatory individual (related) contributions

---

82. The IMF defines reserve assets as: '[...] those external assets that are readily available to and controlled by monetary authorities for meeting balance of payments financing needs, for intervention in exchange markets to affect the currency exchange rate, and for other related purposes (such as maintaining confidence in the currency and the economy, and serving as a basis for foreign borrowing). Reserve assets must be foreign currency assets and assets that actually exist'. See International Monetary Fund, *Balance of Payments and International Investment Position Management*, 6th edn., (Washington D.C.: International Monetary Fund, 2009), Chapter 6, p. 111.
83. P. Kunzel, Y. Lu, I. Petrova & J. Pihlman, 'Investment Objectives of Sovereign Wealth Funds – A Shifting Paradigm' (2011), *IMF Working Paper 11/19*, p. 3.
84. International Monetary Fund, Monetary and Capital Markets Policy Development and Review Departments, 'Sovereign Wealth Funds – A Work Agenda' (29 February 2008), p. 5.
85. Pay-as-you-go pension schemes are unfunded pension arrangements meaning that pension payments are funded by the employer or another sponsor as and when they are paid (i.e., paid on a current disbursement basis).
86. A. Blundell-Wignall, Y. Hu & J. Yermo, 'Sovereign Wealth and Pension Fund Issue' (2008), *OECD Working Papers on Insurance and Private Pensions No. 14*, pp. 4–5, available at: <http://www.oecd.org/finance/private-pensions/40345767.pdf>; J. Yermo, 'Governance and Investment of Public Pension Reserve Funds in Selected OECD Countries' (2008), *OECD Working Papers on Insurance and Private Pensions*, No. 15, p. 3 & p. 5, available at: <http://www.oecd.org/finance/private-pensions/40194872.pdf>.

over current payouts in return for individual entitlements, it can be argued that such pension funds are beneficially owned by individuals and serve individual economic purposes, rather than macroeconomic purposes. On the other hand, SPRFs are most likely regarded as SWFs according to the definition of the IWG, because they are set-up and funded by government-owned funds to cover for expected future deficits of the social security system as a result of an ageing population. Different from SSRFs, individuals have no specified entitlement to payments from SPRFs. Examples of SPRFs are Australia's Future Fund[87] and the New Zealand Superannuation Fund.[88]

These objectives of SWFs can be multiple, overlapping or changing over time. For instance, SWFs that have originally been established for short-term stabilization purposes, may also pursue medium- to long-term savings objectives, due to an (ever) increasing amount of accumulated reserves.

2.3.5 Other Attempts

In literature as well, attempts have been made to define SWFs. For instance, in December 2009, Monk suggested an alternative definition of SWFs on the basis of three commonalities this author identifies among SWFs:[89]

(i) Ownership: ownership and, to a varying degree, (direct or indirect) control of the fund lies with the government, which includes both central and sub-national government.
(ii) Liabilities: in the view of this author, SWFs can have intra-governmental liabilities only (i.e., SWFs can only owe money to other arms of the same government, such as the Ministry of Finance). As SWFs have no external creditors, the entitlement to their assets rests with the government only.
(iii) Beneficiary: the beneficiary of a SWF is '(...) either the government itself, the country's citizenry in abstract, the tax payer generally or is simply left unidentified'.[90] This means that management of SWFs is based on the interest and objectives of the government only.

These three commonalities bring Monk to the following definition:

> SWFs are government-owned and controlled (directly or indirectly) investment funds that have no outside beneficiaries or liabilities (beyond the government or

---

87. <http://www.futurefund.gov.au/about-us>.
88. <https://www.nzsuperfund.co.nz/nz-super-fund-explained/purpose-and-mandate>.
89. A. Monk, 'Recasting the Sovereign Wealth Fund Debate: Trust, Legitimacy, and Governance' (2009) 14 *New Political Economy* 451, p. 456.
90. *Ibid.*

the citizenry in abstract) and that invest their assets, either in the short or long term, according to the interests and objectives of the sovereign sponsor.

2.3.6 Analysis and Working Definition of SWFs

SWFs are in many ways not a homogeneous group. In fact, SWFs 'differ in size, age, structure, funding sources, governance, policy objectives, risk/return profiles, investment horizons, eligible asset classes, and instruments, not to mention levels of transparency and accessibility'.[91] These differences have arguably contributed to the absence of a uniform definition of SWFs. In a research published in January 2014, nineteen different definitions of SWFs were examined from which eleven different criteria were identified.[92] Only two out of the eleven criteria identified were recognized by all nineteen definitions examined; being that SWFs are investment vehicles and that they are government-owned.[93] It is important to keep in mind that definitions of SWFs have been construed for different (home State and investment recipient State) purposes, such as investment law purposes, regulatory purposes, public finance purposes and governance purposes.

This study is concerned with entities and/or arrangements that fit the definition of SWFs as formulated by the IWG. One important reason for adopting this definition is that it has been produced by an international working group (the IWG) comprised of twenty-six IMF Member States working on GAPPs for SWFs, with the support of twelve investment recipient countries, the EC, the OECD and the World Bank, and that it serves multiple (home State and investment recipient State) purposes. It has been argued that this definition of SWFs has now become the 'consensus' definition.[94] Another important reason for adopting this definition is that it has been reflected in the 2010 update of the OECD Commentary. As explained in the introduction to this study, an important part of this study relates to the OECD MTC.

For the sake of convenience, the IWG definition is cited again:

> SWFs are defined as special purpose investment funds or arrangements, owned by the general government. Created by the general government for macroeconomic purposes, SWFs hold, manage, or administer assets to achieve financial objectives, and employ a set of investment strategies which include investing in foreign financial assets. The SWFs are commonly established out of balance of payments surpluses, official foreign currency operations, the proceeds of privatizations, fiscal surpluses, and/or receipts resulting from commodity exports.

---

91. A. Rozanov, 'A Liability-Based Approach to Sovereign Wealth', Chapter 3 in: State Street, *Sovereign Wealth Funds: Assessing the Impact* (2008), Vol. III, Issue 2, p. 15.
92. J. Capapé & T. Blanco, 'More Layers Than an Onion: Looking for a Definition of Sovereign Wealth Funds' (2014), *ESADEgeo Working Paper 21*. The eleven criteria identified were: (1) State-ownership, (2) investment fund, (3) international asset portfolio, (4) absence of explicit pension liabilities, (5) reference to the source of funding, (6) above risk-free rate investors, (7) long-term investors, (8) existence of a defined purpose, (9) explicit financial objective, (10) controlled/owned by a sovereign authority, and (11) independent (legal) structures.
93. *Ibid.*, p. 9.
94. A. Rozanov, 'Definitional Challenges of Dealing with Sovereign Wealth Funds' (2011) 1 *Asian Journal of International Law* 249, p. 256.

The third reason for using the IWG definition is that this definition and the IWG's explanation of this definition captures the author's understanding of the common characteristics which together distinguish these funds or arrangements from State/government-owned enterprises, State/government-owned pension funds, and assets managed for the benefits of individuals other than the population in general. The distinctive features, which together make them an interesting subject of study, are that the funds or arrangements are: (i) controlled and directly or indirectly owned by the State/government/Ministry for Finance, depending on their legal set-up, (ii) used to invest in foreign assets to achieve financial objectives, and (iii) have as a macroeconomic purpose to preserve and accumulate the wealth of a nation. This means that State/government-owned enterprises, State/government-owned pension funds that qualify as SSRFs, and assets managed for the benefit of individuals, are excluded from the definition of SWF:

- State/government-owned enterprises do not fit the IWG definition of SWFs, because they do not represent an investment arm of the State/government/Ministry for Finance, and because their purpose is not always to preserve and accumulate the wealth of a nation.
- State/government-owned pension funds that qualify as SSRFs should not fit the IWG definition, because it can be argued that such pension funds are beneficially owned by individuals and serve individual economic purposes, rather than macroeconomic purposes.
- Assets managed for the benefit of individuals, such as members of the royal family, are excluded from the IWG definition of SWFs, because they do not serve to build up the wealth of a nation as a whole.

Central banks could fit the IWG definition of SWFs, but the IWG has explained that assets used for traditional balance of payments purposes/monetary policy purposes, are not regarded as constituting an SWF. However, reserve assets managed by central banks and not used in exercising the (traditional) central bank functions, can form an SWF according to the definition of the IWG. According to the IWG, (traditional) central bank functions serve a different purpose than SWFs, without elaborating on the difference between the two. Central banks exercise control over key aspects of the financial system.[95] They manage foreign exchange reserves with a view to meet balance of payments needs and deal with issues such as inflation, exchange rates and maintaining financial stability.[96] Although central banks clearly serve macroeconomic purposes, they do not necessarily represent an investment arm of the State.

---

95. For a definition of central bank, *see* International Monetary Fund, *Balance of Payments and International Investment Position Management*, 6th edn., (Washington D.C.: International Monetary Fund, 2009), Chapter 4, p. 62: '[t]he central bank is the financial institution (or institutions) that exercises control over key aspects of the financial system. It carries out such activities as issuing currency, managing international reserves, transacting with the IMF, and providing credit to deposit-taking corporations'.
96. J. Aizenman & R. Glick, 'Assets Class Diversification and Delegation of Responsibilities between Central Banks and Sovereign Wealth Funds' (September, 2010), *Federal Reserve Bank of San Francisco Working Paper Series*, Working Paper 2010-20, p. 2.

2.4 GOVERNANCE STRUCTURE OF SWFs

According to the explanation and commentary on GAPP 6 of the Santiago Principles, the governance structure of SWFs should be set out in its legal framework and a clear distinction between oversight, decision-making and operational responsibilities should be ensured. To that end, the governance structure should clearly distinguish: (i) an owner, (ii) one or more governing bodies, and (iii) operational management. However, in practice the governance of SWFs is not always structured along the lines prescribed by the GAPPs.

2.4.1 Owner

The owner refers to the State/government as the legal and/or beneficial owner of SWFs established as separate legal entities, or of assets constituting SWFs. According to GAPP 7, the owner's responsibilities should determine the SWF's broad objectives, exercise its oversight over the SWF's operations and appoints the members of the governing body/ies.

2.4.2 Governing Body/ies

According to the explanation and commentary on GAPP 8, the governing body/ies should determine the policy and investment strategies in accordance with the SWF's objective(s). The governing body/ies should ultimately be responsible for the performance of the SWF. Furthermore, the governing body/ies may have *inter alia* the responsibility to appoint and remove management.

There can be several governing bodies, and they can take a number of forms, such as a unit in the Ministry for Finance, a board of directors or trustees, a committee or commission or the governing body/ies of the central bank.[97] It follows from an IMF survey that appointments to the governing body/ies are often made by the Minister for Finance or another government official, the appointments are often for a period of five years or more, whilst almost two-third of the respondents indicated that officials represent a minority in the governing body or that there is no government representation at all.[98]

2.4.3 Operational Management

Operational management of SWFs should be responsible for day-to-day operations. In this respect, management should be the one that makes investment decisions, but

---

97. International Working Group of Sovereign Wealth Funds, *Sovereign Wealth Funds: Generally Accepted Principles and Practices 'Santiago Principles'* (October, 2008), Part II, GAPP 8, Explanation and commentary, p. 16.
98. C. Hammer, P. Kunzel & I. Petrova, 'Sovereign Wealth Funds: Current Institutional and Operational Practices' (2008), *IMF Working Paper No. 08/254*, pp. 8–9, available at: <https://www.imf.org/external/pubs/ft/wp/2008/wp08254.pdf>.

should also appoint and remove staff. All this can be subject to direction from the governing body/ies. Many SWFs indicate they make use of external asset managers.[99] Some SWFs have even assigned most or all of their assets to such managers. External asset managers are used when in-house management of assets would be too expensive, or when SWFs lack the knowledge to manage the assets themselves.

2.5 SWFs BY REGION

In several ways, Asia, and the Middle East and North Africa ('MENA'), are the most prominent regions in relation to SWFs. In terms of numbers of SWFs, each region accounted for about 25% in 2013, while 45% of total assets under management is held by Asia based SWFs, mainly China and Singapore, and 28% of total assets is managed by MENA based SWFs, mainly the Gulf States (2013 figures).[100] Europe based SWFs, although very limited in numbers, account for 20% of total assets under management, but this is largely due to Norway's SWF, the GPFG, currently the largest in the world with estimated assets under management of US$ 1.032 billion (February 2018).[101]

2.6 DEFINITION OF SWEs

SWEs are investment vehicles wholly-owned and controlled by an SWF.[102] CIC International Co., Ltd., CIC International (Hong Kong) Co., Ltd., CIC Capital Corporation and Central Huijin Investment Ltd. are examples of SWEs of CIC, one of China's SWFs. SWFs that set-up SWEs do so for a variety of reasons. SWFs can have a strict investment mandate and using SWEs, which may have a different investment mandate, can offer them the flexibility to invest in assets they would otherwise not be allowed to invest in.[103] Another important reason for setting-up SWEs is that it makes it difficult to track the investments, activities and tactics of SWFs, which can help to avoid the public spotlight.[104] It can also avoid being categorized as SWF (e.g., for investment regulation purposes). Yet another reason can be tax driven.[105] SWEs can be established abroad in jurisdictions that provide tax benefits to an SWE that would not have been available had the SWF invested directly. Further, SWEs may be used to centralize investment activities focusing on specific assets classes, such as real estate or government bonds, or focusing on an industry, such as oil & gas, or region, such as Europe.

---

99. *Ibid.*, pp. 16–17.
100. *The 2014 Preqin Sovereign Wealth Fund Review*, p. 13.
101. <http://www.swfinstitute.org/sovereign-wealth-fund-rankings/>.
102. <http://www.swfinstitute.org/statistics-research/sovereign-wealth-enterprise-swe/>.
103. *Ibid.*
104. *Ibid.*
105. *Ibid.*

2.7 INVESTMENT TREND

Whereas sovereign wealth investors have traditionally invested as *passive* investors, e.g., in listed shares or government bonds (portfolio investments), they are increasingly operating as long-term, *active* investors by investing large sums, e.g., in real estate, infrastructure and private companies (direct investments).[106] One example is CIC, one of China's SWFs, which established CIC Capital Corporation in January 2015 for making direct investments.[107] Another example is Temasek, one of Singapore's SWFs, which owns controlling interests in listed and non-listed companies.[108] This move from traditional asset classes to alternative (less liquid) assets is, to a large extent, driven by the current economic environment of low-interest rates and slow economic growth.[109]

2.8 LEGAL FRAMEWORK OF SOVEREIGN WEALTH INVESTORS

2.8.1 SWFs

The legal basis and form of SWFs generally follows one of the following three approaches.[110]

(1) Under the first approach, SWFs are constituted by a pool of assets (arrangement) without a separate legal personality. The legal ownership of the pool of assets rests directly with the State/government[111] or central bank,[112] while the pool of assets is typically governed by specific legislation. Examples include the Botswana Pula Fund and Norway's GPFG.

---

106. M. Castelli & F. Scacciavillani, 'SWFs and State Investments: A Preliminary General Overview', Chapter 1 in: F. Bassan (ed.), *Research Handbook on Sovereign Wealth Funds and International Investment Law* (Cheltenham: Edward Elgar Publishing, 2015), pp. 20–22; PwC, *Sovereign Investors 2020: A growing force* (April, 2016).
107. *See* Section 2.9.4.3.
108. *See* Section 2.9.2.3.
109. M. Castelli & F. Scacciavillani, 'SWFs and State Investments: A Preliminary General Overview', Chapter 1 in: F. Bassan (ed.), *Research Handbook on Sovereign Wealth Funds and International Investment Law* (Cheltenham: Edward Elgar Publishing, 2015), pp. 20–22; PwC, *Sovereign Investors 2020: A Growing Force* (April, 2016).
110. International Working Group of Sovereign Wealth Funds, *Sovereign Wealth Funds: Generally Accepted Principles and Practices 'Santiago Principles'* (October, 2008), Part II, GAPP 1, Explanation and commentary, p. 11.
111. When SWFs have been constituted by a pool of assets within a State, government or Ministry for Finance, the legal owner of the assets often mandates asset management to an asset manager, such as the central bank (in the case of Norway's GPFG), a separate fund management entity owned by the government (such as Singapore's GIC Pte. Ltd.) or to an external asset manager. *See* A. Al-Hassan et al., 'Sovereign Wealth Funds: Aspects of Governance Structures and Investment Management' (2013), *IMF Working Paper No. 13/231*, p. 5.
112. Central banks can take a number of legal forms. In some States the central bank is established as a separate legal entity, in others it forms a part of the State. *See* H. Fox, *The Law of State Immunity*, 2nd edn., (New York: Oxford University Press, 2008), p. 465.

(2) Under the second approach, SWFs are established under public law as legal entities distinct from the State/government or central bank, with full capacity to act. They are the legal owner of the investment assets and governed by a specific constitutive law. Examples include the Abu Dhabi Investment Authority ('ADIA'), Kuwait's KIA and the Qatar Investment Authority.

(3) Under the third approach, SWFs are established as State/government-owned corporations with a separate legal personality. They are the legal owner of the investment assets and typically governed by general company law, although specific laws can (also) apply. Examples include China's CIC, the Korea Investment Corporation and Singapore's Temasek Holdings (Private) Limited.

2.8.2 SWEs

SWEs often have a separate legal identity (derived from public law or company law), but they may also be organized as (legal) entities without a separate legal personality, such as limited partnerships.

2.8.3 SWFs and SWEs Combined

Thus, based on Sections 2.8.1 and 2.8.2, together sovereign wealth investors (i.e., SWFs and SWEs combined) can be divided as follows according to their legal form:

(i) Sovereign wealth investors constituted by a pool of assets within the State (which includes a pool of assets forming a unit within a central bank that has no separate legal personality);
(ii) Sovereign wealth investors established as or within a separate legal entity other than the State itself (comprising SWFs and SWEs established as a separate legal entity under public law or company law, as well as SWFs constituted by a pool of assets within a central bank that has a separate legal personality);
(iii) Sovereign wealth investors organized as a (legal) entity without a separate legal personality, such as limited partnerships (comprising SWEs organized in such manner).

This distinction between sovereign wealth investors according to their legal form is relevant for other parts of this study, such as Chapter 5 (regarding the application of tax treaties) and Chapter 6 (regarding the personal scope of the freedom of capital movement in the EEA Agreement and the freedom of establishment).

2.9 SELECTED EXAMPLES OF SOVEREIGN WEALTH INVESTORS

This section provides an overview of four selected SWFs: Norway's GPFG, Singapore's Temasek, Abu Dhabi's ADIA, and China's CIC. It discusses: (i) their objective(s), (ii) the legal form they take and their governance model, and (iii) the way they are funded and the assets they invest in. These four SWFs have been selected because they are rather well-known, they represent a good mixture in terms of objectives, legal form and activities, and because sufficient information is available about them.

2.9.1 Government Pension Fund Global (Norway)

2.9.1.1 *Incorporation & Objective(s)*

In 1990, the Norwegian Parliament established the Government Petroleum Fund to facilitate the long-term management of its revenue from oil production.[113] In 2006, the Government Petroleum Fund was renamed into the 'GPFG' to underline the fund's (additional) role of financing the expected increase in future public pension costs.[114] Despite its name, the fund is not faced with formal pension liabilities to date.

2.9.1.2 *Legal Form & Governance*

In accordance with the Government Pension Fund Act (no. 123 of 21 December 2005), GPFG has been placed with Norway's central bank, Norges Bank, in the form of a Norwegian krone deposit. Hence, Norway's SWF is constituted by a pool of assets (arrangements). The legal ownership of the assets constituting GPFG is in the hands of the Ministry for Finance (as a representative of the Norwegian State).[115] The primary responsibility for the management of GPFG rests with the Ministry of Finance,[116] but the operational management has been mandated to Norges Bank.[117] Confusingly, the mandate to Norges Bank states that the capital of GPFG shall be invested by the Norges Bank in financial instruments, real estate and cash deposits denominated in foreign

---

113. <http://www.nbim.no/en/the-fund/about-the-fund/>.
114. *Ibid.*
115. Norwegian Ministry of Finance, The Management of the Government Pension Fund in 2012, Meld. St. 27 (2012–2013) Report to the Storting (white paper), p. 16; International Working Group of Sovereign Wealth Funds, *Sovereign Wealth Funds: Generally Accepted Principles and Practices 'Santiago Principles'* (October, 2008), Part III, Appendix III. Background Information on IWG Member Countries' SWFs, p. 41.
116. *See* sec. 2 of the Government Pension Fund Act (no. 123 of 21 December 2005) available at: <https://www.regjeringen.no/contentassets/9d68c55c272c41e99f0bf45d24397d8c/governmentpensionfundact.pdf>.
117. Management mandate for the Government Pension Fund Global, applicable as from 1 January 2011, available at: <https://www.regjeringen.no/globalassets/upload/fin/statens-pensjonsfond/gpfg-management-mandate-14-april-2015.pdf>.

currency *in its own name*.[118] The legal relationship between the Norwegian State, the Ministry for Finance and Norges Bank with respect to (the assets of) GPFG, is therefore not entirely clear.

In its turn, the executive board of Norges Bank has issued an investment mandate to the chief executive officer of the Norges Bank Investment Management ('NBIM').[119] NBIM is allowed to make use of external (investment) managers,[120] which it does in practice.

2.9.1.3 Funding & Portfolio

GPFG is funded by net cash flow from petroleum activities, the net results of financial transactions relating to petroleum activities, and returns on its investments.[121] Its portfolio consists of financial instruments, real estate, and cash deposits denominated in foreign currency.

2.9.2 Temasek Holdings (Private) Limited

2.9.2.1 Incorporation & Objective(s)

Temasek Holdings (Private) Limited was incorporated on 25 June 1974 under the Singapore Companies Act as a private company with the purpose of holding and managing investments, and assets formerly held by the Singapore Government.[122] This way the government could focus on matters other than investing of government money.[123]

2.9.2.2 Legal Form & Governance

Temasek (*sea town*) is a private company owned by the Singapore Government through the Minister for Finance.[124]

Temasek is subject to the Singapore Companies Act, and all other laws and regulations applicable to companies incorporated under Singaporean law. Board members are appointed, removed or renewed by its sole shareholder, subject to the

---

118. Section 1-2(1) of the Management mandate for the Government Pension Fund Global.
119. Available at: < https://www.nbim.no/contentassets/43615da4359c4a47a60ee55e03511589/nbim-ceo-investment-mandate.pdf > .
120. *Ibid.*, sec. 1.5.
121. Section 3 of the Government Pension Fund Act (no. 123 of 21 December 2005).
122. *Temasek Review 2011 (Building for tomorrow)*, p. 42, available at: < https://www.temasek.com.sg/content/dam/temasek-corporate/our-financials/investor-library/annual-review/en-tr-thumbnail-and-pdf/TR11%20Eng_Final_2011-07-06_(low%20res).pdf > .
123. *Temasek Review 2004 (Investing in value)*, p. 34, available at: https://www.temasek.com.sg/content/dam/temasek-corporate/our-financials/investor-library/annual-review/en-tr-thumbnail-and-pdf/TR04_Secured.pdf > .
124. *Temasek Review 2011 (Building for tomorrow)*, p. 42. Under the Singapore Minister for Finance (Incorporation) Act (Chapter 183), the Minister for Finance is a body corporate.

approval of the President of Singapore. The board of directors, consisting of a majority of 'independent private sector business leaders', makes investment, divestment and other business decisions, and provides guidance and policy directions to Temasek's management.

Although Temasek owns and manages assets on a commercial basis independently from the President and Singapore Government,[125] the Singapore Constitution requires the prior approval of the President of Singapore before Temasek can use its past reserves. Past reserves are those reserves that have been accumulated before the current government took office. In line with its custodial role of safeguarding Singapore's past reserves, the President is not involved in directing the investment, divestment and other business decisions of Temasek.

2.9.2.3 Funding & Portfolio

Temasek is financed through proceeds from its investments in portfolio companies and borrowings on the market. Its portfolio is to a large extent equity based, with controlling and non-controlling interests in listed and non-listed companies.[126] Temasek is not represented on the board of its investments, but it exercises its shareholder rights to protect its own financial interests.[127] It does, however, engage with the boards and management to share its perspectives and it does 'look to their boards to drive strategy, and their management to manage day-to-day operations'.[128] Temasek considers itself an active investor.[129] Its assets under management are estimated at US$ 197 billion (February 2018).[130]

2.9.3 Abu Dhabi Investment Authority

2.9.3.1 Incorporation & Objective(s)

ADIA was established in 1976 as an investment institution with the purpose 'to invest funds on behalf of the Government of the Emirate of Abu Dhabi, to make available the necessary financial resources to secure and maintain the future welfare of the Emirate'.[131]

---

125. Ibid.
126. *Temasek Review 2016 (Generational Investing)*, p. 88, available at: < https://www.temasek.com.sg/content/dam/temasek-corporate/our-financials/investor-library/annual-review/en-tr-thumbnail-and-pdf/TR2016_Singles.pdf >.
127. *Temasek Review 2014 (Our journey has just begun)*, p. 65.
128. *Temasek Review 2016 (Generational Investing)*, p. 28.
129. Ibid.
130. < http://www.swfinstitute.org/sovereign-wealth-fund-rankings/ >.
131. *ADIA 2010 Review (Prudent Global Growth)*, p. 4, available at: < http://www.adia.ae/En/pr/Annual_Review_Website_2010.pdf >.

2.9.3.2 Legal Form & Governance

ADIA is a public institution with an independent legal identity that is wholly-owned by the Government of the Emirate of Abu Dhabi.[132] ADIA operates independently from, and without reference to, the Government of the Emirate of Abu Dhabi.[133] ADIA's constitutive document, Law No. (5), provides for a separation of involvement and responsibilities between the owner (the government), the governing entity (the board of directors) and operational management.[134] Its board of directors, appointed by the Ruler of Abu Dhabi, is responsible for the implementation of ADIA's strategy, monitoring ADIA's financial performance and overseeing the activities of ADIA's management.[135] ADIA's managing director, who is one of the board members, is responsible for the fund's investment activities and legally represents ADIA in its external affairs.[136] The managing director is assisted by an Investment Committee, which, in its turn, is assisted by several advisory committees and departments.[137] Furthermore, ADIA uses external managers.[138]

2.9.3.3 Funding & Portfolio

ADIA is funded with government money derived from the government's natural resources.[139] Its portfolio consists, amongst others, of investments in (developed and emerging market) equities, government bonds, real estate and infrastructure.[140] Although ADIA does not actively seek to manage the public companies in which it invests, it does exercise its voting rights in certain circumstances 'to protect its interests or to oppose motions that may be detrimental to shareholders as a body'.[141] Its assets under management are estimated at US$ 828 billion (February 2018).[142]

---

132. < http://www.adia.ae/en/Governance/Santiago_Principles_more.aspx >.
133. *ADIA 2013 Review*, p. 8, available at: < http://www.adia.ae/En/pr/Annual_Review_Website_2013.pdf >.
134. < http://www.adia.ae/en/Governance/Santiago_Principles_more.aspx >.
135. *ADIA 2010 Review (Prudent Global Growth)*, p. 42.
136. *Ibid.*, p. 7.
137. *Ibid.*
138. *ADIA 2013 Review*, p. 33.
139. < http://www.adia.ae/en/Governance/Santiago_Principles_more.aspx >.
140. *ADIA 2016 Review (A Legacy in Motion)*, p. 15, available at: < http://www.adia.ae/En/pr/2016/pdf/ADIA_2016_Review_01_FULL.pdf >.
141. *ADIA 2016 Review (A Legacy in Motion)*, p. 45.
142. < http://www.swfinstitute.org/sovereign-wealth-fund-rankings/ >.

2.9.4 China Investment Corporation

2.9.4.1 Incorporation & Objective(s)

CIC was incorporated on 29 September 2007 as a wholly state-owned company under the Company Law of China with the purpose to 'diversify China's foreign exchange holdings and seek maximum returns for its shareholder within acceptable risk tolerance'.[143]

Its overseas investments are made through CIC International Co., Ltd. (established in September 2011), CIC International (Hong Kong) Co., Ltd. (established in November 2010) and CIC Capital Corporation (established in January 2015). CIC pursues domestic investments through Central Huijin Investment Ltd. (established in December 2003).[144]

2.9.4.2 Legal Form & Governance

CIC is a corporation wholly-owned by the Government of China and governed by the Company Law of China. Its three governing bodies are the Board of Directors (responsible for the overall performance and strategy), the Board of Supervisors (responsible for monitoring the performance of directors and executives) and the Executive Committee (which translates the guidance of the Board of Directors into detailed strategies and oversees day-to-day operations).[145] The chairman and vice-chairman of the board are appointed by the State Council,[146] whereas the appointment and removal of other directors are subject to the approval of the State Council.[147] The Board of Directors is assisted by the International Advisory Council, comprising world-renowned experts.[148]

2.9.4.3 Funding & Portfolio

CIC was funded through issuing special treasury bonds.[149] It has to pay dividends to the State Council, as its owner, to cover the (interest) costs of these bonds.

CIC's portfolio consists of: (i) public market equity and bond investments, hedge fund and real estate investments, private equity fund investments, co-investments, and minority investments (through CIC International); (ii) direct investments and bilateral, multilateral and platform fund investments (through CIC Capital); (iii) global investment-grade corporate bonds and H-shares (through CIC Hong Kong); and (iv)

---

143. *China Investment Corporation Annual Report 2015*, p. 7.
144. *Ibid.*
145. *Ibid.*, p. 11.
146. < http://www.ifswf.org/member-profiles/china-investment-corporation >.
147. < http://www.china-inv.cn/ >.
148. *China Investment Corporation Annual Report 2015*, p. 11.
149. http://www.ifswf.org/member-profiles/china-investment-corporation.

equity investments in key state-owned financial institutions in China (through CIC Huijin).[150] Its assets under management are estimated at US$ 900 billion (February 2018).[151]

2.10 HOME STATE TAX STATUS OF SOVEREIGN WEALTH INVESTORS

As noted in the introduction to this study, the tax treatment of sovereign wealth investors in their home State could be relevant for the international tax analysis of such investors, from a source State perspective. It is often believed that sovereign wealth investors are never taxed in their home State.[152] This does not appear to be correct. A few sovereign wealth investors, including Singapore's Temasek,[153] are taxed in their home State based on a territoriality principle, while China's CIC and Korea Investment Corporation are taxed on their worldwide income.[154] However, these examples are only limited exceptions to the general rule that SWFs and their 'local' SWEs are not taxed in their home State.[155]

From a theoretical point of view, there are three conflicting theories on home State taxation of legal persons of public law and legal persons of private law owned by a legal person of public law – together referred to as State entities –, which could also shed light on the home State taxation of sovereign wealth investors.[156] These theories are discussed below and can be relevant for the analyses in Chapter 5 (tax treaty aspects) and Chapter 6 (European law). The first theory is that home State taxation of public entities is superfluous. That is, there is no need to tax public entities, as the profits already belong to the State owner. Imposing residence taxation on State entities would merely result in a transfer of money from one pocket controlled by the State to another.[157] The State, as the owner, can collect revenue by simply extracting profits through (dividend) distributions, which saves (unnecessary) costs, because there is no need to compute taxable income (under often complex tax rules). In this view, home

---

150. *China Investment Corporation Annual Report 2016*, p. 14 & pp. 36 et seq.
151. < http://www.swfinstitute.org/sovereign-wealth-fund-rankings/ >.
152. For example, M. Desai & D. Dharmapala, 'Taxing the Bandit Kings' (2008) 118 *Yale Law Journal Pocket Part* 98, p. 99; M. Knoll, 'Taxation and the Competitiveness of Sovereign Wealth Funds: Do Taxes Encourage Sovereign Wealth Funds to Invest in the United States?' (2009) 82 *Southern California Law Review* 703, p. 715; M. Kandev, 'Sovereign Wealth Funds: Are They Welcome in Canada?' (2010) 64 *Bulletin for International Taxation* 649, p. 650.
153. *Temasek Review 2012 (Extending Pathways)*, p. 45, available at: < https://www.temasek.com.sg/content/dam/temasek-corporate/our-financials/investor-library/annual-review/en-tr-thumbnail-and-pdf/TR2012_Eng.pdf >.
154. Wei Cui, 'Responding to Sovereign Funds: Are We Looking in the Right Place?' (2009) 123 *Tax Notes* 1237, p. 1241.
155. SWEs which are resident in another State than the home State of SWFs are more likely to be taxed in their residence State.
156. Wei Cui, 'Taxation of State Owned Enterprises: A Review of Empirical Evidence from China' (2015), available at: < http://papers.ssrn.com/sol3/papers.cfm?abstract_id = 2583284 >.
157. M. Knoll, 'Taxation and the Competitiveness of Sovereign Wealth Funds: Do Taxes Encourage Sovereign Wealth Funds to Invest in the United States?' (2009) 82 *Southern California Law Review* 703, p. 715.

State taxes and dividends are seen as functionally equivalent.[158] The first theory, however, also provides an explanation why a State would tax its State entities: it is simply a substitution mechanism for extracting profits through (dividend) distributions. The second theory is completely different from the first one. It holds that home State taxation is necessary to put State entities on equal footing with private investors.[159] In other words, imposing home State taxation on State entities would neutralize the tax-induced competitive advantage of State entities relative to private investors that are liable to home State taxation. Finally, the third theory sees home State taxation as a tool to force payments that is preferable over dividend distributions.[160] The third theory relates to the agency problem with respect to dividend payments, caused by the divergent interests between managers and shareholders.[161] For example, managers may prefer low return investments over dividend distributions to shareholders (i.e., they are payout averse), as this may increase the powers and responsibilities of a manager. To achieve this, managers may use the information asymmetry between themselves and shareholders to their advantage by withholding information from or not providing accurate information to shareholders. In this view, the taxation of State entities is simply a way of dealing with the agency problem by forcing payment of a fixed percentage of annual profits to the State. With respect to private companies, the agency problem regarding dividend distributions can typically be solved by: (i) increasing shareholder monitoring, or (ii) giving the manager an equity stake. However, it has been argued that a State cannot rely on such measures.[162,163]

---

158. R. Gordon, 'Taxes and Privatization' (2001), Discussion Paper No. 2977, Centre for Economic Policy Research, p. 5.
159. This was also the motivation of the EC in its letter of 2 May 2013 in which it invited the Netherlands to take appropriate measures to abolish the corporate income tax-exemption for Dutch public enterprises. In the view of the EC, the former Dutch tax regime for Dutch public enterprises was incompatible (and existing) State aid. Under that regime, Dutch public enterprises which performed economic activities could be exempt from Dutch corporate income tax. The EC argued that this tax-exemption provided an economic advantage to Dutch public enterprises which performed economic activities on the European market in comparison to Dutch private enterprises, as the tax-exemption reduced the charges that are normally included in the operating costs of an undertaking carrying out economic activities.
160. Wei Cui, 'Taxation of State Owned Enterprises: A Review of Empirical Evidence from China' (2015).
161. Wei Cui, 'Taxing State-Owned Enterprises: Towards an Understanding of a Basic Institution of State Capitalism' (2016) 52 *Osgoode Hall Law Journal* 775, available at: <https://papers.ssrn.com/sol3/papers.cfm?abstract_id=2676193>.
162. Wei Cui, 'Taxation of State Owned Enterprises: A Review of Empirical Evidence from China' (2015). This is because: (i) representatives of the State (as the sole shareholder) who are responsible for the monitoring might have less of an incentive than shareholders of private companies, and (ii) because the law may simply not allow another equity holder than the State, while the effectiveness of (other) incentive contracts for managers has been questioned.
163. In 1986, Jensen explained that another way of dealing with agency costs of free cash flow is to use shareholder debt funding as a substitute for dividends. This obliges managers to pay out future cash flows (interest and principle payments) instead of spending the money at discretion of the managers on investment with returns below the cost of capital. M. Jensen, 'Agency Costs of Free Cash Flow, Corporate Finance, and Takeovers' (1986) 76 *American Economic Review* 323. Shareholder debt can also be used as a substitute for taxation as a means to force payments (in relation to sovereign wealth investors).

With respect to SWFs and their 'local' SWEs, the first theory seems clearly dominant, given that, in practice, they are generally not taxed in their home State. With respect to the remaining theories, this could indicate the following. As regards the second theory (level-playing field), the absence of taxation by the residence State could indicate that a State has no interest in creating a level-playing field between domestic sovereign wealth investors and private investors. Why would a State want to tax its own sovereign wealth investors and take away any tax-induced competitive advantage over private investors? It should be noted that imposing home State taxation on domestic sovereign wealth investors in the same way as on private investors is in itself not sufficient to create a level-playing field. Other measures would need to be taken as well. In the author's view, what is required is that the relationship between the owner-State and the domestic sovereign wealth investor becomes such that the tax imposed will be a real cost for the domestic sovereign wealth investor (just like for private investors), i.e., domestic sovereign wealth investors should be made sensitive to home State taxes. This would require, for example, that tax paid by the domestic sovereign wealth investor should not (immediately) flow back, and also that any dividend payout policy should not take into account tax payments. If 'tax' payments would (immediately) flow back or would reduce dividends otherwise due, imposing tax would have no real effect on a sovereign wealth investor. As regards the third theory (agency problem), the absence of taxation in the residence State could indicate that, in relation to many sovereign wealth investors, there is no agency problem, or that a State is simply not aware of an existing agency problem. Given that sovereign wealth investors by definition are created for (a variety of) macroeconomic purposes and established out of public funds, it can be expected that sovereign wealth investors be closely assimilated to the owner-State itself, also when they happen to have a separate legal personality. An agency problem may, therefore, not exist in relation to many sovereign wealth investors.

2.11 CONCLUSIONS

A first purpose of this chapter was to come to a working definition of SWFs and SWEs, to use throughout this study. A second purpose was to get an understanding not only of what sovereign wealth investors are, but also why they exist, what they do and how they look like. As SWEs are merely a component of some SWFs, this chapter mainly focused on SWFs.

Purpose of SWFs. Most SWFs are either established to save funds for future generations by converting non-renewable resources into assets from which future income streams can be derived, or to cover for liabilities that may arise from fluctuations of commodity prices. Other SWFs are established because of a projected shortfall in the public pension system, or simply to increase the returns on reserve assets. It should be noted that the objectives of SWFs could be multiple, overlapping or changing over time.

Definition of SWFs. No universal definition of SWFs exists. This study adopts the definition of SWFs as formulated by the IWG. This definition is widely-followed, has been reflected in the OECD Commentary and captures the common characteristics which distinguish SWFs from other groups of investors.[164] The definition is as follows:

> SWFs are defined as special purpose investment funds or arrangements, owned by the general government. Created by the general government for macroeconomic purposes, SWFs hold, manage, or administer assets to achieve financial objectives, and employ a set of investment strategies which include investing in foreign financial assets. The SWFs are commonly established out of balance of payments surpluses, official foreign currency operations, the proceeds of privatizations, fiscal surpluses, and/or receipts resulting from commodity exports.

SWEs. SWFs sometimes structure investments through separate wholly-owned and controlled investment vehicles, known as SWEs. They do so for a variety of reasons, such as allowing greater flexibility, avoiding public spotlight, creating an efficient tax structure, avoiding being categorized as SWF and centralizing specific investment activities. SWEs can be established in the home State of an SWF or in other States.

Investment trend. Mainly driven by the current economic environment of low-interest rates and slow economic growth, sovereign wealth investors are increasingly proactive and no longer just operate as *passive* (portfolio) investors. As *active* investors, they increasingly make foreign direct investments, including long-term investments in real estate, infrastructure and private companies.

Legal forms. Sovereign wealth investors can have different legal forms and governance structures. Based on their legal form, they can be divided as follows:

(i) Sovereign wealth investors constituted by a pool of assets within the State (which includes a pool of assets forming a unit within a central bank that has no separate legal personality);
(ii) Sovereign wealth investors established as or within a separate legal entity other than the State itself (comprising SWFs and SWEs established as a separate legal entity under public law or company law, as well as SWFs constituted by a pool of assets within a central bank that has a separate legal personality);
(iii) Sovereign wealth investors organized as a (legal) entity without a separate legal personality, such as partnerships (comprising SWEs organized in such manner).

This distinction between sovereign wealth investors according to their legal form is relevant for other parts of this study, such as Chapter 5 (regarding the application of tax treaties) and Chapter 6 (regarding the personal scope of the freedom of capital movement in the EEA Agreement and the freedom of establishment).

Home State tax status of sovereign wealth investors. Sovereign wealth investors are generally not taxed in their home State, because taxation of such investors is seen as superfluous. There are, however, a few exceptions to this rule. Since creating

---

164. *See* Section 1.2 for all developments and distinctive features which together justify addressing sovereign wealth investors separately from other investor groups.

a level-playing field would generally not be in a home State's own interest, the few home States that do impose tax on sovereign wealth investors, would either seem to be dealing with an agency problem, or simply use taxation as a substitute for extracting profits through (dividend) distributions. The tax treatment of sovereign wealth investors in their home State could be relevant for the international tax analysis of such investors, from a source State perspective.

CHAPTER 3
Tax Policy Considerations and Approaches to Taxation of Foreign Sovereign Wealth Investors

3.1 INTRODUCTION

The main purpose of this chapter is to discuss tax policy considerations and to measure approaches to source taxation of foreign sovereign wealth investors against generally accepted principles and objectives of international tax policy. Basic principles and objectives often underlie a State's international tax policy and its design of international tax rules. A State's international tax policy choices, and the underlying basic principles and objectives, may depend on various factors – such as the size and nature of its economy, public interests, societal values, as well as tax policy choices of other States – and may change over time. This study identifies as today's three main 'substantive' attributes of international tax policy: (i) neutrality (efficiency), (ii) equity (fairness), and (iii) international attractiveness. It will discuss and present the key theoretical implications of these policy principles and objectives for the design of international tax rules, focusing on (foreign) sovereign wealth investors. This presentation will enable to measure approaches to source taxation of foreign sovereign wealth investors by their neutrality, equity and international attractiveness. However, this chapter will first consider the taxation of foreign sovereign wealth investors by source States, and how such taxation compares to the taxation of other investor groups, such as CIVs and pension funds. This comparison puts things into perspective, and is relevant for the international law analysis.

3.2 TAX TREATMENT OF FOREIGN SOVEREIGN WEALTH INVESTORS AND OTHER INVESTORS

Section 3.2 will provide a general overview of how States tax investment income derived by investors. In this respect, most States distinguish between resident investors and non-resident investors, as well as between 'regular' investors and types of investors to which special tax rules could apply. These distinctions will be followed in this section.

3.2.1 Tax Treatment of Investment Income Derived by Residents

3.2.1.1 Regular Investors

In most States, residents are, as a general rule, subject to taxation on worldwide income (i.e., from whatever source derived) – residence taxation. The scope of this rule, which applies to both resident individuals and companies, is often effectively limited to passive (investment) income, because active (business) income of residents earned abroad tends to be exempt (or deferred),[165] either unilaterally or under tax treaties. Instead of worldwide taxation, some States impose tax on residents on the basis of territoriality and subject them to taxation on domestic sources of income only – source taxation.[166]

Under both types of tax systems, active (business) income earned domestically and passive (investment) income of residents is combined and subject to the same tax rate (schedule) in some States, and separated and subject to different tax rates in other States. Rather than distinguishing between active and passive income, some States differentiate between ordinary income (which includes both active and passive income) and capital gains, and tax-exempt or subject capital gains to reduced tax rates.[167] In calculating the total taxable income of residents, expenses made to generate the income and, in case of individuals, personal allowances and circumstances, etc., are often taken into account (i.e., taxation on a net-basis).

Taxation of income in the hands of residents could result in double taxation. States have developed various mechanisms to avoid or mitigate (inter)national economic or juridical double taxation, as the case may be, such as exempting dividend income at the (corporate) shareholder level or allowing (foreign) tax credits in respect of passive income.

---

165. R. Avi-Yonah, *International Tax as International Law: An Analysis of the International Tax Regime* (New York: Cambridge University Press, 2007), p. 3.
166. In Singapore, tax is not only imposed on income accruing in and derived from Singapore, but also on income received in Singapore from outside Singapore. See N. Umar, *Singapore – Corporate Taxation*, Country Analyses IBFD, sec. 1.2.1.
167. As a general rule, Singapore does not impose tax on capital gains of resident companies, as well as resident individuals. See N. Umar, *Singapore – Corporate Taxation*, Country Analyses IBFD, sec. 1.7; N. Umar, *Singapore – Individual Taxation*, Country Analyses IBFD, sec. 1.7. In the US, long-term capital gains of resident individuals are subject to reduced federal income tax rates. See J. Rienstra, *United States – Individual Taxation*, Country Analyses IBFD, sec. 1.10.2.

Chapter 3: Tax Policy Considerations and Approaches to Taxation

3.2.1.2 *Sovereign Wealth Investors and Other State Entities*

SWFs and their 'local' SWEs are generally not taxed in their residence State (Section 2.10). In many States, legal persons of public law and legal persons of private law owned by a legal person of public law – together referred to as 'State entities' – are (effectively) not taxed, either entirely or at least to the extent they exercise public functions or do not compete with private economic operators. As explained in Section 2.10, there are three conflicting theories on home State taxation of State entities. The first theory is that home State taxation is superfluous, because the profits of State entities already belong to the owner-State. The second theory holds that home State taxation of State entities is necessary to put them on equal footing with private operators. In the author's view, this would, however, require that State entities be made tax sensitive (just like private operators).[168] The third theory relates to the agency problem with respect to dividend payments, caused by the divergent interests between managers and shareholders. It requires the taxation of State entities simply as a way to deal with this problem by forcing payment of a fixed percentage of annual profits to the State. In Chapter 2, it was concluded that sovereign wealth investors are generally not taxed in their home State, because taxation of such investors is seen as superfluous. Since creating a level-playing field would generally not be in a home State's own interest, the few home States that do impose tax on sovereign wealth investors, would either seem to be dealing with an agency problem, or simply use taxation as a substitute for extracting profits through (dividend) distributions.

3.2.1.3 *Collective Investment Vehicles*

Rather than investing directly, many (smaller) portfolio investors pool their money in and invest collectively through so-called CIVs. CIVs are managed by professional parties and offer investors various benefits as compared to investing directly, such as lower transactions costs, better market access, risk diversification and benefiting from market knowledge of professional managers and advisors.[169] Most States have separate tax rules dealing with CIVs.[170] The common aim of these rules is to achieve neutrality between investing directly and investing indirectly through a CIV, as much as possible.[171] Different States, however, apply different mechanisms to accomplish this neutrality. States typically follow one of the following approaches:[172] (i) disregard CIVs (flow-through) and tax the investors in the CIV directly; (ii) treat CIVs as separate entities, but exempt them under certain conditions, e.g., with regard to the plurality of investors, distribution policy, regulatory requirements and types of assets to be

---

168. *See* Section 2.10 for a more detailed discussion of this matter.
169. OECD (2010), *The Granting of Treaty Benefits with Respect to the Income of Collective Investment Vehicles*, Paras 6-9, available at: < https://www.oecd.org/tax/treaties/45359261.pdf >. The main conclusions of this report have been reflected in Paras 22-48 of the OECD Commentary on Art. 1 (Persons covered).
170. *Ibid.*, Para. 1.
171. *Ibid.* Para. 4.
172. Paragraphs 6.25-6.26 of the OECD Commentary on Art. 1 (Persons covered).

invested in;[173] (iii) subject CIVs to tax, but reduce the tax base by reference to distributions paid to the investors; (iv) tax CIVs at a low or zero rate; or (v) subject CIVs to tax and avoid double taxation at the resident investor level through an exemption or credit method. Under approaches (ii) to (iv), taxation by the State in which the CIV has been established is triggered at the level of the investors – and neutrality may be achieved – when distributions are received from the CIV or when capital gains are realized on the sale of their interests in the CIV. It is noted that neutrality is not achieved if States have different tax rules (and rates) for different categories of passive income and the income received by the CIV (e.g., interest) is classified differently than the distributions received by the participants (e.g., dividend).

3.2.1.4 Pension Funds

Pension schemes can provide a basic level of income for individuals after retirement and can be mandatory, voluntary and linked to an employment relationship or not. Pension funds, being pooling vehicles that manage and invest the contributions on behalf of the participants, offer benefits to participants that are largely similar to CIVs.[174] Many States have special tax rules dealing with pension funds/schemes. In general, pension schemes involve three transactions that could trigger taxation: (i) when contributions to the fund are made, (ii) when investment income and capital gains accrue to the pension fund vehicle, and (iii) when funds are withdrawn.[175] In many States, pension contributions are made by employers and/or employees out of pre-tax income, investment returns of pension funds are tax-exempt and pension payments, including the investment return, are due with tax (so-called exempt-exempt-taxed schemes).[176] In other States, pension contributions are made out of pre-tax income, while investment returns of pension funds as well as pension payments are taxed (so-called exempt-taxed-taxed schemes). Others schemes, ranging from taxed-exempt-exempt to taxed-taxed-taxed schemes, also exist.[177] In many States, the effective tax rate on pension income is (much) lower relative to other types of saving,[178] indicating the social importance that States attribute to (the promotion of) retirement saving. In summary, reasons why pension funds are not, or more

---

173. G. Genta, 'Dividends Received by Investment Funds: An EU Law Perspective – Part 2' (2013) 53 *European Taxation* 141, p. 143.
174. *Notitie Fiscaal Verdragsbeleid 2011*, Tweede Kamer, 2010–2011, 25 087, No. 7, p. 37.
175. K-Y. Yoo & A. de Serres, 'Tax Treatment of Private Pension Savings in OECD Countries and the Net Tax Cost Per Unit of Contribution to Tax-favoured Schemes' (2004), *OECD Working Paper No. 406*, p. 6, available at: < https://www.oecd.org/eco/outlook/35663569.pdf >.
176. *Ibid.*, p. 8.
177. For an overview of the tax treatment of pension schemes by OECD countries, *see* K-Y. Yoo & A. de Serres, 'Tax Treatment of Private Pension Savings in OECD Countries and the Net Tax Cost Per Unit of Contribution to Tax-Favoured Schemes' (2004), *OECD Working Paper No. 406*, pp. 26–28.
178. K-Y. Yoo & A. de Serres, 'Tax Treatment of Private Pension Savings in OECD Countries and the Net Tax Cost Per Unit of Contribution to Tax-favoured Schemes' (2004), OECD Working Paper No. 406.

favourably, taxed is that the investment returns will effectively be taxed when pensions are paid and/or because they fulfil an important social function in society.

3.2.1.5 Not-for-Profit Organizations

A not-for-profit organization is a type of organization that does not aim to earn profit for its owners (shareholders), but uses profit and donations to further a particular social cause, or advocate for a particular point of view. In many States, special tax arrangements are available to not-for-profit organizations.[179] These special rules generally reflect a policy intended to support non-profit activities through tax expenditure.[180] Special tax rules for not-for-profit organizations include reduced tax rates, tax base limitations (e.g., distinguishing between business and non-business income) or a full tax-exemption.[181] To be eligible for these special tax rules, an organization is typically required to further a certain (charitable, public, social and/or political) purpose and/or is prohibited to distribute profits. Additional conditions could apply, for example regarding the level of remuneration of directors or the activities (not) to be performed.

3.2.1.6 Comparison

The discussion above and in Section 2.10 makes it clear that the home State tax treatment of sovereign wealth investors is based on a different rationale, compared to the tax treatment accorded by home States to other resident investor groups. Sovereign wealth investors are generally not taxed in their home State, because taxation of such investors is seen as superfluous. The few home States that do impose tax on sovereign wealth investors, would either seem to be dealing with an agency problem, or simply use taxation as a substitute for extracting profits through (dividend) distributions. On balance, taxes collected from resident sovereign wealth investors do not improve the financial position of the home State, because such investors are already owned, controlled and funded by that home State. Tax-exemptions or tax reductions granted to other groups of resident investors are based on a different rationale, such as achieving neutrality between directly investing and indirectly investing (CIVs), or the social importance attributed to certain resident investors (pension funds and not-for-profit organizations). And imposing or increasing taxes on such resident investors could improve the financial position of the home State. In Chapter 6, it will become apparent that the rationale for taxing or not taxing a resident investor is an important element for the European law analysis.

---

179. D. Gliksberg, 'General Report', in: *Taxation of Non-Profit Organizations*, IFA Cahiers de droit fiscal international, Vol. 84a (Alphen a/d Rijn: Kluwer Law International, 1999).
180. *Ibid.*, p. 36.
181. *Ibid.*, pp. 38–45.

3.2.2 Tax Treatment of Investment Income Derived by Non-residents

3.2.2.1 *Regular Non-resident Investors*

Whereas most States tax their residents on a worldwide basis (i.e., from whatever source derived), non-residents are taxed on (certain items of) domestic-source income only. In this respect, many States have detailed rules to determine where income is (deemed to be) sourced. The right of States to tax income derived from their territory – source taxation – is well established in international law.[182] Here again, many States differentiate between active (business) income and passive (investment) income. With respect to active income, States often tax non-residents in the same way as residents and, therefore, allow taking into account business expenses (i.e., taxation on a net-basis). On the other hand, if passive income of non-residents is taxed, the tax is commonly withheld at source at a flat rate and on a gross basis. Many States have different flat tax rates on different categories of passive income paid to non-residents, and withholding tax rates are often reduced under tax treaties. To illustrate, under OECD MTC based treaties, the source tax rate in respect of dividends is limited to 15% in case of 'portfolio' dividends and 5% in case of 'participation' dividends,[183] whereas the source tax rate in respect of interest is limited to 10%.[184] Non-residents may be indifferent to source taxation if this tax can be fully credited against their tax liability in their residence State. However, since the tax base in the residence State is generally calculated on a net-basis and withholding tax is gross-based, foreign taxes can often not be fully credited.

In an intra-EU context, Member States could be required to exempt from source taxation cross-border dividend as well as interest (and royalty) payments between affiliated entities under the Parent-Subsidiary Directive and Interest & Royalties Directive.[185]

Further, some (source) States do, and others do not tax capital gains of non-residents under domestic law, unless in the case of immovable property situated in their territory.[186] It is noted that OECD MTC based treaties allow source taxation of capital gains derived by a non-resident in a number of situations, without any

---

182. R. Avi-Yonah, *International Tax as International Law: An Analysis of the International Tax Regime* (New York: Cambridge University Press, 2007), p. 27.
183. Article 10 OECD MTC. The rate for 'participation' dividends applies if dividends are paid by a resident subsidiary of one State to a parent company of another State, provided that – in short – the parent owns directly a holding of at least 25%. The rate for 'portfolio' dividends applies in all other cases (provided the tax treaty applies).
184. Article 11 OECD MTC.
185. Discussed in more detail in Section 6.5.
186. This exception to capital gains taxation in the case of immovable property applies in, for example, the US (under the Foreign Investment in Real Property Tax Act). R. Avi-Yonah, *International Tax as International Law: An Analysis of the International Tax Regime* (New York: Cambridge University Press, 2007), pp. 90–92.

Chapter 3: Tax Policy Considerations and Approaches to Taxation

limitation as to the tax rate to be applied, such as capital gains derived from immovable property situated in the source State, as well as capital gains derived from 'immovable property companies'.[187]

3.2.2.2 Foreign Sovereign Wealth Investors

In many States, the tax treatment of foreign sovereign wealth investors follows the tax treatment of regular non-resident corporate investors,[188] both under domestic law and tax treaties. Depending on a source State's tax rules, this could mean that source taxation differentiates between types of income, such as interest and dividends, but it does so without distinction between foreign sovereign wealth investors and other non-resident corporate investors, including CIVs and pension funds. Source taxation imposed by other States represents a net cost to foreign sovereign wealth investors and their home States.

Some States accord specific tax-exemptions or specific tax reductions to foreign sovereign wealth investors, either unilaterally or under tax treaties. A few States even grant a general tax-exemption to foreign sovereign wealth investors, either unilaterally or under tax treaties.[189] Specific tax-exemptions or specific tax reductions refer to exemptions or reductions which conditionally apply to a specific category of income, whereas a general tax-exemption refers to an (un)conditional exemption of all income. These general and specific tax-exemptions or reductions may be available to some foreign sovereign wealth investors, but not to other foreign sovereign wealth investors. They are generally not available to 'regular' non-resident corporate investors.

The unilateral tax-exemptions, both specific and general ones, are granted under domestic law or administrative practice, and are often motivated with reference to sovereign immunity. According to the sovereign immunity principle, States have, as a general rule, no jurisdiction over foreign States and their instrumentalities in civil

---

187. Article 13(4) OECD MTC. Immovable property companies are companies the shares of which derive more than 50% of their value directly or indirectly from immovable property situated in the source State.
188. F. Bassan, 'SWFs and Taxation: National, Bilateral and Multilateral Approach', Chapter 8 in: F. Bassan (ed.), *Research Handbook on Sovereign Wealth Funds and International Investment Law* (Cheltenham: Edward Elgar Publishing, 2015), p. 209.
189. A general exemption from source taxation of income derived by foreign sovereign wealth investors can, for example, be found in the following tax treaties: *Agreement Between Mongolia and the United Arab Emirates for the Avoidance of Double Taxation and the Prevention of Fiscal Evasion with respect to Taxes on Income* (21 February 2001), Treaties IBFD; *Agreement Between the Government of New Zealand and the Government of the United Arab Emirates for the Avoidance of Double Taxation and the Prevention of Fiscal Evasion with respect to Taxes on Income* (22 September 2003), Treaties IBFD; *Agreement Between the Government of the Republic of Mauritius and the Government of the United Arab Emirates for the Avoidance of Double Taxation and the Prevention of Fiscal Evasion with respect to Taxes on Income* (18 September 2006), Treaties IBFD; *Convention Between the Government of the Republic of Azerbaijan and the Government of the United Arab Emirates for the Avoidance of Double Taxation with respect to Taxes on Income and on Capital* (20 November 2006), Treaties IBFD; *Agreement Between the Government of Georgia and the Government of the United Arab Emirates for the Avoidance of Double Taxation and the Prevention of Fiscal Evasion with respect to Taxes on Income and on Capital* (25 November 2010), Treaties IBFD.

proceedings.[190] Some States, including Australia, Canada, the United Kingdom ('UK') and the US, extend the sovereign immunity principle to the taxation of foreign States and their instrumentalities, including foreign sovereign wealth investors.[191] In this respect, most States distinguish between active income and passive income, and only grant tax-exemptions to passive income, as defined. This distinction is explained by the restrictive sovereign immunity theory, according to which immunity cannot be applied to commercial activities, as opposed to governmental activities. These States associate commercial activities with active income (taxed) and governmental activities with passive income (tax-exempt). Sovereign immunity as a motivation for unilateral tax-exemptions by source States vis-à-vis foreign sovereign wealth investors is elaborated on in more detail in Chapter 4 of this study. In a few other States, such as Singapore, unilateral tax-exemptions accorded to foreign sovereign wealth investors are explicitly motivated by international attractiveness.[192]

Tax-exemptions, both specific and general ones, granted to foreign sovereign wealth investors under a tax treaty are sometimes also motivated by reference to sovereign immunity (and perhaps a codification of administrative practice),[193] but more often based on reciprocity, as a leading principle of tax treaty negotiations, or motivated by international attractiveness. Reciprocity is often relied on between two States that are both home to sovereign wealth investors, for example under the tax treaty between Russia and the United Arab Emirates ('UAE').[194] Numerous source States without sovereign wealth investors, such as Germany,[195] the Netherlands[196] and Spain,[197] have also been willing to accord tax benefits to foreign sovereign wealth investors from the other State, either in return for tax benefits by that other State, or simply to attract investments.

In summary, source States have generally adopted one or more of the following five approaches to the taxation of (some) foreign sovereign wealth investors:[198]

---

190. *See* in more detail, Chapter 4 of this study.
191. *See* Section 4.3.1.
192. S-A Joseph, 'Taxing Sovereign Wealth Funds Mark II: Looking to Singapore for Inspiration', Australasian Tax Teachers Association Conference Papers, 2016, p. 15, available at: < https://www.business.unsw.edu.au/About-Site/Schools-Site/Taxation-Business-Law-Site/Documents/Joseph_ATTA-2016-Sally-Joseph.pdf >.
193. For example, the *Agreement Between the Government of New Zealand and the Government of the United Arab Emirates for the Avoidance of Double Taxation and the Prevention of Fiscal Evasion with respect to Taxes on Income* (22 September 2003), Treaties IBFD.
194. *Agreement Between the Government of the Russian Federation and the Government of the United Arab Emirates on Taxation of Income from Investments of the Contracting States or their Financial and Investment Institutions* (7 December 2011), Treaties IBFD.
195. *Agreement Between the Federal Republic of Germany and the United Arab Emirates for the Avoidance of Double Taxation and of Tax Evasion with respect to Taxes on Income* (1 July 2010), Treaties IBFD.
196. *See* the Appendix.
197. *Convention Between the Kingdom of Spain and the United Arab Emirates for the Avoidance of Double Taxation and the Prevention of Fiscal Evasion with respect to Taxes on Income and on Capital* (5 March 2006), Treaties IBFD.
198. Joint Committee on Taxation, *Economic and U.S. Income Tax Issues Raised by Sovereign Wealth Fund Investment in the United States* (June, 2008), JCX-49-08, Appendix One: Foreign Law Tax Treatment of Government Investment; PwC, *Sovereign Wealth Funds: Investment Trends and Global Tax Risks* (May, 2010); F. Bassan, 'SWFs and Taxation: National, Bilateral and

Chapter 3: Tax Policy Considerations and Approaches to Taxation

(1) taxing foreign sovereign wealth investors in the same way as 'regular' non-resident corporate investors.
(2) according a general tax-exemption under domestic law or administrative practice.
(3) according specific tax-exemptions or specific tax reductions under domestic law or administrative practice.
(4) according a general tax-exemption under one or more tax treaties.
(5) according specific tax-exemptions or specific tax reductions under one or more tax treaties.

These approaches will be referred to as Approaches (1) to (5) in this study and will be measured by their neutrality, equity and international attractiveness in Section 3.4 through Section 3.6. The impact international law could have on source States' ability to implement these approaches and to achieve (or promote) tax policy objectives will be examined in Chapter 4 to Chapter 6.

3.2.2.3 *Non-resident Collective Investment Vehicles*

Investment income derived by non-resident CIVs (from a source State perspective) could be subject to regular source taxation under domestic law. Because of the different legal forms that CIVs can take, as well as the different ways that CIVs are treated for tax purposes in the State in which they have been established,[199] it may not be clear whether non-resident CIVs are entitled to tax treaty benefits on investment income derived from a source State. Issues and policy considerations relating to CIVs in a tax treaty context have been discussed by the OECD Committee on Fiscal Affairs in its report *The Granting of Treaty Benefits with Respect to the Income of Collective Investment Vehicles*, the main conclusions of which have been reflected in Paragraphs 22-48 of the OECD Commentary on Article 1 (Persons covered). The report discusses a number of approaches and suggests different treaty provisions that explicitly provide for the treaty entitlement of CIVs under certain conditions. In essence, the ultimate goal is to achieve, as much as possible, neutrality for investors between a direct investment and an indirect investment through a CIV in an international setting.[200] Therefore, the approach that is most in line with this goal is that non-resident CIVs can be entitled to reduced source taxation under treaties, as applicable to each type of income, but the rate cannot generally be lower than the rate that the investor in the CIV could have claimed had it received the income directly. As this would, however, require CIVs to determine the entitlement of every single investor, and these investors could be resident in a third State, other, sometimes more practical, approaches are also discussed in the report.

Multilateral Approach', Chapter 8 in: F. Bassan (ed.), *Research Handbook on Sovereign Wealth Funds and International Investment Law* (Cheltenham: Edward Elgar Publishing, 2015), pp. 206 et seq.
199. *See* Section 3.2.1.3.
200. Paragraph 32 of the OECD Commentary on Art. 1 (Persons covered).

3.2.2.4 Non-resident Pension Funds

As explained in Section 3.2.1.4, many pension funds are tax-exempt in their residence State.[201] As a result, tax imposed by other States on such pension funds as non-residents represents a net cost to them (such pension funds cannot credit foreign taxes). This could distort neutrality with respect to the investment location. That is, pension funds could favour domestic investments over foreign investments. This consideration *mutatis mutandis* applies to foreign sovereign wealth investors, but, surprisingly, does not seem to have played a part for source States (Section 3.2.2.2). In order to promote neutrality, and attract investments, some States have agreed in their tax treaties not to impose source taxation on (certain items of) investment income of a non-resident pension fund in their bilateral relationship, usually on a reciprocity basis.[202] This, in deviation from the regular (domestic and tax treaty) rules that otherwise would have applied and continue to apply to 'regular' non-resident corporate investors. Other States apply a tax treaty to non-resident pension funds without having agreed any special tax treatment, whereas a limited number of States consider a tax treaty not to be applicable (and so disallow its benefits) to non-resident pension funds if they are tax-exempt in their residence State. In the 2017 version of the OECD MTC, 'recognized pension funds'[203] are explicitly mentioned as tax treaty residents, regardless of whether they benefit from a limited or complete exemption from taxation in their residence State.[204]

3.2.2.5 Non-resident Not-for-Profit Organizations

In some States, non-resident not-for-profit organizations are not treated any differently from resident not-for-profit organizations, provided they meet the local requirements, they meet additional requirements, or pursuant to a tax treaty.[205] Such equal treatment may have been forced upon EU Member States and (other) members to the EEA Agreements by the fundamental freedoms. In other States, non-resident not-for-profit organizations are subject to the ordinary corporate tax rules.[206] The comments made above in Section 3.2.2.4 in respect of the application of tax treaties to pension funds, are also relevant to not-for-profit organizations.

---

201. *See also* Para. 13.1 of the OECD Commentary on Art. 10 (Dividends).
202. Paragraph 13.1 of the OECD Commentary on Art. 10 (Dividends); Para. 7.10 of the OECD Commentary on Art. 11 (Interest); Para. 28.8 of the OECD Commentary on Art. 13 (Capital gains); Para. 69 of the OECD Commentary on Art. 18 (Pensions).
203. As defined in Art. 3(1)(i) of the OECD MTC.
204. Paragraphs 8.6–8.10 of the OECD Commentary on Art. 4. *See also* OECD (2016), *Discussion Draft on Changes to the OECD Model Tax Convention Concerning the Treaty Residence of Pension Funds*, available at: <http://www.oecd.org/tax/treaties/discussion-draft-treaty-residence-pension-funds.pdf>.
205. D. Gliksberg, 'General Report', in: *Taxation of Non-Profit Organizations*, IFA Cahiers de droit fiscal international, Vol. 84a (Alphen a/d Rijn: Kluwer Law International, 1999), pp. 56–57.
206. *Ibid.*, p. 57.

Chapter 3: Tax Policy Considerations and Approaches to Taxation

3.2.2.6 Comparison

The discussion regarding resident investors indicated that the home State tax treatment of sovereign wealth investors is based on a different rationale, compared to the tax treatment accorded by home States to other resident investor groups. However, the discussion above regarding non-resident investors shows that the (theoretical) rationales for source States to accord tax-exemptions or tax reductions to foreign sovereign wealth investors and other groups of non-resident investors, overlap to a great extent. This overlap exists, for example, with respect to tax-exemptions and tax reductions which are motivated by achieving neutrality between investing at home and abroad, and those which are motivated by attracting investments. In contrast, no overlap exists in case of tax-exemptions granted to foreign sovereign wealth investors by reference to the doctrine of sovereign immunity.[207] By its nature, this international law doctrine cannot apply to other investor groups, because they are not owned, controlled and funded by a foreign State. Finally, the rationale of achieving neutrality between directly investing and investing indirectly through a vehicle could, to some extent, also be relevant to foreign sovereign wealth investors if the home State – as the sole owner – would have been entitled to a tax-exemption or tax reduction had it invested directly.

3.3 IDENTIFYING THE MAIN ATTRIBUTES OF INTERNATIONAL TAX POLICY

A 2001 OECD study identified three general principles that should underlie 'good' tax policy:

> *First*, so long as taxation affects incentives it may alter economic behaviour (...) in ways that reduce <u>economic efficiency</u>. These effects should be taken into account when the costs and benefits of public expenditure to be funded are being assessed. *Second*, the distribution of taxation's impact across the population raises issues of <u>equity, or fairness</u>, which must be given substantial weight even if it entails costs in terms of economic efficiency. *Third*, the practical <u>enforceability</u> of tax rules and the <u>costs arising from compliance</u> are important considerations, the more so since these are both affected by, and have implications for, the efficiency and public perceptions of the fairness of tax systems.[208] (Emphasis added)

Economic efficiency (neutrality) and equity (fairness) can be seen as 'substantive' policy principles, whereas enforceability and compliance can be seen as 'procedural' policy principles. According to the OECD study, policymakers should find the best possible balance between these tax policy design criteria.[209]

---

207. The application of the sovereign immunity principle in tax matters will be discussed in Chapter 4.
208. OECD (2001), *Tax and the Economy: A Comparative Assessment of OECD Countries*, Tax Policy Studies No. 6, Paris, p. 17.
209. *Ibid.*

Procedural policy principles

In its inquiry into *Principles of tax policy*, the UK House of Commons reports that procedural principles imply that:[210]

- tax laws should be clear, simple and certain;
- tax policy should be stable, i.e., changes to the rules should be kept to a minimum, changes should be justified and this justification and its underlying policy should be made public, while policy shocks should be avoided;
- tax policy should be practicable, in the sense that the tax liability should be easy to calculate, and easy and cheap to collect.

A source State should consider procedural policy principles when introducing new tax policy or reconsidering existing tax policy vis-à-vis foreign sovereign wealth investors. These policy principles will, however, not be further considered in this study, because they do not offer insights as to how foreign sovereign wealth investors should be taxed (in substantive terms) from a source State perspective.

Substantive policy principles

A review of State practice confirms the importance of economic efficiency (neutrality) and equity (fairness) as principles that underlie 'good' international tax policy. Examples of States in which economic efficiency is an important international tax policy driver include Australia,[211] Brazil,[212] Germany,[213] the Netherlands,[214] Norway,[215] the UK[216] and the US. Equity (fairness) considerations have explicitly been referred to as an important tax policy driver in Germany,[217] Norway,[218] the UK[219] and the US,[220] among others. In addition to efficiency and equity (fairness), nowadays international competitiveness of a tax system is considered another important attribute

---

210. House of Commons, Treasury Committee, *Principles of tax policy*, Eight Report of Session 2010–2011, HC 753, pp. 15–25, available at: < https://publications.parliament.uk/pa/cm201 011/cmselect/cmtreasy/753/753.pdf >.
211. R. Krever & P. Mellor, 'Australia', Chapter 2 in: M. Lang et al., *Trends and Players in Tax Policy*, IBFD 2016, Online Books IBFD, sec. 2.7.3.
212. L. Schoueri & M. Barbosa, 'Brazil', Chapter 4 in: M. Lang et al., *Trends and Players in Tax Policy*, IBFD 2016, Online Books IBFD, sec. 4.7.1.
213. G. Müller-Gatermann, 'Germany', Chapter 10 in: M. Lang et al., *Trends and Players in Tax Policy*, IBFD 2016, Online Books IBFD, sec. 10.7.
214. *Notitie Fiscaal Verdragsbeleid 2011, Tweede Kamer*, 2010–2011, 25 087, No. 7.
215. F. Zimmer, A. Scapa Passalacqua & L. Henie, 'Norway', Chapter 14 in: M. Lang et al., *Trends and Players in Tax Policy*, IBFD 2016, Online Books IBFD, sec. 14.7.2.
216. House of Commons, Treasury Committee, *Principles of tax policy*, Eight Report of Session 2010–2011, HC 753, pp. 10–12.
217. G. Müller-Gatermann, 'Germany', Chapter 10 in: M. Lang et al., *Trends and Players in Tax Policy*, IBFD 2016, Online Books IBFD, sec. 10.7.
218. F. Zimmer, A. Scapa Passalacqua & L. Henie, 'Norway', Chapter 14 in: M. Lang et al., *Trends and Players in Tax Policy*, IBFD 2016, Online Books IBFD, sec. 14.2.1.3.
219. House of Commons, Treasury Committee, *Principles of tax policy*, Eight Report of Session 2010–2011, HC 753, p. 10.
220. J. Bird-Pollan, 'The Unjustified Subsidy: Sovereign Wealth Funds and the Foreign Sovereign Tax Exemption' (2012) 17 *Fordham Journal of Corporate & Financial Law* 987, pp. 990–992.

Chapter 3: Tax Policy Considerations and Approaches to Taxation

of international tax policy in many States, including Australia,[221] Austria,[222] Canada,[223] China,[224] Colombia,[225] the Czech Republic,[226] Germany,[227] the Netherlands,[228] New Zealand,[229] Norway[230] and the UK.[231] Given the apparent international importance of: (i) efficiency (neutrality), (ii) equity (fairness), and (iii) international attractiveness, these three attributes of international tax policy, and their relationship with source taxation of sovereign wealth investors, are considered in more detail below.

3.4 INTERNATIONAL NEUTRALITY (EFFICIENCY)

3.4.1 General

Tax neutrality theories are economic theories believed to increase economic efficiency and welfare.[232] Tax neutrality is achieved when economic decisions are not (or, at least, as little as possible) distorted by taxation. In an international context, tax neutrality, referred to as international tax neutrality, is said to promote an efficient allocation of global capital, thus promoting global welfare.[233] The baseline for assessing international tax neutrality is a non-tax world, which is considered to be ideally efficient. The two classic welfare benchmarks for assessing (one side of) international tax neutrality, introduced by Peggy Musgrave[234] and an underlying principle of international tax policy in many States, are capital export neutrality ('CEN') and capital

---

221. R. Krever & P. Mellor, 'Australia', Chapter 2 in: M. Lang et al., *Trends and Players in Tax Policy*, IBFD 2016, Online Books IBFD, sec. 2.7.1.
222. A. Zeiler, 'Austria', Chapter 3 in: M. Lang et al., *Trends and Players in Tax Policy*, IBFD 2016, Online Books IBFD, sec. 3.7.1.1.
223. K. Brooks, 'Canada', Chapter 5 in: M. Lang et al., *Trends and Players in Tax Policy*, IBFD 2016, Online Books IBFD, sec. 5.7.
224. J. Kang & L. Na, 'China', Chapter 6 in: M. Lang et al., *Trends and Players in Tax Policy*, IBFD 2016, Online Books IBFD, sec. 6.7.
225. N. Quiñones, 'Colombia', Chapter 7 in: M. Lang et al., *Trends and Players in Tax Policy*, IBFD 2016, Online Books IBFD, sec. 7.7.
226. D. Nerudová & L. Moravec, 'Czech Republic', Chapter 9 in: M. Lang et al., *Trends and Players in Tax Policy*, IBFD 2016, Online Books IBFD, sec. 9.7.
227. G. Müller-Gatermann, 'Germany', Chapter 10 in: M. Lang et al., *Trends and Players in Tax Policy*, IBFD 2016, Online Books IBFD, sec. 10.7.
228. *Notitie Fiscaal Verdragsbeleid 2011*, Tweede Kamer, 2010–2011, 25 087, No. 7; S. Hemels, 'Netherlands', Chapter 12 in: M. Lang et al., *Trends and Players in Tax Policy*, IBFD 2016, Online Books IBFD, sec. 12.7.
229. A. Sawyer & A. Smith, 'New Zealand', Chapter 13 in: M. Lang et al., *Trends and Players in Tax Policy*, IBFD 2016, Online Books IBFD, sec. 13.7.
230. F. Zimmer, A. Scapa Passalacqua & L. Henie, 'Norway', Chapter 14 in: M. Lang et al., *Trends and Players in Tax Policy*, IBFD 2016, Online Books IBFD, sec. 14.2.1.7.
231. House of Commons, Treasury Committee, *Principles of tax policy*, Eight Report of Session 2010–2011, HC 753, pp. 13–14; C. Wales & C. Turnbull-Hall, 'United Kingdom', Chapter 20 in: M. Lang et al., *Trends and Players in Tax Policy*, IBFD 2016, Online Books IBFD, sec. 20.7.1.
232. F. Shaheen, 'International Tax Neutrality: Reconsiderations' (2007) 27 *Virginia Tax Review* 203, p. 207.
233. R. Mason, 'Tax Discrimination and Capital Neutrality' (2010) 2 *World Tax Journal* 126, p. 126.
234. P. Richman, *Taxation of Foreign Investment Income: An Economic Analysis* (Baltimore: The John Hopkins Press, 1963). Before marrying Richard Musgrave, Peggy Musgrave was Peggy Richman.

import neutrality ('CIN'). As the terminology already suggests, both neutrality concepts are not fully neutral as they address one-sided capital movements only.[235] A third, more recently introduced, global welfare benchmark is capital ownership neutrality ('CON').[236] These three neutrality concepts, their implications for the design of international tax rules and relevant considerations for source State taxation of foreign sovereign wealth investors, are discussed below.

3.4.2 Capital Export Neutrality

3.4.2.1 The Concept Explained

CEN addresses a State taxing in a residence capacity[237] and promotes neutrality with respect to the location of investment.[238] A tax system is said to achieve CEN when tax considerations do not influence a resident investor's decision between investing capital in its home market or abroad (i.e., export neutral), thus allocating capital of residents economically most efficient. This requires resident investors to face the same tax burden on their domestic and outbound investments (investment location neutrality). Under CEN, investors have an incentive to locate investments where pre-tax returns are highest. CEN implies a tax system of worldwide taxation with a full credit for foreign taxes (residence-based taxation).[239] There is no consensus on whether CEN is relevant for the taxation of non-resident investors (i.e., foreign inbound investments). Some authors argue that CEN implies no taxation of non-resident investors,[240] while others argue that CEN appears to have nothing to do with the taxation of non-resident investors.[241] According to the present author, CEN is as such not concerned with a State taxing in a source capacity; CEN does not tell a source State to tax or to forgo tax in relation to non-resident investors. In fact, 'pure' CEN would even require a State acting in a residence capacity to refund foreign source taxation to the extent it exceeds residence taxation (i.e., the responsibility to achieve export neutrality rests with the residence State, as opposed to the source State).

---

235. K. Vogel, 'Worldwide vs. Source Taxation of Income – A Review and Re-evaluation of Arguments (Part II)' (1988) 10 *Intertax* 310, p. 313.
236. Other neutrality concepts, aimed at maximizing national welfare, are national neutrality (allowing residents a deduction for foreign taxes) and national ownership neutrality (exempting foreign income derived by residents). These concepts are not further considered in this study, as they are not concerned with the taxation of non-residents.
237. M. de Wilde, 'Some Thoughts on a Fair Allocation of Corporate Tax in a Globalizing Economy' (2010) 38 *Intertax* 281, p. 294.
238. R. Mason, 'Tax Discrimination and Capital Neutrality' (2010) 2 *World Tax Journal* 126, p. 130.
239. 'Pure' CEN would even require a refund to the extent that the foreign tax exceeds the tax in the residence State.
240. M. Graetz, 'The David R. Tillinghast Lecture Taxing International Income: Inadequate Principles, Outdated Concepts and Unsatisfactory Policies' (2001) 54 *Tax Law Review* 261, p. 271.
241. R. Mason, 'Tax Discrimination and Capital Neutrality' (2010) 2 *World Tax Journal* 126, p. 133.

Chapter 3: Tax Policy Considerations and Approaches to Taxation

3.4.2.2 *Considerations Regarding Foreign Sovereign Wealth Investors*

Although the present author does not consider CEN as such to be concerned with the taxation of non-resident investors, this neutrality concept could provide an argument for a source State not to tax income derived by foreign sovereign wealth investors. This argument is similar to the argument discussed in Section 3.2.2.4 regarding tax-exempt pension funds. As explained in Section 2.10, foreign sovereign wealth investors are generally not taxed in their residence State. Source State taxation of tax-exempt non-resident investors could distort neutrality with respect to the investment location, i.e., it could result in tax-exempt investors favouring domestic investments over foreign investments. In order to promote export neutrality, a source State could consider to exempt from source taxation investment income derived by foreign sovereign wealth investors and other non-resident tax-exempt investors. It could accord such treatment unilaterally or through tax treaties.

Considering the above, Approaches (2) to (5), under which source States grant a general or specific tax-exemptions to (some) foreign sovereign wealth investors, either unilaterally or through tax treaties, could be motivated by referring to promoting CEN. On the other hand, Approach (1), under which source States tax foreign sovereign wealth investors in the same way as 'regular' non-resident corporate investors, does not promote CEN, unless taxation in the same way means no taxation at all.

3.4.3 Capital Import Neutrality

3.4.3.1 *The Concept Explained*

CIN is the flipside of CEN, and promotes neutrality with respect to the location of investors, rather than the location of investment. Musgrave introduced CIN with a view to create 'equal opportunities for expansion' in a particular State for all (foreign) investors.[242] A tax system is said to achieve CIN when tax considerations do not influence which investor, that is, a resident or non-resident investor, makes which investment in one particular State (i.e., import neutral). CIN implies a territorial (or source-based) tax system rather than a residence-based tax system;[243] in other words, a tax system which exempts foreign sourced income and treats domestic sourced income of resident and non-resident investors in the same way. In this respect, the characteristics of investors and place of residence are irrelevant. CIN simply requires equal treatment of investors that perform the same level of investment activities in a source State. Although equal source taxation of all investors investing in one particular jurisdiction, regardless of their residency, promotes CIN, it does not necessarily achieve CIN. Taxes imposed by foreign States may distort import neutrality in the source State, for example when the residence State of a foreign investor applies

---

242. P. Richman, *Taxation of Foreign Investment Income: An Economic Analysis* (Baltimore: The John Hopkins Press, 1963), at 8.
243. K. Vogel, 'Worldwide vs. Source Taxation of Income – A Review and Re-evaluation of Arguments (Part II)' (1988) 10 *Intertax* 310, p. 311.

worldwide taxation (promoting CEN) at rates exceeding those of the source State.[244] It has been said that 'pure' CIN obtains only if *all* States would adopt source-based taxation.[245] Nevertheless, CIN based tax systems at least aim to promote CIN.

There is no consensus in literature on whether CIN is relevant for portfolio investments, i.e., investments that give the investor little or no control over business activities. Some authors argue that CIN only has relevance for direct investments, because taxation of portfolio investments has no, or at most a small, influence on the location of plant or equipment (i.e., location of investment) and, therefore, productivity.[246] The thinking behind this seems to be that capital from portfolio investors is easy to obtain and that portfolio investors are easily replaceable in a global market. Other authors do apply CIN in relation to portfolio investments, because unequal tax treatment of resident and non-resident portfolio investors could impact relative prices, and distort investment decisions and an efficient global allocation of capital.[247] In the present author's view, it is not unlikely that portfolio investments could have influence on the location of business activity. The availability of portfolio capital may vary per country, per region within a country, per sector, per industry and even per company, and may change over time. Currently, portfolio capital may, for example, not be widely available to small and medium-sized enterprises, start-ups and other companies with high-risk profiles. In addition, the distinction between direct investment and portfolio investment, although analytically helpful, is not always clear in practice. For these reasons, this study considers CIN without distinguishing between direct investments and portfolio investments. It is noted, though, that both individuals and companies can make portfolio investments, whereas direct investments are almost always made by companies.[248]

3.4.3.2 *Considerations Regarding Foreign Sovereign Wealth Investors*

CIN is promoted if a State exempts foreign sourced income and taxes domestic sourced income of all investors in the same way, regardless of their residence and characteristics (source-based taxation). In other words, all activity within a State's territory should be treated alike. Equal tax treatment of resident and non-resident investors sounds straightforward, but the actual implementation raises several potential issues. One

---

244. R. Mason, 'Tax Discrimination and Capital Neutrality' (2010) 2 *World Tax Journal* 126, p. 130.
245. F. Shaheen, 'International Tax Neutrality: Reconsiderations' (2007) 27 *Virginia Tax Review* 203, p. 212. This assumes that the location of the investment is fixed.
246. M. Graetz & I. Grinberg, 'Taxing International Portfolio Income' (2003) 56 *Tax Law Review* 537, pp. 554–556.
247. E. Kemmeren, *Principle of Origin in Tax Conventions: A Rethinking of Models* (2001), Dongen: Mr. Eric C.C.M. Kemmeren/Pijnenburg vormgevers, uitgevers, pp. 78–81, available at < https://pure.uvt.nl/portal/files/439888/87428.pdf > ; M.P. Devereux, *Taxation of Outbound Direct Investment: Economic Principles and Tax Policy Considerations*, Research Report Prepared for the Advisory Panel on Canada's System of International Taxation, July 2008, available at: < https://www.sbs.ox.ac.uk/faculty-research/tax/publications/working-papers/taxation-outbound-direct-investment-economic-principles-and-tax-policy-considerations > .
248. M. Graetz & I. Grinberg, 'Taxing International Portfolio Income' (2003) 56 *Tax Law Review* 537, p. 547.

Chapter 3: Tax Policy Considerations and Approaches to Taxation

potential issue relates to the appropriate comparison of investors. If CIN is indeed limited to direct investments, it seems clear that the position of individuals can be disregarded, because, direct investments are almost always made by companies, as indicated. As a consequence, income derived by foreign sovereign wealth investors from direct investment in a source State should receive the same source tax treatment as income derived by other resident and non-resident corporate investors from direct investment in that State. On the other hand, *if* CIN is also relevant for portfolio investments, it seems necessary to consider the position of individuals as well, because individuals can also make portfolio investments. As a consequence, since CIN does not distinguish between types of investors, income derived by foreign sovereign wealth investors from portfolio investment in a source State should receive the same source tax treatment as income *directly* derived by resident and non-resident individuals from portfolio investment in that State. However, as discussed, portfolio investments of individuals are often made *indirectly* through investment vehicles, such as CIVs. As explained, portfolio income can be tax-exempt at the level of these (corporate) vehicles, but subsequent distributions are then usually taxed at the level of the individuals. In the author's view, equal tax treatment as prescribed by CIN requires that resident and non-resident investors that perform the same level of investment activities in a source State are faced with the same overall tax burden *as imposed by the source State*. For resident individuals deriving source income through investment vehicles, this would mean that both corporate level taxes (if any) and personal income tax should be taken into account, and this combined tax burden should be equal to the source tax burden of portfolio income of foreign sovereign wealth investors and other non-resident portfolio investors performing the same level of investment activities in a source State.

Another potential issue relates to the treatment of different categories of investment income. At first sight, the uniform tax treatment of all different categories of income, e.g., a flat rate of 20% on all source income derived by resident and non-resident investors, seems to be neutral. However, dividends are often paid out of profits that already have been or will become subject to corporate tax in a source State, effectively at the expense of the investors-shareholders. This could also apply to capital gains on shares. Imposing a flat tax rate on such dividends and capital gains, as well as other categories of income, could influence investors' behaviour and preference for type of investment income, and produce inefficient outcomes. In the author's view, equal tax treatment as prescribed by CIN also requires neutrality with respect to the type of investment activity, e.g., an investment in loans, shares or immovable property. In other words, the decision to invest in e.g., loans, shares or immovable property should not be influenced by tax considerations. This would require investors with an equal level of investment income from a source State to face equal source State tax burdens, irrespective of the composition of the investment income.

Considering the above, Approaches (2) to (5)[249] regarding the tax treatment of sovereign wealth investors cannot be explained by CIN, because they could result in

---

249. As identified in Section 3.2.2.2. Approaches (2) to (5) are as follows:

different tax treatment *among* foreign sovereign wealth investors, and *between* foreign sovereign wealth investors and other (resident and non-resident) investors, both individuals and companies. On the other hand, Approach (1), under which source States tax foreign sovereign wealth investors in the same way as 'regular' non-resident corporate investors, could be motivated by CIN.

3.4.4 Capital Ownership Neutrality

3.4.4.1 The Concept Explained

Desai and Hines introduced CON, as a benchmark that promotes global welfare, in 2003.[250] They explain that '[t]ax systems satisfy capital ownership neutrality if they do not distort ownership patterns'.[251] The basic assumption underlying CON is that productivity of capital (assets) varies depending on the investor (owner).[252] This means that CON is relevant with respect to direct investments – active investments giving the investor influence on the business decisions and, therefore, productivity –, but not so much with respect to portfolio investments – passive investments giving the investor little or no influence on productivity. CON requires that the most efficient ownership pattern be reached across investors in terms of productivity.[253] According to Desai and Hines, CON would be satisfied if *all* States would adopt either a residence-based tax system or a territorial tax system (source-based taxation).[254]

As explained below, ownership neutrality is achieved when each investor retains the same proportion of the before-tax return across investments. It does not matter when different investors retain different proportions of before-tax returns, as long as each investor retains the same proportion of the before-tax return across investments.

Suppose that two investors, Investor X and Investor Y, are competing for Investment A (the candidate investment), an investment opportunity in source State A.[255] Assume that an investment of 1,000 in Investment A generates 1,120 (or 12%) to Investor X and 1,100 (or 10%) to Investor Y. Let us further assume that the best alternative investment to each investor is another investment in State A, which would

---

(2) according a general tax-exemption under domestic law or administrative practice.
(3) according specific tax-exemptions or specific tax reductions under domestic law or administrative practice.
(4) according a general tax-exemption under one or more tax treaties.
(5) according specific tax-exemptions or specific tax reductions under one or more tax treaties.

250. M. Desai & J. Hines Jr., 'Evaluating International Tax Reform' (2003) 56 *National Tax Journal* 487.
251. *Ibid.*, p. 494.
252. F. Shaheen, 'International Tax Neutrality: Revisited' (2011) 64 *Tax Law Review* 131, p. 136.
253. *Ibid.*, p. 141.
254. M. Desai & J. Hines Jr., 'Evaluating International Tax Reform' (2003) 56 *National Tax Journal* 487, pp. 494–495.
255. The example in this section is inspired by the example in F. Shaheen, 'International Tax Neutrality: Revisited' (2011) 64 *Tax Law Review* 131, pp. 139–143.

Chapter 3: Tax Policy Considerations and Approaches to Taxation

produce a rate of return of 6% to both investors. The rate of return on this alternative investment determines the maximum price each investor is willing to pay for Investment A. Investor X is willing to pay up to 1,056,[256] while Investor Y is willing to pay no more than 1,037.[257] Ownership neutrality requires that Investor X (being the most productive owner) would acquire Investment A for 1,038 and that Investor Y would acquire the alternative investment. Now, taxation is added to the example. Assume that source State A taxes all investors on State A sourced income at a rate of 20%. Source-based taxation by State A does not change the value each investor places on Investment A. This is because each investor retains the same proportion of the before-tax return on both investments. That is, each investor retains 80% across both investments.[258]

Residence-based taxation may also achieve ownership neutrality between investors. For purposes of the example above, assume that Investor X is a resident in State X and taxed on its worldwide income at a rate of 30%, whereas Investor Y is a resident in State Y and taxed on its worldwide income at a rate of 40%. Assume that State A also applies residence-based taxation. Investor X and Investor Y would still value Investment A at 1,056[259] respectively 1,037.[260] As explained, the reason why the value each investor places on Investment A does not change is because each investor retains the same proportion of the before-tax return across investments. That is, the retention rate for Investor X on all investments is 70%, whereas the retention rate for Investor Y on all investments is 60%.

Source-based taxation and residence-based taxation may also achieve ownership neutrality when the alternative investment generates a different rate of return between investors. Recall the original example above where an investment of 1,000 in Investment A, located in State A, generates 1,120 (or 12%) to Investor X and 1,100 (or 10%) to Investor Y. Recall that source State A taxes all investors on State A sourced income at a rate of 20%. Now assume that the alternative investment in State A generates 9% to Investor X and 6% to Investor Y. Both in a non-tax world and in a tax world, Investor

---

256. $1{,}120/1.06 \approx 1{,}056.60$. An investment of 1,056.60 in the alternative investment would generate 1,120 (or 6%) to Investor X. If Investor X would pay more than 1,056.60 for Investment A, the rate of return would be less than 6% and she would prefer the alternative investment.
257. $1{,}100/1.06 \approx 1{,}037.74$. An investment of 1,037.74 in the alternative investment would generate 1,100 (or 6%) to Investor Y. If Investor Y would pay more than 1,037.74 for Investment A, the rate of return would be less than 6% and Investor Y would prefer the alternative investment.
258. For Investor X, the after-tax rate of return on Investment A would be reduced from 7.9% to 6.3% and on the alternative investment from 6% to 4.8%. For Investor Y, the after-tax rate of return on both investments would be reduced from 6% to 4.8%.
259. $1{,}120/1.06 \approx 1{,}056.60$. The after-tax return on the alternative investment for Investor X is 4.2% $((1 - 0.3) * 6\%)$. An investment of 1,056.60 in the alternative investment would generate 1,120 (or 4.2% after taxes) to Investor X. If Investor X would pay more than 1,056.60 for Investment A, the after-tax rate of return would be less than 4.2% and Investor X would prefer the alternative investment.
260. $1{,}100/1.06 \approx 1{,}037.74$. The after-tax return on the alternative investment for Investor Y is 3.6% $((1 - 0.4) * 6\%)$. An investment of 1,037.74 in the alternative investment would generate 1,100 (or 3.6%) to Investor Y. If Investor Y would pay more than 1,037.74 for Investment A, the rate of return would be less than 3.6% and Investor Y would prefer the alternative investment.

X is now willing to pay no more than 1,027[261] for Investment A, while Investor Y is still willing to pay up to 1,037.[262] Thus, Investor Y would outbid Investor X (the most productive owner for Investment A) and acquire Investment A for 1,028, whereas Investor X would acquire the alternative investment. Although Investor X is the most productive owner for Investment A, this outcome of Investor Y acquiring Investment A and Investor X acquiring the alternative investment, is the desired outcome from an ownership neutrality perspective. The overall productivity of such an ownership pattern (10% + 9%) is higher than that of Investor X acquiring Investment A and Investor Y acquiring the alternative investment (12% + 6%). Therefore, the ownership pattern reached across investors is most efficient in terms of productivity. The analysis does not change under residence-based taxation when each investor retains the same proportion of the before-tax return across investments.

In the examples discussed above, ownership neutrality is satisfied. However, the co-existence and interplay of tax systems may distort ownership neutrality. When all States involved would have adopted residence-based tax systems, ownership would be satisfied, since each investor would retain the same proportion of the before-tax return across all investments, also when tax rates differ across States.[263] In contrast, the interplay of source-based tax systems only, or the interplay of residence-based and source-based tax systems, may not satisfy ownership neutrality when tax rates differ across States. The following example illustrates that the interplay of source-based tax systems might not be ownership neutral when tax rates differ across States. Recall the original example above where an investment of 1,000 in Investment A, located in State A, generates 1,120 (or 12%) to Investor X and 1,100 (or 10%) to Investor Y. Recall further that source State A taxes all investors on State A sourced income at a rate of 20%. Now assume that the alternative investment generates 9% to Investor X and 6% to Investor Y, but is now located in State B (instead of State A). State B imposes source taxation on all investors at a rate of 60%. As demonstrated in the previous paragraph, ownership neutrality requires that Investor Y acquires Investment A and Investor X acquires the alternative investment. However, because State B imposes source taxation at a rate of 60% and State A imposes source taxation at a rate of 20%, Investor X would be willing to pay up to 1,071[264] for Investment A and would outbid Investor Y, who

---

261. 1,120/1.09 ≈ 1,027.52. The after-tax return on the alternative investment for Investor X is 7.2% ((1 − 0.2) * 9%). An investment of 1,027.52 in the alternative investment would generate 1,120 (or 7.2% after taxes) to Investor X. If Investor X would pay more than 1,027.52 for Investment A, the after-tax rate of return would be less than 7.2% and Investor X would prefer the alternative investment.
262. 1,100/1.06 ≈ 1,037.74. The after-tax return on the alternative investment for Investor Y is 4.8% ((1 − 0.2) * 6%). An investment of 1,037.74 in the alternative investment would generate 1,100 (or 4.8% after taxes) to Investor Y. If Investor Y would pay more than 1,037.74 for Investment A, the after-tax rate of return would be less than 4.8% and Investor Y would prefer the alternative investment.
263. M. Knoll, 'Reconsidering International Tax Neutrality' (2011) 64 *Tax Law Review* 99.
264. The after-tax return on the alternative investment for Investor X is 3.6% ((1 − 0.6) * 9%). An acquisition price of 1,071.77 for Investment A would generate the same after-tax rate of return for Investor X on Investment A ((1,120 − 1,071.77) * (1 − 0.2) / 1,071.77 * 100 = 3.6%). If Investor X would pay more than 1,071.77 for Investment A, the after-tax rate of return on this investment would be less than 3.6% and Investor X would prefer the alternative investment.

Chapter 3: Tax Policy Considerations and Approaches to Taxation

would be willing to pay no more than 1,068.[265] The reason why Investment A is now worth more to Investor X than to Investor Y, is because being taxed at a lower rate is worth more to a more productive investor (Investor X) than to a less productive investor (Investor Y). Similarly, the interplay of residence-based and source-based tax systems might fail ownership neutrality. For purposes of the example in this paragraph, further assume that Investor X is a resident in State X and taxed on its worldwide income at a rate of 30%, whereas Investor Y is a resident in State Y and taxed on its worldwide income at a rate of 40%. State X and State Y allow foreign tax credits but limited to the level of domestic tax. Investor X and Investor Y would now value Investment A at 1,065[266] respectively 1,057.[267] Hence, Investor X would outbid Investor Y for Investment A and ownership neutrality would not be achieved.

3.4.4.2 *Considerations Regarding Foreign Sovereign Wealth Investors*

The theory behind ownership neutrality is clear: ownership neutrality is achieved when each investor retains the same proportion of the before-tax return across investments; it does not matter when different investors retain different proportions of before-tax returns, as long as each investor retains the same proportion of the before-tax return across investments. Whether this standard is satisfied in an international setting, depends on the interplay of tax systems, the outcome of which is driven by various connected factors, such as tax rates, the location of investments, the location of investors and the nature of the investments. It is argued here that in today's global economy, where investment assets are located in numerous States that may tax investors in different ways at different rates, this neutrality concept has little, if any, practical meaning. And so it will not be further considered in this study.

---

265. The after-tax return on the alternative investment for Investor Y is 2.4% ((1 – 0.6) * 6%). An acquisition price of 1,067.96 for Investment A would generate the same after-tax rate of return for Investor Y on Investment A ((1,100 – 1,067.96) * (1 – 0.2) / 1,067.96 * 100 = 2.4%). If Investor Y would pay more than 1,067.96 for Investment A, the after-tax rate of return on this investment would be less than 2.4% and Investor Y would prefer the alternative investment.
266. The after-tax return on the alternative investment for Investor X is 3.6% ((1 – 0.6) * 9%). An acquisition price of 1,065.21 for Investment A would generate the same after-tax rate of return for Investor X on Investment A ((1,120 – 1,065.21) * (1 – 0.3) / 1,065.21 * 100 = 3.6%). If Investor X would pay more than 1,065.21 for Investment A, the after-tax rate of return on this investment would be less than 3.6% and Investor X would prefer the alternative investment.
267. The after-tax return on the alternative investment for Investor Y is 2.4% ((1 – 0.6) * 6%). An acquisition price of 1,057.69 for Investment A would generate the same after-tax rate of return for Investor Y on Investment A ((1,100 – 1,057.69) * (1 – 0.4) / 1,057.69 * 100 = 2.4%). If Investor Y would pay more than 1,057.69 for Investment A, the after-tax rate of return on this investment would be less than 2.4% and Investor Y would prefer the alternative investment.

3.5 EQUITY (FAIRNESS)

3.5.1 General

Equity is a moral concept, derived from justice (fairness),[268] and an important tax policy principle. The concept of equity has two main elements in a tax policy context: inter-nation equity and inter-taxpayer equity. Inter-nation equity is concerned with a fair (equitable) allocation of national gain (and loss) between States with respect to cross-border activities.[269] On the other hand, inter-taxpayer equity is concerned with a fair (equitable) allocation of tax obligations between taxpayers. Inter-taxpayer equity has two main elements: horizontal equity and vertical equity.[270] Horizontal equity requires that taxpayers who are equals pay equal amounts of tax,[271] whereas vertical equity, in essence, requires that taxpayers who are not equals be taxed differently taking into account their differences.[272] In the author's view, horizontal and vertical inter-taxpayer equity are corollaries of the principle of equality.[273] Aristotle formulated the equality principle as: 'things that are alike should be treated alike, while things that are unalike should be treated unalike in proportion to their unalikeness. (...). Equality and justice are synonymous: to be just is to be equal, to be unjust is to be unequal'.[274] It is fair to say that inter-taxpayer equity deals with (economic) justice between taxpayers, in that it prescribes a just allocation of the tax burden among taxpayers. Inter-taxpayer equity and inter-nation equity, their implications for the design of international tax rules and relevant considerations for source State taxation of foreign sovereign wealth investors, are discussed below.

3.5.2 Inter-taxpayer Equity

3.5.2.1 The Concept Explained

Two theories have dominated discussions on inter-taxpayer equity: the ability-to-pay theory and the benefit theory. Under the ability-to-pay theory, each taxpayer should

---

268. K. Vogel, 'Worldwide vs. Source Taxation of Income – A Review and Re-evaluation of Arguments (Part III)' (1988) 11 *Intertax* 393, p. 393.
269. OECD (2015), *Addressing the Tax Challenges of the Digital Economy, Action 1 – 2015 Final Report*, OECD/G20 Base Erosion and Profit Shifting Project, OECD Publishing, Paris, Chapter 2 – Fundamental Principles of Taxation, p. 21.
270. OECD (2015), *Addressing the Tax Challenges of the Digital Economy, Action 1 – 2015 Final Report*, OECD/G20 Base Erosion and Profit Shifting Project, OECD Publishing, Paris, Chapter 2 – Fundamental Principles of Taxation, p. 21.
271. D. Elkins. 'Horizontal Equity as a Principle of Tax Theory' (2006) 24 *Yale Law & Policy Review* 43.
272. M. de Wilde, *'Sharing the Pie'; Taxing Multinationals in a Global Market* (2015), p. 45, available at: < https://repub.eur.nl/pub/77496/ >.
273. Similarly, M. de Wilde, *'Sharing the Pie'; Taxing Multinationals in a Global Market* (2015), p. 45; D. Herman, *Taxing Portfolio Income in Global Financial Markets*, IBFD Doctoral Series, Vol. 2 (Amsterdam: IBFD, 2002), p. 101.
274. Derived from N. Bammens, *The Principle of Non-discrimination in International and European Tax Law*, IBFD Doctoral Series, Vol. 24 (Amsterdam: IBFD, 2012), p. 5.

Chapter 3: Tax Policy Considerations and Approaches to Taxation

pay tax in accordance with its ability to pay; taxpayers with greater abilities should pay more tax than taxpayers with lesser abilities, while taxpayers with equal abilities should pay an equal amount of tax. Ability-to-pay theory in taxation has become associated with theories of distributive justice, i.e., the redistribution of goods and welfare between persons within a society through taxation.[275] The other theory, the benefit theory, requires that each taxpayer should pay tax in accordance with its level of benefit from governmental goods and services; taxpayers who benefit more from public goods and services should pay more tax than taxpayers who benefit less, while taxpayers who benefit equally should pay an equal amount of tax.

In the tax systems of many States, a basic distinction is made between residents and non-residents, which indicates that residents and non-residents are generally not considered equals. The following discussion about the ability-to-pay theory and the benefit theory also points to a basic difference between residents and non-residents in the context of inter-taxpayer equity. In addition, the benefit theory might indicate a basic equality between non-residents *inter se* when they perform similar activities in the same State.

Residence-based taxation is often associated with the ability-to-pay theory[276] and source-based taxation is not. This is because the source of income is irrelevant to ability to pay[277] and worldwide income of taxpayers serves as a better indication of a taxpayer's ability than does domestic (sourced) income only. Also, the redistribution function attributed to a tax system is better served when worldwide income is used, while redistribution is often limited to residents within a society. Indeed, the ability-to-pay theory points to a basic difference between residents and non-residents and its practical relevance is limited to residents.[278]

Sometimes, the benefit theory is used to explain residence-based taxation, as well as source-based taxation in general and source-based taxation of non-residents.[279] In theory, the benefit principle is relevant for both residents and non-residents. However, general points of criticism about the benefit theory are that the meaning of benefit is unclear and that it is difficult, if not impossible, to measure a taxpayer's benefit (when defined).[280] Given this criticism, it has been argued that source-based taxation of non-residents can perhaps be best explained on the basis of the international law principle of territoriality (entitling a State to impose tax on activities and wealth within

---

275. N. Kaufman, 'Fairness in International Taxation of International Income' (1998) 29 *Law & Policy in International Business* 145, pp. 157–158.
276. N. Kaufman, 'Fairness in International Taxation of International Income' (1998) 29 *Law & Policy in International Business* 145. J. Englisch, 'Ability to Pay', Chapter 19 in: C. Brokelind (ed.), *Principles of Law: Function, Status and Impact in EU Tax Law*, IBFD 2014, Online Books IBFD.
277. J. Fleming, R. Peroni & S. Shay, 'Fairness in International Taxation: The Ability-to-Pay Case for Taxing Worldwide Income' (2001) 5 *Florida Tax Review* 301, p. 311.
278. Similarly, D. Herman, *Taxing Portfolio Income in Global Financial Markets*, IBFD Doctoral Series, Vol. 2 (Amsterdam: IBFD, 2002), p. 130.
279. N. Kaufman, 'Fairness in International Taxation of International Income' (1998) 29 *Law & Policy in International Business* 145.
280. For other points of criticism, *see* N. Kaufman, 'Fairness in International Taxation of International Income' (1998) 29 *Law & Policy in International Business* 145, pp. 183–188.

its territory).²⁸¹ Although the benefit theory has been criticized, often for reasons of practicality, it does offer rules for the taxation of residents and non-residents. Since residents have a stronger personal and generally a stronger economic connection to a State than do non-residents, it can be argued that residents generally benefit more from public goods and services than do non-residents. Unlike non-residents, residents also benefit from public goods and services when they do not perform (economic) activities. In the author's view, this should apply to both individuals and legal entities. The foregoing gives the following practical, rules of thumb under the benefit theory from a single State perspective:²⁸² (1) residents who perform the same economic activities and earn the same level of income might pay a different amount of tax in their home State (as their level of benefit might differ), (2) residents who perform the same economic activities in a State as non-residents and earn the same level of income might pay a higher, but not a lower, amount of tax in that State (as non-residents would never benefit more than residents), (3) non-residents performing the same economic activities in and earning the same level of income from a source State should receive equal tax treatment in that State (as their level of benefit should be the same under such circumstances), and (4) since residents and non-residents always benefit from public goods and services to some extent, forgoing taxation would not make sense from a benefit perspective. The benefit theory not only points to a basic difference between residents and non-residents but also to a basic equality between non-residents *inter se* in case they perform the same economic activities in and earn the same level of income from the same State.

3.5.2.2 *Considerations Regarding Foreign Sovereign Wealth Investors*

As it was argued that the practical relevance of the ability-to-pay theory is limited to residents, the focus is on the benefit principle. This principle, which is relevant for the taxation of both residents and non-residents, requires that each taxpayer should pay tax in accordance with its level of benefit from governmental goods and services. From this principle, three, more practical, rules of thumb can be derived which are relevant for source taxation of non-resident investors. Before discussing these rules, it is noted that these rules apply as much to foreign sovereign wealth investors as they apply to other non-resident investors, both individuals and companies. In fact, the identity of the non-resident investor is completely irrelevant from a benefit perspective. The *first*

---

281. American Law Institute, *Restatement of the Law Third: The Foreign Relations Law of the United States*, Vol. I (St. Paul, Minn.: American Law Institute Publishers, 1987), Para. 402(1); N. Kaufman, 'Fairness in International Taxation of International Income' (1998) 29 *Law & Policy in International Business* 145, pp. 187–188. On this principle, *see also* E. Kemmeren, *Principle of Origin in Tax Conventions: A Rethinking of Models* (2001), Dongen: Mr. Eric C.C.M. Kemmeren/Pijnenburg vormgevers, uitgevers, pp. 21–22, available at: <https://pure.uvt.nl/portal/files/439888/87428.pdf>.
282. Inspired by Vogel, who has argued that the benefit principle requires that an investor investing in another country and thus utilizing 'the other country's facilities (public goods) can be sure of being taxed no more than anyone else who, under the same circumstances, uses these facilities to the same extent.' K. Vogel, 'Worldwide vs. Source Taxation of Income – A Review and Re-evaluation of Arguments (Part II)' (1988) 10 *Intertax* 310, p. 314.

Chapter 3: Tax Policy Considerations and Approaches to Taxation

rule is that a source State should generally not tax non-resident investors less favourably than resident investors when performing the same investment activities in and earning the same level of income from that source State. Under such circumstances, non-resident investors would generally not benefit more from the public goods and services of a source State than resident investors would do. It may, in such circumstances, even require non-resident investors to be taxed more favourably than resident investors. The *second rule* is that a source State should treat and tax all non-resident investors as equals when they perform the same investment activities in and earn the same level of income from that source State (i.e., horizontal non-discriminatory treatment). Under such circumstances, non-resident investors would benefit to the same extent from the public goods and services of a source State. Thus, the benefit principle would require equal tax treatment *among* and *between* them on income derived from similar economic activities. The *third rule*, which applies to both the first and second rule, is that forgoing taxation would not make sense from a benefit perspective, since residents and non-residents that perform investment activities in the source State always benefit from public goods and services to some extent.

Conceptually, the benefit principle could demand a source State to differentiate between different categories of income if it can be demonstrated that different asset classes benefit differently from public goods and services. For instance, it is not unimaginable that investors investing in immovable property benefit more from public goods and services than investors investing in bonds or shares. If so, different tax treatment of such investors would be appropriate from a benefit perspective, because of their different circumstances in this context. However, from a practical point a view, not differentiating between different categories of income could be understandable, subject to the comment in the following paragraph. It is noted that the foregoing consideration applies without distinction to foreign sovereign wealth investors and other (resident and non-resident) investors, including CIVs and pension funds.

The benefit principle could, in addition, demand a source State to differentiate between different categories of income in the case of dividends paid out of, or capital gains relating to, profits that have been or will become subject to corporate tax in a source State. This corporate tax (effectively at the expense of the investors) can already be sufficient from a benefit perspective, so that additional source taxation upon distribution would be unnecessary. Therefore, in the context of the benefit principle, recipients of dividend income could be in different circumstances than recipients of interest income or rental income, requiring different tax treatment. It is noted, again, that the foregoing consideration applies without distinction to foreign sovereign wealth investors and other (resident and non-resident) investors, including CIVs and pension funds.

Considering the above, Approaches (2) to (5)[283] regarding the tax treatment of foreign sovereign wealth investors cannot be motivated by the benefit principle,

---

283. As identified in Section 3.2.2.2. Approaches (2) to (5) are as follows:

   (2) according a general tax-exemption under domestic law or administrative practice.

because they could result in different tax treatment *among* foreign sovereign wealth investors, and *between* foreign sovereign wealth investors and other non-resident investors, be it individuals or companies, that perform the same investment activities in a source State. On the other hand, Approach (1), under which source States tax foreign sovereign wealth investors in the same way as 'regular' non-resident corporate investors that perform the same investment activities in a source State, could be inspired by the benefit principle.

3.5.3 Inter-nation Equity

3.5.3.1 *The Concept Explained*

Inter-nation equity, introduced by Richard and Peggy Musgrave,[284] deals with the allocation of national gain (and loss) between States arising from international activities. These authors use the following example to illustrate what inter-nation equity is about:

> Let X, a resident of A, invest in B. Income earned thereon constitutes a national 'gain' to country A. If country B taxes the income earned by X, the gain accruing to country A as a nation is reduced. This is the issue of inter-nation equity. The fact that the gain accrues to B's treasury is not the crucial point. B may pass this gain on to tax-payers by tax reduction, but it still retains the national gain. Similarly, A has suffered a national loss due to B's tax. This national loss results, whether A gives a credit to X for taxes paid to B, thereby suffering a treasury loss, or whether the income is taxed again and X is left to bear the burden. National gain or loss may or may not be accompanied by a treasury gain or loss; the latter is a matter of intra-nation transfer between treasury and individual and does not affect the existence of national gain or loss. It is thus the national gain or loss (not the treasury gain or loss) that is the subject of inter-nation equity as defined here.[285]

So, inter-nation equity is not about the allocation of revenue between States but is concerned with the allocation of national gain. This allocation is affected when the source State imposes tax on the income derived by non-resident investors; taxation in the residence State has no impact on this allocation[286] (though it could affect inter-

---

        (3) according specific tax-exemptions or specific tax reductions under domestic law or administrative practice.
        (4) according a general tax-exemption under one or more tax treaties.
        (5) according specific tax-exemptions or specific tax reductions under one or more tax treaties.

284. R. Musgrave & P. Musgrave, 'Inter-nation Equity', in: R. Bird & J. Head, *Modern Fiscal Issue: Essays in Honour of Carl. S. Shoup* (Toronto: Toronto University Press, 1972).
285. *Ibid.*, p. 68.
286. K. Brooks, 'Inter-Nation Equity: The Development of an Important but Underappreciated International Tax Policy Objective', Chapter 17 in: J. Head & R. Krever, *Tax Reform in the 21st Century: A Volume in Memory of Richard Musgrave*, Series on International Taxation, Vol. 34 (Alphen a/d Rijn: Kluwer Law International, 2009), p. 474.

Chapter 3: Tax Policy Considerations and Approaches to Taxation

taxpayer equity and capital efficiency).[287] The central question of inter-nation equity is, therefore, whether the source State has a legitimate claim to impose tax on the income derived by non-residents and, if so, how source taxation should be designed. The Musgraves argue that a source State does have a legitimate claim, based on the idea that it should be entitled to charge non-residents for the benefits of public goods and services, as well as the idea that a source State should be entitled to (a share of) pure economic rents derived from activity within its territory.[288] The more difficult issue is how source taxation should be designed, which also involves the question how redistributive a tax system should be in an international setting. However, the 'concept of inter-nation equity will never provide an answer to that question'.[289] A possible approach suggested by the Musgraves is the idea of an internationally coordinated tax rate system where source rates depend on the per capita income of capital importing countries relative to the per capita income of capital exporting countries, and lower-income countries would be allowed to impose higher tax rates relative to higher-income countries.

Since inter-nation equity provides little guidance as to how taxation vis-à-vis non-resident investors should be designed, it is unclear whether inter-nation equity would allow a source State to differentiate between different categories of income, e.g., imposing a heavier tax burden on dividends than on interest, or whether it would require equal treatment of all categories of investment income. In the author's view, an indication can be found in the nature of the legitimate claim for source State taxation. If the legitimate claim is based on the benefit principle, different tax treatment of different categories of income would seem acceptable only if it can be demonstrated that different asset classes benefit differently from public goods and services.[290] On the other hand, if the legitimate claim is based on the idea that a source State should be entitled to (a share of) pure economic rents derived from activity within its territory, it would not seem acceptable to differentiate between different categories of income.

3.5.3.2 *Considerations Regarding Foreign Sovereign Wealth Investors*

Under inter-nation equity, a source State does have a legitimate claim to impose tax on non-resident investors deriving income from its territory. This claim applies as much to foreign sovereign wealth investors as it applies to other non-resident investors, both individuals and companies. The fact that foreign sovereign wealth investors are generally not taxed in their residence State is irrelevant from the perspective of inter-nation equity. Although the concept of inter-nation equity provides little guidance as to how taxation vis-à-vis non-resident investors should be designed, the following

---

287. R. Musgrave & P. Musgrave, 'Inter-nation Equity', in: R. Bird & J. Head, *Modern Fiscal Issue: Essays in Honour of Carl. S. Shoup* (Toronto: Toronto University Press, 1972), pp. 69–70.
288. *Ibid.*, pp. 70–73.
289. K. Brooks, 'Inter-Nation Equity: The Development of an Important but Underappreciated International Tax Policy Objective', Chapter 17 in: J. Head & R. Krever, *Tax Reform in the 21st Century: A Volume in Memory of Richard Musgrave*, Series on International Taxation, Vol. 34 (Alphen a/d Rijn: Kluwer Law International, 2009), p. 493.
290. *See* Section 3.5.2.2.

general rule can, in the author's view, be derived from it. The rule is that non-residents performing the same (investment) activities in a source State should be treated alike in that source State (i.e., horizontal non-discriminatory treatment), unless different treatment can be justified on grounds of international redistribution. In applying this rule, it would seem obvious not to distinguish between non-resident investors from the same State (all-in approach). In other words, if an exemption from source taxation applies to foreign sovereign wealth investors from State A, it should also apply to other investors from that State, but not necessarily to investors from third States. Thus, non-residents from the same State that perform the same (investment) activities in a source State should be treated alike. A different treatment of non-resident investors of different States can be justified on redistribution grounds only.

Considering the above, Approaches (2) to (5)[291] regarding the tax treatment of foreign sovereign wealth investors cannot be explained by inter-nation equity, at least as far as they result in different source taxation between foreign sovereign wealth investors and other non-resident investors from the same State, be it individuals or companies. Approach (1), under which source States tax foreign sovereign wealth investors in the same way as 'regular' non-resident corporate investors, could be motivated by inter-nation equity.

3.6 INTERNATIONAL ATTRACTIVENESS (INSTRUMENTALISM)

3.6.1 General Considerations

Another attribute of international tax policy is the attractiveness of a tax regime in an international setting, i.e., the attractiveness of a State's tax regime vis-à-vis tax regimes of other States. Many States use their tax system, including tax treaties, as an instrument to influence investment decisions and create an attractive investment location in order to stimulate economic growth and to create jobs (tax instrumentalism).[292] Several considerations play a role in deciding on whether or not to use tax

---

291. As identified in Section 3.2.2.2. Approaches (2) to (5) are as follows:

   (2) according a general tax-exemption under domestic law or administrative practice.
   (3) according specific tax-exemptions or specific tax reductions under domestic law or administrative practice.
   (4) according a general tax-exemption under one or more tax treaties.
   (5) according specific tax-exemptions or specific tax reductions under one or more tax treaties.

292. An econometric study performed by the Netherlands Bureau for Economic Policy Analysis concluded that bilateral tax treaties increase bilateral foreign direct investment (FDI) significantly. The study used a very extensive data set covering all bilateral FDI data of 34 OECD countries towards 233 partner countries in the period 1985–2011. It also concluded that lowering dividend withholding tax rates increases bilateral FDI. See A. Lejour & M. van 't Riet, 'De Economische Betekenis van Bilaterale Belastingverdragen' (2013), Annex to; *Bilaterale Belastingverdragen en Buitenlandse Investeringen*, CPB Policy Brief 2013/07, available at: <https://www.cpb.nl/sites/default/files/publicaties/download/cpb-achtergronddocument-de-economische-betekenis-van-bilaterale-belastingverdragen.pdf>. The results of this study have been published in English, *see* A. Lejour, 'The Foreign Investment Effects of Tax Treaties'

Chapter 3: Tax Policy Considerations and Approaches to Taxation

incentives with a view to attract investments. Two important considerations are discussed below. First, because tax incentives are aimed at influencing investment decisions and could result in preferential tax treatment of some investors over others, they could raise capital efficiency and equity concerns. A policy decision should be made as to the relative importance of these policy principles and objectives (*see*, in more detail, Section 3.7). Second, tax incentives do not necessarily have the desired effect of maintaining or attracting additional investments. Although tax considerations play a part in investment decisions, investors are influenced by non-tax factors as well,[293] such as public security, political stability, economic stability and infrastructure.[294] Also, tax incentives by one State may be copied, and can even be accorded more generously, by other States. The specific effects of a tax measure on the international attractiveness of a State's tax system may, therefore, be difficult to predict. Even if a tax incentive increases investment, this comes with a loss of tax revenue on the non-incremental part of the investment (i.e., part that would have occurred without the incentive), which could require further policy measures to counterbalance any deficit,[295] such as shifting part of the tax burden to less mobile factors including labour and immovable property.[296] On the other hand, the incremental part of the investment could increase other sources of tax revenue, such as value-added tax ('VAT') and payroll taxes, and could have social and economic benefits, such as creating new jobs.[297] It is noted that the monetary value of these social and economic benefits may be difficult to determine though.[298]

Various considerations play a role in determining the scope of tax incentives. A first consideration relates to the distinction between direct investment and portfolio investment. Tax incentives are often, but not always, aimed at attracting (foreign) direct investments, as opposed to (foreign) portfolio investments, because direct investments are believed to affect the location of business activity. However, as explained in Section 3.4.3.1 above, where portfolio capital is not widely available, portfolio investments could also influence the location of investment. Furthermore, some States, including the Netherlands, aim to attract foreign portfolio investments

---

(February, 2014), Oxford University Center for Business Taxation, WP 14/03, available at: < http://www.eesc.europa.eu/resources/docs/2014-the-foreign-investment-effects-of-tax-treaties_oxford-univ-centre-for-business-taxation.pdf >.
293. M. Podolny, 'The Limits of Sovereign Immunity: A Study and Analysis of the Canadian Income Taxation of Sovereign Wealth Funds' (2012) 70 *University of Toronto Faculty of Law Review* 90, p. 112.
294. OECD (1998), *Harmful Tax Competition: An Emerging Global Issue*, OECD Publishing, Paris, p. 8.
295. V. Troeger, 'Tax Competition and the Myth of the "Race to the Bottom": Why Governments Still Tax Capital' (2013), *The CAGE-Chatham House Series No. 4*, available at: < https://www.chathamhouse.org/sites/files/chathamhouse/public/Research/International%20Economics/0213bp_troeger.pdf >.
296. OECD (1998), *Harmful Tax Competition: An Emerging Global Issue*, OECD Publishing, Paris, p. 16.
297. A. Easson, 'Tax Incentives for Foreign Direct Investment: Recent Trends and Countertrends (Part I)' (2001) 55 *Bulletin for International Taxation* 266, p. 273.
298. *Ibid.*

through tax incentives, without having regard to the availability of portfolio capital.[299] A second consideration relates to selectivity of tax incentives. Tax incentives are typically narrowly targeted, in that they identify particular types of investments, sectors, industries, etc., and exclude others. The benefit of precise targeting is that it reduces the number of free riders and so the cost of tax incentives.[300] Other relevant considerations are whether tax incentives should be granted automatically (once the conditions have been satisfied) or on a discretionary basis, and whether investment thresholds should apply.[301]

Rather than using a tax system to encourage foreign investments, source States may, in theory, also consider using the tax system to discourage investments (in specific situations) from certain non-resident investors, for example to protect vital economic or infrastructural activities from (indirect) foreign influence. The author did, however, not come across tax measures that are specifically aimed at discouraging investments from (certain) non-resident investors.[302] One could call into question whether tax measures are the appropriate way to achieve this goal. State practice indicates that foreign investment regulation is a more effective and appropriate tool for banning certain non-resident investors;[303] however, non-tax measures are outside the scope of this study and will therefore not be considered.

Finally, proper tax policy requires that the effect of tax incentives is – *ex post* – evaluated.[304]

3.6.2 Considerations Regarding Foreign Sovereign Wealth Investors

Approaches (2) through (5), under which a general tax-exemption or specific tax-exemptions or reductions are granted to (some) foreign sovereign wealth investors, either unilaterally or through tax treaties, could be motivated by international attractiveness. However, as explained in Section 3.2.2.2 above, source States typically

---

299. *Tweede Kamer*, 2011–2012, 33 003, No. 3, p. 38 (concerning the refund of Dutch dividend withholding tax to non-resident tax-exempt portfolio investors resident in third States, including SWFs); *Tweede Kamer*, 2008–2009, 31 591, A/No. 1, p. 5 (concerning the tax treaty entitlement of State entities of Bahrain and related exemption from Dutch source taxation of dividends on both direct investments and portfolio investments).
300. A. Easson, 'Tax Incentives for Foreign Direct Investment: Design Considerations (Part II)' (2001) 55 *Bulletin for International Taxation* 365, p. 366.
301. A. Easson, 'Tax Incentives for Foreign Direct Investment: Design Considerations (Part II)' (2001) 55 *Bulletin for International Taxation* 365.
302. Nor did the author come across situations where certain benefits of a tax system developed to increase attractiveness were denied in such specific situations.
303. For example, in Australia, direct investments by foreign investors, including foreign government investors, require prior approval from the Australian government, *see* Treasurer, *Australia's Foreign Investment Policy* (2016), available at: <https://firb.gov.au/files/2015/09/Australias-Foreign-Investment-Policy-2016-2017.pdf>. In the US, investments by foreign investors, including foreign governments, are regulated through the *Foreign Investment and National Security Act of 2007*.
304. R. Niessen, 'Instrumentalisme en belastingrecht' (1997) Weekblad Fiscaal Recht 653; J. van der Geld, 'Fiscaliteit in een steeds veranderende wereld', in: H. van Arendonk, J. Jansen & L. Stevens (eds), Wetgevingskunsten: Vriendenbundel voor Jan Kees Bartel (Den Haag: Sdu Uitgevers, 2010).

motivate unilateral tax-exemptions by reference to sovereign immunity (i.e., Approaches (2) and (3)), whereas treaty-based tax-exemptions (i.e., Approaches (4) and (5)) are sometimes also motivated by sovereign immunity. One could, therefore, argue that international attractiveness is not the main driver for granting tax-exemptions to foreign sovereign wealth investors which are said to be based on sovereign immunity. The validity of this argument is examined in Chapter 4. Its outcome could be significant, because Approaches (2) through (5)[305] raise capital efficiency concerns since they could influence investment decisions of foreign sovereign wealth investors. They could also raise equity concerns since they could result in preferential tax treatment of (some) foreign sovereign wealth investors over other investors. If the validity of sovereign immunity as a foundation for tax-exemptions for foreign sovereign wealth investors becomes questionable, the justification for treating foreign sovereign wealth investors more favourably than other investors becomes questionable as well. Be that as it may, Approaches (2) through (5)[306] could promote a source State's international attractiveness for foreign sovereign wealth investors, whether motivated by sovereign immunity or not.

In the author's view, as will be explained in Section 3.7 below, equity considerations should play a vital role in relation to international attractiveness. When motivated by international attractiveness (rather than sovereign immunity), source States should only differentiate between investors if – *ex ante* –they have valid (economic) reasons for doing so. One such reason could be the distinctiveness of one or more investors over other investors in terms of stimulating economic growth and creating jobs. This means that a source State which relies on international attractiveness for granting tax-exemptions to (some) foreign sovereign wealth investors (rather than sovereign immunity), but not to other investors, needs to be able to demonstrate the relevant distinctiveness of (some) foreign sovereign wealth investors in terms of stimulating economic growth and creating jobs. The fact that foreign sovereign wealth investors own and invest extremely large amounts of money is not distinctive, because this also applies to other investors, such as CIVs and pension funds. Nor is the fact that foreign sovereign wealth investors are owned, controlled and funded by a foreign State. It is true that foreign sovereign wealth investors 'can bring benefits normally associated with foreign investment such as stimulating business activity and creating jobs',[307] but this applies to other foreign investors as well. In the context of international attractiveness, the distinctiveness must in particular lie in foreign sovereign wealth investors'

---

305. As identified in Section 3.2.2.2. Approaches (2) to (5) are as follows:

> (2) according a general tax-exemption under domestic law or administrative practice.
> (3) according specific tax-exemptions or specific tax reductions under domestic law or administrative practice.
> (4) according a general tax-exemption under one or more tax treaties.
> (5) according specific tax-exemptions or specific tax reductions under one or more tax treaties.

306. *Ibid.*
307. OECD (2008), *Sovereign Wealth Funds and Recipient Country Policies*, p. 2, available at: < https://www.oecd.org/investment/investment-policy/40408735.pdf > .

willingness to make an investment that no, or at least few, others are willing to make, and may, for instance, be found in the very long-term investment strategy of some foreign sovereign wealth investors, or their willingness to make risky investments.[308] This may include certain large infrastructure projects. But even then, a tax incentive may not have the desired effect and could come with a loss of tax revenue for which compensating policy measures may need to be taken. Another valid economic reason to differentiate between sovereign wealth investors and other investors may exist if a source State can demonstrate that according tax-exemptions to sovereign wealth investors promotes good bilateral relations, which could give companies of the source State business opportunities in the home markets of sovereign wealth investors (getting access to these markets can be difficult).[309]

3.7 IS THERE A CLEAR HIERARCHY AMONG THE TAX POLICY PRINCIPLES AND OBJECTIVES?

The question whether a hierarchy exists between the policy principles and objectives is relevant, because they cannot be fully achieved simultaneously. According tax-exemptions to selected investors could increase international attractiveness for such investors, but this would not be equitable and could be inefficient. Equitable tax systems are fair, but they may not be efficient or internationally attractive, while efficient tax systems may be inequitable and internationally unattractive.[310] In the author's view, there is no clear theoretical hierarchy among the policy principles and objectives which applies to all States in all situations.[311] Nevertheless, in practice, individual States have followed an order of priority. For example, in the Carter Report (1966), on Canadian tax policy, it was stated that 'a higher priority [was assigned] to

---

308. PwC, *Sovereign Investors 2020: A growing force* (April, 2016), p. 23; *Sovereign Wealth Funds; gezamenlijke notitie ministeries van Financiën en Economische Zaken*, Tweede Kamer, 2007-2008, 31 350, No. 1, p. 20. Cf. also Report of the Royal Commission on Taxation, *Vol. 2: The use of the tax system to achieve economic and social objectives* (1966), p. 157: 'We believe that there are several considerations which justify the inclusion of special tax incentives to encourage investment in risky ventures. First, the capital markets are by no means "Perfect" in the efficiency of their allocation of resources to highly risky ventures, particularly because such ventures are generally new, small enterprises. Second, while there is need for direct governmental action in assisting new firms to obtain financing, we have concluded that incentives built into the tax system, can provide an efficient means both of making risky investments more profitable and of reducing their need for external funds.'
309. *Notitie Fiscaal Verdragsbeleid 2011*, Tweede Kamer, 2010-2011, 25 087, No. 7, p. 76; *Sovereign Wealth Funds; gezamenlijke notitie ministeries van Financiën en Economische Zaken*, Tweede Kamer, 2007-2008, 31 350, No. 1, p. 20.
310. L. af Ornäs Leijon, 'Tax Policy, Economic Efficiency and the Principle of Neutrality from a Legal and Economic Perspective' *Uppsala Faculty of Law Working Paper 2015:2*, p. 13; Report of the Royal Commission on Taxation, *Vol. 2: The Use of the Tax System to Achieve Economic and Social Objectives* (1966), p. 11 & p. 43.
311. J. van der Geld, 'Fiscaliteit in een steeds veranderende wereld', in: H. van Arendonk, J. Jansen & L. Stevens (eds), *Wetgevingskunsten: Vriendenbundel voor Jan Kees Bartel* (Den Haag: Sdu Uitgevers, 2010).

the objective of equity than to all the others'.[312] The drafters were 'convinced that unless this objective is achieved to a high degree all other achievements are of little account'.[313] Some academic studies, however, have prioritized international tax neutrality (efficiency), but this was because the underlying aim was to maximize global and/or European economic growth; though it was acknowledged that equity considerations could allow for a deviation from this neutrality principle.[314] In other research, it has been argued that neutrality benchmarks are inappropriate tools for designing international tax policy altogether.[315] This study does not purport to develop a tax system aimed at maximizing or promoting (global or national) economic output (efficiency), (inter-taxpayer or inter-nation) equity, or international attractiveness.[316] Rather, its starting point is the individual sovereign State. The State is a product of the people and is charged with (political) authority within a society.[317] Today's functions of the modern State are many; in addition to the classic functions of maintaining peace and security, responsibilities and tasks include the promotion of (social and economic) welfare for its citizens and the protection of liberty and justice. The modern State deeply interferes with the social and economic life and freedom of its citizens. To finance its legal tasks and responsibilities, the State has the legal authority to impose tax.[318] The function of promoting the economic welfare of its citizens arguably calls for an (internally) efficient and attractive tax system, whereas other functions arguably demand an equitable tax system above everything else. However, because the functions of the State co-exist, and no clear hierarchy exists among them, an order of priority as regards tax policy principles and objectives does not logically follow from this perspective.

In a democracy under the rule of law, the legislature determines how the authority to impose tax is exercised. However, a legal system should respect and consider fundamental (legal) values, such as fairness (equity) and the principle of

---

312. Report of the Royal Commission on Taxation, *The Use of the Tax System to Achieve Economic and Social Objectives* (1966), Vol. 2, p. 17.
313. *Ibid.*
314. *See*, for example, E. Kemmeren, *Principle of Origin in Tax Conventions: A Rethinking of Models* (2001), Dongen: Mr. Eric C.C.M. Kemmeren/Pijnenburg vormgevers, uitgevers, Chapter 3; D. Smit, *Freedom of Investment Between EU and Non-EU Member States and Its Impact on Corporate Income Tax Systems within the European Union*, (Tilburg: CentER, 2011), pp. 80–106.
315. D. Weisbach, 'The Use of Neutralities in International Tax Policy' (2014) *Coase-Sandor Institute for Law and Economics*, Working Paper No. 697.
316. *See*, for example, M. de Wilde, *'Sharing the Pie'; Taxing multinationals in a global market* (2015).
317. For a historical review of the rise and development of the concepts of sovereignty and the State, see M. Isenbaert, *EC Law and the Sovereignty of the Member States in Direct Taxation*, IBFD 2009, Online Books IBFD, Chapter 2.
318. A. Christians, 'Sovereignty, Taxation and Social Contract' (2009) 18 *Minnesota Journal of International Law* 99, pp. 104–106; R. Niessen, *Inleiding tot het Nederlands belastingrecht*, Fiscale Handboeken, 9th edn. (Deventer: Kluwer, 2010), Chapters 1, 2, 4 & 5.

equality before the law as derived from this value, in the author's view.[319,320] Indeed, these fundamental (legal) values 'can be regarded as legal translations of important social and cultural values [which] guide the interactions and relations between free and equal people. No other institution than society can be regarded as the author of values'.[321] This understanding is valuable in a tax policy context, because it indicates that the tax legislator should not be able to implement (international) tax policy as it sees fit, without taking into account these fundamental societal values.[322] It also points to the importance of inter-taxpayer equity, as an expression of fairness, in matters of international tax policy. In the context of this study, based on the discussion in Section 3.5.2, the benefit principle, which can apply to both resident and non-resident investors, gives meaning to the concept of fairness. It means that (resident and non-resident) investors should pay tax in accordance with their level of benefit from governmental goods and services. In relation to international attractiveness (instrumentalism), the importance of inter-taxpayer equity (benefit principle) does not imply that a tax incentive should be rejected per se. It implies that a tax incentive must serve a legitimate – i.e., 'rationally defensible'[323] – purpose.[324] In addition, the principle of inter-taxpayer equity should be considered in relation to other tax policy principles and objectives, if adopted, which may also result in conflicts. Ultimately, in case of conflicts, the tax legislator of each individual sovereign State 'has to take into account the relative weight'[325] of the principle of inter-taxpayer equity and any other conflicting tax policy principle or objective it wishes to implement. Although this is not an exact measurement,[326] it should be done in a transparent way, based on rational, convincing arguments.[327] This way, the necessarily subjective choice is being based on objective elements as much as possible and the analysis is verifiable. Otherwise, the legitimacy

---

319. Similarly, R. Niessen, 'Instrumentalisme en belastingrecht' (1997) *Weekblad Fiscaal Recht* 653; H. Gribnau, 'Legislative Instrumentalism vs. Legal Principles in Tax Law' (2013) 16 *Coventry Law Journal* 89; J. Boer, *Sturende belastingheffer een monster? Juridische kanttekeningen bij fiscaal instrumentalisme en 'tax nudging'* (Den Haag: Sdu Uitgevers, 2013).
320. It is noted that in many countries, these fundamental values are enshrined in the constitution. However, in some countries, such as the Netherlands, legislation cannot be tested by the courts against these fundamental values enshrined in the constitution, whereas in other countries these fundamental values may not have been codified. In the author's view, this does not mean that the legislature and policymakers should not take fundamental values into consideration.
321. H. Gribnau, 'Legislative Instrumentalism vs. Legal Principles in Tax Law' (2013) 16 *Coventry Law Journal* 89, p. 106.
322. R. Niessen, 'Instrumentalisme en belastingrecht' (1997) *Weekblad Fiscaal Recht* 653; H. Gribnau, 'Legislative Instrumentalism vs. Legal Principles in Tax Law' (2013) 16 *Coventry Law Journal* 89; J. Boer, *Sturende belastingheffer een monster? Juridische kanttekeningen bij fiscaal instrumentalisme en 'tax nudging'* (Den Haag: Sdu Uitgevers, 2013).
323. H. Gribnau, 'Legislative Instrumentalism vs. Legal Principles in Tax Law' (2013) 16 *Coventry Law Journal* 89, p. 91.
324. On incentives in general, *see* R. Grant, 'Ethics and Incentives: A Political Approach' (2006) 100 *American Political Science Review* 29, p. 32.
325. More in general, *see* R. Dworkin, *Taking Rights Seriously* (Cambridge, Massachusetts: Harvard University Press, 1977), p. 26.
326. *Ibid.*
327. Similarly, H. Gribnau, 'Rechtsbeginselen en evaluatie van belastingwetgeving: rechtvaardigheid hanteerbaar gemaakt', in: A. Rijkers & H. Vording, *Vijf jaar Wet IB* (Deventer: Kluwer, 2006).

Chapter 3: Tax Policy Considerations and Approaches to Taxation

of tax legislation and the morality of taxpayers could be adversely affected.[328] The ultimate outcome may depend on various factors – such as the size and nature of the economy, public interests, societal values as well as tax policy choices of other States – and may change over time.

Finally, in addition to fundamental legal values, the authority to impose tax in an international setting could be further restricted by international law. The impact of international law will be the topic of the following chapters.

3.8 CONCLUSIONS

This chapter has identified five approaches to taxation of (some) foreign sovereign wealth investors by source States. They are as follows:

(1) taxing foreign sovereign wealth investors in the same way as 'regular' non-resident corporate investors.
(2) according a general tax-exemption under domestic law or administrative practice.
(3) according specific tax-exemptions or specific tax reductions under domestic law or administrative practice.
(4) according a general tax-exemption under one or more tax treaties.
(5) according specific tax-exemptions or specific tax reductions under one or more tax treaties.

Each approach has been measured by its neutrality, equity and international attractiveness. The results, which are summarized in the table below, show that each approach could satisfy, at least to some degree, at least two policy principles or objectives. In the absence of a clear theoretical hierarchy among these, often conflicting, international tax policy principles and objectives which applies to all States in all situations, no general judgment can be made about which approach is the 'correct' approach. Nevertheless, the analysis in this chapter indicates that inter-taxpayer equity (benefit principle), as an expression of the fundamental value of fairness, should be an important international policy principle in every democracy under the rule of law. Ultimately, the tax legislator of each individual sovereign State, therefore, has to weigh and balance the principle of inter-taxpayer equity and any other conflicting tax policy principle or objective it wishes to implement.

---

328. C. Alley & D. Bentley, 'A Remodelling of Adam Smith's Tax Design Principles' (2005) 20 *Australian Tax Forum* 579, p. 606; H. Gribnau, 'Legislative Instrumentalism vs. Legal Principles in Tax Law' (2013) 16 *Coventry Law Journal* 89, pp. 94–95; J. Boer, *Sturende belastingheffer een monster? Juridische kanttekeningen bij fiscaal instrumentalisme en 'tax nudging'* (Den Haag: Sdu Uitgevers, 2013), pp. 16–18.

Table 3.1 Approaches to Source Taxation of Foreign Sovereign Wealth Investors Measured by Neutrality, Equity and International Attractiveness

	Neutrality		Equity		International Attractiveness
	(CEN)	(CIN)	(inter-nation)	(inter-taxpayer)	
Approach (1)*	X	✓	✓	✓	X
Approach (2)*	✓	X	X	X	✓
Approach (3)*	✓	X	X	X	✓
Approach (4)*	✓	X	X	X	✓
Approach (5)*	✓	X	X	X	✓

* Approach (1): taxing foreign sovereign wealth investors in the same way as 'regular' non-resident corporate investors.
Approach (2): according a general tax-exemption under domestic law or administrative practice.
Approach (3): according specific tax-exemptions or specific tax reductions under domestic law or administrative practice.
Approach (4): according a general tax-exemption under one or more tax treaties.
Approach (5): according specific tax-exemptions or specific tax reductions under one or more tax treaties.

CHAPTER 4
Sovereign Immunity and Taxation of Foreign Sovereign Wealth Investors

4.1 INTRODUCTION[329]

In the field of international taxation, relations between sovereign States may also be governed by public international law other than (tax) treaties. In its discussion on the application of the OECD MTC to States, their subdivisions and their wholly-owned entities, including SWFs, the OECD Commentary mentions the customary international law principle of sovereign immunity.[330] According to this principle, a sovereign State can be held immune from the jurisdiction of the courts and from the enforcement power of another sovereign State in civil proceedings, and this principle may also apply to State entities. A number of States, including Australia, Canada, the UK and the US, apply the sovereign immunity principle to taxation as well. Foreign sovereign wealth investors might also benefit from these tax immunities.[331]

The purpose of this chapter is to examine what impact the sovereign immunity principle, as a principle of customary international law, could have on the ability of source States to achieve (or promote) tax policy objectives. Since source States often motivate unilateral tax-exemptions by reference to sovereign immunity (i.e., Approaches (2) and (3)), and this motivation may sometimes apply to treaty-based tax-exemptions as well (i.e., Approaches (4) and (5)), the summarizing table at the end of Chapter 3 already indicates how the sovereign immunity principle may have impacted neutrality, equity and international attractiveness in practice. That is,

---

329. Parts of this chapter have originally been published in R. Snoeij, 'Sovereign Immunity and Source State Taxation of Sovereign Wealth Funds: Is It Time to Re-Evaluate?' (2016) 8 *World Tax Journal* 225. Reproduced by kind permission of IBFD.
330. Paragraph 52 of the OECD Commentary on Art. 1.
331. Immunity from taxation could also apply to, *inter alia*, diplomatic and consular officials, and international organizations and their officials. On this topic, *see* M. Lang et al. (eds), *Tax Rules in Non-Tax Agreements*, (Amsterdam: IBFD, 2012).

sovereign immunity could (unintentionally) enhance international attractiveness, while, at the same time, it raises capital efficiency concerns since it could influence investment decisions of foreign sovereign wealth investors. It also raises equity concerns since it results in preferential tax treatment of (some) foreign sovereign wealth investors over other investors.

The more elementary question that will be addressed in this chapter is, however, whether the sovereign immunity principle, as a principle of customary international law, actually requires source States to accord tax immunities to foreign sovereign wealth investors.[332] The answer to this question indicates what impact the sovereign immunity principle could have on source States' ability to achieve (or promote) tax policy objectives (i.e., neutrality, equity and international attractiveness), and to freely implement an approach to taxation of foreign sovereign wealth investors.[333] For example, if the sovereign immunity principle would require source States to accord a general tax-exemption to foreign sovereign wealth investors, it would leave source States no option but to implement Approach (2).[334] This would make it virtually impossible for source States to achieve (or promote) CIN and equity. On the other hand, if the sovereign immunity principle would not require source States to accord any tax-exemption to foreign sovereign wealth investors, it would not restrict the ability of source States to achieve (or promote) tax policy objectives, and to freely implement an approach to taxation of foreign sovereign wealth investors.[335]

The remaining part of this chapter is structured as follows. Section 4.2 will give an introduction to the customary international law principle of sovereign immunity and discusses the rules on jurisdictional immunity in civil proceedings in force in Australia, Canada, the UK and the US. Section 4.3 will discuss the tax immunity regimes of Australia, Canada, the UK and the US, compare each regime with a State's rules on jurisdictional immunity, and examine whether a source State has obligations to accord tax immunity to foreign sovereign wealth investors under customary international law. Section 4.4 will consider immunity from measures of constraint in the context of source taxation of foreign sovereign wealth investors. Based on the analysis in Section 4.3 and Section 4.4, Section 4.5 will examine what impact the sovereign immunity principle, as a principle of customary international law, could have on the ability of source States to achieve (or promote) tax policy objectives. Section 4.6 will end this chapter with the main conclusions.

---

332. Reference is made to footnote 31, where it was noted that, even in many dualist States, customary international law has domestic legal force, or it is applied by courts directly.
333. *See* the five approaches identified in Section 3.2.2.2.
334. Approach (2) has been identified in Section 3.2.2.2 and is as follows: according a general tax-exemption under domestic law or administrative practice.
335. *See* the five approaches identified in Section 3.2.2.2.

4.2 THE SOVEREIGN IMMUNITY PRINCIPLE

4.2.1 Some General Remarks

A basic distinction in the field of sovereign immunity is made between: (i) immunity from jurisdiction, and (ii) immunity from measures of constraint, such as pre-judgment attachment or post-judgment enforcement measures. Immunity from jurisdiction restricts the judicial powers of national courts of a State vis-à-vis foreign States, whereas immunity from measures of constraint restricts the enforcement powers of a State vis-à-vis foreign States. Foreign States that enjoy immunity from jurisdiction cannot be adjudicated by the courts of other States, whereas *property* situated in one State, but belonging to a foreign State, cannot be seized in the first-mentioned State, if the foreign State enjoys immunity from measures of constraint in connection with that property. Immunity typically protects a foreign State (or its property) against claims from private parties.

The international law doctrine of sovereign immunity is mainly derived from judicial practices of States, a development started in the nineteenth century,[336] although national legislation and governmental practice also contributed to the progressive development of rules of international law on this subject matter.[337] Even though the principle of sovereign immunity is (now) generally accepted as a principle of international law, it is not uniformly interpreted and applied by (national courts of) States. And so, at the international level, several attempts have been made to agree on a multilateral treaty on the subject of sovereign immunity. One successful attempt has been the conclusion of the *European Convention on State Immunity* (1972) ('ECSI 1972'), which was signed in Basel in 1972 and is currently in force between eight European States (only).[338] But probably the most extensive international project on sovereign immunity has been conducted under the auspices of the UN, with the UNCSI 2004 as the product of some twenty-two years of work.[339] The UNCSI 2004 will enter

---

336. *Yearbook of the International Law Commission 1980*, Vol. II, Part II, Paras 7–8, p. 143.
337. *Preliminary Report on Jurisdictional Immunities of States and Their Property*, by Mr Sompong Sucharitkul, Special Rapporteur, Doc. A/CN.4/323, published in *Yearbook of the International Law Commission 1979*, Vol. II, Part I, Para. 22 et seq., pp. 231 et seq.
338. The ECSI 1972 is currently in force between Austria, Belgium, Cyprus, Germany, Luxembourg, the Netherlands, Switzerland and the UK.
339. 'Jurisdiction over foreign States' was selected by the ILC in its first session, in 1949, as one of the topics for codification, although it was not on its priority list. Based on the recommendations of the Working Group, as expressed in the report submitted to the ILC in 1978, it was decided by the ILC to include in its programme of work the topic 'Jurisdictional immunities of States and their property.' The first set of draft articles on the topic, including commentaries, was published in 1980. Only in 1991, at its forty-third session, did the ILC adopt the final text of twenty-two *Draft articles on Jurisdictional Immunities of States and Their Property, with commentaries*, which it submitted to the General Assembly. In between the period of the adoption of the draft articles by the ILC in 1991 and the final adoption of the UNCSI 2004, consisting of thirty-three articles, by the General Assembly on 2 December 2004, States as well as the ILC were invited to submit comments, informal consultations were held within the framework of the Sixth Committee and several working groups (of the Sixth Committee), an Ad Hoc Committee and two informative consultative groups were established to solve outstanding issues.

into force once thirty States have deposited an instrument of ratification, acceptance, approval or accession with the Secretary-General of the UN.[340] In March 2018, only twenty-one States have deposited such an instrument, and so this treaty has not yet entered into force. As explained in the preamble to the UNCSI 2004, it is believed 'that an international convention on the jurisdictional immunities of States and their property would enhance the rule of law and legal certainty (...) and would contribute to the codification and development of international law and the harmonization of practice in this area'. The House of Lords has referred to the UNCSI 2004 as the 'the most authoritative statement available on the current international understanding of the limits of state immunity in civil cases'.[341]

The preamble to the UNCSI 2004 also provides that 'the jurisdictional immunities of States and their property are generally accepted as a principle of customary international law'. This statement is supported by court decisions of a great number of States, including Canada,[342] Germany,[343] Greece,[344] Italy,[345] Israel,[346] Portugal,[347] and the UK,[348] to name just a few.

---

340. Article 30 UNCSI 2004.
341. House of Lords, *Jones v. Ministry of the Interior of the Kingdom of Saudi Arabia and Another* (2006) 129 *International Law Reports* 713, at 727.
342. Ontario Court of Appeal, *Bouzari v. Islamic Republic of Iran* (2004) 128 *International Law Reports* 586, at 596.
343. Federal Constitutional Court, *Claim Against the Empire of Iran* (1963) 45 *International Law Reports* 57, at 61: '[t]he general rules of international law on State immunity can only belong to customary international law. There are no treaty rules which might have found general recognition. There are, equally, few general principles of law which – supplementing customary international law – could be authoritative as to the extent of State immunity'.
344. For example, Court of Cassation, *Prefecture of Voiotia v. Germany* (2000) 129 *International Law Reports* 514, at 516: '[t]he extraterritoriality or sovereign immunity of foreign States, meaning their non-submission to the international jurisdiction of the courts of the forum State, is a rule of customary international law and consequently a generally accepted rule of public international law which, according to Article 28(1) of the Constitution, constitutes an integral part of Greek law and takes precedence over any contrary provision'.
345. For example, Court of Cassation, *Kingdom of Greece v. Gamet* (1957) 24 *International Law Reports* 209, at 210. *See also* Court of Appeal of Napels, *United States Government v. Bracale Bicchierai* (1968) 65 *International Law Reports* 273, at 274: '[i]n the opinion of the Italian Supreme Court, together with other generally recognized rules of international law (to which, under Art. 10 of the Constitution, the Italian legal system must conform) there is the customary principle *par in parem non habit imperii* which recognizes the jurisdictional immunity of foreign States'.
346. For example, Supreme Court, *Her Majesty the Queen in Right of Canada v. Edelson and Others* (1997) 131 *International Law Reports* 279, at 287: '[t]he answer is that the rules of sovereign immunity are part of customary international law'.
347. For example, Supreme Court, *Brazilian Embassy Employee Case* (1984) 116 *International Law Reports* 625, at 627: '(...) universally accepted rule of customary international law according to which, given the reciprocal independence of States and in accordance with the old principle of *par in parem non habet juridictionem*, foreign States enjoy immunity in local courts in cases in which proceedings are brought against them.'
348. For example, House of Lords, *Holland v. Lampen-Wolfe* (2000) 119 *International Law Reports* 367, at 378.

4.2.2 Rational Basis and Origin of Sovereign Immunity

As noted by the ILC[349] in its historical and legal review of the doctrine of State (or sovereign) immunity in 1980,[350] even though the rational basis of sovereign immunity is expressed differently in different States:

> [t]he most convincing arguments in support of the principle of State immunity may be found in international law as evidenced in the usage and practice of States and as expressed in terms of the sovereignty, independence, equality and dignity of States. All these notions seem to coalesce, together constituting a firm international legal basis for State immunity. State immunity is derived from sovereignty. Between two co-equals, one cannot exercise sovereign will or authority over the other: *par in parem imperium non habet*.[351]

The origin of the principle of sovereign immunity may be traced to the concept of the modern State-system. The modern State-system is generally regarded as being formally established with the Peace Treaties of Westphalia of 1648,[352] which 'recorded the birth of an international system based on plurality of independent States, recognizing no superior authority over them'.[353] The Westphalian State-system, which aimed to bring peace at last to Western Europe after a long period of conflicts, battles and warfare, was based on the principle of absolute and exclusive jurisdiction within one's own territory – *territorial sovereignty* – and the principle of equality and independence *vis-à-vis* other sovereign States – *national or personal sovereignty*.[354] Whenever one sovereign State enters the exclusive territorial jurisdiction of another sovereign State, these two 'basic principles of international law'[355] would conflict. The principle of territorial sovereignty is generally more absolute so that in most cases of conflict the territorial State does not have to limit its jurisdictional power (or

---

349. The ILC was established by the United Nations General Assembly on 21 November 1947. According to Art. 1(1) of the Statute of the International Law Commission, the 'Commission shall have for its object the promotion of the progressive development of international law and its codification'.
350. *Yearbook of the International Law Commission 1980*, Vol. II, Part II, Paras 9 et seq., pp. 144 et seq. The principle *par in parem non habet imperium* is often referred to by national courts, but also by international courts. For example, the judgment of the ECtHR in *Al-Adsani v. The United Kingdom* (2001) Council of Europe: European Court of Human Rights, Para. 54: '(...) sovereign immunity is a concept of international law, developed out of the principle *par in parem non habet imperium*, by virtue of which one State shall not be subject to the jurisdiction of another State. The Court considers that the grant of sovereign immunity to a State in civil proceedings pursues the legitimate aim of complying with international law to promote comity and good relations between States through the respect of another State's sovereignty'.
351. *Yearbook of the International Law Commission 1980*, Vol. II, Part II, Para. 55, p. 156.
352. For example, C. Warbrick, 'States and Recognition in International Law', in: M. Evans, *International Law*, 2nd edn., (New York: Oxford University Press, 2006), p. 221.
353. A. Cassese, *International Law*, 2nd edn., (New York: Oxford University Press, 2005), p. 24.
354. H. Fox, *The Law of State Immunity*, 2nd edn., (New York: Oxford University Press, 2008), p. 41.
355. *Preliminary Report on Jurisdictional Immunities of States and Their Property*, by Mr Sompong Sucharitkul, Special Rapporteur, Doc. A/CN.4/323, published in *Yearbook of the International Law Commission 1979*, Vol. II, Part I, Para. 56, p. 239.

enforcement power) concerning (assets of) foreign sovereigns.[356] However, this exclusive territorial jurisdiction is understood to be waived in a number of cases to promote comity and good relations between States. In such cases, the personal sovereignty of another State is respected by the territorial State and sovereign immunity is established.[357]

4.2.3 Scope of Sovereign Immunity

4.2.3.1 *Material Scope of Immunity from Jurisdiction*

Prior to the First World War, the practice in most States was to apply the sovereign immunity principle in what has become known as an absolute, or unrestricted manner,

---

356. *Sixth Report on Jurisdictional Immunities of States and Their Property*, by Mr Sompong Sucharitkul, Special Rapporteur, Doc. A/CN.4/376, published in *Yearbook of the International Law Commission 1984*, Vol. II, Part I, Paras 81–82, p. 21.
357. *See also* the 'classic formulation' and explanation of the concept of sovereign immunity by J. Marshall, Chief Justice of the US Supreme Court, in *The Schooner Exchange v. McFaddon & Others* (1813) 11 US Reports 116, pp. 136–137, concerning the question whether the US had jurisdiction over a claim against a French warship of Napoleon:

> (...)
> The jurisdiction of the nation, within its own territory, is necessarily exclusive and absolute; (...).
> All exceptions, therefore, to the full and complete power of a nation within its own territories, must be traced up to the consent of the nation itself. They can flow from no other legitimate source.
> This consent may be either express or implied. In the latter case, it is less determinate, exposed more to the uncertainties of construction; but, if understood, not less obligatory.
> The world being composed of distinct sovereignties, possessing equal rights and equal independence, whose mutual benefit is promoted by intercourse with each other, and by an interchange of those good offices which humanity dictates and its wants require, all sovereigns have consented to a relaxation, in practice, in cases under certain peculiar circumstances, of that absolute and complete jurisdiction within their respective territories which sovereignty confers.
> (...)
> This full and absolute territorial jurisdiction being alike the attribute of every sovereign, and being incapable of conferring extraterritorial power, would not seem to contemplate foreign sovereigns, nor their sovereign rights, as its objects. One sovereign being in no respect amenable to another, and being bound by obligations of the highest character not to degrade the dignity of his nation, by placing himself or its sovereign rights within the jurisdiction of another, can be supposed to enter a foreign territory only under an express license, or in the confidence that the immunities belonging to his independent sovereign station, though not expressly stipulated, are reserved by implication, and will be extended to him.
> This perfect equality and absolute independence of sovereigns, and this common interest impelling them to mutual intercourse, and an interchange of good offices with each other, have given rise to a class of cases in which every sovereign is understood to waive the exercise of a part of that complete exclusive territorial jurisdiction, which has been stated to be the attribute of every nation.

Chapter 4: Sovereign Immunity and Taxation

as opposed to a (more) restrictive, or limited one.[358] The absolute approach meant that foreign States were entitled to immunity for all acts performed by them. But the more States became involved in (international) trade and commerce, the more national courts felt the urge to apply the principle of sovereign immunity in civil cases in a (more) restricted way.[359] The move from an absolute approach of sovereign immunity to a restrictive one was first found in decisions of the national courts of Belgium (since 1907), Egypt (since 1920) and Italy (since 1882),[360] and was subsequently followed by the national courts of Germany, the US, the UK, France, the Netherlands, Austria and a number of developing States.[361] Under the restrictive theory of jurisdictional immunity, immunity applies to sovereign or governmental acts (*acta jure imperii*), but not to commercial or private law acts (*acta jure gestionis*). The legal protection of private parties in their commercial dealings with foreign States is said to be one of the two main foundations of the restrictive theory.[362] Its second main foundation is that requiring a foreign State to answer a claim resulting from a commercial transaction is 'neither a threat to the dignity of that State, nor any interference with its sovereign functions'.[363] The restrictive jurisdictional immunity approach, which is reflected in both the UNCSI 2004 and the ECSI 1972, is now generally accepted.[364] There is, however, continuing controversy on how to distinguish governmental/sovereign acts from commercial acts, partly due to a lack of guidance from international law. In the national practices of States regarding jurisdictional immunities, the following three approaches appear to be most common in distinguishing between the two acts: (i) reference to the nature of the transaction (nature test), (ii) reference to the purpose of the transaction (purpose test), and (iii) reference to the whole context, which includes both nature and purpose of the transaction (mixed approach). The drafting history of the UNCSI 2004 also shows that the question on the method of distinguishing sovereign acts from commercial acts was much disputed.

---

358. For example, in 1912 the Court of Appeal of Paris held: 'No distinction should be made between the (...) public personality which would not be subject to foreign jurisdiction and the legal personality which would, on the contrary, be subject to it, since all the acts of a State can have only one goal and one end, which are always political, and its unity precludes such dualism.' See *Gamen-Humbert v. Etat russe* (1912), quoted in the *Fourth Report on Jurisdictional Immunities of States and Their Property*, by Mr Sompong Sucharitkul, Special Rapporteur, Doc A/CN.4/357, published in *Yearbook of the International Law Commission 1982*, Vol. II, Part I, Para. 62, p. 215.
359. *Claim Against the Empire of Iran* (1963) 45 *International Law Reports* 57, at 61. C. Schmitthoff & F. Wooldridge, 'The Nineteenth Century Doctrine of Sovereign Immunity and the Importance of the Growth of State Trading' (1972) 2 *Denver Journal of International Law & Policy*, p. 199.
360. *Yearbook of the International Law Commission 1991*, Vol. II, Part II, Para. 16, p. 36. For a discussion of the relevant Belgian, Egyptian and Italian case law, see *Yearbook of the International Law Commission 1982*, Vol. II, Part II, Paras 56-61, pp. 214-215.
361. *Yearbook of the International Law Commission 1991*, Vol. II, Part II, Paras 16-18, pp. 36-38.
362. Lord Wilberforce in *Congreso Del Partido* (1981) 64 *International Law Reports* 307, at 314.
363. *Ibid.*
364. H. Fox, *The Law of State Immunity*, 2nd edn., (New York: Oxford University Press, 2008), pp. 201 et seq.

(i) Nature test

Case law of European States shows a strong preference for the nature of the act[365] and this method is probably also used in most States outside of Europe. Preference for the nature test is often motivated by the view that adherence to the purpose test would always result in immunity, as each transaction entered into by a foreign State serves a sovereign purpose, in one way or another, and such outcome is inconsistent with the rationale of restrictive immunity. An influential decision in favour of the nature of the activity is the decision of the German Federal Constitutional Court in *Claim Against the Empire of Iran* (1963):

> [t]he distinction between sovereign and non-sovereign State activities cannot be drawn according to the purpose of the State transaction and whether it stands in a recognizable relation to the sovereign duties of the State. For, ultimately, activities of State, if not wholly then to the widest degree, serve sovereign purposes and duties, and stand in a still recognizable relationship to them. (...) As a means for determining the distinction between acts *jure imperii* and *jure gestionis* one should rather refer to the nature of the State transaction or the resulting legal relationships, and not to the motive or purpose of the State activity. It thus depends on whether the foreign State has acted in exercise of its sovereign authority, that is in public law, or like a private person, that is in private law.[366]

According to the US Supreme Court, which also looks at the nature of the activity rather than its purpose, a foreign State does not act in exercise of its sovereign authority:

> where it exercises 'only those powers that can also be exercised by private citizens,' as distinct from those 'powers peculiar to sovereigns.' Put differently, a foreign state engages in commercial activity for purposes of the restrictive theory only where it acts 'in the manner of a private player within' the market.[367]

As the US Supreme Court already mentioned in 1934, '[w]hen a state enters the market place seeking customers, it divests itself of its *quasi*-sovereignty *pro tanto,* and takes on the character of a trader (...)'.[368] In other words, the relevant question under the nature test is whether a private party could have performed the activity in the same manner (indicating that a foreign sovereign was competing with private parties in the marketplace).[369]

---

365. Council of Europe (G. Hafner, M. Kohen & S. Breau (eds)), *State Practice Regarding State Immunities* (Leiden: Martinus Nijhoff Publishers, 2006), pp. 31 et seq.
366. *Claim Against the Empire of Iran* (1963) 45 *International Law Reports* 57, at 80.
367. US Supreme Court, *Saudi Arabia and Others v. Nelson* (1993) 100 *International Law Reports* 545, at 553.
368. *Ohio v. Helvering* (1934) 292 US 360, at 369.
369. Commissie van Advies inzake Volkenrechtelijke Vraagstukken, *Advies inzake de United Nations Convention on Jurisdictional Immunities of States and their Property*, Advies No. 17, Den Haag, 19 mei 2006, p. 13.

(ii) Purpose test

Examples of court decisions that exclusively focus on the purpose of the transaction, rather than its nature, can be found in Italian case law.[370] The purpose test could in fact be tantamount to absolute immunity, if the reasoning of the German Federal Constitutional in *Claim Against the Empire of Iran* (1963) is followed that 'ultimately, activities of State, if not wholly then to the widest degree, serve sovereign purposes and duties'.[371]

(iii) Mixed approach

In other States, in distinguishing between *acta jure imperii* and *acta jure gestionis*, reference is made to both the nature and the purpose of the transaction. For example, the House of Lords[372] and the Supreme Court of Canada[373] appear to focus on the (whole) context, in which the nature of the transaction is most important, but which also includes the purpose of the transaction. In the UNCSI 2004 the primary focus is on the *nature* of the contract or transaction, but the *purpose* should also be taken into account if: (a) agreed between the parties, or (b) relevant in the national practice of the other State.[374]

With respect to foreign sovereign wealth investors, the activities that require classification will be investment activities. All investment activities of foreign sovereign wealth investors will likely be classified alike, either as commercial activities or governmental activities under the nature test and the purpose test. That is, under the nature test, all investment activities will likely be classified as commercial activities since private parties could have performed the activities in the same manner, whereas, under the purpose test, all investment activities will likely be classified as governmental activities since they serve macroeconomic purposes. Finally, the outcome under the mixed approach will depend on whether the focus is on the nature or the purpose of the activity.

4.2.3.2 Material Scope of Immunity from Measures of Constraint

Interestingly, compared with immunity from jurisdiction, immunity from execution has also developed towards a more restrictive approach, but it has done so at a much slower pace and in a less evident way.[375] The reason for this is that a measure of constraint is considered to have a (far) greater and (far) more direct impact on a foreign

---

370. Council of Europe (G. Hafner, M. Kohen & S. Breau (eds)), *State Practice Regarding State Immunities* (Leiden: Martinus Nijhoff Publishers, 2006), p. 35.
371. *Claim Against the Empire of Iran* (1963) 45 *International Law Reports* 57, at 80.
372. *Congreso Del Partido* (1981) 64 *International Law Reports* 307.
373. Supreme Court of Canada, *Kuwait Airways Corporation v. Republic of Iraq* (2010) 174 *International Law Reports* 303, at 315–316.
374. Article 2(2) and Art. 10 of the UNCSI 2004.
375. Council of Europe (G. Hafner, M. Kohen & S. Breau (eds)), *State Practice Regarding State Immunities* (Leiden: Martinus Nijhoff Publishers, 2006), p. 151.

State's personal sovereignty.[376] A foreign State generally enjoys immunity from measures of constraint in respect of its property situated in another State, if the property is *used for sovereign purposes*. The relevance of immunity from execution for the taxation of foreign sovereign wealth investors is discussed in Section 4.4 below.

4.2.3.3 Personal Scope of Sovereign Immunity

'The very foundation of the institution of immunity resides in the sovereign character of the subject to which it is granted.'[377] Immunity is reserved for sovereign subjects only and this now coincides with the notion of 'State'. The notion of State has been defined for sovereign immunity purposes in international agreements, as well as in the legislation and case law of States. What it shows is that separate entities of States may, under certain circumstances, also enjoy immunity. The development of the notion of 'State' has generally followed the tightening of the material scope of jurisdictional immunity[378] and this development is reflected in Article 2(1)b UNCSI 2004, which defines a 'State' as:

(i) the State and its various organs of government;
(ii) constituent units of a federal State or political subdivisions of the State, which are entitled to perform acts in the exercise of sovereign authority, and are acting in that capacity;
(iii) agencies or instrumentalities of the State or other entities, to the extent that they are entitled to perform and are actually performing acts in the exercise of sovereign authority of the State;
(iv) representatives of the State acting in that capacity.

4.2.4 Jurisdictional Immunity Legislation of Australia, Canada, the UK and the US

The jurisdictional immunity legislation of Australia, Canada, the UK and the US all apply to separate entities of a foreign State under certain conditions, and all follow a

---

376. Council of Europe (G. Hafner, M. Kohen & S. Breau (eds)), *State Practice Regarding State Immunities* (Leiden: Martinus Nijhoff Publishers, 2006), p. 156; H. Fox, *The Law of State Immunity*, 2nd edn., (New York: Oxford University Press, 2008), p. 601.
377. Council of Europe (G. Hafner, M. Kohen & S. Breau (eds)), *State Practice Regarding State Immunities* (Leiden: Martinus Nijhoff Publishers, 2006), p. 2.
378. *Ibid.*, pp. 14–20. Cf. sec. 14(2) of the UK *State Immunity Act 1978*, which provides for immunity from the jurisdiction of the UK courts in relation to separate entities, if: (i) the proceedings relate to anything done by it in the exercise of sovereign authority (*acta jure imperii*), and (ii) the circumstances are such that a State would have been so immune. A separate entity is defined as 'any entity (...) which is distinct from the executive organs of the government of the State and capable of suing or being sued' (sec. 14(1)). This approach to separate entities has been adopted in the sovereign immunity legislation of Pakistan (*The State Immunity Ordinance No. VI of 1981*), Singapore (sec. 16(1)-(2) of the *State Immunity Act 1979*) and South Africa (sec. 2(1)(i) of the *Foreign States Immunities Act 1981*).

Chapter 4: Sovereign Immunity and Taxation

restrictive jurisdictional immunity approach. Nevertheless, their (personal and material) scope is not entirely uniform.

4.2.4.1 Australia

Under Australia's Foreign States Immunities Act 1985 ('AU FSIA 1985'), a separate entity comprises a foreign body corporate or foreign corporation sole that: (i) is an agency or instrumentality of the foreign State, and (ii) is not a department or organ of the executive government of the foreign State.[379] The Federal Court held that an entity is an agency or instrumentality of a foreign State if it is carrying out the foreign State's functions and purposes.[380] In that regard, the court focused on the ownership and control of the entity, the functions performed by the entity, the foreign State's purposes in supporting the entity and the manner in which the entity conducts itself or its business.[381] For purposes of the AU FSIA 1985, the nature test is used to distinguish commercial activities from governmental activities.[382]

4.2.4.2 Canada

In Canada's State Immunity Act 1985, a foreign State includes an agency of a foreign State, which is defined as any legal entity that is an organ of the foreign State but that is separate from the foreign State.[383] Even though the definition of commercial activity in the Canadian legislation exclusively seems to refer to the nature of the activity,[384] the Supreme Court of Canada appears to focus on the (whole) context, in which the nature of the activity is most important, but which also includes its purpose.[385]

4.2.4.3 UK

The UK State Immunity Act 1978 ('UK SIA 1978') applies to separate entities if: (i) the proceedings relate to anything done by it in the exercise of sovereign authority (*acta jure imperii*), and (ii) the circumstances are such that a State would have been so immune.[386] A separate entity is defined as any entity that is distinct from the executive organs of the government of the State and capable of suing or being sued.[387] Just like

---

379. Section 3(1) & sec. 22 AU FSIA 1985.
380. Federal Court of Australia, *PT Garuda Indonesia Ltd v. Australian Competition and Consumer Commission* (2011) FCAFC 52, at 42.
381. Ibid., at 48.
382. Ibid., at 212 (referring to US Supreme Court, *Saudi Arabia and Others v. Nelson* (1993)).
383. Section 2 Canada's State Immunity Act 1985.
384. Ibid.
385. Supreme Court of Canada, *Kuwait Airways Corporation v. Republic of Iraq* (2010) 174 International Law Reports 303, at 315-316.
386. Section 14(2) UK SIA 1978.
387. Section 14(1) UK SIA 1978.

the Supreme Court of Canada, the House of Lords[388] focuses on the (whole) context when characterizing an activity as being commercial or governmental in character.

4.2.4.4 US

The US Foreign Sovereign Immunities Act 1976 ('US FSIA 1976') applies to an agency or instrumentality of a foreign State, which is defined as: (i) a separate legal person, (ii) which is an organ of a foreign State or whose shares or ownership interest is for more than 50% owned by a foreign State, and (iii) which is created under the laws of that foreign State (and not under the laws of any third State).[389] The US FSIA 1976 and the US Supreme Court alike clearly characterize an activity by reference to its nature, rather than by reference to its purpose.[390]

4.3 TAX IMMUNITY AND INCOME DERIVED BY FOREIGN SOVEREIGN WEALTH INVESTORS

As noted in the OECD Commentary, many States do not recognize any application of the sovereign immunity principle in tax matters.[391] And even among States that do recognize the relevance of this principle in the field of taxation, there are differences as regards the scope of application. Section 4.3 will discuss the tax immunity framework in Australia, Canada, the UK and the US, compare each regime with a State's rules on jurisdictional immunity in civil proceedings, and examine whether a source State has obligations to accord tax immunity to foreign sovereign wealth investors under customary international law.

4.3.1 Immunity from Source Taxation in Australia, Canada, the UK and the US

4.3.1.1 Australia

Income derived by foreign governments from the performance of governmental functions within Australia, as opposed to commercial activities, is exempt from Australian tax under the international law doctrine of sovereign immunity. This exemption is based on (administrative) practice[392] as outlined in Interpretative

---

388. *Congreso Del Partido* (1981) 64 *International Law Reports* 307.
389. Section 1603(b) US FSIA 1976.
390. Section 1603(d) US FSIA 1976; US Supreme Court, *Saudi Arabia and Others v. Nelson* (1993) 100 *International Law Reports* 545, at 553.
391. Paragraph 52 of the OECD Commentary on Art. 1.
392. Australia was in the process of adopting tax legislation on this subject matter. It was aimed at: (i) providing foreign governments with greater certainty with regard to the Australian tax implications of their Australian investments, (ii) providing greater certainty as to the withholding obligations for Australian residents, (iii) reducing compliance costs, and (iv) promoting Australia as a regional financial services hub. However, on 14 December 2013, the Australian government announced that it would not proceed with this proposed tax measure. For the

Decision 2002/45 of the Australian Taxation Office ('ATO ID 2002/45'). Whether income is derived from governmental functions (non-commercial activity) or commercial activity depends on the particular facts of each case. With regard to dividend and interest income, ATO ID 2002/45 provides that a tax-exemption applies to a foreign government, if the funds are and will remain government moneys and the income is being derived from a non-commercial activity. Dividend income from a shareholding of 10% or less will generally be accepted as income derived from a non-commercial (or governmental) activity.

ATO ID 2002/45 also applies to foreign government agencies, provided they: (i) perform functions of government, (ii) are owned and controlled by the government, and (iii) do not engage in commercial activities. SWFs can also benefit from ATO ID 2002/45.[393]

4.3.1.2 *Canada*

Canadian sourced income derived by foreign governments, their agencies and central banks is exempt from Canadian taxation under the doctrine of sovereign immunity if:

(1) it can be substantiated that the income is the property of the foreign government, agency or central bank;
(2) the foreign State would provide reciprocal tax-exemptions to the Canadian government and its agencies;
(3) the income is derived in the course of exercising a function of a governmental nature and is not income arising in the course of an industrial or commercial activity carried on by the foreign authority; and
(4) it is interest on an arm's length debt or portfolio dividends on listed company shares (meaning that income such as rentals, royalties or direct dividends from a company in which the foreign government has a substantial or controlling equity interest are excluded from the exemption).[394]

The exemption is based on administrative practice as defined in Information Circular 77–16R4, dated 11 May 1992. The term 'agency of a foreign state' is not

---

latest proposals paper, *see Options to codify the tax treatment of sovereign investments* (April, 2011), available at: < http://archive.treasury.gov.au/documents/2017/PDF/Proposals_Paper. pdf >. This paper was preceded by the consultation papers, *Greater certainty for Sovereign Investment* (November, 2009), available at: < http://archive.treasury.gov.au/documents/166 7/PDF/Consultation_paper.pdf > and *Greater certainty for sovereign investment – the framework rules* (June, 2010).
393. Joint Committee on Taxation, *Economic and U.S. Income Tax Issues Raised by Sovereign Wealth Fund Investment in the United States* (June, 2008), JCX-49-08, Appendix One: Foreign Law Tax Treatment of Government Investment, Australia, A-9 – A-10.
394. For a discussion of the third and fourth condition, *see* M. Kandev, 'Sovereign Wealth Funds: Are They Welcome in Canada?' (2010) 64 *Bulletin for International Taxation* 649, pp. 652–655.

defined; however, SWFs appear to qualify for the exemption if the fund has a public/humanitarian purpose, as opposed to a commercial purpose.[395] It is not clear how to distinguish between the two.

4.3.1.3 UK

The UK tax-exemption for foreign sovereigns is based on administrative practice as defined in *INTM155010 – Sovereign and Crown Immunity* and *INTM368520 – DT applications and claims: Crown Immunity, Sovereign Immunity and Diplomatic Privilege*.[396] The UK exempts from its direct taxes all income arising to, and beneficially owned by, the head of State and the government of a foreign sovereign State. It explains that this tax immunity has its origins in a general principle of international law (i.e., the sovereign immunity principle). Unlike in Australia and Canada, *INTM368520* does not distinguish between income from commercial activities and income from governmental activities. However, it does distinguish between a foreign State and State entities that are legally separate from the foreign State, in that: '[s]overeign [i]mmunity from taxation does not apply to income arising to and beneficially owned by a legal entity that is separate from the foreign Government, even though that government may own the whole of the share capital'. With respect to SWFs this means that they will only enjoy immunity from taxation, if they are an integral part of the foreign State.[397] Foreign sovereign wealth investors that are legally separate from the State do not appear to qualify for the exemption.

4.3.1.4 US

'Since the beginning of the modern federal income tax, the US has treated sovereign immunity from taxation as a corollary to the general principle of sovereign immunity.'[398] The US has detailed and complex rules and regulations to determine the application of income tax-exemption for foreign sovereigns (Section 892 of the Internal

---

395. Joint Committee on Taxation, *Economic and U.S. Income Tax Issues Raised by Sovereign Wealth Fund Investment in the United States* (June, 2008), JCX-49-08, Appendix One: Foreign Law Tax Treatment of Government Investment, Canada, A-4 & A-27.
396. *INTM155010 – Sovereign and Crown Immunity*: 'The United Kingdom recognises the principle of international law known as sovereign immunity whereby one sovereign state does not seek to apply its domestic laws to another sovereign state. In accordance with this principle, current UK practice is to regard as immune from direct taxes all income and gains which are beneficially owned by the head of state and the government of a foreign sovereign state recognised by the UK.'
397. Parliamentary Debates, House of Commons, 28 April 2008, column 143W: '[w]here a sovereign wealth fund is an integral part of the government of a foreign sovereign state it will benefit from immunity from UK tax. As a result of this immunity, no taxation will have been received from sovereign wealth funds'.
398. G. May, 'The Foreign Sovereign Tax Exemption' (2008) 122 *Tax Notes* 389, p. 390.

Revenue Code ('IRC')).[399] Certain passive items of US sourced income[400] received by foreign governments[401] and fully controlled entities of foreign governments[402] can be exempt from US taxation. According to the US Joint Committee on Taxation, SWFs will generally be treated as a foreign government within the meaning of Section 892, because they will either constitute an integral part, or a controlled entity of a foreign sovereign.[403]

To be eligible for the exemption, the income must not be derived from any commercial activity anywhere in the world, or by or from a controlled commercial entity. An entity is a controlled commercial entity if the entity is engaged in commercial activities and if the foreign government holds an interest in that entity of at least 50%, measured by value or vote, or otherwise has effective control.[404] For the purpose of Section 892, commercial activities are generally defined as those activities 'which are ordinarily conducted by the taxpayer or by other persons with a view towards the current or future production of income or gain'.[405] This broad definition is narrowed by excluding five categories of activities from being commercial activities. The first category (*Investments*) is most relevant for foreign sovereign wealth investors as it includes 'investments in stocks, bonds and other securities, loans, [and] investments in

---

399. For more detailed information, *see* G. May, 'The Foreign Sovereign Tax Exemption' (2008) 122 *Tax Notes* 389, pp. 393–401. In relation to SWFs in particular, *see* M. Melone, 'Should the United States Tax Sovereign Wealth Funds?' (2008) 26 *Boston University International Law Journal* 143; V. Fleischer, 'A Theory of Taxing Sovereign Wealth Funds' (2009) 84 *NYU Law Review* 440; V. Fleischer, 'Should We Tax Sovereign Wealth Funds?' (2008) 118 *Yale Law Journal Pocket Part* 93; M. Knoll, 'Taxation and the Competitiveness of Sovereign Wealth Funds: Do Taxes Encourage Sovereign Wealth Funds to Invest in the United States?' (2009) 82 *Southern California Law Review* 703; J. Bird-Pollan, 'The Unjustified Subsidy: Sovereign Wealth Funds and the Foreign Sovereign Tax Exemption' (2012) 17 *Fordham Journal of Corporate & Financial Law* 987.
400. For an elaboration on the eligible items of income, *see* Temporary Treasury Regulations (1988), Subchapter A, § 1.892-3T.
401. For the purpose of sec. 892 IRC, the meaning of the term 'foreign government' is restricted to the integral parts or controlled entities of a foreign sovereign. An integral part of a foreign sovereign is defined as 'any person, body of persons, organization, agency, bureau, fund, instrumentality, or other body, however designated, that constitutes a governing authority of a foreign country. The net earnings of the governing authority must be credited to its own account or to other accounts of the foreign sovereign, with no portion inuring to the benefit of any private person. An integral part does not include any individual who is a sovereign, official, or administrator acting in a private or personal capacity. Consideration of all the facts and circumstances will determine whether an individual is acting in a private or personal capacity'. Temporary Treasury Regulations (1988), Subchapter A, § 1.892-2T(a)(2).
402. A controlled entity of a foreign government is an entity which is (legally) separate in form from a foreign sovereign and which meets the following four conditions: (i) the entity is wholly owned and controlled by a foreign sovereign directly or indirectly through one or more controlled entities, (ii) the entity is organized under the laws of the foreign sovereign by which owned, (iii) the net earnings of the entity are credited to its own account or to other accounts of the foreign sovereign, with no portion of its income inuring to the benefit of any private person, and (iv) the entity's assets vest in the foreign sovereign upon dissolution. *See* Temporary Treasury Regulations (1988), Subchapter A, § 1.892-2T(a)(3). Temporary Treasury Regulations (1988), Subchapter A, § 1.892-2T(a)(2).
403. Joint Committee on Taxation, *Economic and U.S. Income Tax Issues Raised by Sovereign Wealth Fund Investment in the United States* (June, 2008), JCX-49-08, p. 46.
404. Section 892(a)(2)(B) IRC.
405. Temporary Treasury Regulations (1988), Subchapter A, § 1.892-4T(b).

financial instruments held in the execution of governmental financial or monetary policy (...)', as well as 'effecting transactions in stocks, securities, or commodities for a foreign government's own account'.[406] The remaining four categories are certain cultural events, non-profit activities, governmental functions[407] and the purchasing of goods. Income from these five categories of non-commercial activities is, in principle, eligible for the exemption.

4.3.2 Comparison Between the Tax Immunity Regimes and the Rules on Jurisdictional Immunity in Civil Proceedings

When comparing the personal scope of each State's tax immunity regime with a State's rules on jurisdictional immunity, the most notable difference can be found in the UK. Whereas the UK SIA 1978 applies to separate entities which have performed governmental activities, UK tax immunity never applies to legal entities that are separate from the foreign state (even though that foreign state may own the whole of the share capital and even though the separate entity may perform governmental activities). Thus, the personal scope of the UK tax immunity conflicts with the UK rules on jurisdictional immunity in civil proceedings, i.e., it is narrower. No difference in personal scope exists in Australia, while differences in the US context seem to be limited to the ownership threshold (100% versus at least 50% state-owned). With respect to Canada, no difference in personal scope exists, if the term 'agency' has the same meaning in both fields.

As regards the material scope, the tax immunity regimes in Australia, Canada and the US make a basic distinction between commercial activities and governmental activities. This may not come as a surprise, though, given that all three States make a similar basic distinction for jurisdictional immunity purposes in civil proceedings. However, when the tax immunity regimes are further analysed, the distinction in Australia and Canada reveals to be one of 'active' versus 'passive' income, with immunity from tax available for (certain items of) passive income only. What constitutes active and passive income is defined differently in these two states. In the US, it seems that all income from investment activities is considered (passive) income from governmental activities. Neither the active/passive distinction between investments as applied in Australia and Canada, nor the US approach of classifying investment activities of foreign sovereigns as governmental activities, logically follows from the

---

406. *Ibid.*, § 1.892-4T(c)(1)(i) and (iii).
407. According to § 1.892-4T(c)(4), '[g]overnmental functions are not commercial activities. The term "governmental functions" shall be determined under US standards. In general, activities performed for the general public with respect to the common welfare or which relate to the administration of some phase of government will be considered governmental functions. For example, the operation of libraries, toll bridges, or local transportation services and activities substantially equivalent to the Federal Aviation Authority, Interstate Commerce Commission, or United States Postal Service will all be considered governmental functions for purposes of this section'.

Chapter 4: Sovereign Immunity and Taxation

doctrine of sovereign immunity itself.[408] These tax approaches, in fact, conflict with the basic distinction each State makes between *acta jure imperii* and *acta jure gestionis* for jurisdictional immunity purposes in civil proceedings. As explained in Section 4.2.3.1 above, all investment activities of foreign sovereigns and SWFs will likely be classified alike, either as commercial activities or governmental activities under the nature test and purpose test. That is, under the nature test (which is used in both Australia and the US in jurisdictional immunity cases), both active and passive investment activities will likely be classified as commercial activities since private parties could have performed the activities in the same manner. Thus, the tax immunities granted to foreign sovereign wealth investors by Australia and the US are likely broader in scope than would follow from jurisdictional immunity in civil cases.[409] The outcome (of commercial activity or governmental activity) under the mixed approach, which is used in Canada and the UK, will depend on whether the focus is on the nature or the purpose of the activity. Thus, for Canada, its tax immunities could be broader or narrower in scope. In the UK, the personal scope for purposes of the UK tax immunity is narrower, but its subsequent all-in approach of according tax immunity to all activities of a foreign sovereign could be broader in scope than the material scope of the UK rules on jurisdictional immunity, depending on its classification of investment activities of foreign sovereigns as either commercial or governmental in character.

The previous discussion demonstrates significant discrepancies between the tax immunity regimes, on the one hand, and the rules on jurisdictional immunity in civil cases, on the other, in all four States. It strongly suggests that the tax immunities granted to foreign sovereigns and foreign sovereign wealth investors by Australia, Canada, the UK and the US are not (or, at least, are no longer) truly motivated by sovereign immunity. The tax-exemptions seem to be driven by other reasons, such as international attractiveness. As already noted in Section 3.6.2, if the validity of sovereign immunity as a foundation for tax-exemptions for foreign sovereign wealth investors becomes questionable, the justification for treating (some) foreign sovereign wealth investors more favourably than other investors becomes questionable as well. As a result, each State, and any other State in which a comparable situation exists, would either need to align the scope of its tax immunity framework with its rules on jurisdictional immunity in civil proceedings, or abolish any potential preferential tax treatment if such treatment cannot be justified by other good (tax) policy reasons.[410]

---

408. Also, S-A. Joseph, 'Do Tax Treaties Embody Sovereign Immunity? – An Assessment with Regard to Sovereign Wealth Funds' (2015) 69 *Bulletin for International Taxation* 637, p. 643.
409. With respect to the US tax immunities, this view has been presented before by J. Bird-Pollan, 'The Unjustified Subsidy: Sovereign Wealth Funds and the Foreign Sovereign Tax Exemption' (2012) 17 *Fordham Journal of Corporate & Financial Law* 987.
410. R. Snoeij, 'Sovereign Immunity and Source State Taxation of Sovereign Wealth Funds: Is It Time to Re-Evaluate?' (2016) 8 *World Tax Journal* 225, pp. 241–242. *See also* Section 3.7.

4.3.3 Customary International Law Aspects in the Field of Taxation

4.3.3.1 Do Tax Immunities Logically Follow from the Sovereign Immunity Principle?

The sovereign immunity principle is generally accepted as a principle of customary international law. From this principle, binding rules (obligations or prohibitions) for States can be derived. In Section 4.3.3.3 below, it is examined whether a source State is required to accord tax immunity to foreign sovereign wealth investors under customary international law. Before doing so, the author would like to point to two contradictory views on the elementary issue of why the sovereign immunity doctrine should be relevant to taxation (of foreign sovereigns) to begin with.[411] One view holds that sovereign immunity should apply to taxation, whereas the other view denies a connection between sovereign immunity and taxation. The first view can be found in the already mentioned 1978 decision of the Italian Supreme Court. At issue was whether the Association of Italian Knights of the Order of Malta ('AIKOM'), an instrumental body of the Sovereign Military Order of Malta, which was recognized as a sovereign subject of international law, was entitled to immunity from Italian taxation in respect of a loan contract concluded for the financing of the construction of a hospital in Rome. The Italian Supreme Court held as follows:

> A norm of [international law on the fiscal immunity of States and other international legal entities] (...) undoubtedly exists in the general international legal order. It constitutes, in fact, a corollary of the constitutional principle of customary international law which is expressed in the maxim *par in parem non habet jurisdictionem*. On the basis of this principle, out of the respect which is due to the fundamental rights of liberty which that same system recognizes as appertaining to all the members of the international community, each of these members has the duty, equally fundamental, not to interfere in the sphere of freedom which appertains to the others. Each must exercise the powers through which its sovereignty is given expression (and these include the power to impose taxes) in such a way as to comply with the exigencies of this principle. (...). This norm, like the constitutional principle of which it is a corollary, is customary by nature and is generally recognized and accepted by all States. (...). <u>On the basis of this principle, sovereign subjects of international law are, therefore, immune from the fiscal provisions and powers of the Italian State in relation to those same activities in respect of which they are not subject to the jurisdiction of the Italian courts.</u>[412] (Emphasis added)

According to the highest Italian court, fiscal immunity exclusively applied 'in respect of activities which (...) are destined to the realization of the inherent public

---

411. According to one author it is a 'generally accepted principle that one government does not tax another'. *See* J. Taylor, 'Tax Treatment of Income of Foreign Governments and International Organizations', in: U.S. Department of Treasury, *Essays in International Taxation* (Washington: Treasury Department, 1977), p. 154, cited by D. Tillinghast, in 'Sovereign Immunity from the Tax Collector: United States Income Taxation of Foreign Governments and International Organizations' (1978) 10 *Law and Policy in International Business* 495, p. 495.
412. Court of Cassation, *Ministry of Finance v. Association of Italian Knights of the Order of Malta* (1978) 65 *International Law Reports* 321–322.

objectives of the foreign State or other organization of international law'.[413] Although the conclusion of the contract was, in the view of the court, undeniably of a private law nature, the objective pursued was undeniably public in character. It belonged to the internal sovereign order of the AIKOM, with which Italy must not interfere. And so the court concluded that Italy should refrain from imposing tax on the basis of the customary international law principle of sovereign immunity.[414] In determining whether the activity was commercial (*acta jure gestionis*) or governmental (*acta jure imperii*) and, thus, whether Italy was allowed to impose tax or not, the Italian Supreme Court relied on the purpose rather than the nature of the activity. At that time, the purpose test was also repeatedly relied on by Italian courts to characterize an activity in civil proceedings.[415] Apparently, the reasoning behind this decision was that exercising prescriptive jurisdiction in tax matters (i.e., the power to impose tax) and adjudicative jurisdiction in civil proceedings can equally interfere with the dignity and public functions of a foreign sovereign.

The second view can be found in the *Sixth Report on Jurisdictional Immunities of States and Their Property* ('Sixth Report'), published in 1984 by Mr Sompong Sucharitkul, Special Rapporteur to the ILC.[416] This Report forms part of the drafting history of the *Draft articles on Jurisdictional Immunities of States and Their Property, with commentaries* (1991), on which the UNCSI 2004 is based. According to the view expressed in the Sixth Report, sovereign immunity does not prohibit a source State (referred to as the territorial sovereign) from taxing foreign States, because, in the field of international taxation, the territorial sovereignty of a source State is superior to the personal sovereignty of foreign States:

> 81. A State is not normally liable to taxation or customs duties levied by another State, except in cases where it establishes a business – official or commercial – or maintains an office or agency in the territory of another State. The maxim *par in parem imperium non habet* or *jurisdictionem non habet* must be read in the context where there is no overlapping of activities of a State in the territory or under the territorial sovereign authority of another State. It is generally undisputed that the principle of 'territoriality' or 'territorial sovereignty' is more absolute and is not subject to limitations or qualifications by the national or personal sovereignty, or sovereign authority or personality of another State.
> 82. It follows as a matter of course that, in most cases of contact, confrontation, clash or conflict, the territorial sovereign exercises supreme authority over and within its territory. An outside sovereign or extraterritorial power must be presumed to have submitted to the sovereign authority of the territorial State and could only exert or exercise such governmental or sovereign authority as had been previously agreed to by the territorial sovereign, which could either waive its sovereign authority or consent to the exercise

---

413. *Ibid.*, at 323.
414. *Ibid.*, at 324.
415. Council of Europe (G. Hafner, M. Kohen & S. Breau (eds)), *State Practice Regarding State Immunities* (Leiden: Martinus Nijhoff Publishers, 2006), p. 35.
416. *Sixth Report on Jurisdictional Immunities of States and Their Property*, by Mr Sompong Sucharitkul, Special Rapporteur, Doc. A/CN.4/376, published in *Yearbook of the International Law Commission 1984*, Vol. II, Part I.

of a limited governmental power by the visiting extraterritorial authority. Otherwise, it would be tantamount to the recognition of a colonial status or regime, directly against the concept of *jus cogens*.

83. Conceptually, liability in terms of jural relationship is the correlative of power, as opposed to immunity which is the correlative of non-power. Thus to admit the supremacy or superiority of the territorial sovereign is already one big step towards acceptance of liability, once the extraterritorial State projects its image or personality within the territorial sphere of a sovereign authority of another State.

84. The matter has to a large extent been regulated in so far as diplomatic, consular or *ad hoc* missions are concerned. The special regime allowing for special privileges and exemptions from certain categories of taxation is based on functional necessity and justified by the principle of reciprocity. Beyond reciprocity and functional necessity, exemption from taxation is granted as a matter of generosity or courtesy; it stems from the comity of nations, based on considerations of reciprocal treatment rather than *opinio juris* or legal obligation. Besides, there is nothing to prevent two or more States or a group of States from agreeing to accord tax concessions *inter se* (or even unilaterally) as part of a generalized system of special preferences, whether for internal revenues or levies for import of goods or for other tariff or non-tariff barriers. <u>The rationale behind the authority to tax or to collect levies lies in the supremacy of the territorial sovereign</u>.[417] (Emphasis added)

4.3.3.2 Constitutive Elements of Customary International Law

Customary international law is one of the sources of public international law. Article 38(1) of the Statute of the International Court of Justice ('ICJ Statute'), which is generally accepted as the authoritative statement of the sources of public international law,[418] speaks of 'international custom, as evidence of a general practice accepted as law'. From its wording, as well as from decisions of the International Court of Justice ('ICJ'),[419] it follows that customary international law results from a combination of the following two (constitutive) elements:

(i) State practice (*uses* or *diuturnitas*), as the objective element; and

---

417. *Ibid.*, Paras 81–84, pp. 21–22.
418. For example, J. Brierly, *The Law of Nations*, 6th edn., (London: Oxford University Press, 1963), p. 56; H. Meijers, 'On International Customary Law in the Netherlands', in: I. Dekker & H. Post, *On the Foundations and Sources of International Law* (The Hague: T.M.C. Asser Press, 2003), p. 80; T. Buergenthal & S. Murphy, *Public International Law in a Nutshell*, 4th edn., (New York: Thomson/West Group, 2007), p. 19; M. Shaw, *International Law*, 6th edn., (Cambridge: Cambridge University Press, 2008), p. 70; I. Brownlie, *Principles of Public International Law*, 7th edn., (New York: Oxford University Press, 2008), p. 5; H. Thirlway, 'The Source of International Law', in: M. Evans, *International Law*, 3rd edn., (New York: Oxford University Press, 2010), p. 97.
419. ICJ, 20 February 1969, *North Sea Continental Shelf*, I.C.J. Reports 1969, Para. 77, p. 44; ICJ, 3 June 1985, *Continental Shelf*, I.C.J. Reports 1985, Para. 27, pp. 29–30; ICJ, 27 June 1986, *Military and Paramilitary Activities in and against Nicaragua*, I.C.J. Reports 1986, Para. 183, p. 97.

(ii) *Opinio juris sive neccessitatis* ('an opinion of law or necessity'), as the subjective element.

4.3.3.2.1 State Practice

According to Meijers, a rule of custom can only arise through repetition, for which he finds evidence in case law of the ICJ.[420] As pointed out by the ICJ in several of its judgments, the required State practice[421] needs to be 'constant and uniform'.[422] In the 1969 *North Sea Continental Shelf* case, the ICJ considered that 'State practice, including that of States whose interests are specially affected, should have been both extensive and virtually uniform in the sense of the provision invoked.'[423] Indeed, minor inconsistencies in State practice do not prevent this requirement from being met.[424]

4.3.3.2.2 Opinio Juris

According to Article 38(1)b ICJ Statute, a rule of customary international law not only requires 'evidence' of a 'general practice', but also 'evidence' of a general practice that is 'accepted as law' (*opinio juris*).[425] This requirement expresses that States must act in

---

420. H. Meijers, 'On International Customary Law in the Netherlands', in: I. Dekker & H. Post, *On the Foundations and Sources of International Law* (The Hague: T.M.C. Asser Press, 2003), pp. 82–83, arguing that: '[w]ithout the repetition of similar conduct there can be no custom, and without custom no customary law'.
421. According to one author, any activity of the State can contribute to State practice. M. Dixon, *Textbook on International Law*, 6th edn., (New York: Oxford University Press, 2007), p. 31. Another author has proposed the following hierarchy of acts which, in his view, can constitute State practice in the context of customary international law: (a) acts and attitudes of State organs, (b) any national legislation or administrative ruling, (c) a State's participation in and implementation of bilateral and multilateral treaties, (d) a State's participation to treaties on the codification and/or progressive development of rules of customary international law, (e) resolutions adopted by political organs of international organizations, for example the UN General Assembly, and (f) abstract and verbal statements of representatives of a State, diplomatic correspondence as well as their voting in international organizations. V. Degan, *Sources of International Law* (The Hague: Martinus Nijhoff Publishers, 1997), pp. 156–161.
422. ICJ, 20 November 1959, *Colombian-Peruvian Asylum*, I.C.J. Reports 1950, p. 276; ICJ, 12 April 1960, *Right of Passage over Indian Territory*, I.C.J. Reports 1960, p. 40.
423. ICJ, 20 February 1969, *North Sea Continental Shelf*, I.C.J. Reports 1969, Para. 74, p. 43.
424. ICJ, 27 June 1986, *Military and Paramilitary Activities in and against Nicaragua*, I.C.J. Reports 1986, Para. 186, p. 98: 'It is not to be expected that in the practice of States the application of the rules in question should have been perfect, in the sense that States should have refrained, with complete consistency, from the use of force or from intervention in each other's internal affairs. The Court does not consider that, for a rule to be established as customary, the corresponding practice must be in absolutely rigorous conformity with the rule. In order to deduce the existence of customary rules, the Court deems it sufficient that the conduct of States should, in general, be consistent with such rules'.
425. ICJ, 20 February 1969, *North Sea Continental Shelf*, I.C.J. Reports 1969, Para. 77, p. 44: 'Not only must the acts concerned amount to a settled practice, but they must also be such, or be carried out in such a way, as to be evidence of a belief that this practice is rendered obligatory by the existence of a rule of law requiring it. The need for such a belief, i.e., the existence of a subjective element, is implicit in the very notion of the opinio juris sive necessitatis. The States concerned must therefore feel that they are conforming to what amounts to a legal obligation.'

a certain way because they feel obliged to do so by a legal obligation, or because of the existence of a binding rule of law. The requirement of *opinio juris* (i.e., the subjective element)[426] serves to distinguish from acts that are not motivated by a feeling of legal obligation, such as acts of comity or friendship.[427]

4.3.3.3 Analysis

A comparative study that was conducted by the US Directorate of Legal Research for International, Comparative, and Foreign Law of The Law Library of Congress on the *Taxation of the Passive Income of Foreign Governments and Sovereign Wealth Funds in Selected Foreign Countries*, indicates the lack of an extensive and uniform State practice on the taxation of income derived by foreign sovereigns and SWFs. The 2008 report, which forms an appendix to a report that was prepared by the US Joint Committee on Taxation on *Economic and U.S. Income Tax Issues Raised by Sovereign Wealth Fund Investment in the United States*,[428] contains an analysis of the domestic tax legislation, policy or practice of Australia, Canada, Germany, Japan, Norway, Poland, Switzerland and the UK. The practice of Australia, Canada, the UK and the US, all of which apply sovereign immunity in income tax matters, has been discussed in Section 4.3.1 of this chapter. From this discussion it appeared that significant differences exist between these four States, both with respect to who is eligible and what income is eligible. Other examples of States that grant immunity from income taxation to foreign sovereigns include France[429] and Japan. The comparative study shows that Germany, Norway, Poland and Switzerland do not tax-exempt items of passive income derived by foreign governments or SWFs, although benefits may be available under applicable double tax treaties.[430]

The above indicates the lack of an extensive and virtually uniform State practice in this area, as is required for the existence of a rule of customary international (tax) law. It is reasonable to assume that this also applies to SWEs. The OECD Commentary on Article 1 also indicates the absence of an extensive and virtually uniform State

---

426. On the subjective element, *see* R. Walden, 'The Subjective Element in the Formation of Customary International Law' (1977) 12 *Israel Law Review* 344; M. Mendelson, 'The Subjective Element in Customary International Law' (1995) 66 *The British Year Book of International Law* 177.
427. ICJ, 20 February 1969, *North Sea Continental Shelf*, I.C.J. Reports 1969, Para. 77, p. 44: 'The frequency, or even habitual character of the acts is not in itself enough. There are many international acts, e.g., in the field of ceremonial and protocol, which are performed almost invariably, but which are motivated only by considerations of courtesy, convenience or tradition, and not by any sense of legal duty.'
428. Joint Committee on Taxation, *Economic and U.S. Income Tax Issues Raised by Sovereign Wealth Fund Investment in the United States* (June, 2008), JCX-49-08, Appendix One: Foreign Law Tax Treatment of Government Investment.
429. D. Gaukrodger, 'Foreign State Immunity and Foreign Government Controlled Investors' *OECD Working Papers on International Investment*, No. 2010/2, p. 35, available at: <http://www.oecd.org/daf/inv/investment-policy/WP-2010_2.pdf>.
430. Joint Committee on Taxation, *Economic and U.S. Income Tax Issues Raised by Sovereign Wealth Fund Investment in the United States* (June, 2008), JCX-49-08, Appendix One: Foreign Law Tax Treatment of Government Investment, A-3/4.

practice.[431] In addition, the discussion in Section 4.3.2 of this chapter strongly suggests that the tax immunities granted by Australia, Canada, the UK and the US are not (or, at least, no longer) truly motivated by sovereign immunity, indicating the absence of *opinio juris*. So, there is currently no rule of customary international law requiring a source State to accord any immunity from income taxation to foreign States or foreign sovereign wealth investors.[432] On the other hand, there is no rule of customary international law prohibiting a source State from doing so.

4.4 IMMUNITY FROM MEASURES OF CONSTRAINT AND SOURCE STATE TAXATION OF INCOME DERIVED BY FOREIGN SOVEREIGN WEALTH INVESTORS

4.4.1 Introduction

Immunity from measures of constraint limits the enforcement power of (organs of) one State against *property* situated in that State, but belonging to another State, and generally applies to property that is used or intended for use for *sovereign purposes*. Immunity from measures of constraint could (effectively) result in the absence of source State taxation. Consider the situation where a foreign sovereign wealth investor refuses to pay income tax imposed on it by the tax authorities of a source State, or the situation where an SWE situated in a source State fails to comply with withholding tax obligations under the laws of that source State. In these exceptional situations, that source State is often left with the *ultimum remedium* of seeking enforcement measures to be taken against property of that foreign sovereign wealth investor, or possibly the foreign owner-State,[433] to satisfy its tax claim. This property could be situated in the

---

431. Paragraph 52 of the OECD Commentary on Art. 1: '(...) There is no international consensus (...) on the precise limits of the sovereign immunity principle. Most States, for example, would not recognise that the principle applies to business activities and many States do not recognise any application of this principle in tax matters. There are therefore considerable differences between States as regards the extent, if any, to which that principle applies to taxation. Even among States that would recognise its possible application in tax matters, some apply it only to the extent that it has been incorporated into domestic law and others apply it as customary international law but subject to important limitations. (...)'.
432. Similarly, American Law Institute, *Restatement of the Law Third: The Foreign Relations Law of the United States*, Vol. I (St. Paul, Minn.: American Law Institute Publishers, 1987), p. 448: '[u]nder international law, a state may tax not only a foreign state's income from commercial activities or investments in the taxing state's territory but also the foreign state's income from activities that are "governmental" in character, such as interest or gains currency transactions by that state or its central bank'. *See also* B. Kelsey, 'Recent Trends in Sovereign Immunity from Taxation' (1959) 17 *Toronto Faculty of Law Review* 81, p. 95; P. Paone, 'Italian Income Tax and Tax Liability of Foreign States and International Organizations' (1976) 2 *The Italian Yearbook of International Law* 273, p. 276.
433. Under many legal instruments, foreign States and entities of foreign States are shielded against so-called cross-execution. For example, Art. 19(c) UNCSI 2004 provides that post-judgment measures of constraint can only be taken against property which has a connection with the entity against which the proceeding was directed. Therefore, if a creditor (such as a source State) has a claim against an SWF of a foreign State, the assets of that foreign State would be shielded against any post-judgment measures of execution, and vice versa. However, the issue of cross-execution has not yet been settled in State practice. *See* A. van Aaken, *Blurring*

source State itself or in other States. Should a source State decide to take that route, immunity from measures of constraint, and, therefore, immunity from the collection of taxes (rather than immunity from taxation itself), would prevent a source State, or any other State, from taking enforcement measures, thus effectively resulting in the absence of source State taxation. Since a source State may also seek enforcement measures to be taken against property situated in foreign jurisdictions, this effect may depend on how immunity from execution would apply to foreign sovereign wealth investors in one or more foreign jurisdictions. It is important to note that State practice, as well as international instruments, dealing with immunity from execution is typically concerned with situations where the claimant is a private party that is seeking enforcement measures to be taken against property of a foreign State or State entity (*private party v. foreign State/State entity*). However, for present purposes, the claimant is a source State that is seeking enforcement measures to be taken against property of a foreign sovereign wealth investor, or a foreign State (*source State v. foreign sovereign (investor)*). Given this difference in situation, it is uncertain whether immunity from execution enjoyed by foreign sovereign wealth investors in a private law case would still apply in a tax case. Private parties could certainly consider a difference in application, in favour of a source State as claimant, as unfair. On the other hand, it could be argued that the collection of taxes is in the general interest, thus justifying a difference in treatment. In the author's view, based on the rationale of sovereign immunity as expressed in terms of sovereignty, independence, equality and dignity of States,[434] there is much to say for not applying immunity from execution any differently in tax cases.

The legal instruments and case law discussed below, and their potential application to foreign sovereign wealth investors, deal with private law cases. Given that the international law status of immunity from execution in tax cases is unclear, these instruments and case law are nothing more than an indication of how immunity from execution might apply in tax cases. Although the international law status of immunity from execution in tax cases is unsettled, this delicate issue may only occur in rather exceptional circumstances; for example if a foreign sovereign wealth investor refuses to pay income tax imposed on it by a source State, or if an SWE does not comply with withholding tax obligations under the laws of a source State.

4.4.2 Personal Scope

The personal scope of immunity from measures of constraint is generally not different from the personal scope of jurisdictional immunity. As discussed in Section 4.2.3.3 of this chapter, the personal scope is not restricted to the State itself, but also includes separate entities to the extent they are entitled to perform and are actually performing acts in the exercise of sovereign authority.

Boundaries Between Sovereign Acts and Commercial Activities. A Functional View on Regulatory Immunity and Immunity from Execution (March, 2013), Working Paper No. 2013-17, Law & Economics Research Paper Series, U. St. Gallen Law School, pp. 34–36.
434. Section 4.2.2.

Chapter 4: Sovereign Immunity and Taxation

4.4.3 Material Scope

4.4.3.1 *Property Serving Sovereign Purposes*

Different from jurisdictional immunity, the material scope of immunity from measures of constraint is generally determined by reference to the *purpose* of the property against which measures of constraint are sought. In its judgment of 12 April 1983, after an extensive review of State practice, the German Federal Constitutional Court concluded that:

> [a]ccording to established general State practice supported by cogent legal arguments, assets of a foreign State situated or present within the State of the forum cannot be subjected to measures of enforcement or even safeguarding measures without the consent of the foreign State concerned, so long as they serve sovereign purposes of that State.[435]

This distinction between property serving sovereign purposes, and property not serving sovereign purposes, can also be found in subsequent (international) legal instruments and case law of many other States. An example is the decision of the Italian Court of Cassation of 25 May 1989, in which it was held that 'the idea that immunity from execution in the forum State is limited to the assets of the State (and its public entities or agencies) used in the exercise of sovereign functions or devoted to public purposes is now accepted as a rule of the international community'.[436] Another example, of a more recent date, can be found in the UNCSI 2004, which provides that post-judgment measures of constraint are allowed if, *inter alia*, the property 'is specifically in use or intended for use by the State for other than government non-commercial purposes and is in the territory of the State of the forum'. [437]

In determining whether or not property serves sovereign purposes, courts largely follow 'judicially created categories'[438] of property. These categories are also reflected in the UNCSI 2004, which is considered by the House of Lords as 'the most authoritative statement available on the current international understanding of the limits of state immunity in civil cases'.[439] The following categories of property are generally considered to serve sovereign purposes: (1) diplomatic and consular premises and related property, including accounts, (2) military property, (3) property of the central bank or other monetary authority, (4) cultural property, and (5) scientific-historic property. The classification of other categories of property is determined based on the particular facts and circumstances of each case.

---

435. Federal Constitutional Court, *National Iranian Oil Company Revenues from Oil Sales Case* (1983) 65 *International Law Reports* 215, at 242.
436. Court of Cassation, *Libyan Arab Socialist People's Jamahiriya v. Rossbeton Srl* (1989) 87 *International Law Reports* 63, at 66.
437. Article 19(c) of the UNCSI 2004.
438. Council of Europe (G. Hafner, M. Kohen & S. Breau (eds)), *State Practice Regarding State Immunities* (Leiden: Martinus Nijhoff Publishers, 2006), p. 162.
439. House of Lords, *Jones v. Ministry of the Interior of the Kingdom of Saudi Arabia and Another* (2006) 129 *International Law Reports* 713, at 727.

4.4.3.2 Property Belonging to SWFs

Case law concerning SWFs is scarce and inconclusive.[440] In *AIG Capital Partners v. Kazakhstan*,[441] the claimant, AIG, had obtained an arbitration award against the Republic of Kazakhstan, which it sought to enforce against cash and securities held in London by third parties on behalf of the National Bank of Kazakhstan under a custodian agreement. The securities held included UK government bonds and shares in UK listed companies. The cash and securities formed a part of the National Fund of Kazakhstan, an SWF established in 2000, which was managed by the national bank. The purpose of the SWF was to ensure 'stable social and economic development of the country, accumulation of financial resources for future generations, [and] reduction of the vulnerability of the economy to the influence of unfavourable external factors'.[442] The National Bank of Kazakhstan intervened in this procedure and claimed that the assets were immune from execution under the UK SIA 1978. The High Court of England agreed because the assets constituted property of a central bank and such property was always immune from any enforcement process pursuant to Section 14(4) UK SIA 1978.[443] Section 14(4) – dealing with property of a central bank or other monetary authority – grants absolute immunity and does not distinguish between property in use or intended for use for commercial purposes, and property in use or intended for use for sovereign purposes. Interestingly, the court held that, even without Section 14(4), immunity would have been enjoyed, because 'all the London assets were, at all times, in use for sovereign purposes and pursuant to the exercise of sovereign authority of Kazakhstan', acting through the national bank.[444] The court argued that the assets formed part of the SWF and that the SWF was established 'to assist in the management of the economy and government revenues of Kazakhstan', which constituted a sovereign activity. The fact that the investments were aimed at achieving high profits and the securities were actively traded, was not considered relevant, because the aim of the exercise was, at all times, to 'enhance' the SWF, i.e., to assist the sovereign activity.[445] The exercise was considered 'part of the overall exercise of sovereign authority by Kazakhstan'.[446]

In contrast, the Swiss Federal Tribunal[447] has held that immunity from execution did not apply to Swiss assets of the KIA, the SWF of Kuwait, in respect of a debt claim of a Spanish company. Kuwait claimed immunity because the assets (Swiss bank accounts) were part of the SWF that was established to provide for the future needs of

---

440. A. van Aaken, *Blurring Boundaries Between Sovereign Acts and Commercial Activities. A Functional View on Regulatory Immunity and Immunity from Execution* (March, 2013), Working Paper No. 2013-17, Law & Economics Research Paper Series, U. St. Gallen Law School, pp. 28–29.
441. High Court, *AIG Capital Partners Inc. and Another v. Republic of Kazakhstan* (2005) 129 *International Law Reports* 589.
442. Ibid., at 595.
443. Ibid., at 607–616.
444. Ibid., at 625–626.
445. Ibid., at 625.
446. Ibid.
447. *Kuwait v. X* (1994) *Revue Suisse de droit international et européen*, 1995, Vol. 5, p. 593.

Chapter 4: Sovereign Immunity and Taxation

the Kuwaiti people, when the State no longer had oil reserves. The Tribunal decided that immunity was not available, because the SWF could not be assimilated to the State of Kuwait. Based on its constitutive documents and statements by Kuwait, the SWF was considered to be an independent entity. The fact that its funds were provided by and held on behalf of the State of Kuwait, and the fact that its board of directors included representatives of the State of Kuwait, was not considered relevant.

4.4.3.3 *Sovereign Wealth Investors Constituted by a Pool of Assets Within a Central Bank*

Some sovereign wealth investors have been constituted as a unit within a central bank, or other monetary authority. A great number of States apply an absolute immunity approach to measures of constraint in relation to property of foreign central banks. In *AIG Capital Partners v. Kazakhstan*, discussed in Section 4.4.3.2 above, the High Court of England held immune from measures of enforcement 'any asset (…) which is allocated to or held in the name of a central bank, irrespective of the capacity in which the central bank holds it, or the purpose for which the property is held'.[448] Other examples of an absolute immunity approach in relation to property of foreign central banks can be found in the immunity legislation of Pakistan,[449] Singapore[450] and South Africa,[451] which are all based on the UK SIA 1978, making the actual purpose of the property irrelevant. Importantly, the UNCSI 2004 also follows an absolute approach in respect of property of foreign central banks. Under the absolute immunity approach, sovereign wealth investors constituted by a pool of assets within a central bank, enjoy immunity in respect of all property, including property that would otherwise not have been considered as serving sovereign purposes.

But an absolute approach does not prevail in all States. For example, Swiss[452] and German[453] courts do not apply special rules to property of a central bank. Just like other categories of property, it needs to be demonstrated that the relevant property is in use or intended for use for governmental purposes. Such a (more) restrictive approach can also be found in Canada's State Immunity Act 1985.[454] The Special Rapporteur to the ILC also proposed a restrictive approach in relation to property of central banks, but this proposal did not have the general support of the ILC.[455] One member argued that 'central banks were instruments of the sovereign power and all activities conducted by them enjoyed immunity' from execution.[456] However, a (more) restrictive immunity

---

448. High Court, *AIG Capital Partners Inc. and Another v. Republic of Kazakhstan* (2005) 129 *International Law Reports* 589, at 616.
449. Section 15(4) of the Pakistani State Immunity Ordinance No. VI of 1981.
450. Section 16(4) of the Singaporean State Immunity Act 1979.
451. Section 15(3) of the South African Foreign States Immunities Act 1981.
452. Swiss Federal Tribunal, *Libyan Arab Socialist People's Jamahiriya v. Actimon SA* (1985) 82 *International Law Reports* 30, at 35.
453. Provincial Court of Frankfurt, *Central Bank of Nigeria Case* (1975) 65 *International Law Reports* 131, at 135.
454. Section 12(4) of the Canadian State Immunity Act 1985.
455. *Yearbook of the International Law Commission 1991*, Vol. II, Part II, Para. 227, p. 42.
456. *Ibid.*

approach does not necessarily have to limit immunity in relation to property of a sovereign wealth investor constituted as a pool of assets within a central bank, because such property may be considered as serving sovereign purposes, as the decision in *AIG Capital Partners v. Kazakhstan* illustrates.

4.4.4 Analysis

Although immunity from execution in tax cases could (effectively) result in the absence of source State taxation, its impact on achieving tax policy objectives of source States is different in comparison to immunity from taxation. Whereas immunity from taxation raises capital efficiency concerns since it could influence investment decisions of foreign sovereign wealth investors, immunity from execution in tax cases will unlikely influence investment decisions because of the uncertainty that surrounds it. And because of that uncertainty, it cannot be said that immunity from execution in tax cases enhances a source State's international attractiveness. What can be said with certainty, however, is that immunity from execution, once established in a particular tax case, does raise equity concerns since it results in preferential tax treatment of (some) foreign sovereign wealth investors over other investors. Nevertheless, the (potential) overall impact of immunity from execution on source States' ability to achieve (or promote) tax policy objectives, and to freely implement an approach to taxation of foreign sovereign wealth investors,[457] is negligible.

4.5 IMPACT OF THE SOVEREIGN IMMUNITY PRINCIPLE ON ACHIEVING NEUTRALITY (EFFICIENCY), EQUITY (FAIRNESS) AND INTERNATIONAL ATTRACTIVENESS IN RELATION TO FOREIGN SOVEREIGN WEALTH INVESTORS

In this section, it will (shortly) be examined what impact the sovereign immunity principle could have on source States' ability to achieve (or promote) tax policy objectives (i.e., neutrality, equity and international attractiveness), and to freely implement an approach to the taxation of foreign sovereign wealth investors.[458]

In Section 4.3.3.3, it was concluded that there is currently no rule of customary international law requiring a source State to accord any immunity from income taxation to foreign States or foreign sovereign wealth investors. On the other hand, there is no rule of customary international law prohibiting a source State from doing so. Therefore, the principle of jurisdictional immunity has no (negative) impact on source States' ability to achieve (or promote) tax policy objectives, and to freely implement an approach to taxation of foreign sovereign wealth investors.[459]

From the analysis in Section 4.4, it follows that the international law status of immunity from execution in tax cases is unsettled. Immunity from execution in tax

---

457. *See* the five approaches identified in Section 3.2.2.2.
458. *Ibid.*
459. *Ibid.*

cases could (effectively) result in the absence of source State taxation, which would raise equity concerns since it results in preferential tax treatment of (some) foreign sovereign wealth investors over other investors. However, because of the uncertainty that surrounds it and because it may only occur in rather exceptional circumstances, immunity from execution in tax cases should neither influence investment decisions of investors, nor enhance a source State's international attractiveness. Therefore, the (potential) overall impact of immunity from execution on source States' ability to achieve (or promote) tax policy objectives, and to freely implement an approach to taxation of foreign sovereign wealth investors,[460] is negligible.

To conclude, the sovereign immunity principle, as a principle of customary international law, has, at most, a very small impact on source States' ability to achieve (or promote) tax policy objectives, and to freely implement an approach to taxation of foreign sovereign wealth investors.

4.6 CONCLUSIONS

Although many States do not recognize any application of the sovereign immunity principle to taxation, (some) foreign sovereign wealth investors may enjoy immunity from taxation in a number of other States, including Australia, Canada, the UK and the US. The elementary question addressed in this chapter was whether the sovereign immunity principle, as a principle of customary international law, actually requires source States to accord tax immunities to foreign sovereign wealth investors. The answer to this question indicates what impact the sovereign immunity principle could have on source States' ability to achieve (or promote) tax policy objectives (i.e., neutrality, equity and international attractiveness), and to freely implement an approach to taxation of foreign sovereign wealth investors.

The findings of Chapter 4 indicate that there is currently no rule of customary international law requiring a source State to accord any immunity from income taxation to foreign States or foreign sovereign wealth investors. A rule of customary international law requires: (i) evidence of a general State practice, (ii) that is accepted as law (*opinio juris*). As already noted in the OECD Commentary on Article 1, there is no extensive and virtually uniform State practice regarding source taxation of foreign sovereign wealth investors; even among States which do apply sovereign immunity to direct taxation, significant differences exist between them. In addition, an examination of the tax immunity regimes and the rules on jurisdictional immunity in civil proceedings in Australia, Canada, the UK and the US, strongly suggests that the tax-exemptions accorded to foreign sovereign wealth investors are not (or, at least, no longer) truly motivated by sovereignty, indicating the absence of *opinio juris*. Therefore, the principle of jurisdictional immunity has no (negative) impact on source States' ability to achieve (or promote) tax policy objectives, and to freely implement an approach to taxation of foreign sovereign wealth investors.[461]

---

460. *Ibid.*
461. *Ibid.*

Rather than through immunity from taxation, absence of source State taxation could effectively also be achieved when (property of) foreign sovereign wealth investors would enjoy immunity from execution in tax cases and, therefore, immunity from the collection of taxes. Given that a source State may also seek enforcement measures to be taken against property situated in foreign jurisdictions, this effect may depend on how immunity from execution would apply to foreign sovereign wealth investors in one or more foreign jurisdictions. While foreign sovereign wealth investors may enjoy immunity from execution in private law cases in respect of property serving sovereign purposes, it is uncertain whether this would still apply in a tax case. Although the international law status of immunity from execution in tax cases is currently unclear, it can be argued that immunity from execution in tax cases should not apply any differently from immunity from execution in private law cases. This could mean that property of foreign sovereign wealth investors may also enjoy immunity from execution in tax cases. Be that as it may, it should be kept in mind that this delicate issue would only occur in rather exceptional circumstances; for example, if a foreign sovereign wealth investor refuses to pay income tax imposed on it by a source State, or if an SWE does not comply with withholding tax obligations under the laws of a source State. Immunity from execution in tax cases could (effectively) result in the absence of source State taxation, which would raise equity concerns since it results in preferential tax treatment of (some) foreign sovereign wealth investors over other investors. However, because of the uncertainty that surrounds it and because it will only occur in rather exceptional circumstances, immunity from execution in tax cases should neither influence investment decisions of investors, nor enhance a source State's international attractiveness. Therefore, the (potential) overall impact of immunity from execution on source States' ability to achieve (or promote) tax policy objectives, and to freely implement an approach to taxation of foreign sovereign wealth investors, is negligible.

It can be concluded that the sovereign immunity principle, as a principle of customary international law, has, at most, a very small impact on source States' ability to achieve (or promote) tax policy objectives, and to freely implement an approach to taxation of foreign sovereign wealth investors. This is summarized in the table below. The table will be completed with the findings of Chapter 5 (concerning tax treaties) and Chapter 6 (concerning European law).

Chapter 4: Sovereign Immunity and Taxation

Table 4.1 Impact of the Sovereign Immunity Principle on the Ability of Source States to Achieve (or Promote) Tax Policy Objectives, and to Freely Implement an Approach to Taxation of Foreign Sovereign Wealth Investors

	Neutrality		Equity		International Attractiveness
	(CEN)	*(CIN)*	*(Inter-taxpayer)*	*(Inter-nation)*	
Sovereign immunity	No (negative) impact	No (negative) impact	Impact negligible (i.e. only if immunity from execution would apply)	Impact negligible (i.e. only if immunity from execution would apply)	No (negative) impact
OECD/UN MTC based treaties	Chapter 5	Chapter 5	Chapter 5	Chapter 5	Chapter 5
European (Union) law	Chapter 6	Chapter 6	Chapter 6	Chapter 6	Chapter 6
	Potentially underlying Approaches (2) to (5)*	Potentially underlying Approach (1)*	Potentially underlying Approach (1)*	Potentially underlying Approach (1)*	Potentially underlying Approaches (2) to (5)*

* Approach (1): taxing foreign sovereign wealth investors in the same way as 'regular' non-resident corporate investors.
Approach (2): according a general tax-exemption under domestic law or administrative practice.
Approach (3): according specific tax-exemptions or specific tax reductions under domestic law or administrative practice.
Approach (4): according a general tax-exemption under one or more tax treaties.
Approach (5): according specific tax-exemptions or specific tax reductions under one or more tax treaties.

CHAPTER 5
Tax Treaty Aspects of (Foreign) Sovereign Wealth Investors

5.1 INTRODUCTION

The position of sovereign wealth investors is carefully addressed in many bilateral tax treaties.[462] From a source State perspective, many such treaties provide tax-exemptions on items of income derived by foreign sovereign wealth investors.[463] Yet, many other tax treaties currently in force have been concluded between two States at a time where cross-border investments by sovereign wealth investors were not so prominent, and questions have now arisen as to the application of such tax treaties to sovereign wealth investors. Issues relating to the application of tax treaties to State-owned entities, including SWFs, have, to some extent, been considered by the OECD Committee on Fiscal Affairs, through its Working Party 1.[464] The Committee's proposals for additions and changes to the OECD Commentary have been reflected in the 2010 update. In the 2011 revision of the UN MTC and its Commentaries, no such updates have been made.

This chapter will consider the (possible) implications of tax treaties for source State taxation of foreign sovereign wealth investors. Based on these implications, it will be examined what impact tax treaties could have on source States' ability to achieve (or promote) tax policy objectives (i.e., neutrality, equity and international attractiveness), and to freely implement an approach to the taxation of foreign sovereign wealth investors.[465] This chapter will focus on the OECD MTC (2017) and UN MTC (2011), and

---

462. *See*, for example, some of the Dutch tax treaties discussed in the Appendix to this study.
463. *Ibid.*
464. OECD (2009), *Discussion Draft on the Application of Tax Treaties to State-Owned Entities, Including Sovereign Wealth Funds*, available at: < http://www.oecd.org/tax/treaties/44080490.pdf >.
465. *See* the five approaches identified in Section 3.2.2.2.

their Commentaries. Indeed, bilateral tax treaties are often based on, or inspired by, (earlier versions of) the OECD MTC[466] or UN MTC.[467]

After an introduction to the general tax treaty interpretation rule in Section 5.2, Section 5.3–5.6 will first consider the (possible) implications of OECD and UN MTC based treaties for source State taxation of foreign sovereign wealth investors, by focusing on the resident article, the dividend and interest article, the capital gains article and the non-discrimination article. Based on these implications, Section 5.7 will then examine what impact tax treaties could have on the ability of source States to achieve (or promote) neutrality (efficiency), equity (fairness) and international attractiveness, and to freely implement an approach to taxation of foreign sovereign wealth investors. Section 5.8 will end this chapter with the main conclusions.

5.2 THE INTERPRETATION RULE (ARTICLE 3(2))

5.2.1 General

Article 3(2) of the OECD and UN MTC produces a rule of interpretation for any undefined tax treaty term. The interpretation of this interpretation rule will be relevant for the application of OECD and UN MTC based treaties to sovereign wealth investors. For that reason, a more general explanation of Article 3(2) is provided this early in this chapter, followed by a more detailed elaboration in subsequent paragraphs.

Article 3(2) of both model tax conventions provides:

> As regards the application of the Convention at any time by a Contracting State, any term not defined therein shall, unless the context otherwise requires, or the competent authorities agree to a different meaning pursuant to the provisions of Article 25, have the meaning that it has at that time under the law of that State for the purposes of the taxes to which the Convention applies, any meaning under the applicable tax laws of that State prevailing over a meaning given to the term under other laws of that State.

Article 3(2)'s primary reference is to the domestic legislation of the State that is applying the tax treaty, with any domestic tax meaning prevailing over any other domestic meaning. The primary reference to domestic tax law for undefined treaty terms makes sense considering that a tax treaty is concluded against the background of, interacts with and limits the application of the domestic tax laws of the Contracting States.[468] However, the 'context' may require a meaning of a term that is different from the meaning under the domestic (tax) law of the State that is applying the treaty.

---

466. The OECD MTC not only serves as the basic document of reference in tax treaty negotiations between OECD Member States, but it is also used in negotiations between OECD Member States and non-OECD Member States and even between non-OECD Member States. *See* Paras 13–14, Introduction to the OECD MTC.
467. The main difference between the two models is that the UN MTC gives more weight to the source principle compared to the OECD MTC, and this generally favours developing States. *See* Para. 3 and Para. 12, Introduction to the UN MTC. Hence the official title 'United Nations Model Double Taxation Convention between Developed and Developing Countries.'
468. Avery Jones et al., 'The Interpretation of Tax Treaties with Particular Reference to Article 3(2) of the OECD Model – I' (1984) 1 *British Tax Review* 14, p. 17.

Chapter 5: Tax Treaty Aspects

5.2.2 'Unless the Context Otherwise Requires'

As explained, under the interpretation rule of Article 3(2), the domestic (tax) law meaning of the undefined tax treaty term can be 'set aside', if the 'context' so requires. 'Context' in Article 3(2) has not been defined, but the Commentaries on Article 3(2) of both model tax conventions shed (some) light on what 'context' comprises:[469]

> The context is determined in particular by the intention of the Contracting States when signing the Convention as well as the meaning given to the term in question in the legislation of the other Contracting State (an implicit reference to the principle of reciprocity on which the Convention is based). The wording of the Article therefore allows the competent authorities some leeway.

According to the Commentaries, the context comprises *in particular*, but not exclusively: (i) the common intention of the States when signing the treaty, and (ii) the meaning of the term under the domestic (tax) law of the *other* State (an expression of reciprocity).

5.2.3 Relationship Between Article 3(2) and the Vienna Convention on the Law of Treaties (1969)

Article 3(2) is regarded by most authors as *lex specialis* to Articles 31 and 32 of the *Vienna Convention on the Law of Treaties* (1969) ('VCLT 1969').[470] Since *lex specialis derogat generali* in international law, this would seem to imply that Article 3(2) exclusively governs any undefined treaty term.[471] Also, the OECD Commentary and UN Commentary make no reference to the VCLT 1969 and observe that Article 3(2) provides a 'general rule' of interpretation for undefined treaty terms.[472] But this does not mean that the VCLT 1969 has no role to play in relation to Article 3(2). Article 3(2), as a treaty provision, requires interpretation too and cannot be subject to its own rule of interpretation.[473] The interpretation of Article 3(2) is governed by the interpretation rules included in the VCLT 1969.[474] This means that Article 3(2) is to be interpreted in *good faith*, which entails an interpretation that is honest, fair and reasonable, and in

---

469. Paragraph 12 of the OECD Commentary on Art. 3, quoted in Para. 14 of the UN Commentaries on Art. 3.
470. H. Shannon, 'US Income Tax Treaties, Reference to Domestic Law for the Meaning of Undefined Terms' (1989) 17 *Intertax* 453, p. 455; Dutch Advocate-General Wattel in the appendix to his Conclusion preceding *Hoge Raad*, 5 September 2003, No. 37 651, *BNB* 2003/379, Para. 2.15; F. Engelen, *Interpretation of Tax Treaties under International Law*, IBFD Doctoral Series Vol. 7 (Amsterdam: IBFD, 2004), pp. 477–478.
471. F. Engelen, *Interpretation of Tax Treaties under International Law*, IBFD Doctoral Series, Vol. 7 (Amsterdam: IBFD, 2004), p. 478.
472. Paragraph 11 of the OECD Commentary on Art. 3, and Para. 13 of the UN Commentaries on Art. 3.
473. Similarly, Dutch Advocate-General Wattel in the appendix to his Conclusion preceding *Hoge Raad*, 5 September 2003, No. 37 651, *BNB* 2003/379, Para. 2.15.
474. *Ibid.*; F. Engelen, *Interpretation of Tax Treaties under International Law*, IBFD Doctoral Series, Vol. 7 (Amsterdam: IBFD, 2004), p. 478; L. de Broe, *International Tax Planning and Prevention of Abuse*, IBFD Doctoral Series, Vol. 14 (Amsterdam: IBFD, 2008), p. 264.

accordance with the common intention of the parties as expressed in the terms of the tax treaty.[475] In addition, Articles 31 and 32 of the VCLT 1969 come into play when an undefined treaty term has no domestic (tax) law meaning.[476]

5.3 TAX TREATY ACCESS (ARTICLES 1, 3 AND 4)

5.3.1 General

Article 1(1) of the OECD and UN MTC, on the persons covered, are identical and read as follows:

> This convention shall apply to *persons* who are *residents* of one or both of the Contracting States. (Italics added)

Thus, according to the wording of Article 1(1), tax treaty access is generally reserved for someone who or something which qualifies as a 'person' and as a 'resident' (of at least one of the two States).[477] The first term ('person') is defined in Article 3(1)(a), whereas the second term ('resident') is defined in Article 4(1).

As from the 2010 version, the OECD Commentary notices, that issues may arise as to whether SWFs qualify as a 'person' and as a 'resident' for tax treaty purposes.[478] The first aspect is examined in Section 5.3.2 and the second in Section 5.3.3 below.

5.3.2 The Definition of 'Person' (Article 3(1)(a))

5.3.2.1 Introduction

The definition of 'person' in both model tax conventions is identical. The term 'person' is described in Article 3(1)(a) to *include*[479] 'an individual, a company and any other body of persons'. As noted in the Commentaries to both model tax conventions, and as its wording suggests, this definition of 'person' is not exhaustive and is used in a very wide sense.[480] Out of these three categories, the OECD and UN MTC only contain a definition of the term 'company', which is defined as 'any body corporate or any entity

---

475. F. Engelen, *Interpretation of Tax Treaties under International Law*, IBFD Doctoral Series, Vol. 7 (Amsterdam: IBFD, 2004), p. 131.
476. M. Kandev, 'Tax Treaty Interpretation: Determining Domestic Meaning Under Article 3(2) of the OECD Model' (2007) 55 *Canadian Tax Journal* 55.
477. Notwithstanding Art. 1, certain articles of the OECD MTC may, under circumstances, apply to persons who may fail to qualify as resident. On this and the historical background, role and function of Art. 1, *see* P. Hattingh, 'Article 1 of the OECD Model: Historical Background and the Issues Surrounding It' (2010) 57 *Bulletin for International Taxation* 215 et seq.; P. Hattingh, 'The Role and Function of Article 1 of the OECD Model' (2010) 57 *Bulletin for International Taxation* 546 et seq.
478. Paragraph 8.5 of the OECD Commentary on Art. 4.
479. In the OECD Draft Double Taxation Convention of 1963, the word 'comprises' was used instead of 'includes'.
480. Paragraph 2 of the OECD Commentary on Art. 3, and Para. 4 of the UN Commentaries on Art. 3. Similar wording was already used in the 1963 OECD Commentary on Art. 3.

that is treated as a body corporate for tax purposes'.[481] Because of the word *any* in 'any body corporate', the term 'body corporate' appears to be used in a very wide sense too. The definition of company has been formulated with special reference to the article on dividends (Article 10).[482] Article 10 is important to sovereign wealth investors for obtaining relief of source State taxation on cross-border dividends derived from their investments and will be discussed in Section 5.4.2 of this chapter. A sovereign wealth investor qualifying as a 'company' automatically qualifies as a 'person'. The more general term 'person' is relevant for Article 4(1), to be discussed in Section 5.3.3, and Article 11 (Interest), to be discussed in Section 5.4.3. Section 5.3.2 will only consider the application of the tax treaty term 'company' to sovereign wealth investors.

5.3.2.2 'Company' and Article 3(2)

As mentioned, the definition of 'company' is especially relevant to the dividend article (Article 10) and meeting this definition could result in the lowest rate of source State taxation of dividends (paragraph 2(a)).

The OECD and UN MTC are silent whether the perspective of the Contracting State applying the treaty or the perspective of the Contracting State in which the entity is organized is relevant in determining whether an entity is a 'body corporate'. With respect to the term 'national', Article 3(1)(g)(ii) of the OECD MTC and Article 3(1)(f)(ii) of the UN MTC provide that the legal capacity of a person other than an individual is derived from the laws of the Contracting State in which the entity is organized. In the author's view, the same conclusion should apply to the term 'body corporate'. The question whether an entity is a body corporate is a legal question concerning the legal status of an entity. This status can only be derived from, and granted by, the laws of the State under which an entity is incorporated or established. So, it does not make much sense to answer this legal question from the perspective of the source State, not even when that State is applying the tax treaty. In the author's view, the context referred to in Article 3(2) requires this legal question to be answered on the basis of the (company) law of the State under which the entity has been established.[483]

Obviously, whether an entity is treated as a 'body corporate for tax purposes' is a tax question. Unlike the legal question referred to above, this tax question can be answered from the perspective of the State in which the entity is a resident (residence State), as well as from the perspective of the State from which the dividends are paid (source State). One might expect a source State to interpret the term 'body corporate for tax purposes' (as species of the genus 'company') on the basis of its own domestic tax laws, unless the context otherwise requires, pursuant to Article 3(2). However, according to the OECD Commentary, whether an entity is a 'body corporate for tax

---

481. Article 3(1)(b) of the OECD MTC and Art. 3(1)(b) of the UN MTC.
482. Paragraph 3 of the OECD Commentary on Art. 3, and Para. 5 of the UN Commentaries on Art. 3.
483. Also, A. Rust, in Reimer & Rust (eds), *Klaus Vogel on Double Taxation Conventions*, 4th edn., (Alphen a/d Rijn: Kluwer Law International, 2015), p. 186.

purposes' has to be answered according to the tax laws of the State in which the entity is organized.[484] The UN Commentaries are silent on this matter. The OECD Commentary speaks of a 'taxable unit' that is not a body corporate in a legal sense, but is treated as a separate entity for tax purposes in the State in which the entity is organized.[485] An explanation why the OECD Commentary unconditionally chooses the home State perspective to answer this query may be found in the relationship with the 'liable to tax' test. That is, an entity that is not a 'body corporate' in a legal sense will not be 'liable to tax' (and so will not have tax treaty access) if it does not classify as a 'body corporate for tax purposes' in its home State.

From the above, it follows that a 'body corporate' is an entity with a separate legal identity (i.e., a legal person or an entity with legal personality according to laws under which the entity has been incorporated or established), whereas a 'body corporate for tax purposes' is an entity without a separate legal identity that is treated on a par with separate legal entities for tax purposes of the home State.

On a separate note, the use of the word *other* in 'any other body of persons', could suggest that a 'company' is necessarily a body of persons, i.e., a body of at least two persons. This would mean that a separate legal entity with, for example, one shareholder, such as SWFs or SWEs, could never qualify as a 'company'. Surely, this was not the intention of the drafters. The definition of a company does not make any reference to the quality or quantity of (share)holder(s). Around the world many types of corporate bodies exist that can have one (share)holder only.

5.3.2.3 *States, Political Subdivisions and Local Authorities and 'Person'*

A 'resident of a Contracting State' is referred to in Article 4(1) as: (i) any person who is liable to tax under the domestic laws of one of the States by reason of a certain criterion, and (ii) also includes the State itself and any political subdivision or local authority thereof. Under (i) someone or something cannot be a 'resident of a Contracting State' without being a 'person', while the requirement of a 'person' as such is not mentioned under (ii). In the author's view, Articles 1, 3 and 4 of the OECD and UN MTC, when read in conjunction with each other, should be read to say that a 'resident of a Contracting State' under (ii) automatically qualifies as a 'person', or that a 'person' (the definition of which is non-exhaustive) includes a State and any political subdivision or local authority thereof.[486]

---

484. Paragraph 3 of the OECD Commentary on Art. 3. *See also* Para. 24 of the OECD Commentary on Art. 1 (dealing with this matter in relation to collective investment funds).
485. *Ibid.*
486. Cf. P. Hattingh, 'The Role and Function of Article 1 of the OECD Model' (2010) 57 *Bulletin for International Taxation* 546, p. 546, who reads Art. 1, when reading it in conjunction with Arts 3 and 4, as follows: '[t]his Convention shall apply to persons who are residents of a Contracting State, which (a) include an individual, any body corporate or any entity that is treated as a body corporate for tax purposes, and any other body of persons who/which are, under the laws of that State, liable to tax therein by reason of his/its domicile, residence, place of management or any other criterion of a similar nature, and (b) also include that State and any political subdivision or local authority thereof. (...)' In other words, a State and any political subdivision or local authority thereof are persons who are a resident of a Contracting State as mentioned in

5.3.2.4 Application to Sovereign Wealth Investors

Sovereign wealth investors meeting the treaty definition of 'company' qualify as a 'person' under Articles 1(1) and 4(1), and satisfy one of the conditions of Article 10 (Dividends).

The distinction made in Section 2.8.3 between sovereign wealth investors based on their legal form will be followed throughout the remaining part of this chapter, where relevant.

5.3.2.4.1 (i) Sovereign Wealth Investors Constituted by a Pool of Assets Within the State

Sovereign wealth investors constituted by a pool of assets within the State are not corporate bodies 'themselves', but they may be treated as such for home State tax purposes. If not, the relevant question is whether the State qualifies as a 'company' for tax treaty purposes. The term 'company' is defined in a wide sense as '*any* body corporate or *any* entity that is treated as a body corporate for tax purposes' (italics added).[487] So, the word 'any' suggests that the term body corporate includes both corporate bodies/legal persons of *private law* and corporate bodies/legal persons of *public law*. Whether an entity is a body corporate in a legal sense is determined on the basis of the (company) law of the State under which the entity has been established. For example, under Dutch law, the Dutch State (as well as Dutch provinces, Dutch municipalities and other Dutch entities to which public functions have been assigned and which have legal personality by virtue of a specific law)[488] is a corporate body of public law (*publiekrechtelijke rechtspersoon*). Other States can be expected to have legal personality as well,[489] as this enables them to carry out their duties, conduct transactions on their own behalf, hold the ownership of assets, enter into political agreements, etc. So, the State itself will most likely be a body corporate (of public law) and fall within the definition of 'company'. In this respect, the terms 'State' and 'government', as the representative governing body of the State, are interchangeable, as also appears from the Commentaries.[490]

Art. 1. *See also* R. Vann, '"Liable to Tax" and Company Residence under Tax Treaties', in: G. Maisto, *Residence of Companies under Tax Treaties and EC Law*, EC and International Tax Law Series, Vol. 5 (Amsterdam: IBFD, 2009), p. 198, fn. 4.
487. Article 3(1)(b) of the OECD/UN MTC.
488. Cf. Art. 2:1 and Art. 2:3 of the Dutch Civil Code.
489. Bin Cheng, *General Principles of Law as Applied by International Courts and Tribunals*, Grotius Classic Reprint Series, No. 2, (New York: Cambridge University Press, 2006), pp. 182–183, fn. 489. Political subdivisions will also have a separate legal personality (fn. 489). In most European States the local authority itself, and not so much its organs, will have a legal personality, while in other European States, such as Russia and Ukraine, the organs of the local authority carry a separate legal identity (as well). *See* Council of Europe, *Local authority competences in Europe (situation in 2007)*, Study of the European Committee on Local and Regional Democracy, p. 12.
490. Paragraph 8.4 of the OECD Commentary on Art. 4, quoted in Para. 6 of the UN Commentaries on Art. 4, which refers the government of each State.

5.3.2.4.2 (ii) Sovereign Wealth Investors Established as or Within a Separate Legal Entity Other Than the State Itself

Based on its wide definition of '*any* body corporate or *any* entity that is treated as a body corporate for tax purposes', the tax treaty term 'company' includes both corporate bodies/legal persons of private law and corporate bodies/legal persons of public law. So, sovereign wealth investors established as separate legal entities under the laws of a Contracting State should meet the definition of company, whether established under public law or private law.

5.3.2.4.3 (iii) Sovereign Wealth Investors Organized as a (Legal) Entity Without a Separate Legal Personality

SWEs organized as a (legal) entity without a separate legal personality, such as partnerships, will only qualify as a 'company' if they are treated as a body corporate for tax purposes according to the tax laws of the State in which the entity is organized. Otherwise, the sovereign wealth investor that has set-up the SWE would qualify as 'company' (look-through approach).

5.3.3 Residency (Article 4)

5.3.3.1 *Introduction*

Article 4(1) of the OECD MTC defines as a 'resident':

> any *person* who, under the laws of that State, is *liable to tax* therein by reason of his domicile, residence, place of management or any other criterion of a similar nature, *and also includes that State and any political subdivision or local authority thereof* as well as a recognised pension fund of that State. This term however, does not include any person who is liable to tax in that State in respect only of income from sources in that State or capital situated therein. (Italics added)

Article 4(1) of the UN MTC reproduces Article 4(1) OECD MTC, with one relevant exception; place of incorporation has been added as a criterion giving rise to the required tax liability.

The first preliminary remark in the OECD Commentary on Article 4,[491] as reproduced in the UN Commentaries on Article 4,[492] identifies the following functions of the concept of resident for tax treaty purposes:

(1) to determine the personal scope (*ratione personae*) of application of a tax treaty;
(2) to solve issues of double taxation caused by double residence (which is done through the tie-breaker rules); and

---
491. Paragraph 1 of the Preliminary remarks on Art. 4 of the OECD MTC.
492. Paragraph 1 of the UN Commentaries on Art. 4.

(3) to solve issues of double taxation arising from simultaneous taxation in the State of residence and the State of source – which is done in the subsequent articles by means of allocating taxing rights between the State of which the owner of the income is a resident ('residence State') and the State where the income arises ('source State'), and by providing for relief of double taxation. However, tax treaties as such do not create (domestic) taxing rights.

Section 5.3.3 will consider the application of the 'liable to tax' test to sovereign wealth investors (i.e., the first function).

5.3.3.2 Relationship Between 'Liable to Tax' and the Interpretation Rule of Article 3(2)?

From the perspective of a source State, whether a person is a 'resident of the other Contracting State' (cf. Articles 10 and 11), in principle depends on the domestic tax laws of that other Contracting State, because Article 4(1) refers to liable to tax under the laws of that (other) State by reason of a listed criterion. Thus, if a person is not liable to tax under the laws of the other Contracting State, or a person is liable to tax under the laws of the other Contracting State by reason of an unlisted criterion (not of a similar nature), this person is not a 'resident of the other Contracting State'. Does the exclusive reference to the laws of the other Contracting State mean that the source State perspective has no role to play in determining whether a person is a 'resident of the other Contracting State'? The author tends to believe it does have a role to play for the following reasons.

The term 'liable to tax' as referred to in Article 4(1) is an undefined treaty term, which seems to leave room for the application of the interpretation rule of Article 3(2). Pursuant to Article 3(2), the meaning of any undefined treaty term is determined by the meaning under the domestic (tax) laws of the State that is applying the treaty, unless the context otherwise requires. In determining whether the source State needs to provide relief of taxation under the tax treaty (e.g., Articles 10 and 11), the result of this rule of interpretation seems to be that a person needs to be 'liable to tax' from the viewpoint of the State of source as well (as the source State is looking to apply the treaty), unless the context otherwise requires.[493] As explained in Section 5.2.2, according to the Commentaries, the context comprises in particular, but not exclusively: (i) the common intention of the States when signing the treaty, and (ii) the meaning of the term under the domestic (tax) law of the *other* Contracting State (an expression of reciprocity). Although both elements can be relevant to the interpretation of the term 'liable to tax', point (ii) – reference to the meaning of the term under the domestic (tax) law of the other Contracting State – is particularly interesting for the current discussion, also because Article 4(1) refers to liable to tax under the laws of the home State. Does this reference in point (ii) mean that the meaning of the term 'liable

---

493. This is the view of Van Weeghel. *See* Para. 1 of Van Weeghel's comment on *Hoge Raad*, 4 December 2009, No. 07/10383, *BNB* 2010/177.

to tax' from the perspective of the State of source is not relevant in determining whether a person is a 'resident of the other Contracting State' (as referred to in e.g., Articles 10 and 11)? The author tends to believe the source State perspective can be relevant. Article 3(2)'s primary reference is to the domestic (tax) laws of the State that is applying the treaty, so the meaning of an undefined tax treaty term according to the domestic (tax) law of the other Contracting should only have an overriding effect in exceptional circumstances. Otherwise, there is little point in Article 3(2)'s primary reference to the domestic (tax) laws of the State that is applying the treaty. However, one could argue that, because Article 4(1) refers to liable to tax under the laws of the home State, such an exceptional circumstance is present and, consequently, that the interpretation of the term 'liable to tax' by the source State is not relevant. In other words, assuming that Article 3(2) applies, the context would require the source State simply to rely on the home State's understanding of 'liable to tax'. The author did not come across this particular issue and argument in literature or case law. As far as the author could establish, Swedish,[494] Finnish,[495] Indian and French[496] case law dealing with access of foreign tax-exempt entities to OECD MTC based treaties suggests that the 'liable to tax' test is also interpreted from a source State perspective. Also, as far as the author could establish, no explicit reference was made by these courts to the interpretation rule contained in Article 3(2). And so this may have left these courts with the following two means of interpretation: (i) establishing an independent treaty meaning without reference to domestic (tax) law, or (ii) implicit reference to domestic (tax) law based on Article 3(2). Given the limited guidance in the OECD Commentary on the meaning of 'liable to tax' in relation to tax-exempt entities, the courts may implicitly have applied Article 3(2) to determine the meaning of 'liable to tax' from a source State perspective. In addition, the OECD Commentary and UN Commentaries on tax-exempt entities, discussed in Section 5.3.3.7.5 below, also seem to leave room for source State interpretation. However, to avoid discussions, States should preferably clarify the tax treaty status of entities bilaterally.

---

494. *Regeringsrätten*, Supreme Administrative Court, 2 October 1996, RÅ 1996 ref 84 (6301-1994), Tax Treaty Case Law IBFD (summary by M. Hilling), concerning the tax treaty residency of Luxembourg tax-exempt SICAVs.
495. Korkein hallinto-oikeus, Supreme Administrative Court, 22 December 2004, KHO 2004:111, Tax Treaty Case Law IBFD (summary by K. Pettersson), concerning the tax treaty residency of a Luxembourg tax-exempt SICAV.
496. In three decisions dated 6 December 2007, the *Cour Administrative d'Appel de Paris* held that three Dutch pension funds, although subjectively exempt from tax in the Netherlands by virtue of a specific provision, were liable to tax in the Netherlands and could, therefore, be regarded as residents for purposes of the treaty. However, more recently, on 9 November 2015, the *Conseil d'État* held that a German tax-exempt pension fund did not qualify as a tax treaty resident. Regarding the decisions of 6 December 2007, *see* C. Védrine, 'Treaty Between France and Netherlands – French Administrative Court of Appeal Finds Withholding Taxes Applied to Dutch Pension Funds Contrary to Treaty Non-discrimination Clause and EU Free Movement of Capital', 26 June 2008, IBFD Tax News Service. Regarding the decision of 9 November 2015, *see* P. Burg, 'Treaty Between France and Germany – French Administrative Supreme Court Rules That Exempt Pension Fund Is Not Resident Entitled Treaty Benefits,' 11 November 2015, IBFD TNS Online.

Chapter 5: Tax Treaty Aspects

5.3.3.3 *Relevance of the Connecting Criteria for the Meaning of 'Liable to Tax'*

A resident of a Contracting State includes any person who, under the laws of that State, is liable to tax by reason of a certain criterion. The criteria mentioned in Article 4(1) of the OECD MTC are domicile, residence, place of management or any other criterion of a similar nature. In Article 4(1) of the UN MTC, place of incorporation has been added. These criteria are relevant for the interpretation of the term 'liable to tax'. The Supreme Court of Canada has considered in *Crown Forest Industries*[497] what these criteria have in common. Norsk Pacific Steamship Company Limited ('Norsk'), a company incorporated under the laws of the Bahamas with business operations and a place of management in the US, received rental payments from a Canadian resident group company, Crown Forest Industries Limited. The rental payments were subject to Canadian taxation. If the Bahamian incorporated company could be considered a resident of the US for purposes of the Canada – US tax treaty, as claimed by the Canadian company, the statutory rate of 25% would be reduced to 10% under the tax treaty. Norsk was liable to tax in the US as a foreign taxpayer because it was engaged in a trade or business effectively connected with the US. The Supreme Court of Canada held that Norsk's place of management in the US was only one of the factors to be considered to determine whether it was engaged in the conduct of a trade or business in the US. It was liable to tax in the US by reason of this trade or business and not 'by reason' of its place of management, as was required by the tax treaty. The Supreme Court of Canada then considered whether engaged in a trade or business is a criterion of a similar nature. It held that '(...) the most similar element among the enumerated criteria is that, standing alone, they would each constitute a basis on which states generally impose full tax liability on world-wide income'.[498] In more abstract terms, the Canadian court may have been distinguishing between liability to residence taxation and liability to source taxation. The OECD MTC, which served as the basis for the Canada – US tax treaty (1980),[499] and its Commentaries, also assume a distinction between (and a concurrence of) residence taxation and source taxation, and allocate taxing rights over a number of items of income and capital between the residence State (i.e., the State of which the owner of the income or capital is a resident) and the source State (i.e., the State where the income or gain arises).[500] Residence-based taxation refers to taxation based on a principle of residence and principally attaches to the person (subject) instead of the income (object), whereas source-based taxation refers to taxation based on a principle of source and principally attaches to sourced income (object) instead of the person (subject).[501] In general, liability to residence-based taxation (which can take different forms) is more comprehensive as the tax base has no geographical boundaries. In the author's opinion, what all criteria have in common is

---

497. *Crown Forest Industries Ltd. v. Her Majesty the Queen*, Supreme Court of Canada, 22 June 1995, File No.: 23940, Tax Treaty Case Law IBFD.
498. *Ibid.*, at 40.
499. *Ibid.*, at 55.
500. *See*, for example, Paras 19–25, Introduction to the OECD MTC.
501. R. Couzin, *Corporate Residence and International Taxation*, (IBFD Publications BV: Amsterdam, 2002), pp. 148-149.

that they generally serve as a basis for imposing a liability to (some type of) residence taxation by reason of a personal connecting factor, i.e., they attach to a person (subject) rather than income (object). The Commentaries on both model tax conventions also point in this direction:

> Generally the domestic laws of the various States impose a comprehensive liability to tax – 'full tax liability' – based on the taxpayers' personal attachment to the State concerned (the 'State of residence'). This liability to tax is not imposed only on persons who are 'domiciled' in a State in the sense in which 'domicile' is usually taken in the legislations (private law). The cases of full liability to tax are extended to comprise also, for instance, persons who stay continually, or maybe only for a certain period, in the territory of the State.[502]

5.3.3.4 'Liable to Tax' as (the Most) Comprehensive Taxation

The discussion on the connecting criteria has shed some light on the meaning of the 'liable to tax' requirement in Article 4(1). What all criteria have in common is that they generally serve as a basis for imposing a liability to residence taxation, principally attaching to a person (subject) rather than income (object). The Commentary on Article 4(1) reveals what it aims to cover:[503]

> The definition refers to the concept of residence adopted in the domestic laws (...). As far as individuals are concerned, the definition aims at covering the various forms of personal attachment to a State which, in the domestic taxation laws, form the basis of a comprehensive taxation (full liability to tax).

This statement is as relevant for companies as it is for individuals. Therefore, liability to tax in Article 4(1) refers to 'comprehensive liability to tax' or 'full liability to tax' and is relevant for all persons, including companies. Support for this can be found in Canadian[504] and Dutch[505] case law, among others. In many States, comprehensive taxation is understood as taxation on worldwide income and, at first sight, this appears to be supported by the second sentence of Article 4(1), which excludes as a resident

---

502. Paragraph 3 of the OECD Commentary on Art. 4, quoted in Para. 2 of the UN Commentaries on Art. 4.
503. Paragraph 8 of the OECD Commentary on Art. 4, quoted in Para. 5 of the UN Commentaries on Art. 4. Similar wording was already used in Para. 10 of the 1963 OECD Commentary on Art. 4.
504. *Crown Forest Industries Ltd. v. Her Majesty the Queen*, Supreme Court of Canada, 22 June 1995, File No.: 23940, Tax Treaty Case Law IBFD, at 40, concerning the residence status under the Canada – US tax treaty of a company incorporated under the laws of the Bahamas with business operations and a place of management in the US: '(...) the most similar element among the enumerated criteria is that, standing alone, they would each constitute a basis on which states generally impose full tax liability on world-wide income. (...) In this respect, the criteria for determining residence in Article IV, paragraph 1 involve more than simply being liable to taxation on some portion of income (source liability); they entail being subject to as comprehensive a tax liability as is imposed by a state. In the United States and Canada, such comprehensive taxation is taxation on world-wide income'.
505. *Hoge Raad*, 28 February 2001, No. 35 557, BNB 2001/195, Para. 3.7, concerning the residence status under the Netherlands – Belgium tax treaty of a company incorporated under the laws of the Netherlands of which the place of effective management was moved to the Netherlands Antilles.

'any person who is liable to tax in that State in respect only of income from sources in that State or capital situated therein'. This would imply that persons who are 'resident' in a State which has adopted in its income tax system the territoriality principle, would never qualify as a resident under Article 4. The OECD Commentary clarifies that such a result is clearly not intended and also not achieved when the second sentence of Article 4(1) is interpreted in the light of its object and purpose, which is to exclude persons who are not subject to comprehensive taxation.[506] The OECD Commentary implies that comprehensive taxation (full liability to tax) cannot be understood as a universal concept, but should be construed in the light of an individual tax system and the principles upon which that tax system is based (i.e., it should be made country-specific). Comprehensive taxation is therefore sometimes referred to as the 'most comprehensive tax liability' imposed by a State,[507] which then seems to be a more appropriate expression. Thus, persons who are resident in a State that applies a territoriality principle in taxation are liable to the most comprehensive taxation under the laws of that State.

The object and purpose of the second sentence (introduced in the 1977 OECD Model and the 1999 UN MTC) is in particular to exclude persons who, although liable to residence taxation under the *domestic laws* of a State (i.e., liable to tax in the meaning of the first sentence), are in fact liable to tax in that State only on income from sources or capital situated in the receiving State as a consequence of *international law* other than the tax treaty concerned.[508] The original cause for the introduction of the second sentence seems to be to exclude as tax treaty residents diplomatic and consular personnel who are accredited to other States. Such persons are often resident for tax purposes of the receiving State, but the possibility for that receiving State to impose tax on diplomatic and consular staff is (often) restricted by (customary rules of) international law to certain income from sources or capital situated in the receiving State.[509],[510] However, not only diplomats can become excluded residents under the second sentence. In December 1971, after the OECD Draft of 1963, but prior to the OECD Model of 1977, it was first proposed to extend the scope of the excluded resident to 'individuals', not just diplomats and consular staff,[511] while in April 1973, it was agreed

---

506. Paragraph 8.3 of the OECD Commentary on Art. 4. Reference to the object and purpose of the second sentence with respect to the territoriality principle was included in 2008 and changed the Commentary as it was from 1992 onwards, which stated that the second sentence had 'to be interpreted restrictively'. This amendment should be seen as a clarification rather than a material change.
507. *Crown Forest Industries Ltd. v. Her Majesty the Queen*, Supreme Court of Canada, 22 June 1995, File No.: 23940, Tax Treaty Case Law IBFD, at 40; A. de Graaf & F. Pötgens, 'Worrying Interpretation of "Liable to Tax": OECD Clarification Would Be Welcome' (2011) 39 *Intertax* 169, p. 169.
508. H. Pijl, 'Excluded Resident and the Term "Law"/"Laws" in Article 4 of the OECD Draft (1963) and OECD Model (1977/2010)' (2012) 66 *Bulletin for International Taxation* 3, pp. 5–14 & p. 22.
509. Paragraph 8.1 of the OECD Commentary on Art. 4, quoted in Para. 4 of the UN Commentaries on Art. 4.
510. Articles 34(b) and (d) of the *Vienna Convention on Diplomatic Relations 1961*, and Arts 49(b) and (d) of the *Vienna Convention on Consular Relations 1963*.
511. Report on Arts 16, 17 and 19 and the Question Concerning Residence of Diplomats, 23 December 1971, CFA/WP1(71)7, p. 14.

to widen the scope to 'persons',[512] thus including companies as well. Another example of an excluded resident under the second sentence, also mentioned in both Commentaries,[513] is that of dual residents (i.e., residents under the domestic tax laws of two States) who are resident of the loser-State under the tie-breaker rule in the tax treaty between the winner-State and loser-State. Such dual residents do not have access to tax treaties concluded between the loser-State and third States, because, pursuant to the tax treaty between the loser-State and the winner-State (the other international law), they are de facto liable to tax in the loser-State on source income only. The territorial principle applied to the taxation of residents also limits the liability to tax to income from sources or capital situated in that State, but this is the result of domestic tax policy and not of *other international law*.

Couzin has pointed to some of the shortcomings of the 'most comprehensive tax liability' expression.[514] He gives the example, which this author has modified somewhat, of a corporation that is liable to the general territorial regime in its State of residence. This corporation can also elect to become liable to worldwide taxation. In this situation, what is the most comprehensive form of taxation? He also gives the examples of leasing corporations in Canada to whom favourable tax depreciation rules apply and mortgage investment corporations that can deduct dividend payments. Again, what is the most comprehensive form of taxation? According to Couzin, in line with the basic distinction underlying the OECD MTC as a whole, Article 4(1) intends to cover persons who are liable to some type of residence taxation (i.e., taxation by reason of a personal connecting criterion) rather than source taxation.[515] It does not require residence-based taxation to result in 'comprehensive', 'full' or 'the most comprehensive tax liability':

> The attempt to confine Article 4(1) to instances of residence-based taxation on the basis of an implicit requirement that the taxation be comprehensive or full, or the most comprehensive that is imposed by the state, could only succeed if the domestic tax systems were constructed with two simple regimes: 'residence' taxation applied at a single rate or schedule of rates to a defined, invariable, tax base on those who present a particular personal nexus, and 'source' taxation applied to items of income considered to arise in the jurisdiction upon those not subjected to residence taxation. In that case, Article 4(1) would refer to the former, rather than the latter. Since this is not how tax systems actually work, the adjectives ['(the most) comprehensive' or 'full' tax liability] can lead one into error.[516]

The OECD and UN MTC as a whole indeed reflect a distinction between two basic forms of taxation: residence-based taxation and source-based taxation. The connecting criteria listed in Article 4(1) reflect forms of personal attachment commonly used by

---

512. Summary of Discussions at the Seventh Meeting of Working Party No. 1 on Double Taxation, 11 April 1973, DAF/CFA/WP1(73)5, p. 5.
513. Paragraph 8.2 of the OECD Commentary on Art. 4, quoted in Para. 4 of the UN Commentaries on Art. 4.
514. R. Couzin, *Corporate Residence and International Taxation*, (IBFD Publications BV: Amsterdam, 2002), pp. 152–154.
515. *Ibid.*, pp. 147–150 & pp. 154–155.
516. *Ibid.*, p. 154.

States as a basis for imposing residence-based taxation.[517] In the author's opinion, the expression 'a comprehensive taxation (full tax liability)' as adopted in both Commentaries, precisely aims to refer to forms of residence taxation, as opposed to source taxation. Residence taxation (or, in the words of both Commentaries, 'comprehensive taxation (full liability to tax)') can include taxation on worldwide income, but also taxation based on a territoriality principle, as long as the tax liability has been imposed based on a person's subjective attachment to a State. However, when focusing on Article 4(1) of the OECD MTC, the connecting factors seem to contain a territorial, more economic link between a taxpayer and a Contracting State. In contrast, under Article 4(1) of the UN MTC, a more formal link also seems sufficient, as place of incorporation is listed as connecting factor as well. The difference could have implications for the interpretation of the term 'any other criterion of a similar nature' and the scope of both articles. It seems that any domestic feature giving rise to residence taxation is sufficient under Article 4(1) of the UN MTC. However, since it can be argued that Article 4(1) of the OECD MTC requires a more economic link between a taxpayer and a Contracting State, place of incorporation may not qualify as a similar criterion, even when it gives rise to residence taxation.[518] In the author's view, both articles have the same scope and any domestic feature giving rise to residence taxation should be sufficient to qualify as a tax treaty resident. The OECD Commentary indicates that Article 4(1) also covers persons who are deemed to be resident according to the tax laws of a Contracting State.[519]

5.3.3.5 A Source State Perspective on 'Any Other Criterion of a Similar Nature'?

In determining whether a source State needs to provide relief of taxation under the tax treaty (e.g., Articles 10 and 11), the question arises whether the source State perspective on the expression 'any other criterion of a similar nature' is relevant. Different from the term 'liable to tax' (Section 5.3.3.2), the author tends to believe it is not. As an undefined treaty term, this expression seems to be covered by Article 3(2) and so its meaning is in principle determined according to the laws of the State of source, unless the context otherwise requires. Since the term 'any other criterion of a similar nature' itself will not be used or defined in the laws of the State of source, it can be argued that

---

517. This conclusion was also reached by the Income Tax Appellate Tribunal of Mumbai, India in *ITO (IT) v. Rameshkumar Goenka*, I.T.A. No. 3562/Mum/2009: '[t]he expression "liable to tax" is not to read in isolation but in conjunction with the words immediately following it i.e., "by reason of domicile, residence, place of management, place of incorporation or any other criterion of similar nature". (...) These tests of fiscal domicile which are given by way of examples following the expression "liable to tax by reason of" i.e., domicile, residence, place of management, place of incorporation etc. are no more than *examples of locality related attachments that attract residence type taxation*' (Italics added).
518. A. Rust, in Reimer & Rust (eds), *Klaus Vogel on Double Taxation Conventions*, 4th edn., (Alphen a/d Rijn: Kluwer Law International, 2015), p. 261. According to the Dutch explanatory notes to the tax treaty between the Netherlands and Qatar, place of incorporation is a criterion of a similar nature. *Tweede Kamer*, 2008–2009, 31 764, No. 7, p. 3.
519. Paragraph 8 of the OECD Commentary on Art. 4.

the correct approach to determine its domestic law meaning is to establish whether this other criterion would have given rise to residence taxation in the State of source. However, such approach could make an OECD MTC based treaty largely inoperative in the situation where the other State solely imposes residence taxation on companies by reason of their incorporation, while the State of source does not.[520] In this situation, a company incorporated under the laws of the other State would not be liable to tax by reason of a qualifying criterion from the perspective of the State of source. In the author's view, it can be argued that the context requires an alternative interpretation, because the meaning of the expression 'any other criterion of a similar nature' is sufficiently clear from the context of Article 4(1) itself. It refers to forms of 'personal or locative'[521] attachment commonly used by States as a basis for imposing (forms of) residence taxation, as opposed to (forms of) source taxation, but not expressly listed in Article 4(1). If the other Contracting State imposes residence taxation on companies by reason of incorporation, then it is sufficiently clear from the context of Article 4(1) that such companies are liable to tax by reason of a criterion of a similar nature, which leaves no room for a meaning under the domestic tax law of the State of source.

5.3.3.6 *Liable to Tax Versus Subject to Tax*

In the English language, the term 'liable to tax' is distinguished from the term 'subject to tax'. The latter is said to refer to an actual tax liability of a person on all or part of his income, whereas the former is said to refer to a potential, more abstract, tax liability of a person.[522] In this sense, the term 'liable to tax' has a broader meaning and includes the term 'subject to tax', i.e., someone who is subject to tax is always liable to tax, but someone who is liable to tax is not necessarily subject to tax. The conclusion that liable to tax has a broader meaning than subject to tax was also reached during the panel discussion at the IFA Congress in 2004.[523] At this Congress, it was furthermore concluded that 'tax effectively due' was narrower than 'subject to tax' and 'paid tax' was the narrowest term of all.[524] The Commentaries provide no guidance as to whether Article 4(1) requires an actual or a more abstract tax liability, but only observe that '[i]n many States, a person is considered liable to comprehensive taxation even if the Contracting State does not *in fact* impose tax' (italics added).[525] Both Commentaries imply that the term 'liable to tax' is not uniformly interpreted by States, although many

---

520. This problem would not arise under UN MTC based treaties, as place of incorporation is among the listed criteria.
521. R. Couzin, *Corporate Residence and International Taxation*, (IBFD Publications BV: Amsterdam, 2002), p. 134.
522. A. de Graaf & F. Pötgens, 'Worrying Interpretation of "Liable to Tax": OECD Clarification Would Be Welcome' (2011) 39 *Intertax* 169, p. 172.
523. I. Burgers, 'Recente ontwikkelingen in het Nederlands belastingverdragenrecht' (2005) 78 *Tijdschrift voor Fiscaal Ondernemingsrecht*, fn. 11.
524. *Ibid.*
525. Paragraph 8.11 of the OECD Commentary on Art. 4, quoted in Para. 6 of the UN Commentaries on Art. 4.

Chapter 5: Tax Treaty Aspects

States seem to interpret this treaty term as meaning a more abstract tax liability.[526] If liable to tax is understood as a potential, more abstract, tax liability, it seems clear that, for example, exemptions of items of income or tax deductions and losses as a result of which no tax is due in a given year, but otherwise would have been due, do not preclude the application of a tax treaty to a person.[527] If liable to tax is understood as subject to tax, it can be unclear whether in such cases a person is a tax treaty resident.[528] If liable to tax is interpreted as tax effectively due or tax paid, this could have as an absurd consequence that, depending on the nature of the income or the amount of deductions or losses, a person (without any change of its tax status) is a resident for tax treaty purposes in one year, but not in another.

5.3.3.7   Application to Sovereign Wealth Investors

5.3.3.7.1   Tax Treatment of Sovereign Wealth Investors in Their Home State

More often than not, it is believed that sovereign wealth investors are never taxed in their home State.[529] This is probably true in most cases, but certainly not in all. Some sovereign wealth investors, including Singapore's Temasek,[530] are liable to tax based on a territoriality principle, while other sovereign wealth investors, including CIC and

---

526. *See*, for example, India: *ITO (IT) v. Rameshkumar Goenka*, I.T.A. No. 3562/Mum/2009, at 8: '[t]herefore, as long as a person has such locality related attachments which attract residence type taxation, that "person" is to be treated as resident and this status of being a "resident" of the Contracting State is independent of the actual levy of tax on that person. Viewed in this perspective, we are of the considered opinion that being "liable to tax" in the Contracting State *does not necessarily imply that the person should actually be liable to tax* in that Contracting State by the virtue of an existing legal provision but would also cover the cases where that other Contracting State has the right to tax such persons – irrespective of whether or not such a right is exercised by the Contracting State' (Italics added); Sweden: *Regeringsrätten* (Supreme Administrative Court), 2 October 1996, RÅ 1996 ref 84 (6301–1994), Tax Treaty Case Law IBFD (summary by M. Hilling). This interpretation has also found support in international literature. *See*, for example, D. Ward et al., 'A Resident of a Contracting State for Tax Treaty Purposes: A Case Comment on Crown Forest Industries' (1996) 44 *Canadian Tax Journal* 408, pp. 419–422; A. de Graaf & F. Pötgens, 'Worrying Interpretation of "Liable to Tax": OECD Clarification Would Be Welcome' (2011) 39 *Intertax* 169, pp. 172–173; N. Bammens, 'Belgium', in: *Residence of Companies under Tax Treaties and EC Law*, EC and International Tax Law Series, Vol. 5 (Amsterdam: IBFD, 2009), p. 393.
527. A. Scapa & L. Henie, 'Avoidance of Double Non-Taxation under the OECD Model Tax Convention' (2005) 33 *Intertax* 266, p. 271.
528. According to the International Manual, which can be used by HM Revenue & Customs staff for guidance, a person would be regarded as subject to tax for UK tax treaty purposes if, for example, they do not pay any UK tax because their income is covered by personal allowances and reliefs. *See* INTM162020 – UK residents with foreign income or gains: double taxation relief – claims and procedures – 'Subject to tax'.
529. For example, M. Desai & D. Dharmapala, 'Taxing the Bandit Kings' (2008) 118 *Yale Law Journal Pocket Part* 98, p. 99; M. Knoll, 'Taxation and the Competitiveness of Sovereign Wealth Funds: Do Taxes Encourage Sovereign Wealth Funds to Invest in the United States?' (2009) 82 *Southern California Law Review* 703, p. 715; M. Kandev, 'Sovereign Wealth Funds: Are They Welcome in Canada?' (2010) 64 *Bulletin for International Taxation* 649, p. 650.
530. *Temasek Review 2012 (Extending Pathways)*, p. 45, available at: < https://www.temasek.com .sg/content/dam/temasek-corporate/our-financials/investor-library/annual-review/en-tr-thu mbnail-and-pdf/TR2012_Eng.pdf > .

the Korea Investment Corporation, appear to be liable to tax on their worldwide income.[531] In Section 2.10, three conflicting views were discussed regarding the issue of home State taxation of sovereign wealth investors: (i) home State taxation is superfluous, because taxes and dividends are functionally equivalent, (ii) home State taxation is necessary as its puts sovereign wealth investors on equal footing with private investors, and (iii) home State taxation is necessary to deal with the agency problem.

Some argue that taxing resident entities wholly-owned by a State, including SWFs and SWEs, makes no sense, as the profits of such entities already belong to that State. Imposing tax on its own SWFs and SWEs would merely result in a transfer of money from one pocket controlled by the State to another.[532] The State, as its owner, can collect revenue by simply extracting profits through (dividend) distributions, which saves (unnecessary) costs, because there is no need to compute taxable income (under often complex tax rules). In this view, which is relevant for State entities in general, home State taxes and dividends are seen as functionally equivalent.[533] Most home States are not convinced by the arguments to tax their own SWFs and SWEs. To the author's knowledge, many sovereign wealth investors are not taxed in their home State, because they are carved out/excluded from the tax statute as a person, because they have been established in a State (or political subdivision) with no or a very limited (corporate) income tax system in place[534] (e.g., the Future Generations Reserve Fund of Bahrain), or because income tax legislation has been enacted, but is not (yet) enforced upon them (e.g., the UAE).[535] Sovereign wealth investors could also not be taxed in their home State because they are subjectively exempt from tax, just like many (other) State entities.

In summary, some sovereign wealth investors may be taxed in their home State, because they are:

(1) liable to tax on their worldwide income; or
(2) liable to tax under a territorial tax system.

However, most sovereign wealth investors are not taxed in their home State, because:

(3) they are subjectively exempt from tax;
(4) income tax legislation has been enacted, but is not (yet) enforced upon them;

---

531. Wei Cui, 'Responding to Sovereign Funds: Are We Looking in the Right Place?' (2009) 123 *Tax Notes* 1237, p. 1241.
532. M. Knoll, 'Taxation and the Competitiveness of Sovereign Wealth Funds: Do Taxes Encourage Sovereign Wealth Funds to Invest in the United States?' (2009) 82 *Southern California Law Review* 703, p. 715.
533. R. Gordon, 'Taxes and privatization' (2001), Discussion Paper No. 2977, Centre for Economic Policy Research, p. 5.
534. Bahrain only levies income tax on oil companies. *See* S. Gueydi, *Bahrain – Corporate Taxation*, Country Surveys IBFD.
535. H. Hull, 'United Arab Emirates: Tax Treaty Relief on International Investment' (2009) 63 *Bulletin for International Taxation* 52, p. 52.

(5) they are carved out/excluded from the tax statute as a person; or
(6) they have been established in a State (or political subdivision) with no or a very limited (corporate) income tax system in place.

Below, it is examined for each of these categories whether the 'liable to tax' test would be satisfied.

5.3.3.7.2 Relationship Between 'Liable to Tax' and the Interpretation Rule of Article 3(2)?

From the discussion in Section 5.3.3.2 above, it appears to be somewhat unclear whether the source State perspective on the undefined term 'liable to tax' is relevant in determining whether the source State needs to provide relief of taxation (e.g., Articles 10 and 11). The author tends to believe it is relevant and finds support for this view in literature, case law and the OECD Commentary and UN Commentaries.[536]

5.3.3.7.3 (1) Liable to Home State Taxation on Worldwide Income

Sovereign wealth investors being liable to home State taxation on worldwide income by reason of a listed criterion should qualify as a resident under Article 4(1). In the view of most States this would be no different if the income of a sovereign wealth investors would be wholly or partly tax-exempt.

5.3.3.7.4 (2) Liable to Territorial Based Home State Taxation

Some sovereign wealth investors are liable to tax in their home State, but only to the extent they derive (certain items of) income or profit from that State. One might argue that since sovereign wealth investors only invest abroad they de facto will never pay any tax in their home State. However, not paying tax in the State of residence does not necessarily mean that a person is not regarded as a resident under Article 4(1). Also, some sovereign wealth investors do invest in and pay tax in their home State on profits from domestic investments.[537] One might further argue that the term 'liable to tax' in Article 4(1) refers to a comprehensive tax liability and that comprehensive tax liability should be understood as taxation of worldwide income and, therefore, territoriality-based income tax systems are excluded from its scope. However, as explained in more detail in Section 5.3.3.4, this view conflicts with the principles underlying the OECD and UN MTC itself, the nature of the connecting factors, as well as the Commentaries. Therefore, sovereign wealth investors set-up in States that have adopted a territorial tax system can be a resident under Article 4(1), as long as the tax liability has been imposed

---

536. Reference is made to Section 5.3.3.2.
537. Singapore's Temasek pays taxes to the Singapore Government and, as on 31 March 2012, 30% of its funds were invested domestically. *See Temasek Review 2012 (Extending Pathways)*, p. 16 & p. 45.

by reason of a personal or locative attachment to that State. This would also apply if the sovereign wealth investor in fact does not pay tax in its home State, because it enjoys foreign sourced income or domestic tax-exempt income only.

5.3.3.7.5 (3) Subjectively Exempt from Home State Taxation

Paragraph 8.5 of the OECD Commentary on Article 4 points to the relevance of Paragraphs 8.11 and 8.12 in cases where SWFs are not (considered) an integral part of the State. Paragraphs 8.11 and 8.12, quoted in Paragraph 6 of the UN Commentaries on Article 4, are concerned with tax treaty residency of tax-exempt entities and express the views of States taken on this matter. The majority view can be found in Paragraph 8.11, where the Commentary observes that:

> In many States, a person is considered liable to comprehensive taxation even if the Contracting State does not in fact impose tax. For example, charities and other organisations may be exempted from tax, but they are exempt only if they meet all of the requirements for exemption specified in the tax laws. They are, thus, subject to the tax laws of a Contracting State. Furthermore, if they do not meet the standards specified, they are also required to pay tax. Most States would view such entities as residents for purposes of the Convention (see, for example, paragraph 1 of Article 10 and paragraph 5 of Article 11).

The minority view can be found in Paragraph 8.12:

> In some States, however, these entities are not considered liable to tax if they are exempt from tax under domestic tax laws. These States may not regard such entities as residents for purposes of a convention unless these entities are expressly covered by the convention.

The Commentaries do not take sides, but only observe that States understand the term 'liable to tax' differently when it comes to tax-exempt entities. The majority view, among others expressed by the US Treasury Department and the US tax authorities,[538] the Swedish and Finnish Administrative Supreme Court[539] and the French Administrative Court of Appeal[540] is that tax-exempt entities which would have been taxable but for the exemption, to which conditions are attached, are considered liable to tax. The Commentaries introduce the expression 'subject to the tax laws' of a State, which probably means to say that these entities have a personal attachment to a State that would have given rise to residence taxation in the absence of the exemption. The State could have imposed tax on the entity as a resident, but chose not to. The minority view,

---

538. For example, Revenue Ruling 2000-59, p. 8: 'While the 1981 U.S. Model does not specifically provide that persons organized under the laws of a state that are generally exempt from tax and established and maintained exclusively to provide pension or other similar benefits are residents of that state (and the 1996 U.S. Model does so provide), the Treasury Department's Technical Explanation to the 1996 U.S. Model confirms that the specific provision in the 1996 U.S. Model merely clarifies the generally accepted practice that these entities are residents even though they may be entitled to a complete or partial exemption from tax.'
539. *See* Section 5.3.3.2.
540. *Ibid.*

Chapter 5: Tax Treaty Aspects

among others expressed by the Canada Revenue Agency,[541] the Supreme Court of Canada,[542] the Dutch Supreme Court,[543] the French Administrative Supreme Court,[544] the French tax authorities,[545] is that tax-exempt entities are not 'liable to tax' as referred in Article 4(1). States adhering to the majority view interpret the term 'liable to tax' as a potential, more abstract, tax liability of a person. Couzin aptly refers to such potential liability as 'liable to be liable'.[546] To conclude, subjectively tax-exempt sovereign wealth investors will be considered 'liable to tax' by many States, but certainly not by all.

5.3.3.7.6 *(4) Income Tax Legislation Has Been Enacted, but Is Not Enforced*

Most emirates of the UAE have enacted corporate income tax decrees for the taxation of income earned by corporate bodies. However, in practice, these decrees are currently only enforced upon oil and gas companies and branches of foreign banks.[547] Most sovereign wealth investors from the UAE have been set-up as corporate bodies under the laws of the UAE[548] and so it seems likely that they are covered by the relevant income tax decree. The issue whether UAE entities (other than oil and gas companies and branches of foreign banks) are 'liable to tax' for model based tax treaty purposes was considered by the Indian Income-tax Appellate Tribunal in *Green Emirate*

---

541. Canada Revenue Agency, Income Tax Technical News No. 35, 26 February 2007, as discussed by K. Brooks, 'Canada', in: G. Maisto, *Residence of Companies under Tax Treaties and EC Law*, EC and International Tax Law Series, Vol. 5 (Amsterdam: IBFD, 2009), p. 429.
542. *Crown Forest Industries Ltd. v. Her Majesty the Queen*, Supreme Court of Canada, 22 June 1995, File No.: 23940, Tax Treaty Case Law IBFD. From this decision, learned authors have drawn the conclusion that: '(...) if the broad sweep of statements of the Supreme Court in *Crown Forest Industries* were to be applied, [tax-exempt charitable organizations and pension funds] would be considered not to be residents of a contracting state and therefore would not be entitled to the treaty-reduced rates of tax.' See D. Ward et al., 'A Resident of a Contracting State for Tax Treaty Purposes: A Case Comment on Crown Forest Industries' (1996) 44 *Canadian Tax Journal* 408, p. 419.
543. *Hoge Raad*, 4 December 2009, No. 07/10383, *BNB* 2010/177. Admittedly, there is no consensus in Dutch literature on this point. The Supreme Court decision of 4 December 2009 involved a Dutch resident association which was not subjectively tax-exempt, but carved out from the Dutch tax statute because it did not carry on a business. The Dutch Supreme Court held that the Dutch association was not 'liable to tax' under the US – Netherlands tax treaty (1992). The author agrees with De Graaf & Pötgens' view that, based on the reasoning in this decision, the Dutch Supreme Court would not consider subjectively tax-exempt entities as being liable to tax either. *See* A. de Graaf & F. Pötgens, 'Worrying Interpretation of "Liable to Tax": OECD Clarification Would Be Welcome' (2011) 39 *Intertax* 169, p. 169. For a different view, *see* H. Pijl, 'De additionele inwonerseis in het verdrag met de Verenigde Staten: HR 4 december 2009, BNB 2010/177' (2010) *Weekblad voor Fiscaal Recht* 1371, Para. 1.
544. *Conseil d'État*, 9 November 2015, Case 370054, Tax Treaty Case Law IBFD, concerning the tax treaty residency of a German tax-exempt pension fund.
545. N. de Boynes, 'France', in: G. Maisto, *Residence of Companies under Tax Treaties and EC Law*, EC and International Tax Law Series, Vol. 5 (Amsterdam: IBFD, 2009), p. 453.
546. R. Couzin, *Corporate Residence and International Taxation*, (IBFD Publications BV: Amsterdam, 2002), p. 107.
547. United Arab Emirates – Corporate Taxation – Country Surveys – Introduction, IBFD Database.
548. *See* Section A.3.2 of this study.

Shipping & Travels Ltd.[549] It held that the enumerated criteria in Article 4(1) are examples of 'locality-related attachments' which attract residence type taxation and that 'liable to tax':

> does not necessarily imply that the person should actually be liable to tax in that Contracting State by virtue of an existing legal provision but would also cover the cases where that other Contracting State has the right to tax such persons irrespective of whether or not such a right is exercised by the Contracting State.

As a result, this UAE entity was considered 'liable to tax' for purposes of the tax treaty between the UAE and India (1993).

Similar to subjectively tax-exempt entities, it can be argued that UAE corporate bodies (other than oil and gas companies and branches of foreign banks) are 'subject to the tax laws' of the UAE, because they are covered by the relevant income tax decree. Therefore, many States would probably view such entities, including UAE sovereign wealth investors, as being 'liable to tax' for tax treaty purposes.

5.3.3.7.7 *(5) Carved Out from Their Home State's Tax Statute as a Person*

Entities, including sovereign wealth investors, that are excluded from the tax statute from the start, appear not to be considered liable to tax for tax treaty purposes. In comparison with subjectively tax-exempt entities and entities that are covered by income tax legislation that is not enforced upon them, it cannot be said that entities excluded from the reach of a tax system are subject to the tax laws of a State. The 'subject to the tax laws' argument is presented by a majority of States to grant tax treaty entitlement to subjectively tax-exempt entities. The rationale behind this reasoning is that such entities have the required personal connection to a State which would have resulted in residence taxation in the absence of the exemption. Not only do such entities have the required connection to a State (*the personal connection*), they also fall within reach of that State's tax system (*the tax (law) connection*). Although entities that have been carved out from the tax statute can have the required personal attachment to a State, it cannot be said they are governed by or subject to the tax laws of that State. The term 'liable to tax' implies at least some sort of tax connection between the entity and the State. In this respect, a connection to the tax laws (subject to or governed by) is considered sufficient in most sources States, and this is where the term 'liable to tax' appears to find its limit. Since carved out entities, including carved out sovereign wealth investors, have no such connection, they would most likely not meet the 'liable to tax' test in the view of most States.

---

549. *Green Emirate Shipping & Travels Ltd v. Assistant Director of Income Tax*, Income-tax Appellate Tribunal, 30 November 2005, (2006) 99 TTJ Mum 988.

5.3.3.7.8 (6) No or a Very Limited (Corporate) Income Tax System in Place

Just like sovereign wealth investors which have been carved out from the statute, sovereign wealth investors resident in a State with no or a very limited income tax system in place, do not have the required tax (law) connection. As a result, such sovereign wealth investors would most likely not meet the 'liable to tax' test in the view of most States. It, therefore, seems unlikely that States with no or a very limited income tax system in place would adopt the 'liable to tax' test in a tax treaty.

5.3.3.7.9 Comment

Many States choose not to tax their sovereign wealth investors. Many States also choose, for a number of reasons, not to tax certain private investors, such as pension funds and CIVs. However, as demonstrated, the way this non-taxation of sovereign wealth investors and private investors is achieved in the legislation of the home State can make a difference for the outcome of the 'liable to tax' test.[550] This is a major point of criticism about the 'liable to tax' test. The 'liable to tax' test fulfils a key function within the traditional main purpose of a tax treaty according to both the OECD Commentary and UN Commentaries:[551] the avoidance of international juridical double taxation.[552] It identifies and solves potential situations of international juridical double taxation by allocating taxing rights between two States. This is the system underlying the OECD and UN MTC as a whole. If a person is liable to tax, there is, at least, a risk of international juridical double taxation. In situations (3) to (6), discussed in Sections 5.3.3.7.5–5.3.3.7.8 above, there is, in principle, no risk of international juridical double taxation, but (source) States may still consider the 'liable to tax' test to be satisfied in one situation but not in another. However, this is done so without distinction among and between sovereign wealth investors and other investors.

The author argues that the 'liable to tax' test generally has no proper meaning in relation to sovereign wealth investors. A State can simply choose to impose tax on its own sovereign wealth investors and let these funds immediately flow back, or reduce the amount of dividends otherwise due with the amount of tax. In these cases, imposing tax on sovereign wealth investors would have no impact on that State's revenue, or on its sovereign wealth investor.

---

550. Van Weeghel has also observed this in more general terms in his comment on *Hoge Raad*, 4 December 2009, No. 07/10383, *BNB* 2010/177. *See also*, J. Wheeler, 'The Missing Keystone of Income Tax Treaties' (2011) 3 *World Tax Journal* 247, p. 252.
551. Paragraph 1 of the Preliminary remarks on Art. 4 of the OECD MTC, and Para. 1 of the UN Commentaries on Art. 4. *See* Section 5.3.3.1.
552. Paragraphs 1–3, Introduction of the Commentary on the OECD MTC. International juridical double taxation is defined as the imposition of comparable taxes by at least two States on the same taxpayer with respect to the same item of income or capital during the same period. Reference to this main purpose could also be found in the title of the 1963 OECD Draft Double Taxation Convention, as well as the 1977 Model Double Taxation Convention, but was dropped in the 1992 version because it was recognized that the avoidance of (international juridical) double taxation was not the only purpose of the OECD MTC.

5.3.4 '[T]hat State and Any Political Subdivision or Local Authority Thereof' (Article 4(1))

5.3.4.1 Introduction

The term 'resident of a Contracting State' in Article 4(1) also includes *that State and any political subdivision or local authority thereof*. Section 5.3.4 will consider how this phrase applies to sovereign wealth investors.

5.3.4.2 History

The phrase *that State and any political subdivision or local authority thereof* was added to Article 4(1) of the OECD MTC in 1995 and Article 4(1) of the UN MTC in 1999. The OECD Commentary explains that, even without this phrase, *most* (hence, not all) OECD Member States would have considered the State and its political subdivisions and local authorities as tax treaty residents.[553] This explanation has been copied into the Commentaries of the UN MTC.[554] Unfortunately, neither of the Commentaries explains why most Member States would consider them a 'resident of a Contracting State'. The addition cannot be explained on the basis of the traditional main purpose of a tax treaty according to both the OECD Commentary and UN Commentaries: the avoidance of international juridical double taxation. Because of the unique position of the State as legislator, tax recipient and investor, there is de facto never a risk of international juridical double taxation in relation to States themselves (in a bilateral relation), not even if a State decides to tax itself. Nor can the addition of the phrase be explained on the basis of the customary international law principle of sovereign immunity.[555] Further, the purpose of attracting investments is unlikely the reason behind the special treatment, because cross-border investments by States were not so prominent at that time. Perhaps the addition of the phrase *that State and any political subdivision or local authority thereof* can be explained, because the personal attachment as expressed in the 'liable to tax' test is by definition not in question. However, it would then further be required that a tax (law) connection can be established (Section 5.3.3.7.7), which would depend on the way the non-taxation is achieved in the tax legislation of a State. Perhaps the best explanation for the addition is that the 'liable to tax' test has no proper meaning in relation to States themselves (or political subdivisions and local authorities), as a State can simply choose to impose tax on itself without this having any (financial) impact on that State. However, this would require a State to compute taxable income, file a tax return and pay tax to itself (through the tax

---

553. Paragraph 8.4 of the OECD Commentary on Art. 4 (added in 1995): 'It has been the general understanding of most member countries that the government of each State, as well as any political subdivision or local authority thereof, is a resident of that State for purposes of the Convention. Before 1995, the Model did not explicitly state this; in 1995, Art. 4 was amended to conform the text of the Model to this understanding.'
554. Paragraph 6 of the UN Commentaries on Art. 4.
555. *See* Chapter 4; S-A. Joseph, 'Do Tax Treaties Embody Sovereign Immunity? – An Assessment with Regard to Sovereign Wealth Funds' (2015) 69 *Bulletin for International Taxation* 637.

office). To keeps things simple, States may simply have decided to grant tax treaty access to each other (reciprocity), and allocate taxing jurisdiction between them.

5.3.4.3 Integral Part of the State, Etc.

As noted in Paragraph 8.5 of the OECD Commentary on Article 4 (added in 2010), the phrase *that State and any political subdivision or local authority thereof* may be relevant for sovereign wealth investors:[556]

> [w]hether a sovereign wealth fund qualifies as a 'resident of a Contracting State' depends on the facts and circumstances of each case. For example, when a sovereign wealth fund is *an integral part of the State*, it will likely fall within the scope of the expression '[the] State and any political subdivision or local authority thereof' in Article 4. In other cases, paragraphs 8.11 and 8.12 below will be relevant. States may want to address the issue in the course of bilateral negotiations, particularly in relation to whether a sovereign wealth fund qualifies as a 'person' and is 'liable to tax' for purposes of the relevant tax treaty (see also paragraphs 50 to 53 of the Commentary on Article 1). (Italics added)

This and other OECD Commentary on State-owned entities has not been reflected in the Commentaries on the UN MTC. On the one hand, this might cause surprise, because the UN MTC is sometimes used by States that are home to SWFs, such as the UAE,[557] and may very well be used by a source State for treaty negotiations (developing countries). On the other hand, the Commentary on the OECD MTC dealing with State-owned entities, in general, and SWFs, in particular, adds little and raises new questions. Although the OECD Commentary on SWFs and State-owned entities has not been adopted in the Commentaries on the UN MTC, the author does not see why sovereign wealth investors cannot form an integral part of a State under UN MTC based treaties, given the reproduction of the OECD definition of resident in the UN MTC.

5.3.4.4 Application to Sovereign Wealth Investors

5.3.4.4.1 When Are Sovereign Wealth Investors an Integral Part of a State?

As discussed in Section 5.3.4.3 above, the OECD Commentary indicates that *when* an SWF is an integral part of the State, it will likely be covered by expression *that State and any political subdivision or local authority thereof*. The OECD Commentary only points to a possibility, but it lacks any guidance as to when a sovereign wealth investor forms an integral part of the State. This Commentary can be interpreted from three perspectives: (1) a legal perspective, (2) a tax perspective, or (3) a material/functional

---

556. S. Janssen, 'How to Treat(y) Sovereign Wealth Funds? The Application of Tax Treaties to State-Owned Entities, Including Sovereign Wealth Funds', in: D. Weber & S. van Weeghel, *The 2010 OECD Updates, Model Tax Convention & Transfer Pricing Guidelines, A Critical Review*, Series on International Taxation, Vol. 38 (Alphen a/d Rijn: Kluwer Law International, 2011).
557. H. Hull, 'United Arab Emirates: Tax Treaty Relief on International Investment' (2009) 63 *Bulletin for International Taxation* 52, p. 53.

perspective. It is unlikely, though, that the relevant Commentary is intended to be interpreted from a tax perspective; if so intended, the use of different wording, such as SWFs which are tax transparent, would have been more appropriate. When interpreted from a legal perspective, as is done under the UK tax immunity regime,[558] the relevant Commentary will have very limited effect given that the vast majority of sovereign wealth investors have been established as separate legal entities (other than the State). When interpreted from a material/functional perspective, which seems to be the most appropriate way, the question arises under which circumstances a sovereign wealth investor can materially/functionally be identified with the State. For purposes of the US tax-exemption for foreign sovereigns, an integral part of a foreign sovereign is defined as 'any person, body of persons, organization, agency, bureau, fund, instrumentality, or other body, however designated, that constitutes a governing authority of a foreign country'.[559] In addition, '[t]he net earnings of the governing authority must be credited to its own account or to other accounts of the foreign sovereign, with no portion inuring to the benefit of any private person. An integral part does not include any individual who is a sovereign, official, or administrator acting in a private or personal capacity (...)'.[560] What is relevant under this US approach is whether the entity constitutes a governing authority; the legal design of the entity is not relevant. There is, however, no guidance when an entity constitutes a governing authority. A mixture between a legal and material/functional approach can be found in a decision of the Swiss Federal Tribunal dealing with the issue of whether KIA, the SWF of Kuwait, was entitled to immunity.[561] The tribunal took into consideration various documents, including the SWF's constitutional law and its articles, statements from the SWF and its representatives, the fact that the SWF had brought suit in its own name in previous proceedings, the composition of the SWF's board and the purpose of its investments. According to the Tribunal, the SWF was not entitled to immunity, because it had an independent status based on the decree by which the SWF was established (which referred to its 'autonomous status'), its articles, letters and statements by Kuwait (which considered the SWF as an 'independent public authority') and the fact that the SWF had brought suit in its own name in previous proceedings. The fact that its funds were provided by and held on behalf of the State of Kuwait, and the fact that its board of directors included representatives of the State of Kuwait, was not considered relevant. In the author's view, the elements that the Swiss Federal Tribunal took into consideration are indeed useful in determining whether a sovereign wealth investor is an integral part of the State under Article 4(1), if interpreted from a material/functional perspective. The Swiss Federal Tribunal had to determine whether the SWF could (materially/functionally) be identified with the State, and this also seems to be the most appropriate test under Article 4(1). Whether a sovereign wealth investor is an integral part of a State needs to be determined a case-by-case basis.

---

558. See Section 4.3.1.3.
559. Temporary Treasury Regulations (1988), Subchapter A, § 1.892-2T(a)(2).
560. *Ibid.*
561. *Kuwait v. X* (1994) *Revue Suisse de droit international et européen*, 1995, Vol. 5, p. 593.

5.3.4.4.2 (i) Sovereign Wealth Investors Constituted by a Pool of Assets Within a State

Whether interpreted from a legal, tax or material/functional perspective, sovereign wealth investors constituted by a pool of assets will most likely be considered an integral part of the State, as the pool of assets (arrangement) has no separate legal identity. The absence of a separate legal personality usually points to the close relationship with the State itself. The same conclusion should apply to sovereign wealth investors constituted by a pool of assets within a central bank that has no separate legal identity.

5.3.4.4.3 (ii) Sovereign Wealth Investors Established as or Within a Separate Legal Entity Other Than the State Itself

It is unclear from the OECD Commentary whether sovereign wealth investors established as a separate legal entity (other than the State) can be covered by the expression *that State and any political subdivision or local authority thereof*, and whether a further distinction should be made between legal persons of public law and legal persons of private law owned by a legal person of public law. The OECD Commentary on Article 1 observes that some States have modified Article 4(1) by including as a 'resident of a Contracting State', a 'statutory body', an 'agency or instrumentality' or a 'legal person of public law' of *a State, a political subdivision or local authority*.[562] Such terminology indeed clarifies that sovereign wealth investors set-up as a separate legal entity under public law qualify as a tax treaty resident, but it may still leave doubt for sovereign wealth investors established as corporations under company law.

As explained Section 5.3.4.4.1, it is unlikely that Paragraph 8.5 of the OECD Commentary on Article 4 is intended to be interpreted from a tax perspective. When Paragraph 8.5 of the OECD Commentary on Article 4 intends to follow a legal approach, sovereign wealth investors established as a separate legal entity (other than the State) are not covered by the expression *that State and any political subdivision or local authority thereof*. Since the vast majority of sovereign wealth investors have been established in that way, the relevant Commentary will then have very limited effect in practice. Finally, the outcome under the material/functional approach will depend on which element(s) is/are considered decisive.

The phrase *that State and any political subdivision or local authority thereof* is interpreted broadly by the Dutch government in the Dutch Explanatory Note to the tax treaty between the Netherlands and Bahrain (which precedes the introduction of Paragraph 8.5 of the OECD Commentary on Article 4 in 2010).[563] In the agreed minutes, it has been made explicit that this phrase includes 'a governmental agency, national bank (which is a commercial bank and not a central bank) and a wholly owned

---

562. Paragraph 50 of the OECD Commentary on Art. 1.
563. *Convention Between the Government of the Kingdom of the Netherlands and the Government of the Kingdom of Bahrain for the Avoidance of Double Taxation and the Prevention of Fiscal Evasion with respect to Taxes on Income* (16 April 2008), Treaties IBFD.

company' of a State, a political subdivision or a local authority thereof.[564] Notably, it was mentioned in the Dutch Explanatory Note that, even without the phrase from the agreed minutes, it would have been clear to the Netherlands that these governmental and State-owned entities would qualify as a resident under this tax treaty.[565] Put differently, even without the phrase from the agreed minutes, the Netherlands would have considered these entities as an integral part of the State of Bahrain, etc. This interpretation was motivated by saying that tax treaty entitlement of these entities is of importance, because of possible investments into the Netherlands.[566] In other words, this interpretation was motivated by an economic reason (international attractiveness). The Dutch Explanatory Note to other treaties does not refer to a similar interpretation, though.

In some tax treaties, sovereign wealth investors are expressly recognized as an integral part of the State. An example can be found in the protocol to the tax treaty between Mauritius and the UAE,[567] in which a sovereign wealth investor of the Emirate of Abu Dhabi, ADIA, and a sovereign wealth investor of the Emirate of Dubai, Dubai Investment Corporation, are expressly recognized as an integral part of the (local) government.

5.3.4.4.4 (iii) Sovereign Wealth Investors Organized as a (Legal) Entity Without a Separate Legal Personality

SWEs organized as a (legal) entity without a separate legal personality, such as partnerships, could be considered an integral part of the State when the SWF that holds an SWE is considered an integral part of the State.

5.4 DIVIDENDS (ARTICLE 10) AND INTEREST (ARTICLE 11)

5.4.1 Introduction

Article 10, concerning dividends, and Article 11, concerning interest, are of particular importance to sovereign wealth investors. Both articles apply to payments by a resident of a Contracting State to a resident of the other Contracting State, and allocate taxing rights between the Contracting States. The primary taxing right is allocated to the residence State, and the source State has been allocated a limited taxing right only. Article 10 limits the rate of tax to be applied by a source State to the lowest rate if a certain threshold is met and if the recipient of the dividends is the beneficial owner and a company.

---

564. *Tweede Kamer*, 2008–2009, 31 591, No. A/1, p. 5.
565. *Ibid.*
566. *Ibid.*
567. *Agreement Between the Government of the Republic of Mauritius and the Government of the United Arab Emirates for the Avoidance of Double Taxation and the Prevention of Fiscal Evasion with respect to Taxes on Income* (18 September 2006), Treaties IBFD.

5.4.2 Dividends

The first two paragraphs of Article 10 read as follows:

1. Dividends paid by a company which is a resident of a Contracting State to a resident of the other Contracting State may be taxed in that other State.
2. However, such dividends may also be taxed in the Contracting State of which the company paying the dividends is a resident and according to the laws of that State, but if the beneficial owner of the dividends is a resident of the other Contracting State, the tax so charged shall not exceed:
   a) [OECD MTC: 5 per cent][UN MTC: (...) per cent] (...) of the gross amount of the dividends if the beneficial owner is a company (other than a partnership) which holds directly at least [OECD MTC: 25][UN MTC: 10] per cent of the capital of the company paying the dividends (...);
   b) [OECD MTC: 15 per cent][UN MTC: (...) per cent] (...) of the gross amount of the dividends in all other cases. (...) .

The OECD Commentary explains the allocation of tax jurisdiction between the State of residence and the State as follows:

> Taxation of dividends exclusively in the State of source is not acceptable as a general rule. (...)
> On the other hand, taxation of dividends exclusively in the State of the beneficiary's residence is not feasible as a general rule. It would be more in keeping with the nature of dividends, which are investment income, but it would be unrealistic to suppose that there is any prospect of it being agreed that all taxation of dividends at the source should be relinquished.[568]

The OECD rate structure is motivated as follows:

> the rate of tax is limited to 15 per cent, which appears to be a reasonable maximum figure. A higher rate could hardly be justified since the State of source can already tax the company's profits.
> On the other hand, a lower rate (5 per cent) is expressly provided in respect of dividends paid by a subsidiary company to its parent company. If a company of one of the States owns directly (...) a holding of at least 25 per cent in a company of the other State, it is reasonable that the payment of that dividend by the subsidiary to the foreign parent company should be taxed less heavily to avoid recurrent taxation and to facilitate international investment. (...) .[569]

The UN MTC leaves these rates to be established through bilateral negotiations.[570]

Both the OECD Commentary and UN Commentaries indicate that some tax treaties provide for an exemption from source taxation on dividends paid to tax-exempt pension funds, in order to achieve (greater) neutrality between domestic and foreign

---

568. Paragraphs 5–6 of the OECD Commentary on Art. 10.
569. Paragraphs 9–10 of the OECD Commentary on Art. 10.
570. Paragraph 5 of the UN Commentaries on Art. 10.

investments by these investors.[571] Also, some treaties provide for an exemption from source taxation on dividends paid to other States and their wholly-owned entities.[572]

5.4.3 Interest

The first two paragraphs of Article 11 read as follows:

> 1. Interest arising in a Contracting State and paid to a resident of the other Contracting State may be taxed in that other State.
> 2. However, such interest may also be taxed in the Contracting State in which it arises and according to the laws of that State, but if the beneficial owner of the interest is a resident of the other Contracting State, the tax so charged shall not exceed [OECD MTC: 10 per cent][UN MTC: (...) per cent] (...) of the gross amount of the interest. (...).

The OECD Commentary on the interest article does not contain an explanation for the prescribed allocation of tax jurisdiction between the State of residence and the State of source. As regards the maximum source rate, the OECD Commentary considers a rate of 10% to be 'a reasonable maximum bearing in mind that the State of source is already entitled to tax profits or income produced on its territory by investments financed out of borrowed capital'.[573] The UN MTC leaves the source rate to be established through bilateral negotiations.[574]

Similar to the OECD Commentary on Article 10, the OECD Commentary on Article 11 indicates that some tax treaties provide for an exemption from source taxation on interest paid to tax-exempt pension funds,[575] as well as interest paid to other States and their wholly-owned entities.[576]

5.4.4 Application to Sovereign Wealth Investors

As appeared from Section 5.3, qualifying as a resident of a Contracting State is of key importance for the entitlement to tax treaty benefits. Foreign sovereign wealth investors will only be entitled to reduced treaty rates on dividends and interest if they qualify as a tax treaty resident. As indicated in the OECD Commentary on Articles 10 and 11 (added in 2010), some source States even accord tax-exemptions to foreign States and (some of) their wholly-owned entities. Foreign sovereign wealth investors might also be entitled to such exemptions from source taxation.

The beneficial ownership test should generally play no role in relation to sovereign wealth investors. If sovereign wealth investors should, for some reason, not

---

571. Paragraph 13.1 of the OECD Commentary on Art. 10, quoted in Para. 13 of the UN Commentaries on Art. 10.
572. Paragraph 13.2 of the OECD Commentary on Art. 10, quoted in Para. 13 of the UN Commentaries on Art. 10.
573. Paragraph 7 of the OECD Commentary on Art. 11.
574. Paragraph 5 of the UN Commentaries on Art. 10.
575. Paragraph 7 of the OECD Commentary on Art. 11.
576. Paragraph 7.4 of the OECD Commentary on Art. 11.

Chapter 5: Tax Treaty Aspects

be considered the beneficial owner of the income themselves, the owner-State should be considered so and, therefore, be entitled to the tax treaty benefits.

5.5 CAPITAL GAINS (ARTICLE 13)

5.5.1 Introduction

Article 13 allocates taxing rights between Contracting States – the residence State and the source State – regarding capital gains on property. The allocation depends on the type of property concerned. Article 13 of the UN MTC is broadly in line with Article 13 of the OECD MTC, except for capital gains derived from 'non-immovable property companies'. Whereas the OECD MTC allocates the taxing right over gains from such companies exclusively to the residence State, the UN MTC allocates the primary taxing right over gains from such companies to the source State in case of a substantial participation (the percentage to be established during negotiations, but commonly set at 25% or more[577]). The UN MTC only allocates the taxing right over gains from non-immovable property companies exclusively to the residence State in the absence of a substantial participation.[578]

Both the OECD and UN MTC allocate the primary taxing right to the source State in respect of gains derived by a resident of the other Contracting State from the alienation of: (i) immovable property (Article 6)[579], (ii) business assets forming part of a permanent establishment (and, in case of the UN MTC, movable property pertaining to a fixed base for performing independent personal services), (iii) shares (and, in case of the UN MTC, an interest in a partnership, trust or estate) that derive value for more than 50% from immovable property situated in the source State (the UN MTC provides for an exception in respect of immovable property used by entities in their business activities).

Where Article 13 allocates the primary taxing right to the source State, the residence State's taxing rights are residual in that it is allowed to tax the capital gain, but must provide relief of double taxation. Article 13 neither specifies the tax rate, nor the method of taxation.

5.5.2 Application to Sovereign Wealth Investors

As appeared from Section 5.3, qualifying as a resident of a Contracting State is of key importance for the entitlement to tax treaty benefits. Foreign sovereign wealth investors will only be entitled to exclusive residence taxation (i.e., the absence of source taxation) on the listed categories of capital gains if they qualify as a tax treaty resident.

---

577. Global Tax Treaty Commentaries, Art. 13: Capital Gains, para. 3.1.5.2, IBFD Database.
578. Article 13(5) of the UN MTC.
579. The taxing right on income from immovable property is exclusively allocated to the source State, based on Art. 6.

5.6 NON-DISCRIMINATION (ARTICLE 24)

5.6.1 Introduction

Article 24 is aimed at eliminating tax discrimination in very specific situations.[580] That is, 'the various provisions of Article 24 prevent differences in tax treatment that are solely based on certain specific grounds'.[581] Section 5.6 will examine whether the non-discrimination rules of Article 24 could have special implications in relation to foreign sovereign wealth investors. The focus will be on Article 24(1) and Article 24(5), as these provisions might contain elements specifically relevant vis-à-vis sovereign wealth investors.

5.6.2 Sovereign Wealth Investors and Article 24(1)

Article 24(1) reads as follows:

> 1. Nationals of a Contracting State shall not be subjected in the other Contracting State to any taxation or any requirement connected therewith, which is other or more burdensome than the taxation and connected requirements to which nationals of that other State in the same circumstances, in particular with respect to residence, are or may be subjected. This provision shall, notwithstanding the provisions of Article 1, also apply to persons who are not residents of one or both of the Contracting States.

Article 24(1) prohibits tax discrimination between two persons in the same circumstances on the grounds of *nationality*. This provision applies to individuals possessing the nationality or citizenship of a Contracting State, as well as legal persons deriving their status from the laws of a Contracting State.[582] The OECD Commentary explains that Article 24(1) does not sanction a difference in tax treatment of two persons based on a *different residence* because such persons are not in the same circumstances.[583] So, Article 24(1) does not forbid a source State to tax resident companies and non-resident companies differently based on a different (place of) residence, as many source States do. Article 24(1) does forbid a situation where a State taxes a resident investor of that State which is incorporated in that State more favourably than *another resident* investor of that State because that other resident investor is incorporated in the other Contracting State (absent other relevant different circumstances). In such case, the two investors are in the same circumstances, also with respect to their residence, but one of them is treated less favourably on the basis of its nationality (i.e., its legal status derived from the laws of the other Contracting

---
580. Paragraph 1 of the OECD Commentary on Art. 24, reproduced in the UN Commentaries.
581. Paragraph 3 of the OECD Commentary on Art. 24, reproduced in the UN Commentaries.
582. Article 24(1) in conjunction with Art. 3(1)(g)(ii) of the OECD MTC and Art. 3(1)(f)(ii) of the UN MTC.
583. Paragraphs 7, 17–18 of the OECD Commentary on Art. 24(1), reproduced in the UN Commentaries.

State). The following parts of the OECD Commentary on Article 24(1), dealing with public bodies and services, should be read against this background:

> the provisions of paragraph 1 are not to be construed as obliging a State which accords special taxation privileges to its own public bodies or services as such, to extend the same privileges to the public bodies and services of the other State.[584]
> if a State accords immunity from taxation to its own public bodies and services, this is justified because such bodies and services are integral parts of the State and at no time can their circumstances be comparable to those of the public bodies and services of the other State. Nevertheless, this reservation is not intended to apply to State corporations carrying on gainful undertakings. To the extent that these can be regarded as being on the same footing as private business undertakings, the provisions of paragraph 1 will apply to them.[585]

The relevance of these comments is limited to public bodies (and services) of one State that are comparable to public bodies (and services) of the other State. The OECD Commentary explains that public bodies (and services) of one State can never be comparable to public bodies (and services) of the other State to the extent they do not carry on gainful undertakings (public tasks). And to the extent that these public bodies (and services) do carry on gainful undertakings, Article 24(1) will only apply if public bodies (and services) of the Contracting State are in the same circumstances. They will be in different circumstances if a (source) State taxes its own public bodies (and services) and those of the other State differently based on a different (place of) residence, as many (source) States do. This also applies to non-resident private investors. Therefore, Article 24(1) should have very limited practical relevance for both sovereign wealth investors and non-resident private investors.

5.6.3 Sovereign Wealth Investors and Article 24(5)

Article 24(5) reads as follows:

> 5. Enterprises of a Contracting State, the capital of which is wholly or partly owned or controlled, directly or indirectly, by one or more residents of the other Contracting State, shall not be subjected in the first-mentioned State to any taxation or any requirement connected therewith which is other or more burdensome than the taxation and connected requirements to which other similar enterprises of the first-mentioned State are or may be subjected.

Article 24(5) forbids tax discrimination between two similar resident enterprises of the same Contracting State which is solely based on the (direct or indirect) ownership or control by a resident of the other Contracting State.[586] Article 24(5) is only concerned with the position of the enterprise itself and *not* with the position of its

---

584. Paragraph 10 of the OECD Commentary on Art. 24(1), reproduced in the UN Commentaries.
585. Paragraph 12 of the OECD Commentary on Art. 24(1), reproduced in the UN Commentaries.
586. Paragraph 79 of the OECD Commentary on Art. 24(5), reproduced in the UN Commentaries.

non-resident shareholders. It requires equal tax treatment of similar enterprises residing in the same State, as opposed to equal treatment of resident shareholders and non-resident shareholders.[587]

Resident entities wholly-owned by a State, including sovereign wealth investors, are often not taxed in an internal situation. A State may also exempt its wholly-owned resident entities to the extent they do not carry on gainful undertakings, or to the extent they are not in competition with private-owned businesses. In contrast, resident entities wholly-owned by a *foreign* State are (often) taxed in their residence State. Based on Article 24(5), the residence State is required to give equal tax treatment to a similar resident entity wholly-owned by a foreign State, if the difference in tax treatment is solely based on the fact that the resident entity is (directly or indirectly) owned or controlled by a foreign State. Equal treatment of a resident entity owned by a foreign State could benefit that foreign State, as a (partial) tax-exemption leaves more distributable profits in the resident entity. In the author's view, whether or not the difference in tax treatment is based on the ownership of or control by a foreign State depends on the (true) motivation for not taxing the State entity in a domestic situation.

Often, the difference in tax treatment is based on the unique tax position of State entities in a domestic situation. That is, in relation to domestic State entities, revenue does not necessarily has to be collected through taxation, as a State can extract profits from such entities instead. This unique tax position of domestic State entities, including sovereign wealth investors, is often the reason for the difference in tax treatment of State entities in a domestic situation and resident entities owned by a foreign State. If the resident entity had been held by a resident private investor, or by a non-resident private investor, it would have been taxed similar to a resident entity owned by a foreign State. This comparison makes it clear that the different tax treatment is based on the unique tax position of domestic State entities, rather than the ownership of or control by a foreign State. Therefore, Article 24(5) should have very limited practical relevance for sovereign wealth investors as well.

5.7 IMPACT OF TAX TREATIES ON ACHIEVING NEUTRALITY (EFFICIENCY), EQUITY (FAIRNESS) AND INTERNATIONAL ATTRACTIVENESS IN RELATION TO FOREIGN SOVEREIGN WEALTH INVESTORS

In this section, it will be examined what impact tax treaties could have on source States' ability to achieve (or promote) tax policy objectives (i.e., neutrality, equity and international attractiveness), and to freely implement an approach to the taxation of foreign sovereign wealth investors. For the sake of convenience, the different approaches as identified in Chapter 3, and their relationship with the tax policy objectives, are repeated below:

---

587. Paragraph 76 of the OECD Commentary on Art. 24(5), reproduced in the UN Commentaries.

(1) taxing foreign sovereign wealth investors in the same way as 'regular' non-resident corporate investors.
(2) according a general tax-exemption under domestic law or administrative practice.
(3) according specific tax-exemptions or specific tax reductions under domestic law or administrative practice.
(4) according a general tax-exemption under one or more tax treaties.
(5) according specific tax-exemptions or specific tax reductions under one or more tax treaties.

Table 5.1 *Approaches to Source Taxation of Foreign Sovereign Wealth Investors Measured by Neutrality, Equity and International Attractiveness*

	Neutrality		Equity		International Attractiveness
	(CEN)	(CIN)	(inter-nation)	(inter-taxpayer)	
Approach (1)*	X	✓	✓	✓	X
Approach (2)*	✓	X	X	X	✓
Approach (3)*	✓	X	X	X	✓
Approach (4)*	✓	X	X	X	✓
Approach (5)*	✓	X	X	X	✓

* Approach (1): taxing foreign sovereign wealth investors in the same way as 'regular' non-resident corporate investors.
Approach (2): according a general tax-exemption under domestic law or administrative practice.
Approach (3): according specific tax-exemptions or specific tax reductions under domestic law or administrative practice.
Approach (4): according a general tax-exemption under one or more tax treaties.
Approach (5): according specific tax-exemptions or specific tax reductions under one or more tax treaties.

5.7.1 Neutrality (Efficiency)

5.7.1.1 Capital Export Neutrality

Foreign sovereign wealth investors are generally not taxed in their residence State.[588] Source State taxation of tax-exempt non-resident investors could distort neutrality with respect to the investment location, i.e., it could result in tax-exempt investors favouring domestic investments over foreign investments.[589] In order to promote export neutrality (from a residence State perspective), a source State could consider to exempt from source taxation investment income derived by foreign sovereign wealth investors and other non-resident tax-exempt investors. It could accord such treatment through tax treaties. Reference is made to Approaches (4) and (5), under which source States grant a general or specific tax-exemptions to (some) foreign sovereign wealth investors on the basis of a tax treaty. As such, OECD and UN MTC based treaties have no (negative) impact on source States' ability to promote CEN through Approaches (2) to (5) by according exemptions from source taxation to tax-exempt foreign sovereign wealth investors (i.e., tax treaties do not impose restrictions on source States to do so).

5.7.1.2 Capital Import Neutrality

CIN requires equal treatment of investors that perform the same level of investment activities in a source State, which implies a territorial (or source-based) tax system; in other words, a tax system which exempts foreign sourced income and treats domestic sourced income of resident and non-resident investors in the same way.[590]

Qualifying as a resident of a Contracting State is of key importance for the entitlement to tax treaty benefits. Investors have access to a tax treaty and its benefits if they are 'liable to tax'. Many States choose not to tax their sovereign wealth investors.[591] Many States also choose, for a number of reasons, not to tax certain private resident investors, such as pension funds and CIVs.[592] However, as demonstrated in this chapter, the way this non-taxation of sovereign wealth investors and private resident investors is achieved in the legislation of the home State can make a difference for the outcome of the 'liable to tax' test.[593] This is a major point of criticism about the 'liable to tax' test. In addition to the 'liable to tax' test, sovereign wealth investors could also be a tax treaty resident if they are covered by the expression *that State and any political subdivision or local authority thereof*. Thus, Article 4(1) of the OECD and UN MTC not only creates a distinction among sovereign wealth investors, on

---

588. *See* Section 2.10 and Section 3.2.1.2.
589. *See* Section 3.4.2.2.
590. *See* Section 3.4.3.1.
591. *See* Section 2.10 and Section 3.2.1.2.
592. *See* Section 3.2.1.
593. Van Weeghel has also observed this in more general terms in his comment on *Hoge Raad*, 4 December 2009, No. 07/10383, *BNB* 2010/177. *See also*, J. Wheeler, 'The Missing Keystone of Income Tax Treaties' (2011) 3 *World Tax Journal* 247, p. 252.

the one hand, and among private investors, on the other hand, but also between sovereign wealth investors and private investors. In summary, Article 4(1) creates the following distinctions between investors:

(1) private investors which are 'liable to tax' vs. private investors which are not 'liable to tax';
(2) sovereign wealth investors which are 'liable to tax' vs. sovereign wealth investors which are not 'liable to tax' and also not covered by the phrase *State and any political subdivision or local authority thereof*;
(3) sovereign wealth investors which are not 'liable to tax', yet covered by the phrase *State and any political subdivision or local authority thereof* vs. sovereign wealth investors which are not 'liable to tax' and also not covered by the phrase *State and any political subdivision or local authority thereof*;
(4) sovereign wealth investors which are 'liable to tax' vs. private investors which are not 'liable to tax';
(5) sovereign wealth investors which are not 'liable to tax', yet covered by the phrase *State and any political subdivision or local authority thereof* vs. private investors which are not 'liable to tax';
(6) sovereign wealth investors which are not 'liable to tax' and also not covered by the phrase *State and any political subdivision or local authority thereof* vs. private investors which are 'liable to tax'.

These distinctions created by Article 4(1) entitle some investors to tax treaty benefits (e.g., reduced tax rates under Articles 10 and 11), while excluding others. This could give rise to tax differences and different tax burdens, from a source State perspective, between investors that perform the same level of investment activities in a source State, which would not promote CIN. Article 24 (non-discrimination) does not change this outcome. Tax differences and different tax burdens between investors that are and investors that are not entitled to tax treaty benefits could also occur under tax treaties which deviate from the OECD and UN MTC. Tax treaties, including those based on the OECD or UN MTC, could not only result in tax differences and distortions between investors that do and investors that do not have treaty access, but also among investors that do have tax treaty access (even though a tax treaty applies in the same way to all treaty residents in similar circumstances). First, the different source rates under treaties for the same category of income could result in different tax burdens, such as in case of dividends. Second, the different source rates under treaties for different categories of income could result in different tax burdens, for example for dividends and interest. Third, the different allocation rules for different categories of income could result in different tax burdens, for example capital gains on shares (exclusive allocation to the residence State) and dividends (allowing limited source taxation). Different source rates for the same category of income, different source rates for different categories of income, and different allocation rules for different categories of income, could result in different tax burdens between investors that perform the same level of investment activities in a source State, which would not promote CIN. In determining the tax burden, the fact that dividends and capital gains can relate to profits that have been or will become subject to corporate tax in a source State should, however, be taken into account.

Chapter 5: Tax Treaty Aspects

Source States wishing to promote CIN by introducing equal treatment between investors could be required to *reduce* and/or *increase* the current level of taxation of foreign sovereign wealth investors (and other investors). However, its obligations under existing tax treaties – with respect to maximum tax rates and allocation rules – could restrict a source State to follow the second route (*increase*), as opposed to the first route (*reduction*), while the first route may not always be realistic from a revenue perspective. This would generally leave a State with the option to amend or terminate existing tax treaties. But tax treaties are rarely renegotiated, or unilaterally terminated. Once a tax treaty enters into force, it will generally apply for a long period of time. Based on the above, it can be concluded that tax treaties could restrict source States' ability to promote CIN, and to implement Approach (1).

Source States wishing to promote CIN through tax treaties would need to implement more CIN driven tax treaties, based on the principle of exclusive source jurisdiction, non-discrimination, as well as neutrality for all categories of investment income. Since investors' tax status and characteristics are irrelevant from the perspective of CIN, tax treaty access should not be determined on the basis of the 'liable to tax' test, as used in the current models. Rather, tax treaty access should be granted to investors from the other Contracting State that have derived income from the source State, irrespective of their tax status and characteristics. The exact design of CIN driven tax treaties is outside the scope of this study, but reference is made to the comprehensive research of Kemmeren, who has advocated and outlined a tax treaty model based on the principle of origin, rather than the principle of source.[594] Different from the principle of source, traditionally associated with CIN, the principle of origin requires a causal relationship between the production of income and the territory of a State for establishing tax jurisdiction.[595] If income arises from a State, but is not generated from activities within the territory of that State, tax jurisdiction can be established under the principle of source but not under the principle of origin.[596]

5.7.2 Equity (Fairness)

5.7.2.1 *Inter-taxpayer Equity*

The benefit theory, which, unlike the ability-to-pay theory, is also relevant for the taxation of non-residents, requires that each taxpayer should pay tax in accordance with its level of benefit from governmental goods and services.[597] From this general rule, three, more practical, rules of thumb were derived which are relevant for the taxation of foreign sovereign wealth investors, from a source State perspective.[598] The *first rule* is that a source State should generally not tax non-resident investors less

---

594. E. Kemmeren, *Principle of Origin in Tax Conventions: A Rethinking of Models* (2001), Dongen: Mr Eric C.C.M. Kemmeren/Pijnenburg vormgevers, uitgevers, available at: < https://pure.uvt.nl/portal/files/439888/87428.pdf > .
595. *Ibid.*, pp. 35–36.
596. *Ibid.*
597. *See* Section 3.5.2.1.
598. *See* Section 3.5.2.2.

favourably than resident investors when performing the same investment activities in and earning the same level of income from that source State. It may, in such circumstances, even require non-resident investors to be taxed more favourably than resident investors. The *second rule* is that a source State should treat and tax all non-resident investors as equals when they perform the same investment activities in and earn the same level of income from that source State (i.e., horizontal non-discriminatory treatment). The *third rule*, which applies to both the first and second rule, is that forgoing taxation would not make sense from a benefit perspective, since residents and non-residents that perform investment activities in the source State always benefit from public goods and services to some extent.

OECD and UN MTC based treaties may achieve, but do not guarantee compliance with the first rule, and may produce effects incompatible with the second and third rule. As regards the first rule, it is noted that the primary aim of OECD and UN MTC based treaties is to prevent international juridical double taxation, rather than guaranteeing that non-residents are not taxed less favourably than residents (in similar circumstances). The allocation provisions of a tax treaty may achieve that tax treaty resident foreign sovereign wealth investors (and other non-resident investors) are not taxed less favourably than resident investors performing the same investment activities in and earning the same level of income from the same source State, but Article 24 (non-discrimination provision) would normally not prohibit non-residents from being taxed less favourably than resident investors, regardless of whether they perform the same investment activities in and earn the same level of income from the same source State. Therefore, tax treaties may achieve, but do not guarantee that foreign sovereign wealth investors (and other non-resident investors) do not pay more source State tax than resident investors performing the same investment activities in the same source State.

The analysis regarding the second rule is largely similar to the analysis above in respect of CIN, but limited to non-resident investors. Article 4(1) of OECD and UN MTC based treaties potentially creates the following distinctions among and between non-resident investors:

(1) non-resident private investors which are 'liable to tax' vs. non-resident private investors which are not 'liable to tax';
(2) foreign sovereign wealth investors which are 'liable to tax' vs. foreign sovereign wealth investors which are not 'liable to tax' and also not covered by the phrase *State and any political subdivision or local authority thereof*;
(3) foreign sovereign wealth investors which are not 'liable to tax', yet covered by the phrase *State and any political subdivision or local authority thereof* vs. foreign sovereign wealth investors which are not 'liable to tax' and also not covered by the phrase *State and any political subdivision or local authority thereof*;
(4) foreign sovereign wealth investors which are 'liable to tax' vs. non-resident private investors which are not 'liable to tax';
(5) foreign sovereign wealth investors which are not 'liable to tax', yet covered by the phrase *State and any political subdivision or local authority thereof* vs. non-resident private investors which are not 'liable to tax';

(6) foreign sovereign wealth investors which are not 'liable to tax' and also not covered by the phrase *State and any political subdivision or local authority thereof* vs. non-resident private investors which are 'liable to tax'.

These distinctions created by Article 4(1) entitle some non-resident investors to tax treaty benefits (e.g., reduced tax rates under Articles 10 and 11), while excluding others. This could give rise to tax differences and different tax burdens among foreign sovereign wealth investors and among non-resident private investors, as well as between foreign sovereign wealth investors and non-resident private investors, that perform the same investment activities in a source State, which would be in conflict with inter-taxpayer equity. Article 24 (non-discrimination) does not change this outcome, since it does not prohibit horizontal discrimination between non-resident investors. Tax differences and different tax burdens between non-resident investors that are and non-resident investors that are not entitled to tax treaty benefits could also occur under tax treaties which deviate from the OECD and UN MTC.

As explained in Section 3.5.2.2, the benefit principle would prescribe different treatment of different categories of income if it can be demonstrated that different asset classes benefit differently from public goods and services. If, however, this cannot be demonstrated, tax differences and different tax burdens that tax treaties, including those based on the OECD or UN MTC, could create among non-resident investors that do have tax treaty access, would also be in conflict with the second rule. As explained in Section 5.7.1.2, these tax differences and different tax burdens could result from different source rates for the same category of income, different source rates for different categories of income, and different allocation rules for different categories of income. In determining the tax burden, the fact that dividends and capital gains can relate to profits that have been or will become subject to corporate tax in a source State should, however, be taken into account. This final remark is also relevant for the application of the third rule.

Source States wishing to promote inter-taxpayer equity would need to *reduce* the current level of taxation of foreign sovereign wealth investors (and other investors) paying too much tax from a benefit perspective, and *increase* the current level of taxation of foreign sovereign wealth investors (and other investors) paying too little. However, obligations under existing tax treaties – with respect to tax rates and allocation rules – could restrict a source State to follow the second route (*increase*), as opposed to the first route (*reduction*), while the first route may not always be realistic from a revenue perspective. This would generally leave a State with the option to amend or terminate existing tax treaties. But tax treaties are rarely renegotiated, or unilaterally terminated. Once a tax treaty enters into force, it will generally apply for a long period of time. Based on the above, it can be concluded that tax treaties could restrict source States' ability to achieve inter-taxpayer equity, and to implement Approach (1).

Including a horizontal non-discrimination rule in a tax treaty – stipulating that investors from the other Contracting State receive equal treatment in the source State – would serve inter-taxpayer equity. In this respect, tax treaty access should (also) be granted to investors from the other Contracting State that have derived income from the source State, irrespective of their tax status and characteristics. In addition, including a MFN rule in a tax treaty – ensuring equal source State treatment of investors from different States – would also serve inter-taxpayer equity.

5.7.2.2 Inter-nation Equity

Under inter-nation equity, non-resident investors from the same State that perform the same (investment) activities in a source State should be treated alike in that source State.[599] A different treatment of non-resident investors from different States can be justified on redistribution grounds only.[600] The analysis regarding the impact of tax treaties on States' ability to achieve inter-nation equity is largely similar to the analysis above in respect of CIN, but limited to non-resident investors from the same State. Article 4(1) of OECD and UN MTC based treaties potentially creates the following distinctions among and between non-resident investors from the same State:

(1) non-resident private investors which are 'liable to tax' vs. non-resident private investors which are not 'liable to tax';
(2) foreign sovereign wealth investors which are 'liable to tax' vs. foreign sovereign wealth investors which are not 'liable to tax' and also not covered by the phrase *State and any political subdivision or local authority thereof*;
(3) foreign sovereign wealth investors which are not 'liable to tax', yet covered by the phrase *State and any political subdivision or local authority thereof* vs. foreign sovereign wealth investors which are not 'liable to tax' and also not covered by the phrase *State and any political subdivision or local authority thereof*;
(4) foreign sovereign wealth investors which are 'liable to tax' vs. non-resident private investors which are not 'liable to tax';
(5) foreign sovereign wealth investors which are not 'liable to tax', yet covered by the phrase *State and any political subdivision or local authority thereof* vs. non-resident private investors which are not 'liable to tax';
(6) foreign sovereign wealth investors which are not 'liable to tax' and also not covered by the phrase *State and any political subdivision or local authority thereof* vs. non-resident private investors which are 'liable to tax'.

These distinctions created by Article 4(1) entitle some non-resident investors to tax treaty benefits (e.g., reduced tax rates under Articles 10 and 11), while excluding other non-resident investors from the same State. This could give rise to tax differences and different tax burdens among foreign sovereign wealth investors and among non-resident private investors from the same State, as well as between foreign sovereign wealth investors and non-resident private investors from the same State, that perform the same investment activities in a source State, which would be in conflict with inter-nation equity. Article 24 (non-discrimination) does not change this outcome, since it does not prohibit horizontal discrimination between non-resident investors from the same State. Tax differences and different tax burdens between non-resident

---

599. *See* Section 3.5.3.2.
600. *Ibid.*

Chapter 5: Tax Treaty Aspects

investors that are and non-resident investors from the same State that are not entitled to tax treaty benefits, could also occur under tax treaties which deviate from the OECD and UN MTC.

As explained in Section 3.5.3.1, it is unclear whether inter-nation equity would allow a source State to differentiate between different categories of investment income, or whether it would require equal treatment of all categories of investment income. If inter-nation equity would not allow a source State to differentiate, tax differences and different tax burdens that tax treaties, including those based on the OECD or UN MTC, could create among non-resident investors from the same State that do have tax treaty access, would also be in conflict with inter-nation equity. As explained in Section 5.7.1.2 above, these tax differences and different tax burdens could result from different source rates for the same category of income, different source rates for different categories of income, and different allocation rules for different categories of income. In determining the tax burden, the fact that dividends and capital gains can relate to profits that have been or will become subject to corporate tax in a source State should be taken into account.

Source States wishing to promote inter-nation equity by introducing equal treatment between non-resident investors from the same State could be required to *reduce* and/or *increase* the current level of taxation of foreign sovereign wealth investors (and other non-resident investors). However, obligations under existing tax treaties – with respect to maximum tax rates and allocation rules – could restrict a source State to follow the second route (*increase*), as opposed to the first route (*reduction*), while the first route may not always be realistic from a revenue perspective. This would generally leave a State with the option to amend or terminate existing tax treaties. But tax treaties are rarely renegotiated, or unilaterally terminated. Once a tax treaty enters into force, it will generally apply for a long period of time. Based on the above, it can be concluded that tax treaties could restrict source States' ability to achieve inter-nation equity, and to implement Approach (1).

Including a horizontal non-discrimination rule in a tax treaty – stipulating that investors from the other Contracting State receive equal treatment in the source State – would serve inter-nation equity. In this respect, tax treaty access should (also) be granted to investors from the other Contracting State that have derived income from the source State, irrespective of their tax status and characteristics.

5.7.3 International Attractiveness

States can use a tax treaty as an instrument to enhance the international attractiveness of their tax system for foreign sovereign wealth investors.[601] Recently, the OECD has recognized that 'there are also many non-tax factors that can lead to the conclusion of a tax treaty and that each country has a sovereign right to decide to enter into tax

---

601. *See* Section 3.6.

treaties with any jurisdiction with which it decides to do so.'[602] Nowadays, many tax treaties are (also) concluded for a specific economic purpose. The memorandum on Dutch tax treaty policy (2011) gives two examples of a specific economic purpose for concluding a tax treaty: (i) facilitating cross-border investments by Dutch tax-exempt pension funds, and (ii) attracting investments from SWFs.[603] The Netherlands, and many other States, have, in more recent times, concluded tax treaties with a purpose of attracting investments from sovereign wealth investors[604] and protecting their competitiveness position vis-à-vis other States.[605] Offering tax benefits through tax treaties, rather than unilaterally, might give a source State the possibility to obtain tax (or other) benefits in return (reciprocal approach).

In a tax treaty context, any restrictions on source States' ability to pursue international attractiveness must come from a treaty provision that is based on Article 24 (non-discrimination) of the OECD or UN MTC. However, Article 24 does not prohibit *reverse* discrimination, i.e., it does not prohibit non-resident investors from being treated more favourably than resident investors. Nor does it prohibit horizontal discrimination between non-resident investors from the same State, or between non-resident investors from different States, i.e., Article 24 does not prohibit one non-resident investor from being treated more favourably than other non-resident investors from the same State, or from different States. Therefore, OECD and UN MTC based treaties have no (negative) impact on source States' ability to pursue international attractiveness through Approaches (2) to (5).

5.8 CONCLUSIONS

This chapter has considered the (possible) implications of tax treaties for source State taxation of foreign sovereign wealth investors. Based on these implications, it was examined what impact tax treaties could have on source States' ability to achieve (or promote) tax policy objectives (i.e., neutrality, equity and international attractiveness), and to freely implement an approach to taxation of foreign sovereign wealth investors.[606] This chapter has focused on the OECD and UN MTC, and their Commentaries.

Qualifying as a resident of a Contracting State (Article 4(1)) is of key importance for the entitlement to tax treaty benefits. Investors have access to a tax treaty and its benefits if they are 'liable to tax' – i.e., a comprehensive taxation (full tax liability). Many States choose not to tax their sovereign wealth investors. Many States also choose, for a number of reasons, not to tax certain private resident investors, such as pension funds and CIVs. However, as demonstrated in this chapter, the way this non-taxation of sovereign wealth investors and private resident investors is achieved in

---

602. OECD (2015), *Preventing the Granting of Treaty Benefits in Inappropriate Circumstances, Action 6 – 2015 Final Report*, OECD/G20 Base Erosion and Profit Shifting Project, OECD Publishing, Paris, Para. 76, p. 94.
603. *Notitie Fiscaal Verdragsbeleid 2011*, Tweede Kamer, 2010–2011, 25 087, No. 7, p. 17.
604. *See*, for example, the Dutch tax treaties discussed in the Appendix to this study.
605. *Tweede Kamer*, 2009–2010, 32 346, No. 3, p. 6 (Discussion notes to the tax treaty with the UAE, referring to the favourable tax treaty concluded between the UAE and Belgium and between the UAE and Austria).
606. *See* the five approaches identified in Section 3.2.2.2.

the legislation of the home State, can make a difference in the outcome of the 'liable to tax' test. The phrase *State or any political subdivision or local authority thereof* in Article 4(1) of both the OECD and UN MTC offers sovereign wealth investors an additional possibility to get tax treaty access. Sovereign wealth investors constituted by a pool of assets can most likely be considered an integral part of the State. It is, however, unclear whether sovereign wealth investors with a separate legal identity are covered by this expression, and whether a further distinction should be made between legal persons of public law and legal persons of private law owned by a legal person of public law.

Tax treaty benefits include reduced treaty rates on outbound dividends and interest payments. As indicated by the OECD Commentary on Articles 10 (Dividends) and 11 (Interest), some source States even accord tax-exemptions to foreign States and (some of) their wholly-owned entities. And these exemptions from source taxation might also be available to foreign sovereign wealth investors. Tax treaty benefits could also include the absence of source taxation on the listed categories of capital gains, including capital gains derived from non-immovable property companies. In the author's view, the non-discrimination article (Article 24) has no impact on source taxation of sovereign wealth investors.

Article 4(1) creates distinctions between investors which entitle some investors to tax treaty benefits (e.g., reduced tax rates under Articles 10 and 11), while excluding others. From a source State perspective, this could give rise to tax differences and different tax burdens:

- between investors that perform the same level of investment activities in a source State; which would not promote CIN;
- among foreign sovereign wealth investors and among non-resident private investors, as well as between foreign sovereign wealth investors and non-resident private investors, that perform the same investment activities in and earn the same level of income from a source State; which would be in conflict with inter-taxpayer equity;
- among foreign sovereign wealth investors and among non-resident private investors from the *same* State, as well as between foreign sovereign wealth investors and non-resident private investors from the *same* State, that perform the same investment activities in a source State; which would be in conflict with inter-nation equity.

Article 24 (non-discrimination) does not change these outcomes.

Tax treaties, including those based on the OECD or UN MTC, could not only result in tax differences and different tax burdens between investors that do and investors that do not have treaty access, but also among investors that do have tax treaty access (even though a tax treaty applies in the same way to all treaty residents in similar circumstances). These tax differences and different tax burdens could result from different source tax rates for the same category of income, different source tax rates for different categories of income, and different allocation rules for different categories of income, which would not promote CIN and might be in conflict with both inter-taxpayer equity and inter-nation equity.

Source States wishing to promote CIN by introducing equal treatment between investors could be required to *reduce* and/or *increase* the current level of taxation of foreign sovereign wealth investors (and other investors). Source States wishing to promote inter-taxpayer equity would need to *reduce* the current level of taxation of foreign sovereign wealth investors (and other investors) paying too much tax from a benefit perspective, and *increase* the current level of taxation of foreign sovereign wealth investors (and other investors) paying too little. Source States wishing to promote inter-nation equity by introducing equal treatment between non-resident investors from the same State could be required to *reduce* and/or *increase* the current level of taxation of foreign sovereign wealth investors (and other non-resident investors). However, obligations under existing tax treaties – with respect to maximum tax rates and allocation rules – could restrict a source State to follow the second route (*increase*), as opposed to the first route (*reduction*), while the first route may not always be realistic from a revenue perspective. This would generally leave a State with the option to amend or terminate existing tax treaties. But tax treaties are rarely renegotiated, or unilaterally terminated. Once a tax treaty enters into force, it will generally apply for a long period of time. Considering the above, OECD and UN MTC based treaties could restrict source States' ability to promote CIN, inter-taxpayer equity and inter-nation equity, and to implement Approach (1).[607]

On the other hand, tax treaties have no (negative) impact, as such, on source States' ability to promote CEN through Approaches (2) to (5)[608] by according exemptions from source taxation to tax-exempt foreign sovereign wealth investors (i.e., tax treaties do not impose restrictions on source States to do so).

Finally, OECD and UN MTC based treaties, as such, have no (negative) impact on source States' ability to pursue international attractiveness through Approaches (2) to (5).[609]

It can be concluded that OECD and UN MTC based treaties could restrict source States' ability to pursue CIN, inter-taxpayer equity and inter-nation equity, and to implement Approach (1). However, they have no (negative) impact on the ability of source States to promote CEN in relation to foreign sovereign wealth investors, nor on their ability to pursue international attractiveness through Approaches (2) to (5). This is summarized in the table below.

---

607. Approach (1) has been identified in Section 3.2.2.2 and is as follows: taxing foreign sovereign wealth investors in the same way as 'regular' non-resident corporate investors.
608. Approaches (2) to (5) have been identified in Section 3.2.2.2 and are as follows:

   (2) according a general tax-exemption under domestic law or administrative practice.
   (3) according specific tax-exemptions or specific tax reductions under domestic law or administrative practice.
   (4) according a general tax-exemption under one or more tax treaties.
   (5) according specific tax-exemptions or specific tax reductions under one or more tax treaties.

609. *Ibid.*

Chapter 5: Tax Treaty Aspects

Table 5.2 Impact of OECD/UN MTC Based Treaties on the Ability of Source States to Achieve (or Promote) Tax Policy Objectives, and to Freely Implement an Approach to Taxation of Foreign Sovereign Wealth Investors

	Neutrality		Equity		International Attractiveness
	(CEN)	*(CIN)*	*(Inter-taxpayer)*	*(Inter-nation)*	
Sovereign immunity	No (negative) impact	No (negative) impact	Impact negligible (i.e. only if immunity from execution would apply)	Impact negligible (i.e. only if immunity from execution would apply)	No (negative) impact
OECD/UN MTC based treaties	No (negative) impact	Restrict Approach (1) (but only where an increase in level of taxation is required)	Restrict Approach (1) (but only where an increase in level of taxation is required)	Restrict Approach (1) (but only where an increase in level of taxation is required)	No (negative) impact
European (Union) law	Chapter 6	Chapter 6	Chapter 6	Chapter 6	Chapter 6
	Potentially underlying Approaches (2) to (5)*	Potentially underlying Approach (1)*	Potentially underlying Approach (1)*	Potentially underlying Approach (1)*	Potentially underlying Approaches (2) to (5)*

* Approach (1): taxing foreign sovereign wealth investors in the same way as 'regular' non-resident corporate investors.
Approach (2): according a general tax-exemption under domestic law or administrative practice.
Approach (3): according specific tax-exemptions or specific tax reductions under domestic law or administrative practice.
Approach (4): according a general tax-exemption under one or more tax treaties.
Approach (5): according specific tax-exemptions or specific tax reductions under one or more tax treaties.

CHAPTER 6
European Tax Law Aspects of Foreign Sovereign Wealth Investors

6.1 INTRODUCTION

This chapter will consider the (possible) implications of European law for source State taxation of foreign sovereign wealth investors. Based on these implications, it will be examined what impact European law could have on the ability of source States to achieve (or promote) neutrality (efficiency), equity (fairness) and international attractiveness, and to freely implement an approach to taxation of foreign sovereign wealth investors.[610]

From a source State perspective, the European law analysis will only be relevant to EU Member States and (other) members to the EEA Agreement. This chapter will consider primary European law, notably the fundamental freedoms and State aid rules included in the TFEU[611] and the EEA Agreement,[612] which can all apply in (direct) tax matters. An important reason for including the EEA Agreement is that Norway, a member to this agreement, hosts currently the largest sovereign wealth investor in the world in terms of assets under management. As regards the fundamental freedoms, it is noted that the freedom of capital movement, rather than the freedom of establishment, potentially has the most relevance in relation to foreign sovereign wealth investors. The first reason for this is that, although sovereign wealth investors increasingly operate as long-term, *active* investors, they are still predominantly (passive) portfolio investors (to which the free movement of capital has the most relevance). The second reason is that most sovereign wealth investors reside outside the EU. Importantly, the personal and territorial scope of the free movement of capital in the TFEU is not limited to EU Member States; it has universal personal and territorial

---

610. *See* the five approaches identified in Section 3.2.2.2.
611. Official Journal of the European Union, Vol. 55, C 326, 26 October 2012.
612. Official Journal of the European Communities, Vol. 37, L 1, 3 January 1994.

scope. As a result, the free movement of capital in the TFEU, as opposed to its counterpart in the EEA Agreement, may be relevant in relation to sovereign wealth investors from so-called third countries. Nevertheless, because sovereign wealth investors are increasingly operating as *active* investors, and may reside inside EU Member States and (other) members to the EEA Agreement, the freedom of establishment will be considered as well. With respect to the State aid rules, the analysis will be a first general analysis in the context of foreign sovereign wealth investors, aimed at identifying potential issues in this complex area of European law. As regards secondary EU law, the focus will be on the Parent-Subsidiary Directive[613] and Interest & Royalties Directive.[614]

After a basic introduction to European law in Section 6.2, Section 6.3 will first consider the (possible) implications of the freedom of capital movement and the freedom of establishment for source State taxation of foreign sovereign wealth investors. Section 6.4 concerns the State aid rules and will provide a first general analysis in the context of foreign sovereign wealth investors, which will be aimed at identify potential issues in this complex area of European law. Section 6.5 will briefly consider the Parent-Subsidiary Directive and Interest & Royalties Directive. Based on the findings of Section 6.3–6.5, Section 6.6 will examine what impact European law could have on source States' ability to achieve (or promote) neutrality (efficiency), equity (fairness) and international attractiveness, and to freely implement an approach to taxation of foreign sovereign wealth investors. Section 6.7 will end this chapter with the main conclusions.

6.2 EUROPEAN LAW: A BASIC INTRODUCTION

6.2.1 The EU and the Internal Market

The EU is founded on the TFEU.[615] A principal aim of the EU is to further the economic and social progress of its Member States, currently twenty-eight in total, by eliminating the barriers that divide Europe, and to improve the living and working conditions of their peoples.[616] The establishment and the progressive development of the internal market serve this aim. The TFEU provides that the 'internal market shall comprise an area without internal frontiers in which the free movement of goods, persons, services and capital is ensured in accordance with the provisions of the Treaties'.[617] The internal market refers to an economic market striving for free competition between economic operators.

---

613. *Council Directive 2011/96/EU of 30 November 2011 on the common system of taxation applicable in the case of parent companies and subsidiaries of different Member States*, Official Journal of the European Union, Vol. 54, L 345, 29 December 2011, as amended by Council Directive (EU) 2015/121 of 27 January 2015, Official Journal of the European Union, Vol. 58, L 21, 28 January 2015.
614. *Council Directive 2003/49/EC of 3 June 2003 on a common system of taxation applicable to interest and royalty payments made between associated companies of different Member States*, Official Journal of the European Union, Vol. 46, L 157, 29 June 2003.
615. Official Journal of the European Union, Vol. 55, C 326, 26 October 2012. Art. 1(2) TFEU.
616. Preamble to the TFEU.
617. Article 26(2) TFEU.

6.2.2 How the Internal Market Is Achieved

6.2.2.1 Integration

The internal market between the currently twenty-eight Member States is being developed by positive and negative integration in accordance with the TFEU. Positive integration (policy integration) is achieved through the harmonization and coordination/unification of national legislation or national policies of EU Member States. Negative integration (market integration) is mainly achieved through the fundamental freedoms, as interpreted by the Court of Justice of the European Union ('CJEU'), the judicial institution of the EU, and through the State aid rules. The fundamental freedoms and State aid rules prohibit national measures that are incompatible with the TFEU.[618] In the field of direct taxation, negative integration was clearly dominant until not so long ago. However, more recently, positive integration in direct tax matters is clearly on the rise with the EU Directive on country-by-country reporting,[619] the EU Anti-Tax Avoidance Directives,[620] and the proposals for a European corporate tax system,[621] as major contributors.

6.2.2.2 Fundamental Freedoms

The most important contributors to negative tax integration are the four fundamental freedoms – the free movement of goods, persons, services and capital – as laid down in the TFEU. These fundamental freedoms are (specific) expressions of the general principle of non-discrimination,[622] which prescribes that 'comparable situations must not be treated differently and different situations must not be treated in the same way unless such treatment is objectively justified'.[623] The fundamental freedoms traditionally prohibit cross-border situations from being treated less favourably than comparable domestic situations. They not only prohibit overt discrimination on the basis of

---

618. The CJEU's primary responsibility is to examine the compatibility of EU measures and national measures of EU Member States with EU law, including the fundamental freedoms, and ensure the uniform interpretation and application of EU law.
619. These rules, which are based on OECD BEPS Action 13: Guidance on Transfer Pricing Documentation and Country-by-Country Reporting, will require large multinational enterprises to report to their local tax authorities of EU Member States certain information on a country-by-country basis as from the 2016 fiscal year. The country-by-country reports will subsequently be exchanged between relevant EU Member States.
620. These directives, which build on OECD recommendations to address tax base erosion and profit shifting, lay down anti-tax avoidance rules in the following five fields: (i) interest deductibility, (ii) exit taxation, (iii) general anti-abuse, (iv) low-taxed controlled foreign companies, and (v) hybrid mismatches.
621. On 25 October 2016, the EC published a Proposal for a Council Directive on a Common Corporate Tax Base, COM(2016) 685 final, and a Proposal for a Council Directive on a Common Consolidated Corporate Tax Base, COM(2016) 683 final. The proposals need to be approved unanimously by all EU Member States.
622. N. Bammens, *The Principle of Non-discrimination in International and European Tax Law*, IBFD Doctoral Series, Vol. 24 (Amsterdam: IBFD, 2012), pp. 501–502.
623. CJEU, 13 December 1984, Case C-106/83 (*Sermide SpA v. Cassa Conguaglio Zucchero*), Para. 28. According to Bammens, the CJEU's concept of non-discrimination reflects the Aristotelian

nationality, 'but also all covert forms of discrimination which, by the application of other criteria of differentiation, lead in fact to the same result'.[624] A different treatment based on a person's 'residence' could result in indirect discrimination. These concepts of direct and indirect discrimination also apply in the field of direct taxation, which means that (foreign) nationality and (foreign) residence as such cannot be relied on to explain a different tax treatment of otherwise comparable persons (comparable *subjects* from a source State perspective).[625] While prohibiting discrimination on the basis of nationality or residence of taxpayers, the fundamental freedoms also prohibit discrimination on the basis of place or destination of activity.[626] This means that a taxpayer's cross-border activity (e.g., investment) must not be treated less favourably than a domestic activity in comparable circumstances (comparable *objects* from a residence State perspective).[627] Clearly, the focus in this study is on the first perspective. Although the fundamental freedoms typically prohibit cross-border situations from being treated less favourably than comparable internal situations (i.e., vertical discrimination), recent case law indicates that the freedoms may also prohibit discrimination between comparable non-residents (i.e., horizontal discrimination).

All fundamental freedoms have direct effect; they are an integral part of the legal systems of the EU Member States, and nationals of an EU Member State can directly rely upon the freedoms before their national courts.[628] The free movement of persons, one of the four fundamental freedoms, includes the right of citizens of the EU to move and reside freely within the EU,[629] the free movement of workers,[630] and the freedom of establishment for self-employed persons, companies and firms.[631] The freedom of establishment (Articles 49–55 TFEU) and freedom of capital movement (Articles 63–66 TFEU) are the relevant freedoms in the context of this study.

6.2.2.3 *State Aid Rules*

An increasingly important contributor to negative tax integration is the State aid framework (Articles 107–108 TFEU). Both the free movement provisions and State aid rules prohibit certain national tax measures affecting free competition within the internal market. Whereas rules on free movement traditionally deal with distinctions between cross-border positions and internal positions (inter-State distinctions), State

---

concept of non-discrimination. See N. Bammens, *The Principle of Non-discrimination in International and European Tax Law*, IBFD Doctoral Series, Vol. 24 (Amsterdam: IBFD, 2012), pp. 501–502.
624. CJEU, 12 February 1974, Case 152/73 (*Sotgiu*), Para. 11.
625. For an overview of relevant case law, *see* S. Douma, *Optimization of Tax Sovereignty and Free Movement* (2011), PhD. Thesis, pp. 26–27 and case law cited in footnotes 53–66, available at: <https://openaccess.leidenuniv.nl/handle/1887/17973>.
626. CJEU, 27 September 1988, Case 81/87 (*Daily Mail*), Para. 16.
627. For an overview of relevant case law, *see* S. Douma, *Optimization of Tax Sovereignty and Free Movement* (2011), PhD. Thesis, pp. 28–29 and case law cited in footnotes 67–83.
628. CJEU, 5 February 1963, Case 26-62 (*van Gend & Loos*); CJEU, 15 July 1964, Case 6/64 (*Costa v. ENEL*).
629. Articles 21 TFEU et seq.
630. Articles 45–48 TFEU.
631. Articles 49–55 TFEU.

aid rules are concerned with distinctions between economic operators operating within the same State (intra-State distinctions).[632] While the free movement rules traditionally aim to remove *disadvantages* (negative discrimination) in cross-border situations as compared to comparable domestic situations, State aid rules aim to remove certain *benefits* (positive discrimination) that economic operators enjoy over other economic operators operating within the same State.[633]

The EC is the exclusive administrative body in charge of ensuring that Member States comply with State aid rules. All decisions of the EC in State aid matters can be challenged (ultimately) before the CJEU.

6.2.2.4 Directives in the Field of Direct Taxation

A directive is one of the legal instruments of the EU and an important contributor to positive integration in the field of direct taxation. The adoption of a tax directive requires the unanimous consent of all EU Member States[634] and, once adopted, the directive must be incorporated into the national legal order of EU Member States.[635] In this respect, an EU Member State is free to choose form and methods, as long as the results of the directive are achieved.[636] Examples of European directives in the field of direct taxation are the Parent-Subsidiary Directive, Interest & Royalties Directive, Merger Directive and Anti-Tax Avoidance Directives.

6.2.3 The European Economic Area and the Extension of the Internal Market

In some respects, the internal market within the EU is extended to Iceland, Norway and Liechtenstein (three of the four members of the European Free Trade Association ('EFTA'))[637] through the EEA Agreement, by adopting the four fundamental freedoms.[638] The EEA Agreement provides for the free movement of goods, persons, services and capital between Iceland, Norway and Liechtenstein ('EEA-EFTA States'), on the one hand, and between the EU (Member States) and the EEA-EFTA States, on the other. The fundamental freedoms included in the EEA Agreement have direct effect.[639] The CJEU has recognized that, in order to realize the extension of the internal market to the EEA-EFTA States, the rules of the EEA Agreement that are identical in

---

632. P. Wattel, 'Interaction of State Aid, Free Movement, Policy Competition and Abuse Control in Direct Tax Matters' (2013) 5 *World Tax Journal* 128.
633. *Ibid.*, pp. 128–129.
634. Article 114(2) in conjunction with Art. 115 TFEU.
635. Article 288 TFEU.
636. *Ibid.*
637. The other EFTA State, Switzerland, did not accede the EEA due to a negative referendum in December 1992.
638. CJEU, 23 September 2003, Case C-452/01 (*Margarethe Ospelt*), Para. 29; EFTA Court, 23 November 2004, Case E-1/04 (*Fokus Bank*), Para. 23. *See also* Art. 1(2) EEA Agreement.
639. D. Smit, *Freedom of Investment Between EU and Non-EU Member States and Its Impact on Corporate Income Tax Systems Within the European Union*, (Tilburg: CentER, 2011), pp. 346–347, available at: <https://pure.uvt.nl/portal/files/5897717/Smit_freedom_02_12_2011_emb_tot_01_09_2013.pdf>.

substance to those of the TFEU, are to be interpreted uniformly.[640] Further, based on its constitutional rules, the EFTA Court, which has jurisdiction with respect to the EEA-EFTA States, has to take due account of case law of the CJEU concerning the interpretation of rules of the TFEU that are identical in substance to those of the EEA Agreement.[641] As will be discussed in more detail in this chapter, the freedom of establishment and freedom of capital movement, the focus of this chapter, are (substantially) identical in substance. Thus, both courts seek to interpret the relevant provisions in the TFEU and the EEA Agreement uniformly, although there may be differences in reality.

The EEA Agreement also contains State aid rules (Articles 61–64 EEA Agreement), which are broadly in line with State aid rules in the TFEU. The EFTA Surveillance Authority is in charge of ensuring that EEA-EFTA States comply with State aid rules. The Authority has similar powers and functions as the EC as far as the enforcement of State aid rules is concerned. All decisions of the Authority on State aid can be challenged before the EFTA Court, which has jurisdiction with respect to the EEA-EFTA States.

The directives discussed in this study, namely the Parent-Subsidiary Directive and Interest & Royalties Directive, do not apply to EEA-EFTA States.

6.2.4 Code of Conduct for Business Taxation

In December 1997, a Code of Conduct for Business Taxation was adopted within the EU to curb harmful tax competition between the EU Member States.[642] The Code is a political agreement between the EU Member States to counter harmful tax measures; it is, however, not a legally binding instrument. The Code covers those tax measures (legislative, regulatory and administrative) in the area of business taxation 'which affect, or may affect, in a significant way the location of business activity'[643] in the EU. Within this parameter, the defining characteristic of a (potentially) harmful tax measure is a tax measure that provides 'for a significantly lower effective level of taxation, including zero taxation, than those levels which generally apply in the Member State in question'.[644] The Code sets out criteria for assessing whether a tax measure is potentially harmful, including: (i) whether advantages are accorded only to non-residents or in respect of transactions carried out with non-residents; (ii) whether advantages are ring-fenced from the domestic market, so that they do not affect the national tax base; (iii) whether advantages are granted without any real economic

---

640. CJEU, 23 September 2003, Case C-452/01 (*Margarethe Ospelt*), Para. 29; EFTA Court, 12 December 2003, Case E-1/03 (*EFTA Surveillance Authority v. The Republic of Iceland*), Para. 27; CJEU, 20 October 2011, Case C-284/09 (*European Commission v. Federal Republic of Germany*), Para. 95.
641. Article 3(2) of the *Agreement between the EFTA States on the Establishment of a Surveillance Authority and a Court of Justice (Surveillance and Court Agreement)*.
642. *Code of Conduct for Business Taxation*, Annex to the Conclusions of the ECOFIN Council Meeting on 1 December 1997 concerning taxation policy (98/C 2/01), Official Journal of the European Union, Vol. 41, C 2, 6 January 1998.
643. *Ibid*.
644. *Ibid*.

activity and substantial economic presence within the Member State offering such tax advantage; (iv) whether transfer pricing rules depart from internationally accepted principles, notably the rules agreed upon within the OECD; (v) whether the tax measures lack transparency.

The Code is enforced by a group of representatives of the EU Member States, known as the Code of Conduct Group on Business Taxation.[645] The Group – which meets regularly and is assisted by several subgroups – selects, reviews and assesses tax measures against the criteria of the Code. In November 1999, the Group presented its first final report, known as the Primarolo Report, in which sixty-six tax measures were identified as potentially harmful.[646] Since then, the Group reports regularly to the Council and many other tax measures have been found harmful. Although the Code is a soft law instrument, it has achieved significant negative integration in the area of business taxation. Relying on peer pressure, the Code has resulted in the abolishment of many existing tax measures and has held back the introduction of new harmful tax measures. Since the criteria of the Code require interpretation, consensus is not always achieved within the Group though.

The Code of Conduct will not be further considered in this study, but it could impose restrictions, in a political sense, on an EU Member State to introduce tax policy in relation to foreign sovereign wealth investors. In the author's view, the main question to be answered is whether tax-exemptions or reductions accorded to foreign sovereign wealth investors – i.e., Approaches (2) through (5)[647] – affect, or may affect, in a *significant way* the location of business activity in the EU. In Section 3.4.3.1, it was explained that not only direct investments, but also portfolio investments could, under circumstances, have influence on the location of business activity. However, the question remains whether tax-exemptions or reductions accorded to foreign sovereign wealth investors may influence the location of business activity in the EU in a *significant way*. In this respect, tax-exemptions or reductions through a tax treaty – i.e., Approaches (4) and (5) – may have less of an impact than unilateral tax-exemptions or reductions – i.e., Approaches (2) and (3).

---

645. Council Conclusions of 9 March 1998 concerning the establishment of the Code of Conduct Group (business taxation) (98/C 99/01), Official Journal of the European Union, Vol. 41, C 99, 1 April 1998, p. 1. For an overview of issues the Group is currently dealing with, *see* M. Nouwen, 'The European Code of Conduct Group Becomes Increasingly Important in the Fight Against Tax Avoidance: More Openness and Transparency is Necessary' (2017) 45 *Intertax* 138.
646. Code of Conduct Group, Council of the European Union, *Report on the Code of Conduct (Business Taxation)*, SN 4901/99, 23 November 1999.
647. Approaches (2) to (5) have been identified in Section 3.2.2.2 and are as follows:

   (2) according a general tax-exemption under domestic law or administrative practice.
   (3) according specific tax-exemptions or specific tax reductions under domestic law or administrative practice.
   (4) according a general tax-exemption under one or more tax treaties.
   (5) according specific tax-exemptions or specific tax reductions under one or more tax treaties.

6.3 FREEDOM OF ESTABLISHMENT, FREEDOM OF CAPITAL MOVEMENT AND FOREIGN SOVEREIGN WEALTH INVESTORS

6.3.1 Introduction

Section 6.3 will consider the (possible) implications of the freedom of establishment and freedom of capital movement for the taxation of foreign sovereign wealth investors, from a source State perspective. The CJEU and the EFTA Court have developed a decision tree to examine whether a national measure in the field of direct taxation is (in)compatible with the fundamental freedoms. The courts generally apply the following order of steps:

(1) Does the person invoking the fundamental freedoms have access to the TFEU or EEA Agreement and its fundamental freedoms?
(2) If so, does the national measure distinguish between cross-border situations and domestic situations in a manner incompatible with the fundamental freedoms? Are the cross-border situations and the domestic situations comparable, but treated differently, or are they different, but treated in the same way (comparability test)?
(3) If so, is this justified by overriding reasons in the public interest?[648]
(4) If so, is the national measure appropriate to achieve the objective?
(5) If so, does it go beyond what is necessary to achieve that objective (steps (3) to (5) are referred to as the justification test)?

6.3.2 Step (1): Access to the TFEU or EEA Agreement and the Freedom of Establishment and Freedom of Capital Movement

6.3.2.1 Purely Domestic Situations

The fundamental freedoms are aimed at contributing to the internal market by eliminating obstacles to the cross-border movement of goods, persons, services and capital. This implicates that the fundamental freedoms do not apply to purely domestic situations; i.e., situations not involving a cross-border element.[649] It also implicates

---

648. The CJEU does not always distinguish between step two and step three, in that it sometimes treats incomparability as a justification. Cf., for example, CJEU, 20 October 2011, Case C-284/09 (*European Commission v. Federal Republic of Germany*) with CJEU, 10 May 2012, Joined Cases C-338/11 to C-347/11 (*Santander Asset Management*). See also B. Terra & P. Wattel, *European Tax Law*, 6th edn., (Deventer: Kluwer, 2012), p. 45.
649. CJEU, 3 October 1990, Joined Cases C-54/88 (*Nino*), C-91/88 and C-14/89, Para. 11; CJEU, 27 June 1996, Case C-107/94 (*Asscher*), Para. 32. However, a purely internal situation is not considered present in cases where nationals of a Member State are, by reason of their conduct and with regard to their Member State of origin, in a situation which may be regarded as equivalent to that of any other person enjoying access to the fundamental freedoms.

that the freedoms do not prohibit *reverse* discrimination: residents of a Member State who are treated less favourably than comparable cross-border situations cannot rely upon EU law.[650]

6.3.2.2 Freedom of Establishment

6.3.2.2.1 Personal and Territorial Scope

Article 49 TFEU prohibits restrictions on the freedom of establishment of nationals of an EU Member State in the territory of another EU Member State. Although the concept of establishment is interpreted broadly by the CJEU,[651] its territorial scope is 'limited' to acts of establishment within the EU. In terms of personal scope, according to Article 54 TFEU, the freedom of establishment not only applies to natural persons (individuals) who are nationals of Member States,[652] but also to '[c]ompanies or firms formed in accordance with the law of a Member State and having their registered office, central administration or principal place of business within the [European] Union'. 'Companies or firms formed in accordance with the law of a Member State' refers to '[c]ompanies or firms constituted under civil or commercial law, including cooperative societies, and other legal persons governed by public or private law, save for those which are non-profit-making'.[653] So, companies and firms with the required nexus to an EU Member State are treated on equal footing with individuals who are nationals of an EU Member State.[654]

The CJEU has held that the freedom of establishment guaranteed by the Article 31 EEA Agreement is identical in substance to the freedom of establishment laid down in the TFEU.[655] The EEA Agreement uses the same definition of company or firm. As a result, the provisions dealing with the freedom of establishment in the TFEU and EEA Agreement need to be interpreted uniformly.

6.3.2.2.2 Material Scope (Acts of Establishment)

The CJEU and the EFTA Court interpret the concept of establishment broadly:

> The concept of establishment within the meaning of the [TFEU and EEA Agreement] is therefore a very broad one, allowing a Community [or EEA] national to

---

650. CJEU, 23 February 2006, Case C-513/03 (*Van Hilten-van der Heijden*); P. Matos, 'Reverse Discrimination and Direct Taxation in the EU', Chapter 9 in: D. Weber (ed.), *EU Income Tax Law: Issues for the Years Ahead*, IBFD 2013, Online Books IBFD.
651. CJEU, 30 November 1995, Case C-55/94 (*Reinhard Gebhard*), Para. 25.
652. Whether a natural person (individual) possesses the nationality of a Member State is determined solely by reference to the national law of the Member State concerned. *See* the *Final Act and Declarations of the Intergovernmental Conferences on the European Union, 7 February 1992, Declaration on nationality of a Member State*, Official Journal of the European Union, Vol. 35, C 191, 29 July 1992, p. 98.
653. Article 54 TFEU.
654. *Ibid.*
655. CJEU, 19 July 2012, Case C-48/11 (*A Oy*), Para. 21 and case law cited.

participate, on a stable and continuous basis, in the economic life of a Member State other than his State of origin and to profit therefrom, so contributing to economic and social interpenetration within the Community [or within the EEA] (...).[656]

The freedom of establishment includes the right for companies and firms with the required nexus to a Member State to set-up and manage agencies, branches or subsidiaries in another Member State.

According to constant case law, establishment involves the pursuit of a real and genuine economic activity by a national of one Member State through a fixed establishment in another Member State for an indefinite period.[657] Whether an entity conducts a real and genuine activity depends on the facts and circumstances, although some general guidelines can be derived from case law. The concept of 'economic activity' is used in other areas of EU law as well, such as the competition rules and the VAT Directive. It is, however, not entirely clear whether this concept has an identical meaning in different areas of EU law.[658] In the context of both the competition rules[659] and the VAT Directive,[660] the CJEU has repeatedly held that the mere acquisition, holding and sale of shares and other negotiable securities does not constitute an economic activity, basically because any returns are merely the fruits of the (passive) ownership of an asset. On the other hand, being directly or indirectly involved in the management of a company is sufficient to constitute an economic activity for VAT purposes,[661] whereas 'an entity which, owning controlling shareholdings in a company, actually exercises that control by involving itself directly or indirectly in the management thereof must be regarded as taking part in the economic activity carried on by the controlled undertaking'[662] under the EU competition rules. These concepts, which clearly require a more active ownership of assets, do not fully resemble the criterion the CJEU introduced in *Baars*, where it held that a situation involving a 'national of a Member State who has a holding in the capital of a company established in another Member State which gives him *definite influence* over the company's decisions and allows him to determine its activities'[663] falls within the material scope of the freedom of establishment. Different from the relevant test for purposes of the VAT Directive and the EU competition rules, the *Baars* criterion does not appear to require that the influence is *actually* exercised; instead, it is sufficient that a holding

---

656. CJEU, 30 November 1995, Case C-55/94 (*Reinhard Gebhard*), Para. 25; EFTA Court, 9 July 2014, Cases E-3/13 and E-20/13 (*Fred Olsen and Others and The Norwegian State*), Para. 94.
657. CJEU, 11 December 2007, Case C-438/05 (*International Transport Workers' Federation*), Para. 70; EFTA Court, 9 July 2014, Cases E-3/13 and E-20/13 (*Fred Olsen and Others and The Norwegian State*), Paras 95-97.
658. Different views can be found in D. Smit, *Freedom of Investment Between EU and Non-EU Member States and Its Impact on Corporate Income Tax Systems Within the European Union*, (Tilburg: CentER, 2011), p. 46.
659. CJEU, 10 January 2006, Case C-222/04 (*Cassa di Risparmio di Firenze SpA*), Para. 111.
660. CJEU, 12 January 2017, Case C-28/16 (*MVM Magyar Villamos Művek Zrt.*), Para. 31 and case law cited.
661. *Ibid.*, Paras 32-33 and case law cited.
662. CJEU, 10 January 2006, Case C-222/04 (*Cassa di Risparmio di Firenze SpA*), Para. 112.
663. CJEU, 13 April 2000, Case C-251/98 (*Baars*), Para. 22 (Italics added).

enables a national to exercise influence.[664] However, a shareholder that is able to exercise influence will normally do so in practice, so that the *Baars* criterion is typically associated with (more) active shareholders. Whether a holding allows definite influence has to be determined on a case-by-case basis; a holding of less than 50% could still constitute definite influence.[665] The EFTA Court has held that not only the involvement 'in the management of a group's companies', but also the involvement in '*other activities for a group*, such as managing a pool of resources (...) has to be regarded as a real and genuine economic activity, which constitutes establishment' (italics added).[666] It is, however, unclear whether the CJEU would follow this interpretation.

With respect to the purchasing and holding of immovable property, the CJEU has held that the freedom of establishment can only apply if the property is actively managed.[667] The mere holding of immovable property is insufficient to constitute an economic activity.

Further, it may not always be clear whether a situation is covered by the (material scope of the) freedom of establishment or the freedom of capital movement, particularly in case of cross-border shareholdings. This distinction, and its relevance in relation to foreign sovereign wealth investors, is discussed in more detail in Section 6.3.2.4 below.

6.3.2.2.3 Application to Sovereign Wealth Investors

As regards its material scope, it is noted that the framework discussed above equally applies to foreign sovereign wealth investors and other non-resident investors. An act of establishment involves the pursuit of a real and genuine economic activity by a national of one Member States through a fixed establishment in another Member State for an indefinite period. Whether an entity conducts a real and genuine activity depends on the facts and circumstances. In any case, sovereign wealth investors owning shares of a company established in a Member State that give them *definite influence* over the company's decisions and allow them to determine its activities, are regarded to conduct a real and genuine economic activity. This so-called *Baars* criterion is typically associated with (more) *active* foreign sovereign wealth investors.

Whether sovereign wealth investors are covered by the personal and territorial scope of the freedom of establishment is analysed below. In this respect, the distinction made in Section 2.8.3 between sovereign wealth investors based on their legal form is relevant and will be followed.

---

664. F. Pötgens & M. Straathof, 'Establishment and Substance of Intermediate and Other Holding Companies from an EU Law Perspective' (2016) 44 *Intertax* 608, p. 619.
665. For a discussion of relevant case law, *see* D. Smit, *Freedom of Investment Between EU and Non-EU Member States and Its Impact on Corporate Income Tax Systems Within the European Union*, (Tilburg: CentER, 2011), pp. 53–57.
666. EFTA Court, 9 July 2014, Cases E-3/13 and E-20/13 (*Fred Olsen and Others and The Norwegian State*), Para. 99.
667. CJEU, 14 September 2006, Case C-386/04 (*Centro di Musicologia Walter Stauffer*), Para. 19.

(i) Sovereign wealth investors constituted by a pool of assets within the State

In relation to sovereign wealth investors constituted by a pool of assets within the State, such as Norway's GPFG, the question arises whether a Member State and its government can be considered a national of a Member State for purposes of the freedom of establishment. This concerns the question whether or not a Member State can be a national of itself.[668] As explained in Section 6.3.2.2.1 above, the term 'companies or firms formed in accordance with the law of a Member State' includes (other) legal persons governed by public law.[669] Member States themselves can be expected to be legal persons governed by public law[670] and to have legal personality,[671] as this enables them to carry out their duties, conduct transactions on their own behalf, hold the ownership of assets, enter into (political) agreements, etc. For purposes of the freedom of establishment, a legal person governed by public law is furthermore required to have its registered office (*statutaire zetel*), central administration (*hoofdbestuur*) or principal place of business (*hoofdvestiging*) within a Member State. These criteria, which together establish the required nexus of a company or firm to the EU/EEA-EFTA,[672] have probably been drafted without having in mind a Member State itself as a legal person governed by public law, unless the reference to central administration includes the central government. One might argue that, in the absence of a registered office, central administration or principal place of business, a Member State does not have access to the freedom of establishment. In contrast, others might argue that such a strict interpretation would not only be contrary to the purpose of the three criteria, namely to establish a connection to the EU or EEA-EFTA States, but also to the purpose of the freedom of establishment in general, namely to contribute to an internal market with free competition. In the author's view, a Member State has a 'natural' connection to the EU/EEA-EFTA and as an economic operator within the internal market it should be protected by the freedom of establishment in the same way as its competitors in similar circumstances. This interpretation, under which a Member State is treated as a national of an EU Member State respectively EEA-EFTA State, would best serve the freedom of establishment and the internal market.

(ii) Sovereign wealth investors established as or within a separate legal entity other than the State itself

Sovereign wealth investors established as a separate legal identity under public law or private law of a Member State should have the required nexus, provided they

---

668. It is noted that a State, having a separate legal personality, can be the subject of (its 'own') national (tax) legislation.
669. Article 54 TFEU/Art. 34 EEA Agreement.
670. For example, under the laws of the Netherlands, the (Dutch) State, provinces, municipalities and other entities that exercise public functions are legal persons of public law (*publiekrechtelijke rechtspersonen*), have a separate legal personality.
671. Bin Cheng, *General Principles of Law as Applied by International Courts and Tribunals*, Grotius Classic Reprint Series, No. 2, (New York: Cambridge University Press, 2006), pp. 182–183, fn. 489.
672. CJEU, 14 December 2006, Case C-170/05 (*Denkavit Internationaal BV*), Para. 22.

have their registered office, central administration or principal place of business within a Member State.

(iii) Sovereign wealth investors organized as a (legal) entity without a separate legal personality

In relation to sovereign wealth investors organized as a (legal) entity without a separate legal personality, the question arises whether an entity without a legal personality, such as a partnership, qualifies as a 'company or firm'. The EFTA Court has held that the right of establishment is not restricted to legal entities having a legal personality.[673] In a recent case, the CJEU was asked the question whether a UK trust could rely on the freedom of establishment. This is a question as to the scope of the concept of 'other legal persons governed by public or private law'. The CJEU explained that this concept 'extends to an entity which, under national law, possesses rights and obligations that enable it to act in its own right within the legal order concerned, notwithstanding the absence of a particular legal form, and which is profit-making'.[674] This reasoning is in line with the purpose of the freedom of establishment to contribute to an internal market with free competition. Based on the above, sovereign wealth investors without a separate legal identity, but formed in accordance with the law of a Member State, possessing rights and obligations that enable it to act in its own right and performing an act of establishment in another Member State, should be covered by the personal, territorial and material scope of the freedom of establishment.

6.3.2.3 *Freedom of Capital Movement*

6.3.2.3.1 *Personal and Territorial Scope*

Article 63(1) TFEU, in principle, not only prohibits restrictions on the movement of capital and payments between EU Member States, but also between EU Member States and non-EU Member States/third countries. Unlike the freedom of establishment, the TFEU (unilaterally) extends the free movement of capital and payments to third countries (i.e., universal territorial scope) and does not require an eligible entity or person (i.e., universal personal scope). According to the CJEU, the objectives of the liberalization of the free movement of capital with third countries include, in particular, 'that of ensuring the credibility of the single Community currency on world financial markets and maintaining financial centers with a world-wide dimension within the Member States'.[675] In literature, the unilateral extension of free movement of capital towards third countries is further explained by the wish to create a global capital

---

673. EFTA Court, 9 July 2014, Cases E-3/13 and E-20/13 (*Fred Olsen and Others and The Norwegian State*), Para. 93.
674. CJEU, 14 September 2017, Case C-646/15 (*Trustees of the P Panayi Accumulation & Maintenance Settlements*), Para. 29.
675. CJEU, 18 December 2007, Case C-101/05 (*A*), Para. 31.

market with free competition for capital.[676] The freedom of capital movement included in the TFEU has direct effect, also in relation to third countries.[677]

Different from Article 63(1) TFEU, Article 40 EEA Agreement does not accord universal territorial and personal scope to the freedom of capital movement. Its territorial scope is limited to the EEA-EFTA States/EU Member States, while its personal scope is limited to (capital belonging to) persons resident in an EU Member State/EEA-EFTA State.[678]

6.3.2.3.2 Material Scope (Capital Movements)

It follows from case law of the CJEU that the term capital movement is interpreted broadly. In the absence of a definition of 'movement of capital' in the TFEU, the CJEU has recognized that the – non-exhaustive – nomenclature annexed to an old Council Directive[679] has indicative value. Although profit distributions (dividends) are not expressly mentioned as capital movements, the CJEU has held in *Verkooijen*, concerning a Dutch resident individual who received dividends from a company listed on the Belgian stock exchange, that receipt of dividends 'necessarily presupposes participation in new or existing undertakings referred to in (...) the nomenclature'[680] and that receipt of dividends from the Belgian company could 'also be linked to "Acquisition by residents of foreign securities dealt in on a stock exchange" as referred to in (...) the nomenclature'.[681] This judgment seems to indicate that income from a capital movement according to the nomenclature, itself qualifies as a capital movement. In more recent case law concerning the taxation of outbound cross-border dividends, the CJEU no longer referred to the nomenclature in examining the free movement of capital.[682] As such, the classification of profit distributions as capital movements appears to be a given.[683] This makes sense for the nomenclature is non-exhaustive[684] and should 'not be interpreted as restricting the scope of the principle of full liberalization of capital movements'.[685]

---

676. For an overview of relevant literature, *see* D. Smit, *Freedom of Investment Between EU and Non-EU Member States and its Impact on Corporate Income Tax Systems Within the European Union*, (Tilburg: CentER, 2011), pp. 401–402.
677. CJEU, 18 December 2007, Case C-101/05 (*Skatteverket v. A*), Para. 26.
678. Article 40 EEA Agreement.
679. *Council Directive 88/361 EEC of 24 June 1988 for the implementation of Article 67 of the Treaty*, Official Journal of the European Union, Vol. 31, L 178, 8 July 1988, p. 5.
680. CJEU, 6 June 2000, Case C-35/98 (*Verkooijen*), Para. 28 (referring to Heading I(2)); Opinion of Advocate General Sharpston, 19 July 2012, Case C-342/10 (*European Commission v. Republic of Finland*), Para. 28.
681. *Ibid.* (*Verkooijen*), Para. 29 (referring to Heading III.A(2)).
682. For instance, CJEU, 8 November 2007, Case C-379/05 (*Amurta*); CJEU, 3 June 2010, Case C-487/08 (*European Commission v. Kingdom of Spain*); CJEU, 20 October 2011, Case C-284/09 (*European Commission v. Federal Republic of Germany*); CJEU, 8 November 2012, Case C-342/10 (*European Commission v. Republic of Finland*).
683. Cf. CJEU, 13 November 2012, Case C-35/11 (*Test Claimants in the FII Group Litigation*), Para. 103.
684. CJEU, 17 September 2008, Case C-182/08 (*Glaxo Welcome*), Para. 39 and case law cited.
685. *Council Directive 88/361 EEC of 24 June 1988 for the implementation of Article 67 of the Treaty*, Official Journal of the European Union, Vol. 31, L 178, 8 July 1988, p. 5.

Chapter 6: European Tax Law Aspects

The concept of capital movement is in particular concerned with two main categories: direct investments and portfolio investments.[686] According to the Explanatory Notes to the nomenclature, *direct investments* are '[i]nvestments of all kinds by natural persons or commercial, industrial or financial undertakings, and which serve to establish or to maintain lasting and direct links between the person providing the capital and the entrepreneur to whom or the undertaking to which the capital is made available in order to carry on an economic activity'. The nomenclature further provides a list of examples of direct investments.[687] In assessing whether a direct investment exists, the CJEU primarily focuses on whether it concerns a shareholding that gives the shareholder the *possibility* to participate effectively in the management and control of the company.[688] Such a possibility also constitutes an act of establishment for the purpose of the freedom of establishment (Section 6.3.2.2.2 of this chapter). Thus, the concept of direct investment and the concept of establishment overlap to a large extent.[689] Whether an investor is able to effectively participate in the management and control depends on the facts and circumstances, taking into account company law and other factors.[690] Based on the above, the concept of direct investment is typically associated with (more) *active* investors. On the other hand, *portfolio investments* are described by the CJEU as the acquisition of securities on the capital market solely with the intention of making a financial investment without any intention to influence the management and control of the undertaking.[691] The concept of portfolio investment is typically associated with *passive* investors. Examples of portfolio investments listed in the nomenclature include securities dealt in and not dealt in on a stock exchange, bonds, investments in real estate, credits, financial loans, and others. In the author's view, by analogy with *Verkooijen*, income from portfolio investments should also qualify as capital movements for the purposes of the TFEU.

---

686. CJEU, 21 October 2010, Case C-81/09 (*Idrima Tipou*), Para. 48; D. Smit, *Freedom of Investment Between EU and Non-EU Member States and Its Impact on Corporate Income Tax Systems Within the European Union*, (Tilburg: CentER, 2011), p. 67.
687. (1) Establishment and extension of branches or new undertakings belonging solely to the person providing the capital, and the acquisition in full of existing undertakings; (2) Participation in new or existing undertaking with a view to establishing or maintaining lasting economic links; (3) Long-term loans with a view to establishing or maintaining lasting economic links; (4) Reinvestment of profits with a view to companies limited by shares or otherwise, to maintaining lasting economic links.
688. CJEU, 13 November 2012, Case C-35/11 (*Test Claimants in the FII Group Litigation*), Para. 102 and case law cited. This terminology seems to be derived from the Explanatory Notes to Heading I-2 of the nomenclature (Participation in new or existing undertaking with a view to establishing or maintaining lasting economic links) in which it is stated that 'there is participation in the nature of direct investment where the block of shares held by a natural person of another undertaking or any other *holder enables the shareholder*, either pursuant to the provisions of national laws relating to companies limited by shares or otherwise, *to participate effectively in the management of the company or in its control*' (Italics added).
689. D. Smit, *Freedom of Investment Between EU and Non-EU Member States and Its Impact on Corporate Income Tax Systems Within the European Union*, (Tilburg: CentER, 2011), p. 68.
690. *Ibid.*, pp. 69–71.
691. CJEU, 21 October 2010, Case C-81/09 (*Idrima Tipou*), Para. 48 and case law cited.

The nomenclature referred to by the CJEU applies to the free movement of capital in the EEA Agreement as well.[692] Since the CJEU has held that the relevant provisions on the free movement of capital in the TFEU and the EEA Agreement[693] are substantially identical, having the same legal scope,[694] the analysis for the EEA Agreement and the TFEU is the same.

6.3.2.3.3 Standstill Provision TFEU

In relation to capital movements to and from *third countries*, Article 64(1) TFEU allows restrictions on the free movement of capital imposed by national legislation which already existed on 31 December 1993, involving: (i) direct investment (including in real estate), (ii) establishment, (iii) the provision of financial services, or (iv) the admission of securities to capital markets.[695] The concept of direct investment versus portfolio investment was discussed in Section 6.3.2.3.2 of this chapter.

The list of capital movements mentioned in Article 64(1) TFEU is exhaustive and must be interpreted strictly.[696] Article 64(1) TFEU, which can also apply in the field of taxation, expresses the wish of EU Member States to partially maintain sovereignty with respect to capital movements to and from third countries.[697]

National tax measures adopted after 31 December 1993 may also fall under the scope of the grandfathering rule, provided that the new tax measure is, in essence, identical to the previous measure, or the new tax measure merely reduces or eliminates EU law infringements that existed under the previous measure.[698] In contrast, new tax measures which are different in approach than the previous measure and establish new procedures, are excluded from Article 64(1) TFEU.[699]

A national tax measure of an EU Member State can simultaneously impose restrictions on the free movement of capital involving direct investment, establishment, the provision of financial services, etc., and on the free movement of capital not involving such situations. In such case, an EU Member State can rely on Article 64(1) TFEU, but only to the extent that it concerns capital movements referred to in that provision.[700]

National measures which relate to capital movements and restrict *the provision of financial services*, can also be safeguarded by the standstill provision. The effect of this

---

692. Article 40 EEA Agreement refers to the application of Annex XII (Free movement of capital) to the EEA Agreement which, in its turn, refers to the nomenclature of capital movements in Annex I to Directive 88/361/EEC, as relied upon by the CJEU for the interpretation of Art. 63 TFEU.
693. Article 63 TFEU and Art. 40 EEA Agreement (and Annex XII).
694. CJEU, 20 October 2011, Case C-284/09 (*European Commission v. Federal Republic of Germany*), Para. 96 and case law cited.
695. For Bulgaria, Estonia and Hungary, the relevant date is 31 December 1999.
696. CJEU, 21 May 2015, Case C-560/13 (*Wagner-Raith*), Para. 21 and case law cited.
697. D. Smit, *Freedom of Investment Between EU and Non-EU Member States and Its Impact on Corporate Income Tax Systems Within the European Union*, (Tilburg: CentER, 2011), pp. 668–672.
698. CJEU, 10 April 2014, Case C-190/12 (*Emerging Markets Series*), Para. 48 and case law cited.
699. *Ibid.*
700. CJEU, 15 February 2017, Case C-317/15 (*X*), Paras 20–25.

particular derogation can be that portfolio investments, although not listed as a particular category in Article 64(1) TFEU, could effectively be safeguarded by the standstill provision. The application of this particular derogation requires that 'the national measure (...) relate[s] to capital movements that have a sufficiently close link with the provision of financial services, which requires that there be a causal link between the movement of capital and the provision of financial services'.[701] Because the scope of Article 64(1) is defined by particular capital movements, rather than particular persons, this provision could still apply to national measures which are (primarily) directed at the investor and not the financial service provider, on condition that the causal link can be established.[702] In *Wagner-Raith* (2015) and *X* (2017), the CJEU concluded that a causal link between the capital movements concerned and the provision of financial services was present. *Wagner-Raith* concerned a German tax measure under which income from a non-EU collective investment fund was under conditions taxed on a notional instead of an actual basis. According to the CJEU, both the acquisition by German residents of units in foreign investment funds and the receipt of dividends from the investment funds qualify as capital movement,[703] and both involve the existence of financial services provided by the funds to the investors.[704] The court added that the investment in a collective investment fund must be distinguished from a direct acquisition of company shares on the market, because investors investing directly do not benefit from such services.[705] Thus, in case of investors investing directly, there does not appear to be a (sufficient) link with the provision of financial services. Finally, the CJEU held that the German measure was 'liable to deter resident investors from acquiring units in non-resident investment funds and therefore results in those investors having recourse to the services of such funds less frequently'.[706] In *X*, a Dutch resident had opened a securities account with a banking institution outside the EU (Switzerland). The Dutch taxpayer had not reported the account to the Dutch tax authorities. According to the CJEU, there was a causal link in this case because the Dutch account holder transferred capital (money) to the Swiss securities account in order to benefit from management services of the Swiss bank.[707] As a result of this decision, the Dutch tax office was able to impose additional assessments under the extended recovery period applicable to foreigners.

It is obvious that these decisions have widened the scope of the standstill provision, to the detriment of the freedom of capital movement. As a result of these judgments, portfolio investments, although not listed as a category of capital movement in Article 64(1), could effectively be covered by the standstill provision if a causal link with the provision of financial services can be established. In both *Wagner-Raith* and *X*, the services were provided to resident investors of a Member State by service providers outside the EU (i.e., inbound financial services). In the author's view, it is

---

701. CJEU, 15 February 2017, Case C-317/15 (*X*), Para. 28 and case law cited.
702. *Ibid.*, Paras 32–33 and case law cited.
703. CJEU, 21 May 2015, Case C-560/13 (*Wagner-Raith*), Paras 23–26.
704. *Ibid.*, Para. 46.
705. *Ibid.*
706. CJEU, 21 May 2015, Case C-560/13 (*Wagner-Raith*), Para. 47.
707. CJEU, 15 February 2017, Case C-317/15 (*X*), Paras 29–30.

clear from *Wagner-Raith*, which concerned outbound investments in non-EU investment funds, that inbound portfolio investments by non-EU collective investment funds, including non-EU pension funds, should come within the concept of a capital movement involving the provision of financial services, irrespective of the location of the participants.[708] This means that discriminatory tax treatment of inbound investments by such funds could be safeguarded by the standstill clause of Article 64(1), also in respect of portfolio investments. Furthermore, there seems to be a tension between *Wagner-Raith* and *X*. In *Wagner-Raith*, the CJEU noted that the direct acquisition of company shares on the market does not involve the existence of financial services. However, in *X*, the mere opening by a resident of a Member State of a securities account with a Swiss bank was enough for the court to establish a causal link between the movement of capital and the provision of financial services. An investor investing directly, rather than through an investment fund, can use a securities account. It is unclear whether a tax measure that applies to such investments made through a securities account could be considered to involve the provision of financial services. This is even more so if such investments are made through an ordinary bank account. Finally, it is noted that a broad interpretation of the financial services exception in Article 64(1) TFEU, as was the case in *X*, carries the risk that the freedom of capital movement would to a large extent be deprived of its practical effect in relation to third countries.

The EEA Agreement does not contain a general grandfathering provision which allows tax measures that restrict the free movement of capital. In the author's opinion, this means that EU Member States should not be able to rely on Article 64(1) TFEU in relation to the EEA-EFTA States, as the EEA Agreement is more restrictive in this respect.

6.3.2.3.4 Application to Sovereign Wealth Investors

As regards its material scope, it is noted that the framework discussed above equally applies to foreign sovereign wealth investors and other non-resident investors. Since sovereign wealth investors are still predominately *passive* investors their investments will often be regarded as portfolio investments. However, since sovereign wealth investors are increasingly operating as *active* investors their investments could increasingly be regarded as direct investments.

Whether sovereign wealth investors are covered by the personal and territorial scope of the freedom of capital movement is analysed below. In this respect, the distinction made in Section 2.8.3 between sovereign wealth investors based on their legal form is relevant and will be followed.

---

708. Similarly, W. Egelie, Case note on CJEU, 15 February 2017, Case C-317/15 (*X*), *Nederlands Tijdschrift voor Fiscaal Recht* 2017/637.

Chapter 6: European Tax Law Aspects

(i) Sovereign wealth investors constituted by a pool of assets within the State

Sovereign wealth investors constituted by a pool of assets (arrangement) within the State are covered by the (universal) personal and territorial scope of the freedom of capital movement in the TFEU, whether established inside or outside the EU.

Article 40 EEA Agreement makes reference to a person resident in a Member State. Such reference gives rise to a question similar as under the freedom of establishment: does the personal scope include Member States and their governments themselves? Can a Member State be a resident in that Member State? The provisions dealing with the free movement of capital in the EEA Agreement have probably been drafted without having regard to a State itself and its government. One might argue that it would be impossible and contradictory for a State to meet this condition. In contrast, others might argue that such a strict interpretation would not only be contrary to the purpose of this condition, namely to establish the required nexus between that (legal) person and the EU or EEA-EFTA States, but also to the purpose of the freedom of capital movement in general, namely to contribute to an internal market with free competition. In the author's view, a Member State has that 'natural' connection and as an operator within the internal market it should be protected by the freedom of capital movement in the same way as other operators in similar circumstances. This interpretation, under which a Member State is treated as a resident in a Member State, would best serve the freedom of capital movement and the internal market. Moreover, the CJEU has held that, *in the context of the relations governed by the EEA Agreement*,[709] the relevant provision on the free movement of capital in the TFEU and EEA Agreement[710] are substantially identical provisions having the same legal scope.[711] Both provisions would not have the same legal scope if an Member State itself and its government cannot be a person resident in an EU Member State/EEA-EFTA State for purposes of the free movement of capital in the EEA Agreement. Based on the above, it is argued that an EU Member State/EEA-EFTA State needs to be treated as a resident under Article 40 EEA Agreement.

(ii) Sovereign wealth investors established as or within a separate legal entity other than the State itself

SWFs, central banks and SWEs established as a separate legal identity under public law or private law fall within the personal and territorial scope of the freedom of capital movement in the TFEU, whether established inside or outside the EU.

Such sovereign wealth investors will be covered by the personal scope of the freedom of capital movement in the EEA Agreement (Article 40 EEA Agreement), if they qualify as a person resident in an EU Member State/EEA-EFTA State. The EEA Agreement does not indicate when a person meets this condition. The purpose of this condition is to establish personal nexus, something not required under Article 63(1)

---

709. Being capital movements between EEA-EFTA States and between EU Member States and EEA-EFTA States.
710. Article 63 TFEU and Art. 40 EEA Agreement (and Annex XII).
711. CJEU, 20 October 2011, Case C-284/09 (*European Commission v. Federal Republic of Germany*), Para. 96 and case law cited.

TFEU because of its universal scope. As the EEA Agreement distinguishes between natural persons and legal persons, the more general term 'person' seems to include legal persons – of public law and private law – as well. However, it is not clear when a legal person is a resident in an EU Member State/EEA-EFTA State. Be that as it may, EU Member States should in the author's view, in any case, be bound by the wider (and universal) personal scope of Article 63(1) TFEU, also vis-à-vis EEA-EFTA States. This limits any potential issue to the application of Article 40 EEA Agreement by the EEA-EFTA States. Nevertheless, the author expects sovereign wealth investors established and managed and controlled in a Member State to have the required personal nexus, and so to be covered by the personal scope of Article 40 EEA Agreement.

(iii) Sovereign wealth investors organized as a (legal) entity without a separate legal personality

Sovereign wealth investors organized as a (legal) entity without a separate legal personality, such as partnerships, are covered by the universal personal and territorial scope of the freedom of capital movement in the TFEU.

With respect to the freedom of capital movement in the EEA Agreement, the question arises whether an entity without legal personality, such as a partnership, can be a person that is a resident in an EU Member State/EEA-EFTA State. Based on the fact that the CJEU has held that, *in the context of the relations governed by the EEA Agreement*,[712] Article 63(1) TFEU and Article 40 EEA Agreement are substantially identical provisions having the same legal scope, and in order to give full effect to the freedom of capital movement and the rights that it grants, the author answers this question affirmatively.

6.3.2.4 *Freedom of Establishment Versus Freedom of Capital Movement: Order of Precedence*

According to European case law, the tax treatment of dividends may fall within the scope of the freedom of establishment and freedom of capital movement.[713] As regards sovereign wealth investors, the relevance of the applicable freedom in third country situations (excluding EEA-EFTA situations) is obvious; only the freedom of capital movement has universal scope. In intra-EU/EEA situations, its relevance is less obvious, because the CJEU interprets the freedoms in a similar fashion (creating legal certainty).[714] However, as will be explained in this section below, also in intra-EU/EEA situations the applicable freedom can be relevant as regards sovereign wealth investors.

---

712. Being capital movements between EEA-EFTA States and between EU Member States and EEA-EFTA States.
713. CJEU, 10 February 2011, Joined Cases C-436/08 and C-437/08 (*Haribo Lakritzen and Österreichische Salinen*), Para. 89 and case law cited; CJEU, 18 June 2009, Case C-303/07 (*Aberdeen Property Fininvest*), Para. 30.
714. B. Terra & P. Wattel, *European Tax Law*, 6th edn., (Deventer: Kluwer, 2012), p. 49.

From *Test Claimants in the FII Group Litigation*,[715] concerning dividends received by a UK resident company from non-EU resident companies, and *Emerging Markets Series*,[716] concerning dividends paid by a Polish resident company to a US investment fund, rules can be derived regarding the issue of precedence.[717] In this respect, it is necessary to look at the purpose of a domestic tax measure, and to distinguish between: (i) direct investments; shareholdings that enable the shareholder a definite influence over the decisions of the company and to determine its activities, and (ii) portfolio investments; shareholdings acquired solely with the intention of making a financial investment, with no intention of influencing the management and control of the company. In addition, a distinction should be made between intra-EU/EEA situations and third country situations.

In intra-EU/EEA situations, the following rules apply regarding the order of precedence:

(1) if a domestic tax measure exclusively applies to direct investments, it is exclusively governed by the freedom of establishment (purpose approach);[718]
(2) if a domestic tax measure exclusively applies to portfolio investments, it falls exclusively within the scope of the freedom of capital movement (purpose approach);[719]
(3) if a domestic tax measure applies to both direct investments and portfolio investments – i.e., a general tax measure – it must be examined in the light of the freedom of establishment in case of a direct investment, and in the light of the free movement of capital in case of a portfolio investment (factual approach).[720]

In non-EU/EEA situations, the following rules apply regarding the order of precedence:

(1) if a domestic tax measure exclusively applies to direct investments, neither the freedom of establishment, nor the freedom of capital movement applies (purpose approach);[721]
(2) if a domestic tax measure exclusively applies to portfolio investments, it must be examined in the light of the freedom of capital movement (purpose approach);[722]

---

715. CJEU, 13 November 2012, Case C-35/11 (*Test Claimants in the FII Group Litigation*).
716. CJEU, 10 April 2014, Case C-190/12 (*Emerging Markets Series*), Para. 32.
717. *See also*, E. Nijkeuter & M. de Wilde, 'FII 2 and the Applicable Freedoms of Movement in Third Country Situations' (2013) 22 *EC Tax Review* 250.
718. CJEU, 13 November 2012, Case C-35/11 (*Test Claimants in the FII Group Litigation*), Para. 91.
719. *Ibid.*, Para. 92.
720. *Ibid.*, Paras 93–94.
721. *Ibid.*, Para. 98.
722. *Ibid.*, Para. 92.

(3) if a domestic tax measure applies to both direct investments and portfolio investments – i.e., a general tax measure – it must be examined in the light of the free movement of capital (purpose approach).[723]

The rules regarding the order of precedence in intra-EU/EEA situations could put more emphasis on the personal scope of the freedom of establishment in situations involving *direct investments*. In intra-EU/EEA situations involving direct investments, tax measures aimed at such investments, as well as general tax measures, must exclusively be examined in the light of the freedom of establishment. However, the freedom of establishment does not apply if a taxpayer falls outside its personal scope. The analysis in Section 6.3.2.2.3 shows that the application of the concept of 'companies and firms' is not entirely clear regarding sovereign wealth investors constituted by a pool of assets within a State. As regards general tax measures, falling outside the personal scope of the freedom of establishment might have as an absurd consequence that an EU/EEA resident sovereign wealth investor would enjoy less protection than a non-EU/EEA resident sovereign wealth investor in similar circumstances; the latter would have access to the freedom of capital movement, whereas the former would not. If a sovereign wealth investor would fall outside the personal scope of the freedom of establishment, it would need to be able to rely on the general non-discrimination provision of Article 18 TFEU/Article 4 EEA Agreement in order to enjoy protection.

6.3.3 Step (2): Comparability

The general principle underlying the comparability analysis under European law is that 'discrimination can arise only through the application of different rules to comparable situations or the application from the same rule to different situations'.[724] Based on recent case law, it is now clear that discrimination of non-residents is not only possible in relation to residents (*vertical comparability*), but also in relation to other

---

723. *Ibid.*, Paras 99–104. According to the CJEU, taking account of the particular facts and circumstances with respect to general tax measures in third country situations, as suggested by the UK, Germany, France and the Netherlands, 'would produce effects incompatible with Article 64(1) TFEU' (the standstill provision). In this respect, the CJEU finds that the standstill provision for the free movement of capital is relevant for the interpretation of the material scope of the free movement of capital. The standstill provision refers to the movement of capital involving establishment or direct investment. Such capital movements are characterized by the possibility for the shareholder to effectively participate in the management and control of the company. The author believes the CJEU's line of reasoning to be the following. Capital movements involving establishment or direct investment are acts of establishment as well as capital movements. However, since the freedom of establishment is not capable of applying to third country situations, there is no need to determine which freedom of movement takes precedence in case of general tax measures, unlike in intra-EU situations. Consequently, the freedom of capital movement is relied upon. Capital movements not involving establishment or direct investment are not acts of establishment and, therefore, covered by the freedom of capital movement. In summary, in third country situations, the paths always lead to the free movement of capital when tax measures with a general purpose are involved.
724. CJEU, 14 February 1995, Case C-279/93 (*Schumacker*), Para. 30.

non-residents (*horizontal comparability*).⁷²⁵ This distinction is followed below when discussing the general guidelines in regard to the comparability analysis, and their application to sovereign wealth investors.

It is important to note from the outset that, in the context of the free movement of capital, the CJEU addresses the issue of comparability in intra-EU situations and third country situations in the same way.⁷²⁶ Furthermore, the CJEU and the EFTA Court do not distinguish between the freedom of establishment and freedom of capital movement in addressing the comparability question.

6.3.3.1 *Vertical Comparability*

The CJEU and the EFTA Court (often) use a two-step comparability analysis.⁷²⁷ As a first step, the courts determine whether the cross-border situation is prima facie comparable to a domestic situation at all (prima facie comparison). National (tax) measures which treat such cross-border situations less favourably than domestic situations are, in principle, prohibited, because such measures may, for example, discourage non-residents from acquiring, creating or maintaining a subsidiary in another State (inbound investments), or from making investments in another State (outbound investments). In the context of direct taxes, the courts have constantly held that, as a general rule, residents and non-residents are not comparable.⁷²⁸ However, once a Member State, either unilaterally or by way of a convention, imposes tax on income, not only of residents, but also on income of non-residents, their situation becomes prima facie comparable.⁷²⁹ This also applies if a Member State tax-exempts payments to its residents, while creating a risk of a series of tax charges or economic double taxation by imposing tax on payments to non-residents.⁷³⁰ In this respect, the (absence of) taxation in another State is irrelevant, since 'it is solely because of the exercise by [the Member] State of its taxing powers that (...) a risk of a series of charges to tax may arise'.⁷³¹ Thus, once a Member State chooses to exercise its taxing jurisdiction over non-residents, these non-residents find themselves in a situation

---

725. CJEU, 24 February 2015, Case C-512/13 (*Sopora*).
726. For a discussion of relevant case law, *see* D. Smit, *Freedom of Investment Between EU and Non-EU Member States and Its Impact on Corporate Income Tax Systems Within the European Union*, (Tilburg: CentER, 2011), pp. 527–540.
727. P. Wattel, 'Non-Discrimination *à la Cour*: The ECJ's (Lack of) Comparability Analysis in Direct Tax Cases' (2015) 55 *European Taxation* 542.
728. CJEU, 14 February 1995, Case C-279/93 (*Schumacker*), Para. 31; CJEU, 12 June 2003, Case C-234/01 (*Arnoud Gerritse*), Paras 43–45; CJEU, 14 December 2006, Case C-170/05 (*Denkavit Internationaal BV*), Para. 24; CJEU, 22 December 2008, Case C-282/07 (*Truck Center*), Para. 38.
729. CJEU, 17 September 2015, Joined Cases C-10/14, C-14/14 and C-17/14 (*Miljoen, X, Société Générale*), Para. 67; CJEU, 10 April 2014, Case C-190/12 (*Emerging Markets Series*), Para. 58 and case law cited; CJEU, 19 November 2009, Case C-540/07 (*European Commission v. Italian Republic*), Paras 51–52 and case law cited; CJEU, 18 June 2009, Case C-303/07 (*Aberdeen Property Fininvest*), Paras 42–43 and case law cited, and Para. 54.
730. CJEU, 17 September 2015, Joined Cases C-10/14, C-14/14 and C-17/14 (*Miljoen, X, Société Générale*), Para. 68; CJEU, 10 April 2014, Case C-190/12 (*Emerging Markets Series*), Para. 58 and case law cited.
731. CJEU, 12 December 2006, Case C-374/04 (*Test Claimants in Class IV of the ACT Group Litigation*), Para. 70; CJEU, 8 November 2007, Case C-379/05 (*Amurta*), Para. 39; CJEU, 18

prima facie comparable to that of residents as regards the risk of a series of charges to tax.[732] Further, a Member State cannot rely on a neutralizing measure granted unilaterally by another (Member or third) State to justify its more burdensome taxation of non-residents.[733] However, a Member State can rely on a (bilateral) tax treaty, provided this treaty guarantees *full* neutralization[734] in the other State.[735]

As a second step, if a cross-border situation is prima facie comparable to a domestic situation, and treated less favourably, the courts focus on whether a cross-border situation is *objectively comparable* to a domestic situation.[736] Whether a non-resident is in an objectively (in)comparable situation to that of residents is determined in the light of the purpose of the national tax measure at issue,[737] and by taking account of any relevant distinguishing criteria or characteristics established by the national tax measure in question.[738] In *Hein Persche*,[739] Germany refused to allow tax deductions in respect of gifts in kind made by a German resident individual to a Portuguese resident organization which had charitable status according to Portuguese law. According to Germany, the recipient of the gift was not established in Germany and the German individual failed to produce a donation certificate in proper form. According to the CJEU:

> a body which is established in one Member State but satisfies the requirements imposed for [the] purpose [of determining the charitable status] by another Member State for the grant of tax advantages, is, in respect of the grant by the latter Member State of tax advantages intended to encourage the charitable activities

---

June 2009, Case C-303/07 (*Aberdeen Property Fininvest*), Paras 51 and 54; CJEU, 10 April 2014, Case C-190/12 (*Emerging Markets Series*), Para. 59.
732. CJEU, 17 September 2015, Joined Cases C-10/14, C-14/14 and C-17/14 (*Miljoen, X, Société Générale*), Para. 69 and case law cited.
733. CJEU, 8 November 2007, Case C-379/05 (*Amurta*), Para. 78; CJEU, 3 June 2010, Case C-487/08 (*European Commission v. Kingdom of Spain*), Para. 66.
734. Meaning that 'the tax withheld at source under national legislation can be set off against the tax due in the other Member State in the full amount of the difference in treatment arising under the national legislation'. See CJEU, 17 September 2015, Joined Cases C-10/14, C-14/14 and C-17/14 (*Miljoen, X, Société Générale*), Para. 79.
735. CJEU, 17 September 2015, Joined Cases C-10/14, C-14/14 and C-17/14 (*Miljoen, X, Société Générale*), Paras 77–80.
736. With respect to Art. 49 TFEU (which is identical in substance to Art. 31 EEA Agreement), see e.g., CJEU, 18 June 2009, Case C-303/07 (*Aberdeen Property Fininvest*), Para. 32 and case law cited. With respect to Art. 63 TFEU and Art. 65 TFEU, see e.g., CJEU, 10 April 2014, Case C-190/12 (*Emerging Markets Series*), Paras 54–57 and case law cited; CJEU, 10 May 2012, Joined Cases C-338/11 to C-347/11 (*Santander Asset Management*), Paras 20–23 and case law cited. With respect to Art. 40 EEA Agreement, see e.g., EFTA Court, 23 November 2004, Case E-1/04 (*Fokus Bank*), Para. 28 and case law cited.
737. Cf. CJEU, 8 November 2012, Case C-342/10 (*European Commission v. Republic of Finland*), Para. 36 and case law cited; CJEU, 20 October 2011, Case C-284/09 (*European Commission v. Federal Republic of Germany*), Para. 53; CJEU, 3 June 2010, Case C-487/08 (*European Commission v. Kingdom of Spain*), Para. 48; CJEU, 19 November 2009, Case C-540/07 (*European Commission v. Italian Republic*), Para. 50; CJEU, 27 January 2009, Case C-318/07 (*Hein Persche*), Paras 50–52.
738. CJEU, 10 April 2014, Case C-190/12 (*Emerging Markets Series*), Para. 61 and case law cited; CJEU, 10 May 2012, Joined Cases C-338/11 to C-347/11 (*Santander Asset Management*), Para. 27 and case law cited.
739. CJEU, 27 January 2009, Case C-318/07 (*Hein Persche*).

concerned, in a situation comparable to that of bodies recognised as having charitable purposes which are established in the latter Member State.[740]

Hein Persche is consistent with previous and subsequent other European case law:[741] objective comparability is determined, unilaterally and rather strictly, in the light of the objective of the national tax measure at issue, and by the conditions laid down in the national tax legislation of a State as imposed on its residents. In this respect, 'only the relevant distinguishing criteria established by the legislation in question must be taken into account in determining whether the difference in treatment resulting from that legislation reflects an objectively different situation'.[742] This substantive approach regarding comparability applies without distinction to non-resident 'shareholders', 'share companies', 'pension funds' or 'investment funds'.[743] In the context of CIVs, this substantive approach means that, if the position of the participants in the fund is not a relevant element under the national tax measure in question, comparability between resident and non-resident funds needs to be carried out only at the level of the fund vehicle, and vice versa.[744] As regards other types of non-resident taxpayers, this rule implies that comparability generally takes place at the level of the non-resident taxpayer itself.[745] Furthermore, from case law it can be derived that the conditions (distinguishing criteria) may not be such that they would deprive the freedoms of all effectiveness, such as requiring a legal form unknown to the legal systems of other States (Aberdeen),[746] or requiring that non-residents (fully) comply with local source State regulations, such as the EU directive on undertakings for collective investment in transferable securities (Emerging Markets Series). In the latter case, Poland required a US resident investment fund to comply with an EU directive, which the fund could not since the directive does not apply to investment funds established in third countries. The CJEU held that 'a requirement that [non-resident]

---

740. Ibid., Para. 50. Based on Hein Persche and other European case law, the Dutch Supreme Court decided that the Netherlands is not obliged to recognize the Finnish tax-exempt status of a Finnish resident CIV for Dutch tax purposes. Since the Finnish CIV did not satisfy the conditions imposed on Dutch resident entities for obtaining a tax-exempt status, relating to the nature of their activities or the destination of their profit, it was not comparable to a Dutch resident tax-exempt entity, according to the Dutch Supreme Court. Therefore, the Finnish CIV was not entitled to a refund of Dutch dividend withholding, unlike Dutch tax-exempt entities. Hoge Raad, 15 November 2013, No. 12/01866, BNB 2014/20.
741. CJEU, 14 September 2006, Case C-386/04 (Centro di Musicologia Walter Stauffer), Paras 40–42; CJEU, 8 November 2007, Case C-379/05 (Amurta); CJEU, 10 April 2014, Case C-190/12 (Emerging Markets Series), Paras 73 and 87; CJEU, 2 June 2016, Case C-252/14 (Pensioenfonds Metaal en Techniek), Para. 48.
742. CJEU, 2 June 2016, Case C-252/14 (Pensioenfonds Metaal en Techniek), Para. 49 and case law cited.
743. G. Hippert, 'The TFEU Eligibility of Non-EU Investment Funds Subjected to Discriminatory Dividend Withholding Taxes' (2016) 25 EC Tax Review 77.
744. CJEU, 10 May 2012, Joined Cases C-338/11 to C-347/11 (Santander Asset Management), Paras 39–40; CJEU, 10 April 2014, Case C-190/12 (Emerging Markets Series), Para. 62.
745. CJEU, 14 December 2006, Case C-170/05 (Denkavit Internationaal BV); CJEU, 8 November 2007, Case C-379/05 (Amurta); CJEU, 17 September 2015, Joined Cases C-10/14, C-14/14 and C-17/14 (Miljoen, X, Société Générale), Para. 69 and case law cited.
746. CJEU, 18 June 2009, Case C-303/07 (Aberdeen Property Fininvest), Para. 50. In the author's view, the consideration that the legal form unknown to the legal system of another Member State does not create an objective difference also applies to the free movement of capital.

investment funds be regulated in the same way as resident investment funds would deprive the principle of free movement of capital of any practical effect'.[747] In the author's view, based on *Emerging Markets Series*, the rule which prohibits requiring a legal form unknown to the legal systems of other States should apply without distinction between EU Member States and third countries.

The purpose of a national tax measure at issue can result in non-residents being in a situation incomparable to that of residents. Notably, in the Swedish case *Pensioenfonds Metaal en Techniek*, the CJEU concluded that a non-resident (Dutch) pension fund was not comparable to a (Swedish) resident pension fund in the light of the aim pursued by the Swedish national tax measure as regards resident pension funds.[748] Although both were subject to Swedish taxation at a rate of 15%, this rate was applied to a different tax base. A notional yield applicable to all asset classes, irrespective of the actual receipt of income, was used to calculate the tax base for Swedish pension funds, whereas the Dutch pension fund was subject to Swedish withholding tax on distributed dividends. The aim of the calculation method for Swedish pension funds was to achieve 'neutral taxation independent of the economic climate surrounding various kinds of assets and all of the kinds of pension products concerned'.[749] The CJEU held that such an aim, which presupposes taxation on the entire asset base, cannot be achieved in relation to non-resident pension funds pursuant to the limited taxing powers of Sweden under the tax treaty with the Netherlands.[750] The CJEU therefore held in that particular case that – in the light of the aim pursued by the Swedish national measure – a non-resident pension fund was not comparable to a Swedish pension fund. Although this decision seems to conflict with previous decisions of the court,[751] it does illustrate that a national tax measure, despite being capable of imposing a heavier tax burden on non-residents and discouraging non-residents from making investments in a Member State, can be compatible with EU law.

When a non-resident is objectively *comparable* to a resident, a Member State is, in principle, not allowed to tax that non-resident more heavily. That is to say, a State is allowed to apply a different tax method or different tax base and tax rate to non-residents as compared to *comparable* residents, but it is not allowed to impose a higher final tax burden, as defined, on those non-residents.[752] As a result, the taxation at the level of a non-resident must be compared with the overall taxation at the level of a comparable resident, which could consist of (a gross-based) withholding tax and (a net-based) income tax combined.[753] The relevant period for comparing the tax burden

---

747. CJEU, 10 April 2014, Case C-190/12 (*Emerging Markets Series*), Para. 67.
748. CJEU, 2 June 2016, Case C-252/14 (*Pensioenfonds Metaal en Techniek*), Paras 47–63.
749. *Ibid.*, Para. 53.
750. *Ibid.*, Paras 53–62.
751. In particular, CJEU, 17 September 2015, Joined Cases C-10/14, C-14/14 and C-17/14 (*Miljoen, X, Société Générale*).
752. CJEU, 14 December 2006, Case C-170/05 (*Denkavit Internationaal BV*); CJEU, 17 May 2017, Case C-68/15 (*X*), Para. 41.
753. CJEU, 17 September 2015, Joined Cases C-10/14, C-14/14 and C-17/14 (*Miljoen, X, Société Générale*), Paras 73–74.

is the period taken into account for residents; usually one tax year.[754] In comparing the tax burden, only expenses that are directly linked to an activity that has generated taxable income can be taken into account when calculating the tax burden of a comparable resident.[755] In this respect, the CJEU seems to distinguish between expenses related to business income and expenses related to passive (portfolio) income, and to follow a stricter approach in respect of the latter category.[756] For passive (portfolio) income, a direct link only exists for expenses directly linked to the actual payment of the passive income itself.[757] As a result, financing cost related to the acquisition of portfolio assets should not be taken into account when calculating the tax burden of a comparable resident (since such financing costs are not directly linked to the actual payment of the income itself). On the other hand, it seems much easier for the CJEU to establish a direct link between financing costs and business income.[758]

6.3.3.2 Horizontal Comparability

The previous discussion shows that the freedoms prohibit non-residents from being treated less favourably than objectively comparable residents (vertical comparability). The question has been raised before the CJEU whether the freedoms also prohibit discrimination among objectively comparable non-residents (horizontal comparability).

In *D.*[759] and subsequent case law, the CJEU ruled that the freedoms do not entitle residents of one Member State to the benefits that a second Member State has made available to residents of a third Member State *under a bilateral tax treaty*. It considered that a tax treaty is a product of reciprocal rights and obligations confined to residents of one of the two Member States, and that a specific tax treaty benefit is an integral part of the overall tax treaty, and contributes to its overall balance. In *Riskin & Timmermans*, the CJEU made explicit that this reasoning similarly applies to tax treaties concluded with third States.[760] So, from a source State perspective, non-residents

---

754. CJEU, 2 June 2016, Case C-252/14 (*Pensioenfonds Metaal en Techniek*), Para. 37 and case law cited.
755. CJEU, 17 September 2015, Joined Cases C-10/14, C-14/14 and C-17/14 (*Miljoen, X, Société Générale*), Para. 57.
756. Compare, CJEU, 12 June 2003, Case C-234/01 (*Arnoud Gerritse*) and CJEU, 15 February 2007, Case C-345/04 (*Centro Equestre da Lezíria Grande*), Paras 22–26, on the one hand, and CJEU, 17 September 2015, Joined Cases C-10/14, C-14/14 and C-17/14 (*Miljoen, X, Société Générale*), Para. 58 and CJEU, 2 June 2016, Case C-252/14 (*Pensioenfonds Metaal en Techniek*), on the other.
757. CJEU, 17 September 2015, Joined Cases C-10/14, C-14/14 and C-17/14 (*Miljoen, X, Société Générale*), Para. 58.
758. CJEU, 13 July 2016, Case C-18/15 (*Brisal*), Para. 48.
759. CJEU, 5 July 2005, Case C-376/03 (*D.*), Paras 53–63. For different views on this case, see D. Weber, 'Most-Favoured-Treatment under Tax Treaties Rejected in the European Community: Background and Analysis of the *D* Case: A Proposal to Include a Most-Favoured-Nation Clause in the EC Treaty' (2005) 33 *Intertax* 429; A. de Graaf & G. Janssen, 'The Implications of the Judgment in the *D* Case: The Perspective of Two Non-believers' (2005) 14 *EC Tax Review* 173.
760. CJEU, 30 June 2016, Case C-176/15 (*Riskin & Timmermans*), Para. 31; A. Dourado, 'The EU Free Movement of Capital and Third Countries: Recent Developments' (2017) 45 *Intertax* 192, p. 203.

covered by different tax treaties are not in an objectively comparable situation due the bilateral character of a tax treaty. With these decisions, the CJEU refuses to apply MFN treatment in case of bilateral tax treaty benefits (i.e., horizontal inter-State comparison). The question whether non-residents from the same State that are, and those that are not entitled to the same benefit under a tax treaty with a Member State can be objectively comparable (i.e., horizontal intra-State comparison), has not been explicitly answered by the CJEU. The issue of horizontal intra-State comparison in case of tax treaty benefits was at stake in *ATC Group Litigation*.[761] The question referred to the CJEU was whether the 'limitation of benefits' clause under the UK – Netherlands tax treaty could constitute discrimination.[762] Based on this clause, some tax treaty residents of the Netherlands were denied a UK tax treaty benefit, while other tax treaty residents of the Netherlands were entitled to this benefit, thus resulting in different treatment between tax treaty residents from the same Member State. The CJEU answered that the 'limitation of benefits' provision did not constitute (horizontal) discrimination, by referring to *D*.[763] However, in doing so, the court wrongly referred to non-residents from different States, rather than to non-residents from the same Member State.[764] In another case, *Riskin & Timmermans*,[765] concerning two Belgian resident individuals who had received dividends from a company established in Poland, the CJEU had to deal with the issue of horizontal intra-State comparison, but this time in an inbound situation. Mr Riskin and Ms Timmermans were denied to credit Polish dividend withholding tax against Belgian income tax, pursuant to the conditions of the Belgium – Poland tax treaty. Under tax treaties concluded with third States, Belgium would have allowed foreign tax to be credited against Belgian income tax, without imposing similar conditions. The CJEU concluded that Belgian residents covered by the tax treaty with Poland are not objectively comparable to Belgian residents covered by other tax treaties.[766] It held, by referring to *D.*, that:

> [i]n the context of bilateral tax conventions, it follows from the case-law of the Court that the scope of such a convention is limited to the natural or legal persons defined by it. Likewise, the benefits granted by it are an integral part of all the rules under the convention and contribute to the overall balance of mutual relations between the two contracting States (…). It must be noted (…) that that situation is the same with regard to double taxation conventions concluded with Member States or with third States.[767]

---

761. CJEU, 12 December 2006, Case C-374/04 (*Test Claimants in Class IV of the ACT Group Litigation*), Paras 82–93.
762. On the topic of the EU law compatibility of limitation of benefit clauses, *see* F. Debelva et al., 'LOB Clauses and EU-Law Compatibility: A Debate Revived by BEPS?' (2015) 24 *EC Tax Review* 132; J. Calejo Guerra, 'Limitation on Benefits Clauses and EU Law' 51 (2011) *European Taxation* 85.
763. CJEU, 12 December 2006, Case C-374/04 (*Test Claimants in Class IV of the ACT Group Litigation*), Paras 88–94.
764. *Ibid.*, Paras 91–94.
765. CJEU, 30 June 2016, Case C-176/15 (*Riskin & Timmermans*).
766. *Ibid.*, Para. 34.
767. *Ibid.*, Para. 31.

Chapter 6: European Tax Law Aspects

In the author's view, this strongly indicates that non-residents from the same State that are, and those that are not entitled to the same tax treaty benefit, will not be held objectively comparable by the CJEU. The only difference with both *D.* and *Riskin & Timmermans* is that the taxpayers in these cases were covered by a tax treaty, but claimed benefits of other tax treaties. The issue of horizontal comparability between non-residents from the same Member State that are, and those that are not entitled to the same benefit under a tax treaty with another Member State, involves one tax treaty only. However, based on *Riskin & Timmermans*, this difference does not appear to be relevant, because a tax treaty benefit accorded to one non-resident but not to another non-resident from the same State, is also an integral part of the wider treaty and contributes to its overall balance. The previous discussion should be distinguished from decisions such as *Saint-Gobain*[768] and *Gottardo*.[769] These judgments do not concern the issue of horizontal discrimination (MFN treatment) but deal with vertical discrimination (NT of non-residents). Based on *Sain-Gobain*, a company of Member State A with a permanent establishment in Member State B could be entitled to benefits under tax treaties concluded by Member State B with other States, on the same conditions applicable to companies of Member State B. Based on *Gottardo*, residents of other Member States could be entitled to the same benefits as those enjoyed by residents of Member State A under a treaty between Member State A and third States.

In the beginning of 2015, in *Sopora*,[770] the CJEU for the first time explicitly accepted that a freedom, the freedom of movement of workers in this case, could prohibit discrimination between non-residents (horizontal comparability). This case concerned a Dutch wage tax facility, which allowed a fixed exemption of 30% of employment income and was open only to foreign high-skilled expatriates who had lived outside a certain radius from the Dutch border during a certain period prior to their employment in the Netherlands. The court mainly based its decision on the wording of Article 45(2) TFEU, which prohibits discrimination 'between workers of the Member States', but also referred to Article 26 TFEU, which instructs the EU to establish and develop the functioning of the internal market.[771] In *Sopora*, horizontal comparability under a tax treaty was not at stake. The question arises whether the *Sopora* decision also applies to the other freedoms. The freedom of establishment and freedom to provide services clearly lack language similar to Article 45(2); they both focus on vertical comparability. The language used in the free movement of capital leaves more room for a horizontal comparability. In literature, several arguments have been identified in favour of extending the *Sopora* decision to all other freedoms, including:[772]

– the CJEU's converging interpretation of the freedoms;

---

768. CJEU, 21 September 1999, Case C-307/97 (*Saint-Gobain*).
769. CJEU, 15 January 2002, Case C-55/00 (*Elide Gottardo*).
770. CJEU, 24 February 2015, Case C-512/13 (*Sopora*).
771. *Ibid.*, Para. 25.
772. CFE ECJ Task Force, Opinion Statement ECJ-TF 3/2015 on the Decision of the European Court of Justice in *C.G. Sopora* (Case C-512/13), on 'Horizontal Discrimination' (2016) 56 *European Taxation*; E. Kemmeren, 'Sopora: *A Welcome Landmark Decision on Horizontal Comparison*' (2015) 24 *EC Tax Review* 178.

- the CJEU's reference to Article 26 TFEU, paragraph 2 which provides that the 'internal market shall comprise an area without internal frontiers in which the free movement of goods, persons, services and capital is ensured (...)'. All freedoms appear to contribute to the internal market and not extending *Sopora* to the other freedoms would be contrary to the establishment and functioning of the internal market;
- Article 18 TFEU, which prohibits any discrimination on grounds of nationality and is broad enough to cover 'horizontal discrimination'. Since the fundamental freedoms are *lex specialis* to Article 18 TFEU, this general provision should govern any discrimination not covered by a fundamental freedom, including horizontal discrimination.

However, in the context of the free movement of capital, the CJEU currently does not seem to allow the possibility of horizontal comparability in relation to third States. Four years prior to *Sopora*, the CJEU already held in *Haribo and Salinen* that 'the different treatment of income from one non-member State compared to income from another non-member State is not concerned, as such, by' the free movement of capital.[773] Also, the CJEU explicitly justified horizontal comparability in *Sopora* with reference to the establishment and functioning of the internal market (Article 26 TFEU). Based on these decisions, horizontal comparability seems confined to intra-EU/EEA situations, which would mean that the freedom of capital movement in the TFEU has no universal scope when it comes to horizontal comparability. Although *Sopora* was concerned with non-resident workers from different States, the author does not see why the concept of horizontal comparability would apply any differently to non-residents from the same Member State. Further, horizontal comparability under a tax treaty was not at stake in *Sopora*, so the rule laid down in *D.* should continue to apply, i.e., no MFN treatment in case of tax treaty benefits.

6.3.3.3 *Application to Sovereign Wealth Investors*

There is currently no European tax case law dealing with the issue of comparability as regards foreign sovereign wealth investors. To whom, if any, should foreign sovereign wealth investors that have access to either the freedom of capital movement or the freedom of establishment be compared? This question has not been answered before, but becomes relevant when foreign sovereign wealth investors are treated differently than other investors. Below, the issue of comparability as regards foreign sovereign wealth investors is addressed by applying existing guidelines as discussed above, and by relying on common features of direct tax systems.

---

773. CJEU, 10 February 2011, Joined Cases C-436/08 and C-437/08 (*Haribo Lakritzen and Österreichische Salinen*), Para. 48.

6.3.3.3.1 Vertical Comparability

In accordance with the rules on prima facie comparability as discussed in Section 6.3.3.1 above, if a Member State imposes tax on a foreign sovereign wealth investor, as well as resident investors, their situation should become prima facie comparable. This should also apply if a Member State tax-exempts payments to its residents, while creating a risk of a series of tax charges or economic double taxation by imposing tax on payments to foreign sovereign wealth investors. In this respect, the (absence of) taxation in a foreign State is of no relevance, whereas a Member State can only rely on a neutralizing measure granted under a (bilateral) tax treaty, provided this treaty guarantees *full* neutralization in that other State.

If a foreign sovereign wealth investor is prima facie comparable to a resident, the next step is to determine whether a foreign sovereign wealth investor is *objectively comparable* to any resident (investor). Objective comparability is determined, unilaterally and rather strictly, in the light of the objective of the national tax measure at issue, and by the relevant conditions laid down in the national tax legislation of a State as imposed on its residents. In the direct tax system of many Member States, including the Netherlands, a basic distinction is made between the following categories of residents: (1) the State and State entities, (2) CIVs, (3) pension funds, (4) not-for-profit organizations, (5) regular corporate shareholders, and (6) individuals. Their common features, tax status and comparability (or not) to foreign sovereign wealth investors is discussed below. The analysis below is at a more abstract level and relies to a large extent on the information from Section 3.2.

(1) The State and State entities

In many States, legal persons of public law and legal persons of private law owned by a legal person of public law – together referred to as 'State entities' – are (effectively) not taxed, either entirely or at least to the extent they exercise public functions or do not compete with private economic operators. As explained in Section 2.10, there are three conflicting theories on home State taxation of State entities. The first theory is that home State taxation is superfluous because the profits of State entities already belong to the owner-State. The second theory holds that home State taxation of such entities is necessary to put them on equal footing with private operators. In the author's view, this would, however, require that they are made tax sensitive (just like private operators).[774] The third theory relates to the agency problem with respect to dividend payments, caused by the divergent interests between managers and shareholders. It requires taxation of State entities simply as a way to deal with this problem by forcing payment of a fixed percentage of annual profits to the State.

As explained, comparability must be examined by having regard to the purpose of and taking into account the relevant distinguishing criteria established by the national tax measure in question. Thus, if legal persons of public law and legal persons of private law owned by a legal entity of public law are not taxed, because taxation is

---

774. *See* Section 2.10 for a more detailed discussion of this matter.

considered to be superfluous, it could be argued that a foreign sovereign wealth investor is not comparable to such resident entities in the light of the objective of a national tax measure and the tax system as a whole; that is, source State taxation of foreign sovereign wealth investors is not superfluous. On the other hand, if resident State entities are not taxed to the extent they exercise public functions or do not compete with private economic operators, the type of functions and activities become relevant. In such cases, it can be argued that, having regard to the aim pursued by the national measure at issue, as well as its purpose and content and taking into account the relevant distinguishing criteria, a foreign sovereign wealth investor is objectively comparable to resident State entities, if it performs a similar function and/or similar activities, and meets any other relevant conditions imposed on resident State entities.[775] Thus, if resident State entities are not taxed to the extent they exercise public functions or do not compete with private economic operators, the tax treatment of investment activities of a foreign sovereign wealth investor should in principle follow the treatment of similar activities performed by resident State entities. However, the (remaining) conditions cannot be such that they would deprive the freedoms of all effectiveness, such as requiring a legal form unknown to the legal systems of other States. In the author's view, based on *Emerging Markets Series*, the rule which prohibits requiring a legal form unknown to the legal systems of other States should apply without distinction between EU Member States and third countries. Furthermore, the fact that a foreign sovereign wealth investor is not taxed in its home State is irrelevant for the comparability analysis.

In this context, a certain level of interaction exists between the fundamental freedoms and the State aid rules. As will be discussed in Section 6.4, the State aid rules could require a Member State to impose tax on economic (business) activities of resident State entities in a manner similar to private companies, without being superfluous. Furthermore, passive investment activities should fall outside the scope of the State aid rules. Therefore, the distinction between economic (business) activities and passive investment activities, and the tax treatment of such activities performed by resident State entities, could become relevant for the required treatment of foreign sovereign wealth investors by Member States.

(2) Collective investment vehicles

Rather than investing directly, many (smaller) portfolio investors pool their money in and invest collectively through CIVs. CIVs are managed by professional parties and offer investors various benefits as compared to investing directly, such as lower transactions costs, better market access, risk diversification and benefiting from market knowledge of professional managers and advisors. Most Member States have separate tax rules dealing with CIVs. The common aim of these rules is to achieve neutrality between investing directly and investing indirectly through a CIV, as much as possible. Different States, however, apply different mechanisms to accomplish this neutrality.

---

775. This reasoning was followed by the Dutch Court of Appeal in a case concerning the refund of Dutch dividend withholding tax claimed by a German entity created under public law. *Gerechtshof 's-Hertogenbosch*, 12 October 2017, No. 14/00640-00645, V-N 2017/57.9.

Tax neutrality may be achieved in different ways, such as through subjective tax-exemptions, objective tax-exemptions or a 0% tax rate.[776] Eligibility is typically subject to certain conditions, e.g., in terms of a plurality of investors, distribution policy, regulatory requirements, and types of assets to be invested in.[777] Because foreign sovereign wealth investors are not established to achieve tax neutrality between direct and indirect investment for a wider group of investors, they are unlikely to meet these conditions. For instance, a foreign sovereign wealth investor will not meet a condition regarding plurality of investors, since it has one single (ultimate) shareholder only, namely the owner-State. Therefore, in the light of the objective pursued and the relevant conditions imposed under a domestic tax measure, a foreign sovereign wealth investor is unlikely to be objectively comparable to resident CIVs.

(3) Pension funds

Many States do not tax funds which facilitate and organize the investment of contributions by the employer and employees for retirement purposes,[778] provided they comply with local pension fund regulations and/or meet other specific conditions. These regulations and/or conditions will typically require, amongst others, that the aim of the fund is to facilitate and organize private retirement saving plans. One reason why pension funds are not taxed is that the investment returns will effectively be taxed when pensions are paid; in most countries, pension contributions are made out of pre-tax income, investment returns of pension funds are tax-exempt and pension payments, including the profit component, are due with tax.[779] Another reason why many States do not tax pension funds is because they fulfil an important social function in society.[780] Based on *Hein Persche*, it can be argued that foreign sovereign wealth investors that do not comply with similar or comparable regulations at home and/or do not meet other conditions imposed on resident pension funds, are not objectively comparable to resident pension funds. However, the conditions cannot be such that they would deprive the freedoms of all effectiveness, such as requiring a legal form unknown to the legal systems of other States, or requiring full compliance with local pension fund regulations. As most foreign sovereign wealth investors will have a different, or less specific, purpose than the purpose required under the legislation of many Member States to qualify for the status of tax-exempt pension fund, most foreign sovereign wealth investors will unlikely meet the conditions imposed on resident pension funds under domestic (tax) law. Therefore, having regard to the purpose of and taking into account the relevant distinguishing criteria established by a national tax

---

776. J. Lynne & P. Bongaarts, *The Taxation of Investment Funds*, General Report, IFA Cahiers de Droit Fiscal International Vol. 8ba (Periodicals Service Company, 1997), Online Books IBFD, p. 38.
777. G. Genta, 'Dividends Received by Investment Funds: An EU Law Perspective – Part 2' (2013) 53 *European Taxation* 141, p. 143.
778. K-Y. Yoo & A. de Serres, 'Tax Treatment of Private Pension Savings in OECD Countries and the Net Tax Cost Per Unit of Contribution to Tax-favoured Schemes' (2004), *OECD Working Paper No. 406*, available at: <https://www.oecd.org/eco/outlook/35663569.pdf>.
779. *Ibid*.
780. *See* Section 3.2.1.4.

measure in question, a foreign sovereign wealth investor will unlikely be objectively comparable to such resident pension funds.

Other pension funds, known as SPRFs, are set-up and funded by the government to cover for expected future deficits of the social security system as a result of an ageing population.[781] Given that the objective of SPRFs is less specific, and perhaps of a more macroeconomic nature, than that of pension funds which facilitate and organize private retirement saving plans, a foreign sovereign wealth investor is arguably more likely to be objectively comparable to resident SPRFs.

(4) Not-for-profit organizations

A not-for-profit organization is a type of organization that does not aim to earn profit for its owners (shareholders), but uses profit and donations to further a particular social cause, or advocate for a particular point of view. In many States, special tax arrangements are available to not-for-profit organizations.[782] These special rules generally reflect a policy intended to support non-profit activities through tax expenditure.[783] Special tax rules for not-for-profit organizations include reduced tax rates, tax base limitations (e.g., distinguishing between business and non-business income) or a full tax-exemption.[784] To be eligible for these special tax rules, an organization is typically required to further a certain (charitable, public, social and/or political) purpose and/or is prohibited to distribute profits. Additional conditions could apply, e.g., regarding the level of remuneration of directors or the activities (not) to be performed. Member States have discretion to determine which activities qualify as charitable and are to be tax incentivized.[785] In *Hein Persche*, the CJEU indicated that Member States '(…) are free to define the interests of the general public that they wish to promote by granting benefits to associations and bodies which pursue objects linked to such interests in a disinterested manner and comply with the requirements relating to the implementation of those objects'.[786] However, a Member State cannot refuse the benefit to an entity 'solely on the ground that it is not established in its territory'.[787]

According to the 'consensus' definition,[788] foreign sovereign wealth investors are established to achieve financial objectives (i.e., earn profit) for macroeconomic purposes. It could be argued that foreign sovereign wealth investors fulfil a public or social function, since they benefit the home population as a whole. However, this function will unlikely qualify under the legislation of source States. Furthermore, foreign sovereign wealth investors are not prohibited from distributing profits to its

---

781. *See* Section 2.3.4.2.
782. D. Gliksberg, 'General Report', in: *Taxation of Non-Profit Organizations*, IFA Cahiers de droit fiscal international, Vol. 84a (Alphen a/d Rijn: Kluwer Law International, 1999).
783. *Ibid.*, p. 36.
784. *Ibid.*, pp. 38–45.
785. A. Yevgenyeva, 'The Taxation of Non-profit Organizations after *Stauffer*', Chapter 11: in W. Haslehner et al. (eds), *Landmark Decisions of the ECJ in Direct Taxation*, (Alphen a/d Rijn: Kluwer Law International, 2015).
786. CJEU, 27 January 2009, Case C-318/07 (*Hein Persche*), Para. 48 (referring to CJEU, 14 September 2006, Case C-386/04 (*Centro di Musicologia Walter Stauffer*), Para. 39).
787. CJEU, 14 September 2006, Case C-386/04 (*Centro di Musicologia Walter Stauffer*), Para. 40.
788. *See* Section 2.3.6.

Chapter 6: European Tax Law Aspects

owner. It is, thus, very unlikely that foreign sovereign wealth investors will meet the conditions imposed by source States on resident not-for-profit organizations. As a result, having regard to the purpose of and taking into account the relevant distinguishing criteria established by a national tax measure in question, a foreign sovereign wealth investor is very likely not objectively comparable to resident not-for-profit organizations.

(5) Regular corporate shareholders

The fundamental freedoms have largely contributed to national tax treatment of non-resident regular shareholders in intra-EU/EEA situations, often resulting in the absence or reduction of source taxation on outbound dividends (in particular).[789] Furthermore, the freedom of capital movement could require EU Member States to accord national tax treatment to non-EU corporate shareholders in respect of outbound portfolio dividends.[790] When a Member State has a system for preventing or mitigating a series of charges to tax or economic double taxation in a domestic situation, non-resident corporate shareholders are objectively comparable to resident corporate shareholders and could be entitled to similar tax treatment, provided they meet the relevant conditions which apply in a domestic situation. In the light of the purpose to avoid or mitigate economic double taxation, foreign sovereign wealth investors that are taxed by a Member State on income derived from that State, could be objectively comparable to regular resident corporate shareholders, provided they meet the relevant conditions which apply in a domestic situation. The conditions, however, cannot be such that they would deprive the freedoms of all effectiveness, such as requiring a legal form unknown to the legal systems of other States. In the author's view, based on *Emerging Markets Series*, the rule which prohibits requiring a legal form unknown to the legal systems of other States should apply without distinction between EU Member States and third countries. It does not matter when foreign sovereign wealth investors are not taxed in their home State, since, according to settled case law:

> it is solely because of the exercise by [a Member State] of its power to tax that, irrespective of any taxation in another non-Member State or [another Member State], a risk of a series of charges to tax or economic double taxation may arise, [the freedom of establishment and the freedom of capital movement] obliges that [first-mentioned] Member State, which establishes a tax exemption, with regard to dividends paid to resident traders by companies which are also resident, to accord equivalent treatment to dividends paid to traders established in non-Member States [and other Member States].[791]

---

789. CJEU, 8 November 2007, Case C-379/05 (*Amurta*); CJEU, 17 September 2015, Joined Cases C-10/14, C-14/14 and C-17/14 (*Miljoen, X, Société Générale*).
790. By analogy, CJEU, 10 February 2011, Joined Cases C-436/08 and C-437/08 (*Haribo Lakritzen and Österreichische Salinen*), Para. 50; CJEU, 10 April 2014, Case C-190/12 (*Emerging Markets Series*), Para. 39.
791. CJEU, 10 April 2014, Case C-190/12 (*Emerging Markets Series*), Para. 59, in relation to non-Member States. Similarly, CJEU, 12 December 2006, Case C-374/04 (*Test Claimants in Class IV of the ACT Group Litigation*), Para. 70, in relation to Member States.

Based on the above analysis, a foreign sovereign wealth investor could very well be objectively comparable to regular resident corporate shareholders and entitled to similar tax treatment. In fact, foreign sovereign wealth investors might already have received NT as a result of the fundamental freedoms (notably in EU Member States, based on the freedom of capital movement).

(6) Individuals

The author would not expect a foreign sovereign wealth investor to be objectively comparable to resident individuals, simply because of their difference in nature. This difference in nature between legal entities and individuals has resulted in separate tax regimes for each group.

To conclude, State entities or regular corporate shareholders are likely the best candidates in terms of objective vertical comparability with a foreign sovereign wealth investor. If a foreign sovereign wealth investor is comparable to both a regular resident corporate shareholder and a resident State entity, and both are taxed differently, it seems reasonable that a foreign sovereign wealth investor would be entitled to the most favourable tax treatment. It is unlikely that a foreign sovereign wealth investor is objectively comparable to any of the remaining categories of residents, essentially because the tax treatment of these other categories of residents is based on a different rationale, such as achieving neutrality between directly investing and indirectly investing or their social importance, as expressed in the relevant distinguishing criteria.

6.3.3.3.2 Horizontal Comparability

A foreign sovereign wealth investor may be able to rely on the fundamental freedoms vis-à-vis Member States, if it is treated less favourably than other objectively comparable non-resident investors, including other foreign sovereign wealth investors. In the author's view, the framework for vertical comparability (Section 6.3.3.1 of this chapter) should be applied as much as possible to assess horizontal comparability of investors in outbound situations. Importantly, horizontal comparability seems confined to intra-EU/EEA situations,[792] and should not apply in case of tax treaty benefits. Within these limitations, this means that horizontal comparability should be examined by having regard to the purpose of and taking into account the relevant distinguishing criteria established by the national tax measure in question. Horizontal comparability is a new, unexplored and interesting area of European law. Therefore, a first general analysis for foreign sovereign wealth investors is made below, relying on information from Section 3.2. But before doing so, the author would like to make a general remark. In many Member States, the tax treatment of non-resident investors has been and continues to be impacted, often in their favour, by the fundamental freedoms as a result of vertical comparability. In its turn, and as the analysis below will show, the impact

---

792. Which would mean that the freedom of capital movement in the TFEU has no universal scope when it comes to horizontal comparability.

vertical comparability has had on the tax treatment of non-resident investors could have an impact on the outcome of the horizontal comparability analysis.

(1) Other foreign sovereign wealth investors and other non-resident State entities

In many States, the tax treatment of foreign sovereign wealth investors (and other non-resident State entities) follows the regular source taxation under domestic tax law. However, some States accord unilateral tax-exemptions (or tax reductions) to such non-residents, often with reference to sovereign immunity (Chapter 4), motivated by international attractiveness and/or based on reciprocity. Especially when an individual Member State relies on reciprocity, it is not unlikely that foreign sovereign wealth investors (or other non-resident State entities) from different States receive a different tax treatment under the national tax laws of that Member State. In the author's view, a Member State should not be protected by reciprocity under national tax law, because this would deprive the freedoms of their practical effect. Therefore, when reciprocity did not find its way into a tax treaty, foreign sovereign wealth investors (and other non-resident State entities) from different States could be objectively comparable under the freedoms in an intra-EU/EEA context.

(2) Non-resident collective investment vehicles

Investment income of non-resident CIVs could be subject to regular source taxation. In order to achieve neutrality between investing directly and investing through a CIV in an international setting, many Member States have included special provisions in tax treaties. However, these treaty provisions are irrelevant for the horizontal comparability analysis, because the prohibition of horizontal discrimination should not apply in a tax treaty context. In many Member States, the tax treatment of non-resident CIVs has been impacted by the fundamental freedoms as a result of vertical comparability.[793] The impact is often such that a Member State will impose conditions on non-resident CIVs that are similar or comparable to those imposed on resident CIVs, e.g., regarding the plurality of investors, distribution policy and the types of assets to be invested in. Foreign sovereign wealth investors are unlikely to meet the relevant conditions imposed on non-resident CIVs. For instance, a foreign sovereign wealth investor will not meet a condition regarding plurality of investors, since it has one single (ultimate) shareholder only, namely the owner-State. It is, therefore, unlikely that foreign sovereign wealth investors will be objectively comparable to non-resident CIVs.

(3) Non-resident pension funds

Many pension funds are tax-exempt in their residence State. As a result, source taxation imposed by Member States on such pension funds as non-residents represents a net cost to them (such pension funds cannot credit foreign taxes). This could distort neutrality with respect to the investment location. That is, pension funds could favour

---

793. CJEU, 18 June 2009, Case C-303/07 (*Aberdeen Property Fininvest*); CJEU, 10 May 2012, Joined Cases C-338/11 to C-347/11 (*Santander Asset Management*); CJEU, 10 April 2014, Case C-190/12 (*Emerging Markets Series*); G. Hippert, 'The TFEU Eligibility of Non-EU Investment Funds Subjected to Discriminatory Dividend Withholding Taxes' (2016) 25 *EC Tax Review* 77.

domestic investments over foreign investments. In order to promote neutrality, many Member States have agreed in their tax treaties not to impose source taxation on (certain items of) investment income of a non-resident pension fund in their bilateral relationship, usually on a reciprocity basis. However, these treaty provisions are irrelevant for the horizontal comparability analysis, because the prohibition of horizontal discrimination should not apply in a tax treaty context. The national tax legislation of Member States could have been impacted by the fundamental freedoms as a result of vertical comparability.[794] The impact could have been such that a Member State unilaterally accords a tax-exemption to non-resident pension funds. European law allows to impose conditions on non-resident pension funds that are similar or comparable to those imposed on resident pension funds, notably the aim to facilitate and organize private retirement saving plans. However, the conditions cannot be such that they would deprive the freedoms of all effectiveness, such as requiring a legal form unknown to the legal systems of other States, or requiring full compliance with local pension fund regulations. Sovereign wealth investors will unlikely meet these conditions, simply because they do not facilitate and organize private retirement saving plans. Therefore, foreign sovereign wealth investors will unlikely be objectively comparable to non-resident pension funds.

(4) Non-resident not-for-profit organizations

The analysis in relation to non-resident not-for-profit organizations is similar to the analysis above in respect of non-resident pension funds. Thus, foreign sovereign wealth investors will unlikely be objectively comparable to non-resident not-for-profit organizations.

(5) Non-resident regular corporate shareholders

The fundamental freedoms have largely contributed to national tax treatment of non-resident regular shareholders in intra-EU/EEA situations, often resulting in the absence or reduction of source taxation on outbound dividends (in particular).[795] When a Member State has a system for preventing or mitigating a series of charges to tax or economic double taxation in a domestic situation, non-resident corporate shareholders are objectively comparable to resident corporate shareholders and could be entitled to similar tax treatment, provided they meet the relevant conditions which apply in a domestic situation.[796] In the light of the purpose to avoid or mitigate economic double taxation, foreign sovereign wealth investors could be objectively comparable to non-resident regular corporate shareholders in intra-EU/EEA situations, provided they meet the relevant conditions which apply to non-resident regular corporate shareholders. In fact, foreign sovereign wealth investors might already have received similar horizontal treatment as a result of the impact of vertical comparability.

---

794. *See* Section 6.3.3.1.
795. CJEU, 8 November 2007, Case C-379/05 (*Amurta*); CJEU, 17 September 2015, Joined Cases C-10/14, C-14/14 and C-17/14 (*Miljoen, X, Société Générale*).
796. By analogy, CJEU, 12 December 2006, Case C-374/04 (*Test Claimants in Class IV of the ACT Group Litigation*), Paras 56–57.

The fact that a foreign sovereign wealth investor is not taxed in its home State, and non-resident corporate shareholders could be taxed in their home State, is, in principle, irrelevant for the comparability analysis.

(6) Non-resident individuals

The author would not expect a foreign sovereign wealth investor to be objectively comparable to non-resident individuals, simply because of their difference in nature. This difference in nature between legal entities and individuals has resulted in separate tax regimes for each group.

To conclude, non-resident regular corporate shareholders or other foreign sovereign wealth investors (and non-resident State entities) are likely the best candidates in terms of objective horizontal comparability with a foreign sovereign wealth investor in intra-EU/EEA situations. It is unlikely that a foreign sovereign wealth investor is objectively comparable to any of the other categories of non-residents. These outcomes are in line with the outcomes in the context of vertical comparability, because horizontal comparability is to a large extent influenced by vertical comparability. In the context of vertical comparability, the freedoms have impacted the tax treatment of non-residents by Member States, and they prescribe, in principle, to impose conditions on non-residents that are similar or comparable to those imposed on residents. As a result, when a non-resident is comparable to a category of residents, it will often be comparable to the same category of non-residents.

6.3.4 Steps (3)–(5): Justification Test

6.3.4.1 *Relevant Justification Grounds*

To date, the CJEU has only accepted a limited number of justification grounds for different tax treatment of comparable situations.[797] Regarding foreign sovereign wealth investors, the following justifications could be relevant: (i) the need to prevent international tax avoidance,[798] (ii) the need to protect a balanced allocation of taxing powers, (iii) the need to safeguard fiscal coherence,[799] and (iv) the need for effective fiscal supervision.[800] The first three justification grounds should not apply any differently to foreign sovereign wealth investors than to other non-resident investors, and do not give rise to any particularities regarding foreign sovereign wealth investors. The fourth justification ground is in particular relevant for third country situations (which can only be examined in the light of Article 63(1) TFEU), and, in the author's view, its application to foreign sovereign wealth investors shows that a refinement of this justification ground is appropriate. The focus will, therefore, be on the need for effective fiscal supervision.

---

797. B. Terra & P. Wattel, *European Tax Law*, 6th edn., (Deventer: Kluwer, 2012), pp. 42–44.
798. For example, CJEU, 12 September 2006, Case C-196/04 (*Cadbury Schweppes*).
799. For example, CJEU, 28 January 1992, Case C-204/90 (*Bachmann*).
800. E. Nijkeuter, 'Exchange of Information and the Free Movement of Capital Between Member States and Third Countries' (2011) 20 *EC Tax Review* 232.

6.3.4.2 *Need for Effective Fiscal Supervision in Relation to Third States*

With respect to Article 63(1) TFEU, the CJEU has held that capital movements between EU Member States and third States take place in a 'different legal context'.[801] Because of this different legal context, restrictions on capital movements between EU Member States and third States may be justified where they would not be justified in an intra-Union situation.[802] For one thing, the framework of EU Directive 2011/16/EU on administrative cooperation between EU Member States in the field of taxation, which provides for the exchange of information, does not apply to third States. The CJEU has ruled that restrictions on capital movements to and from third States are justified – based on the need to guarantee the effectiveness of fiscal supervision – in case: (i) the national tax measure at issue imposes conditions for obtaining a tax advantage,[803] (ii) compliance with these conditions can only be verified by obtaining confirmation/information from the competent authorities of a third State, and (iii) that third State is not obliged under an agreement to exchange the information required for tax purposes.[804] In such circumstances, the CJEU rules out *a priori* the possibility that the taxpayer resident in a third State himself can provide the relevant information.[805] The reason behind ruling out such possibility seems that an EU Member State cannot verify the correctness of the information received from a taxpayer in the absence of an appropriate exchange of information mechanism. Apparently, only information or confirmation received from the (competent) authorities of a third State is presumed to be correct. It should be noted that this justification ground is becoming less significant, since the international developments against base erosion and profit shifting have resulted in an overall increase of applicable exchange of information frameworks between EU Member States and third countries.[806]

6.3.4.3 *Application to Foreign Sovereign Wealth Investors from Third States*

In the author's opinion, the application to foreign sovereign wealth investors of the justification ground regarding the need to guarantee the effectiveness of fiscal supervision shows that a refinement of this justification ground is appropriate. The mere absence of the obligation for a third State to exchange information to an EU Member State cannot rule out *a priori* the possibility to demonstrate to that EU Member State

---

801. CJEU, 18 December 2007, Case C-101/05 (*Skatteverket v. A*), Para. 36.
802. *Ibid.*, Para. 37.
803. These conditions cannot, of course, be discriminatory or restrictive themselves, e.g., CJEU, 10 April 2014, Case C-190/12 (*Emerging Markets Series*), Para. 67.
804. CJEU, 10 February 2011, Joined Cases C-436/08 and C-437/08 (*Haribo Lakritzen and Österreichische Salinen*), Para. 131 and case law cited; CJEU, 19 July 2012, Case C-48/11 (*Veronsaajien oikeudenvalvontayksikkö v. A Oy*), Para. 36; CJEU, 10 April 2014, Case C-190/12 (*Emerging Markets Series*), Para. 84.
805. CJEU, 10 April 2014, Case C-190/12 (*Emerging Markets Series*), Para. 85.
806. For example, as on 24 January 2018, one hundred seventeen jurisdictions, including all EU Member States, participate in the OECD's Multilateral Convention on Mutual Administrative Assistance in Tax Matters, providing a legal basis for the exchange of information between States.

Chapter 6: European Tax Law Aspects

that the conditions for obtaining a tax advantage have been satisfied. Even in the absence of an existing obligation to exchange information, a third State could still be (very much) willing to voluntarily provide the necessary information to an EU Member State regarding a taxpayer; particularly so in relation to foreign sovereign wealth investors that reside in the owner-State/third State, because a reduction of taxation in an EU Member State would benefit that third State. An EU Member State should trust that the information voluntarily provided by the owner-State is accurate and reliable, based on the international law principle of mutual trust, also in the absence of an information exchange instrument. In such circumstances, it would not be appropriate for an EU Member State to successfully rely on the need for effective fiscal supervision. Admittedly, the CJEU may have recently introduced the refinement mentioned above. In *SECIL*, it held that, if:

> the legislation of a Member State makes a more advantageous tax system dependent on the satisfaction of requirements, compliance with which can be verified only by obtaining information from the competent authorities of a non-member State, it is, in principle, legitimate for that Member State to refuse to grant that advantage if, *in particular*, because that non-member State is not under any obligation pursuant to a convention or agreement to provide information, it proves impossible to obtain such information from that non-member State[807] (Italics added).

Based on this decision, it could be argued that a Member State cannot rely on the need to ensure the effectiveness of fiscal supervision if a third State would be willing to voluntarily provide the necessary information.[808]

6.4 STATE AID AND FOREIGN SOVEREIGN WEALTH INVESTORS

6.4.1 General Aspects

If a domestic measure constitutes unlawful State aid, the EC or EFTA Surveillance Authority will order a Member State to recover the aid, including interest, from the beneficiary, so that the advantage enjoyed over its competitors on the market is forfeited, and the situation prior to payment of the aid is restored.[809] However, under the *de minimis* rule, aid granted per Member State to a single undertaking is not considered to have satisfied the State aid criteria if it does not exceed EUR 200,000 over any period of three fiscal years.[810] The recovery of State aid is limited to a period of ten

---

807. CJEU, 24 November 2016, Case C-464/14 (*SECIL*), Para. 64.
808. J. van Eijsden, B. Kiekebeld & D. Smit (eds), *Nederlands belastingrecht in Europees perspectief*, 2nd edn., (Deventer: Kluwer, 2014), pp. 197–198.
809. For example, CJEU, 15 December 2005, Case C-148/04 (*Unicredito Italiano*), Para. 113 and case law cited.
810. Article 3 of the *Commission Regulation (EU) No 1407/2013 of 18 December 2013 on the application of Articles 107 and 108 of the Treaty on the Functioning of the European Union to de minimis aid*, Official Journal of the European Union, Vol. 56, L 352, 24 December 2013; Art. 63 EEA Agreement in conjunction with Annex XV of the EEA Agreement.

years.[811] With respect to existing aid, such as aid which existed prior to the entry into force of the TFEU or EEA Agreement in the respective Member State,[812] which is not or no longer compatible with the internal market, the EC or EFTA Surveillance Authority will issue a recommendation proposing appropriate measures to the Member State concerned, such as amendments to or abolition of the aid scheme.[813]

The TFEU and EEA Agreement provide for specific exceptions to the application of State aid rules. Article 107(2) TFEU and Article 61(2) EEA Agreement list aid that is disregarded for State aid purposes, such as: (i) aid having a social character, granted to individual consumers, provided that such aid is granted without discrimination related to the origin of the products concerned, and (ii) aid to make good the damage caused by natural disasters or exceptional occurrences. Article 107(3) TFEU and Article 61(3) EEA Agreement provide for exceptions which the EC or EFTA Surveillance Authority could consider as not constituting State aid, such as: (i) aid to promote the economic development of areas where the standard of living is abnormally low or where there is serious underemployment, in view of their structural, economic and social situation, (ii) aid to facilitate the development of certain economic activities or of certain economic areas, where such aid does not adversely affect trading conditions to an extent contrary to the common interest, (iii) aid to promote culture and heritage conservation where such aid does not affect trading conditions and competition in the EU to an extent that is contrary to the common interest, and (iv) other categories of aid as may be specified by decision of the Council on a proposal from the EC or the EEA Joint Committee. The EC has adopted a regulation,[814] known as the General Block Exemption Regulation,[815] which permits certain specific categories of State aid and exempts Member States from the requirement of prior notification to the EC.[816] This regulation, which is also applied by the EFTA Surveillance Authority,[817] contains detailed (and sometimes complex) rules and imposes general and specific conditions –

---

811. Article 17(1) of the *Council Regulation (EU) 2015/1589 of 13 July 2015 laying down detailed rules for the application of Article 108 of the Treaty on the Functioning of the European Union* ('Procedural Regulation'), Official Journal of the European Union, Vol. 58, L 248, 24 September 2015, p. 9; Art. 15(1) of Part II of Protocol 3 to the Agreement between the EFTA States on the Establishment of a Surveillance Authority and a Court of Justice.
812. Article 1(b) of the Procedural Regulation; Art. 1(b) of Part II of Protocol 3 to the Agreement between the EFTA States on the Establishment of a Surveillance Authority and a Court of Justice.
813. Article 22 of the Procedural Regulation; Art. 18 of Part II of Protocol 3 to the Agreement between the EFTA States on the Establishment of a Surveillance Authority and a Court of Justice.
814. Based on Art. 108(4) TFEU.
815. *Commission Regulation No 651/2014 of 17 June 2014 declaring certain categories of aid compatible with the internal market in application of Articles 107 and 108 of the Treaty*, Official Journal of the European Union, Vol. 57, L 187, 26 June 2014, p. 1; *Commission Regulation (EU) 2017/1084 of 14 June 2017 amending Regulation (EU) No 651/2014 as regards aid for port and airport infrastructure, notification thresholds for aid for culture and heritage conservation and for aid for sport and multifunctional recreational infrastructures, and regional operating aid schemes for outermost regions and amending Regulation (EU) No 702/2014 as regards the calculation of eligible costs*, Official Journal of the European Union, Vol. 60, L 156, 20 June 2017, p. 1.
816. Article 107(3) TFEU.
817. Article 63 EEA Agreement in conjunction with Annex XV of the EEA Agreement.

in particular regarding eligible categories, beneficiaries, maximum aid and eligible expenses – aimed at ensuring that the exemptions have a limited effect on trade and competition. The eligible categories include aid to small- and medium-sized enterprises, aid for research and development and innovation, aid for local infrastructure, investment aid for regional airports and investment aid for ports.[818] In addition, based on Article 106(2) TFEU and Article 59(2) EEA Agreement, aid granted to an undertaking entrusted by a Member State with the operation of services of general economic interest may also be compatible with State aid rules.

6.4.2 Constitutive Elements

Article 107(1) TFEU provides:

> Save as otherwise provided in the Treaties, any aid granted by a Member State or through State resources in any form whatsoever which distorts or threatens to distort competition by favouring certain undertakings or the production of certain goods shall, in so far as it affects trade between Member States, be incompatible with the internal market.

Article 61(1) EEA Agreement contains similar wording.

From their wording and from case law it follows that Article 107(1) TFEU and Article 61(1) EEA Agreement, in principle, prohibit:

(i) an advantage;
(ii) granted by a Member State or through State resources in any form whatsoever;
(iii) which is selective in that it favours certain undertakings or the production of certain goods;
(iv) which cannot be justified by the inner logic of the system; and
(v) which distorts or threatens to distort competition, and trade between Member States.

6.4.2.1 *Advantage*

An advantage is any economic benefit resulting from State intervention.[819] This is assessed by comparing the financial situation of an undertaking with and without State intervention. An advantage can be a positive economic advantage, but also any mitigation of charges normally included in the budget of an undertaking,[820] such as taxes, as they are similar in character and have the same effect.[821]

---

818. Article 1(1) General Block Exemption Regulation.
819. Commission Notice on the notion of State aid as referred to in Art. 107(1) TFEU, Official Journal of the European Union, Vol. 59, C 262, 19 July 2016, Para. 66 and case law referred to in footnote 99. The EFTA Surveillance Authority has adopted similar guidelines.
820. *Ibid.*, Paras 67–68 and case law referred to in footnotes 100–109.
821. EFTA Court, 10 May 2011, Joined Cases E-4/10, E-6/10 and E-7/10 (*Principality of Liechtenstein et. al*), Para. 69.

Direct beneficiaries are entities to which State resources are directly 'transferred'. However, a measure can also confer an advantage on entities to which State resources are not directly transferred (indirect beneficiaries).[822] An indirect advantage is present if a measure indirectly benefits (a group of) identifiable entities; general secondary economic effects do not constitute State aid.[823] In this respect, case law in the context of CIVs indicates that: (i) external asset managers of such vehicles, and (ii) potential EU/EEA targets (EU/EEA investment opportunities) are potential indirect beneficiaries.[824]

6.4.2.2 State Resources

A 'shortfall' in tax revenue normally accruing to the budget, due to tax-exemptions or reductions granted by an EU Member State/EEA-EFTA State, fulfils this condition.[825]

6.4.2.3 Undertaking (and Economic Activity)

According to settled case law, the concept of undertaking covers 'any entity engaged in economic activity, regardless of the legal status of the entity or way in which it is financed'.[826] In that respect, it does not matter whether an entity is part of the State or structured as a separate legal body, as long as it carries on economic activities.[827] It is possible that several separate legal entities are considered to form one economic unit based on a controlling share and other functional, economic and organic links.[828] Such an economic unit is treated as an undertaking for State aid purposes.

An economic activity is broadly defined as 'any activity consisting in offering goods or services on a given market'.[829] For the meaning of the term economic activity in State aid matters, the EC refers to EU case law in the field of VAT, from which it can be derived that the 'simple acquisition and the mere sale of shares'[830] and other negotiable securities does not constitute an economic activity, basically because any

---

822. Commission Notice on the notion of State aid as referred to in Art. 107(1) TFEU, Official Journal of the European Union, Vol. 59, C 262, 19 July 2016, Para. 115 and case law referred to in footnotes 178–180.
823. Ibid., Para. 115 and case law referred to in footnote 78.
824. CFI, 4 March 2009, Case T-445/05 (*Fineco Asset Management*).
825. Commission Notice on the notion of State aid as referred to in Art. 107(1) TFEU, Official Journal of the European Union, Vol. 59, C 262, 19 July 2016, Para. 51 and case law referred to in footnote 78.
826. CJEU, 23 April 1991, Case C-41/90 (*Klaus Höfner and Fritz Elser v. Macrotron GmbH*), Para. 21; CJEU, 22 January 2002, Case C-218/00 (*Cisal di Battistello Venanzio & C. Sas*), Para. 22 and case law cited.
827. CJEU, 16 June 1987, Case 118/85 (*Commission v. Italy*), Paras 8–10; CJEU, 18 March 1997, Case C-343/95 (*Servizi Ecologici Porto di Genova SpA*), Para. 17.
828. Commission Notice on the notion of State aid as referred to in Art. 107(1) TFEU, Official Journal of the European Union, Vol. 59, C 262, 19 July 2016, Para. 11 and case law referred to in footnote 8.
829. CJEU, 1 July 2008, Case C-49/07 (*Motosykletistiki Omospondia Ellados NPID (MOTOE)*), Para. 22.
830. CJEU, 21 October 2004, Case C-8/03 (*BBL*), Para. 38.

Chapter 6: European Tax Law Aspects

returns are merely the fruits of the (passive) ownership of an asset and are not the product of any economic activity.[831] From the State aid decision in *Cassa di Risparmio di Firenze SpA* it can be derived that even the holding of controlling shareholdings is 'insufficient to characterise as economic an activity (...), when it gives rise only to the exercise of the rights attached to the status of shareholder or member, as well as, if appropriate, the receipt of dividends, which are merely the fruits of the ownership of an asset'.[832] However, this is different when the owner of a controlling shareholding in an undertaking actually exercises that control by involving itself (directly or indirectly) in the management of that company. In such case, the owner must be regarded as taking part in that company's economic activity and itself be considered as an undertaking (economic unit approach).[833] In the author's view, it cannot *a contrario* be derived from this decision that non-controlling shareholdings can never amount to an economic activity. An investor and a non-controlling shareholding in a company may not be considered to form an economic unit, but an investor with a non-controlling shareholding in a company could still be involved in the management of that company. It cannot be excluded that such *active* investors with non-controlling shareholdings must themselves be regarded as conducting an economic activity for State aid purposes. This would also be more in line with the concept of economic activity in the context of VAT and the freedom of establishment. For VAT purposes, being directly or indirectly involved in the management of a company is sufficient to constitute an economic activity, without the need to have a controlling shareholding.[834] Transactions carried out in the course of a business trading in securities can also constitute an economic activity for VAT purposes.[835] In the context of the freedom of establishment, in order to constitute an economic activity, it is even sufficient that a shareholding *enables* a national to exercise definite influence on the company; the *Baars* criterion does not appear to require that the influence is *actually* exercised.[836] Nor does it necessarily require the presence of a controlling (more than 50%) shareholding.

State aid case law in the context of CIVs also indicates that the holding of non-controlling shareholdings can constitute an economic activity. In the State aid case *Fineco Asset Management*, concerning an Italian tax scheme for specialized CIVs, the EC relied on case law dealing with the VAT status of open-ended investment companies (*societés d'investissement à capital variable*) ('SICAVs') in Luxembourg to demonstrate that the investment vehicles performed economic activities and therefore constituted undertakings. According to that VAT case law (*BBL*),[837] the activities of SICAVs – which consisted of raising of capital from the public, purchasing of shares, and

---

831. *Ibid.*; CJEU, 29 April 2004, Case C-77/01 (*EDM*), Para. 57 (and case law cited); CJEU, 12 January 2017, Case C-28/16 (*MVM Magyar Villamos Művek Zrt.*), Para. 31.
832. CJEU, 10 January 2006, Case C-222/04 (*Cassa di Risparmio di Firenze SpA*), Para. 111.
833. *Ibid.*, Paras 112–113.
834. CJEU, 12 January 2017, Case C-28/16 (*MVM Magyar Villamos Művek Zrt.*), Paras 32–33 and case law cited.
835. CJEU, 21 October 2004, Case C-8/03 (*BBL*), Para. 41 and case law cited.
836. F. Pötgens & M. Straathof, 'Establishment and Substance of Intermediate and Other Holding Companies from an EU Law Perspective' (2016) 44 *Intertax* 608, p. 619.
837. CJEU, 21 October 2004, Case C-8/03 (*BBL*), Paras 42–43.

assembling and managing transferable securities on behalf of the subscribers for a fee – constitute an economic activity within the meaning of the VAT Directive, because they go 'beyond the compass of the simple acquisition and the mere sale of securities' and aim 'to produce income on a continuing basis.' The Court of First Instance ('CFI') did not dismiss the EC's reference to this VAT case law for State aid purposes, but it indicated that the EC's demonstration that the investment vehicles qualify as undertakings 'may in some aspects appear questionable or ambiguous' and 'must not be read out of context but in the light of the [EC's] contested decision as a whole and its enacting terms'.[838] In *Fineco Asset Management*, the CFI acknowledged that investment vehicles – which typically hold non-controlling shareholdings – might qualify as undertakings themselves.[839] It did not, however, indicate how this must be determined. In literature, it has been suggested that the qualification of CIVs as undertakings themselves 'will depend on what kind of investment activities they carry on themselves and on whether or not they themselves are to be considered relatively *passive* investors'.[840] This basic distinction between *passive* investors – involved in the simple acquisition and sale of assets – and *active* investors – performing activities that go beyond the compass of the simple acquisition and sale of assets – indeed seems to be relevant for State aid purposes. Whether an investor qualifies as active or passive depends on the facts and circumstances, but an investor that holds a controlling shareholding in an undertaking and actually exercises that control by involving itself (directly or indirectly) in the management of that company must, in any case, be regarded as an *active* investor and therefore as an undertaking.

In VAT case law, the definition of economic activity is broadly interpreted. In *EDM*, the CJEU pointed out that the granting of interest-bearing loans by a holding company to companies in which it holds shares, as well as placements in bank deposits or securities, such as treasury notes or certificates of deposit, constitute economic activities for VAT purposes, because the interest income is not merely the fruit of simple ownership of the asset, but the consideration for making capital available for the benefit of somebody else.[841] Although the CFI did not dismiss the EC's reference in *Fineco Asset Management* to VAT case law for the interpretation of the term economic activity in relation to investment vehicles, it is unclear whether the broad interpretation of the concept of economic activity in *EDM* – where interest-bearing loans and placements in bank deposits and securities were classified as economic activities – would similarly apply in a State aid context.

With respect to activities performed by States (directly or through a separate legal body), a further distinction must be made between 'a situation where the State acts in the exercise of official authority [directly or through a separate legal body] and that where it carries on economic activities of an industrial or commercial nature by offering

---

838. CFI, 4 March 2009, Case T-445/05 (*Fineco Asset Management*), Para. 96.
839. *Ibid.*, Para. 150 and Para. 153.
840. R. Luja, 'Fiscal Autonomy, Investment Funds and State Aid: A Follow-Up' (2009) 47 *European Taxation*.
841. CJEU, 29 April 2004, Case C-77/01 (*EDM*), Paras 65–70.

goods or services on the market'.[842] This distinction is relevant because for State aid purposes 'the conduct of the State can never be compared to that of an operator or private investor in a market economy'.[843] When a State is considered to exercise its public powers, no economic activity and therefore no undertaking is considered present, and the State aid rules do not apply. Case law indicates that an activity is part of State conduct if it forms part of the essential functions of the State or if it is connected to such functions by its nature, its aim and the rules to which the activity is subject.[844] According to the EC's Notice on State aid, in general, activities performed by States which intrinsically form part of the prerogatives of official authority are not economic activities, such as: (a) the army or the police, (b) air navigation safety and control, (c) maritime traffic control and safety, (d) anti-pollution surveillance, (e) the organization, financing and enforcement of prison sentences, and (f) the development and revitalization of public land by public authorities.[845]

In a somewhat similar context, the CJEU explained in *Congregación de Escuelas Pías Provincia Betania* that educational services do not constitute an economic activity if provided by institutions which are integrated into a public education system and financed, mainly or fully, by the State. According to the court, in such case, 'the State is not seeking to engage in gainful activity, but is fulfilling its social, cultural and educational obligations towards its population'.[846] In contrast, educational activities which are essentially financed by private funds do classify as economic activities, because the aim is to offer a service against remuneration.[847] Therefore, the presence of a remuneration strongly indicates the presence of an economic activity for State aid purposes.[848] The element of remuneration was also decisive, or at least very important, in the VAT cases *BBL* (concerning CIVs) and *EDM* (concerning financing activities of a holding company).

---

842. CJEU, 18 March 1997, Case C-343/95 (*Servizi Ecologici Porto di Genova SpA*), Para. 16.
843. CFI, 17 December 2008, Case T-196/04 (*Ryanair v. European Commission*), Para. 85; General Court, 11 September 2012, Case T-565/08 (*Corsica Ferries France v. European Commission*), Para. 79.
844. CJEU, 19 January 1994, Case C-364/92 (*SAT/Eurocontrol*), Para. 30: '[t]aken as a whole, Eurocontrol's activities, by their nature, their aim and the rules to which they are subject, are connected with the exercise of powers relating to the control and supervision of air space which are typically those of a public authority. They are not of an economic nature justifying the application of the Treaty rules of competition'; CJEU, 18 March 1997, Case C-343/95 (*Servizi Ecologici Porto di Genova SpA*), Paras 22–23.
845. Commission Notice on the notion of State aid as referred to in Art. 107(1) TFEU, Official Journal of the European Union, Vol. 59, C 262, 19 July 2016, Para. 17 and case law and EC decisions cited in footnotes 16–22.
846. CJEU, 27 June 2017, Case C-74/16 (*Congregación de Escuelas Pías Provincia Betania*), Para. 50 and case law cited.
847. *Ibid.*, Para. 48 and case law cited.
848. J. Luts, 'Congregación de Escuelas Pías Provincia Betania: Tax Exemption for Education Services by Religious Congregation Not Sacrosanct from State Aid Perspective' (2017) 26 *EC Tax Review* 292, pp. 297–298.

6.4.2.4 Selectivity and Justification

When a measure benefits one or more identified undertakings, selectivity is normally given.[849] However, in more complex situations, when a measure benefits all undertakings fulfilling certain conditions, a three-step analysis should normally be taken. As a first step, the reference system must be identified. According to the EC's Notice on State aid, the '(...) reference system is composed of a consistent set of rules that generally apply – on the basis of objective criteria – to all undertakings falling within its scope as defined by its objective. Typically, those rules define not only the scope of the system, but also the conditions under which the system applies, the rights and obligations of undertakings subject to it and the technicalities of the functioning of the system'.[850] In direct tax cases, the reference system typically is the general tax regime,[851] although a different reference system in a particular situation, such as a special tax regime or a tax treaty,[852] cannot *a priori* be excluded. As a second step, it needs to be determined whether a measure favours certain undertakings in derogation from the reference system as compared to other undertakings 'which are in a legal and factual situation that is comparable in the light of the objective pursued by the measure at issue'.[853] A similar substantive approach regarding comparability is followed in free movement cases (Section 6.3.3.1 of this chapter); the State aid rules are, therefore, the 'flip side' of the fundamental freedoms.[854] It should be noted, however, that the implications of

---

849. Commission Notice on the notion of State aid as referred to in Art. 107(1) TFEU, Official Journal of the European Union, Vol. 59, C 262, 19 July 2016, Para. 126 and case law cited in footnote 196.
850. *Ibid.*, Para. 133.
851. CJEU, 15 December 2005, Case C-148/04 (*Unicredito Italiano*), Para. 50; EC, 12 May 2010, State Aid No. N131/2009 – Finland – Residential Real Estate Investment Trust (REIT) Scheme, C(2010) 2974 final, Paras 24–25; EC, 9 July 2014, State aid SA.25338 (2014/C, ex E 3/2008, CP 115/2004 and CP 120/2006) – The Netherlands – Corporate tax exemption for public undertakings, C(2014) 4480 final, Para. 35, Official Journal of the European Union, Vol. 57, C 280, 22 August 2014; EFTA Court, 10 May 2011, Joined Cases E-4/10, E-6/10 and E-7/10 (*Principality of Liechtenstein et. al*), Para. 69; EC, 3 December 2015, State aid SA. 38945 (2015/C) (ex 2015/NN) – Luxembourg – Alleged aid to McDonald's, C(2015) 8343 final, Para. 69, Official Journal of the European Union, Vol. 59, C 258, 15 July 2016.
852. J. Vleggeert, 'Dutch CV-BV Structures: Starbucks-Style Tax Planning and State Aid Rules' (2016) 70 *Bulletin for International Taxation* 3.
853. For example, CFI, 4 March 2009, Case T-445/05 (*Fineco Asset Management*), Para. 148. *See also* CJEU, 21 December 2016, Cases C-20/15 P and C-21/15 P (*World Duty Free Group*), Para. 54 and case law cited.
854. Opinion of Advocate General Kokott, 2 July 2009, Case C-169/08 (*Presidente del Consiglio dei Ministri v. Regione Sardegna*), Paras 133–134; P. Wattel, 'Interaction of State Aid, Free Movement, Policy Competition and Abuse Control in Direct Tax Matters' (2013) 5 *World Tax Journal* 128, p. 130; Opinion of Advocate General Wathelet, 28 July 2016, Cases C-20/15 P and C-21/15 P (*World Duty Free Group*), Para. 137; Opinion of Advocate General Bobek, 21 April 2016, Case C-270/15 P (*Kingdom of Belgium v. Commission*), Para. 29, expresses this eloquently: 'There is no doubt that the heart of the selectivity test is establishing the "reference framework". However, as far as the relationship between its textual expression and its genuine content are concerned, that heart reminds one of a Russian doll: only by opening the external layer does one see that the key notion is in fact that of discrimination. And again, hidden further within the notion of discrimination is comparability. Thus, when searching for the genuine content of selectivity, one arrives at the notion intimately known from other areas of EU law: comparability.'

tax treaties for the selectivity test under State aid rules are currently less clear.[855] If a measure does favour certain undertakings that are in a comparable legal and factual situation, the third, and final, step is to determine whether the derogation is justified by the nature or general scheme of the (reference) system. In addition, a measure should be proportionate as regards the objective being pursued. Examples of justification grounds in the field of direct taxation according to the EC include the need to fight tax evasion, the principle of tax neutrality (as regards CIVs), the progressive nature of income tax and its redistribution purpose, as well as the need to avoid double taxation.[856] Measures of purely general application that do not favour certain undertakings only, do not fall within the scope of Article 107(1) TFEU.[857]

6.4.2.5 Effect on Trade and Competition

The EC is not required to demonstrate that a measure has a real effect on competition, and on trade between Member States, but only that a measure is liable to do so.[858] The effect on trade and competition, however, cannot be merely hypothetical or presumed. According to settled case law, a measure will be regarded to be liable to affect competition, and trade between Member States, 'when State financial aid strengthens the position of an undertaking compared with other undertakings competing in intra-[Union] trade'.[859] Furthermore, there is no requirement that the beneficiary undertaking itself be involved in intra-Union trade.[860] In *Cassa di Risparmio di Firenze SpA*, concerning a domestic undertaking not involved in intra-Union trade, it was held that a measure is liable to affect trade between Member States when it may have helped 'to maintain or increase domestic activity, with the result that undertakings established in other Member States (...) [may have had] less chance of penetrating the market of the Member State concerned'.[861]

6.4.3 EC Decision on the Former Dutch Corporate Income Tax Regime for Public Enterprises and the Belgian and French Corporate Income Tax Regime for State-Owned Ports

In the context of State aid and source State taxation of foreign sovereign wealth investors, it could be helpful to look at the EC's reasoning in its provisional decision on

---

855. R. Luja, 'Tax Treaties and State Aid: Some Thoughts' (2004) 44 *European Taxation* 234; L. De Broe, 'Can Tax Treaties Confer State Aid?' (2017) 26 *EC Tax Review* 228.
856. Commission Notice on the notion of State aid as referred to in Art. 107(1) TFEU, Official Journal of the European Union, Vol. 59, C 262, 19 July 2016, Para. 139.
857. *Ibid.*, Para. 118.
858. CJEU, 15 December 2005, Case C-148/04 (*Unicredito Italiano*), Para. 54 and case law cited.
859. CFI, 15 June 2000, Joined Cases T-298/97, T-312/97, etc. (*Mauro Alzetta*), Para. 81; CFI, 4 April 2001, Case T-288/97 (*Regione autonoma Friuli-Venezia Giulia*), Para. 41.
860. CJEU, 10 January 2006, Case C-222/04 (*Cassa di Risparmio di Firenze SpA*), Para. 143.
861. *Ibid.*

the former Dutch corporate income tax regime for Dutch public enterprises. This regime, which was abolished on 1 January 2016 as a direct result of this decision, granted tax-exemptions for (many) Dutch public enterprises carrying out economic activities, including enterprises of the Dutch State and legal entities wholly-owned by the Dutch State. The EC argued that the tax-exemptions disturbed the level-playing field between Dutch public enterprises performing economic activities on the European market in comparison to Dutch private companies.[862] According to the EC, the former Dutch corporate income tax regime for Dutch public enterprises constituted State aid, because:

(i) the measure provides an **advantage** to those public **undertakings** benefiting from the exemption, as it reduces the charges normally included in the operating costs of an undertaking carrying out economic activities;[863]
(ii) although the tax-exemption does not involve a transfer of State resources, it is **funded by State resources** as the Dutch authorities forgo revenue, while it places those public undertakings to whom the exemption applies in a better position;[864]
(iii) the measure grants a **selective advantage to public undertakings carrying out economic activities** and constitutes a derogation from the general corporate income tax regime;
(iv) the tax-exemption **distorts or threatens to distort competition and trade between Member States**, as it applies to public undertakings which are and may be involved in intra-Union trade;
(v) the derogation from the general corporate income tax regime **cannot be justified by the inner logic of the (Dutch) corporate tax regime**, which is to tax profits.

The EC has followed a similar line of reasoning in its provisional decisions on the Belgian and French corporate income tax regime for State-owned ports.[865]

---

862. EC, 9 July 2014, State aid SA.25338 (2014/C, ex E 3/2008, CP 115/2004 and CP 120/2006) – The Netherlands – Corporate tax exemption for public undertakings, C(2014) 4480 final, Official Journal of the European Union, Vol. 57, C 280, 22 August 2014.
863. Similarly, Capobianco, A. & Christiansen, H., 'Competitive Neutrality and State-Owned Enterprises: Challenges and Policy Options' (2011), *OECD Corporate Governance Working Papers No. 1*, p. 5, available at: < http://www.oecd-ilibrary.org/governance/competitive-neutrality-and-state-owned-enterprises_5kg9xfgjdhg6-en >.
864. CJEU, 15 March 1994, Case C-387/92 (*Banco de Crédito Industrial SA*), Para. 14.
865. EC, 8 July 2016, State aid SA.38393 (2016/C) (ex 2015/E) – Ports taxation in Belgium, Official Journal of the European Union, Vol. 59, C 302, 19 August 2016, p. 5; EC, 8 July 2016, State aid SA.38398 (2016/C) (ex 2015/E) – Ports taxation in France, Official Journal of the European Union, Vol. 59, C 302, 19 August 2016, p. 23.

Chapter 6: European Tax Law Aspects

6.4.4 Could Preferential Tax Treatment Accorded to a Sovereign Wealth Investor Constitute State Aid?

6.4.4.1 *Preferential Tax Treatment*

To begin with, a tax measure cannot constitute State aid if it does not distinguish between (groups of) investors. For purposes of the State aid analysis below, it is, therefore, assumed that a Member State either accords:

(i) preferential tax treatment to a foreign sovereign wealth investor over (resident or non-resident) private investors in derogation from the general tax regime; or
(ii) preferential tax treatment to a foreign sovereign wealth investor over other foreign sovereign wealth investors (or non-resident State entities) in derogation from the general tax regime.

Such preferential tax treatment of a foreign sovereign wealth investor can be achieved through domestic legislation, administrative practice or specific tax treaty provisions (in this respect, reference is made to Approaches (2) through (5)[866]).[867] It is clear that such preferential tax treatment provides an advantage to a foreign sovereign wealth investor and is funded through State resources. The analysis below is a first general analysis in the context of foreign sovereign wealth investors, aimed at identifying potential issues in the complex area of State aid.

6.4.4.2 *Foreign Sovereign Wealth Investor as a Direct Beneficiary*

A foreign sovereign wealth investor that has a separate legal personality is itself a direct beneficiary of a source State tax measure which results in preferential tax treatment. In case of a foreign sovereign wealth investor without legal personality, the owner-State or central bank that has a corporate form,[868] can be considered the direct beneficiary of such a tax measure. In such cases, the first two State aid conditions are satisfied. The remaining three constitutive elements of State aid in relation to foreign sovereign

---

866. Approaches (2) to (5) have been identified in Section 3.2.2.2 and are as follows:

   (2) according a general tax-exemption under domestic law or administrative practice.
   (3) according specific tax-exemptions or specific tax reductions under domestic law or administrative practice.
   (4) according a general tax-exemption under one or more tax treaties.
   (5) according specific tax-exemptions or specific tax reductions under one or more tax treaties.

867. Although there is currently no State aid case law dealing with the issue of the relationship between State aid and tax treaties, *communis opinio* in literature seems that specific tax treaty provisions could indeed constitute State aid. *See* R. Luja, 'Tax Treaties and State Aid: Some Thoughts' (2004) 44 *European Taxation* 234; L. De Broe, 'Can Tax Treaties Confer State Aid?' (2017) 26 *EC Tax Review* 228.
868. *See* Section 2.8.

wealth investors are analysed below. However, before doing so, the issue of State aid recovery and sovereign immunity will be touched upon briefly.

6.4.4.2.1 State Aid Recovery and Sovereign Immunity

Property of foreign sovereign wealth investors can enjoy immunity from measures of constraint in civil cases. In Section 4.5, it was concluded that it cannot be excluded that such immunity would also apply in tax cases. The question arises whether immunity from measures of constraint could prevent a Member State to recover unlawful fiscal State aid from a foreign sovereign wealth investor. If a foreign sovereign wealth investor has received unlawful fiscal State aid, the EC will order a Member State to take all necessary measures to recover this aid,[869] including interest, so that the advantage enjoyed over competitors on the market is forfeited, and the situation prior to payment of the aid is restored. In the event that a foreign sovereign wealth investor refuses to repay the aid, the respective Member State is left with the *ultimum remedium* of seeking enforcement measures to be taken against property of that foreign sovereign wealth investor, or possibly the foreign-owner State,[870] to satisfy its claim. This property could be situated in the respective Member State itself, but also in other States. A State would be prevented from taking enforcement measures if property of a foreign sovereign wealth investor would enjoy immunity from such measures. The EC shall not require recovery of the aid if this would be contrary to a general principle of Union law.[871] It is unclear whether immunity from measures of constraint, as an element of the customary international law principle of sovereign immunity, can be regarded as a general principle of Union law. Depending on the answer to that question, immunity from measures of constraint could prevent a Member State to recover fiscal State aid granted to a foreign sovereign wealth investor.

6.4.4.2.2 Undertaking (and Economic Activity)

From the discussion in Section 6.4.2.3, it follows that investors involved in the simple acquisition and sale of assets – i.e., *passive* investors – are not regarded to perform an economic activity and conduct an undertaking for State aid purposes. On the other hand, investors performing activities that go beyond the compass of the simple

---

869. Article 16(1) of the Procedural Regulation.
870. Under many legal instruments, foreign States and entities of foreign States are shielded against so-called cross-execution. For example, Art. 19(c) UNCSI 2004 provides that post-judgment measures of constraint can only be taken against property which has a connection with the entity against which the proceeding was directed. Therefore, if a creditor (such as a source State) has a claim against an SWF of a foreign State, the assets of that foreign State would be shielded against any post-judgment measures of execution, and vice versa. However, the issue of cross-execution has not yet been settled in State practice. See A, van Aaken, *Blurring Boundaries Between Sovereign Acts and Commercial Activities. A Functional View on Regulatory Immunity and Immunity from Execution* (March, 2013), Working Paper No. 2013-17, Law & Economics Research Paper Series, U. St. Gallen Law School, pp. 34–36.
871. Article 16(1) of the Procedural Regulation.

Chapter 6: European Tax Law Aspects

acquisition and sale of assets – i.e., *active* investors – do seem to qualify as an undertaking. Whether an investor qualifies as active or passive depends on the facts and circumstances, but an investor that holds a controlling shareholding in an undertaking and actually exercises that control by involving itself (directly or indirectly) in the management of that company must, in any case, be regarded as an *active* investor and therefore as an undertaking.

From the discussion in Section 6.4.2.3 it appears that the concept of economic activity is broadly interpreted in VAT case law, and could also include passive investment activities. VAT case law points out that the granting of interest-bearing loans, as well as placements in bank deposits or securities, such as treasury notes or certificates of deposit, constitute economic activities for VAT purposes, because the interest income is not merely the fruit of simple ownership of the asset, but the consideration for making capital available for the benefit of somebody else. If such a broad interpretation of the concept of economic activity, which clearly encompasses passive activities, would similarly apply for State aid purposes, it is clear from Section 2.9 that many foreign sovereign wealth investors would be considered to conduct an undertaking. However, although the CFI did not dismiss the EC's reference in *Fineco Asset Management* to VAT case law for the interpretation of the term economic activity in relation to investment vehicles, it is unclear whether the granting of interest-bearing loans, or placements in bank deposits or securities, would constitute an economic activity for State aid purposes. VAT case law also indicates that transactions carried out in the course of a business trading in securities can constitute an economic activity. This could fit the description above of *active* investors, but it is unclear what is required to be regarded as a business trading in securities.

The concept of economic activity for State aid purposes in relation to investors needs to be further crystallized, and its relationship with VAT case law (and other areas of European law) needs to be clarified. If this concept would be similar for State aid purposes and VAT purposes and therefore encompass passive investment activities, such as the granting of interest-bearing loans, or placements in bank deposits or securities, the investment activities of many foreign sovereign wealth investors would constitute economic activities. Otherwise, foreign sovereign wealth investors would seem to qualify as an undertaking when performing activities that go beyond the compass of the simple acquisition and sale of assets, which depends on the facts and circumstances. An investor that holds a controlling shareholding in an undertaking and actually exercises that control by involving itself (directly or indirectly) in the management of that company must, in any case, be regarded as an *active* investor and therefore as an undertaking. Based on the above, it is not unlikely that a foreign sovereign wealth investor performs economic activities and conducts an undertaking for State aid purposes.

With respect to activities performed by States (directly or through a separate legal body), a further distinction must be made between acts in the exercise of official authority and the pursuit of economic activities of an industrial or commercial nature. This distinction is relevant because acts in the exercise of official authority can never constitute State aid. All case law dealing with this issue is concerned with the classification of *activities of the Member State* (performed directly or through a separate legal body) *that has granted the alleged aid*. It is not concerned with the activities performed by foreign (Member) States. Given this difference, it is unclear to the author whether this distinction between governmental activities and commercial activities would similarly apply to activities of foreign Member States, or even third States. In many cases, this question has no practical relevance, because the activities of bodies that enjoy prerogatives of official authority (i.e., bodies that exercise an activity typical of public authority)[872] often do not extend beyond the territory of their home State. However, this question could become relevant in relation foreign sovereign wealth investors, because they are engaged in cross-border investments. Although the wording of the case law does not indicate that the distinction between acts in the exercise of official authority and economic activities of an industrial or commercial nature should not similarly apply to foreign Member States, or even third States, the outcome would probably be that investment activities of foreign sovereign wealth investors do not classify as acts in the exercise of official authority, because they can be performed by private (profit-making) investors as well. Indeed, the CJEU has held that 'the fact that an activity may be exercised by a private undertaking amounts to further evidence that the activity in question may be described as a business activity'.[873]

The fact that the activities of sovereign wealth investors are entirely financed by a State, and probably not being remunerated, does not mean that such investors cannot perform economic activities, in the author's view. In *Congregación de Escuelas Pías Provincia Betania*, this particular element was, in essence, decisive in classifying educational services as economic activities or not, because a service was only remunerated if the institutions were financed by private funds, rather than public funds. However, the issue of classifying activities of foreign sovereign wealth investors is of a different nature and takes place in a different context, since sovereign wealth investors invest instead of offering (educational) services. Based on the analysis above, sovereign wealth investors, although entirely financed by a State, and probably not being remunerated, could still qualify as *active* investors and therefore as undertakings.

6.4.4.2.3 Selectivity and Justification

A measure is selective if it favours certain undertakings as compared to other undertakings that are in a legal and factual situation that is comparable in the light of the objective pursued by the measure (reference system) at issue. A similar substantive approach regarding comparability is followed in free movement cases; the State aid rules are, therefore, the 'flip side' of the fundamental freedoms. As noted before,

---

[872]. This terminology is derived from the Opinion of Advocate General Cosmas, 10 December 1996, Case C-343/95 (*Servizi Ecologici Porto di Genova SpA*), Para. 41.
[873]. CJEU, 24 October 2002, Case C-82/01 P (*Aéroports de Paris*), Para. 82. *See* further, in the context of the VAT status of bodies governed by public law, CJEU, 19 January 2017, Case C-344/15 (*National Roads Authority*), Para. 39: '(...) what is envisaged here is the situation in which bodies governed by public law engage in activities which may also be engaged in, in competition with them, by private economic operators. The aim is to ensure that those private operators are not placed at a disadvantage because they are taxed while those bodies are not (...)'.

Chapter 6: European Tax Law Aspects

however, the implications of tax treaty benefits for the selectivity test under State aid rules are currently less clear. To date, this issue has not reached the CJEU. It would be consistent with the free movement cases *D.*[874] and *Riskin & Timmermans*,[875] if a tax treaty benefit accorded to a non-resident investor from one State, but not to a non-resident investor from another State (i.e., *horizontal* comparability), would not be considered selective for State aid purposes.[876] If the CJEU would reach the opposite conclusion under the State aid rules, the overall balance of a Member State's tax treaties could likewise be upset. The judgment in the State aid case *Congregación de Escuelas Pías Provincia Betania* does not have to set aside *D.* and *Riskin & Timmermans*. This case did not involve a benefit on the basis of a tax treaty, but it concerned a tax-exemption accorded by Spain to an establishment of the Catholic Church pursuant to an order of the Ministry of Finance that was based on a non-tax treaty between Spain and the Holy See. The CJEU seemed to have avoided the issue of the relationship between a treaty and State aid law by assuming that the order of the Ministry was the cause of the aid, rather than the treaty between Spain and the Holy See.[877] Advocate General Kokott was of the view that the tax benefit embedded in the treaty between Spain and the Holy See could be selective.[878] In the author's view, the tax benefit embedded in this non-tax treaty is 'a rather specific phenomenon'.[879] Furthermore, since this case did not concern a tax treaty benefit, the judgment in *Congregación de Escuelas Pías Provincia Betania* does not have to set aside *D.* and *Riskin & Timmermans*. Of course, the judgment in *D.* and *Riskin & Timmermans* can be criticized from the perspective of an internal market without borders and with free competition.[880]

A tax treaty benefit accorded by a Member State to particular non-resident investors could also result in more favourable treatment as compared to resident investors of that Member State (i.e., *reverse* comparability). This issue has not been

---

874. CJEU, 5 July 2005, Case C-376/03 (*D.*), Paras 53–63.
875. CJEU, 30 June 2016, Case C-176/15 (*Riskin & Timmermans*), Paras 29–35.
876. L. De Broe, 'Can Tax Treaties Confer State Aid?' (2017) 26 *EC Tax Review* 228, p. 230.
877. CJEU, 27 June 2017, Case C-74/16 (*Congregación de Escuelas Pías Provincia Betania*), Para. 69; J. Luts, 'Congregación de Escuelas Pías Provincia Betania: Tax Exemption for Education Services by Religious Congregation Not Sacrosanct from State Aid Perspective' (2017) 26 *EC Tax Review* 292.
878. Opinion of Advocate General Kokott, 16 February 2017, Case C-74/16 (*Congregación de Escuelas Pías Provincia Betania*), Para. 71: 'Under the "general system" concerned in this case, in Spain, a tax in favour of the municipality is levied on all constructions, installations and works. The fact that under the 1979 Agreement [between Spain and the Holy See] only the Catholic Church does not have to pay this tax constitutes an advantage for it which puts it in a better financial position than other economic operators, to the extent to which it is economically and therefore entrepreneurially active. In no way is it an advantage founded on a general measure applicable without distinction to all economic operators and available to anyone satisfying the conditions for it to be granted.'
879. Similarly, R. Luja, Case note on Case C-74/16 (*Congregación de Escuelas Pías Provincia Betania*), *Highlights & Insights on European Taxation* 2017/260.
880. For different views on this case, see D. Weber, 'Most-Favoured-Treatment under Tax Treaties Rejected in the European Community: Background and Analysis of the *D* Case: A Proposal to Include a Most-Favoured-Nation Clause in the EC Treaty' (2005) 33 *Intertax* 429; A. de Graaf & G. Janssen, 'The Implications of the Judgment in the *D* Case: The Perspective of Two Non-believers' (2005) 14 *EC Tax Review* 173.

dealt with under the freedoms, because the freedoms do not prohibit reverse discrimination. This may be an argument to use the State aid instrument in situations concerning reverse discrimination. On the other hand, the reasoning that tax treaty benefits are an integral part of a tax treaty and contribute to the overall balance of mutual relations between two States, applies similarly vis-à-vis a Member State which treats its residents less favourably than its non-residents pursuant to tax treaty benefits accorded to those non-residents.

It remains to be seen how the CJEU will deal with the issue of the relationship between tax treaty benefits and State aid law. The fact remains that the State aid rules are not identical to the fundamental freedoms. Differences are, therefore, possible, and it cannot be excluded that tax treaty benefits could be selective.

In addition, based on *Sopora*,[881] non-treaty benefits that favour particular non-resident investors as compared to other non-resident investors, could be selective. Different from horizontal comparability under the freedoms, horizontal comparability under the State aid rules is not limited to intra-EU/EEA situations.

A tax benefit can only be selective if it favours economic operators relative to other economic operators which are comparable in the light of the objective pursued by the reference system. The reference system is driven by the taxpayers that claim to be discriminated against.[882] In case of an alleged *reverse discrimination*, whether by means of a tax treaty or not, this means that the reference system should be a Member State's domestic tax system.[883] It also means that the general analysis in Section 6.3.3.3.1 above can be used, indicating that State entities or regular corporate shareholders are likely the best candidates in terms of vertical comparability with a foreign sovereign wealth investor. In case of an alleged *horizontal discrimination*, a distinction needs to be made between a tax treaty benefit and a tax benefit under domestic law. For the second, the reference system should a Member State's domestic tax system, so that the general analysis in Section 6.3.3.3.2 above can be relied upon. This analysis indicates that non-resident regular corporate shareholders or other foreign sovereign wealth investors (and non-resident State entities) are likely the best candidates in terms of horizontal comparability with a foreign sovereign wealth investor. In case of an alleged horizontal discrimination based on a tax treaty, the tax treaty as a whole or a particular tax treaty provision should be the reference system.[884] In the author's view, the distinction made in both the OECD and UN MTC between, for example, portfolio dividends and non-portfolio dividends is not selective, or can be justified, because it reflects a generally accepted allocation of taxing rights that can be considered a part of the general tax system of a State.[885] Following this line of thought would mean that the more special a tax treaty benefit becomes, the greater the chance it no longer reflects a

---

881. CJEU, 24 February 2015, Case C-512/13 (*Sopora*).
882. L. De Broe, 'Can Tax Treaties Confer State Aid?' (2017) 26 *EC Tax Review* 228, p. 229.
883. *Ibid.*
884. *Ibid.*, pp. 230–231.
885. Cf. CJEU, 12 May 1998, Case C-336/96 (*Gilly*), Para. 31, where it was held, in the context of the fundamental freedoms that, 'in the allocation of fiscal jurisdiction, (…) it [is not] unreasonable for the Member States to base their agreements on international practice and the model convention drawn up by the OECD.'

Chapter 6: European Tax Law Aspects

generally accepted allocation of taxing rights, and could be considered selective.[886] In her Opinion to *Congregación de Escuelas Pías Provincia Betania*, Advocate General Kokott also used the limited scope of the treaty benefit as an indication for selectivity.[887] In fact, the more special a tax treaty benefit becomes, the greater the chance it has nothing to do with the allocation of taxing rights and it has more to do with attracting investments from particular investors. Therefore, special tax treaty benefits which favour a sovereign wealth investor as compared to other non-resident investors, may be selective in some cases, but not in others.

A selective measure does not constitute State aid if it is justified by the nature or general scheme of the (reference) system (*see also* above). A tax measure aimed at attracting capital from (some) foreign sovereign wealth investors should not meet this justification test. Member States which accord preferential tax treatment to a foreign sovereign wealth investor, should bring forward other arguments to demonstrate that a particular selective tax measure is justified by the nature or general scheme of the (reference) system. For instance, a State could argue that a tax-exemption accorded to a foreign sovereign wealth investor is motivated by the sovereign immunity principle, which forms a part of the general tax scheme, as a result of which governmental activities are immune from its taxing jurisdiction. However, this argument must, in any case, be rejected if the tax-exemption is not truly motivated by sovereign immunity. In this regard, reference is made to Section 4.3.2 where it was argued that the tax-exemptions accorded to foreign sovereign wealth investors by Australia, Canada, the UK and the US seem to be motivated by other reasons than sovereign immunity, such as international attractiveness.

In any case, the selective advantage needs to be more than the *de minimis* threshold of EUR 200,000 over any period of three fiscal years.

6.4.4.2.4 Effect on Trade and Competition

It is obvious that preferential tax treatment of a foreign sovereign wealth investor is liable to improve its competitiveness position, thus to distort competition with other investors. However, it is less clear whether preferential tax treatment of a foreign sovereign wealth investor is liable to affect *trade between Member States*. On the one hand, it could be argued that (foreign sovereign wealth) investors are not involved in any trade, because they do not offer goods and services, but only invest money, so that a selective tax benefit accorded by a Member State to (foreign sovereign wealth) investors, although liable to affect competition, is not liable to affect trade between Member States. And even if foreign sovereign wealth investors are involved in any trade, it could be argued that the benefit has no major effect on trade between Member States, since most foreign sovereign wealth investors are based outside the Member

---

886. Similarly, R. Luja, 'Tax Treaties and State Aid: Some Thoughts' (2004) 44 *European Taxation* 234; E. Raingeard, *The Relationship Between EC Law and International Tax Law*, European Academic Tax Thesis Award, 2009, p. 28.
887. Opinion of Advocate General Kokott, 16 February 2017, Case C-74/16 (*Congregación de Escuelas Pías Provincia Betania*), Para. 71.

States. On the other hand, there is no requirement that the beneficiary undertaking itself be involved in intra-Union trade.[888] In *Cassa di Risparmio di Firenze SpA*, concerning an Italian banking foundation not involved in intra-Union trade, it was held that a measure is liable to affect trade between Member States when it may have helped 'to maintain or increase domestic activity, with the result that undertakings established in other Member States (...) [may have had] less chance of penetrating the market of the Member State concerned'.[889] Based on this consideration, it could be argued that a selective tax benefit accorded to a foreign sovereign wealth investor, although itself not involved in intra-Union trade, may have helped to maintain or increase domestic activity and may have given undertakings of other Member States less chance of investing in and penetrating the market of the Member State which offered the tax benefit. In *Cassa di Risparmio di Firenze SpA*, the court also observed, in the context of affecting trade between Member States, that the tax advantage in that case could 'strengthen, in terms of financing and/or funding, the position of the economic unit'.[890] It could, therefore, also be argued that, when an investor is considered to form one economic unit with its controlling shareholding in an undertaking, the tax benefit is liable to benefit the economic unit as a whole, which may affect trade between Member States *if at least part of the unit is involved in intra-Union trade*. It could, furthermore, be argued that a selective tax benefit accorded to foreign sovereign wealth investors, whether located inside or outside the Member States, is still potentially liable to affect trade between Member States as it could result in higher demand for assets (target companies) located in the respective Member State, increased liquidity and/or favourable financing conditions, thus strengthening the position of domestic economic operators compared with economic operators of other Member States. In the situations described above, the effect of the aid on intra-Union trade may be 'less immediate and even less discernible', which could require a 'greater effort to state reasons on the part of the [European] Commission'.[891]

Although surrounded with uncertainty, in particular in relation to foreign sovereign wealth investors that are based outside the Member States, it cannot, in the author's view, be excluded that preferential tax treatment of a foreign sovereign wealth investor, whether located inside or outside the Member States, would be regarded as being liable to affect trade between Member States. In this respect, it is noted that the magnitude of the aid on trade between the Member States has no impact on the amount of aid to be recovered. The recovery is aimed at restoring the situation prior to payment of the aid. According to settled fiscal State aid case law, this means that transactions must be subject to the tax treatment that would have applied in the absence of the unlawful fiscal aid.[892] Therefore, the 'calculation of the aid (...) simply involves determining the sum owing to the [Member] State which has not been collected and does not require complex assessments of an economic nature, or, in principle, an

---

888. CJEU, 10 January 2006, Case C-222/04 (*Cassa di Risparmio di Firenze SpA*), Para. 143.
889. *Ibid.*
890. *Ibid.*, Para. 145 (second indent).
891. CJEU, 30 April 2009, Case 494/06 P (*Wam SpA*), Para. 62.
892. CJEU, 21 December 2016, Joined Cases C-164/15 P and C-165/15 P (*Aer Lingus & Ryanair*), Para. 93 and case law cited.

analysis of the conditions of competition on the market in question or of the conduct of the operators concerned on that market'.[893]

6.4.4.3 Indirect Beneficiaries

If a foreign sovereign wealth investor does not conduct an undertaking, preferential tax treatment granted to a foreign sovereign wealth investor might constitute an indirect advantage and State aid for other natural or legal persons.[894] In this regard, State aid case law in the context of CIVs indicates that: (i) external asset managers of foreign sovereign wealth investors, and (ii) potential EU/EEA targets (EU/EEA investment opportunities) are potential indirect beneficiaries.[895]

6.4.4.3.1 External Asset Managers

External asset managers are indirect beneficiaries of a measure if that measure inevitably leads to an increase of their fees.[896] This could be so, for example, when the fees depend on the amount of assets under the management and this amount has increased as a result of a measure. A measure could also lead to an increase in fees when the fees depend on the net return on investment. A preferential tax measure accorded to a foreign sovereign wealth investor could lead to an increase in fees for their external asset managers, which could constitute State aid if the remaining conditions are satisfied, but only if the aid would exceed EUR 200,000 per undertaking over any period of three fiscal years.[897]

6.4.4.3.2 Investment Targets

EU/EEA investment targets are indirect beneficiaries of a preferential tax measure accorded to a foreign sovereign wealth investor if that measure has led to higher demand (and liquidity) for them.[898] However, any such (indirect) benefit is not selective, hence no State aid for such targets, if the preferential tax measure applies to investments (targets) in general and not to specific undertakings, sectors or industries, so that it could benefit targets (companies) in general. There is a tension between the consideration in Section 3.6.2 in the context of international attractiveness to accord special tax treatment to a foreign sovereign wealth investor only for investments that

---

893. Opinion of Advocate General Mengozzi, 5 July 2016, Joined Cases C-164/15 P and C-165/15 P (*Aer Lingus & Ryanair*), Para. 66.
894. CFI, 4 March 2009, Case T-445/05 (*Fineco Asset Management*), Para. 127 and case law cited.
895. CFI, 4 March 2009, Case T-445/05 (*Fineco Asset Management*).
896. *Ibid.*, Para. 143.
897. Article 3 of the *Commission Regulation (EU) No 1407/2013 of 18 December 2013 on the application of Articles 107 and 108 of the Treaty on the Functioning of the European Union to de minimis aid*, Official Journal of the European Union, Vol. 56, L 352, 24 December 2013, p. 1; Art. 15(1) of Part II of Protocol 3 to the Agreement between the EFTA States on the Establishment of a Surveillance Authority and a Court of Justice.
898. CFI, 4 March 2009, Case T-445/05 (*Fineco Asset Management*), Paras 159 et seq.

no, or at least few, others are willing to make, and the selectivity issue regarding indirect beneficiaries. Even if an indirect benefit is selective, all or part of the aid granted to individual indirect beneficiaries might fall within the scope of the rules on *de minimis* aid.

With respect to the recovery of aid, it is noted that indirect beneficiaries could be required to pay to a Member State an amount not corresponding to the actual benefit they have indirectly derived from the aid measure. In *Fineco Asset Management*, the court ordered the indirect beneficiaries (i.e., the investment vehicles and the fund managers) to pay to the Italian Republic an amount corresponding to the tax reduction enjoyed by the direct beneficiaries (i.e., the investors) of the aid, because only then the situation prior to payment of the aid could be restored.[899]

6.4.4.4 *Conclusion*

Although uncertain in many situations, the analysis in this chapter demonstrates, in the author's view, that preferential tax treatment accorded to a foreign sovereign wealth investor by a Member State could constitute (unlawful) State aid for such an investor, regardless of whether it resides inside or outside the Member States. The three key elements involved are: (i) whether a foreign sovereign wealth investor would be regarded to perform an economic activity and therefore to conduct an undertaking, (ii) whether a tax benefit accorded to a foreign sovereign wealth investor would be regarded as selective, and (iii) whether a tax benefit accorded to a foreign sovereign wealth investor would be liable to affect trade between Member States.

If the concept of economic activity would be similar for State aid and VAT purposes, and therefore comprise passive investment activities, such as the granting of interest-bearing loans, or placements in bank deposits or securities, the investment activities of many foreign sovereign wealth investors would constitute economic activities. Otherwise, foreign sovereign wealth investors would seem to qualify as an undertaking when performing activities that go beyond the compass of the simple acquisition and sale of assets (i.e., *active* investors). This depends on the facts and circumstances. However, an investor that holds a controlling shareholding in an undertaking and actually exercises that control by involving itself (directly or indirectly) in the management of that company, must, in any case, be regarded as an *active* investor and therefore as an undertaking.

The selectivity test under State aid rules is, in principle, similar to the comparability approach in free movement cases; the State aid rules are, therefore, the 'flip side' of the fundamental freedoms. A tax benefit can only be selective if it favours economic operators relative to other economic operators which are comparable in the light of the objective pursued by the reference system. The reference system is driven by the taxpayers that claim to be discriminated against. Although the State aid rules follow the comparability approach in free movement cases, the implications of tax treaty benefits

---

899. *Ibid.*, Paras 198–204.

Chapter 6: European Tax Law Aspects

are currently less clear. Therefore, it cannot be excluded that tax treaty benefits which favour a sovereign wealth investor over other investors, will be considered selective by the CJEU in a State aid context.

The question whether a tax benefit accorded to a foreign sovereign wealth investor would be liable to affect trade between Member States arises in particular in relation to foreign sovereign wealth investors that are based outside the Member States. It could, for example, be argued that a selective tax benefit accorded to foreign sovereign wealth investors, whether located inside or outside the Member States, is still potentially liable to affect trade between Member States, as it could result in higher demand for assets (target companies) located in the respective Member State, increased liquidity and/or favourable financing conditions, and thus strengthening the position of domestic economic operators compared with economic operators of other Member States, or it could maintain or increase domestic activity.

Member States wishing to introduce new or change existing tax policy vis-à-vis foreign sovereign wealth investors could consider notifying the EC respectively the EFTA Surveillance Authority in case of doubt as regards to the application of the State aid rules.

In addition, a preferential tax measure accorded by Member States to foreign sovereign wealth investors which are not undertakings themselves could amount to State aid for external asset managers (as indirect beneficiaries), if that measure inevitably leads to an increase of their fees, but only if it would exceed EUR 200,000 per undertaking over any period of three fiscal years. Although a preferential tax measure accorded to foreign sovereign wealth investors by Member States could also benefit EU/EEA investment targets through higher demand and liquidity, any such (indirect) benefit is not selective, and hence no State aid for such targets, if that measure applies to targets in general and not just to specific undertakings, sectors or industries.

6.5 PARENT-SUBSIDIARY DIRECTIVE AND INTEREST & ROYALTIES DIRECTIVE

6.5.1 Parent-Subsidiary Directive

6.5.1.1 *Main Features*

In essence, the Parent-Subsidiary Directive abolishes the taxation[900] of outbound profit distributions (dividends) from a subsidiary of one EU Member State to its parent

---

900. The directive refers to 'withholding tax', but contains no definition of this term. The CJEU uses a substantive definition of 'withholding tax': '(...) every tax on income received by a parent company from a subsidiary established in another Member State, the chargeable event being the payment of dividends or of any other income from shares, where the taxable amount is the income from those shares and the taxable person is the holder of those shares.' (CJEU, 12 December 2006, Case C-446/04 (*Test Claimants in the FII Group Litigation*), Para. 109). This definition can also include taxes levied by assessment.

company in another EU Member State,[901] and eliminates double taxation on inbound dividends in the EU Member State of the parent company. To that end, key conditions to be satisfied include:

- the parent and subsidiary are a company of an EU Member State as listed in the Annex to the directive;
- the parent and subsidiary are resident for tax purposes in an EU Member State according to the national tax laws of that Member State, and cannot be considered a resident outside the EU pursuant to a tax treaty with a third country;
- the parent and subsidiary are subject to one of the taxes listed in the Annex to the directive, without being exempt and without the possibility of an option to be exempt;
- the parent holds at least 10% of the capital of the subsidiary; and
- anti-abuse rules do not apply.

6.5.1.2 *Some Comments Regarding Foreign Sovereign Wealth Investors*

As explained in Section 2.8, foreign sovereign wealth investors can take a number of different legal forms, such as separate legal entities under public law, as well as separate legal entities under company law. The focus in the Annex is on a wide range of legal forms under company law, whereas legal forms under public law may not qualify. However, since the vast majority of SWFs reside outside the EU,[902] the (potential) application of the Parent-Subsidiary Directive is often limited to SWEs (of SWFs) that have been established under the laws of an EU Member State. And if these EU based SWEs will have a separate legal personality, their legal form will generally be listed in the Annex, and they will be entitled to the benefits of the Parent-Subsidiary Directive if the remaining conditions are satisfied. These conditions will not be satisfied if the SWE has been set-up with the main purpose or one of the main purposes of obtaining the benefits of the directive.[903]

6.5.2 Interest & Royalties Directive

6.5.2.1 *Main Features*

In essence, the Interest & Royalties Directive aims to avoid juridical double taxation[904] and abolishes the taxation of outbound interest and royalty payments from a company

---

901. The Parent-Subsidiary Directive (Art. 1) also covers certain situations involving permanent establishments.
902. *See* Section 2.5.
903. Article 1(2)-(3) Parent-Subsidiary Directive.
904. CJEU, 21 July 2011, Case C-397/09 (*Scheuten Solar Technology GmbH*), Para. 28.

of one EU Member State to an associated company of another EU Member State.[905] To that end, key conditions to be satisfied include:

- the debtor and the recipient are a company of an EU Member State as listed in the Annex to the directive;
- the debtor and the recipient are resident for tax purposes in an EU Member State according to the national tax laws of that Member State, and cannot be considered a resident outside the EU pursuant to a tax treaty with a third country;
- the debtor and the recipient are subject to one of the taxes listed in the Annex to the directive, without being exempt;
- the debtor and the recipient are associated companies, which means that either: (i) the recipient directly holds at least 25% of the capital (or voting rights) of the debtor, or vice versa, or (ii) a third company directly holds at least 25% in both the debtor and the recipient;
- the recipient is the beneficial owner of the interest or royalties; and
- (other) anti-abuse rules do not apply.

In November 2011, the EC proposed to amend the Interest & Royalties Directive. Key elements of this proposal were to: (i) extend the currently limited list of qualifying entities in line with the Parent-Subsidiary Directive, (ii) replace the 25%-threshold by a 10%-threshold that also covers indirect holdings, and (iii) not require a tax-exemption on outbound interest and royalty payments if the payments are exempt from corporate income tax in the Member State of the recipient.[906] On 26 and 30 May 2017, the Maltese Presidency proposed compromise texts, but no agreement could be reached among the Member States.[907] Therefore, this file is still pending.

6.5.2.2 Some Comments Regarding Foreign Sovereign Wealth Investors

The comments made above in respect of the Parent-Subsidiary Directive largely apply to the Interest & Royalties Directive as well. However, given the (far) more limited list of qualifying legal forms under the Interest & Royalties Directive, chances that EU based SWEs will have a legal form that is not listed in the Annex could be greater.

---

905. The Interest & Royalties Directive (Art. 1) also covers certain situations involving permanent establishments.
906. Proposal for a Council Directive on a common system of taxation applicable to interest and royalty payments made between associated companies of different Member States (COM(2011) 714 final).
907. ECOFIN Report to the European Council on Tax issues, 10397/17, 16 June 2017, pp. 9–11.

6.6 IMPACT OF EUROPEAN LAW ON ACHIEVING NEUTRALITY (EFFICIENCY), EQUITY (FAIRNESS) AND INTERNATIONAL ATTRACTIVENESS IN RELATION TO FOREIGN SOVEREIGN WEALTH INVESTORS

In this section, it will be examined what impact European law could have on source States' ability to achieve (or promote) tax policy objectives (i.e., neutrality, equity and international attractiveness), and to freely implement an approach to the taxation of foreign sovereign wealth investors. For the sake of convenience, the different approaches as identified in Chapter 3, and their relationship with the tax policy objectives, are repeated below:

(1) taxing foreign sovereign wealth investors in the same way as 'regular' non-resident corporate investors;
(2) according a general tax-exemption under domestic law or administrative practice;
(3) according specific tax-exemptions or specific tax reductions under domestic law or administrative practice;
(4) according a general tax-exemption under one or more tax treaties;
(5) according specific tax-exemptions or specific tax reductions under one or more tax treaties.

Chapter 6: European Tax Law Aspects

Table 6.1 Approaches to Source Taxation of Foreign Sovereign Wealth Investors Measured by Neutrality, Equity and International Attractiveness

	Neutrality		Equity		International Attractiveness
	(CEN)	(CIN)	(inter-nation)	(inter-taxpayer)	
Approach (1)*	X	✓	✓	✓	X
Approach (2)*	✓	X	X	X	✓
Approach (3)*	✓	X	X	X	✓
Approach (4)*	✓	X	X	X	✓
Approach (5)*	✓	X	X	X	✓

* Approach (1): taxing foreign sovereign wealth investors in the same way as 'regular' non-resident corporate investors.
Approach (2): according a general tax-exemption under domestic law or administrative practice.
Approach (3): according specific tax-exemptions or specific tax reductions under domestic law or administrative practice.
Approach (4): according a general tax-exemption under one or more tax treaties.
Approach (5): according specific tax-exemptions or specific tax reductions under one or more tax treaties.

6.6.1 Neutrality (Efficiency)

6.6.1.1 *Capital Export Neutrality*

Foreign sovereign wealth investors are generally not taxed in their residence State.[908] Source State taxation of tax-exempt non-resident investors could distort neutrality with respect to the investment location, i.e., it could result in tax-exempt investors favouring domestic investments over foreign investments.[909] In order to promote export neutrality (from a residence State perspective), a Member State could consider to exempt from source taxation investment income derived by foreign sovereign wealth investors and other non-resident tax-exempt investors. It could accord such treatment unilaterally – i.e., Approaches (2) and (3) – or through tax treaties – i.e., Approaches (4) and (5).

Primary European law

According tax-exemptions to foreign sovereign wealth investors, but not to resident investors – i.e., reverse discrimination – is not prohibited by the fundamental freedoms.[910] It could, however, constitute (unlawful) State aid, even when this different treatment is based on a tax treaty, but a State aid risk will probably be limited to *active* foreign sovereign wealth investors.[911] In the event of State aid, the Member State would need to recover the aid granted. Thus, the State aid rules could, under circumstances, restrict Member States' ability to promote CEN.

According unilateral tax-exemptions to foreign sovereign wealth investors, but not to comparable other non-resident investors, could constitute horizontal discrimination under the freedoms in intra-EU/EEA situations (but unlikely in non-EU/EEA situations).[912] In that case, other non-resident investors would be entitled to the tax-exemptions as well. According unilateral tax-exemptions to foreign sovereign wealth investors, but not to comparable other non-resident investors, could also constitute (unlawful) State aid, even in non-EU/EEA situations, but this risk will probably be limited to *active* foreign sovereign wealth investors.[913] In the event of State aid, other non-resident investors would not be entitled to the tax-exemptions, but the Member State would need to recover the aid granted. Thus, the freedoms as well as the State aid rules could, under circumstances, restrict Member States' ability to promote CEN through Approaches (2) and (3).

In contrast, according tax-exemptions to foreign sovereign wealth investors through tax treaties but not to non-resident investors from other States, or from the same State, should not constitute horizontal discrimination under the freedoms, not even in intra-EU/EEA situations.[914] It may, however, constitute (unlawful) State aid

---

908. *See* Section 2.10 and Section 3.2.1.2.
909. *See* Section 3.4.2.2.
910. *See* Section 6.3.2.1.
911. *See* Section 6.4.4.2.2 and Section 6.4.4.2.3.
912. *See* Section 6.3.3.3.2.
913. *See* Section 6.4.4.2.2 and Section 6.4.4.2.3.
914. *See* Section 6.3.3.2.

under rather strict circumstances.[915] Thus, primary European law may restrict Member States' ability to promote CEN through Approaches (4) and (5).

Secondary EU law

If the conditions of the Parent-Subsidiary Directive and Interest & Royalties Directive are satisfied, an EU Member State is obliged to tax-exempt outbound dividend, interest and royalty payments between affiliated entities in cross-border intra-EU situations. These directives have no (negative) impact on EU Member States' ability to promote CEN in relation to foreign sovereign wealth investors.

6.6.1.2 Capital Import Neutrality

CIN requires equal treatment of investors that perform the same level of investment activities in a source State, which implies a territorial (or source-based) tax system; in other words, a tax system which exempts foreign sourced income and treats domestic sourced income of resident and non-resident investors in the same way.[916]

Primary European law

In principle, neither the fundamental freedoms, nor the State aid rules, prohibit a Member State from implementing a (territorial based) tax system which would promote CIN by adopting equal treatment of investors that perform the same level of investment activities in a source State, irrespective of their place of residence and characteristics.[917] Thus, primary European law has no (negative) impact on Member States' ability to promote CIN, and to implement Approach (1). In fact, the fundamental freedoms even contribute to CIN to the extent that they require similar source State taxation between non-resident investors and resident investors (vertical comparison), and among non-resident investors (horizontal comparison). They would only do so if investors are held to be objectively comparable (and a different treatment cannot be justified), which is determined, unilaterally and rather strictly, in the light of the objective of the national tax measure at issue, and by the relevant conditions laid down in the national tax legislation of a State as imposed on its residents.[918] Although it was argued that State entities or regular corporate shareholders are likely the best candidates in terms of objective vertical comparability with a foreign sovereign wealth investor,[919] many other non-resident investors will be held incomparable to any resident investor under this test. In such cases, the fundamental freedoms do not

---

915. *See* Section 6.4.4.2.3.
916. *See* Section 3.4.3.1.
917. It should, however, be noted that the freedom of establishment would require a Member State of a parent company to take into account 'definitive losses' of a foreign subsidiary of another Member State under rather strict conditions, also known as the *Marks & Spencer* exception, or the 'final losses' doctrine. *See* CJEU, 13 December 2005, Case C-446/03 *(Marks & Spencer)*, Para. 55; as specified in subsequent case law, such as CJEU 3 February 2015, Case C-172/13 *(European Commission v. United Kingdom)*.
918. *See* Section 6.3.3.1.
919. *See* Section 6.3.3.3.

enforce equal treatment. In this respect, it is noted that, due to its universal scope, the freedoms of capital movement in the TFEU has greater potential to contribute to CIN than its counterpart in the EEA Agreement.

As regards horizontal comparability, the impact of the fundamental freedoms seems further confined to intra-EU/EEA situations,[920] and the prohibition of horizontal discrimination should not apply in case of tax treaty benefits.[921] The State aid rules could (effectively) also contribute to CIN to the extent that these rules prohibit different taxation of non-resident investors and resident investors (vertical comparability), or among non-resident investors (horizontal comparability). However, since the selectivity test under State aid rules seems similar to the comparability approach in free movement cases,[922] it is possible that non-resident investors are held not to be objectively comparable to any resident investor, or to any other non-resident investor. Different from the fundamental freedoms, horizontal comparability under the State aid rules is not limited to intra-EU/EEA situations. To conclude, both the fundamental freedoms and the State aid rules could contribute to CIN to a certain extent, but they may still allow various situations which are in conflict with CIN.

Secondary EU law

If the conditions of the Parent-Subsidiary Directive and Interest & Royalties Directive are satisfied, an EU Member State is obliged to tax-exempt outbound dividend, interest and royalty payments between affiliated entities in cross-border intra-EU situations. This could give rise to preferential tax treatment of (some) EU based foreign sovereign wealth investors (and other EU based non-resident investors) over other investors. An EU Member State wishing to promote CIN by introducing equal treatment between investors could be required to *reduce* and/or *increase* the current level of taxation of EU based foreign sovereign wealth investors and other non-resident investors. However, its obligations under the Parent-Subsidiary Directive and Interest & Royalties Directive could restrict an EU Member State to follow the second route (*increase*), as opposed to the first route (*reduction*), while the first route may not always be realistic from a revenue perspective. Thus, secondary EU law could restrict an EU Member State's ability to promote CIN, and to implement Approach (1).

6.6.2 Equity (Fairness)

6.6.2.1 *Inter-taxpayer Equity*

The benefit theory, which, unlike the ability-to-pay theory, is also relevant for the taxation of non-residents, requires that each taxpayer should pay tax in accordance with its level of benefit from governmental goods and services.[923] From this general

---

920. Which would mean that the freedom of capital movement in the TFEU has no universal scope when it comes to horizontal comparability.
921. *See* Section 6.3.3.2.
922. *See* Section 6.4.4.2.3.
923. *See* Section 3.5.2.1.

rule, three, more practical, rules of thumb were derived which are relevant for the taxation of foreign sovereign wealth investors, from a source State perspective.[924] The *first rule* is that a source State should generally not tax non-resident investors less favourably than resident investors when performing the same investment activities in and earning the same level of income from that source State. It may, in such circumstances, even require non-resident investors to be taxed more favourably than resident investors. The *second rule* is that a source State should treat and tax all non-resident investors as equals when they perform the same investment activities in and earn the same level of income from that source State (i.e., horizontal non-discriminatory treatment). The *third rule*, which applies to both the first and second rule, is that forgoing taxation would not make sense from a benefit perspective, since residents and non-residents that perform investment activities in the source State always benefit from public goods and services to some extent.

Primary European law

The analysis regarding inter-taxpayer equity in the light of primary European law is similar to the analysis above in respect of CIN, but needs to be completed for the situation in which the benefit principle would prescribe foreign sovereign wealth investors (and other non-resident investors) to be taxed more favourably than resident investors (i.e., the first rule). More favourable treatment of foreign sovereign wealth investors (and other non-resident investors) over resident investors is not prohibited by the fundamental freedoms, since the freedoms do not prohibit reverse discrimination,[925] but it may constitute (unlawful) State aid. However, this State aid risk will probably be limited to *active* foreign (sovereign wealth) investors. Thus, primary European law could restrict Member States' ability to achieve inter-taxpayer equity, but only if the benefit principle would prescribe foreign sovereign wealth investors (and other non-resident investors) to be taxed more favourably than resident investors. This conclusion has no impact on Member States' ability to implement Approach (1)[926] though because this approach is concerned with the relationship among non-resident investors, rather than the relationship between non-resident and resident investors. Thus, primary European law, notably the State aid rules, could restrict Member States' ability to achieve inter-taxpayer equity, but this conclusion does not impact Approach (1).

Secondary EU law

The analysis regarding inter-taxpayer equity in the light of secondary EU law is similar to the analysis above in respect of CIN, but the following should be added regarding the third rule. At first sight, the Parent-Subsidiary Directive and Interest & Royalties Directive both seem to conflict with the essence of the benefit principle, i.e., that everyone should pay tax in accordance with its benefit from public goods and services.

---

924. *See* Section 3.5.2.2.
925. *See* Section 6.3.2.1.
926. Approach (1) has been identified in Section 3.2.2.2 and is as follows: taxing foreign sovereign wealth investors in the same way as 'regular' non-resident corporate investors.

However, in the author's view, this does not necessarily apply to the Parent-Subsidiary Directive. As explained in Chapter 3, taxation of (undistributed) profits at the level of the subsidiary is effectively at the expense of the shareholder/investor. It can, therefore, be argued that the application of the Parent-Subsidiary Directive to outbound dividend payments between affiliated entities in cross-border intra-EU situations does not necessarily contradict the benefit principle[927] (unless the benefit principle would require additional taxation on outbound dividends). This cannot be said about the Interest & Royalties Directive. Arm's length interest and royalties generally reduce the tax base in the source State, and the abolition of source State taxation on deductible outbound interest and royalty payments in cross-border intra-EU situations leaves the source State empty-handed. This outcome would conflict with the benefit principle, because the creditor/investor has benefitted from public goods and services, at least to some extent. Based on the above, the Interest & Royalties Directive seems to impose greater restrictions on an EU Member State to implement the benefit principle than the Parent-Subsidiary Directive would do.

6.6.2.2 Inter-nation Equity

Under inter-nation equity, non-resident investors from the same State that perform the same (investment) activities in a source State should be treated alike in that source State.[928] A different treatment of non-resident investors from different States can be justified on redistribution grounds only.[929] The concept of inter-nation equity is, to a large extent, associated with the concept of horizontal comparability.

Primary European law

In principle, neither the fundamental freedoms, nor the State aid rules, impose restrictions on a Member State to treat non-resident investors from the same State that perform the same (investment) activities in a source State alike. Thus, primary European law has no impact on Member States' ability to achieve inter-nation equity, and to implement Approach (1) if it would not be required to treat non-resident investors from different States differently, based on redistribution grounds. In fact, the fundamental freedoms could even contribute to inter-nation equity to the extent that they require similar source State taxation between non-resident investors from the same State (horizontal comparability). Although *Sopora*[930] was concerned with non-resident workers from different States, the author does not see why the concept of horizontal comparability would apply any differently to non-residents from the same State.[931] The fundamental freedoms would, therefore, require equal source State taxation between non-resident investors from the same State, provided they are held to

---

927. Similarly, E. Kemmeren, *Principle of Origin in Tax Conventions: A Rethinking of Models* (2001), Dongen: Mr Eric C.C.M. Kemmeren/Pijnenburg vormgevers, uitgevers, p. 218.
928. See Section 3.5.3.2.
929. *Ibid.*
930. CJEU, 24 February 2015, Case C-512/13 (*Sopora*).
931. *See* Section 6.3.3.2.

Chapter 6: European Tax Law Aspects

be objectively comparable (and a different treatment cannot be justified), which is determined, unilaterally and rather strictly, in the light of the objective of the national tax measure at issue, and by the relevant conditions laid down in the national tax legislation of a State.[932] The scope of the prohibition of horizontal discrimination under the fundamental freedoms seems further confined to intra-EU/EEA situations,[933] and should not apply to tax treaty benefits.[934] The State aid rules could (effectively) also contribute to inter-nation equity to the extent that they prohibit different taxation among non-resident investors from the same State (horizontal comparability). The selectivity test under State aid rules is similar to the comparability approach in free movement cases.[935] However, the scope of horizontal comparability under the State aid rules is not limited to intra-EU/EEA situations, but it will probably be limited to *active* investors. Based on the above, both the fundamental freedoms and the State aid rules could contribute to inter-nation equity to a certain extent, but they may still allow various situations which are in conflict with this concept.

From the discussion above, it is now also clear that both the fundamental freedoms and the State aid rules could impose restrictions on a Member State if inter-nation equity would require to treat non-resident investors from different States differently, based on redistribution grounds. However, as discussed, in the context of horizontal comparability, the impact of the fundamental freedoms seems confined to intra-EU/EEA situations, is limited to non-treaty benefits, and is further limited by the comparability standard. In the context of horizontal comparability, the impact of the State aid rules should not be confined to intra-EU/EEA situations and may or may not be limited to non-treaty benefits, but it does seem limited to *active* investors. Therefore, treating non-resident investors from different States differently based on redistribution grounds should still be achieved through tax treaties as much as possible.

To conclude, primary European law could restrict Member States' ability to achieve inter-nation equity, but only if inter-nation equity would require to treat non-resident investors from different States differently, based on redistribution grounds. To limit the impact as much as possible, different treatment of non-resident investors from different States should be achieved through tax treaties as much as possible. Whereas both the fundamental freedoms and the State aid rules could restrict Member States' ability to achieve inter-nation equity, this conclusion has no impact on Member States' ability to implement Approach (1)[936] though because this approach implies equal treatment between non-resident investors from different States (as opposed to different treatment).

---

932. *See* Section 6.3.3.3.2.
933. Which would mean that the freedom of capital movement in the TFEU has no universal scope when it comes to horizontal comparability.
934. *See* Section 6.3.3.2.
935. *See* Section 6.4.4.2.3.
936. Approach (1) has been identified in Section 3.2.2.2 and is as follows: taxing foreign sovereign wealth investors in the same way as 'regular' non-resident corporate investors.

Secondary EU law

The Parent-Subsidiary Directive and Interest & Royalties Directive could result in different tax burdens for non-resident investors from the same EU Member State, which could be in conflict with inter-nation equity. Source States wishing to promote inter-nation equity by introducing equal treatment between non-resident investors from the same State could be required to *reduce* and/or *increase* the current level of taxation of EU based foreign sovereign wealth investors and other non-resident investors. However, its obligations under Parent-Subsidiary Directive and Interest & Royalties Directive could restrict an EU Member State to follow the second route (*increase*), as opposed to the first route (*reduction*), while the first route may not always be realistic from a revenue perspective. Thus, secondary EU law could restrict an EU Member State's ability to achieve inter-nation equity, and to implement Approach (1).

6.6.3 International Attractiveness

In order to enhance international attractiveness, a Member State could consider to accord (a general or specific) tax-exemptions or reductions to (one or more) foreign sovereign wealth investors.[937] It could accord such treatment unilaterally – i.e., Approaches (2) and (3) – or through tax treaties – i.e., Approaches (4) and (5).[938]

Primary European law

The analysis regarding international attractiveness in the light of primary European law is similar to the analysis above in respect of CEN, but is repeated below for the sake of convenience.

According tax-exemptions to foreign sovereign wealth investors, but not to resident investors – i.e., reverse discrimination – is not prohibited by the fundamental freedoms.[939] It could, however, constitute (unlawful) State aid, even when this different treatment is based on a tax treaty, but a State aid risk will probably be limited to *active* foreign sovereign wealth investors.[940] In the event of State aid, the Member State would need to recover the aid granted. Thus, the State aid rules could, under circumstances, restrict Member States' ability to promote international attractiveness.

According unilateral tax-exemptions (or tax reductions) to foreign sovereign wealth investors, but not to comparable other non-resident investors, could constitute

---

937. *See* Section 3.6.2.
938. Approaches (2) to (5) have been identified in Section 3.2.2.2 and are as follows:

    (2) according a general tax-exemption under domestic law or administrative practice.
    (3) according specific tax-exemptions or specific tax reductions under domestic law or administrative practice.
    (4) according a general tax-exemption under one or more tax treaties.
    (5) according specific tax-exemptions or specific tax reductions under one or more tax treaties.

939. *See* Section 6.3.2.1.
940. *See* Section 6.4.4.2.2 and Section 6.4.4.2.3.

horizontal discrimination under the freedoms in intra-EU/EEA situations (but unlikely in non-EU/EEA situations).[941] In that case, other non-resident investors would be entitled to the tax-exemptions (or tax reductions) as well. According unilateral tax-exemptions (or tax reductions) to foreign sovereign wealth investors, but not to comparable other non-resident investors, could also constitute (unlawful) State aid, even in non-EU/EEA situations, but this risk will probably be limited to *active* foreign sovereign wealth investors.[942] In the event of State aid, other non-resident investors would not be entitled to the tax-exemptions (or tax reductions), but the Member State would need to recover the aid granted. Thus, the freedoms as well as the State aid rules could, under circumstances, restrict Member States' ability to promote international attractiveness through Approaches (2) and (3).

In contrast, according tax-exemptions (or tax reductions) to foreign sovereign wealth investors through tax treaties but not to non-resident investors from other States, or from the same State, should not constitute horizontal discrimination under the freedoms, not even in intra-EU/EEA situations.[943] It may, however, constitute (unlawful) State aid under rather strict circumstances.[944] Thus, primary European law may restrict Member States' ability to promote international attractiveness through Approaches (4) and (5).

Secondary EU law

If the conditions of the Parent-Subsidiary Directive and Interest & Royalties Directive are satisfied, an EU Member State is obliged to tax-exempt outbound dividend, interest and royalty payments between affiliated entities in cross-border intra-EU situations, which could enhance international attractiveness in relation to EU based foreign sovereign wealth investors. The Parent-Subsidiary Directive and Interest & Royalties Directive have no (negative) impact on EU Member States' ability to promote international attractiveness in relation to foreign sovereign wealth investors through Approaches (2) to (5) (i.e., they do not impose restrictions on EU Member States to do so).

6.7 CONCLUSIONS

This chapter considered the (possible) implications of European law for source State taxation of foreign sovereign wealth investors. Based on these implications, it was examined what impact European law could have on source States' ability to achieve (or promote) tax policy objectives (i.e., neutrality, equity and international attractiveness), and to freely implement an approach to taxation of foreign sovereign wealth investors.[945]

The (possible) key implications of European law for source State taxation of foreign sovereign wealth investors are the following:

---

941. *See* Section 6.3.3.3.2.
942. *See* Section 6.4.4.2.2 and Section 6.4.4.2.3.
943. *See* Section 6.3.3.2.
944. *See* Section 6.4.4.2.3.
945. *See* the five approaches identified in Section 3.2.2.2.

(1) The freedom of capital movement and freedom of establishment do not prohibit *reverse discrimination*: a Member State is allowed to tax a foreign sovereign wealth investor more favourably than resident investors. However, the State aid rules could prohibit reverse discrimination, even if more favourable treatment of non-residents is achieved through a tax treaty.
(2) The freedom of establishment in both the TFEU and EEA Agreement does not apply to foreign sovereign wealth investors not formed in accordance with the law of a Member State and not having their registered office, central administration or principal place of business in a Member State. The scope of the freedom of capital movement enshrined in the EEA Agreement is limited to residents of the EU Member States/EEA-EFTA States. However, importantly, the TFEU accords universal territorial and personal scope to the freedom of capital movement, although certain restrictions which already existed before 1994 in relation to third countries may be allowed under the grandfathering rule. The precise implications of this standstill provision for the taxation of inbound portfolio investments from third countries are currently uncertain. As noted, most sovereign wealth investors reside in third countries.
(3) The freedom of capital movement and freedom of establishment prohibit *vertical discrimination*: a Member State is not allowed to tax a foreign sovereign wealth investor less favourably than resident investors, but only if their situations are objectively comparable. Objective comparability is determined, unilaterally and rather strictly, in the light of the objective of the national tax measure at issue, and by the relevant conditions laid down in the national tax legislation of a State as imposed on its residents. A similar substantive approach regarding comparability is followed for State aid purposes (selectivity test); the State aid rules are, therefore, the 'flip side' of the fundamental freedoms. It was argued that State entities or regular corporate shareholders are likely the best candidates in terms of objective vertical comparability with a foreign sovereign wealth investor.
(4) The freedom of capital movement and freedom of establishment may also prohibit *horizontal discrimination*, in which case a Member State would not be allowed to tax a foreign sovereign wealth investor less favourably than an objectively comparable other foreign sovereign wealth investor or other non-resident investor. In the author's view, the framework for vertical comparability should be applied as much as possible to assess horizontal comparability of investors in outbound situations. Importantly, the prohibition of horizontal discrimination under the freedoms seems to be limited to intra-EU/EEA situations (*Haribo and Salinen* and *Sopora*),[946] and should not apply in case of tax treaty benefits (*D.* and *Riskin & Timmermans*). The framework for horizontal comparability under the State aid rules and the freedoms seems similar, although horizontal comparability under the former is not limited to intra-EU/EEA situations and may or may not apply in case of

---

946. Which would mean that the freedom of capital movement in the TFEU has no universal scope when it comes to horizontal comparability.

Chapter 6: European Tax Law Aspects

tax treaty benefits. It was argued that other foreign sovereign wealth investors (and non-resident State entities) or non-resident regular corporate shareholders are likely the best candidates in terms of objective horizontal comparability with a foreign sovereign wealth investor. These outcomes are in line with the outcomes in the context of vertical comparability, because horizontal comparability is to a large extent influenced by vertical comparability.

(5) Although uncertain in many situations, it cannot, in the author's view, be excluded that preferential tax treatment accorded to a foreign sovereign wealth investor by a Member State could constitute (unlawful) State aid for such an investor, regardless of whether it resides inside or outside Member States. The three key elements involved are: (i) whether a foreign sovereign wealth investor would be regarded to perform an economic activity and therefore to conduct an undertaking, (ii) whether a tax benefit accorded to a foreign sovereign wealth investor would be regarded as selective, and (iii) whether a tax benefit accorded to a foreign sovereign wealth investor would be liable to affect trade between Member States.

If the concept of economic activity would be similar for State aid and EU VAT purposes, and therefore encompass passive investment activities, such as the granting of interest-bearing loans, or placements in bank deposits or securities, the investment activities of many foreign sovereign wealth investors would constitute economic activities. Otherwise, foreign sovereign wealth investors would seem to qualify as an undertaking when performing activities that go beyond the compass of the simple acquisition and sale of assets (i.e., *active* investors). This depends on the facts and circumstances. However, an investor that holds a controlling shareholding in an undertaking and actually exercises that control by involving itself (directly or indirectly) in the management of that company, must, in any case, be regarded as an *active* investor and therefore as an undertaking.

A tax benefit can only be selective if it favours economic operators relative to other economic operators which are comparable in the light of the objective pursued by the reference system. The reference system is driven by the taxpayers that claim to be discriminated against. Although the State aid rules follow the comparability approach in free movement cases, the implications of tax treaty benefits are currently less clear. Therefore, it cannot be excluded that tax treaty benefits which favour a sovereign wealth investor over other investors, will be considered selective by the CJEU in a State aid context.

The question whether a tax benefit accorded to a foreign sovereign wealth investor would be liable to affect trade between Member States arises in particular in relation to foreign sovereign wealth investors that are based outside the Member States. It could, for example, be argued that a selective tax benefit accorded to foreign sovereign wealth investors, whether located inside or outside the Member States, is still potentially liable to affect trade between Member States, as it could result in higher demand for assets (target companies) located in the respective Member State, increased liquidity and/or favourable financing conditions, and thus strengthening the position of domestic economic operators compared with economic operators of other Member States, or it could maintain or increase domestic activity.

Member States wishing to introduce new or change existing tax policy vis-à-vis foreign sovereign wealth investors could consider notifying the EC respectively the EFTA Surveillance Authority in case of doubt as regards to the application of the State aid rules.

(6) In addition, a preferential tax measure accorded by a Member State to foreign sovereign wealth investors which are not undertakings could amount to State aid for external asset managers (as indirect beneficiaries). Although a preferential tax measure accorded to foreign sovereign wealth investors by Member States could also benefit EU/EEA investment targets through higher demand and liquidity, any such (indirect) benefit is not selective, and hence no State aid for such targets, if that measure applies to targets in general and not just to specific undertakings, sectors or industries.

(7) Foreign sovereign wealth investors, in particular SWEs established under the laws of an EU Member State, could be entitled to the benefits of the Parent-Subsidiary Directive and Interest & Royalties Directive. It is noted that these directives do not apply to EEA-EFTA States.

These key implications could have the following impact on the ability of Member States (as source States) to achieve (or promote) tax policy objectives in relation to foreign sovereign wealth investors:

Capital import neutrality

Neither the fundamental freedoms, nor the State aid rules, prohibit a Member State from implementing a (territorial based) tax system that would promote CIN by adopting equal treatment of investors that perform the same level of investment activities in a source State, irrespective of their place of residence and characteristics. Thus, neither the fundamental freedoms, nor the State aid rules, have a (negative) impact on the ability of Member States to promote CIN, and to implement Approach (1).[947]

However, its obligations under the Parent-Subsidiary Directive and Interest & Royalties Directive could restrict an EU Member State to promote CIN and achieve equal taxation, by increasing the current level of taxation of EU based foreign sovereign wealth investors and other non-resident investors. Thus, secondary EU law could restrict an EU Member State's ability to promote CIN, and to implement Approach (1).[948]

Inter-taxpayer equity

The State aid rules, but not the fundamental freedoms, could restrict Member States' ability to achieve inter-taxpayer equity, but only if the benefit principle would

---

947. Approach (1) has been identified in Section 3.2.2.2 and is as follows: taxing foreign sovereign wealth investors in the same way as 'regular' non-resident corporate investors.
948. *Ibid.*

prescribe foreign sovereign wealth investors (and other non-resident investors) to be taxed more favourably than resident investors (i.e., reverse discrimination). This conclusion has no impact on Member States' ability to implement Approach (1)[949] though because this approach is concerned with the relationship among non-resident investors, rather than the relationship between non-resident and resident investors.

Its obligations under the Parent-Subsidiary Directive and Interest & Royalties Directive could restrict an EU Member State to promote inter-taxpayer equity and increase the current level of taxation of EU based foreign sovereign wealth investors (and other non-resident investors) paying too little from a benefit perspective. Thus, secondary EU law could restrict an EU Member State's ability to achieve inter-taxpayer equity, and to implement Approach (1).

Inter-nation equity

Both the fundamental freedoms and the State aid rules could restrict Member States' ability to achieve inter-nation equity, but only if inter-nation equity would require to treat non-resident investors from different States differently, based on redistribution grounds (i.e., horizontal discrimination). To limit the impact as much as possible, different treatment of non-resident investors from different States should still be achieved through tax treaties as much as possible. Whereas both the fundamental freedoms and the State aid rules could restrict Member States ability to achieve inter-nation equity, this conclusion has no impact on Member States' ability to implement Approach (1) though because this approach implies equal treatment between non-resident investors from different States (as opposed to different treatment).

Its obligations under the Parent-Subsidiary Directive and Interest & Royalties Directive could restrict an EU Member State to promote inter-nation equity and achieve equal taxation between non-resident investors from the same EU Member State, by increasing the current level of taxation of EU based foreign sovereign wealth investors and other non-resident investors. Thus, secondary EU law could restrict an EU Member State's ability to achieve inter-nation equity, and to implement Approach (1).[950]

Capital export neutrality & International attractiveness

According tax-exemptions to foreign sovereign wealth investors, but not to resident investors – i.e., reverse discrimination – is not prohibited by the fundamental freedoms. It could, however, constitute (unlawful) State aid, even if this different treatment is based on a tax treaty, but a State aid risk will probably be limited to *active* foreign sovereign wealth investors. Thus, the State aid rules could, under circumstances, restrict Member States' ability to promote CEN in relation to foreign sovereign wealth investors and to promote international attractiveness.

---

949. *Ibid.*
950. *Ibid.*

According unilateral tax-exemptions (or tax reductions) to foreign sovereign wealth investors, but not to comparable other non-resident investors – i.e., Approaches (2) and (3)[951] – could constitute horizontal discrimination under the freedoms in intra-EU/EEA situations (but unlikely in non-EU/EEA situations), as well as State aid, even in non-EU/EEA situations. However, the State aid risk will probably be limited to *active* foreign sovereign wealth investors. Thus, the freedoms as well as the State aid rules could, under circumstances, restrict Member States' ability to promote CEN in relation to foreign sovereign wealth investors and to promote international attractiveness through Approaches (2) and (3).[952]

In contrast, according tax-exemptions (or tax reductions) to foreign sovereign wealth investors through tax treaties but not to non-resident investors from other States, or from the same State – i.e., Approaches (4) and (5)[953] – should not constitute horizontal discrimination under the freedoms, not even in intra-EU/EEA situations. It may, however, constitute (unlawful) State aid under rather strict circumstances. Thus, primary European law may restrict Member States' ability to promote CEN and international attractiveness through Approaches (4) and (5).[954]

The Parent-Subsidiary Directive and Interest & Royalties Directive have no (negative) impact on an EU Member State's ability to promote CEN or international attractiveness in relation to foreign sovereign wealth investors through Approaches (2) to (5).[955]

The impact European law could have on source States' ability to achieve (or promote) neutrality, equity and international attractiveness, and to freely implement an approach to taxation of foreign sovereign wealth investors, is summarized in the table below.

---

951. Approaches (2) and (3) have been identified in Section 3.2.2.2 and are as follows:

    (2) according a general tax-exemption under domestic law or administrative practice.
    (3) according specific tax-exemptions or specific tax reductions under domestic law or administrative practice.
952. *Ibid.*
953. Approaches (4) and (5) have been identified in Section 3.2.2.2 and are as follows:

    (4) according a general tax-exemption under one or more tax treaties.
    (5) according specific tax-exemptions or specific tax reductions under one or more tax treaties.
954. *Ibid.*
955. Approaches (2) to (5) have been identified in Section 3.2.2.2 and are as follows:

    (2) according a general tax-exemption under domestic law or administrative practice.
    (3) according specific tax-exemptions or specific tax reductions under domestic law or administrative practice.
    (4) according a general tax-exemption under one or more tax treaties.
    (5) according specific tax-exemptions or specific tax reductions under one or more tax treaties.

Chapter 6: European Tax Law Aspects

Table 6.2 Impact of European (Union) Law on the Ability of Source States to Achieve (or Promote) Tax Policy Objectives, and to Freely Implement an Approach to Taxation of Foreign Sovereign Wealth Investors

	Neutrality			Equity			International Attractiveness
	(CEN)	(CIN)	(inter-taxpayer)		(inter-nation)	
Sovereign immunity	No (negative) impact	No (negative) impact	Impact negligible (i.e. only if immunity from execution would apply)		Impact negligible (i.e. only if immunity from execution would apply)		No (negative) impact
OECD/UN MTC based treaties	No (negative) impact	Restrict Approach (1) (but only where an increase in level of taxation is required)	Restrict Approach (1) (but only where an increase in level of taxation is required)		Restrict Approach (1) (but only where an increase in level of taxation is required)		No (negative) impact
European (Union) law							
fundamental freedoms	Could restrict Approaches (2) and (3), but not Approaches (4) and (5)	No (negative) impact	No impact		Could restrict inter-nation equity if it would be required to treat non-resident investors from different States differently based on redistribution grounds, but do not restrict Approach (1) though		Could restrict Approaches (2) and (3), but not Approaches (4) and (5)
State aid rules	Could restrict Approaches (2) to (5)**	No (negative) impact	Could restrict inter-taxpayer equity if it would be required to treat non-resident investors more favourably than resident investors, but do not restrict Approach (1) though		Could restrict inter-nation equity if it would be required to treat non-resident investors from different States differently based on redistribution grounds, but do not restrict Approach (1) though		Could restrict Approaches (2) to (5)**
Directives (not applicable to EEA-EFTA States)	No (negative) impact	Restrict Approach (1) (but only where an increase in level of taxation is required, and limited to outbound dividend, interest and royalty payments in certain intra-EU situations)	Restrict Approach (1) (but only where an increase in level of taxation is required, and limited to outbound dividend, interest and royalty payments in certain intra-EU situations)		Restrict Approach (1) (but only where an increase in level of taxation is required, and limited to outbound dividend, interest and royalty payments in certain intra-EU situations)		No (negative) impact
	Potentially underlying Approaches (2) to (5)*	Potentially underlying Approach (1)*	Potentially underlying Approach (1)*		Potentially underlying Approach (1)*		Potentially underlying Approaches (2) to (5)*

* Approach (1): taxing foreign sovereign wealth investors in the same way as 'regular' non-resident corporate investors.
Approach (2): according a general tax-exemption under domestic law or administrative practice.
Approach (3): according specific tax-exemptions or specific tax reductions under domestic law or administrative practice.
Approach (4): according a general tax-exemption under one or more tax treaties.
Approach (5): according specific tax-exemptions or specific tax reductions under one or more tax treaties.
** But probably limited to *active* foreign sovereign wealth investors.

CHAPTER 7
The Framework Applied to The Netherlands

7.1 INTRODUCTION

In this chapter, the conceptual framework developed in this study regarding foreign sovereign wealth investors will be applied to the Netherlands, as an illustration.[956] The Netherlands has been selected for several reasons. First, as will become apparent in this chapter, the primacy of Dutch international tax policy in relation to sovereign wealth investors is international attractiveness. This policy has found its way into Dutch tax treaties; the Netherlands has concluded several tax treaties containing favourable provisions for sovereign wealth investors, and Dutch tax (treaty) policy, as well as Dutch tax treaties, are approved by Dutch parliament. Second, the Netherlands is an OECD Member State, as well as an EU Member State, which means that the international law analysis will have to be considered in full. Third, the application of the framework requires in-depth knowledge of a tax system and a certain level of information. The author is familiar with Dutch tax law, whereas political decision-making in the Netherlands happens in a transparent way, and tax policy information, legislative information and other relevant information is publicly available.

Given the primacy of international attractiveness as a Dutch tax policy objective in relation to sovereign wealth investors, the conceptual framework is primarily used in this chapter to answer the following question: *What impact, if any, does international law have on the Netherlands' ability to achieve (or promote) international tax attractiveness in relation to foreign sovereign wealth investors?*

Section 7.2 will first discuss the leading Dutch international tax policy principles in general, and identify the leading Dutch tax policy principle(s) applicable to foreign sovereign wealth investors in particular. This will be followed by some remarks on the

---

956. As the constituent country within the Kingdom of the Netherlands, excluding the Caribbean island territories.

impact of the sovereign immunity principle and OECD MTC based treaties in Section 7.3 and Section 7.4. In Section 7.5, the impact of European law on the ability of the Netherlands to pursue international attractiveness in relation to sovereign wealth investors will be considered, by focusing on the application of the Dutch Corporate Income Tax Act (1969) ('DCITA 1969'), the Dutch Dividend Withholding Tax Act (1965) ('DDWTA 1965') and Dutch tax treaties, as in force on 1 January 2018. Section 7.6 will end this chapter with its conclusions.

7.2 DUTCH INTERNATIONAL TAX POLICY CONSIDERATIONS

The Netherlands has a small and open economy with a big foreign market. Therefore, the tax competitiveness position of the Netherlands vis-à-vis other relevant States is constantly monitored.[957] Tax treaties concluded by the Netherlands stimulate international activities of Dutch enterprises (outbound investments) and contribute to an attractive investment climate, economic growth and employment in the Netherlands (inbound investments).[958] According to the memorandum on Dutch tax treaty policy (2011), at least four important considerations play a role for entering into a tax treaty with another State.[959] First, the structure of the tax system of the other State and its interaction with the Dutch tax system. This also involves an analysis of the tax treaty network of the other State. Second, the nature and the extent of the economic relations between the Netherlands and the other State. The effect of concluding a tax treaty on these existing economic relations and the expected future impact will be considered. The conclusion of a tax treaty can also serve a *specific* economic goal, such as facilitating foreign outbound investments by Dutch pension funds or facilitating foreign inbound investments by foreign sovereign wealth investors. Third, the competitiveness position of Dutch employees, businesses and investors in the other State. Finally, economic, political or diplomatic factors may make it desirable to enter into a tax treaty with another State. In this respect, the memorandum notes that honouring the wish of another State to conclude a tax treaty can (also) solve a bilateral political or diplomatic issue.

Dutch international tax policy contains elements of both CEN and CIN. With respect to 'passive' (portfolio) income, such as portfolio dividends, interest and royalties, the underlying policy is CEN, whereas CIN is followed as regards 'active' (business) income. These policy principles are, to a greater or lesser extent, applied to both resident and non-resident investors, and produce the following general picture. For Dutch resident investors with 'passive' income, the policy of CEN means that the aim is to include passive foreign income in the Dutch tax base and allow foreign taxes to be credited against the Dutch tax. For Dutch resident investors with 'active' income, the policy of CIN means that active foreign income is exempt from Dutch taxation and active income from Dutch activities is taxed. As regards non-resident investors, it should be noted upfront that currently the Netherlands does not levy a withholding tax

---
957. *Notitie Fiscaal Verdragsbeleid 2011*, Tweede Kamer, 2010–2011, 25 087, No. 7, p. 76, pp. 15–16.
958. Ibid., p. 16.
959. Ibid., pp. 16–17.

Chapter 7: The Framework Applied to The Netherlands

on interest or royalties, but it does levy a withholding tax on dividends.[960] The absence of a withholding tax on interest and royalties has, among others, been motivated with reference to CEN, which may raise eyebrows,[961] but the better explanation seems to be the wish to stimulate the free movement of funds and to attract know-how.[962] On the other hand, dividends paid by Dutch companies to non-resident investors are, in principle, subject to Dutch dividend withholding tax at a rate of 15%. However, in keeping with CIN, Dutch tax treaty policy is not to tax non-resident companies in respect of dividends derived from shareholdings in Dutch companies of at least 10%.[963] For tax treaty policy purposes, the threshold of 10% is the distinction between 'active' income and 'passive' income, as far as corporate shareholders are concerned (dividends paid to non-resident individuals are always considered passive income). Because dividends are paid out of local profits that have already been subject to Dutch corporate income tax, this tax-exemption for non-resident companies achieves – in accordance with CIN – equal treatment with Dutch resident corporate investors, i.e., both being subject to Dutch tax on Dutch sourced active income only. In case of 'passive' portfolio dividends (i.e., shareholdings of less than 10%), non-resident companies are, in principle, not entitled to an exemption or reduction of Dutch dividend withholding tax under tax treaties. Basically, the Netherlands finds that in this situation the other State should grant a credit for the Dutch dividend withholding tax, like the Netherlands does in the reversed situation, based on the principle of CEN. As will be discussed in this section and in the following sections, a number of exceptions apply to the general picture outlined above, both under bilateral tax treaties and domestic tax law. The exceptions under bilateral tax treaties are often motivated by international attractiveness, whereas the exceptions under domestic tax law are often the result of EU law.

The Netherlands is very much aware of the (increasing) significance of foreign sovereign wealth investors in the global economy. The memorandum on Dutch tax treaty policy (2011) recognizes sovereign wealth investors as important capital providers in the global economy[964] and welcomes their investments into the Netherlands.[965] It even pronounces the ambition of the Netherlands to become a regional investment centre for sovereign wealth investors through its tax treaty policy and the existing Dutch financial and tax infrastructure.[966] It also notes that good fiscal relations with countries that are rich in oil and gas, could give business opportunities to Dutch

---

960. However, on 10 October 2017, the new Dutch government announced the plan to abolish the dividend withholding tax, except in cases of abusive situations and in relation to low tax jurisdictions, and to introduce a withholding tax on interest and royalties in cases of abusive situations and in relation to low tax jurisdictions. Regeerakkoord 2017-2021, *Vertrouwen in de toekomst* (10 October 2017), pp. 35-36 & pp. 67-68.
961. *See* the discussion in Section 3.4.2, where it was argued that CEN is not concerned with source taxation of non-residents.
962. *Uitgangspunten van het beleid op het terrein van het internationaal fiscaal (verdragen)recht*, Tweede Kamer, 1997-1998, 25 087, No. 4, p. 44 & pp. 46-47.
963. *Ibid.*, pp. 39-41.
964. *Notitie Fiscaal Verdragsbeleid 2011*, Tweede Kamer, 2010-2011, 25 087, No. 7, p. 33.
965. *Ibid.*, p. 76.
966. *Ibid.*

companies. The parts of the memorandum that deal with sovereign wealth investors strongly resemble parts of an earlier non-tax memorandum (2008) on sovereign wealth investors from the Ministry of Finance and the Ministry of Economic Affairs.[967] One of the conclusions of this non-tax memorandum was that investments of sovereign wealth investors bring, or could bring, important economic benefits to the Netherlands, among others because these investors generally appear to be stable, long-term shareholders.[968] Another conclusion was that investments by sovereign wealth investors were not politically motivated, and that the public interests of the Netherlands were sufficiently protected through the existing legal framework.[969] Nonetheless, some additional non-tax measures were announced to optimize the level of protection. It was also concluded that investments of sovereign wealth investors in the Netherlands could improve access of Dutch companies to the home markets of these investors.[970] It was, furthermore, noted that the Netherlands can benefit if assets of sovereign wealth investors are managed in the Netherlands.[971] In line with specific Dutch tax treaty policy regarding sovereign wealth investors, but in deviation from general Dutch tax treaty policy, sovereign wealth investors of tax treaty partners of the Netherlands are very often entitled to an exemption or reduction of Dutch source taxation on dividends. In this respect, reference is made to the Dutch tax treaties discussed in the Appendix. In addition, sovereign wealth investors which do not benefit from an exemption of Dutch source taxation on portfolio dividends under a tax treaty, may be entitled to a full refund under Dutch tax law, as will discussed in more detail in Sections 7.5.3.3 and 7.5.3.4 below. The extension of the Dutch refund regime to portfolio investors from third countries in 2012 was motivated by EU law (the freedom of capital movement), and by increasing the attractiveness for non-resident pension funds and foreign sovereign wealth investors.[972] Based on the above, it can be concluded that the primacy of Dutch international tax policy vis-à-vis foreign sovereign wealth investors is international attractiveness.

The tax-exemptions or reductions accorded to sovereign wealth investors by the Netherlands, in particular those accorded through tax treaties, are most often aimed at attracting investments. With respect to the tax treaty between the Netherlands and the UAE,[973] the Netherlands furthermore argued that the tax-exemption for dividends paid to sovereign wealth investors was necessary to protect the Netherlands' competitiveness position vis-à-vis other source States, including Belgium and Austria.[974] It follows from the discussion of the Dutch tax rules in this chapter and the discussion of the Dutch tax treaties in the Appendix, that some of the tax-treaty-based exemptions accorded to sovereign wealth investors are (far) more generous as compared to general

---

967. *Sovereign Wealth Funds; gezamenlijke notitie ministeries van Financiën en Economische Zaken*, Tweede Kamer, 2007–2008, 31 350, No. 1.
968. *Ibid.*, p. 25.
969. *Ibid.* pp. 38–39.
970. *Ibid.*, p. 20.
971. *Ibid.*, p. 8.
972. *Tweede Kamer*, 2011–2012, 33 003, No. 3, p. 38 & p. 113.
973. See Section A.3.2 of this study.
974. *Tweede Kamer*, 2009–2010, 32 346, No. 3, p. 6.

Chapter 7: The Framework Applied to The Netherlands

Dutch tax treaty policy and Dutch domestic tax law. Notably, sovereign wealth investors from the UAE, Oman and Norway are entitled to a wide and general exemption of Dutch taxation on dividends under the tax treaty. With regard to these and other tax treaties, there is no publicly available information indicating that attention was paid to the other international tax policy principles and objectives. This may come as a surprise, in particular because tax-exemptions or reductions accorded through tax treaties could conflict with inter-taxpayer equity (benefit principle). The analysis in Section 3.7 indicates that inter-taxpayer equity, as an expression of the fundamental value of fairness, should be an important international policy principle in every democracy under the rule of law. In the context of international attractiveness, the importance of inter-taxpayer equity does not mean that a tax incentive should be rejected per se. It means that a tax incentive must serve a legitimate – i.e., 'rationally defensible' – purpose. Ultimately, the tax legislator of each individual sovereign State, therefore, has to weigh and balance the principle of inter-taxpayer equity and any other conflicting tax policy principle or objective it wishes to implement. Although this is not an exact measurement, it should be done in a transparent way, based on rational, convincing arguments, and its ultimate outcome may depend on various factors – such as the size and nature of the economy, public interests, societal values as well as tax policy choices of other States – and may change over time. Admittedly, the memorandum on Dutch tax treaty policy (2011) and the non-tax memorandum on sovereign wealth investors (2008) have both been discussed with Dutch parliament, and Dutch tax treaties are approved by, and increasingly discussed in, Dutch parliament. In addition, it is true that favourable tax treaty provisions are an integral part of the entire tax treaty and contribute to the overall balance of mutual relations between two States. Nevertheless, given the tension with inter-taxpayer equity, a separate, more detailed and in-depth analysis – *ex ante* – for each favourable tax treaty provision regarding sovereign wealth investors would have been appropriate, in the author's view. Indeed, as indicated in Chapter 2, sovereign wealth investors are in many ways not a homogeneous group. In addition, the Netherlands does not get (any meaningful) direct tax benefits in return when sovereign wealth investors reside in States that do not levy (corporate) income tax (Norway being an exception). (Why) is it likely that these favourable tax treaty provisions will attract additional investments which will benefit the Dutch economy? Why are these tax treaty benefits not available to other investors? (Why) is it likely that tax treaties concluded with States that are home to sovereign wealth investors will improve access of Dutch companies to the home markets of these investors? Is there any relevant data available on the impact of existing tax treaties? After all, proper tax policy requires that the effect of tax incentives are properly evaluated. This economic information can be used for the benefit of future policy decisions, such as the inclusion of special provisions in future tax treaties. Why are these favourable tax treaty provisions designed as a general tax-exemption, rather than more specific tax-exemptions directed at industries or sectors where capital is/was scarcely available, such as small- and medium-sized enterprises, start-ups and other companies with high-risk profiles?[975/976] An additional reason why a separate, more detailed and in-depth analysis for each favourable tax treaty provision for sovereign wealth investors would have been appropriate, is that tax treaties are rarely renegotiated, or unilaterally terminated. Once a tax treaty enters into force, it will generally apply for a long period of time.

7.3 SOVEREIGN IMMUNITY

The issue of the application of the sovereign immunity principle to taxation was raised in Dutch parliament in 2015 during the legislative process on the new corporate tax regime for public enterprises (*overheidsondernemingen*). This regime will be discussed in more detail in Section 7.5.2.2 below. According to the Dutch government, the Netherlands follows the restrictive immunity theory, and applies this theory in tax matters as well, meaning that governmental acts of foreign States will enjoy immunity from Dutch (corporate income) taxation.[977] The new corporate tax regime contains a specific tax-exemption for income from activities involving the exercise of a public function or public authority, which can also apply to foreign public enterprises. Based on this tax-exemption, the Dutch government indicated that the tax rules for foreign public enterprises do not conflict with the sovereign immunity principle. It should be noted that the scope of this tax-exemption will be limited in practice, because it does not apply to activities which are being exercised in competition with private undertakings. In Chapter 4, it was concluded that source States are not obliged under customary international law to accord any immunity from income taxation to foreign States or foreign sovereign wealth investors. On the other hand, there is no rule of customary international law prohibiting a source State from doing so. Therefore, the sovereign immunity principle has (had) no (negative) impact on the ability of the Netherlands to promote international attractiveness in relation to (one or more) foreign sovereign wealth investors.

7.4 OECD MTC BASED TREATIES

Dutch tax treaties are based on the OECD MTC. In Chapter 5, it was concluded that OECD MTC based treaties have no (negative) impact on source States' ability to pursue international attractiveness in relation to (one or more) foreign sovereign wealth investors.

In Section 5.7.3, it was noted that, nowadays, many tax treaties are (also) concluded for a specific economic purpose. Sovereign wealth investors of tax treaty partners of the Netherlands are very often entitled to a generous exemption or reduction of Dutch source taxation on dividends, in deviation from entitlements under domestic law and from a generally accepted allocation of taxing rights as expressed in

---

975. *See* Section 3.6.
976. It should be noted that, in a State aid context, tax benefits aimed at specific undertakings, sectors or industries could be selective. *See* Section 6.4.4.3.2.
977. *Eerste Kamer*, 2014–2015, 34 003, No. D, p. 20.

the OECD and UN MTC, as well as general Dutch tax treaty policy.[978] As indicated, these tax-exemptions or reductions are most often aimed at attracting investments.

7.5 EUROPEAN LAW

7.5.1 Introduction

In Chapter 6, the following situations were identified where European law could restrict the ability of Member States to enhance international attractiveness in relation to foreign sovereign wealth investors:

(1) according tax-exemptions (or tax reductions) under domestic law to foreign sovereign wealth investors, but not to comparable other non-resident investors; because this could constitute horizontal discrimination under the freedoms in intra-EU/EEA situations.[979]
(2) according tax-exemptions (or tax reductions) under domestic law or a tax treaty to foreign sovereign wealth investors, but not to comparable resident investors; because this could constitute State aid in relation to *active* investors, even in third country situations.[980]
(3) according tax-exemptions (or tax reductions) under domestic law or a tax treaty to foreign sovereign wealth investors, but not to comparable other non-resident investors; because this could constitute State aid in relation to *active* investors, even in third country situations.[981]

Below, it will be examined whether one or more of these situations exist in the Netherlands. To that end, it is first necessary to analyse in more detail how sovereign wealth investors and other investors are treated in the Netherlands under domestic tax legislation. In case of differences in treatment, it will then be examined whether sovereign wealth investors could be objectively comparable to other investors, or whether the standstill provision of Article 64(1) TFEU or a justification ground could apply in the context of the freedom of capital movement. The focus will be on the application of the DCITA 1969 in Section 7.5.2 and the DDWTA 1965 in Section 7.5.3, as in force on 1 January 2018. In Section 7.5.4, pursuing international attractiveness through tax treaties is considered.

---

978. *See* the Dutch tax treaties discussed in the Appendix.
979. *See* Section 6.3.3.3.2.
980. *See* Section 6.4.4.2.
981. *See* Section 6.4.4.2.

7.5.2 Dutch Corporate Income Tax Regime

7.5.2.1 Introduction

Entities resident in the Netherlands and listed in Article 2(1) DCITA 1969 are, in principle, subject to Dutch corporate income tax on their worldwide profits. Article 2(1) DCITA 1969 includes legal persons of private law, such as private companies limited by shares (*besloten vennootschappen*), public limited companies (*naamloze vennootschapen*), associations and foundations, as well as non-transparent limited partnerships. Unlike private companies limited by shares and public limited companies, associations and foundations are only subject to corporate income tax to the extent that they carry on a business enterprise.[982] Article 2(1)(g) DCITA 1969 refers to legal persons of public law (*publiekrechtelijke rechtspersonen*). Similar to associations and foundations, legal persons of public law are subject to corporate income tax to the extent that they carry on a business enterprise.[983] In relation to the Dutch State, business enterprises within each Ministry are together subject to corporate income tax.[984]

Entities resident outside the Netherlands and listed in Article 3(1) DCITA 1969 are subject to Dutch corporate income tax on their Dutch income as referred to in Articles 17 and 17a DCITA 1969 only. Article 3(1) DCITA 1969 includes foreign body corporates (*rechtspersonen*). Dutch income typically includes profits from a Dutch permanent establishment, income from Dutch immovable property, as well as income from shareholdings in Dutch resident companies of at least 5% in abusive situations. Associations and foundations established under foreign law as well as foreign legal persons of public law with Dutch income, are only subject to Dutch corporate income tax insofar as they carry on a business enterprise.

7.5.2.2 Public Enterprises

Until 1 January 2016, the tax liability of legal persons of public law (*directe overheidsbedrijven*) and legal persons of private law owned/controlled by a legal person of public law (*indirecte overheidsbedrijven*) was limited to income from certain listed activities, which included farms, industrial undertakings, mining undertakings and transport undertakings.[985] In addition, certain entities owned/controlled by a legal person of public law were expressly mentioned as being subject to Dutch corporate income tax.[986] This regime was abolished in response to the decision of the EC that it constituted existing State aid.[987]

---

982. Article 2(1)(e) DCITA 1969.
983. Article 2(1)(g) DCITA 1969.
984. Article 2(2) DCITA 1969.
985. Article 2(3) (old) DCITA 1969.
986. Article 2(7) (old) DCITA 1969.
987. Section 6.4.3.

Chapter 7: The Framework Applied to The Netherlands

As from 1 January 2016, a new corporate tax regime applies to legal persons of public law and legal persons of private law owned by a legal person of public law. Since then, legal persons of public law are subject to Dutch corporate income tax insofar as they carry on a business enterprise (*publiekrechtelijke overheidslichamen* c.q. *directe overheidsondernemingen*).[988] This rule *mutatis mutandis* applies to foreign legal persons of public law,[989] while the tax liability of such non-resident entities is further limited to Dutch income as referred to in Articles 17 and 17a DCITA 1969.[990] In relation to the Dutch State, business enterprises within each Ministry are together subject to corporate income tax.[991] A business enterprise requires the existence of an organization of labour and capital, which participates in economic traffic with the purpose of making profit. On the other hand, legal persons of private law which are owned/controlled by a legal person of public law (*privaatrechtelijke overheidslichamen* c.q. *indirecte overheidsondernemingen*) are, as a general rule, subject to the ordinary rules applicable to legal persons of private law, as discussed in Section 7.5.2.1. For example, a Dutch private company limited by shares and owned by a legal person of public law is taxable on its worldwide income, whereas a Dutch foundation controlled by a legal person of public law is taxable to the extent that it carries on a business enterprise. This rule *mutatis mutandis* applies to foreign legal persons of private law owned by a foreign legal person of public law, while the tax liability of such non-resident entities is further limited to Dutch sourced income. The rationale behind the different tax principles applicable to legal persons of public law, on the one hand, and legal persons of private law owned by a legal person of public law, on the other, is that legal persons of public law, unlike legal persons of private law (except for associations and foundations), usually lack the purpose of making profit.[992]

The new regime contains tax-exemptions for income from activities as listed in Articles 8e and 8f DCITA 1969. Article 8e DCITA 1969 is directed at legal persons of public law, whereas Article 8f DCITA 1969 is directed at legal persons of private law owned/controlled by a legal person of public law. The income-based tax-exemptions provided in Article 8e DCITA 1969 only become relevant if the legal person of public law carries on a business enterprise. The purpose of Articles 8e and 8f DCITA 1969 is to achieve (more) tax neutrality in the choice between conducting activities by means of a legal person of public law or a legal person of private law.[993] The activities listed in these provisions include activities performed for the legal person of public law itself, and activities performed between a legal person of public law and a legal person of private law owned by that legal person of public law (i.e., internal activities). Also listed are activities involving the exercise of a public function or public authority. Such activities can also be exercised by legal persons of private law which are owned/controlled by a legal person of public law. However, income from activities involving the exercise of a public function or public authority is not tax-exempt if they are being

---

988. Article 2(1)(g) DCITA 1969.
989. Article 3(3) DCITA 1969.
990. Article 3(1) DCITA 1969.
991. Article 2(2) DCITA 1969.
992. *Tweede Kamer*, 2014–2015, 34 003, No. 3, p. 9.
993. *Ibid.*, p. 15.

exercised in competition with private undertakings (in order not to disturb the level-playing field[994]). The tax-exemptions provided in Articles 8e and 8f DCITA 1969 apply by analogy to foreign legal persons of public law and foreign legal persons of private law owned by a foreign legal person of public law.[995]

7.5.2.3 Collective Investment Vehicles

7.5.2.3.1 Fiscale beleggingsinstelling *(Fiscal Investment Institution)*

The tax regime for *fiscale beleggingsinstellingen* (fiscal investment institutions ('FBIs')) came into existence in 1969 and has been modified often since then. FBIs are investment vehicles. The relevant rules are contained in Article 28 DCITA 1969 and in a decree *(Besluit beleggingsinstellingen)*.[996] The original purpose of the tax regime for FBIs was to facilitate collective investment by individuals (portfolio investors) in order to benefit from risk diversification and achieve higher returns.[997] However, nowadays, the tax regime for FBIs is not only open to individuals (portfolio investors), but also to corporate investors (entities), even to single ones.

FBIs are liable to Dutch corporate income tax at a rate of 0%, under certain conditions.[998] A key feature of this regime is the obligation to distribute most profits to the participants within a short timeframe.[999] It is not required that the entity has a legal or statutory obligation to distribute most profits within a short timeframe; it suffices that the entity actually distributes profits within this timeframe.[1000] The distribution requirement does not apply to gains from the alienation of assets if they are allocated to a reinvestment reserve.[1001] The 0% rate and the distribution requirement express that FBIs are merely intermediaries and that the aim of the regime is to achieve, as much as possible, tax neutrality for portfolio investors between investing directly and investing indirectly through an FBI,[1002] or at least to achieve taxation at the level of the investors.[1003] In order to achieve this aim, dividend distributions by an FBI are, in principle, subject to 15% Dutch dividend withholding tax (but may, under Article 11a DDWTA 1965, be reduced with dividend withholding tax and foreign tax on income derived by the FBI itself). Therefore, Article 28 DCITA 1969 cannot be seen separately

---

994. *Ibid.*, p. 47.
995. *Eerste Kamer*, 2014–2015, 34 003, No. D, p. 20; Art. 18(1) DCITA 1969.
996. For a more detailed description of the tax regime for FBIs, *see* H. Vermeulen, *Het regime voor de fiscale beleggingsinstelling*, 3rd edn., (Deventer: Kluwer, 2012).
997. *Tweede Kamer*, 2000–2001, 27 466, No. 3, pp. 4–5.
998. Article 9 *Besluit beleggingsinstellingen*.
999. Article 28(2)(b) DCITA 1969.
1000. *Hoge Raad*, 3 March 2017, No. 16/03954, *BNB* 2017/86, Para. 7.14.
1001. Article 4 *Besluit beleggingsinstellingen*.
1002. *Tweede Kamer*, 1989–1990, 20 701, No. 9, p. 9; *Tweede Kamer*, 2000–2001, 27 466, No. 3, pp. 4–5; *Hoge Raad*, 10 July 2015, No. 14/03956, *BNB* 2015/203.
1003. *Hoge Raad*, 18 December 1991, No. 27 362, *BNB* 1992/288.

Chapter 7: The Framework Applied to The Netherlands

from the levy of Dutch dividend withholding tax. The statutory purpose and the actual activities of FBIs must be limited to (passively) investing funds (*beleggen van vermogen*).[1004]

Article 28 DCITA 1969 imposes certain shareholders requirements, depending on whether the FBI qualifies as a 'listed/regulated' FBI or as a 'non-listed/non-regulated' FBI. As regards 'listed/regulated' FBIs, a resident or non-resident single individual is not allowed to hold an interest in the FBI of 25% or more, while a resident or non-resident entity which is subject to a profit tax is not allowed to own a shareholding in the FBI of 45% or more.[1005] Corporate participants which are not subject to a profit tax fall outside the scope of this restriction. Such resident and non-resident corporate participants are, therefore, allowed to hold an interest in a 'listed/regulated' FBI of more than 45%. With respect to 'non-listed/non-regulated' FBIs, a resident or non-resident single individual is never allowed to own a shareholding in the FBI of 5% or more.[1006] In addition, at least 75% of the shares of the 'non-listed/non-regulated' FBI must be held – together or alone – by: (i) resident or non-resident individuals, (ii) resident and non-resident corporate entities which are not subject to a profit tax,[1007] and (iii) 'listed/regulated' FBIs.[1008] Therefore, participants which *are* subject to a profit tax cannot hold more than 25% in a 'non-listed/non-regulated' FBI. On the other hand, corporate participants which are not subject to a profit tax are allowed to own a shareholding in such an FBI of more than 75%.

The FBI regime is open to Dutch resident *besloten vennootschappen, naamloze vennootschappen, open fondsen voor gemene rekening* ('non-transparent' funds for joint account), as well Dutch resident foreign law equivalents established under the laws of an EU Member State or entitled to non-discriminatory treatment under a tax treaty concluded by the Netherlands.[1009] The FBI regime is furthermore open to such foreign law equivalents resident outside the Netherlands, but with a Dutch permanent establishment, provided they meet the conditions of Article 28 DCITA 1969, including the distribution requirement.[1010]

7.5.2.3.2 Vrijgestelde beleggingsinstelling *(Tax-Exempt Investment Institution)*

On 1 January 2007, a new tax regime for CIVs was introduced in Article 6a DCITA 1969, to improve the competitiveness for this industry, namely the *vrijgestelde beleggingsinstelling* (tax-exempt investment institution ('VBI')). The tax regime for VBIs exists alongside the tax regime for FBIs. Article 6a DCITA 1969 provides for an entity-based exemption from Dutch corporate income tax for investment entities, the purpose and actual activities of which consist of collective investment in financial instruments, as

---

1004. Article 28(2) DCITA 1969.
1005. Article 28(2)(c) DCITA 1969. In case of tax transparent entities this condition needs to be tested at the upper level.
1006. Article 28(2)(d)(1°) DCITA 1969.
1007. In case of tax transparent entities this condition needs to be tested at the upper level.
1008. Article 28(2)(d)(2°) DCITA 1969.
1009. Article 28(2) DCITA 1969.
1010. *Eerste Kamer*, 2006–2007, 30 533, No. C, p. 4; Art. 28(2) DCITA 1969.

defined, and which operate on the principle of risk-spreading. Furthermore, the tax regime for VBIs is limited to open-ended vehicles, i.e., vehicles with units which are, at the request of holders, repurchased or redeemed out of those vehicles' assets. The definition of investment vehicles in Article 6a(3) DCITA 1969 and the foregoing imply that the tax regime for VBIs is open for vehicles which perform asset management for a group of investors, rather than asset management for individual investors (*individueel vermogensbeheer*).[1011]

The VBI regime is open to Dutch resident *naamloze vennootschappen* and *open fondsen voor gemene rekening* ('non-transparent' funds for joint account), as well Dutch resident foreign law equivalents established under the laws of an EU Member State or entitled to non-discriminatory treatment under a tax treaty concluded by the Netherlands.[1012] The VBI regime is furthermore open to such foreign law equivalents resident outside the Netherlands, but with a Dutch permanent establishment, provided they meet the conditions of Article 6a DCITA 1969, including the requirement to perform asset management for a group of investors and the requirement to be open-ended.[1013]

7.5.2.4 Pension Funds

Based on Article 5(1)(b) DCITA 1969, entities which for at least 90% aim to facilitate – in short – retirement saving plans for employees under a regulated pension scheme, are subjectively exempt from Dutch corporate income tax in respect of activities directly related to this purpose. This entity related tax-exemption is based on the idea that pension funds, by their nature, do not make profits, because profits de facto benefit the participants.[1014] Another reason is that pension funds fulfil an important social function.[1015] Non-resident pension funds can similarly be entitled to this tax-exemption, provided that the non-resident pension funds implements a pension regulation which, by its nature and scope, is similar to a Dutch pension regulation.[1016]

7.5.2.5 Not-for-Profit Organizations

Resident entities which did not aim to earn profit, and which either represented an interest of the community (*algemeen maatschappelijk belang*) or furthered a social cause (*sociaal belang*), could have been subjectively exempt from Dutch corporate income tax, under certain conditions.[1017] However, this entity-based tax-exemption was abolished on 1 January 2012. Since then, not-for-profit organizations are in principle governed by the general rules as discussed in Section 7.5.2.1. Since not-for-

---

1011. Decree of 10 March 2008, No. CPP2008/291M, *BNB* 2008/141.
1012. Article 6a(2) DCITA 1969.
1013. Ibid.
1014. *Tweede Kamer*, 2003–2004, 29 210, No. 3, p. 23.
1015. Ibid.
1016. Article 5(3)(a) DCITA 1969.
1017. Article 6 (old) DCITA 1969.

Chapter 7: The Framework Applied to The Netherlands

profit organizations typically take the legal form of an association or foundation, they will only be subject to Dutch corporate income tax insofar as they carry on a business enterprise. A business enterprise requires the existence of an organization of labour and capital, which participates in economic traffic with the purpose of making profit.

7.5.2.6 Application to Foreign Sovereign Wealth Investors and Comparison to Other Investors

From the discussion of the DCITA 1969, it is clear that different categories of investors are governed by different corporate income tax rules, which could result in different taxation. The conditions imposed on a category of resident investors generally apply to the same category of non-resident investors in a similar way (notwithstanding the different territorial scope of the tax liability between residents and non-residents). Below, the application of the DCITA 1969 to sovereign wealth investors will be analysed, and it will be examined whether (or not) sovereign wealth investors could be objectively comparable to other investors in the context of the DCITA 1969. It is noted that the Netherlands has no SWF itself. As explained in Chapter 6, comparability is determined, unilaterally and rather strictly, in the light of the objective of the national tax measure at issue, and by the relevant conditions laid down in the national tax legislation. This comparability standard is relevant under the freedoms and State aid rules, for both vertical and horizontal comparability. However, unlike the State aid rules, the freedoms do not prohibit *reverse discrimination*. Furthermore, unlike the State aid rules, the prohibition of horizontal discrimination under the freedoms should not apply in case of tax treaty benefits and seems further confined to intra-EU/EEA situations. The application of the State aid rules is, in any case, limited to undertakings.

7.5.2.6.1 Tax Regime for Public Enterprises

Based on the new tax regime for public enterprises, sovereign wealth investors constituted by a pool of assets within the State, being a legal person of public law (*buitenlands publiekrechtelijk overheidslichaam*), are subject to Dutch taxation on their Dutch income as referred to in Articles 17 and 17a DCITA 1969, but only to the extent that they carry on a business enterprise. The same rule applies to sovereign wealth investors established as a separate legal person of public law. A business enterprise requires the existence of an organization of labour and capital, which participates in economic traffic with the purpose of making profit. *Active* investors are more likely to meet these criteria than *passive* investors. Even if sovereign wealth investors established as or within a legal person of public law carry on a business enterprise, Dutch income derived from activities listed in Article 8e DCITA 1969 is exempt from Dutch corporate income tax. Article 8e DCITA 1969, most notably, exempts income from activities involving the exercise of a public function or public authority, unless such activities are being exercised in competition with private undertakings (in order not to disturb the level-playing field).[1018] In the author's view, the investment activities of sovereign wealth investors should not be covered by this particular tax-exemption, even if they are connected to the exercise of a public function or public authority, because such activities are being exercised in competition with private undertakings.

Sovereign wealth investors established as a legal person of private law referred to in Article 3(1) DCITA 1969 (*buitenlands privaatrechtelijk overheidslichaam*), are subject to Dutch corporate income tax on their Dutch income similar to regular non-resident corporate investors, except for Dutch income derived from activities listed in Article 8f DCITA 1969. Similar to Article 8e DCITA 1969, Article 8f DCITA 1969 exempts, most notably, income from activities involving the exercise of a public function or public authority, unless such activities are being exercised in competition with private undertakings. As explained, this particular tax-exemption should, in the author's view, not apply to investment activities of sovereign wealth investors, because they are being exercised in competition with private undertakings.

The new tax regime for public enterprises accords different tax treatment between sovereign wealth investors, depending on the legal form and activities of these investors. In the author's view, this different treatment does not constitute horizontal discrimination under the freedoms, nor does it constitute State aid. The rationale behind the different tax principles applicable to legal persons of public law, on the one hand, and legal persons of private law owned by a legal person of public law, on the other, is that legal persons of public law, unlike legal persons of private law (except for associations and foundations), usually lack the purpose of making profit.[1019] It is, therefore, reasonable to distinguish between business activities and other activities of legal persons of public law, and to apply this distinction *mutatis mutandis* to foreign legal persons of public law, but not to foreign legal persons of private law (owned by a foreign legal person of public law). Admittedly, Articles 8e and 8f DCITA 1969 could increase the difference in tax treatment between legal persons of private law owned by a legal person of public law and those not owned by a legal person of public law, but these exemptions reflect that the first-mentioned entities can closely resemble a legal person of public law. Based on the rationale behind the different tax principles, (sovereign wealth) investors established as or within a legal person of public law should, in principle, not be objectively comparable to (sovereign wealth) investors established as a legal person of private law (owned by a legal person of public law). In contrast, (sovereign wealth) investors established as or within a legal person of public law should be objectively comparable to other legal persons of public law, whereas

---

1018. Cf. CJEU, 24 October 2002, Case C-82/01 P (*Aéroports de Paris*), Para. 82: '(...) the fact that an activity may be exercised by a private undertaking amounts to further evidence that the activity in question may be described as a business activity.'; CJEU, 19 January 2017, Case C-344/15 (*National Roads Authority*), Para. 39: '(...) what is envisaged here is the situation in which bodies governed by public law engage in activities which may also be engaged in, in competition with them, by private economic operators. The aim is to ensure that those private operators are not placed at a disadvantage because they are taxed while those bodies are not (...)'.

1019. *Tweede Kamer*, 2014–2015, 34 003, No. 3, p. 9.

(sovereign wealth) investors established as a legal person of private law (owned by a legal person of public law) should be objectively comparable to other similar legal persons of private law.[1020]

7.5.2.6.2 Tax Regimes for Collective Investment Vehicles

The DCITA 1969 contains two separate tax regimes for CIVs, namely the FBI regime and the VBI regime. Both regimes are open to certain non-resident entities established under foreign law with a Dutch permanent establishment, provided they meet the conditions of Article 28 DCITA 1969 respectively Article 6a DCITA 1969, as also imposed on resident entities. In the author's view, sovereign wealth investors with a Dutch permanent establishment will unlikely qualify for the FBI regime if only because they will unlikely meet the key requirement to distribute most profits within a short timeframe. Failing the distribution requirement was reason for the Dutch Supreme Court to conclude, in 2013, that a Luxembourg resident CIV was not objectively comparable to a Dutch FBI, in the context of the DDWTA 1965.[1021] In March 2017, the Dutch Supreme Court decided to refer a number of questions to the CJEU in two cases, again in the context of the DDWTA 1965, including the subsidiary question whether its decision in 2013 is (still) compatible with EU law.[1022] The highest court still thinks it does,[1023] but nevertheless has some doubt, in particular because a Danish court has referred questions to the CJEU in an apparently similar case.[1024] In the author's view, there is no reason for this doubt. The author agrees with Wattel,[1025] Vleggeert[1026] and Gerechtshof 's-Hertogenbosch[1027] that, based on constant EU case law and taking into account the purpose of the FBI regime and the relevant conditions, a foreign entity that does not satisfy the distribution requirement is, for that reason alone, not objectively comparable to a Dutch FBI. In addition, sovereign wealth investors may fail the statutory purpose requirement, and may not be objectively comparable to a Dutch FBI because they are not required to withhold Dutch dividend withholding tax. The fact that a Luxembourg investment fund was not required to withholding Dutch dividend withholding tax was reason for the Dutch Supreme Court to conclude, in 2015, that this fund was not objectively comparable to a Dutch FBI.[1028] However, the court is also not sure whether this decision is (still) compatible with EU law, in particular because of the

---

1020. *Gerechtshof 's-Hertogenbosch*, 12 October 2017, No. 14/00640-00645, *V-N* 2017/57.9.
1021. *Hoge Raad*, 15 November 2013, No. 12/01866, *BNB* 2014/20.
1022. *Hoge Raad*, 3 March 2017, No. 16/03954, *BNB* 2017/86; *Hoge Raad*, 3 March 2017, No. 16/03955, *BNB* 2017/87.
1023. *Hoge Raad*, 3 March 2017, No. 16/03954, *BNB* 2017/86, Paras 7.4.2 & 7.12.
1024. Request for a preliminary ruling from the Østre Landsret (Denmark) lodged on 5 September 2016 – *Fidelity Funds v. Skatteministeriet* (Case C-480/16).
1025. Opinion of the Dutch Advocate General P. Wattel, 9 November 2016, *BNB* 2017/86, Para. 5.44.
1026. J. Vleggeert, Case note on *Hoge Raad*, 3 March 2017, No. 16/03954, *Nederland Tijdschrift voor Fiscaal Recht* 2017/686.
1027. *Gerechtshof 's-Hertogenbosch*, 24 November 2017, No. 16/03761-03770, *V-N Vandaag* 2017/2851.
1028. *Hoge Raad*, 10 July 2015, No. 14/03956, *BNB* 2015/203.

questions referred to the CJEU by a Danish court. Therefore, in March 2017, the Dutch Supreme Court, requested the CJEU for a preliminary ruling on this matter as well.[1029]

Sovereign wealth investors with a Dutch permanent establishment will not be entitled to the VBI regime, because they perform asset management for an individual investor (*individueel vermogensbeheer*) and they are not open-ended.

Based on the above, sovereign wealth investors will unlikely be comparable to resident and non-resident FBIs and VBIs, based on the purpose of the national tax measure and taking into account the relevant distinguishing criteria.

7.5.2.6.3 Tax Regime for Pension Funds

Dutch resident entities as well as non-resident entities which for at least 90% aim to facilitate – in short – retirement saving plans for employees under a regulated pension scheme, are subjectively exempt from Dutch corporate income tax in respect of activities directly related to this purpose. Sovereign wealth investors should not meet this requirement, simply because they do not facilitate retirement saving plans for employees under a (comparable) regulated pension scheme. This should also apply to sovereign wealth investors that have been set-up to cover for expected future deficits of the social security system as a result of an aging population. These sovereign wealth investors could be regarded as SPRFs.[1030] However, because SPRFs are entirely government-funded, have no superannuation liabilities, and individuals have no specified entitlement to future payments (i.e., SPRFs have no members/participants),[1031] they do not facilitate retirement saving plans for employees under a regulated pension scheme that is comparable to a Dutch one, in the author's view. As a result, sovereign wealth investors should not be comparable to resident and non-resident pension funds, based on the purpose of the national tax measure and taking into account the relevant distinguishing criteria.

7.5.2.6.4 Not-for-Profit Organizations

Not-for-profit organizations are in principle governed by the general rules as discussed in Section 7.5.2.1. Since not-for-profit organizations typically take the legal form of an association or foundation, they will only be subject to Dutch corporate income tax insofar as they carry on a business enterprise. A business enterprise requires the existence of an organization of labour and capital, which participates in economic traffic with the purpose of making profit. From the discussion in Section 2.8, it follows that sovereign wealth investors do not take the legal form of an association or

---

1029. *Hoge Raad*, 3 March 2017, No. 16/03954, *BNB* 2017/86; *Hoge Raad*, 3 March 2017, No. 16/03955, *BNB* 2017/87.
1030. *See* the discussion in Section 2.3.4.2.
1031. *See* < http://www.futurefund.gov.au/about-us > and < https://www.nzsuperfund.co.nz/nz-super-fund-explained/purpose-and-mandate >.

foundation. And unlike not-for-profit organizations, sovereign wealth investors aim to make profit. Therefore, sovereign wealth investors should not be objectively comparable to not-for-profit organizations.

7.5.2.6.5 Tax Regime for Regular Corporate Investors

Under the new corporate tax regime for public enterprises, sovereign wealth investors established as or within a legal person of public law are subject to Dutch corporate income tax insofar as they carry on a business enterprise. These sovereign wealth investors are, therefore, not taxed like a regular investor. In contrast, sovereign wealth investors established as a legal person of private law as referred to in Article 3(1) DCITA 1969, are subject to Dutch corporate income tax similar to a regular corporate investor. As explained above, the rationale behind these different tax principles is that legal persons of public law, unlike legal persons of private (except for associations and foundations), usually lack the purpose of making profit. Based on this, it was argued that (sovereign wealth) investors established as or within a legal person of public law should, in principle, not be objectively comparable to (sovereign wealth) investors established as a legal person of private law (owned by a legal person of public law). In contrast, (sovereign wealth) investors established as a legal person of private law (owned by a legal person of public law) should be objectively comparable to other similar legal persons of private law.

7.5.2.6.6 Tax Regime for Individuals

Income or a fixed rate of return on the value of assets of Dutch resident individuals would be subject to Dutch personal income tax. The author would not expect sovereign wealth investors to be objectively comparable to Dutch resident individuals, simply because of their difference in nature.

7.5.2.7 Conclusion

The Dutch corporate income tax treatment of foreign sovereign wealth investors is determined by their legal form and their activities. Sovereign wealth investors established as or within a legal person of public law are governed by the rules of the DCITA 1969 that apply (by analogy) to Dutch resident legal persons of public law, whereas sovereign wealth investors established as a legal person of private law are governed by the rules that apply (by analogy) to similar Dutch resident legal persons of private law. As a result, the former are only subject to Dutch corporate income tax on Dutch income insofar as they carry on a business enterprise, whereas the latter are subject to Dutch corporate income tax on Dutch income regardless of whether they carry on a business enterprise. This treatment could result in differences among sovereign wealth investors, as well as differences between sovereign wealth investors, on the one hand, and other categories of resident investors, on the other. These differences in tax treatment should, however, not be in conflict with European law, since it concerns situations which are not objectively comparable within the framework of the DCITA 1969, essentially because the different tax treatment is based on a different rationale, as reflected in the distinguishing criteria applicable to each category. Indeed, in the context of the DCITA 1969, sovereign wealth investors established as or within a legal person of public law should only be objectively comparable to other legal persons of public law, whereas sovereign wealth investors established as a legal person of private law should only be objectively comparable to other similar legal persons of private law. Therefore, the current Dutch corporate income tax treatment of foreign sovereign wealth investors is in accordance with European law. However, the comparability analysis indicates that, if the Netherlands wishes to increase international attractiveness for sovereign wealth investors in the future, by means of the DCITA 1969, the fundamental freedoms could impose restrictions in intra-EU/EEA situations (because this could constitute horizontal discrimination), whereas the State aid rules could impose restrictions in both intra-EU/EEA and third country situations (because this could constitute reverse and horizontal discrimination).

7.5.3 Dutch Dividend Withholding Tax Regime

7.5.3.1 *Introduction*

Based on the DDWTA 1965, dividends paid by a company resident in the Netherlands are, in principle, subject to 15% withholding tax.[1032] In domestic situations, this withholding tax has the character of an advance levy and can be offset against the Dutch corporate (and personal) income tax due by the Dutch shareholder/recipient. Where the amount of corporation income tax is not sufficient to offset the amount of dividend withholding tax, the excess dividend withholding tax will be reimbursed.[1033] In cross-border situations, Dutch dividend withholding tax can, however, be a final levy for foreign shareholders/recipients. The DDWTA 1965 provides for an exemption regime and a refund regime, which could both apply to domestic and cross-border situations. Both regimes are discussed below. However, before doing so, it is noted that FBIs, VBIs and their foreign law equivalents, as shareholders/recipients, are never entitled to an exemption or refund of dividend withholding tax. With respect to FBIs, this is, in essence, because dividend withholding tax to be withheld by FBIs, as dividend distributors, may, under Article 11a DDWTA 1965, be reduced with dividend withholding tax and foreign tax on income derived by the FBI. With respect to VBIs, this is because VBIs, as dividend distributors, have no obligation to withhold dividend withholding tax.[1034]

1032. Article 1(1) DDWTA 1965.
1033. Article 25 DCITA 1969.
1034. Article 1(4) DDWTA 1965.

The new Dutch government has announced the plan to abolish the DDWTA 1965 as from 1 January 2020, except in cases of abusive situations and in relation to low tax jurisdictions.[1035]

7.5.3.2 The Dividend Withholding Tax-Exemption Regime (Article 4 DDWTA 1965)

Article 4 DDWTA 1965 provides for an exemption to withhold Dutch dividend withholding tax in domestic situations and intra-EU/EEA situations, under certain conditions. As from 1 January 2018, the withholding exemption was extended to shareholders from third countries, under certain conditions, basically to further reduce tax barriers within international groups.[1036]

In domestic situations, the exemption to withhold Dutch dividend withholding tax can be applied if the participation exemption regime[1037] (or credit regime[1038]) applies. This means, in essence, that the shareholder must be a resident company subject to Dutch corporate income tax and own a shareholding of at least 5%. Thus, resident entities which are subjectively exempt from Dutch corporate income tax, such as pension funds, are not entitled to the exemption from Dutch dividend withholding tax.

In intra-EU/EEA situations, based on Article 4(2) DDWTA 1965, the exemption to withhold dividend withholding tax applies in relation to shareholders which are resident of an EU Member State or EEA-EFTA State according to the tax legislation of that State, provided the participation exemption regime (or credit regime) would have applied if the non-resident shareholder had been tax resident in the Netherlands (and in the absence of abuse). This means, in essence, that the EU/EEA shareholder would have been subject to Dutch corporate income tax if they had been tax resident in the Netherlands, and must own a shareholding in a Dutch resident company of at least 5%.[1039] Thus, non-resident entities which would have been subjectively exempt from Dutch corporate income tax if they had been tax resident in the Netherlands, are not entitled to the exemption from Dutch dividend withholding tax. This dividend withholding tax-exemption in intra-EU/EEA situations is based on the Parent-Subsidiary Directive, and its design has been influenced by decisions of the CJEU.[1040]

As from 1 January 2018, the withholding exemption, under conditions similar to intra-EU/EEA situations, applies in relation to shareholders from third countries,

---

1035. Regeerakkoord 2017–2021, *Vertrouwen in de toekomst* (10 October 2017), pp. 35–36 & p. 68.
1036. *Tweede Kamer*, 2017–2018, 34 788, No. 3, pp. 2–3.
1037. Article 13 DCITA 1969.
1038. Article 13aa DCITA 1969.
1039. The exemption can also be applied to non-resident corporate taxpayers with a Dutch permanent establishment, provided the shares can be allocated to that permanent establishment.
1040. For example, CJEU, 11 June 2009, Case C-521/07 (*European Commission v. Kingdom of the Netherlands*); CJEU, 18 June 2009, Case C-303/07 (*Aberdeen Property Fininvest*).

provided they are tax resident in a country with which the Netherlands has concluded a tax treaty containing a dividend article.[1041]

7.5.3.3 The Dividend Withholding Tax Refund Regime (Articles 10 and 10a DDWTA 1965)

Articles 10 and 10a DDWTA 1965 provide for a refund of Dutch dividend withholding tax to shareholders falling within one of the following three categories, under certain conditions: (1) resident and non-resident entities which are not subject to corporate income tax, (2) legal persons of public law, as well as legal persons of private law owned by a legal person of public law, and (3) non-resident individuals and non-resident entities faced with an amount of dividend withholding tax that is higher than the amount of Dutch tax that would have been due if they had been tax resident in the Netherlands. The refund regime has to a large extent been influenced by EU law, and applies to both intra-EU/EEA and third country situations. The different provisions of the refund regime are discussed in more detail below.

7.5.3.3.1 Entities Which Are Not Subject to Corporate Income Tax

In domestic situations, resident entities which are not subject to Dutch corporate income tax, such as pension funds, are not entitled to an exemption from dividend withholding tax. Such entities are not able to offset the dividend withholding tax against corporate income tax, and the dividend withholding tax loses its function as an advance levy.[1042] Without further regulation, the dividend withholding tax would become a final levy for such tax-exempt resident investors. Article 10(1) DDWTA 1965, therefore, entitles these residents to a full refund.

As from 1 January 2007, based on EU law, this refund regime for tax-exempt entities was extended to entities resident in other EU Member States. As from 1 January 2010, the refund regime was also applied to Norway and Iceland. One year later, the refund regime for tax-exempt entities was further extended to entities resident in Liechtenstein. In intra-EU/EEA situations, based on Article 10(2) DDWTA 1965, a non-resident entity is entitled to a refund of Dutch dividend withholding tax, if that entity: (i) is not subject to a profit tax in its country of residence, and (ii) would also not have been subject to Dutch corporate tax if it had been tax resident in the Netherlands. The requirement of not being subject to a profit tax locally is not in accordance with EU law, in the author's view.[1043]

1041. Article 4(2)(a)(2°) DDWTA 1965.
1042. Cf. *Hoge Raad*, 15 November 2013, No. 12/01866, *BNB* 2014/20.
1043. CJEU, 12 December 2006, Case C-374/04 (*Test Claimants in Class IV of the ACT Group Litigation*), Para. 70; CJEU, 8 November 2007, Case C-379/05 (*Amurta*), Para. 39; CJEU, 18 June 2009, Case C-303/07 (*Aberdeen Property Fininvest*), Paras 51 and 54; CJEU, 10 April 2014, Case C-190/12 (*Emerging Markets Series*), Para. 59; Similarly, J. van Eijsden, B. Kiekebeld & D. Smit (eds), *Nederlands belastingrecht in Europees perspectief*, 2nd edn., (Deventer: Kluwer, 2014), p. 195.

As from 1 January 2012, the refund regime for tax-exempt entities applies to entities resident in third countries as well. This extension was motivated by the freedom of capital movement, and by increasing the attractiveness for non-resident pension funds and sovereign wealth investors.[1044] In addition to the conditions which apply in intra-EU/EEA situations, based on Article 10(3) DDWTA 1965, entities resident in third countries will only be entitled to a refund, if: (iii) they are resident of a country with which sufficient means for the exchange of information are available, and (iv) the dividend qualifies as a return on a 'portfolio investment'[1045] as meant in Articles 63 and 64 TFEU. In the author's view, the third requirement needs to be refined. In Section 6.3.4.3, it was argued that a Member State should not be able rely on the need to ensure the effectiveness of fiscal supervision if a third State would be willing to voluntarily provide the necessary information.

7.5.3.3.2 Legal Persons of Public Law and Legal Persons of Private Law Owned by a Legal Person of Public Law

Due to the new corporate income tax regime for public enterprises, many legal persons of public law, and legal persons of private law owned by a legal person of public law, became subject to Dutch corporate income tax, as from 1 January 2016. However, income derived by such investors may be exempt from corporate income tax under Article 8e or 8f DCITA 1969.[1046] Without any further regulation, many such investors would not have been entitled to a refund of dividend withholding tax under Article 10 DDWTA 1965, even if the dividend income would be exempt from corporate income tax under Article 8e or 8f DCITA 1969. In such cases, legal persons of public law and legal persons of private law owned by a legal person of public law would (eventually) have received back, as part of the corporate income tax assessment procedure, any dividend withholding tax that could not be offset, but this would have resulted in a cash flow disadvantage compared to the situation prior to 1 January 2016.[1047] Therefore, as from 1 January 2016, Article 10(5) DDWTA 1965 provides for a refund of dividend withholding tax to legal persons of public law and legal persons of private law owned by a legal person of public law which are subject to Dutch corporate income tax, provided the withholding tax relates to dividend income that is exempt from corporate income tax under Article 8e or 8f DCITA 1969. This refund regime for legal persons of public law, and legal persons of private law owned by a legal person of public law, can also apply in intra-EU/EEA and third country situations.

In intra-EU/EEA situations, legal persons of public law, and legal persons of private law owned by a legal person of public law, are entitled to a refund of Dutch dividend withholding tax, if: (i) the dividend income is not included in the taxable

---

1044. *Tweede Kamer*, 2011–2012, 33 003, No. 3, p. 38 & p. 113.
1045. The concept of portfolio investment and direct investment was discussed in Section 6.3.2.3.2.
1046. Articles 8e and 8f DCITA 1969 were discussed in Section 7.5.2.6.1.
1047. *Tweede Kamer*, 2014–2015, 34 220, No. 3, p. 5.

profit in the other State, and (ii) the dividend income would also not have been taxed pursuant to Article 8e or 8f DCITA 1969 if the entity had been tax resident in the Netherlands.

In third country situations, these two conditions apply *mutatis mutandis*, supplemented by the requirements that: (iii) the entity is a resident of a country with which sufficient means for the exchange of information are available,[1048] and (iv) the dividend qualifies as a return on a 'portfolio investment'[1049] as meant in Articles 63 and 64 TFEU.

7.5.3.3.3 Non-resident Individuals and Non-resident Entities Faced with a Higher Dutch Tax Burden

Article 10a DDWTA 1965 was introduced on 1 January 2017 in response to the judgment of the CJEU in the joined cases *Miljoen, X* and *Société Générale*.[1050] These cases concerned two non-resident individuals and one non-resident company who were subject to a final 15% Dutch dividend withholding tax on dividends from Dutch shareholdings of less than 5%. Resident individuals and resident entities are also subject to 15% dividend withholding tax on dividends from such shareholdings; however, the withholding tax for residents is not final, but can be offset against personal income tax (maximum rate of 52%) or corporate income tax (maximum rate of 25%). Where the amount of personal income tax or corporate income tax is not sufficient to offset the amount of dividend withholding tax, the excess dividend withholding tax will be reimbursed to residents. According to the CJEU, the freedom of capital movement prohibits national tax legislation which imposes a heavier final tax burden on non-residents compared to residents for the same dividends. As a result, the taxation at the level of a non-resident investor must be compared with the overall taxation at the level of a comparable resident investor. The relevant period for comparing the tax burden is the period taken into account for residents; usually one tax year. The CJEU furthermore held that, in comparing the tax burden, only expenses that are directly linked to an activity that has generated taxable income can be taken into account when calculating the tax burden of a comparable resident.[1051] This refund regime for non-resident individuals and non-resident entities applies in intra-EU/EEA situations, as well as third country situations.

In intra-EU/EEA situations, Article 10a(1) DDWTA 1965 provides for a refund of Dutch dividend withholding tax to an individual or entity resident in another EU Member State or EEA-EFTA State, to the extent that the amount of dividend withholding tax, after the application of a tax treaty, is higher than the amount of (corporate) income tax that would have been due if the individual or entity had been tax resident

---

1048. In Section 6.3.4.3, it was argued that a Member State should not be able rely on the need to ensure the effectiveness of fiscal supervision if a third State would be willing to voluntarily provide the necessary information.
1049. The concept of portfolio investment and direct investment was discussed in Section 6.3.2.3.2.
1050. CJEU, 17 September 2015, Joined Cases C-10/14, C-14/14 and C-17/14 (*Miljoen, X, Société Générale*).
1051. *Ibid.*, Para. 57.

Chapter 7: The Framework Applied to The Netherlands

in the Netherlands. For non-resident entities, Article 10a(1) DDWTA 1965 is relevant in intra-EU/EEA situations where the withholding tax-exemption of Article 4(2) DDWTA 1965 does not apply. For non-resident entities, only expenses that are directly linked to an activity that has generated taxable income can be taken into account. It is noted that, because the corporate income tax rate is 25% and the dividend withholding tax rate is 15%, the directly linked expenses of non-resident entities would need to be more than 40% of the dividend income to be able to benefit from Article 10a DDWTA 1965. Therefore, the practical relevance of Article 10a(1) DDWTA 1965 for non-resident entities is rather limited.

In third country situations, based on Article 10a(2) DDWTA 1965, the same condition applies, supplemented by the requirements that: (ii) the individual or entity is a resident of a country with which sufficient means for the exchange of information are available,[1052] and (iii) the dividend qualifies as a return on a 'portfolio investment'[1053] as meant in Articles 63 and 64 TFEU. With respect to non-resident entities that would have been subject to Dutch corporate income tax, the practical relevance of Article 10a(2) DDWTA 1965, in 2017, seems limited to shareholdings in Dutch resident companies of at least 5%, because a resident for corporate tax purposes would have been entitled to the participation exemption regime, resulting in no corporate income taxation on the dividend income and, therefore, in a lower tax burden than the dividend withholding tax burden for the non-resident entity. In 2018, with respect to non-resident entities that would have been subject to Dutch corporate income tax, the practical relevance of Article 10a(2) DDWTA 1965 seems even further limited to shareholdings in Dutch resident companies of at least 5% held by shareholders resident in a non-tax treaty third country (due to the extension of the withholding tax regime to third countries). In case of shareholdings of less than 5%, the participation exemption would not have applied, so that the directly linked expenses would need to be more than 40% of the taxable dividend income to be able to benefit from Article 10a DDWTA 1965. With respect to non-resident entities that would *not* be subject to Dutch corporate income tax, Article 10a(2) DDWTA 1965 may apply as long as the shareholding qualifies as a 'portfolio investment'.[1054]

In line with EU case law,[1055] a refund will not be granted if the individual or entity is entitled to a full deduction of the Dutch dividend withholding tax in its country of residence, pursuant to a tax treaty concluded between the Netherlands and the country of residence.[1056]

1052. In Section 6.3.4.3, it was argued that a Member State should not be able rely on the need to ensure the effectiveness of fiscal supervision if a third State would be willing to voluntarily provide the necessary information.
1053. The concept of portfolio investment and direct investment was discussed in Section 6.3.2.3.2.
1054. *Ibid.*
1055. CJEU, 17 September 2015, Joined Cases C-10/14, C-14/14 and C-17/14 (*Miljoen, X, Société Générale*), Paras 77–80.
1056. Article 10a(5) DDWTA 1965.

7.5.3.4 Application to Foreign Sovereign Wealth Investors and Comparison to Other Investors

From the discussion of the DDWTA 1965, it is clear that different categories of investors are governed by different dividend withholding tax rules. Below, the application of the DDWTA 1965 to sovereign wealth investors and other investors will be analysed and compared.

Dividend payments by Dutch resident companies to foreign sovereign wealth investors are, in principle, subject to 15% Dutch dividend withholding tax. The application of both the dividend withholding tax-exemption regime and dividend withholding tax refund regime to non-resident investors, depends for an important part on the Dutch corporate income tax status or treatment of such entities if they had been tax resident in the Netherlands. This test resembles the comparability standard under the freedoms and the State aid rules, and produces the following picture. Non-resident investors may only be entitled to:

- an exemption from Dutch dividend withholding tax if they would have been subject to Dutch corporate income tax, if the participation exemption would have applied, and, in relation to third countries, if the shareholder is resident in a tax treaty country;
- a refund of Dutch dividend withholding tax under Articles 10(2) and 10(3) DDWTA 1965 if they would not have been subject to Dutch corporate income tax;
- a refund of Dutch dividend withholding tax under Article 10(5) DDWTA 1965 if they would have been subject to Dutch corporate income tax and if the withholding tax relates to dividend income that would have been exempt from corporate income tax under Article 8e or 8f DCITA 1969;
- a refund of Dutch dividend withholding tax under Article 10a DDWTA 1965 to the extent that the amount of dividend withholding tax, after the application of a tax treaty, is higher than the amount of (corporate) income tax that would have been due if they had been tax resident in the Netherlands.

The reference to the Dutch corporate income tax status or treatment applies to all categories of non-resident investors, including foreign sovereign wealth investors. This reference makes it necessary to compare non-resident investors to resident investors in the context of the DCITA 1969. This exercise was already performed in Section 7.5.2 from the perspective of sovereign wealth investors. The outcome was that sovereign wealth investors can be objectively comparable to legal persons of public law, or to similar legal persons of private law, depending on their legal form and their activities. In the context of the DCITA 1969, sovereign wealth investors should not be objectively comparable to the other categories of resident investors, essentially because the different tax treatment is based on a different rationale, as reflected in the distinguishing criteria applicable to these categories. The Dutch corporate income tax treatment of sovereign wealth investors, if they would have been tax resident in the Netherlands, can be summarized as follows. Pursuant to Article 2(1)(g) DCITA 1969, sovereign wealth investors established as or within a legal person of public law would have been subject to Dutch corporate income tax insofar as they carry on a business enterprise. Thus, sovereign wealth investors taking this legal form, would not be subject to Dutch corporate income tax if they do not carry on a business enterprise, and vice versa. On the other hand, sovereign wealth investors established as a legal person of private law as referred to in Article 2(1) DCITA 1969, would have been subject to Dutch corporate income tax, similar to regular corporate investors, regardless of whether a business enterprise is being carried on. Sovereign wealth investors will probably not be entitled to the exemptions provided for in Articles 8e and 8f DCITA 1969.

Withholding Tax-Exemption Regime

In intra-EU/EEA situations, sovereign wealth investors which would have been subject to Dutch corporate income tax if they had been tax resident in the Netherlands, are entitled to an exemption from dividend withholding tax under Article 4(2) DDWTA 1965 in case of shareholdings in Dutch resident companies of at least 5% and in the absence of abuse. Sovereign wealth investors which would *not* have been subject to Dutch corporate income tax if they had been tax resident in the Netherlands, are not covered by Article 4(2) DDWTA 1965.

In 2017, Article 4 DDWTA 1965 did not apply to third country situations. This restriction in relation to third countries should be covered by the standstill provision, but only to the extent that it concerns direct investments.[1057] Article 4 DDWTA 1965 could, however, conflict with the freedom of capital movement in case of portfolio investments that would qualify for the participation exemption.[1058] In 2018, Article 4(2) DDWTA 1965 applies in relation to shareholders from third countries, under conditions similar to intra-EU/EEA situations, provided they are tax resident in a country with which the Netherlands has concluded a tax treaty containing a dividend article. Therefore, in third country situations, sovereign wealth investors which: (i) would have been subject to Dutch corporate income tax if they had been tax resident in the Netherlands, (ii) are tax resident in a country with which the Netherlands has concluded a tax treaty containing a dividend article, and (iii) own a shareholding in a Dutch company of at least 5%, could be entitled to an exemption from Dutch dividend withholding tax, as from 1 January 2018, based on Article 4(2) DDWTA 1965. Article 4 DDWTA 1965 (new) could still conflict with the freedom of capital movement in third country, non-tax treaty situations involving portfolio investments that would qualify for the participation exemption.

Withholding Tax Refund Regime for Non-resident Entities Which Are Not Subject to Corporation Tax

In intra-EU/EEA situations, sovereign wealth investors which would *not* have been subject to Dutch corporate income tax if they had been tax resident in the Netherlands, are entitled to a refund of dividend withholding tax under Article 10(2) DDWTA 1965,

---

1057. Section 6.3.2.3.3.
1058. Similarly, J. van Eijsden, B. Kiekebeld & D. Smit (eds), *Nederlands belastingrecht in Europees perspectief*, 2nd edn., (Deventer: Kluwer, 2014), p. 192.

and vice versa, provided they are *not* subject to a profit tax in their country of residence, and regardless of the size of the shareholding. This requirement of not being subject to a profit tax locally is not in accordance with EU law, in the author's view.[1059]

In third country situations, sovereign wealth investors which would *not* have been subject to Dutch corporate income tax if they been tax resident in the Netherlands, are entitled to a refund of dividend withholding tax under Article 10(3) DDWTA 1965 if: (i) they are *not* subject to a profit tax in their country of residence, (ii) they are resident of a country with which sufficient means for the exchange of information are available, and (iii) the shareholding in a Dutch resident company qualifies as a 'portfolio investment'[1060] (i.e., shareholdings which do not enable the shareholder to participate effectively in the management and control of the company). As indicated in Section 7.5.3.3.1, in the author's view, the first requirement is not in accordance with EU law. In addition, the second requirement needs to be refined.[1061] The third requirement is based on the standstill provision and means that the size of the shareholding could be relevant. Although being based on the standstill, the 'portfolio investment' requirement may carry the risk of constituting State aid in relation to Dutch resident investors, because they would be entitled to a refund in case of 'direct investments'.

Withholding Tax Refund Regime for Legal Persons of Public Law and Legal Persons of Private Law Owned by a Legal Person of Public Law

In both intra-EU/EEA situations and third country situations, sovereign wealth investors which would have been subject to Dutch corporate income tax if they had been tax resident in the Netherlands, should probably not be entitled to a refund of dividend withholding tax under Article 10(5) DDWTA 1965, because the income is often not taxed in their country of residence[1062] and/or because Article 8e or 8f DCITA 1969 are unlikely applicable to sovereign wealth investors.[1063] Article 10(5) DDWTA 1965 cannot apply to sovereign wealth investors which would *not* have been subject to Dutch corporate income tax if they had been tax resident in the Netherlands.

Withholding Tax Refund Regime for Non-resident Individuals and Non-resident Entities Faced with a Higher Dutch Tax Burden

In intra-EU/EEA situations, sovereign wealth investors which would have been subject to Dutch corporate income tax if they had been tax resident in the Netherlands, should unlikely be entitled to a refund of dividend withholding tax under Article 10a(1) DDWTA 1965 in case of shareholdings in Dutch companies of less than 5%, because directly linked expenses would need to be more than 40% of the taxable dividend income. As explained, in case of shareholdings of at least 5%, such sovereign wealth

---

1059. *Ibid.*, p. 195.
1060. The concept of portfolio investment and direct investment was discussed in Section 6.3.2.3.2.
1061. *See* Section 6.3.4.3, where it was argued that a Member State should not be able rely on the need to ensure the effectiveness of fiscal supervision if a third State would be willing to voluntarily provide the necessary information.
1062. *See* Section 2.10.
1063. *See* the discussion in Section 7.5.2.6.1.

Chapter 7: The Framework Applied to The Netherlands

investors would already be covered by the dividend withholding exemption of Article 4(2) DDWTA 1965. In intra-EU/EEA situations, sovereign wealth investors which would *not* have been subject to Dutch corporate income tax if they had been tax resident in the Netherlands, could also be entitled to a full refund under Article 10a(1) DDWTA 1965, but they will likely already be entitled to a refund under Article 10(2) DDWTA 1965 (unless they are subject to a profit tax in their country of residence).[1064]

In third country situations, sovereign wealth investors which would have been subject to Dutch corporate income tax if they had been tax resident in the Netherlands, may be entitled to a refund of dividend withholding tax under Article 10a(2) DDWTA 1965, in particular in case of shareholdings in Dutch companies of at least 5% not covered by the withholding exemption regime. As explained, in case of shareholdings of at least 5%, a resident for corporate income tax purposes would have been entitled to the participation exemption, resulting in no corporation income taxation on the dividend income and, therefore, in a lower tax burden than the dividend withholding tax burden for these sovereign wealth investors. In case of shareholdings of less than 5%, the directly linked expenses would need to be more than 40% of the taxable dividend income to be able to benefit from Article 10a(2) DDWTA 1965. It is noted that a shareholding of at least 5% would still need to qualify as a 'portfolio investment', and the sovereign wealth investors needs to be a resident of a country with which sufficient means for the exchange of information are available.[1065] Although the requirement of 'portfolio investment' is based on the standstill provision, it may carry the risk of constituting State aid in relation to Dutch resident investors, because they could have been entitled to a refund in case of 'direct investments'. As explained in Section 6.3.4.3, the information exchange requirement needs to be refined, in the author's view.[1066] In third country situations, sovereign wealth investors which would *not* have been subject to Dutch corporate income tax could also be entitled to a full refund under Article 10a(2) DDWTA 1965, but they will likely already be entitled to a refund under Article 10(3) DDWTA 1965 (unless they are subject to a profit tax in their country of residence).[1067]

In summary, sovereign wealth investors which would have been subject to Dutch corporate income tax if they had been tax resident in the Netherlands, are (likely) not entitled to an exemption or refund of Dutch dividend withholding tax under the DDWTA 1965, in the following situations:

1064. Note that Art. 10a(1) DDWTA 1965 effectively sets aside the condition in Art. 10(2) DDWTA 1965 that a non-resident investor should be subject to a profit tax in its country of residence.
1065. Section 7.5.3.3.3.
1066. In Section 6.3.4.3, it was argued that a Member State should not be able rely on the need to ensure the effectiveness of fiscal supervision if a third State would be willing to voluntarily provide the necessary information.
1067. Note that Art. 10a(2) DDWTA 1965 effectively sets aside the condition in Art. 10(3) DDWTA 1965 that a non-resident investor should be subject to a profit tax in its country of residence.

- sovereign wealth investors resident inside and outside the EU/EEA with shareholdings in Dutch companies of less than 5%, because the directly related expenses will unlikely account for more than 40% of the dividend income;
- sovereign wealth investors resident outside the EU/EEA in a non-tax treaty country and owning a shareholding in a Dutch company of at least 5% which qualifies as 'direct investment';
- sovereign wealth investors resident outside the EU/EEA in a non-tax treaty country and owning a shareholding in a Dutch company of at least 5% which qualifies as 'portfolio investment', in case the sovereign wealth investor is resident of a country with which no sufficient means for the exchange of information are available.

Sovereign wealth investors which would *not* have been subject to Dutch corporate income tax if they had been tax resident in the Netherlands, are not entitled to an exemption or refund of Dutch dividend withholding tax under the DDWTA 1965, in the following situations:

- sovereign wealth investors resident outside the EU/EEA with shareholdings in Dutch companies of at least 5% which qualify as 'direct investment';
- sovereign wealth investors resident outside the EU/EEA with shareholdings in Dutch companies of at least 5% which qualify as 'portfolio investment', in case the sovereign wealth investor is either resident of a country with which no sufficient means for the exchange of information are available, or entitled to a full deduction of the Dutch dividend withholding tax in its country of residence pursuant to a tax treaty concluded between the Netherlands and the country of residence.

7.5.3.5 *Conclusion*

In domestic situations, the withholding tax-exemption and withholding tax refund apply if the dividend income is not taxed at the level of the Dutch shareholder, either because the shareholder is subjectively exempt from Dutch corporate income tax, or because the dividend income is exempt from Dutch corporate income tax under the participation exemption or Article 8e or 8f DCITA 1969. In these situations, the dividend withholding tax has lost its function as an advance levy. Put differently, whether the dividend withholding tax has a function as an advance levy for entities, depends on the Dutch corporate income tax status or treatment of such entities. The withholding tax-exemption regime and withholding tax refund regime have been gradually extended to non-resident investors over the years, mainly under the influence of EU law. For many non-resident entities, the Dutch dividend withholding tax does not function as an advance levy to be offset against Dutch corporate income tax, because the dividend income of many non-resident entities is not subject to Dutch corporate income tax. This could be an argument not to impose dividend withholding tax at all in such situations.

The technique followed in the DDWTA 1965 is to connect the application of the exemption and refund regime for non-resident investors to the Dutch corporate income tax status or treatment if they would have been tax resident in the Netherlands. Therefore, the conclusion that was reached in Section 7.5.2.7 in the context of the DCITA 1969, similarly applies in the context of the DDWTA 1965: sovereign wealth investors established as or within a legal person of public law should be objectively comparable to other legal persons of public law, but not to other categories of investors, whereas sovereign wealth investors established as a legal person of private law should be objectively comparable to other similar legal persons of private law, but not to other categories of investors. However, with respect to investors resident outside the EU/EEA in a non-tax treaty country, the Netherlands does not accord NT in case of 'direct investments' (based on the standstill provision of Article 64(1) TFEU), or in case of 'portfolio investments' under the conditions mentioned above. As a result of the technique followed in the DDWTA 1965, the dividend withholding tax treatment could differ *among* sovereign wealth investors, depending on their legal form and activities, as well as their place of residence and type of shareholding. It could, furthermore, result in sovereign wealth investors being taxed more favourably, but also less favourably, than other categories of investors, in the context of the DDWTA 1965. However, to the extent that these differences result from the technique of connecting to the DCITA 1969, they should not be in conflict with EU law, because this technique ensures that the dividend withholding tax treatment of non-resident investors is, in general, similar to that of resident and other non-resident investors in similar circumstances. Such differences in treatment, therefore, concern situations which are not objectively comparable in the context of the DDWTA 1965.

With respect to the remaining differences, the standstill provision (relied on in Articles 4(2), 10(3), 10(5) and 10a(2) DDWTA 1965) allows the Netherlands to refuse NT to sovereign wealth investors resident in third countries, in case of 'direct investments'. Although this may carry the risk of constituting State aid in relation to Dutch resident investors, because they could be entitled to an exemption or refund, it would have no *negative* impact on the ability of the Netherlands to pursue international attractiveness in relation to foreign sovereign wealth investors through the DDWTA 1965.

In case of 'portfolio investments', the Netherlands should not, in the author's view, be able to rely on the need to ensure the effectiveness of fiscal supervision if a third country would be willing to voluntarily provide the necessary information (Articles 10(3), 10(5) and 10a(2) DDWTA 1965). Furthermore, the requirement of not being subject to a profit tax locally (relied on in Articles 10(2)-(3) DDWTA 1965) is not in accordance with EU law, in the author's view. In addition, Article 4 DDWTA 1965 (new) could conflict with the freedom of capital movement in third country, non-tax treaty situations involving 'portfolio investments' that would qualify for the participation exemption. All these restrictive conditions would need to be removed or amended, and would likely have a positive, rather than a negative impact on the international attractiveness of the Netherlands for foreign sovereign wealth investors.

Considering the above, European law should not impose restrictions on the Netherlands to the extent that it currently pursues international attractiveness in relation to foreign sovereign wealth investors through the DDWTA 1965. However, the comparability analysis indicates that, if the Netherlands wishes to increase international attractiveness for sovereign wealth investors in the future, by means of the DDWTA 1965, the fundamental freedoms could impose restrictions in intra-EU/EEA situations (because this could constitute horizontal discrimination), whereas the State aid rules could impose restrictions in both intra-EU/EEA and third country situations (because this could constitute reverse and horizontal discrimination).

7.5.4 Dutch Tax Treaties

7.5.4.1 *General*

In line with Dutch tax treaty policy, sovereign wealth investors of tax treaty partners of the Netherlands are very often entitled to an exemption or reduction of Dutch source taxation on dividends. Reference is made to the Dutch tax treaties discussed in the Appendix. In Chapter 6, it was concluded that tax treaty benefits accorded by a Member State to (one or more) foreign sovereign wealth investors and resulting in more favourable treatment as compared to resident investors of that Member State (i.e., *reverse* discrimination), should not constitute discrimination under the freedoms,[1068] but it may constitute State aid under rather strict circumstances.[1069] The same conclusion applies in case of tax treaty benefits accorded to (one or more) foreign sovereign wealth investors, but not to other non-resident investors (i.e., horizontal discrimination). To be clear, the implications of tax treaty benefits for the selectivity test under State aid rules are currently unclear.[1070] To date, this issue has not reached the CJEU. The fact remains that the State aid rules are not identical to the fundamental freedoms. Differences are, therefore, possible, and it cannot be excluded that tax treaty benefits could be selective in a State aid context. Assuming that tax treaty benefits can indeed amount to State aid, application of the State aid rules would then require a sovereign wealth investor to qualify as an *active* investor.[1071] It would also require such sovereign wealth investors to be treated more favourably than other economic operators which are comparable in the light of the objective pursued by the reference system.

1068. Section 6.3.3.2.
1069. Section 6.4.4.
1070. *See* the discussion in Section 6.4.4.2.3.
1071. Section 6.4.4.2.2.

7.5.4.2 *Selectivity*

In case of reverse discrimination based on a tax treaty, Dutch domestic tax law is the reference system,[1072] and the analysis in Sections 7.5.2.6 and 7.5.3.4 above can be used. This analysis indicates that, for Dutch tax purposes, sovereign wealth investors established as or within a legal person of public law should be objectively comparable to another legal persons of public law, whereas sovereign wealth investors established as a legal person of private law should be objectively comparable to other similar legal persons of private law. Dividends paid to such comparable resident investors may be subject to Dutch corporation income tax and dividend withholding tax, whereas sovereign wealth investors may be entitled to a general exemption of Dutch taxation on dividends pursuant to a tax treaty, for example under the tax treaties with the UAE, Oman and Norway (discussed in the Appendix). Without these general tax-treaty-based exemptions, dividends paid to sovereign wealth investors may have been subject to Dutch dividend withholding tax under the DDWTA 1965, as the analysis in Section 7.5.3.4 demonstrates. Therefore, general tax-treaty-based exemptions may not be justified by the nature or general scheme of the (reference) system. Nor can they be justified by the need to avoid international double taxation if sovereign wealth investors are not taxed in their home State. Instead, general tax-treaty-based exemptions accorded to sovereign wealth investors are most often aimed at attracting investments from these investors, and could, therefore, be selective. Nonetheless, since tax treaty provisions are generally not aimed at specific investment targets (as potential indirect beneficiaries),[1073] the State aid rules should only come into play if these sovereign wealth investors would qualify as *active* investors, and if the tax treaty benefit would be more than the *de minimis* threshold of EUR 200,000 over any period of three fiscal years. In the author's view, it is not entirely clear how the tax treaty benefit should be calculated; though it would seem to make sense to take into account (non-selective) entitlements that exist under the DDWTA 1965.

In case of horizontal discrimination based on a tax treaty, the tax treaty as a whole or a particular tax treaty provision should be the reference system.[1074] In the author's view, the more limited (defined) a tax treaty benefit becomes in terms of eligible persons, the greater the chance it no longer reflects a generally accepted allocation of taxing rights, and could be considered selective. Generous tax-exemptions accorded to sovereign wealth investors under tax treaties carry the risk of being selective, in particular if they are limited to (a) selected (group of) investors and deviate significantly from a generally accepted allocation of taxing rights as expressed in the OECD and UN MTC, as well as general Dutch tax treaty policy. In this regard, the tax treaties between the Netherlands and the UAE, Oman and Norway (discussed in the Appendix) catch the eye. Nonetheless, since tax treaty provisions are generally not aimed at specific investment targets (as potential indirect beneficiaries),[1075] the State

---

1072. L. De Broe, 'Can Tax Treaties Confer State Aid?' (2017) 26 *EC Tax Review* 228, p. 229.
1073. *See* the discussion in Section 6.4.4.3.2.
1074. L. De Broe, 'Can Tax Treaties Confer State Aid?' (2017) 26 *EC Tax Review* 228, pp. 230–231.
1075. *See* the discussion in Section 6.4.4.3.2.

aid rules could typically only come into play if the relevant sovereign wealth investors would qualify as *active* investors, and if the tax treaty benefit would be more than the *de minimis* threshold of EUR 200,000 over any period of three fiscal years. In the author's view, it is not entirely clear how the tax treaty benefit should be calculated; though it would seem to make sense to take into account (non-selective) entitlements that exist under the DDWTA 1965.

The EC shall not require recovery of the aid if this would be contrary to a general principle of Union law.[1076] In Section 6.4.4.2.1, it was noted, however, that it is unclear whether immunity from measures of constraint, as an element of the customary international law principle of sovereign immunity, can be regarded as a general principle of Union law. Depending on the answer to that question, immunity from measures of constraint could prevent a Member State to recover fiscal State aid granted to a foreign sovereign wealth investor.

7.5.4.3 *Conclusion*

The Netherlands mainly pursues international attractiveness in relation to foreign sovereign wealth investors through tax treaties. Tax-treaty-based benefits accorded by the Netherlands to sovereign wealth investors, in deviation from (non-selective) entitlements under domestic law or from a generally accepted allocation of taxing rights, carry the risk of being selective, and may, therefore, constitute State aid. Thus, European law, notably the State aid rules, may, under rather strict circumstances, (have) impose(d) restrictions on the Netherlands' ability to pursue international attractiveness in relation to foreign sovereign wealth investors. Nonetheless, the analysis in this section indicates that, if the Netherlands wishes to grant (further) tax benefits to (other) foreign sovereign wealth investors in the future, but not to other (comparable) investors, it would probably still be best to continue do so through tax treaties as much as possible. However, the downside of implementing a tax policy through tax treaties is that it may leave little leeway to give effect to a tax policy change. Tax treaties are rarely renegotiated, or unilaterally terminated. Once a tax treaty enters into force, it will generally apply for a long period of time.

7.6 CONCLUSIONS

In this chapter, the conceptual framework as developed in Chapters 3–6 has been applied to the Netherlands, as an illustration. After a review of Dutch international tax policy principles and objectives, it was concluded that the Netherlands largely adheres to the objective of international tax attractiveness vis-à-vis sovereign wealth investors. This policy appears particularly from Dutch tax treaties, which often provide extensive tax benefits to sovereign wealth investors of the other contracting State. Given the tension with inter-taxpayer equity, as an expression of the fundamental value of

---

1076. Article 16(1) of the Procedural Regulation.

Chapter 7: The Framework Applied to The Netherlands

fairness, a separate, more detailed and in-depth analysis for each favourable tax treaty provision regarding sovereign wealth investors would have been appropriate, in the author's view.

Nonetheless, given the primacy of international attractiveness as a Dutch tax policy objective in relation to sovereign wealth investors, the conceptual framework was primarily used in this chapter to answer the following question: *What impact, if any, does international law have on the Netherlands' ability to achieve (or promote) international tax attractiveness in relation to foreign sovereign wealth investors?* In this respect, the impact of the sovereign immunity principle, OECD MTC based treaties and European law was considered.

Based on Chapters 4 and 5, it was concluded that neither the sovereign immunity principle, nor OECD based treaties concluded by the Netherlands have (had) a (negative) impact on the ability of the Netherlands to pursue international attractiveness in relation to foreign sovereign wealth investors.

European law should not impose restrictions on the Netherlands to the extent that it currently pursues international attractiveness in relation to foreign sovereign wealth investors through the DDWTA 1965 (or the DCITA 1969). However, the Netherlands mainly pursues international attractiveness through tax treaties. Tax-treaty-based benefits accorded by the Netherlands to sovereign wealth investors, in deviation from (non-selective) entitlements under domestic law or from a generally accepted allocation of taxing rights, carry the risk of being selective, and may, therefore, constitute State aid. Thus, European law, notably the State aid rules, may, under rather strict circumstances, (have) impose(d) restrictions on the Netherlands' ability to pursue international attractiveness in relation to foreign sovereign wealth investors. Nonetheless, if the Netherlands wishes to grant (further) tax benefits to (other) foreign sovereign wealth investors in the future, but not to other (comparable) investors, it would probably still be best to continue to do so through tax treaties as much as possible. However, the downside of implementing a tax policy through tax treaties is that it may leave little leeway to give effect to a tax policy change. Tax treaties are rarely renegotiated, or unilaterally terminated. Once a tax treaty enters into force, it will generally apply for a long period of time.

CHAPTER 8
Summary and Conclusions

8.1 INTRODUCTION TO THIS STUDY

In more recent years, an increasing number of States have entered the market looking to invest government funds in domestic and, even more so, foreign assets. Their investments are, more often than not, structured through special purpose investment funds or arrangements, known as SWFs, or investment entities owned by SWFs, known as SWEs. The total value of assets under the management of SWFs and SWEs – together referred to as 'sovereign wealth investors' in this study – is currently estimated at US$ 7.6 trillion (February 2018), which is an increase from US$ 5.8 trillion as in March 2012 and US$ 3.9 trillion as in March 2008. This development of States acting as investors, managing the wealth of a nation, and competing in the marketplace with other (private) investors, raises many interesting questions in various fields. This study is concerned with international tax aspects of sovereign wealth investors.

SWFs and their 'local' SWEs[1077] are generally not taxed in their home State, whereas income (including capital gains) derived from another State may be taxed in that investment recipient State ('the source State'). The more tax a foreign sovereign wealth investor pays in a source State, the smaller the return and revenue available to its home State. Therefore, this study primarily focuses on international income tax aspects of sovereign wealth investors, from a source State perspective. But that does not mean that the tax treatment of sovereign wealth investors in their home State cannot be relevant to the international tax analysis of such investors, from the viewpoint of a source State. Thus, the home State tax treatment of sovereign wealth investors is also considered.

In recent years, sovereign wealth investors have established themselves as an important class of investors and will continue to be so. They are widely regarded as a

---

1077. A 'local' SWE of an SWF is an SWE which has been established in the same State as the SWF which owns the SWE.

separate group of investors in various fields of law, including international investment law and international tax law, by academics and policymakers. Addressing sovereign wealth investors separately from other investor groups can essentially be traced back to the following developments and distinctive features. First, sovereign wealth investors own and invest extreme amounts of money, and their investment activity increases rapidly. They have increased in both number and size and will continue to look for cross-border investment opportunities in the years to come. Second, sovereign wealth investors are owned, controlled and funded by States. This link has not only raised political and security concerns in source States, but also raises questions as to the scope of the international law doctrine of sovereign immunity. Based on this doctrine, a foreign State, and its entities, can be held immune from the jurisdiction or enforcement power of a source State. A number of source States also apply the doctrine of sovereign immunity to taxation. By its nature, this doctrine cannot apply to other investor groups. In addition, the fact that sovereign wealth investors are owned, controlled and funded by States, means that the home State tax treatment of such investors is based on a different rationale, compared to the tax treatment accorded by home States to other groups of resident investors, such as pension funds and CIVs. A third reason for addressing sovereign wealth investors separately, may be found in a recent investment trend concerning this group of investors. Whereas sovereign wealth investors traditionally invested as *passive* investors, for example in listed shares or government bonds (portfolio investments), they are increasingly operating as *active* investors by making long-term investments, for example in real estate, infrastructure and private companies (direct investments). This move from traditional asset classes to alternative (less liquid) assets is, to a large extent, driven by the current economic environment of low-interest rates and slow economic growth.

Given the increasing significance of sovereign wealth investors and taking into account their distinctive features, source States may wish to introduce new tax policy, or evaluate or reconsider their existing tax policy vis-à-vis foreign sovereign wealth investors. The purpose of this study is to assist source States in doing so, by developing a conceptual framework.

This study uses two main ingredients to develop the conceptual framework: (i) international tax policy principles and objectives, and (ii) international law. Basic principles and objectives often underlie a State's international tax policy and its international tax rules design. A State's international tax policy choices, and the underlying basic principles and objectives, may depend on various factors – such as the size and nature of its economy, public interests, societal values, as well as tax policy choices of other States – and may change over time. International tax policy principles and objectives can serve as a useful and important starting point for source States when introducing new tax policy or reconsidering existing tax policy vis-à-vis foreign sovereign wealth investors. This study identifies as today's three main 'substantive' attributes of international tax policy: (i) neutrality (efficiency), (ii) equity (fairness), and (iii) international attractiveness. It discusses and presents the key theoretical implications of these policy principles and objectives for the design of international tax rules, focusing on foreign sovereign wealth investors. This presentation was then used to measure approaches to source taxation of foreign sovereign wealth investors by their

Chapter 8: Summary and Conclusions

neutrality, equity and international attractiveness. Before being able to do so, it was necessary to consider the taxation of foreign sovereign wealth investors by source States, and how such taxation compared to the taxation of other investor groups, such as CIVs and pension funds. This comparison put things into perspective and is relevant for the international law analysis, the second main ingredient.

International law may impact the ability of source States to achieve tax policy objectives. Because of the obligations it can impose on a source State in the field of taxation, international law could restrict or limit, to a greater or lesser extent, a source State's sovereign power (i.e., its ability) to implement (or promote) a tax policy principle. So, this study examines and, sometimes, explores its possible impact on source States' ability to achieve tax policy objectives in relation to foreign sovereign wealth investors. With respect to the international law analyses, this study considers the (possible) impact of: (1) the sovereign immunity principle, (2) tax treaties, and (3) European law.

The approach of measuring a source State's tax treatment of foreign sovereign wealth investors against the three main 'substantive' attributes of international tax policy, and examining the possible impact international law could have on achieving tax policy objectives based on these attributes, produces the conceptual framework.

The central question in this study is as follows:

> What impact, if any, does international law have on source States' ability to achieve (or promote) tax policy objectives in relation to foreign sovereign wealth investors?

This question is answered by discussing the following five sub-questions in Chapters 2–6:

(1) Who are sovereign wealth investors, why do they exist, what do they do, what (legal) forms can they take, and what is their home State tax status? (Chapter 2)
(2) How do source States tax foreign sovereign wealth investors (in comparison to other investors), and how does such taxation relate to generally accepted attributes of international tax policy? (Chapter 3)
(3) What impact, if any, does the sovereign immunity principle have on source States' ability to achieve tax policy objectives in relation to foreign sovereign wealth investors? (Chapter 4)
(4) What impact, if any, do tax treaties (in particular those based on the OECD and UN Model) have on source States' ability to achieve tax policy objectives in relation to foreign sovereign wealth investors? (Chapter 5)
(5) What impact, if any, does European law have on source States' ability to achieve tax policy objectives in relation to foreign sovereign wealth investors? (Chapter 6)

In Chapter 7, the conceptual framework as developed in Chapters 3–6 is applied to the Netherlands, as an illustration.

8.2 SOVEREIGN WEALTH INVESTORS

A first purpose of Chapter 2 is to come to a working definition of SWFs and SWEs, to use throughout this study. A second purpose is to get a better understanding of sovereign wealth investors. As SWEs are merely a component of some SWFs, Chapter 2 mainly focuses on SWFs. The main findings are summarized below.

Purpose of SWFs. Most SWFs are either established to save funds for future generations by converting non-renewable resources into assets from which future income streams can be derived, or to cover for liabilities that may arise from fluctuations of commodity prices. Other SWFs are established because of a projected shortfall in the public pension system, or simply to increase the returns on reserve assets. It should be noted that the objectives of SWFs could be multiple, overlapping or changing over time.

Definition of SWFs. No universal definition of SWFs exists. This study adopts the definition of SWFs as formulated by the IWG. This definition is widely-followed, has been reflected in the OECD Commentary and captures the common characteristics which distinguish SWFs from other groups of investors. The definition is as follows:

> SWFs are defined as special purpose investment funds or arrangements, owned by the general government. Created by the general government for macroeconomic purposes, SWFs hold, manage, or administer assets to achieve financial objectives, and employ a set of investment strategies which include investing in foreign financial assets. The SWFs are commonly established out of balance of payments surpluses, official foreign currency operations, the proceeds of privatizations, fiscal surpluses, and/or receipts resulting from commodity exports.

SWEs. SWFs sometimes structure investments through separate wholly-owned and controlled investment vehicles, known as SWEs. They do so for a variety of reasons, such as allowing greater flexibility, avoiding public spotlight, creating an efficient tax structure, avoiding being categorized as SWF and centralizing specific investment activities. SWEs can be established in the home State of an SWF or in other States.

Investment trend. Mainly driven by the current economic environment of low-interest rates and slow economic growth, sovereign wealth investors are increasingly proactive and no longer just operate as *passive* (portfolio) investors. As *active* investors, they increasingly make foreign direct investments including long-term investments in real estate, infrastructure and private companies.

Legal forms. Sovereign wealth investors can have different legal forms and governance structures. Based on their legal form, they can be divided as follows:

(i) Sovereign wealth investors constituted by a pool of assets within the State (which includes a pool of assets forming a unit within a central bank that has no separate legal personality);

(ii) Sovereign wealth investors established as or within a separate legal entity other than the State itself (comprising SWFs and SWEs established as a separate legal entity under public law or company law, as well as SWFs constituted by a pool of assets within a central bank that has a separate legal personality);

(iii) Sovereign wealth investors organized as a (legal) entity without a separate legal personality, such as partnerships (comprising SWEs organized in such manner).

This distinction between sovereign wealth investors according to their legal form is relevant for other parts of this study, such as Chapter 5 (regarding the application of tax treaties) and Chapter 6 (regarding the personal scope of the freedom of capital movement in the EEA Agreement and the freedom of establishment).

Home State tax status of sovereign wealth investors. Sovereign wealth investors are generally not taxed in their home State, because taxation of such investors is seen as superfluous. There are, however, a few exceptions to this rule. Since creating a level-playing field would generally not be in a home State's own interest, the few home States that do impose tax on sovereign wealth investors, would either seem to be dealing with an agency problem, or simply use taxation as a substitute for extracting profits through (dividend) distributions. The tax treatment of sovereign wealth investors in their home State could be relevant for the international tax analysis of such investors, from a source State perspective.

8.3 TAX POLICY CONSIDERATIONS AND APPROACHES TO TAXATION OF FOREIGN SOVEREIGN WEALTH INVESTORS

8.3.1 Introduction

Approaches to source taxation of foreign sovereign wealth investors

The main purpose of Chapter 3 is to discuss tax policy considerations and to measure source States' tax treatment of foreign sovereign wealth investors against generally accepted attributes of international tax policy. To that end, Chapter 3 first identifies five approaches to taxation of (some) foreign sovereign wealth investors by source States. They are as follows:

(1) taxing foreign sovereign wealth investors in the same way as 'regular' non-resident corporate investors.
(2) according a general tax-exemption under domestic law or administrative practice.
(3) according specific tax-exemptions or specific tax reductions under domestic law or administrative practice.
(4) according a general tax-exemption under one or more tax treaties.
(5) according specific tax-exemptions or specific tax reductions under one or more tax treaties.

These approaches are referred to as Approaches (1) to (5) in this study.

International tax policy attributes

Chapter 3 identifies as today's three main attributes of international tax policy: (i) neutrality (efficiency), (ii) equity (fairness), and (iii) international attractiveness. These 'substantive' policy attributes should be distinguished from 'procedural' policy principles. The latter imply that:

- tax laws should be clear, simple and certain;
- tax policy should be stable, i.e., changes to the rules should be kept to a minimum, changes should be justified and this justification and its underlying policy should be made public, while policy shocks should be avoided;
- tax policy should be practicable, in the sense that the tax liability should be easy to calculate, and easy and cheap to collect.

A source State should also consider procedural policy principles when introducing new tax policy or reconsidering existing tax policy vis-à-vis foreign sovereign wealth investors. These policy principles are, however, not further considered in this study, because they do not offer insights as to how foreign sovereign wealth investors should be taxed (in substantive terms) from a source State perspective.

Approaches (1) to (5) are measured by their neutrality, equity and international attractiveness. The meaning of these concepts and the main findings of this exercise are summarized below.

8.3.2 Neutrality (Efficiency)

Tax neutrality theories are economic theories believed to increase economic efficiency and welfare. Tax neutrality is achieved when economic decisions are not (or, at least, as little as possible) distorted by taxation. In an international context, tax neutrality, known as international tax neutrality, is said to promote an efficient allocation of global capital, thus promoting global welfare. This study considers three international tax neutrality benchmarks: CEN, CIN and CON.

8.3.2.1 *Capital Export Neutrality*

CEN addresses a State taxing in a residence capacity and promotes neutrality with respect to the location of investment. A tax system is said to achieve CEN when tax considerations do not influence a resident investor's decision between investing in its home market or abroad (i.e., export neutral). This requires resident investors to face the same tax burden on their domestic and outbound investments. CEN implies a tax system of worldwide taxation with a full credit for foreign taxes (residence-based taxation). There is no consensus in literature on whether CEN is relevant for the taxation of non-resident investors (i.e., foreign inbound investments). Some authors argue that CEN implies no taxation of non-resident investors, while others argue that CEN appears to have nothing to do with the taxation of non-resident investors. In the present author's view, CEN is as such not concerned with a State taxing in a source capacity; CEN does not tell a source State to tax or to forgo tax in relation to non-resident investors. In fact, 'pure' CEN would even require a State acting in a resident capacity to refund foreign source taxation to the extent it exceeds residence taxation (i.e., the responsibility to achieve export neutrality rests with the residence State, as opposed to the source State).

Although the present author does not consider CEN as such to be concerned with the taxation of non-resident investors, this neutrality concept could provide an argument for a source State not to tax income derived by foreign sovereign wealth investors. As explained, foreign sovereign wealth investors are generally not taxed in their residence State. Source State taxation of tax-exempt non-resident investors could distort neutrality with respect to the investment location, i.e., it could result in tax-exempt investors favouring domestic investments over foreign investments. In order to promote export neutrality, a source State could consider to exempt from source taxation investment income derived by foreign sovereign wealth investors and other non-resident tax-exempt investors. It could accord such treatment unilaterally or through tax treaties.

Considering the above, Approaches (2) to (5), under which source States grant a general or specific tax-exemptions to (some) foreign sovereign wealth investors, either unilaterally or through tax treaties, could be motivated by referring to promoting CEN. On the other hand, Approach (1), under which source States tax foreign sovereign wealth investors in the same way as 'regular' non-resident corporate investors, does not promote CEN, unless taxation in the same way means no taxation at all.

8.3.2.2 *Capital Import Neutrality*

CIN is the flipside of CEN and promotes neutrality with respect to the location of investors, rather than the location of investment. A tax system is said to achieve CIN when tax considerations do not influence which investor, that is, a resident or non-resident investor, makes which investment in one particular State (i.e., import neutral). CIN implies a territorial (or source-based) tax system rather than a residence-based tax system; in other words, a tax system which exempts foreign sourced income and treats domestic sourced income of resident and non-resident investors in the same way. In this respect, the characteristics of investors and place of residence are irrelevant. CIN simply requires equal tax treatment of investors that perform the same level of investment activities in a source State. There is no consensus in literature on whether CIN is relevant for portfolio investments, i.e., investments that give the investor little or no control over business activities. Some authors argue that CIN is not relevant for portfolio investments because such investments, as opposed to direct investments, have no, or at most a small, influence on the location of plant and equipment and therefore productivity. According to the present author, as explained in Section 3.4.3.1, where portfolio capital is not widely available, portfolio investments could also influence the location of business activity. In addition, the distinction between direct investment and portfolio investment, although analytically helpful, is not always clear in practice. For these reasons, CIN is considered in this study without distinguishing between direct investments and portfolio investments.

In the author's view, equal tax treatment as prescribed by CIN also requires neutrality with respect to the type of investment activity, e.g., an investment in loans, shares or immovable property. In other words, the decision to invest in e.g., loans, shares or immovable property should not be influenced by tax considerations. This would require investors with an equal level of investment income from a source State to face equal source State tax burdens, irrespective of the composition of the investment income.

Considering the above, Approaches (2) to (5)[1078] regarding the tax treatment of foreign sovereign wealth investors cannot be explained by CIN, because they could result in different tax treatment *among* foreign sovereign wealth investors, and *between* foreign sovereign wealth investors and other (resident and non-resident) investors, both individuals and companies. On the other hand, Approach (1), under which source States tax foreign sovereign wealth investors in the same way as 'regular' non-resident corporate investors, could be motivated by CIN.

8.3.2.3 *Capital Ownership Neutrality*

The basic assumption underlying CON is that productivity of capital (assets) varies depending on the investor (owner). Tax systems satisfy CON if they do not distort ownership patterns. CON is relevant with respect to direct investments – active investments giving the investor influence on the business decisions and, therefore, productivity–, but not so much with respect to portfolio investments – passive investments not giving the investor influence on productivity. CON is achieved when each investor retains the same proportion of the before-tax return across (the candidate and alternative) investments. It does not matter when different investors retain different proportions of the before-tax returns, as long as each investor retains the same proportion across investments. Whether this standard is satisfied in an international setting, depends on the interplay of tax systems, the outcome of which is driven by various connected factors, such as tax rates, the location of investments, the location of investors and the nature of the investments. Although the theory behind CON is clear, it was argued that in today's global economy, where investment assets are located in numerous States which may tax investors in different ways at different rates, this neutrality concept has little, if any, practical meaning. And so it is not further considered in this study.

1078. As identified in Section 3.2.2.2. Approaches (2) to (5) are as follows:

    (2) according a general tax-exemption under domestic law or administrative practice.
    (3) according specific tax-exemptions or specific tax reductions under domestic law or administrative practice.
    (4) according a general tax-exemption under one or more tax treaties.
    (5) according specific tax-exemptions or specific tax reductions under one or more tax treaties.

8.3.3 Equity (Fairness)

Equity is a moral concept, derived from justice (fairness), and an important tax policy principle. It has two main elements in a tax policy context: inter-nation equity and inter-taxpayer equity. Inter-nation equity is concerned with a fair (equitable) allocation of national gain (and loss) between States with respect to cross-border activities. On the other hand, inter-taxpayer equity is concerned with a fair (equitable) allocation of tax obligations between taxpayers.

8.3.3.1 Inter-taxpayer

Inter-taxpayer equity has two main elements: horizontal equity and vertical equity. Horizontal equity requires that taxpayers who are equals pay equal amounts of tax, whereas vertical equity, in essence, requires that taxpayers who are not equals be taxed differently taking into account their differences. Inter-taxpayer equity, as an expression of the fundamental value of fairness, should be an important (international) policy principle in every democracy under the rule of law.

Two theories have dominated discussions on inter-taxpayer equity: the ability-to-pay theory and the benefit theory. Under the ability-to-pay theory, each taxpayer should pay tax in accordance with its ability to pay; taxpayers with greater abilities should pay more tax than taxpayers with lesser abilities, while taxpayers with equal abilities should pay an equal amount of tax. Ability-to-pay theory in taxation has become associated with theories of distributive justice, i.e., the redistribution of goods and welfare between persons within a society through taxation. As it was argued that the practical relevance of the ability-to-pay theory is limited to residents, the focus was on the benefit principle. The benefit theory, which, unlike the ability-to-pay theory, is relevant for the taxation of both residents and non-residents, requires that each taxpayer should pay tax in accordance with its level of benefit from governmental goods and services. From this general rule, three, more practical, rules of thumb can be derived which are relevant for the taxation of foreign sovereign wealth investors, from a source State perspective. The *first rule* is that a source State should generally not tax non-resident investors less favourably than resident investors when performing the same investment activities in and earning the same level of income from that source State. It may, in such circumstances, even require non-resident investors to be taxed more favourably than resident investors. The *second rule* is that a source State should treat and tax all non-resident investors as equals when they perform the same investment activities in and earn the same level of income from that source State (i.e., horizontal non-discriminatory treatment). The *third rule*, which applies to both the first and second rule, is that forgoing taxation would not make sense from a benefit perspective, since residents and non-residents that perform investment activities in the source State always benefit from public goods and services to some extent.

Conceptually, the benefit principle could demand a source State to differentiate between different categories of income if it can be demonstrated that different asset classes benefit differently from public goods and services. However, from a practical point of view, not differentiating between different categories of income is understandable. The benefit principle could, in addition, demand a source State to differentiate between different categories of income in the case of dividends paid out, or capital gains relating to, profits that have been or will become subject to corporate tax in a source State. This corporate tax (effectively at the expense of the investor) can already be sufficient from a benefit perspective.

Considering the above, Approaches (2) to (5)[1079] regarding the tax treatment of foreign sovereign wealth investors cannot be motivated by the benefit principle, because they could result in different tax treatment *among* foreign sovereign wealth investors, and *between* foreign sovereign wealth investors and other non-resident investors, be it individuals or companies, that perform the same investment activities in a source State. On the other hand, Approach (1), under which source States tax foreign sovereign wealth investors in the same way as 'regular' non-resident corporate investors that perform the same investment activities in a source State, could be inspired by the benefit principle.

8.3.3.2 Inter-nation Equity

Inter-nation equity is not about the allocation of revenue between States, but is concerned with the allocation of national gain (or loss) in the context of cross-border activities. This allocation is affected when the source State imposes tax on the income derived by non-residents; taxation in the residence State has no impact on this allocation (as it does not affect the gain accruing to that State). The central question of inter-nation equity is whether the source State has a legitimate claim to impose tax on the income derived by non-residents and, if so, how source taxation should be designed. Source States have a legitimate claim, based on the benefit principle, as well as the idea that source State should be entitled to (a share of) pure economic rents derived from activity within its territory. However, inter-nation equity provides little guidance as to how taxation vis-à-vis non-resident investors should be designed. Nevertheless, the following general rule can be derived from it, in the author's view: non-residents from the *same State* performing the same (investment) activities in a source State should be treated alike in that source State (i.e., horizontal non-discriminatory treatment); a different treatment of non-resident investors from *different States* can be justified on redistribution grounds only.

Considering the above, Approaches (2) to (5)[1080] regarding the tax treatment of foreign sovereign wealth investors cannot be explained by inter-nation equity, at least

---

1079. As identified in Section 3.2.2.2. Approaches (2) to (5) are as follows:

    (2) according a general tax-exemption under domestic law or administrative practice.
    (3) according specific tax-exemptions or specific tax reductions under domestic law or administrative practice.
    (4) according a general tax-exemption under one or more tax treaties.
    (5) according specific tax-exemptions or specific tax reductions under one or more tax treaties.

1080. *Ibid.*

as far as they result in different source taxation between foreign sovereign wealth investors and other non-resident investors from the *same* State, be it individuals or companies. Approach (1), under which source States tax foreign sovereign wealth investors in the same way as 'regular' non-resident corporate investors, could be motivated by inter-nation equity.

8.3.4 International Attractiveness

Another attribute of international tax policy is the attractiveness of a tax regime in an international setting, i.e., the attractiveness of a State's tax regime vis-à-vis tax regimes of other States. A State may want to use its tax system, including tax treaties, as an instrument to influence investment decisions and create an attractive investment location for foreign sovereign wealth investors in order to stimulate economic growth and to create jobs. However, such a State needs to be aware that a tax reduction does not necessarily have the desired effect (e.g., an increase of investments from these investors), and may often result in a loss of tax revenue for which compensating policy measures may need to be taken.

Tax incentives are often aimed at attracting (foreign) direct investments, as opposed to (foreign) portfolio investments, because direct investments are believed to affect the location of business activity. However, as explained in Section 3.4.3.1, where portfolio capital is not widely available, portfolio investments could also influence the location of investment. Furthermore, some States, including the Netherlands, aim to attract foreign portfolio investments through tax incentives, without having regard to the availability of portfolio capital.

In the author's view, inter-taxpayer equity (benefit principle), as an expression of the fundamental value of fairness, should play a vital role in relation to international attractiveness in every democracy under the rule of law. When motivated by international attractiveness, source States should only differentiate between investors if they have valid (economic) reasons for doing so – i.e., a rationally defensible purpose. That is, they need be able to demonstrate the distinctiveness of one or more investors over other investors in terms of stimulating economic growth and creating jobs. In the context of international attractiveness, the distinctiveness must in particular lie in foreign sovereign wealth investors' willingness to make an investment that no, or at least few, others are willing to make, and could, for instance, be found in the very long-term investment strategy of some foreign sovereign wealth investors, or their willingness to make risky investments.

Considering the above, Approaches (2) to (5)[1081] regarding the tax treatment of foreign sovereign wealth investors could promote a source State's international attractiveness for foreign sovereign wealth investors.

1081. *Ibid.*

8.3.5 Conclusion

Approaches (1) to (5)[1082] regarding the taxation of foreign sovereign wealth investors have been measured by their neutrality, equity and international attractiveness. The results, which are summarized in the table below, point out that each approach could satisfy, at least to some degree, at least two policy principles or objectives. In the absence of a clear theoretical hierarchy among these, often conflicting, international tax policy principles and objectives which applies to all States in all situations, no general judgment can be made about which approach is the 'correct' approach. Nevertheless, inter-taxpayer equity (benefit principle), as an expression of the fundamental value of fairness, should be an important international policy principle in every democracy under the rule of law. Ultimately, the tax legislator of each individual sovereign State, therefore, has to weigh and balance the principle of inter-taxpayer equity and any other conflicting tax policy principle or objective it wishes to implement.

1082. *Ibid.*

Table 8.1 *Approaches to Source Taxation of Foreign Sovereign Wealth Investors Measured by Neutrality, Equity and International Attractiveness*

	Neutrality		Equity		International Attractiveness
	(CEN)	(CIN)	(inter-nation)	(inter-taxpayer)	
Approach (1)*	X	✓	✓	✓	X
Approach (2)*	✓	X	X	X	✓
Approach (3)*	✓	X	X	X	✓
Approach (4)*	✓	X	X	X	✓
Approach (5)*	✓	X	X	X	✓

* Approach (1): taxing foreign sovereign wealth investors in the same way as 'regular' non-resident corporate investors.
Approach (2): according a general tax-exemption under domestic law or administrative practice.
Approach (3): according specific tax-exemptions or specific tax reductions under domestic law or administrative practice.
Approach (4): according a general tax-exemption under one or more tax treaties.
Approach (5): according specific tax-exemptions or specific tax reductions under one or more tax treaties.

8.4 Sovereign Immunity Principle

8.4.1 Introduction

Chapter 4 addresses the elementary question whether the sovereign immunity principle, as a principle of customary international law, actually requires source States to accord tax immunities to foreign sovereign wealth investors. The question to that answer indicates what impact the sovereign immunity principle, as a principle of customary international law, has on source States' ability to achieve (or promote) tax policy objectives, and to freely implement an approach to taxation of foreign sovereign wealth investors.[1083] For example, if the sovereign immunity principle would require source States to accord a general tax-exemption to foreign sovereign wealth investors, it would leave source States no option but to implement Approach (2).

8.4.2 Main Findings

According to the customary international law principle of sovereign immunity, a foreign sovereign State (and its property) can be held immune from the jurisdiction of the courts (jurisdictional immunity) and from the enforcement power of another sovereign State (immunity from execution) in civil proceedings, and this principle may also apply to State entities.

The findings of Chapter 4 indicate that there is currently no rule of customary international law requiring a source State to accord any immunity from income taxation to foreign States or foreign sovereign wealth investors. A rule of customary international law requires: (i) evidence of a general State practice, (ii) that is accepted as law (*opinio juris*). As already noted in the OECD Commentary on Article 1, there is no extensive and virtually uniform State practice regarding source taxation of foreign sovereign wealth investors; even among States which do apply sovereign immunity to direct taxation, significant differences exist between them. In addition, an examination of the tax immunity regimes and the rules on jurisdictional immunity in civil proceedings in Australia, Canada, the UK and the US, strongly suggests that the tax-exemptions accorded to foreign sovereign wealth investors are not (or, at least, no longer) truly motivated by sovereignty, indicating the absence of *opinio juris*. Therefore, the principle of jurisdictional immunity has no (negative) impact on source States' ability to achieve (or promote) tax policy objectives, and to freely implement an approach to taxation of foreign sovereign wealth investors.[1084]

Rather than through immunity from taxation, absence of source State taxation could effectively also be achieved when (property of) foreign sovereign wealth investors would enjoy immunity from execution in tax cases and, therefore, immunity from the collection of taxes. Given that a source State may also seek enforcement measures to be taken against property situated in foreign jurisdictions, this effect may

---

1083. *See* the five approaches identified in Section 3.2.2.2.
1084. *Ibid.*

Chapter 8: Summary and Conclusions

depend on how immunity from execution would apply to foreign sovereign wealth investors in one or more foreign jurisdictions. While foreign sovereign wealth investors may enjoy immunity from execution in private law cases in respect of property serving sovereign purposes, it is uncertain whether this would still apply in a tax case. Although the international law status of immunity from execution in tax cases is currently unclear, it can be argued that immunity from execution in tax cases should not apply any differently from immunity from execution in private law cases. This could mean that property of foreign sovereign wealth investors may also enjoy immunity from execution in tax cases. Be that as it may, it should be kept in mind that this delicate issue would only occur in rather exceptional circumstances; for example, if a foreign sovereign wealth investor refuses to pay income tax imposed on it by a source State, or if an SWE does not comply with withholding tax obligations under the laws of a source State. Immunity from execution in tax cases could (effectively) result in the absence of source State taxation, which would raise equity concerns since it results in preferential tax treatment of (some) foreign sovereign wealth investors over other investors. However, because of the uncertainty that surrounds it and because it may only occur in rather exceptional circumstances, immunity from execution in tax cases should neither influence investment decisions of investors, nor enhance a source State's international attractiveness. Therefore, the (potential) overall impact of immunity from execution on source States' ability to achieve (or promote) tax policy objectives, and to freely implement an approach to taxation of foreign sovereign wealth investors,[1085] is negligible.

8.4.3 Conclusion

It was concluded in Chapter 4 that the sovereign immunity principle, as a principle of customary international law, has, at most, a very small impact on source States' ability to achieve (or promote) tax policy objectives, and to freely implement an approach to taxation of foreign sovereign wealth investors.

8.5 Tax Treaties

8.5.1 Introduction

Chapter 5 considers the (possible) implications of tax treaties for source State taxation of foreign sovereign wealth investors. Based on these implications, it examines what impact tax treaties could have on source States' ability to achieve (or promote) tax policy objectives (i.e., neutrality, equity and international attractiveness), and to freely implement an approach to taxation of foreign sovereign wealth investors.[1086] The focus in Chapter 5 is on the OECD and UN MTC, and their Commentaries.

1085. *Ibid.*
1086. *Ibid.*

8.5.2 Main Findings

Qualifying as a resident of a Contracting State (Article 4(1)) is of key importance for the entitlement to tax treaty benefits. Investors have access to a tax treaty and its benefits if they are 'liable to tax' – i.e., a comprehensive taxation (full tax liability). Many States choose not to tax their sovereign wealth investors. Many States also choose, for a number of reasons, not to tax certain private resident investors, such as pension funds and CIVs. However, the way this non-taxation of sovereign wealth investors and private resident investors is achieved in the legislation of the home State can make a difference in the outcome of the 'liable to tax' test. The phrase *State or any political subdivision or local authority thereof* in Article 4(1) of both the OECD and UN MTC offers sovereign wealth investors an additional possibility to get tax treaty access. Sovereign wealth investors constituted by a pool of assets can most likely be considered an integral part of the State. It is, however, unclear whether sovereign wealth investors with a separate legal identity are covered by this expression, and whether a further distinction should be made between legal persons of public law and legal persons of private law owned by a legal person of public law.

Tax treaty benefits include reduced treaty rates on outbound dividends and interest payments. As indicated by the OECD Commentary on Articles 10 (Dividends) and 11 (Interest), some source States even accord tax-exemptions to foreign States and (some of) their wholly-owned entities. And these exemptions from source taxation might also be available to foreign sovereign wealth investors. Tax treaty benefits could also include the absence of source taxation on the listed categories of capital gains, including capital gains derived from non-immovable property companies. The non-discrimination article (Article 24) has no impact on source taxation of sovereign wealth investors.

Article 4(1) creates distinctions between investors which entitle some investors to tax treaty benefits (e.g., reduced tax rates under Articles 10 and 11), while excluding others. From a source State perspective, this could give rise to tax differences and different tax burdens:

- between investors that perform the same level of investment activities in a source State; which would not promote CIN;
- among foreign sovereign wealth investors and among non-resident private investors, as well as between foreign sovereign wealth investors and non-resident private investors, that perform the same investment activities in and earn the same level of income from a source State; which would be in conflict with inter-taxpayer equity;
- among foreign sovereign wealth investors and among non-resident private investors from the *same* State, as well as between foreign sovereign wealth investors and non-resident private investors from the *same* State, that perform the same investment activities in a source State; which would be in conflict with inter-nation equity.

Article 24 (non-discrimination) does not change these outcomes.

Chapter 8: Summary and Conclusions

Tax treaties, including those based on the OECD or UN MTC, could not only result in tax differences and different tax burdens between investors that do and investors that do not have treaty access, but also among investors that do have tax treaty access (even though a tax treaty applies in the same way to all treaty residents in similar circumstances). These tax differences and different tax burdens could result from different source tax rates for the same category of income, different source tax rates for different categories of income, and different allocation rules for different categories of income, which would not promote CIN and might be in conflict with both inter-taxpayer equity and inter-nation equity.

Source States wishing to promote CIN by introducing equal treatment between investors could be required to *reduce* and/or *increase* the current level of taxation of foreign sovereign wealth investors (and other investors). Source States wishing to promote inter-taxpayer equity would need to *reduce* the current level of taxation of foreign sovereign wealth investors (and other investors) paying too much tax from a benefit perspective, and *increase* the current level of taxation of foreign sovereign wealth investors (and other investors) paying too little. Source States wishing to promote inter-nation equity by introducing equal treatment between non-resident investors from the same State could be required to *reduce* and/or *increase* the current level of taxation of foreign sovereign wealth investors (and other non-resident investors). However, obligations under existing tax treaties – with respect to maximum tax rates and allocation rules – could restrict a source State to follow the second route (*increase*), as opposed to the first route (*reduction*), while the first route may not always be realistic from a revenue perspective. This would generally leave a State with the option to amend or terminate existing tax treaties. But tax treaties are rarely renegotiated, or unilaterally terminated. Once a tax treaty enters into force, it will generally apply for a long period of time. Thus, tax treaties could restrict source States' ability to pursue CIN, inter-taxpayer equity and inter-nation equity, and to implement Approach (1).[1087]

On the other hand, tax treaties have no (negative) impact, as such, on source States' ability to promote CEN through Approaches (2) to (5)[1088] by according exemptions from source taxation to tax-exempt foreign sovereign wealth investors (i.e., tax treaties do not impose restrictions on source States to do so).

1087. Approach (1) has been identified in Section 3.2.2.2 and is as follows: taxing foreign sovereign wealth investors in the same way as 'regular' non-resident corporate investors.
1088. Approaches (2) to (5) have been identified in Section 3.2.2.2 and are as follows:

   (2) according a general tax-exemption under domestic law or administrative practice.
   (3) according specific tax-exemptions or specific tax reductions under domestic law or administrative practice.
   (4) according a general tax-exemption under one or more tax treaties.
   (5) according specific tax-exemptions or specific tax reductions under one or more tax treaties.

Finally, OECD and UN MTC based treaties, as such, have no (negative) impact on source States' ability to pursue international attractiveness through Approaches (2) to (5).[1089]

8.5.3 Conclusion

It was concluded in Chapter 5 that OECD and UN MTC based treaties could restrict source States' ability to pursue CIN, inter-taxpayer equity and inter-nation equity, and to implement Approach (1).[1090] However, they have no (negative) impact on the ability of source States to promote CEN in relation to foreign sovereign wealth investors, nor on their ability to pursue international attractiveness through Approaches (2) to (5).

8.6 European Law

8.6.1 Introduction

Chapter 6 considers the (possible) implications of European law for source State taxation of foreign sovereign wealth investors. Based on these implications, it examines what impact European law could have on source States' ability to achieve (or promote) tax policy objectives (i.e., neutrality, equity and international attractiveness), and to freely implement an approach to taxation of foreign sovereign wealth investors.[1091]

From a source State perspective, the European law analysis is only relevant to EU Member States and (other) members to the EEA Agreement. Chapter 6 considers primary European law, notably the fundamental freedoms and State aid rules included in the TFEU and the EEA Agreement, which can all apply in (direct) tax matters. An important reason for including the EEA Agreement is that Norway, a member to this agreement, hosts currently the largest sovereign wealth investor in the world in terms of assets under management (US$ 1,032 billion as in February 2018).[1092] As regards the fundamental freedoms, the freedom of capital movement, rather than the freedom of establishment, potentially has the most relevance in relation to foreign sovereign wealth investors. The first reason for this is that, although sovereign wealth investors increasingly operate as long-term, *active* investors, they are still predominantly (passive) portfolio investors (to which the free movement of capital has the most relevance). The second reason is that most sovereign wealth investors reside outside the EU. Importantly, the personal and territorial scope of the free movement of capital in the TFEU is not limited to EU Member States; it has universal personal and territorial scope. As a result, the free movement of capital in the TFEU, as opposed to its counterpart in the EEA Agreement, may be relevant in relation to sovereign wealth investors from so-called third countries. Nevertheless, because sovereign wealth

---
1089. *Ibid.*
1090. *Ibid.*
1091. *See* the five approaches identified in Section 3.2.2.2.
1092. < http://www.swfinstitute.org/sovereign-wealth-fund-rankings/ >.

investors are increasingly operating as *active* investors and may reside inside EU Member States and (other) members to the EEA Agreement, the freedom of establishment is considered as well. With respect to the State aid rules, the analysis is a first general analysis in the context of foreign sovereign wealth investors, aimed at identifying potential issues in this complex and rapidly developing area of European law. As regards secondary EU law, the focus is on the Parent-Subsidiary Directive and Interest & Royalties Directive.

8.6.2 Main Findings

The (possible) key implications of European law for source State taxation of foreign sovereign wealth investors are the following:

(1) The freedom of capital movement and freedom of establishment do not prohibit *reverse discrimination*: a Member State is allowed to tax a foreign sovereign wealth investor more favourably than resident investors. However, the State aid rules could prohibit reverse discrimination, even if more favourable treatment of non-residents is achieved through a tax treaty.

(2) The freedom of establishment in both the TFEU and EEA Agreement does not apply to foreign sovereign wealth investors not formed in accordance with the law of a Member State and not having their registered office, central administration or principal place of business in a Member State. The scope of the freedom of capital movement enshrined in the EEA Agreement is limited to residents of the EU Member States/EEA-EFTA States. However, importantly, the TFEU accords universal territorial and personal scope to the freedom of capital movement, although certain restrictions which already existed before 1994 in relation to third countries may be allowed under the grandfathering rule. The precise implications of this standstill provision for the taxation of inbound portfolio investments from third countries are currently uncertain. As noted, most sovereign wealth investors reside in third countries.

(3) The freedom of capital movement and freedom of establishment prohibit *vertical discrimination*: a Member State is not allowed to tax a foreign sovereign wealth investor less favourably than resident investors, but only if their situations are objectively comparable. Objective comparability is determined, unilaterally and rather strictly, in the light of the objective of the national tax measure at issue, and by the relevant conditions laid down in the national tax legislation of a State as imposed on its residents. A similar substantive approach regarding comparability is followed for State aid purposes (selectivity test); the State aid rules are, therefore, the 'flip side' of the fundamental freedoms. It was argued that State entities or regular corporate shareholders are likely the best candidates in terms of objective vertical comparability with a foreign sovereign wealth investor.

(4) The freedom of capital movement and freedom of establishment may also prohibit *horizontal discrimination*, in which case a Member State would not

be allowed to tax a foreign sovereign wealth investor less favourably than an objectively comparable other foreign sovereign wealth investor or other non-resident investor. In the author's view, the framework for vertical comparability should be applied as much as possible to assess horizontal comparability of investors in outbound situations. Importantly, the prohibition of horizontal discrimination under the freedoms seems to be limited to intra-EU/EEA situations (*Haribo and Salinen* and *Sopora*),[1093] and should not apply in case of tax treaty benefits (*D.* and *Riskin & Timmermans*). The framework for horizontal comparability under the State aid rules and the freedoms seems similar, although horizontal comparability under the former is not limited to intra-EU/EEA situations and may or may not apply in case of tax treaty benefits. It was argued that other foreign sovereign wealth investors (and non-resident State entities) or non-resident regular corporate shareholders are likely the best candidates in terms of objective horizontal comparability with a foreign sovereign wealth investor. These outcomes are in line with the outcomes in the context of vertical comparability, because horizontal comparability is to a large extent influenced by vertical comparability.

(5) Although uncertain in many situations, it cannot, in the author's view, be excluded that preferential tax treatment accorded to a foreign sovereign wealth investor by a Member State could constitute (unlawful) State aid for such an investor, regardless of whether it resides inside or outside Member States. The three key elements involved are: (i) whether a foreign sovereign wealth investor would be regarded to perform an economic activity and therefore to conduct an undertaking, (ii) whether a tax benefit accorded to a foreign sovereign wealth investor would be regarded as selective, and (iii) whether a tax benefit accorded to a foreign sovereign wealth investor would be liable to affect trade between Member States.

If the concept of economic activity would be similar for State aid and EU VAT purposes, and therefore encompass passive investment activities, such as the granting of interest-bearing loans, or placements in bank deposits or securities, the investment activities of many foreign sovereign wealth investors would constitute economic activities. Otherwise, foreign sovereign wealth investors would seem to qualify as an undertaking when performing activities that go beyond the compass of the simple acquisition and sale of assets (i.e., *active* investors). This depends on the facts and circumstances. However, an investor that holds a controlling shareholding in an undertaking and actually exercises that control by involving itself (directly or indirectly) in the management of that company must, in any case, be regarded as an *active* investor and therefore as an undertaking.

A tax benefit can only be selective if it favours economic operators relative to other economic operators which are comparable in the light of the objective pursued by the reference system. The reference system is driven by the

---

1093. Which would mean that the freedom of capital movement in the TFEU has no universal scope when it comes to horizontal comparability.

taxpayers that claim to be discriminated against. Although the State aid rules follow the comparability approach in free movement cases, the implications of tax treaty benefits are currently less clear. Therefore, it cannot be excluded that tax treaty benefits which favour a sovereign wealth investor over other investors, will be considered selective by the CJEU in a State aid context.

The question whether a tax benefit accorded to a foreign sovereign wealth investor would be liable to affect trade between Member States arises in particular in relation to foreign sovereign wealth investors that are based outside the Member States. It could, for example, be argued that a selective tax benefit accorded to foreign sovereign wealth investors, whether located inside or outside the Member States, is still potentially liable to affect trade between Member States, as it could result in higher demand for assets (target companies) located in the respective Member State, increased liquidity and/or favourable financing conditions, and thus strengthening the position of domestic economic operators compared with economic operators of other Member States, or it could maintain or increase domestic activity.

Member States wishing to introduce new or change existing tax policy vis-à-vis foreign sovereign wealth investors could consider notifying the EC respectively the EFTA Surveillance Authority in case of doubt as regards to the application of the State aid rules.

(6) In addition, a preferential tax measure accorded by a Member State to foreign sovereign wealth investors which are not undertakings could amount to State aid for external asset managers (as indirect beneficiaries). Although a preferential tax measure accorded to foreign sovereign wealth investors by Member States could also benefit EU/EEA investment targets through higher demand and liquidity, any such (indirect) benefit is not selective, and hence no State aid for such targets, if that measure applies to targets in general and not just to specific undertakings, sectors or industries.

(7) Foreign sovereign wealth investors, in particular SWEs established under the laws of an EU Member State, could be entitled to the benefits of the Parent-Subsidiary Directive and Interest & Royalties Directive. It is noted that these directives do not apply to EEA-EFTA States.

These key implications could have the following impact on the ability of Member States (as source States) to achieve (or promote) tax policy objectives in relation to foreign sovereign wealth investors:

Capital import neutrality

Neither the fundamental freedoms, nor the State aid rules, prohibit a Member State from implementing a (territorial based) tax system that would promote CIN by adopting equal treatment of investors that perform the same level of investment activities in a source State, irrespective of their place of residence and characteristics.

Thus, neither the fundamental freedoms, nor the State aid rules, have a (negative) impact on the ability of Member States to promote CIN and to implement Approach (1).[1094]

However, its obligations under the Parent-Subsidiary Directive and Interest & Royalties Directive could restrict an EU Member State to promote CIN and achieve equal taxation, by increasing the current level of taxation of EU based foreign sovereign wealth investors and other non-resident investors. Thus, secondary EU law could restrict an EU Member State's ability to promote CIN, and to implement Approach (1).[1095]

Inter-taxpayer equity

The State aid rules, but not the fundamental freedoms, could restrict Member States' ability to achieve inter-taxpayer equity, but only if the benefit principle would prescribe foreign sovereign wealth investors (and other non-resident investors) to be taxed more favourably than resident investors (i.e., reverse discrimination). This conclusion has no impact on Member States' ability to implement Approach (1) though[1096] because this approach is concerned with the relationship among non-resident investors, rather than the relationship between non-resident and resident investors.

Its obligations under the Parent-Subsidiary Directive and Interest & Royalties Directive could restrict an EU Member State to promote inter-taxpayer equity and increase the current level of taxation of EU based foreign sovereign wealth investors (and other non-resident investors) paying too little from a benefit perspective. Thus, secondary EU law could restrict an EU Member State's ability to achieve inter-taxpayer equity, and to implement Approach (1).

Inter-nation equity

Both the fundamental freedoms and the State aid rules could restrict Member States' ability to achieve inter-nation equity, but only if inter-nation equity would require to treat non-resident investors from different States differently, based on redistribution grounds (i.e., horizontal discrimination). To limit the impact as much as possible different treatment of non-resident investors from different States should still be achieved through tax treaties as much as possible. Whereas both the fundamental freedoms and the State aid rules could restrict Member States ability to achieve inter-nation equity, this conclusion has no impact on Member States' ability to implement Approach (1) though because this approach implies equal treatment between non-resident investors from different States (as opposed to different treatment).

Its obligations under the Parent-Subsidiary Directive and Interest & Royalties Directive could restrict an EU Member State to promote inter-nation equity and achieve

---

1094. Approach (1) has been identified in Section 3.2.2.2 and is as follows: taxing foreign sovereign wealth investors in the same way as 'regular' non-resident corporate investors.
1095. *Ibid.*
1096. *Ibid.*

Chapter 8: Summary and Conclusions

equal taxation between non-resident investors from the same EU Member State, by increasing the current level of taxation of EU based foreign sovereign wealth investors and other non-resident investors. Thus, secondary EU law could restrict an EU Member State's ability to achieve inter-nation equity, and to implement Approach (1).[1097]

Capital export neutrality & International attractiveness

According tax-exemptions to foreign sovereign wealth investors, but not to resident investors – i.e., reverse discrimination – is not prohibited by the fundamental freedoms. It could, however, constitute (unlawful) State aid, even if different treatment is based on a tax treaty, but a State aid risk will probably be limited to *active* foreign sovereign wealth investors. Thus, the State aid rules could, under circumstances, restrict Member States' ability to promote CEN in relation to foreign sovereign wealth investors and to promote international attractiveness.

According unilateral tax-exemptions (or tax reductions) to foreign sovereign wealth investors, but not to comparable other non-resident investors – i.e., Approaches (2) and (3)[1098] – could constitute horizontal discrimination under the freedoms in intra-EU/EEA situations (but unlikely in non-EU/EEA situations), as well as State aid, even in non-EU/EEA situations. However, the State aid risk will probably be limited to *active* foreign sovereign wealth investors. Thus, the freedoms as well as the State aid rules could, under circumstances, restrict Member States' ability to promote CEN in relation to foreign sovereign wealth investors and to promote international attractiveness through Approaches (2) and (3).[1099]

In contrast, according tax-exemptions (or tax reductions) to foreign sovereign wealth investors through tax treaties but not to non-resident investors from other States, or from the same State – i.e., Approaches (4) and (5)[1100] – should not constitute horizontal discrimination under the freedoms, not even in intra-EU/EEA situations, but it may constitute (unlawful) State aid under rather strict circumstances. Thus, primary European law may restrict Member States' ability to promote CEN and international attractiveness through Approaches (4) and (5).[1101]

The Parent-Subsidiary Directive and Interest & Royalties Directive have no (negative) impact on an EU Member State's ability to promote CEN or international

---

1097. *Ibid.*
1098. Approaches (2) and (3) have been identified in Section 3.2.2.2 and are as follows:

   (2) according a general tax-exemption under domestic law or administrative practice.
   (3) according specific tax-exemptions or specific tax reductions under domestic law or administrative practice.

1099. *Ibid.*
1100. Approaches (4) and (5) have been identified in Section 3.2.2.2 and are as follows:

   (4) according a general tax-exemption under one or more tax treaties.
   (5) according specific tax-exemptions or specific tax reductions under one or more tax treaties.

1101. *Ibid.*

attractiveness in relation to foreign sovereign wealth investors through Approaches (2) to (5) (i.e., they do not impose restrictions on EU Member States to do so).

8.7 The Framework Applied to the Netherlands

In Chapter 7, the conceptual framework as developed in Chapters 3–6 is applied to the Netherlands, as an illustration. The Netherlands has been selected for several reasons. First, the primacy of Dutch international tax policy in relation to sovereign wealth investors is international attractiveness. This policy has found its way into Dutch tax treaties; the Netherlands has concluded several tax treaties containing favourable provisions for sovereign wealth investors, and Dutch tax (treaty) policy, as well as Dutch tax treaties, are approved by Dutch parliament. Second, the Netherlands is an OECD Member State, as well as an EU Member State, which means that the international law analysis will have to be considered in full. Third, the application of the framework requires in-depth knowledge of a tax system and a certain level of information. The author is familiar with Dutch tax law, whereas political decision-making in the Netherlands happens in a transparent way, and tax policy information, legislative information and other relevant information is publicly available.

After a review of Dutch international tax policy principles and objectives, it is concluded that the Netherlands largely adheres to the objective of international tax attractiveness vis-à-vis sovereign wealth investors. This policy appears particularly from Dutch tax treaties, which often provide extensive tax benefits to sovereign wealth investors of the other contracting State. Given the tension with inter-taxpayer equity, as an expression of the fundamental value of fairness, a separate, more detailed and in-depth analysis for each favourable tax treaty provision regarding sovereign wealth investors would have been appropriate, in the author's view.

Nonetheless, given the primacy of international attractiveness as a Dutch tax policy objective in relation to sovereign wealth investors, the conceptual framework is primarily used in Chapter 7 to answer the following question: *What impact, if any, does international law have on the Netherlands' ability to achieve (or promote) international tax attractiveness in relation to foreign sovereign wealth investors?* In this respect, the impact of the sovereign immunity principle, OECD MTC based treaties and European law is considered.

Based on Chapters 4 and 5, it is concluded that neither the sovereign immunity principle, nor OECD based treaties concluded by the Netherlands have (had) a (negative) impact on the ability of the Netherlands to pursue international attractiveness in relation to foreign sovereign wealth investors.

European law should not impose restrictions on the Netherlands to the extent that it currently pursues international attractiveness in relation to foreign sovereign wealth investors through the DDWTA 1965 (or the DCITA 1969). However, the Netherlands mainly pursues international attractiveness through tax treaties. Tax-treaty-based benefits accorded by the Netherlands to sovereign wealth investors, in deviation from (non-selective) entitlements under domestic law or from a generally accepted allocation of taxing rights, carry the risk of being selective, and may, therefore, constitute State aid. Thus, European law, notably the State aid rules, may, under rather strict circumstances, (have) impose(d) restrictions on the Netherlands' ability to pursue international attractiveness in relation to foreign sovereign wealth investors. Nonetheless, if the Netherlands wishes to grant (further) tax benefits to (other) foreign sovereign wealth investors in the future, but not to other (comparable) investors, it would probably still be best to continue to do so through tax treaties as much as possible. However, the downside of implementing a tax policy through tax treaties is that it may leave little leeway to give effect to a tax policy change. Tax treaties are rarely renegotiated, or unilaterally terminated. Once a tax treaty enters into force, it will generally apply for a long period of time.

8.8 Final Conclusion and Final Remarks

The impact the sovereign immunity principle, tax treaties and European law could have on source States' ability to achieve (or promote) neutrality, equity and international attractiveness, and to freely implement an approach to taxation of foreign sovereign wealth investors,[1102] is summarized in the table below.

1102. *See* the five approaches identified in Section 3.2.2.2.

Table 8.2 Impact of the Sovereign Immunity Principle, OECD/UN MTC Based Treaties and European (Union) Law on the Ability of Source States to Achieve (or Promote) Tax Policy Objectives, and to Freely Implement an Approach to Taxation of Foreign Sovereign Wealth Investors

	Neutrality (CEN)	Neutrality (CIN)	Equity (inter-taxpayer)	Equity (inter-nation)	International Attractiveness
Sovereign immunity	No (negative) impact	No (negative) impact	Impact negligible (i.e. only if immunity from execution would apply)	Impact negligible (i.e. only if immunity from execution would apply)	No (negative) impact
OECD/UN MTC based treaties	No (negative) impact	Restrict Approach (1) (but only where an increase in level of taxation is required)	Restrict Approach (1) (but only where an increase in level of taxation is required)	Restrict Approach (1) (but only where an increase in level of taxation is required)	No (negative) impact
European (Union) law fundamental freedoms	Could restrict Approaches (2) and (3), but not Approaches (4) and (5)	No (negative) impact	No impact	Could restrict inter-nation equity if it would be required to treat non-resident investors from different States differently based on redistribution grounds, but do not restrict Approach (1) though	Could restrict Approaches (2) and (3), but not Approaches (4) and (5)
State aid rules	Could restrict Approaches (2) to (5)**	No (negative) impact	Could restrict inter-taxpayer equity if it would be required to treat non-resident investors more favourably than resident investors, but do not restrict Approach (1) though	Could restrict inter-nation equity if it would be required to treat non-resident investors from different States differently based on redistribution grounds, but do not restrict Approach (1) though	Could restrict Approaches (2) to (5)**
Directives (not applicable to EEA-EFTA States)	No (negative) impact	Restrict Approach (1) (but only where an increase in level of taxation is required, and limited to outbound dividend, interest and royalty payments in certain intra-EU situations)	Restrict Approach (1) (but only where an increase in level of taxation is required, and limited to outbound dividend, interest and royalty payments in certain intra-EU situations)	Restrict Approach (1) (but only where an increase in level of taxation is required, and limited to outbound dividend, interest and royalty payments in certain intra-EU situations)	No (negative) impact
	Potentially underlying Approaches (2) to (5)*	Potentially underlying Approach (1)*	Potentially underlying Approach (1)*	Potentially underlying Approach (1)*	Potentially underlying Approaches (2) to (5)*

* Approach (1): taxing foreign sovereign wealth investors in the same way as 'regular' non-resident corporate investors.
Approach (2): according a general tax-exemption under domestic law or administrative practice.
Approach (3): according specific tax-exemptions or specific tax reductions under domestic law or administrative practice.
Approach (4): according a general tax-exemption under one or more tax treaties.
Approach (5): according specific tax-exemptions or specific tax reductions under one or more tax treaties.

** But probably limited to *active* foreign sovereign wealth investors.

Chapter 8: Summary and Conclusions

For non-EU/EEA-EFTA Member States, the impact international law could have on their ability to achieve (or promote) tax policy objectives in relation to foreign sovereign wealth investors depends on the policy objective that is being pursued. The international law considered has no (negative) impact on their ability to enhance international attractiveness and promote CEN in relation to foreign sovereign wealth investors – both potentially underlying Approaches (2) to (5).[1103] However, OECD and UN MTC based treaties could restrict the ability of non-Member States to promote CIN, inter-taxpayer equity and/or inter-nation equity – all three potentially underlying Approach (1)[1104] – should it be required to increase the current level of taxation of foreign sovereign wealth investors (and other investors).

For EU Member States and EEA-EFTA States, the picture is more complicated. In general terms, due to the impact of European law, the ability of EU Member States and EEA-EFTA States to achieve (or promote) tax policy objectives, and to freely implement an approach to taxation of foreign sovereign wealth investors, is more restricted than that of non-EU Member States/non-EEA-EFTA States, whereas the ability of EU Member States is restricted the most. The latter is due to the European tax directives, which do not apply to EEA-EFTA States, and the freedom of capital movement under the TFEU, which has universal scope unlike its counterpart in the EEA Agreement. The actual impact of European law can vary depending on the policy objective that is being pursued, and may further depend on a number of other variables, most notably the type and size of investment, as well as the type of sovereign wealth investor and its place of residence. However, as demonstrated in this study, the implications of European law for foreign sovereign wealth investors are not always clear, in particular in the area of State aid, so that its exact impact on the ability to achieve (or promote) tax policy objectives, and to freely implement an approach to taxation of these investors, may be difficult to determine. The relevant European law issues have been discussed in this study, and EU Member States and EEA-EFTA States wishing to introduce new tax policy, or evaluate or reconsider existing tax policy vis-à-vis foreign sovereign wealth investors, could consider notifying the EC respectively the EFTA Surveillance Authority in case of doubt as regards to the application of the State aid rules.

1103. Approaches (2) to (5) have been identified in Section 3.2.2.2 and are as follows:

  (2) according a general tax-exemption under domestic law or administrative practice.
  (3) according specific tax-exemptions or specific tax reductions under domestic law or administrative practice.
  (4) according a general tax-exemption under one or more tax treaties.
  (5) according specific tax-exemptions or specific tax reductions under one or more tax treaties.

1104. Approach (1) has been identified in Section 3.2.2.2 and is as follows: taxing foreign sovereign wealth investors in the same way as 'regular' non-resident corporate investors.

APPENDIX
Dutch Tax Treaties

A.1. INTRODUCTION

Dutch international tax policy vis-à-vis foreign sovereign wealth investors is largely aimed at enhancing the attractiveness of the Netherlands as an investment location. The memorandum on Dutch tax treaty policy recognizes sovereign wealth investors as important capital providers in the global economy[1105] and welcomes their investments into the Netherlands.[1106] It even pronounces the ambition of the Netherlands to become a regional investment centre for sovereign wealth investors through its tax treaty policy and the existing Dutch financial and tax infrastructure.[1107] In line with this policy, sovereign wealth investors of tax treaty partners of the Netherlands are very often entitled to an exemption or reduction of Dutch source taxation on dividends, in deviation from regular tax treaty policy. This appendix sets out and discusses selected tax treaties concluded between the Netherlands and States that are home to sovereign wealth investors. The focus will be on the dividend article, because the Netherlands currently does not levy interest or royalty withholding tax. Before doing so, it is noted that regular Dutch tax treaty policy aims to agree upon a tax rate of 0% in respect of dividends paid to companies resident of the other Contracting State in case of shareholdings of at least 10% (referred to as 'non-portfolio dividends').[1108] In all other cases (referred to as 'portfolio dividends'), the Netherlands aims to agree upon a tax rate of 15% (equal to the current Dutch domestic withholding tax rate).[1109]

1105. *Notitie Fiscaal Verdragsbeleid 2011*, Tweede Kamer, 2010–2011, 25 087, No. 7, p. 33.
1106. *Ibid.*, p. 76.
1107. *Ibid.*
1108. *Ibid.*, p. 45. Similarly, *Uitgangspunten van het beleid op het terrein van het internationaal fiscaal (verdragen)recht*, Tweede Kamer, 1997–1998, 25 087, No. 4, p. 41.
1109. *Notitie Fiscaal Verdragsbeleid 2011*, Tweede Kamer, 2010–2011, 25 087, No. 7, p. 47. Similarly, *Uitgangspunten van het beleid op het terrein van het internationaal fiscaal (verdragen)recht*, Tweede Kamer, 1997–1998, 25 087, No. 4, p. 42.

Appendix

A.2. TAX TREATY BETWEEN THE NETHERLANDS AND KUWAIT (2001)

A.2.1 Resident article

The tax treaty with Kuwait[1110] is the oldest tax treaty in force between the Netherlands and a Persian Gulf State. KIA, the SWF of Kuwait, which has been established as a legal identity under public law,[1111] will undoubtedly qualify as a resident under the tax treaty between the Netherlands and Kuwait, pursuant to Art. 4(2), which states that a 'resident of a Contracting State' shall include:

(a) the Government of that Contracting State or any political subdivision or local authority thereof; and
(b) any governmental institution created in that Contracting State under public law such as a corporation, Central Bank, fund, authority, foundation, agency or other similar entity, provided that its capital is beneficially and exclusively owned by the Government of that Contracting State or any political subdivision or local authority thereof.[1112]

A.2.2 Dividend article

Based on Art. 10(2)(a), companies resident of Kuwait are entitled to an exemption from Dutch taxation on dividends in case of shareholdings of at least 10% in Dutch resident companies. From Art. 5 of the Protocol, it can be derived that residents referred to in Art. 4(2), and companies resident in Kuwait and exclusively owned by a resident referred to in Art. 4(2), will also be entitled to this exemption from Dutch taxation. In all other cases, the Netherlands is allowed to tax dividends at a maximum rate of 10%, based on Art. 10(2)(b). The SWF of Kuwait will be entitled to an exemption from Dutch taxation on dividends in case of shareholdings of at least 10%.

A.3. TAX TREATY BETWEEN THE NETHERLANDS AND THE UAE (2007)

A.3.1 Resident article

The tax treaty between the Netherlands and the UAE[1113] contains both a separate definition of resident for each Contracting State and a general definition of resident that

---

1110. *Agreement Between the Government of the Kingdom of the Netherlands and the Government of the State of Kuwait for the Avoidance of Double Taxation and the Prevention of Fiscal Evasion with respect to Taxes on Income* (29 May 2001), Treaties IBFD.
1111. International Working Group of Sovereign Wealth Funds, *Sovereign Wealth Funds: Generally Accepted Principles and Practices 'Santiago Principles'* (October, 2008), Part II, GAPP 1, Explanation and commentary, p. 11.
1112. Article 4(2).
1113. *Convention Between the Kingdom of the Netherlands and the United Arab Emirates for the Avoidance of Double Taxation and the Prevention of Fiscal Evasion with respect to Taxes on Income* (8 May 2007), Treaties IBFD.

applies to both Contracting States. In the case of the UAE, the tax treaty with the Netherlands applies to companies that have their place of effective management in the UAE.[1114] The general treaty definition of resident includes 'that State and any political subdivision or local authority thereof', as well as a 'government institution'.[1115] The treaty provides that any institution shall be deemed to be a government institution if (i) 'created, wholly owned and controlled by the government of one of the Contracting States or of its political subdivisions, for the fulfilment of public functions' and if (ii) recognized as such by mutual agreement. The Dutch Minister of Finance has indicated that SWFs of the UAE, such as ADIA and the Abu Dhabi Investment Council, qualify as government institution under this tax treaty.[1116]

A.3.2 Dividend article

Based on Art. 10(2)(a), the tax rate on dividends paid by Dutch resident companies to companies resident of the UAE is maximized at 5% in case of shareholdings of at least 10%. In all other cases, the Netherlands is, in principle, allowed to tax dividends at a maximum rate of 10%, based on Art. 10(2)(b). However, pursuant to Art. 10(3), the following shareholders are entitled to an exemption from Dutch taxation on dividends, regardless of the size of the shareholding:

> the beneficial owner is that State itself, a political subdivision, local government, or the Central Bank thereof, a pension fund, the <u>Abu Dhabi Investment Authority, Abu Dhabi Investment Council</u> or any other institution created by the Government of, a political subdivision, local authority of that other State which is recognised as an integral part of that Government as shall be agreed by mutual agreement of the competent authorities of the Contracting States. (underline added)

ADIA, the second largest SWF of the world,[1117] has explicitly been named as a fund in relation to which the Netherlands in principle has no right to tax dividends paid by a Dutch resident company, regardless of the size of the shareholding, provided the application of Art. 10(3) has been settled by mutual agreement. The wording of Art. 10(3) leaves open the possibility to include in its scope those sovereign wealth investors of the UAE which have not been explicitly mentioned, but which are nonetheless considered an integral part of an Emirate or the UAE.

1114. Article 4(1)b.
1115. Article 4(2).
1116. *Tweede Kamer*, 2009-2010, 32 346, No. 3, p. 6.
1117. *See* Section 2.9.3.

Appendix

A.4. TAX TREATY BETWEEN THE NETHERLANDS AND BAHRAIN (2008)

A.4.1 Resident article

The tax treaty between the Netherlands and Bahrain[1118] follows the 1995 OECD MTC definition of resident. However, as explained in Section 5.3.4.4.3, for purposes of this tax treaty, the expression *that State and any political subdivision or local authority thereof* in Art. 4(2) is interpreted by the Netherlands as including 'a governmental agency, national bank (which is a commercial bank and not a central bank) and a wholly owned company' of a State, a political subdivision or a local authority thereof.[1119] This broad interpretation was motivated by the purpose of attracting investments from such sovereign wealth investors.[1120] The SWF of Bahrain (Mumtalakat Holding Company) was established as an independent holding company[1121] and should therefore qualify as a tax treaty resident of Bahrain.

A.4.2 Dividend article

Based on Art. 10(2)(a), companies resident of Bahrain with a capital divided into shares are entitled to an exemption from Dutch taxation on dividends in case of shareholdings of at least 10% in Dutch resident companies. From Art. 10(10), it can be derived that residents referred to in Art. 4(2), and companies resident in Bahrain and exclusively owned by a resident referred to in Art. 4(2), will also be entitled to this exemption from Dutch taxation. In all other cases, the Netherlands is allowed to tax dividends at a maximum rate of 10%, based on Art. 10(2)(b). The SWF of Bahrain will be entitled to an exemption from Dutch taxation on dividends in case of shareholdings of at least 10%.

A.5. TAX TREATY BETWEEN THE NETHERLANDS AND OMAN (2009)

A.5.1 Resident article

The tax treaty between the Netherlands and Oman[1122] replicates the OECD MTC definition of resident[1123] and, based on the protocol, this definition is extended to 'any statutory body of a Contracting State'.[1124]

1118. *Convention Between the Government of the Kingdom of the Netherlands and the Government of the Kingdom of Bahrain for the Avoidance of Double Taxation and the Prevention of Fiscal Evasion with respect to Taxes on Income* (16 April 2008), Treaties IBFD.
1119. *Tweede Kamer*, 2008–2009, 31 591, No. A/1, p. 5.
1120. *Ibid.*
1121. < http://www.mumtalakat.bh/our-story/ > .
1122. *Agreement Between the Kingdom of the Netherlands and the Sultanate of Oman for the Avoidance of Double Taxation and the Prevention of Fiscal Evasion with respect to Taxes on Income* (5 October 2009), Treaties IBFD.
1123. Article 4(1).
1124. Article III.

Appendix

A.5.2 Dividend article

Based on Art. 10(2)(a), companies resident of Oman are entitled to an exemption from Dutch taxation on dividends in case of shareholdings of at least 10% in Dutch resident companies. In all other cases, the Netherlands is, in principle, allowed to tax dividends at a maximum rate of 10%, based on Art. 10(2)(b). However, pursuant to Art. 10(4), the following entities are also entitled to an exemption from Dutch taxation, regardless of the size of the shareholding:

> that other State, a political subdivision, local government, a pension fund, or the Central Bank of either Contracting State, <u>the State General Reserve Fund of the Sultanate of Oman, the Omani Investment Fund</u>, the Omani Development bank, and any other statutory body or institution wholly or mainly owned by the Government of the Sultanate of Oman as may be agreed from time to time between the competent authorities of the Contracting States. (underline added)

Therefore, dividends paid by a Dutch resident company to the two SWFs of Oman are exempt from Dutch tax, regardless of the size of the shareholding. The wording of Art. 10(4) leaves open the possibility to include in its scope any new sovereign wealth investors of Oman in the future.

A.6. TAX TREATY BETWEEN THE NETHERLANDS AND NORWAY (1990) AND ITS NEW PROTOCOL (2013)

A.6.1 Resident article

The new protocol, concluded on 23 April 2013,[1125] has introduced a number of changes to the tax treaty between the Netherlands and Norway (1990).[1126] The resident article has been aligned with Art. 4(1) of the OECD MTC and now includes as a tax treaty resident the *State and any political subdivision or local authority thereof*. Furthermore, the new protocol deals with the application of the tax treaty to tax-exempt entities. A new article has been introduced in the protocol, which expresses the understanding of both States that a person (other than an individual) that is a subject *of* the tax laws of one of the States, is considered to be 'liable to tax' as meant in Art. 4(1), 'even when all elements of income attributable to that person are exempted from tax where the person meets all the requirements for exemption specified in the domestic tax law'. However, whether and, if so, to which extent a resident that is subject to a preferential regime will be entitled to tax treaty benefits, shall be decided by mutual agreement. According to the Dutch Explanatory Note to the new protocol, the aim is to apply the

---

1125. *Protocol Amending the Convention Between the Kingdom of Norway and the Kingdom of the Netherlands for the Avoidance of Double Taxation and the Prevention of Fiscal Evasion with respect to Taxes on Income and on Capital* (23 April 2013), Treaties IBFD.
1126. *Convention Between the Kingdom of Norway and the Kingdom of the Netherlands for the Avoidance of Double Taxation and the Prevention of Fiscal Evasion with respect to Taxes on Income and on Capital* (12 January 1990), Treaties IBFD.

Appendix

tax treaty in principle to all persons that are treated as body corporates (i.e., separate entities) for Dutch corporate income tax purposes.[1127]

A.6.2 Dividend article

As a general rule, the Netherlands is allowed to tax outbound dividends at a maximum rate of 15%, based on Art. 10(2). However, companies resident of Norway are entitled to an exemption from Dutch taxation on dividends in case of shareholdings of at least 10% in Dutch resident companies. Pursuant to the new Protocol, the following entities are also entitled to an exemption from Dutch taxation, regardless of the size of the shareholding: a pension fund, the central bank of Norway, Norway's SWF (the Government Pension Fund Global),[1128] and any statutory body or any institution wholly or mainly owned by the government of Norway as may be agreed from time to time between the competent authorities.[1129]

A.7. TAX TREATY BETWEEN THE NETHERLANDS AND CHINA (2013)

A.7.1 Resident article

Art. 4 of the tax treaty between the Netherlands and China (2013)[1130] is almost an exact copy of the 1995 version of Art. 4 of the OECD MTC. The Netherlands proposed to deviate from Art. 4(1) of the OECD MTC in line with Dutch tax treaty policy, but China's model did not allow such deviation.[1131] China recognized the difficulties that Art. 4(1) of the OECD MTC could give rise to, but did not expect interpretation differences between China and the Netherlands, because both States recognize (foreign) resident pension funds, not-for-profit organizations and government institutions (*overheidsinstellingen*) as a resident for purposes of this tax treaty.[1132]

A.7.2 Dividend article

Based on Art. 10(2)(a), the maximum Dutch tax rate on dividends paid to companies resident of China is 5% in case of shareholdings of at least 25%. In all other cases, the maximum tax rate is, in principle, 10%, based on Art. 10(2)(b). However, pursuant to Art. 10(3), the following entities are entitled to an exemption from Dutch taxation on dividends, regardless of the size of the shareholding: the government of China, any of

---

1127. *Staten Generaal*, 2012–2013, 33 731, No. 1, p. 6.
1128. *See* Section 2.9.1.
1129. Article X of the Protocol.
1130. *Agreement Between the Government of the Kingdom of the Netherlands and the Government of the People's Republic of China for the Avoidance of Double Taxation and the Prevention of Fiscal Evasion with respect to Taxes on Income* (31 May 2013), Treaties IBFD.
1131. *Tweede Kamer*, 2012–2013, 33 718, No. 3, p. 8.
1132. *Ibid.*

its institutions or any other entity the capital of which is wholly owned directly or indirectly by China. The two main SWFs of China, CIC[1133] and SAFE Investment Company, are established under company law and wholly-owned by the government of China. They should, therefore, be entitled to an exemption from Dutch taxation on dividends, regardless of the size of the shareholding. It is noted that, for purposes of Art. 11 (Interest), CIC is explicitly mentioned as a financial institution wholly-owned by China.

1133. *See* Section 2.9.4.

Bibliography

Books / Articles and Chapters / Reports

Oppenheim's International Law (ed. by R. Jennings & A. Watts), Vol. I, 9th edn., (London: Longman, 1992).

A. van Aaken, *Blurring Boundaries Between Sovereign Acts and Commercial Activities. A Functional View on Regulatory Immunity and Immunity from Execution* (March, 2013), Working Paper No. 2013-17, Law & Economics Research Paper Series, U. St. Gallen Law School.

J. Aizenman & R. Glick, 'Assets Class Diversification and Delegation of Responsibilities Between Central Banks and Sovereign Wealth Funds' (September, 2010), *Federal Reserve Bank of San Francisco Working Paper Series*, Working Paper 2010-20.

A. Albrecht, 'The Taxation of Aliens Under International Law' (1952) 28 *British Yearbook of International Law* 145.

C. Alley & D. Bentley, 'A Remodelling of Adam Smith's Tax Design Principles' (2005) 20 *Australian Tax Forum* 579.

Aristotle, *Politics*, trans. H. Rackman, in *Aristotle: In Twenty-Three Volumes*, Vol. XXI, (Cambridge, Massachusetts: Harvard University Press, 1967).

R. Attard, 'Discriminatory Taxation and the European Convention on Human Rights', Chapter 9 in: D. Weber & P. Pistone (eds.) *Non-Discrimination in Tax Treaties: Selected Issues from a Global Perspective*, IBFD 2016, Online Books IBFD.

R. Avi-Yonah, *International Tax as International Law: An Analysis of the International Tax Regime* (New York: Cambridge University Press, 2007).

P. Baker, 'Taxation and the European Convention on Human Rights' (2000) 4 *British Tax Review* 211.

N. Bammens, 'Belgium', in: *Residence of Companies under Tax Treaties and EC Law*, EC and International Tax Law Series, Vol. 5 (Amsterdam: IBFD, 2009).

N. Bammens, *The Principle of Non-discrimination in International and European Tax Law*, IBFD Doctoral Series, Vol. 24 (Amsterdam: IBFD, 2012).

F. Bassan, 'SWFs and Taxation: National, Bilateral and Multilateral Approach', Chapter 8 in: F. Bassan (ed.), *Research Handbook on Sovereign Wealth Funds and International Investment Law* (Cheltenham: Edward Elgar Publishing, 2015).

Bibliography

R. Beck & M. Fidora, 'The Impact of Sovereign Wealth Funds on Global Financial Markets' (2008), *ECB Occasional Paper No. 91*. Online at www.ecb.europa.eu/pub/pdf/scpops/ecbocp91.pdf.

J. Bird-Pollan, 'The Unjustified Subsidy: Sovereign Wealth Funds and the Foreign Sovereign Tax Exemption' (2012) 17 *Fordham Journal of Corporate & Financial Law* 987.

A. Blundell-Wignall, Y. Hu, & J. Yermo, 'Sovereign Wealth and Pension Fund Issue' (2008), *OECD Working Papers on Insurance and Private Pensions No. 14*. Online at www.oecd.org/finance/private-pensions/40345767.pdf.

J. Boer, *Sturende belastingheffer een monster? Juridische kanttekeningen bij fiscaal instrumentalisme en 'tax nudging'* (Den Haag: Sdu Uitgevers, 2013).

N. de Boynes, 'France', in: G. Maisto, *Residence of Companies under Tax Treaties and EC Law*, EC and International Tax Law Series, Vol. 5 (Amsterdam: IBFD, 2009).

J. Brierly, *The Law of Nations*, 6th edn., (London: Oxford University Press, 1963).

L. De Broe, *International Tax Planning and Prevention of Abuse*, IBFD Doctoral Series, Vol. 14 (Amsterdam: IBFD, 2008).

L. De Broe, 'Can Tax Treaties Confer State Aid?' (2017) 26 *EC Tax Review* 228.

K. Brooks, 'Canada', in: G. Maisto, *Residence of Companies under Tax Treaties and EC Law*, EC and International Tax Law Series, Vol. 5 (Amsterdam: IBFD, 2009).

K. Brooks, 'Canada', Chapter 5 in: M. Lang et al., *Trends and Players in Tax Policy*, IBFD 2016, Online Books IBFD.

K. Brooks, 'Inter-Nation Equity: The Development of an Important but Underappreciated International Tax Policy Objective', Chapter 17 in: J. Head & R. Krever, *Tax Reform in the 21st Century: A Volume in Memory of Richard Musgrave*, Series on International Taxation, Vol. 34 (Alphen a/d Rijn: Kluwer Law International, 2009).

I. Brownlie, *Principles of Public International Law*, 7th edn., (New York: Oxford University Press, 2008).

T. Buergenthal & S. Murphy, *Public International Law in a Nutshell*, 4th edn., (New York: Thomson/West Group, 2007).

P. Burg, 'Treaty Between France and Germany – French Administrative Supreme Court Rules that Exempt Pension Fund Is Not Resident Entitled Treaty Benefits', 11 November 2015, IBFD TNS Online.

I. Burgers, 'Recente ontwikkelingen in het Nederlands belastingverdragenrecht' (2005) 78 *Tijdschrift voor Fiscaal Ondernemingsrecht* 45.

J. Capapé, & T. Blanco, 'More Layers Than an Onion: Looking for a Definition of Sovereign Wealth Funds' (2014), *ESADEgeo Working Paper 21*.

A. Cassese, *International Law*, 2nd edn., (New York: Oxford University Press, 2005).M. Castelli & F. Scacciavillani, 'SWFs and State Investments: A Preliminary General Overview', Chapter 1 in: F. Bassan (ed.), *Research Handbook on Sovereign Wealth Funds and International Investment Law* (Cheltenham: Edward Elgar Publishing, 2015).

A. Capobianco & H. Christiansen, 'Competitive Neutrality and State-Owned Enterprises: Challenges and Policy Options' (2011), *OECD Corporate Governance*

Working Papers No. 1. Online at www.oecd-ilibrary.org/governance/competitive-neutrality-and-state-owned-enterprises_5kg9xfgjdhg6-en.

A. Christians, 'Sovereignty, Taxation and Social Contract' (2009) 18 *Minnesota Journal of International Law* 99.

CFE ECJ Task Force, Opinion Statement ECJ-TF 3/2015 on the Decision of the European Court of Justice in *C.G. Sopora* (Case C-512/13), on 'Horizontal Discrimination' (2016) 56 *European Taxation* 2/3.

B. Cheng, *General Principles of Law as Applied by International Courts and Tribunals*, Grotius Classic Reprint Series, No. 2, (New York: Cambridge University Press, 2006).

Cicero, *De Re Publica, De Legibus*, trans. C.W. Keyes, (Cambridge, Massachusetts: Harvard University Press, 1966).

Council of Europe (G. Hafner, M.G. Kohen & S. Breau (eds.)), *State Practice Regarding State Immunities* (Leiden: Martinus Nijhoff Publishers, 2006).

R. Couzin, *Corporate Residence and International Taxation*, (IBFD Publications BV: Amsterdam, 2002).

U. Das, Y. Lu, C. Mulder & A. Sy, 'Setting Up a Sovereign Wealth Fund: Some Policy and Operational Considerations' (2009), *IMF Working Paper No. 09/179*. Online at https://www.imf.org/external/pubs/ft/wp/2009/wp09179.pdf.

A. De Luca, 'The EU and Member States: FDI, Portfolio Investments, Golden Powers and SWFs', Chapter 7 in: F. Bassan (ed.), *Research Handbook on Sovereign Wealth Funds and International Investment Law* (Cheltenham: Edward Elgar Publishing, 2015).

V. Degan, *Sources of International Law* (The Hague: Martinus Nijhoff Publishers, 1997).

F. Debelva et al., 'LOB Clauses and EU-Law Compatibility: A Debate Revived by BEPS?' (2015) 24 *EC Tax Review* 132.

M. Desai & D. Dharmapala, 'Taxing the Bandit Kings' (2008) 118 *Yale Law Journal Pocket Part* 98.

M. Desai & J. Hines Jr., 'Evaluating International Tax Reform' (2003) 56 *National Tax Journal* 487.

M. Devereux, *Taxation of Outbound Direct Investment: Economic Principles and Tax Policy Considerations*, Research Report Prepared for the Advisory Panel on Canada's System of International Taxation, July 2008. Online at www.sbs.ox.ac.uk/faculty-research/tax/publications/working-papers/taxation-outbound-direct-investment-economic-principles-and-tax-policy-considerations.

M. Dixon, *Textbook on International Law*, 6th edn., (New York: Oxford University Press, 2007).

S. Douma, *Optimization of Tax Sovereignty and Free Movement* (2011), PhD. Thesis. Online at openaccess.leidenuniv.nl/handle/1887/17973.

A. Dourado, 'The EU Free Movement of Capital and Third Countries: Recent Developments' (2017) 45 *Intertax* 192.

R. Dworkin, *Taking Rights Seriously* (Cambridge, Massachusetts: Harvard University Press, 1977).

Bibliography

A. Easson, 'Tax Incentives for Foreign Direct Investment: Recent Trends and Countertrends (Part I)' (2001) 55 *Bulletin for International Taxation* 266.

A. Easson, 'Tax Incentives for Foreign Direct Investment: Design Considerations (Part II)' (2001) 55 *Bulletin for International Taxation* 365.

C. Ebrahim-Zadeh, 'Dutch Disease: Too Much Wealth Managed Unwisely' (2003) 40 *Finance & Development*, International Monetary Fund. Online at www.imf.org/external/pubs/ft/fandd/2003/03/ebra.htm.

W. Egelie, Case note on CJEU, 15 February 2017, Case C-317/15 (*X*), *Nederlands Tijdschrift voor Fiscaal Recht* 2017/637.

J. van Eijsden, B. Kiekebeld & D. Smit (eds.), *Nederlands belastingrecht in Europees perspectief*, 2nd edn., (Deventer: Kluwer, 2014).

D. Elkins. 'Horizontal Equity as a Principle of Tax Theory' (2006) 24 *Yale Law & Policy Review* 43.

F. Engelen, *Interpretation of Tax Treaties under International Law*, IBFD Doctoral Series, Vol. 7 (Amsterdam: IBFD, 2004).

J. Englisch, 'Ability to Pay', Chapter 19 in: C. Brokelind (ed.), *Principles of Law: Function, Status and Impact in EU Tax Law*, IBFD 2014, Online Books IBFD.

V. Fleischer, 'Should We Tax Sovereign Wealth Funds?' (2008) 118 *Yale Law Journal Pocket Part* 93.

V. Fleischer, 'A Theory of Taxing Sovereign Wealth Funds' (2009) 84 *NYU Law Review* 440. Online at www.nyulawreview.org/sites/default/files/pdf/NYULawReview-84-2-Fleischer.pdf.

J. Fleming, R. Peroni & S. Shay, 'Fairness in International Taxation: The Ability-to-Pay Case for Taxing Worldwide Income' (2001) 5 *Florida Tax Review* 301.

H. Fox, *The Law of State Immunity*, 2nd edn., (New York: Oxford University Press, 2008).

D. Gaukrodger, 'Foreign State Immunity and Foreign Government Controlled Investors' *OECD Working Papers on International Investment*, No. 2010/2. Online at http://www.oecd.org/daf/inv/investment-policy/WP-2010_2.pdf.

J. van der Geld, 'Fiscaliteit in een steeds veranderende wereld', in: H. van Arendonk, J. Jansen & L. Stevens (eds.), *Wetgevingskunsten: Vriendenbundel voor Jan Kees Bartel* (Den Haag: Sdu Uitgevers, 2010).

G. Genta, 'Dividends Received by Investment Funds: An EU Law Perspective – Part 2' (2013) 53 *European Taxation* 141.

R. Gilson & C. Milhaupt, 'Sovereign Wealth Funds and Corporate Governance: A Minimalist Response to the New Mercantilism' (2008) 60 *Stanford Law Review* 1345.

D. Gliksberg, 'General Report', in: *Taxation of Non-Profit Organizations*, IFA Cahiers de droit fiscal international, Vol. 84a (Alphen a/d Rijn: Kluwer Law International, 1999).

R. Gordon, 'Taxes and Privatization' (2001), Discussion Paper No. 2977, Centre for Economic Policy Research.

A. de Graaf & F. Pötgens, 'Worrying Interpretation of "Liable to Tax": OECD Clarification Would Be Welcome' (2011) 39 *Intertax* 169.

Bibliography

A. de Graaf & G. Janssen, 'The Implications of the Judgment in the *D* Case: The Perspective of Two Non-believers' (2005) 14 *EC Tax Review* 173.

M. Graetz, 'The David R. Tillinghast Lecture Taxing International Income: Inadequate Principles, Outdated Concepts and Unsatisfactory Policies' (2001) 54 *Tax Law Review* 261.

M. Graetz & I. Grinberg, 'Taxing International Portfolio Income' (2003) 56 *Tax Law Review* 537.

R. Grant, 'Ethics and Incentives: A Political Approach' (2006) 100 *American Political Science Review* 29.

H. Gribnau, 'Legislative Instrumentalism vs. Legal Principles in Tax Law' (2013) 16 *Coventry Law Journal* 89.

H. Gribnau, 'Rechtsbeginselen en evaluatie van belastingwetgeving: rechtvaardigheid hanteerbaar gemaakt', in: A. Rijkers & H. Vording, *Vijf jaar Wet IB* (Deventer: Kluwer, 2006).

J. Calejo Guerra, 'Limitation on Benefits Clauses and EU Law' (2011) 51 *European Taxation* 85.

C. Hammer, P. Kunzel & I. Petrova, 'Sovereign Wealth Funds: Current Institutional and Operational Practices' (2008), *IMF Working Paper No. 08/254*. Online at www.imf.org/external/pubs/ft/wp/2008/wp08254.pdf.

A. Al-Hassan et al., 'Sovereign Wealth Funds: Aspects of Governance Structures and Investment Management' (2013), *IMF Working Paper No. 13/231*. Online at www.imf.org/en/Publications/WP/Issues/2016/12/31/Sovereign-Wealth-Funds-Aspects-of-Governance-Structures-and-Investment-Management-41046.

P. Hattingh, 'Article 1 of the OECD Model: Historical Background and the Issues Surrounding It' (2010) 57 *Bulletin for International Taxation* 215.

P. Hattingh, 'The Role and Function of Article 1 of the OECD Model' (2010) 57 *Bulletin for International Taxation* 546.

S. Hemels, 'Netherlands', Chapter 12 in: M. Lang et al., *Trends and Players in Tax Policy*, IBFD 2016, Online Books IBFD.

D. Herman, *Taxing Portfolio Income in Global Financial Markets*, IBFD Doctoral Series, Vol. 2 (Amsterdam: IBFD, 2002).

G. Hippert, 'The TFEU Eligibility of Non-EU Investment Funds Subjected to Discriminatory Dividend Withholding Taxes' (2016) 25 *EC Tax Review* 77.

C. Hoyos Jiménez, 'Non-Discrimination on the Basis of Nationality in IIAs: A Latin American Tax Perspective', Chapter 2 in: D. Weber & P. Pistone (eds.) *Non-Discrimination in Tax Treaties: Selected Issues from a Global Perspective*, IBFD 2016, Online Books IBFD.

H. Hull, 'United Arab Emirates: Tax Treaty Relief on International Investment' (2009) 63 *Bulletin for International Taxation* 52.

M. Isenbaert, *EC Law and the Sovereignty of the Member States in Direct Taxation*, IBFD 2009, Online Books IBFD.

S. Janssen, 'How to Treat(y) Sovereign Wealth Funds? The Application of Tax Treaties to State-Owned Entities, Including Sovereign Wealth Funds', in: D. Weber & S. van Weeghel, *The 2010 OECD Updates, Model Tax Convention & Transfer Pricing*

Bibliography

Guidelines, A Critical Review, Series on International Taxation, Vol. 38 (Alphen a/d Rijn: Kluwer Law International, 2011).

A. Jones et al., 'The Interpretation of Tax Treaties with Particular Reference to Article 3(2) of the OECD Model – I' (1984) 1 *British Tax Review* 14.

S-A. Joseph, 'Do Tax Treaties Embody Sovereign Immunity? – An Assessment with Regard to Sovereign Wealth Funds' (2015) 69 *Bulletin for International Taxation* 637.

S-A. Joseph, M. Walpole & R. Deutsch, 'Taxation of Sovereign Wealth Funds – A Suggested Approach' (2015) 10 *Journal of the Australasian Tax Teachers Association* 119. Online at www.business.unsw.edu.au/About-Site/Schools-Site/Taxation-Business-Law-Site/Journal%20of%20The%20Australasian%20Tax%20Teachers%20Associati/JATTA-2015_all_articles.pdf.

S-A. Joseph, 'Jurisdictional Taxing Rights of Sovereign Wealth Funds' (2016) 70 *Bulletin for International Taxation* 146.

S-A. Joseph, 'Taxing Sovereign Wealth Funds Mark II: Looking to Singapore for Inspiration', Australasian Tax Teachers Association Conference Papers, 2016. Online at www.business.unsw.edu.au/About-Site/Schools-Site/Taxation-Business-Law-Site/Documents/Joseph_ATTA-2016-Sally-Joseph.pdf.

M. Kandev, 'Tax Treaty Interpretation: Determining Domestic Meaning Under Article 3(2) of the OECD Model' (2007) 55 *Canadian Tax Journal* 31.

M. Kandev, 'Sovereign Wealth Funds: Are They Welcome in Canada?' (2010) 64 *Bulletin for International Taxation* 649.

J. Kang & L. Na, 'China', Chapter 6 in: M. Lang et al., *Trends and Players in Tax Policy*, IBFD 2016, Online Books IBFD.

A. Kardachaki, 'Tax Aspects of International Non-Tax Agreements' (2012-2013), *IFA Research Paper*. Online at www.ifa.nl/Document/Research%20Papers/IFA%20Research%20paper%20-%20Tax%20Aspects%20of%20Int%20non-tax%20agreements.pdf.

N. Kaufman, 'Fairness in International Taxation of International Income' (1998) 29 *Law & Policy in International Business* 145.

B. Kelsey, 'Recent Trends in Sovereign Immunity from Taxation' (1959) 17 *Toronto Faculty of Law Review* 81.

E. Kemmeren, *Principle of Origin in Tax Conventions: A Rethinking of Models* (2001), Dongen: Mr. Eric C.C.M. Kemmeren/Pijnenburg vormgevers, uitgevers. Online at pure.uvt.nl/portal/files/439888/87428.pdf.

E. Kemmeren, 'Sopora: *A Welcome Landmark Decision on Horizontal Comparison*' (2015) 24 *EC Tax Review* 178.

R. Kimmitt, 'Public Footprints in Private Markets: Sovereign Wealth Funds and the World Economy' (2008) 87 *Foreign Affairs* 119.

M. Knoll, 'Taxation and the Competitiveness of Sovereign Wealth Funds: Do Taxes Encourage Sovereign Wealth Funds to Invest in the United States?' (2009) 82 *Southern California Law Review* 703. Online at scholarship.law.upenn.edu/cgi/viewcontent.cgi?article=1236&context=faculty_scholarship.

M. Knoll, 'Reconsidering International Tax Neutrality' (2011) 64 *Tax Law Review* 99.

Bibliography

R. Krever & P. Mellor, 'Australia', Chapter 2 in: M. Lang et al., *Trends and Players in Tax Policy*, IBFD 2016, Online Books IBFD.

P. Kunzel, Y. Lu, I. Petrova & J. Pihlman, 'Investment Objectives of Sovereign Wealth Funds – A Shifting Paradigm' (2011), *IMF Working Paper No. 11/19*. Online at www.imf.org/en/Publications/WP/Issues/2016/12/31/Investment-Objectives-of-Sovereign-Wealth-Funds-A-Shifting-Paradigm-24598.

M. Lang et al. (eds.), *Tax Rules in Non-Tax Agreements*, (Amsterdam: IBFD, 2012).

A. Lejour & M. van 't Riet, 'De Economische Betekenis van Bilaterale Belastingverdragen' (2013), Annex to; *Bilaterale Belastingverdragen en Buitenlandse Investeringen*, CPB Policy Brief 2013/07. Online at www.cpb.nl/sites/default/files/publicaties/download/cpb-achtergronddocument-de-economische-betekenis-van-bilaterale-belastingverdragen.pdf.

A. Lejour, 'The Foreign Investment Effects of Tax Treaties' (2014), Oxford University Center for Business Taxation, WP 14/03. Online at www.eesc.europa.eu/resources/docs/2014-the-foreign-investment-effects-of-tax-treaties_oxford-univ-centre-for-business-taxation.pdf.

J. Locke, *Two Treatises of Government*, ed. P. Laslett, (Cambridge: Cambridge University Press, 1988).

R. Luja, 'Fiscal Autonomy, Investment Funds and State Aid: A Follow-Up' (2009) 47 *European Taxation*.

R. Luja, 'Tax Treaties and State Aid: Some Thoughts' (2004) 44 *European Taxation* 234.

R. Luja, Case note on Case C-74/16 (*Congregación de Escuelas Pías Provincia Betania*), *Highlights & Insights on European Taxation* 2017/260.

J. Luts, 'Congregación de Escuelas Pías Provincia Betania: Tax Exemption for Education Services by Religious Congregation Not Sacrosanct from State Aid Perspective' (2017) 26 *EC Tax Review* 292.

E. Lynne & P. Bongaarts, *The Taxation of Investment Funds, General Report*, IFA Cahiers de Droit Fiscal International Vol. 8ba (Periodicals Service Company, 1997), Online Books IBFD.

G. Maisto, *Residence of Companies under Tax Treaties and EC Law*, EC and International Tax Law Series, Vol. 5 (Amsterdam: IBFD, 2009).

P. Malanczuk, *Akehurst's Modern Introduction to International Law*, 7th edn., (London: Routledge, 1997).

D. Markheim, 'Sovereign Wealth Funds: New Voluntary Principles a Step in the Right Direction' (2008), The Heritage Foundation, WebMemo No. 2175.

K. Marx, 'On the Jewish Question', ed. D. McLellan, in *Karl Marx: Selected Writings* (Oxford: Oxford University Press, 1977).

M. Maslakovic, 'Sovereign Wealth Funds 2010' (2010) *International Financial Services London Research*.

R. Mason, 'Tax Discrimination and Capital Neutrality' (2010) 2 *World Tax Journal* 126.

P. Matos, 'Reverse Discrimination and Direct Taxation in the EU', Chapter 9 in: D. Weber (ed.), *EU Income Tax Law: Issues for the Years Ahead*, IBFD 2013, Online Books IBFD.

G. May, 'The Foreign Sovereign Tax Exemption' (2008) 122 *Tax Notes* 389.

H. Meijers, 'On International Customary Law in the Netherlands', in: I. Dekker & H. Post, *On the Foundations and Sources of International Law* (The Hague: T.M.C. Asser Press, 2003).

M. Melone, 'Should the United States Tax Sovereign Wealth Funds?' (2008) 26 *Boston University International Law Journal* 143. Online at www.bu.edu/law/journals-archive/international/volume26n2/documents/melone.pdf.

M. Mendelson, 'The Subjective Element in Customary International Law' (1995) 66 *The British Year Book of International Law* 177.

A. Monk, 'Recasting the Sovereign Wealth Fund Debate: Trust, Legitimacy, and Governance' (2009) 14 *New Political Economy* 451.

G. Müller-Gatermann, 'Germany', Chapter 10 in: M. Lang et al., *Trends and Players in Tax Policy*, IBFD 2016, Online Books IBFD.

R. Musgrave & P. Musgrave, 'Inter-nation Equity', in: R. Bird & J. Head, *Modern Fiscal Issue: Essays in Honour of Carl. S. Shoup* (Toronto: Toronto University Press, 1972).

D. Nerudová & L. Moravec, 'Czech Republic', Chapter 9 in: M. Lang et al., *Trends and Players in Tax Policy*, IBFD 2016, Online Books IBFD.

R. Niessen, *Inleiding tot het Nederlands belastingrecht*, Fiscale Handboeken, 9th edn. (Deventer: Kluwer, 2010).

R. Niessen, 'Instrumentalisme en belastingrecht' (1997) *Weekblad Fiscaal Recht* 653.

E. Nijkeuter, 'Exchange of Information and the Free Movement of Capital Between Member States and Third Countries' (2011) 20 *EC Tax Review* 232.

E. Nijkeuter & M. de Wilde, 'FII 2 and the Applicable Freedoms of Movement in Third Country Situations' (2013) 22 *EC Tax Review* 250.

M. Nouwen, 'The European Code of Conduct Group Becomes Increasingly Important in the Fight Against Tax Avoidance: More Openness and Transparency is Necessary' (2017) 45 *Intertax* 138.

J. Nugée, 'The Growing Role of Sovereign Wealth Funds', Chapter 2 in: State Street, *Sovereign Wealth Funds: Assessing the Impact* (2008), Vol. III, Issue 2.

L. af Ornäs Leijon, 'Tax Policy, Economic Efficiency and the Principle of Neutrality From a Legal and Economic Perspective' *Uppsala Faculty of Law Working Paper 2015:2*.

P. Paone, 'Italian Income Tax and Tax Liability of Foreign States and International Organizations' (1976) 2 *The Italian Yearbook of International Law* 273.

H. Pijl, 'De additionele inwonerseis in het verdrag met de Verenigde Staten: HR 4 december 2009, BNB 2010/177' (2010) *Weekblad voor Fiscaal Recht* 1371.

H. Pijl, 'Excluded Resident and the Term "Law"/"Laws" in Article 4 of the OECD Draft (1963) and OECD Model (1977/2010)' (2012) 66 *Bulletin for International Taxation* 3.

M. Podolny, 'The Limits of Sovereign Immunity: A Study and Analysis of the Canadian Income Taxation of Sovereign Wealth Funds' (2012) 70 *University of Toronto Faculty of Law Review* 90.

F. Pötgens & M. Straathof, 'Establishment and Substance of Intermediate and Other Holding Companies from an EU Law Perspective' (2016) 44 *Intertax* 608.

N. Quiñones, 'Colombia', Chapter 7 in: M. Lang et al., *Trends and Players in Tax Policy*, IBFD 2016, Online Books IBFD.E. Raingeard, *The Relationship Between EC Law and International Tax Law*, European Academic Tax Thesis Award, 2009.

H. Reisen, 'How to Spend It: Commodity and Non-Commodity Sovereign Wealth Funds' (2008), *OECD Development Centre Policy Brief No. 38*.

P. Richman, *Taxation of Foreign Investment Income: An Economic Analysis* (Baltimore: The John Hopkins Press, 1963).

J. Rienstra, *United States – Individual Taxation*, Country Analyses IBFD.

A. Rozanov, 'Who Holds the Wealth of Nations?' (2005) 15 *Central Banking Journal* 52.

A. Rozanov, 'A Liability-Based Approach to Sovereign Wealth', Chapter 3 in: State Street, *Sovereign Wealth Funds: Assessing the Impact* (2008), Vol. III, Issue 2.

A. Rozanov, 'Definitional Challenges of Dealing with Sovereign Wealth Funds' (2011) 1 *Asian Journal of International Law* 249.

A. Rust, in Reimer & Rust (eds), *Klaus Vogel on Double Taxation Conventions*, 4th edn., (Alphen a/d Rijn: Kluwer Law International, 2015).

A. Sandor, 'Leveraging International Law to Incentivize Value-Added Shareholding: Why Foreign Sovereign Wealth Funds *Still* Matter and How They Can Improve Shareholder Governance' (2015) 46 *Georgetown Journal of International Law* 948.

J. Santiso, 'Sovereign Development Funds: Key Financial Actors of the Shifting Wealth of Nations' (2008), *OECD Emerging Markets Network Working Paper*. Online at http://www.oecd.org/dev/41944381.pdf.

A. Sawyer & A. Smith, 'New Zealand', Chapter 13 in: M. Lang et al., *Trends and Players in Tax Policy*, IBFD 2016, Online Books IBFD.

A. Scapa & L. Henie, 'Avoidance of Double Non-Taxation under the OECD Model Tax Convention' (2005) 33 *Intertax* 266.

C. Schmitthoff & F. Wooldridge, 'The Nineteenth Century Doctrine of Sovereign Immunity and the Importance of the Growth of State Trading' (1972) 2 *Denver Journal of International Law & Policy* 199.

L. Schoueri & M. Barbosa, 'Brazil', Chapter 4 in: M. Lang et al., *Trends and Players in Tax Policy*, IBFD 2016, Online Books IBFD.

F. Shaheen, 'International Tax Neutrality: Reconsiderations' (2007) 27 *Virginia Tax Review* 203.

F. Shaheen, 'International Tax Neutrality: Revisited' (2011) 64 *Tax Law Review* 131.

H. Shannon, 'US Income Tax Ttreaties, Reference to Domestic Law for the Meaning of Undefined Terms' (1989) 17 *Intertax* 453.

M. Shaw, *International Law*, 6th edn., (Cambridge: Cambridge University Press, 2008).

D. Sloss, 'Domestic Application of Treaties' (2011). Online at digitalcommons.law.scu.edu/facpubs/635/.

A. Smith, *The Theory of Moral Sentiments*, (1759, 1799, 6th edn.), ed. D Rapheal & A. Macfie, (Glasgow Edition, Vol. I), (Oxford: Clarendon Press, 1976).

D. Smit, *Freedom of Investment Between EU and Non-EU Member States and its Impact on Corporate Income Tax Systems Within the European Union*, (Tilburg: CentER, 2011). Online at pure.uvt.nl/portal/files/5897717/Smit_freedom_02_12_2011_emb_tot_01_09_2013.pdf.

Bibliography

R. Snoeij, 'Sovereign Immunity and Source State Taxation of Sovereign Wealth Funds: Is It Time to Re-Evaluate?' (2016) 8 *World Tax Journal* 225.

J. Taylor, 'Tax Treatment of Income of Foreign Governments and International Organizations', in: US Department of Treasury, *Essays in International Taxation* (Washington: Treasury Department, 1977).

B. Terra & P. Wattel, *European Tax Law*, 6th edn., (Deventer: Kluwer, 2012).

H. Thirlway, 'The Source of International Law', in: M. Evans, *International Law*, 3rd edn., (New York: Oxford University Press, 2010).

D. Tillinghast, 'Sovereign Immunity from the Tax Collector: United States Income Taxation of Foreign Governments and International Organizations' (1978) 10 *Law and Policy in International Business* 495.

V. Troeger, 'Tax Competition and the Myth of the "Race to the Bottom": Why Governments Still Tax Capital' (2013), *The CAGE-Chatham House Series No. 4*. Online at www.chathamhouse.org/sites/files/chathamhouse/public/Research/International%20Economics/0213bp_troeger.pdf.

N. Umar, *Singapore – Corporate Taxation*, Country Analyses IBFD.

C. Védrine, '*Treaty Between France and Netherlands – French Administrative Court of Appeal Finds Withholding Taxes Applied to Dutch Pension Funds Contrary to Treaty Non-discrimination Clause and EU Free Movement of Capital*', 26 June 2008, IBFD Tax News Service.

H. Vermeulen, *Het regime voor de fiscale beleggingsinstelling*, 3rd edn., (Deventer: Kluwer, 2012).

J. Vleggeert, 'Dutch CV-BV Structures: Starbucks-Style Tax Planning and State Aid Rules' (2016) 70 *Bulletin for International Taxation* 3.

J. Vleggeert, Case note on *Hoge Raad*, 3 March 2017, No. 16/03954, *Nederland Tijdschrift voor Fiscaal Recht* 2017/686.

K. Vogel, 'Worldwide vs. Source Taxation of Income – A Review and Re-evaluation of Arguments (Part II)' (1988) 10 *Intertax* 310.

R. Walden, 'The Subjective Element in the Formation of Customary International Law' (1977) 12 *Israel Law Review* 344.

C. Wales & C. Turnbull-Hall, 'United Kingdom', Chapter 20 in: M. Lang et al., *Trends and Players in Tax Policy*, IBFD 2016, Online Books IBFD.

C. Warbrick, 'States and Recognition in International Law', in: M. Evans, *International Law*, 2nd edn., (New York: Oxford University Press, 2006).

D. Ward et al., 'A Resident of a Contracting State for Tax Treaty Purposes: A Case Comment on Crown Forest Industries' (1996) 44 *Canadian Tax Journal* 408.

P. Wattel, 'Interaction of State Aid, Free Movement, Policy Competition and Abuse Control in Direct Tax Matters' (2013) 5 *World Tax Journal* 128.

P. Wattel, 'Non-Discrimination à la Cour: The ECJ's (Lack of) Comparability Analysis in Direct Tax Cases' (2015) 55 *European Taxation* 542.

D. Weber, 'The New Common Minimum Anti-Abuse Rule in the EU Parent-Subsidiary Directive: Background, Impact, Applicability, Purpose and Effect' (2016) 44 *Intertax* 98.

D. Weber, 'Most-Favoured-Treatment under Tax Treaties Rejected in the European Community: Background and Analysis of the *D* Case: A proposal to include a most-favoured-nation clause in the EC Treaty' (2005) 33 *Intertax* 429.

D. Weisbach, 'The Use of Neutralities in International Tax Policy' (2014) *Coase-Sandor Institute for Law and Economics*, Working Paper No. 697.

J. Wheeler, 'The Missing Keystone of Income Tax Treaties' (2011) 3 *World Tax Journal* 247.

Wei Cui, 'Responding to Sovereign Funds: Are We Looking in the Right Place?' (2009) 123 *Tax Notes* 1237.

Wei Cui, 'Taxing State-Owned Enterprises: Towards an Understanding of a Basic Institution of State Capitalism' (2016) 52 *Osgoode Hall Law Journal* 775. Online at papers.ssrn.com/sol3/papers.cfm?abstract_id = 2676193.

Wei Cui, *'Taxation of State Owned Enterprises: A Review of Empirical Evidence from China'* (2015). Online at papers.ssrn.com/sol3/papers.cfm?abstract_id = 2583284.

M. de Wilde, 'Some Thoughts on a Fair Allocation of Corporate Tax in a Globalizing Economy' (2010) 38 *Intertax* 281.

M. de Wilde, *'Sharing the Pie'; Taxing Multinationals in a Global Market* (2015). Online at repub.eur.nl/pub/77496/.

L. Wildhaber & S. Breitenmoser, 'The Relationship Between Customary International Law and Municipal Law in Western European Countries' (1988) 48 *Zeitschrift für ausländisches öffentliches Recht und Völkerrecht* 163.

J. Yermo, 'Governance and Investment of Public Pension Reserve Funds in Selected OECD Countries' (2008), *OECD Working Papers on Insurance and Private Pensions*, No. 15. Online at http://www.oecd.org/finance/private-pensions/40194872.pdf.

A. Yevgenyeva, 'The Taxation of Non-profit Organizations after *Stauffer*', Chapter 11: in W. Haslehner et al. (eds.), *Landmark Decisions of the ECJ in Direct Taxation*, (Alphen a/d Rijn: Kluwer Law International, 2015).

K-Y. Yoo & A. de Serres, 'Tax Treatment of Private Pension Savings in OECD Countries and the Net Tax Cost Per Unit of Contribution to Tax-Favoured Schemes' (2004), *OECD Working Paper No. 406*. Online at www.oecd.org/eco/outlook/35663569.pdf.

F. Zimmer, A. Scapa Passalacqua & L. Henie, 'Norway', Chapter 14 in: M. Lang et al., *Trends and Players in Tax Policy*, IBFD 2016, Online Books IBFD.

A. Zeiler, 'Austria', Chapter 3 in: M. Lang et al., *Trends and Players in Tax Policy*, IBFD 2016, Online Books IBFD.

Table of Cases

Table of International Cases

Court of Justice of the European Union

CJEU, 18 December 2007, Case C-101/05 (*A*), **167**, **168**, **194**
CJEU, 19 July 2012, Case C-48/11 (*A Oy*), **163**, **194**
CJEU, 18 June 2009, Case C-303/07 (*Aberdeen Property Fininvest*), **174**, **177–179**, **191**, **253**, **254**
CJEU, 21 December 2016, Joined Cases C-164/15 P and C-165/15 P (*Aer Lingus & Ryanair*), **212**
Opinion of Advocate General Mengozzi, 5 July 2016, Joined Cases C-164/15 P and C-165/15 P (*Aer Lingus & Ryanair*), **213**
CJEU, 24 October 2002, Case C-82/01 P (*Aéroports de Paris*), **208**, **248**
CJEU, 8 November 2007, Case C-379/05 (*Amurta*), **168**, **177–179**, **189**, **192**, **254**
CJEU, 12 June 2003, Case C-234/01 (*Arnoud Gerritse*), **177**, **181**
CJEU, 27 June 1996, Case C-107/94 (*Asscher*), **162**
CJEU, 13 April 2000, Case C-251/98 (*Baars*), **164**
CJEU, 28 January 1992, Case C-204/90 (*Bachmann*), **193**
CJEU, 15 March 1994, Case C-387/92 (*Banco de Crédito Industrial SA*), **204**
CJEU, 21 October 2004, Case C-8/03 (*BBL*), **198**, **199**
CJEU, 13 July 2016, Case C-18/15 (*Brisal*), **181**
CJEU, 12 September 2006, Case C-196/04 (*Cadbury Schweppes*), **193**
CJEU, 10 January 2006, Case C-222/04 (*Cassa di Risparmio di Firenze SpA*), **164**, **199**, **203**, **212**
CJEU, 14 September 2006, Case C-386/04 (*Centro di Musicologia Walter Stauffer*), **165**, **179**, **188**
CJEU, 15 February 2007, Case C-345/04 (*Centro Equestre da Lezíria Grande*), **181**
CJEU, 22 January 2002, Case C-218/00 (*Cisal di Battistello Venanzio & C. Sas*), **198**
CJEU, 16 June 1987, Case 118/85 (*Commission v. Italy*), **198**
CJEU, 27 June 2017, Case C-74/16 (*Congregación de Escuelas Pías Provincia Betania*), **201**, **209**

Table of Cases

Opinion of Advocate General Kokott, 16 February 2017, Case C-74/16 (*Congregación de Escuelas Pías Provincia Betania*), **209, 211**
General Court, 11 September 2012, Case T-565/08 (*Corsica Ferries France v. European Commission*), **201**
CJEU, 15 July 1964, Case 6/64 *(Costa v. ENEL)*, **158**
CJEU, 5 July 2005, Case C-376/03 *(D.)*, **181**
CJEU, 27 September 1988, Case 81/87 (*Daily Mail*), **158**
CJEU, 14 December 2006, Case C-170/05 (*Denkavit Internationaal BV*), **166, 177, 179, 180**
CJEU, 29 April 2004, Case C-77/01 (*EDM*), **199, 200**
CJEU, 15 January 2002, Case C-55/00 (*Elide Gottardo*), **183**
CJEU, 10 April 2014, Case C-190/12 (*Emerging Markets Series*), **170, 175, 177–180, 189, 191, 194, 254**
CJEU, 20 October 2011, Case C-284/09 (*European Commission v. Federal Republic of Germany*), **160, 162, 168, 170, 173, 178**
CJEU, 19 November 2009, Case C-540/07 (*European Commission v. Italian Republic*), **177, 178**
CJEU, 11 June 2009, Case C-521/07 (*European Commission v. Kingdom of the Netherlands*), **253**
CJEU, 3 June 2010, Case C-487/08 (*European Commission v. Kingdom of Spain*), **168, 178**
Opinion of Advocate General Sharpston, 19 July 2012, Case C-342/10 (*European Commission v. Republic of Finland*), **168**
CJEU, 8 November 2012, Case C-342/10 (*European Commission v. Republic of Finland*), **168, 178**
CFI, 4 March 2009, Case T-445/05 (*Fineco Asset Management*), **198, 200, 202, 213**
CJEU, 12 May 1998, Case C-336/96 (*Gilly*), **210**
CJEU, 17 September 2008, Case C-182/08 (*Glaxo Welcome*), **168**
CJEU, 10 February 2011, Joined Cases C-436/08 and C-437/08 (*Haribo Lakritzen and Österreichische Salinen*), **174, 184, 189, 194**
CJEU, 27 January 2009, Case C-318/07 (*Hein Persche*), **178, 188**
CJEU, 21 October 2010, Case C-81/09 (*Idrima Tipou*), **169**
CJEU, 11 December 2007, Case C-438/05 (*International Transport Workers' Federation*), **164**
Opinion of Advocate General Bobek, 21 April 2016, Case C-270/15 P (*Kingdom of Belgium v Commission*), **202**
CJEU, 23 April 1991, Case C-41/90 (*Klaus Höfner and Fritz Elser v. Macrotron GmbH*), **198**
CJEU, 23 September 2003, Case C-452/01 (*Margarethe Ospelt*), **159, 160**
CJEU, 13 December 2005, Case C-446/03 (*Marks & Spencer plc*), **221**
CFI, 15 June 2000, Joined Cases T-298/97, T-312/97, etc. (*Mauro Alzetta*), **203**
CJEU, 17 September 2015, Joined Cases C-10/14, C-14/14 and C-17/14 (*Miljoen, X, Société Générale*), **177–181, 189, 192, 256, 257**
CJEU, 1 July 2008, Case C-49/07 (*Motosykletistiki Omospondia Ellados NPID (MOTOE)*), **198**

Table of Cases

CJEU, 12 January 2017, Case C-28/16 (*MVM Magyar Villamos Művek Zrt.*), **164, 199**
CJEU, 19 January 2017, Case C-344/15 (*National Roads Authority*), **208, 248**
CJEU, 3 October 1990, Joined Cases C-54/88 (*Nino*), C-91/88 and C-14/89, **162**
CJEU, 2 June 2016, Case C-252/14 (*Pensioenfonds Metaal en Techniek*), **179–181**
Opinion of Advocate General Kokott, 2 July 2009, Case C-169/08 (*Presidente del Consiglio dei Ministri v. Regione Sardegna*), **202**
CFI, 4 April 2001, Case T-288/97 (*Regione autonoma Friuli-Venezia Giulia*), **203**
CJEU, 30 November 1995, Case C-55/94 (*Reinhard Gebhard*), **163, 164**
Request for a preliminary ruling from the Østre Landsret (Denmark) lodged on 5 September 2016–*Fidelity Funds v Skatteministeriet* (Case C-480/16), **249**
CJEU, 30 June 2016, Case C-176/15 (*Riskin & Timmermans*), **181, 182, 209**
CFI, 17 December 2008, Case T-196/04 (*Ryanair v. European Commission*), **201**
CJEU, 21 September 1999, Case C-307/97 (*Saint-Gobain*), **183**
CJEU, 10 May 2012, Joined Cases C-338/11 to C-347/11 (*Santander Asset Management*), **162, 178, 179, 191**
CJEU, 19 January 1994, Case C-364/92 (*SAT/Eurocontrol*), **201**
CJEU, 21 July 2011, Case C-397/09 (*Scheuten Solar Technology GmbH*), **216**
CJEU, 14 February 1995, Case C-279/93 (*Schumacker*), **176, 177**
CJEU, 24 November 2016, Case C-464/14 (*SECIL*), **195**
CJEU, 13 December 1984, Case C-106/83 (*Sermide SpA v. Cassa Conguaglio Zucchero*), **157**
Opinion of Advocate General Cosmas, 10 December 1996, Case C-343/95 (*Servizi Ecologici Porto di Genova SpA*), **208**
CJEU, 18 March 1997, Case C-343/95 (*Servizi Ecologici Porto di Genova SpA*), **198, 201**
CJEU, 18 December 2007, Case C-101/05 (*Skatteverket v. A*), **167, 168, 194**
CJEU, 24 February 2015, Case C-512/13 (*Sopora*), **177, 183, 210, 224**
CJEU, 12 February 1974, Case 152/73 (*Sotgiu*), **158**
CJEU, 12 December 2006, Case C-374/04 (*Test Claimants in Class IV of the ACT Group Litigation*), **177, 182, 189, 192, 254**
CJEU, 12 December 2006, Case C-446/04 (*Test Claimants in the FII Group Litigation*), **215**
CJEU, 13 November 2012, Case C-35/11 (*Test Claimants in the FII Group Litigation*), **168, 169, 175**
CJEU, 22 December 2008, Case C-282/07 (*Truck Center*), **177**
CJEU, 14 September 2017, Case C-646/15 (*Trustees of the P Panayi Accumulation & Maintenance Settlements*), **167**
CJEU, 15 December 2005, Case C-148/04 (*Unicredito Italiano*), **195, 202, 203**
CJEU, 5 February 1963, Case 26-62 *(Van Gend & Loos)*, **158**
CJEU, 23 February 2006, Case C-513/03 (*Van Hilten-van der Heijden*), **163**
CJEU, 6 June 2000, Case C-35/98 (*Verkooijen*), **168**
CJEU, 19 July 2012, Case C-48/11 (*Veronsaajien oikeudenvalvontayksikkö v. A Oy*), **163, 194**
CJEU, 21 May 2015, Case C-560/13 (*Wagner-Raith*), **170, 171**
CJEU, 30 April 2009, Case 494/06 P (*Wam SpA*), **212**

Table of Cases

Opinion of Advocate General Wathelet, 28 July 2016, Cases C-20/15 P and C-21/15 P (*World Duty Free Group*), **202**
CJEU, 21 December 2016, Cases C-20/15 P and C-21/15 P (*World Duty Free Group*), **202**
CJEU, 15 February 2017, Case C-317/15 (*X*), **170–172**
CJEU, 17 May 2017, Case C-68/15 (*X*), **180**

EFTA Court

EFTA Court, 23 November 2004, Case E-1/04 (*Fokus Bank*), **159, 178**
EFTA Court, 12 December 2003, Case E-1/03 (*EFTA Surveillance Authority v. The Republic of Iceland*), **160**
EFTA Court, 10 May 2011, Joined Cases E-4/10, E-6/10 and E-7/10 (*Principality of Liechtenstein et. al*), **197, 202**
EFTA Court, 9 July 2014, Cases E-3/13 and E-20/13 (*Fred Olsen and Others and The Norwegian State*), **164, 165**

European Court of Human Rights

Case of Darby v. Sweden, 17/1989/177/233, Council of Europe: European Court of Human Rights, 23 October 1990, **7**
Della Ciaja et al. against Italy, 46757/99, Council of Europe: European Court of Human Rights, 22 June 1999, **8**
Al-Adsani v. The United Kingdom, 35763/97, Council of Europe: European Court of Human Rights, 21 November 2001, **79**
Victor Jones against the UK, 42639/04, Council of Europe: European Court of Human Rights, 13 September 2005, **8**

International Court of Justice

Asylum Case (Colombia v. Peru), I.C.J. Reports 1950, p. 276, International Court of Justice (ICJ), 20 November 1950, **95**
Case Concerning Military and Paramilitary Activities In and Against Nicaragua (Nicaragua v. United States of America); Merits, I.C.J. Reports 1986, International Court of Justice (ICJ), 27 June 1986, **94, 95**
Case concerning Right of Passage over Indian Territory (Portugal v. India); Judgment, I.C.J. Reports 1960, International Court of Justice (ICJ), 12 April 1960, **95**
Continental Shelf (Libyan Arab Jarnahiriya/Malta), Judgment, I.C.J. Reports 1985, International Court of Justice (ICJ), 3 June 1985, **94**
North Sea Continental Shelf Cases (Federal Republic of Germany v. Denmark; Federal Republic of Germany v. Netherlands), I.C.J. Reports 1969, International Court of Justice (ICJ), 20 February 1969, **94–96**

Human Rights Committee

HRC, 30 March 1989, No. 273/1988 (*B. d. B. et al. v. The Netherlands*), **8**
HRC, 9 April 1987, No. 172/1984 (*Broeks*), **8**
HRC, 25 July 2005, No. 1192/2003 (*De Vos*), **8**

European Commission

EC, 12 May 2010, State Aid No. N131/2009–Finland–Residential Real Estate Investment Trust (REIT) Scheme, C(2010) 2974 final, **202**
EC, 9 July 2014, State aid SA.25338 (2014/C, ex E 3/2008, CP 115/2004 and CP 120/2006)–The Netherlands–Corporate tax exemption for public undertakings, C(2014) 4480 final, Official Journal of the European Union, Vol. 57, C 280, 22 August 2014, **202, 204**
EC, 3 December 2015, State aid SA. 38945 (2015/C) (ex 2015/NN)–Luxembourg–Alleged aid to McDonald's, C(2015) 8343 final, Official Journal of the European Union, Vol. 59, C 258, 15 July 2016, **202**
EC, 8 July 2016, State aid SA.38393 (2016/C) (ex 2015/E)–Ports taxation in Belgium, Official Journal of the European Union, Vol. 59, C 302, 19 August 2016, **204**
EC, 8 July 2016, State aid SA.38398 (2016/C) (ex 2015/E)–Ports taxation in France, Official Journal of the European Union, Vol. 59, C 302, 19 August 2016, **204**

Table of National Cases

Canada

Bouzari v. Islamic Republic of Iran, Ontario Court of Appeal, 30 June 2004, 128 ILR 586, **78**
Crown Forest Industries Ltd. v. Her Majesty the Queen, Supreme Court of Canada, 22 June 1995, File No.: 23940, Tax Treaty Case Law IBFD, **117–119, 127**
Her Majesty the Queen in Right of Canada v. Edelson and Others, Supreme Court, 3 June 1997, 131 ILR 279, **78**
Kuwait Airways Corporation v Republic of Iraq, Supreme Court of Canada, 21 October 2010, 174 ILR 303, **83, 85**

Germany

Central Bank of Nigeria Case, Provincial Court of Frankfurt, 2 December 1975, 65 ILR 131, **101**
Claim Against the Empire of Iran Case, Federal Republic of Germany, Federal Constitutional Court, 30 April 1963, 45 ILR *(1973)* 57, **78, 81–83**
National Iranian Oil Company Revenues from Oil Sales Case, Federal Constitutional Court, 12 April 1983, 65 ILR 215, **99**

Table of Cases

Greece

Kingdom of Greece v. Gamet, Court of Cassation, 8 June 1957, 24 ILR 209, **78**
Prefecture of Voiotia v. Germany, Court of Cassation, 4 May 2000, 129 ILR 514, **78**

France

Conseil d'État, 9 November 2015, Case 370054, Tax Treaty Case Law IBFD, **127**

India

ITO (IT) v. Rameshkumar Goenka, Income Tax Appellate Tribunal of Mumbai, India, I.T.A. No. 3562/Mum/2009, **121, 123**
Green Emirate Shipping & Travels Ltd v. Assistant Director of Income Tax, Income-tax Appellate Tribunal, 30 November 2005, (2006) 99 TTJ Mum 988, **128**

Italy

Libyan Arab Socialist People's Jamahiriya v. Rossbeton Srl, Court of Cassation, 25 May 1989, 87 ILR 63, **99**
Ministry of Finance v. Association of Italian Knights of the Order of Malta, Italian Court of Cassation, 3 May 1978, 65 ILR 320, **92**
United States Government v. Bracale Bicchierai, Court of Appeal of Napels, 18 November 1968, 65 ILR 273, **78**

Netherlands

Gerechtshof 's-Hertogenbosch, 12 May 2000, No. 97/0437, BNB 2001/426, **8**
Gerechtshof 's-Hertogenbosch, 12 October 2017, No. 14/00640-00645, V-N 2017/57.9, **186, 249**
Gerechtshof 's-Hertogenbosch, 24 November 2017, No. 16/03761-03770, V-N Vandaag 2017/2851, **249**
Hoge Raad, 18 December 1991, No. 27 362, BNB 1992/288, **244**
Hoge Raad, 28 February 2001, No. 35 557, BNB 2001/195, **118**
Hoge Raad, 5 September 2003, No. 37 651, BNB 2003/379, **109**
Hoge Raad, 2 March 2007, No. 42.144, BNB 2007/240, **8**
Hoge Raad, 4 December 2009, No. 07/10383, BNB 2010/177, **115, 127, 129, 143**
Hoge Raad, 15 November 2013, No. 12/01866, BNB 2014/20, **179, 249, 254**
Hoge Raad, 22 November 2013, No. 13/016222, BNB 2014/30, **8**
Hoge Raad, 10 July 2015, No. 14/03956, BNB 2015/203, **244, 249**
Hoge Raad, 3 March 2017, No. 16/03954, BNB 2017/86, **244, 249, 250**
Hoge Raad, 3 March 2017, No. 16/03955, BNB 2017/87, **249, 250**
Opinion of the Dutch Advocate General P. Wattel, 9 November 2016, BNB 2017/86, **249**

Portugal

Brazilian Embassy Employee Case, Supreme Court, 11 May 1984, 116 ILR 625, **78**

Sweden

Korkein hallinto-oikeus, Supreme Administrative Court, 22 December 2004, KHO 2004:111, Tax Treaty Case Law IBFD, **116**
Regeringsrätten, Supreme Administrative Court, 2 October 1996, RÅ 1996 ref 84 (6301-1994), Tax Treaty Case Law IBFD, **116, 123**

Switzerland

Kuwait v. X (1994) *Revue Suisse de droit international et européen,* 1995, Vol. 5, **100, 132**
Libyan Arab Socialist People's Jamahiriya v. Actimon SA, Swiss Federal Tribunal, 24 April 1985, 82 ILR 30, **101**

United Kingdom

AIG Capital Partners Inc. and Another v. Republic of Kazakhstan, High Court, 20 October 2005, 129 ILR 589, **100, 101**
Congreso Del Partido (1981) 64 ILR 307, **81, 83, 86**
Jones v. Ministry of the Interior of the Kingdom of Saudi Arabia and Another, House of Lords, 14 June 2006, 129 ILR 713, **78, 99**
Holland v. Lampen-Wolfe, House of Lords, 20 July 2000, 119 ILR 367, **78**

United States

Ohio v. Helvering (1934) 292 U.S. 360, **82**
Saudi Arabia and Others v. Nelson, United States Supreme Court, 23 March 1993, 100 ILR 545, **82, 86**
The Schooner Exchange v. McFaddon & Others (1813) 11 U.S. Reports 116, **80**

Table of Treaties and Other Instruments

Agreement between the EFTA States on the Establishment of a Surveillance Authority and a Court of Justice (Surveillance and Court Agreement) (1994), **160, 196, 213**

Agreement Between the Federal Republic of Germany and the United Arab Emirates for the Avoidance of Double Taxation and of Tax Evasion with respect to Taxes on Income (1 July 2010), Treaties IBFD, **46**

Agreement Between the Government of Georgia and the Government of the United Arab Emirates for the Avoidance of Double Taxation and the Prevention of Fiscal Evasion with respect to Taxes on Income and on Capital (25 November 2010), Treaties IBFD, **45**

Agreement Between the Government of the Kingdom of the Netherlands and the Government of the State of Kuwait for the Avoidance of Double Taxation and the Prevention of Fiscal Evasion with respect to Taxes on Income (29 May 2001), Treaties IBFD, **298**

Agreement Between the Government of the Kingdom of the Netherlands and the Government of the People's Republic of China for the Avoidance of Double Taxation and the Prevention of Fiscal Evasion with respect to Taxes on Income (31 May 2013), Treaties IBFD, **302**

Agreement Between the Government of New Zealand and the Government of the United Arab Emirates for the Avoidance of Double Taxation and the Prevention of Fiscal Evasion with respect to Taxes on Income (22 September 2003), Treaties IBFD, **45, 46**

Agreement Between the Government of the Republic of Mauritius and the Government of the United Arab Emirates for the Avoidance of Double Taxation and the Prevention of Fiscal Evasion with respect to Taxes on Income (18 September 2006), Treaties IBFD, **45, 134**

Agreement Between the Kingdom of the Netherlands and the Sultanate of Oman for the Avoidance of Double Taxation and the Prevention of Fiscal Evasion with respect to Taxes on Income (5 October 2009), Treaties IBFD, **300**

Agreement Between Mongolia and the United Arab Emirates for the Avoidance of Double Taxation and the Prevention of Fiscal Evasion with respect to Taxes on Income (21 February 2001), Treaties IBFD, **45**

Agreement Between the Government of the Russian Federation and the Government of the United Arab Emirates on Taxation of Income from Investments of the

Contracting States or their Financial and Investment Institutions (7 December 2011), Treaties IBFD, **46**

Agreement on the European Economic Area, Official Journal of the European Union, Vol. 37, L 1, 3 January 1994, **7**

Convention Between the Government of the Kingdom of the Netherlands and the Government of the Kingdom of Bahrain for the Avoidance of Double Taxation and the Prevention of Fiscal Evasion with respect to Taxes on Income (16 April 2008), Treaties IBFD, **133**

Convention Between the Government of the Republic of Azerbaijan and the Government of the United Arab Emirates for the Avoidance of Double Taxation with respect to Taxes on Income and on Capital (20 November 2006), Treaties IBFD, **45**

Convention Between the Kingdom of the Netherlands and the United Arab Emirates for the Avoidance of Double Taxation and the Prevention of Fiscal Evasion with respect to Taxes on Income (8 May 2007), Treaties IBFD, **298**

Convention Between the Kingdom of Norway and the Kingdom of the Netherlands for the Avoidance of Double Taxation and the Prevention of Fiscal Evasion with respect to Taxes on Income and on Capital (12 January 1990), Treaties IBFD, **301**

Convention Between the Kingdom of Spain and the United Arab Emirates for the Avoidance of Double Taxation and the Prevention of Fiscal Evasion with respect to Taxes on Income and on Capital (5 March 2006), Treaties IBFD, **46**

Convention for the Protection of Human Rights and Fundamental Freedoms (Council of Europe, Rome, 4.XI.1950), **7**

Council Directive 2015/121 of 27 January 2015 amending Directive 2011/96/EU on the common system of taxation applicable in the case of parent companies and subsidiaries of different Member States, Official Journal of the European Union, Vol. 58, L 21, 28 January 2015, **156**

Council Directive 2011/96/EU of 30 November 2011 on the common system of taxation applicable in the case of parent companies and subsidiaries of different Member States, Official Journal of the European Union, Vol. 54, L 345, 29 December 2011, as amended by Council Directive (EU) 2015/121 of 27 January 2015, Official Journal of the European Union, Vol. 58, L 21, 28 January 2015, **156**

Council Directive 2003/49/EC of 3 June 2003 on a common system of taxation applicable to interest and royalty payments made between associated companies of different Member States, Official Journal of the European Union, Vol. 46, L 157, 29 June 2003, **156**

Council Directive 88/361 EEC of 24 June 1988 for the implementation of Article 67 of the Treaty, Official Journal of the European Union, Vol. 31, L 178, 8 July 1988, **168**

Council Regulation (EU) 2015/1589 of 13 July 2015 laying down detailed rules for the application of Article 108 of the Treaty on the Functioning of the European Union, Official Journal of the European Union, Vol. 58, L 248, 24 September 2015, **196**

Commission Regulation (EU) No 1407/2013 of 18 December 2013 on the application of Articles 107 and 108 of the Treaty on the Functioning of the European Union to de minimis aid, Official Journal of the European Union, Vol. 56, L 352, 24 December 2013, **195, 213**

Table of Treaties and Other Instruments

Commission Regulation No 651/2014 of 17 June 2014 declaring certain categories of aid compatible with the internal market in application of Articles 107 and 108 of the Treaty, Official Journal of the European Union, Vol. 57, L 187, 26 June 2014, **196**

Commission Regulation (EU) 2017/1084 of 14 June 2017 amending Regulation (EU) No 651/2014 as regards aid for port and airport infrastructure, notification thresholds for aid for culture and heritage conservation and for aid for sport and multifunctional recreational infrastructures, and regional operating aid schemes for outermost regions and amending Regulation (EU) No 702/2014 as regards the calculation of eligible costs, Official Journal of the European Union, Vol. 60, L 156, 20 June 2017, **196**

Commission Notice on the notion of State aid as referred to in Article 107(1) TFEU, Official Journal of the European Union, Vol. 59, C 262, 19 July 2016, **197, 198, 201–203**

Proposal for a Council Directive on a Common Corporate Tax Base, 25 October 2016, COM(2016) 685 final, **157**

Proposal for a Council Directive on a Common Consolidated Corporate Tax Base, 25 October 2016, COM(2016) 683 final, **157**

Draft articles on Jurisdictional Immunities of States and Their Property, with commentaries (1991), **77, 93**

Draft Double Taxation Convention on Income and Capital, OECD, Paris, 1963, **110**

European Union, *Consolidated version of the Treaty on the Functioning of the European Union,* Official Journal of the European Union, Vol. 55, C 326, 26 October 2012, **155, 156**

Final Act and Declarations of the Intergovernmental Conferences on the European Union, 7 February 1992, Declaration on nationality of a Member State, Official Journal of the European Union, Vol. 35, C 191, 29 July 1992, **163**

General Assembly resolution 174 (II), *Establishment of an International Law Commission,* A/RES/174(II) (21 November 1947)

Article 1(1), **79**

International Covenant on Civil and Political Rights (General Assembly of the United Nations, 16 December 1966), **7**

OECD (2017), *Model Tax Convention on Income and on Capital.*

Article 1, **6, 47, 96, 103, 110**

Article 3, **109, 111**

Article 4, **11, 18, 48, 114, 129, 302**

Article 10, **11, 44, 135, 136, 147, 284**

Article 11, **11, 44, 136, 147, 284**

Article 13, **11, 137**

Article 24, **11, 138, 146, 148, 150, 151**

Protocol Amending the Convention Between the Kingdom of Norway and the Kingdom of the Netherlands for the Avoidance of Double Taxation and the Prevention of Fiscal Evasion with respect to Taxes on Income and on Capital (23 April 2013), Treaties IBFD, **301**

UN General Assembly, *United Nations Convention on Jurisdictional Immunities of States and Their Property,* 2 December 2004, A/RES/59/38.

Table of Treaties and Other Instruments

Article 2(2), **83**
Article 10, **83**
Article 19(c), **97, 99, 206**
Article 30, **78**
United Nations, *United Nations Double Taxation Convention between Developed and Developing Countries* (2001), ST/ESA/PAD/SER.E/21.
Article 3(1)(b), **111, 113**
Article 3(1)(f)(ii), **111**
Article 4(1), **114, 117, 120, 121, 125, 130, 143, 144, 148, 150, 151, 284**
United Nations, *Vienna Convention on Consular Relations*, 24 April 1963, 596 U.N.T.S. 261.
Article 49(b), **119**
Article 49(d), **119**
United Nations, *Vienna Convention on Diplomatic Relations*, 18 May 1961, 500 U.N.T.S. 95.
Article 34(b), **119**
Article 34(d), **119**

Table of National Instruments

Australia

Foreign States Immunities Act 1985.
Section 22, **85**
Section 3(1), **85**

Canada

State Immunity Act 1985.
Section 2, **85**
Section 12(4), **101**

Netherlands

Burgerlijk Wetboek (Civil Code).
Article 2:1, **113**
Article 2:3, **113**
Wet op de dividendbelasting 1965 (Dividend Withholding Tax Act 1965).
Article 1, **252**
Article 4, **253–254, 259, 263**
Article 10, **254–257**
Article 10a, **254–258**
Article 11a, **244, 252**
Wet op de vennootschapsbelasting 1969 (Corporate Income Tax Act 1969).
Article 2, **242**
Article 3, **195, 213**
Article 5, **298**
Article 6a, **245, 246**
Article 8e, **248, 255, 256, 259, 260, 262**
Article 8f, **248, 255, 256, 259, 260, 262**
Article 13, **253**

Table of National Instruments

Article 13aa, **253**
Article 17, **242, 243, 247**
Article 17a, **242, 243, 247**
Article 18, **245**
Article 25, **252**
Article 28, **244, 249**

Norway

Government Pension Fund Act (no. 123 of 21 December 2005).
Section 2, **29**
Section 3, **30**
Management Mandate for the Government Pension Fund Global.
Section 1-2(1), **30**

Pakistan

The State Immunity Ordinance No. VI of 1981.
Section 15(4), **101**

Singapore

State Immunity Act 1979.
Section 16(1)-(2), **84**
Section 16(4), **101**

South Africa

Foreign States Immunities Act 1981.
Section 2(1)(i), **84**
Section 15(3), **101**

United Kingdom

INTM155010 – Sovereign and Crown Immunity, **88**
INTM368520 – DT Applications and Claims: Crown Immunity, Sovereign Immunity and Diplomatic Privilege, **88**
INTM162020 – UK residents with foreign income or gains: double taxation relief – claims and procedures – 'Subject to tax'., **123**
State Immunity Act 1978.
Section 14(1), **85**
Section 14(2), **85**

United States

Internal Revenue Code.
Section 892, **88, 89**
Section 892(a)(2)(B), **89**
Temporary Treasury Regulations (1988).
Subchapter A, § 1.892-2T(a)(2), **89, 132**
Subchapter A, § 1.892-3T, **89**
Subchapter A, § 1.892-4T(b), **89**
Subchapter A, § 1.892-4T(c)(1)(i), **90**
Subchapter A, § 1.892-4T(c)(1)(iii), **90**

Miscellaneous

Abu Dhabi Investment Authority

Abu Dhabi Investment Authority (ADIA). *The Santiago Principles*. Online at www.adia.ae/en/Governance/Santiago_Principles_more.aspx, **32**

Abu Dhabi Investment Authority (ADIA). *2016 Review (A Legacy in Motion)*. Online at www.adia.ae/En/pr/2016/pdf/ADIA_2016_Review_01_FULL.pdf, **32**

Abu Dhabi Investment Authority (ADIA). *2013 Review*. Online at www.adia.ae/En/pr/Annual_Review_Website_2013.pdf, **32**

Abu Dhabi Investment Authority (ADIA). *2010 Review (Prudent Global Growth*. Online at www.adia.ae/En/pr/Annual_Review_Website_2010.pdf, **31, 32**

International Law Commission

International Law Commission, *Yearbook of the International Law Commission 1991*, **81, 101**

International Law Commission, *Yearbook of the International Law Commission 1984*, **80, 93**

International Law Commission, *Yearbook of the International Law Commission 1982*, **81**

International Law Commission, *Yearbook of the International Law Commission 1980*, **77, 79**

Sixth Report on Jurisdictional Immunities of States and Their Property, by Mr. Sompong Sucharitkul, Special Rapporteur, Doc. A/CN.4/376, published in *Yearbook of the International Law Commission 1984*, Vol. II, Part I, **80, 93**

Fourth Report on Jurisdictional Immunities of States and Their Property, by Mr. Sompong Sucharitkul, Special Rapporteur, Doc A/CN.4/357, published in *Yearbook of the International Law Commission 1982*, Vol. II, Part I, **81**

Preliminary Report on Jurisdictional Immunities of States and Their Property, by Mr. Sompong Sucharitkul, Special Rapporteur, Doc. A/CN.4/323, published in *Yearbook of the International Law Commission 1979*, Vol. II, Part I, **77, 79**

International Monetary Fund

International Monetary Fund, *Global Financial Stability Report: Financial Market Turbulence: Causes, Consequences, and Policies* (October, 2007), **19**

Miscellaneous

International Monetary Fund, *Balance of Payments and International Investment Position Management*, 6th edn., (Washington D.C.: International Monetary Fund, 2009), **21, 24**

International Monetary Fund (2008), *Communiqué of the International Monetary and Financial Committee of the Board of Governors of the International Monetary Fund*, **15**

International Monetary Fund (2008), Monetary and Capital Markets Policy Development and Review Departments, *'Sovereign Wealth Funds – A Work Agenda'*, **20, 21**

International Working Group of Sovereign Wealth Funds

International Working Group of Sovereign Wealth Funds (April, 2009), *'Kuwait Declaration': Establishment of the International Forum of Sovereign Wealth Funds'*, **15**

International Working Group of Sovereign Wealth Funds (October, 2008), *Sovereign Wealth Funds: Generally Accepted Principles and Practices 'Santiago Principles'*. Online at http://www.ecgi.org/codes/documents/iwg_santiago_principles_oct2008_en.pdf, **14, 15, 19, 25, 27, 29, 298**

International Working Group of Sovereign Wealth Funds (May, 2008), *'International Working Group of Sovereign Wealth Funds is Established to Facilitate Work on Voluntary Principles'*, Press Release No. 08/97, **14**

Organisation for Economic Co-operation and Development (OECD)

OECD (2016), *Discussion Draft on Changes to the OECD Model Tax Convention Concerning the Treaty Residence of Pension Funds*. Online at http://www.oecd.org/tax/treaties/discussion-draft-treaty-residence-pension-funds.pdf, **48**

OECD (2015), *Addressing the Tax Challenges of the Digital Economy, Action 1 – 2015 Final Report*, OECD/G20 Base Erosion and Profit Shifting Project, OECD Publishing, Paris. Online at http://www.oecd.org/tax/addressing-the-tax-challenges-of-the-digital-economy-action-1-2015-final-report-9789264241046-en.htm, **60**

OECD (2015), *Preventing the Granting of Treaty Benefits in Inappropriate Circumstances, Action 6 – 2015 Final Report*, OECD/G20 Base Erosion and Profit Shifting Project, OECD Publishing, Paris. Online at http://www.oecd.org/tax/preventing-the-granting-of-treaty-benefits-in-inappropriate-circumstances-action-6-2015-final-report-9789264241695-en.htm, **150**

OECD, Commentaries on the Articles of the Model Tax Convention 2017, **48**

OECD (2010), *The Granting of Treaty Benefits with Respect to the Income of Collective Investment Vehicles*. Online at https://www.oecd.org/tax/treaties/45359261.pdf, **41, 47**

OECD Working Papers on International Investment, No. 2010/2. Online at http://www.oecd.org/daf/inv/investment-policy/WP-2010_2.pdf, **96**

OECD (2009), *Discussion Draft on the Application of Tax Treaties to State-Owned Entities, Including Sovereign Wealth Funds*. Online at www.oecd.org/tax/treaties/44080490.pdf, **4, 107**

OECD (2009), 'Foreign Government-Controlled Investors and Recipient Country Investment Policy: A Scoping Paper'. Online at https://www.oecd.org/daf/inv/investment-policy/42022469.pdf, **14, 19**

OECD (2008), *Sovereign Wealth Funds and Recipient Country Policies*. Online at https://www.oecd.org/investment/investment-policy/40408735.pdf, **69**

OECD (2001), *Tax and the Economy: A Comparative Assessment of OECD Countries*, Tax Policy Studies No. 6, Paris, **49**

OECD (1998), *Harmful Tax Competition: An Emerging Global Issue*, OECD Publishing, Paris, **67**

Temasek

Temasek. *Review 2016 (Generational Investing)*. Online at https://www.temasek.com.sg/content/dam/temasek-corporate/our-financials/investor-library/annual-review/en-tr-thumbnail-and-pdf/TR2016_Singles.pdf, **31**

Temasek, *Review 2014 (Our journey has just begun)*, **31**

Temasek. *Review 2012 (Extending Pathways)*. Online at https://www.temasek.com.sg/content/dam/temasek-corporate/our-financials/investor-library/annual-review/en-tr-thumbnail-and-pdf/TR2012_Eng.pdf, **34, 123, 125**

Temasek. *Review 2011 (Building for tomorrow)*. Online at https://www.temasek.com.sg/content/dam/temasek-corporate/our-financials/investor-library/annual-review/en-tr-thumbnail-and-pdf/TR11%20Eng_Final_2011-07-06_(low%20res).pdf, **30**

Temasek. *Review 2004 (Investing in value)*. Online at https://www.temasek.com.sg/content/dam/temasek-corporate/our-financials/investor-library/annual-review/en-tr-thumbnail-and-pdf/TR04_Secured.pdf, **30**

Other

African Development Bank (2013), *The boom in African Sovereign Wealth Funds*. Online at www.afdb.org, **13**

American Law Institute, *Restatement of the Law Third: The Foreign Relations Law of the United States*, Vol. I (St. Paul, Minn. American Law Institute Publishers, 1987), **62, 97**

Australian Government (April, 2011), *Options to codify the tax treatment of sovereign investments*. Online at archive.treasury.gov.au/documents/2017/PDF/Proposals_Paper.pdf, **87**

Australian Government (November, 2009), *Greater certainty for Sovereign Investment*. Online at archive.treasury.gov.au/documents/1667/PDF/Consultation_paper.pdf, **87**

Miscellaneous

Australian Government (June, 2010), *Greater certainty for sovereign investment – the framework rules*. Online at archive.treasury.gov.au/documents/1842/PDF/Sovereign_Immunity_Consultation_paper.pdf, **87**

Besluit Staatssecretaris van Financiën, 10 March 2008, *CPP2008/291M*, **246**

China Investment Corporation. *Annual Report 2015*. Online at http://www.china-inv.cn/wps/wcm/connect/62e332fc-8ddd-4eb9-b21c-b5cc3585e82a/CICAnnualReport2015.pdf?MOD=AJPERES&CACHEID=62e332fc-8ddd-4eb9-b21c-b5cc3585e82a, **33**

China Investment Corporation. *Annual Report 2016*, **34**

Commissie van Advies inzake Volkenrechtelijke Vraagstukken, *Advies inzake de United Nations Convention on Jurisdictional Immunities of States and their Property*, Advies No. 17, Den Haag, 19 mei 2006, **82**

Council of Europe, *Local authority competences in Europe (situation in 2007)*, Study of the European Committee on Local and Regional Democracy, **113**

Code of Conduct for Business Taxation, Annex to the Conclusions of the ECOFIN Council Meeting on 1 December 1997 concerning taxation policy (98/C 2/01), Official Journal of the European Union, Vol. 41, C 2, 6 January 1998, **160**

Code of Conduct Group, Council of the European Union, *Report on the Code of Conduct (Business Taxation)*, SN 4901/99, 23 November 1999, **161**

Council Conclusions of 9 March 1998 concerning the establishment of the Code of Conduct Group (business taxation) (98/C 99/01), Official Journal of the European Union, Vol. 41, C 99, 1 April 1998, **161**

ECOFIN Report to the European Council on Tax issues, 10397/17, 16 June 2017, **217**

European Commission, SA.25338 (E 3/2008, ex CP 115/2004 and CP 120/2006) – The Netherlands Corporate Tax, **202, 204**

Exemption of Dutch Public Enterprises, Letter of 2 May 2013 to Zijne Excellentie de Heer Frans TIMMERMANS, **35**

House of Commons, Treasury Committee, *Principles of tax policy*, Eight Report of Session 2010-11, HC 753. Online at publications.parliament.uk/pa/cm201011/cmselect/cmtreasy/753/753.pdf, **50, 51**

Joint Committee on Taxation, *Economic and U.S. Income Tax Issues Raised by Sovereign Wealth Fund Investment in the United States* (June, 2008), JCX-49-08, Appendix One: Foreign Law Tax Treatment of Government, **4, 14, 16, 46, 87–89, 96**

Investment, Australia, A-9 – A-10. JCX-49-08. Online at www.jct.gov/x-49-08.pdf, **87**

Norwegian Government, *Government Pension Fund Global Management Mandate* (translated form the Norwegian version). Online at www.regjeringen.no/globalassets/upload/fin/statens-pensjonsfond/gpfg-management-mandate-14-april-2015.pdf, **29**

Norges Bank Investment Management, *About the Fund*. Online at www.nbim.no/en/the-fund/about-the-fund/, **29, 30**

Parliamentary Debates, House of Commons, 28 April 2008, column 143W, **88**

Preqin, *The 2014 Preqin Sovereign Wealth Fund Review*, **26**

Regeerakkoord 2017-2021, *Vertrouwen in de toekomst* (10 October 2017), **237, 253**

Report of the Royal Commission on Taxation, *Vol. 2: The use of the tax system to achieve economic and social objectives* (1966), **70, 71**
Summary of Discussions at the Seventh Meeting of Working Party No. 1 on Double Taxation, 11 April 1973, DAF/CFA/WP1(73)5, **120**
SWFI, *Sovereign Wealth Enterprise (SWE)*. Online at www.swfinstitute.org/statistics-research/sovereign-wealth-enterprise-swe/, **14, 26**
SWFI, *SWF Rankings*. Online at www.swfinstitute.org/sovereign-wealth-fund-rankings/, **2, 7, 13, 26, 31, 32, 34, 286**
Treasurer (2016), *Australia's Foreign Investment Policy*. Online at firb.gov.au/files/2015/09/Australias-Foreign-Investment-Policy-2016-2017.pdf, **68**
Eerste Kamer der Staten-Generaal, 2006-2007, 30 533, No. C, **245**
Eerste Kamer der Staten-Generaal, 2014-2015, 34 003, No. D., **240, 244**
Staten-Generaal, 2012-2013, 33 731, No. 1, **302**
Tweede Kamer der Staten-Generaal, 1989-1990, 20 701, No. 9, **244**
Tweede Kamer der Staten-Generaal, 2000-2001, 27 466, No. 3, **244**
Tweede Kamer der Staten-Generaal, 2003-2004, 29 210, No. 3, **246**
Tweede Kamer der Staten-Generaal, 2008-2009, 31 591, No. A/1, **134, 300**
Tweede Kamer der Staten-Generaal, 2008–2009, 31 764, No. 7, **121**
Tweede Kamer der Staten-Generaal, 2009-2010, 32 346, No. 3, **150, 238, 299**
Tweede Kamer der Staten-Generaal, 2011-2012, 33 003, No. 3, **68, 238, 255**
Tweede Kamer der Staten-Generaal, 2012-2013, 33 718, No. 3, **302**
Tweede Kamer der Staten-Generaal, 2014-2015, 34 003, No. 3, **243, 248**
Tweede Kamer der Staten-Generaal, 2014-2015, 34 220, No. 3, **255**
Notitie Fiscaal Verdragsbeleid 2011, Tweede Kamer der Staten-Generaal, 2010-2011, 25 087, No. 7, **3, 42, 50, 51, 70, 150, 236, 237, 297**
Sovereign Wealth Funds; gezamenlijke notitie ministeries van Financiën en Economische Zaken, Tweede Kamer der Staten-Generaal, 2007-2008, 31 350, No. 1, **70, 238**
Uitgangspunten van het beleid op het terrein van het internationaal fiscaal (verdragen)recht, Tweede Kamer der Staten-Generaal, 1997-1998, 25 087, No. 4, **237, 297**
United Nations Conference on Trade and Development, *Bilateral Investment Treaties 1995-2006: Trends in Investment Rulemaking* (UN, 2007). Online at unctad.org/en/docs/iteiia20065_en.pdf, **9**

Index

A

Ability-to-pay theory, 60–62, 145, 222, 277
Abu Dhabi Investment Authority (ADIA), 28, 29, 31–32, 134, 299
Abu Dhabi Investment Council (ADIC)
acta jure gestionis, 81, 83, 91, 93
acta jure imperii, 81, 83, 85, 91, 93
agency problem, 31
ADIA. *See* Abu Dhabi Investment Authority (ADIA)
AIG Capital Partners v. Kazakhstan case, 100–102
Association of Italian Knights of the Order of Malta (AIKOM), 92, 93
Australian Taxation Office (ATO), 87
Australia's Future Fund, 22

B

Benefit principle, 61–65, 72, 73, 147, 223, 224, 230, 239, 277–280, 290
Benefit theory, 60–62, 145, 222, 277
Bilateral investment treaty (BIT), 9
Body corporate, 85, 110–114, 242, 302
Business enterprise, 242, 243, 247, 250, 251, 259

C

Capital export neutrality (CEN), 51–54, 143, 152, 220–221, 226, 231, 232, 236, 237, 274–275, 285, 286, 291–292, 295
Capital gains article, 11, 108, 137
Capital import neutrality (CIN), 53–56, 76, 143–146, 148, 151, 152, 221–223, 230, 236, 237, 274–276, 284–286, 289–290, 295
Capital ownership neutrality (CON), 52, 56–59, 274, 276
Cassa di Risparmio di Firenze SpA case, 199, 203, 212
CEN. *See* Capital export neutrality (CEN)
Central banks, 16, 17, 19, 24, 25, 27–29, 37, 87, 99–102, 133, 173, 205, 272, 273, 298–302
China Investment Corporation (CIC), 17, 26–29, 33–34, 123–124, 303
CIN. *See* Capital import neutrality (CIN)
Code of Conduct for Business Taxation, 160–161
Collective investment vehicles (CIVs), 3, 5, 39, 41–43, 45, 47, 55, 63, 69, 129, 143, 150, 179, 185–187, 191, 198–201, 203, 213, 244–246, 249–250, 270, 271, 284

Comparability, 11, 162, 176-193, 202, 208-210, 214, 221, 222, 224, 225, 228, 229, 247, 252, 258, 264, 287-289
Comprehensive tax liability, 119-121, 125, 150, 284
CON. *See* Capital ownership neutrality (CON)
Congregación de Escuelas Pías Provincia Betania case, 201, 208, 209, 211
Contingent pension reserve funds, 21-22
Crown Forest Industries case, 117
Customary international law, 6, 75, 76, 78, 86, 92-97, 102-104, 130, 206, 240, 266, 282, 283

D

D. case, 181, 209
De minimis rule, 195
Development funds, 21
Dividend article, 111, 254, 259, 297-303

E

ECHR. *See* European Convention on Human Rights (ECHR)
ECSI. *See* European Convention on State Immunity (ECSI)
EEA. *See* European Economic Area (EEA)
EFTA. *See* European Free Trade Association (EFTA)
Emerging Markets Series case, 175, 179, 180, 186, 189
Enforcement measures, 77, 97, 98, 104, 206, 282
Equity, 5, 9, 10, 20, 31-35, 39, 47, 49-51, 60-67, 69, 71-73, 75, 76, 87, 102-104, 107, 108, 140-152, 155, 156, 218-227, 230-232, 239, 266, 270-271, 274, 277-280, 283-286, 290-293, 295
European Convention on Human Rights (ECHR), 7
European Convention on State Immunity (ECSI), 77, 81
European Economic Area (EEA), 7, 11, 48, 155, 156, 159-160, 162-176, 184, 189-193, 196-198, 210, 213, 215, 220, 222, 225, 227, 228, 230, 232, 241, 247, 252-257, 259-264, 286-289, 291, 295
European Free Trade Association (EFTA), 159, 160, 162, 163, 165-168, 172-174, 177, 195, 196, 198, 215, 228, 230, 253, 256, 287, 289, 295

F

Fairness, 5, 10, 39, 49-51, 60-66, 72, 73, 102-103, 145-149, 155, 156, 218-227, 239, 266-267, 270, 274, 277-280, 292
Fineco Asset Management case, 199, 200, 207, 214
Fiscale beleggingsinstelling (FBI), 244-245, 249, 250, 252
Freedom of capital movement, 7, 11, 28, 37, 155, 156, 158, 160, 162-195, 222, 228, 238, 241, 255, 256, 259, 263, 273, 286, 287, 295
Freedom of establishment, 7, 11, 28, 37, 155, 156, 158, 160, 162-195, 199, 228, 273, 286, 287
Full tax liability, 117, 118, 120, 121, 150, 284
Fundamental freedoms, 7, 48, 155, 157-159, 162, 184, 186, 189-192, 202, 208, 210, 214, 220-226, 228, 230, 231, 252, 264, 286, 287, 289-291

Index

Fundamental (legal) values, 71, 72
Future Generations Reserve Fund of Bahrain, 124

G

Government Pension Fund Global (Norway) (GPFG), 17, 26, 27, 29–30, 166, 302

H

Haribo and Salinen case, 184, 228, 288
Hein Persche case, 178, 179, 187, 188
Horizontal comparability, 177, 181–184, 190–193, 209, 210, 222, 224, 225, 228, 229, 247, 288
Horizontal discrimination, 147, 148, 150, 158, 182–184, 191, 192, 210, 220, 222, 225–228, 231, 232, 241, 247, 248, 252, 264, 265, 287, 288, 290, 291
Horizontal equity, 60, 277

I

ICCPR. *See* International Covenant on Civil and Political Rights (ICCPR)
IFSWF. *See* International Forum of Sovereign Wealth Funds (IFSWF)
ILC. *See* International Law Commission (ILC)
IMF. *See* International Monetary Fund (IMF)
Immunity from jurisdiction, 10, 77, 80–83
Immunity from measures of constraint, 10, 76, 77, 83–84, 97–102, 206, 266
Immunity from taxation, 10, 88, 90, 98, 102–104, 139, 282

Indirect beneficiaries, 198, 213–215, 230, 265, 289
Instrumentalism, 66–70, 72
Integral part of the State, 126, 131–134, 139, 151, 284
Interest article, 11, 108, 136
Interest & Royalties Directive, 7, 11, 44, 156, 159, 160, 215–217, 221–224, 226, 227, 230–232, 241, 287, 289–291
Internal Revenue Code (IRC), 88–89
International attractiveness, 5, 9–11, 39, 46, 47, 51, 66–73, 75–76, 91, 102–104, 107, 108, 134, 140–150, 152, 155, 156, 191, 211, 213, 218–227, 231–233, 235–241, 252, 263, 264, 266, 267, 270, 271, 274, 279, 280, 283, 286, 291–293, 295
International Covenant on Civil and Political Rights (ICCPR), 7
International Forum of Sovereign Wealth Funds (IFSWF), 15
International Law Commission (ILC), 10–11, 79, 93, 101
International Monetary Fund (IMF), 10, 14, 18–22
International tax neutrality, 51, 71, 274
International Working Group of Sovereign Wealth Funds (IWG), 14, 15, 18–24, 36, 272
Inter-nation equity, 60, 64–66, 71, 148–149, 151, 152, 224–226, 231, 277–279, 284–286, 290–291, 295
Interpretation rule, 108–110, 115–116, 125, 160
Inter-taxpayer equity, 60–65, 72, 73, 145–148, 151, 152, 222–224, 230–231, 239, 266–267, 277, 279, 280, 284–286, 290, 292, 295
IRC. *See* Internal Revenue Code (IRC)

341

Index

J

Justification grounds, 11, 193, 194, 203, 241

K

Kuwait Investment Authority (KIA), 16, 28, 100, 132, 298

L

Legal persons of private law, 34, 41, 113, 114, 133, 151, 185, 242–244, 248, 249, 251, 252, 254–256, 258, 260, 263, 265, 284
Legal persons of public law, 34, 41, 113, 114, 133, 151, 185, 242–244, 248, 251, 252, 254–256, 258, 260, 263, 265, 284
Level-playing field, 36–38, 41, 204, 244, 248, 273
Liable to tax test, 112, 115, 116, 125, 128–130, 143, 145, 151, 284

M

Memorandum on Dutch tax treaty policy (2011), 150, 236, 237, 239, 297
Miljoen, X and *Société Générale* case, 256
Most-favoured-nation (MFN), 8, 9

N

National Fund of Kazakhstan, 100
National treatment (NT), 9, 183, 190, 263
New Zealand Superannuation Fund, 22
Nomenclature, 168–170
Non-discrimination article, 11, 108, 151, 284
Not-for-profit organization, 43, 48, 185, 188–189, 192, 246–247, 250–251, 302
NT. *See* National treatment (NT)

O

Objectively comparable, 11, 178, 180–183, 185–193, 221, 222, 224–225, 228, 241, 247–249, 251, 252, 258, 263, 265, 287–288
Omani Investment Fund, 301
Opinio juri, 94–97, 103, 282

P

Parent-Subsidiary Directive, 7, 11, 44, 156, 159, 160, 215–217, 221–224, 226, 227, 230–232, 241, 253, 287, 289–291
Pension funds, 3, 5, 17, 19, 21, 22, 24, 39, 42–43, 45, 48, 53, 63, 69, 114, 129, 135, 136, 143, 150, 172, 179, 180, 185, 187–188, 191–192, 236, 238, 246, 250, 253–255, 270, 271, 284, 299, 301, 302
Personal sovereignty, 79, 80, 84, 93
Pool of assets, 27–29, 37, 101–102, 113, 133, 151, 166, 173, 176, 247, 272, 273, 284
Procedural policy principles, 49, 50, 274
Public enterprise, 203–204, 240, 242–244, 247–249, 251, 255

R

Reciprocity, 6, 46, 48, 94, 109, 115, 131, 191, 192
Redistribution, 61, 65, 66, 148, 203, 224, 225, 231, 277, 278, 290
Reserve investment corporations, 21
Resident article, 11, 108, 298–302
Reverse discrimination, 150, 161–162, 209–210, 220, 223, 226, 228, 231, 247, 264, 265, 287, 290, 291
Riskin & Timmermans case, 181–183, 209, 228, 288

Index

S

SAFE Investment Company, 303
Santiago Principles, 14–15, 25
Savings funds, 20
Selectivity test, 202–203, 209, 214, 222, 225, 228, 264, 287
Social security reserve fund (SSRF), 21, 22, 24
Sopora case, 183, 184, 210, 224, 228, 288
Sovereign immunity, 3–6, 10, 11, 45, 46, 49, 69, 75–105, 130, 191, 206, 211, 236, 240, 266, 267, 270, 271, 282–283, 292, 293
Sovereign pension reserve fund (SPRF), 21, 22, 188, 250
Sovereign wealth enterprise (SWE), 2, 10, 13, 14, 26, 28, 34, 36, 37, 41, 96–98, 104, 112, 114, 124, 134, 173, 216, 217, 230, 269, 272, 273, 283, 289
Sovereign wealth fund (SWF), 2, 4, 10, 13–29, 34, 36, 37, 41, 75, 87–89, 91, 96, 100–101, 107, 110, 112, 124, 126, 131, 132, 134, 150, 173, 216, 247, 269, 272, 273, 298–303
Sovereign wealth investors, 2–11, 13–105, 107–153, 155–233, 235–241, 247–252, 255, 258–267, 269–293, 295, 297, 299–301
Special Rapporteur, 93, 101
SPRF. *See* Sovereign pension reserve fund (SPRF)
SSRF. *See* Social security reserve fund (SSRF)
Stabilization funds, 18, 20
Standstill provision, 170–172, 228, 241, 259–261, 263, 287
State entities, 34, 35, 41, 75, 79, 82, 88, 98, 124, 140, 185–186, 190, 191, 193, 205, 210, 221, 228, 229, 282, 287, 288
State General Reserve Fund of Oman, 301
State practice, 10, 50, 68, 94–96, 98, 99, 103, 282
Subject to tax, 40, 122–123
Substantive policy principles, 49–51
SWE. *See* Sovereign wealth enterprise (SWE)
SWF. *See* Sovereign wealth fund (SWF)

T

Tax incentives, 67–68, 70, 72, 239, 279
Temasek, 27–31, 34, 123
Territorial sovereignty
  territoriality, 40, 125
  territoriality principle, 34, 61, 119, 121, 123
Test Claimants in the FII Group Litigation case, 175

U

U.S. Department of Treasury, 10, 16–17
U.S. Joint Committee on Taxation, 89, 96
UNCSI. *See* United Nations Convention on Jurisdictional Immunities of States and their Property (UNCSI)
Undertaking, 139, 140, 164, 168, 169, 179, 195, 197–204, 206–208, 212–215, 229, 230, 240, 242, 244, 247–248, 288, 289
United Arab Emirates (U.A.E.), 46
United Nations Convention on Jurisdictional Immunities of States and their Property (UNCSI), 10, 77, 78, 81, 83, 84, 93, 99, 101

Index

V

VBI. *See Vrijgestelde beleggingsinstelling* (VBI)
Vertical comparability, 176–181, 183, 185–193, 210, 221, 222, 228, 229, 287, 288

Vertical discrimination, 158, 183, 228, 287
Vertical equity, 60, 277
Vrijgestelde beleggingsinstelling (VBI), 245–246, 249, 250, 252

SERIES ON INTERNATIONAL TAXATION

1. Alberto Xavier, *The Taxation of Foreign Investment in Brazil*, 1980 (ISBN 90-200-0582-0).
2. Hugh J. Ault & Albert J. Rädler, *The German Corporation Tax Law with 1980 Amendments*, 1981 (ISBN 90-200-0642-8).
3. Paul R. McDaniel & Hugh J. Ault, *Introduction to United States International Taxation*, 1981 (ISBN 90-6544-004-6).
4. Albert J. Rädler, *German Transfer Pricing/Prix de Transfer en Allemagne*, 1984 (ISBN 90-6544-143-3).
5. Paul R. McDaniel & Stanley S. Surrey, *International Aspects of Tax Expenditures: A Comparative Study*, 1985 (ISBN 90-654-4163-8).
6. Kees van Raad, *Nondiscrimination in International Tax Law*, 1986 (ISBN 90-6544-266-9).
7. Sijbren Cnossen (ed.), *Tax Coordination in the European Community*, 1987 (ISBN 90-6544-272-3).
8. Ben Terra, *Sales Taxation. The Case of Value Added Tax in the European Community*, 1989 (ISBN 90-6544-381-9).
9. Rutsel S.J. Martha, *The Jurisdiction to Tax in International Law: Theory and Practice of Legislative Fiscal Jurisdiction*, 1989 (ISBN 90-654-4416-5).
10. Paul R. McDaniel & Hugh J. Ault, *Introduction to United States International Taxation* (3rd revised edition), 1989 (ISBN 90-6544-423-8).
11. Manuel Pires, *International Juridicial Double Taxation of Income*, 1989 (ISBN 90-6544-426-2).
12. A.H.M. Daniels, *Issues in International Partnership Taxation*, 1991 (ISBN 90-654-4577-3).
13. Arvid A. Skaar, *Permanent Establishment: Erosion of a Tax Treaty Principle*, 1992 (ISBN 90-6544-594-3).
14. Cyrille David & Geerten M.M. Michielse (eds), *Tax Treatment of Financial Instruments*, 1996 (ISBN 90-654-4666-4).
15. Herbert H. Alpert & Kees van Raad (eds), *Essays on International Taxation*, 1993 (ISBN 90-654-4781-4).
16. Wolfgang Gassner, Michael Lang & Eduard Lechner (eds), *Tax Treaties and EC Law*, 1997 (ISBN 90-411-0680-4).
17. Glória Teixeira, *Taxing Corporate Profits in the EU*, 1997 (ISBN 90-411-0703-7).
18. Michael Lang et al. (eds), *Multilateral Tax Treaties*, 1998 (ISBN 90-411-0704-5).
19. Stef van Weeghel, *The Improper Use of Tax Treaties*, 1998 (ISBN 90-411-0737-1).
20. Klaus Vogel (ed.), *Interpretation of Tax Law and Treaties and Transfer Pricing in Japan and Germany*, 1998 (ISBN 90-411-9655-2).
21. Bertil Wiman (ed.), *International Studies in Taxation: Law and Economics; Liber Amicorum Leif Mutén*, 1999 (ISBN 90-411-9692-7).
22. Alfonso J. Martín Jiménez, *Towards Corporate Tax Harmonization in the European Community*, 1999 (ISBN 90-411-9690-0).

23. Ramon J. Jeffery, *The Impact of State Sovereignty on Global Trade and International Taxation*, 1999 (ISBN 90-411-9703-6).
24. A.J. Easson, *Taxation of Foreign Direct Investment*, 1999 (ISBN 90-411-9741-9).
25. Marjaana Helminen, *The Dividend Concept in International Tax Law: Dividend Payments Between Corporate Entities*, 1999 (ISBN 90-411-9765-6).
26. Paul Kirchhof, Moris Lehner, Kees van Raad, Arndt Raupach & Michael-Rodi (eds), *International and Comparative Taxation: Essays in Honour of Klaus Vogel*, 2002 (ISBN 90-411-9841-5).
27. Krister Andersson, Peter Melz & Christer Silfverberg (eds), *Liber Amicorum Sven-Olof Lodin*, 2001 (ISBN 90-411-9850-4).
28. Juan Martín Jovanovich, *Customs Valuation and Transfer Pricing: Is It Possible to Harmonize Customs and Tax Rules?*, Second Edition, 2018 (ISBN 978-90-411-6134-5).
29. Stefano Simontacchi, *Taxation of Capital Gains under the OECD Model Convention: With Special Regard to Immovable Property*, 2007 (ISBN 978-90-411-2549-1).
30. Michael Lang, Josef Schuch, & Claus Staringer (eds), *Tax Treaty Law and EC Law*, 2007 (ISBN 978-90-411-2629-0).
31. Duncan Bentley, *Taxpayers' Rights: Theory Origin and Implementation*, 2007 (ISBN 978-90-411-2650-4).
32. Sergio André Rocha, *Interpretation of Double Taxation Conventions: General Theory and Brazilian Perspective*, 2008 (ISBN 978-90-411-2822-5).
33. Robert F. van Brederode, *Systems of General Sales Taxation: Theory, Policy and Practice*, 2009 (ISBN 978-90-411-2832-4).
34. John G. Head & Richard Krever (eds), *Tax Reform in the 21st Century: A Volume in Memory of Richard Musgrave*, 2009 (ISBN 978-90-411-2829-4).
35. Jens Wittendorff, *Transfer Pricing and the Arm's Length Principle in International Tax Law*, 2010 (ISBN 978-90-411-3270-3).
36. Marjaana Helminen, *The International Tax Law Concept of Dividend*, Second Edition, 2017 (ISBN 978-90-411-8394-1).
37. Robert F. van Brederode (ed.), *Immovable Property under VAT: A Comparative Global Analysis*, 2011 (ISBN 978-90-411-3126-3).
38. Dennis Weber & Stef van Weeghel, *The 2010 OECD Updates: Model Tax Convention & Transfer Pricing Guidelines - A Critical Review*, 2011 (ISBN 978-90-411-3812-5).
39. Yariv Brauner & Martin James McMahon, Jr. (eds), *The Proper Tax Base: Structural Fairness from an International and Comparative Perspective—Essays in Honour of Paul McDaniel*, 2012 (ISBN 978-90-411-3286-4).
40. Robert F. van Brederode (ed.), *Science, Technology and Taxation*, 2012 (ISBN 978-90-411-3125-6).
41. Oskar Henkow, *The VAT/GST Treatment of Public Bodies*, 2013 (ISBN 978-90-411-4663-2).
42. Jean Schaffner, *How Fixed Is a Permanent Establishment?*, 2013 (ISBN 978-90-411-4662-5).

43. Miguel Correia, *Taxation of Corporate Groups*, 2013 (ISBN 978-90-411-4841-4).
44. Veronika Daurer, *Tax Treaties and Developing Countries*, 2014 (ISBN 978-90-411-4982-4).
45. Claire Micheau, *State Aid, Subsidy and Tax Incentives under EU and WTO Law*, 2014 (ISBN 978-90-411-4555-0).
46. Robert F. van Brederode & Richard Krever (eds), *Legal Interpretation of Tax Law*, 2014 (ISBN 978-90-411-4945-9).
47. Radhakishan Rawal, *Taxation of Cross-border Services*, 2014 (ISBN 978-90-411-4947-3).
48. João Dácio Rolim, *Proportionality and Fair Taxation*, 2014 (ISBN 978-90-411-5838-3).
49. Paulo Rosenblatt, *General Anti-avoidance Rules for Major Developing Countries*, 2015 (ISBN 978-90-411-5839-0).
50. Gaspar Lopes Dias V.S., *Tax Arbitrage through Cross-Border Financial Engineering*, 2015 (ISBN 978-90-411-5875-8).
51. Geerten M.M. Michielse & Victor Thuronyi (eds), *Tax Design Issues Worldwide*, 2015 (ISBN 978-90-411-5610-5).
52. Oktavia Weidmann, *Taxation of Derivatives*, 2015 (ISBN 978-90-411-5977-9).
53. Chris Evans, Richard Krever & Peter Mellor (eds), *Tax Simplification*, 2015 (ISBN 978-90-411-5976-2).
54. Reuven Avi-Yonah & Joel Slemrod (eds), *Taxation and Migration*, 2015 (ISBN 978-90-411-6136-9).
55. Alexander Bosman, *Other Income under Tax Treaties: An Analysis of Article 21 of the OECD Model Convention*, 2015 (ISBN 978-90-411-6610-4).
56. John Abrahamson, *International Taxation of Manufacturing and Distribution*, 2016 (ISBN 978-90-411-6664-7).
57. Frederik Boulogne, *Shortcomings in the EU Merger Directive*, 2016 (ISBN 978-90-411-6713-2).
58. Angelika Meindl-Ringler, *Beneficial Ownership in International Tax Law*, 2016 (ISBN 978-90-411-6833-7).
59. Andreas Waltrich, *Cross-Border Taxation of Permanent Establishments: An International Comparison*, 2016 (ISBN 978-90-411-6832-0).
60. Sergio André Rocha & Allison Christians (eds), *Tax Sovereignty in the BEPS Era*, 2017 (ISBN 978-90-411-6707-1).
61. Peter Antony Wilson, *BRICS and International Tax Law*, 2018 (ISBN 978-90-411-9435-0).
62. Louise Otis, Brigitte Alepin & Blanca Moreno-Dodson (eds), *Winning the Tax Wars: Tax Competition and Cooperation*, 2018 (ISBN 978-90-411-9460-2).
63. Marta Castelon, *International Taxation of Income from Services under Double Taxation Conventions: Development, Practice and Policy*, 2018 (ISBN 978-90-411-9594-4).
64. D.M. Broekhuijsen, *A Multilateral Tax Treaty: Designing an Instrument to Modernise International Tax Law*, 2018 (ISBN 978-90-411-9872-3).

65. John Abrahamson, *International Taxation of Energy Production and Distribution*, 2018 (ISBN 978-90-411-9101-4).
66. Leopoldo Parada, *Double Non-taxation and the Use of Hybrid Entities: An Alternative Approach in the New Era of BEPS*, 2018 (ISBN 978-90-411-9991-1).
67. Richard Snoeij, *International Tax Aspects of Sovereign Wealth Investors: A Source State Perspective*, 2018 (ISBN 978-90-411-9431-2).